WRITING, KINGSHIP
IN ANGLO-SAXON

The workings of royal and ecclesiastical authority in Anglo-Saxon England can only be understood on the basis of direct engagement with original texts and material artefacts. This book, written by leading experts, brings together new research that represents the best of current scholarship on the nexus between authority and written sources from Anglo-Saxon England. Ranging from the seventh to the eleventh century, the chapters in this volume offer fresh approaches to a wide range of linguistic, historical, legal, diplomatic and palaeographical evidence. Central themes include the formation of power in early Anglo-Saxon kingdoms during the age of Bede (d. 735) and Offa of Mercia (757–96), authority and its articulation in the century from Edgar (959–75) to 1066 and the significance of books and texts in expressing power across the period. *Writing, Kingship and Power* represents a critical resource for students and scholars alike with an interest in early medieval history from political, institutional and cultural perspectives.

RORY NAISMITH is a lecturer in medieval history at King's College London. He is a Fellow of the Royal Historical Society and author of *Money and Power in Anglo-Saxon England: The Southern English Kingdoms 757–865* (Cambridge University Press, 2012) and *Medieval European Coinage, with a Catalogue of Coins in the Fitzwilliam Museum, Cambridge*, Volume 8: *Britain and Ireland c. 400–1066* (Cambridge University Press, 2017).

DAVID A. WOODMAN is Fellow of Robinson College, Cambridge, where he is Director of Studies in History and Anglo-Saxon, Norse and Celtic. He is a Fellow of the Royal Historical Society and author of *Charters of Northern Houses* (2012) and co-editor of *The Long Twelfth-Century View of the Anglo-Saxon Past* (2015).

Professor Simon Keynes

WRITING, KINGSHIP AND POWER IN ANGLO-SAXON ENGLAND

EDITED BY

RORY NAISMITH
King's College London

DAVID A. WOODMAN
Robinson College, Cambridge

CAMBRIDGE
UNIVERSITY PRESS

CAMBRIDGE
UNIVERSITY PRESS

University Printing House, Cambridge CB2 8BS, United Kingdom

One Liberty Plaza, 20th Floor, New York, NY 10006, USA

477 Williamstown Road, Port Melbourne, VIC 3207, Australia

314-321, 3rd Floor, Plot 3, Splendor Forum, Jasola District Centre, New Delhi - 110025, India

79 Anson Road, #06-04/06, Singapore 079906

Cambridge University Press is part of the University of Cambridge.

It furthers the University's mission by disseminating knowledge in the pursuit of education, learning and research at the highest international levels of excellence.

www.cambridge.org
Information on this title: www.cambridge.org/9781108744782
DOI: 10.1017/9781316676066

© Cambridge University Press 2018

First published 2018
First paperback edition 2020

A catalogue record for this publication is available from the British Library

ISBN 978-1-107-16097-2 Hardback
ISBN 978-1-108-74478-2 Paperback

Contents

Figures

Contributors

JULIA CRICK Professor of Palaeography and Manuscript Studies at King's College London

CATHERINE CUBITT Professor of Medieval History at the University of East Anglia

DAVID N. DUMVILLE Sixth-Century Professor in History, Palaeography and Celtic at the University of Aberdeen

SARAH FOOT Regius Professor of Ecclesiastical History at Christ Church, Oxford

HELEN FOXHALL FORBES Senior Lecturer in Early Medieval History at Durham University

RORY NAISMITH Lecturer in Early Medieval British History at King's College London

JINTY NELSON Emeritus Professor of Medieval History at King's College London

OLIVER PADEL Formerly Reader in Cornish and Celtic in the Department of Anglo-Saxon, Norse and Celtic, University of Cambridge, and former President of the English Place-Name Society

DAVID PRATT Fellow and Director of Studies in History at Downing College, Cambridge

LEVI ROACH Lecturer in Medieval History at the University of Exeter

PAULINE STAFFORD Professor Emerita of Early Medieval History at the University of Liverpool and Visiting Professor in the Institute of Medieval Studies, University of Leeds

FRANCESCA TINTI Ikerbasque Research Professor at the University of the Basque Country UPV/EHU

DAVID A. WOODMAN Fellow and Director of Studies in History and Anglo-Saxon, Norse and Celtic at Robinson College, Cambridge

Abbreviations

Anglo-Saxon charters are cited using the conventions laid down in
S. Keynes, 'Church Councils, Royal Assemblies, and Anglo-Saxon Royal
Diplomas', in *Kingship, Legislation and Power in Anglo-Saxon England*, ed.
G. R. Owen-Crocker and B. W. Schneider (Woodbridge, 2013),
pp. 17–182, at 180–2. References to the *Anglo-Saxon Chronicle* use the
conventional lettering for individual manuscript witnesses, where appropriate. References to Domesday Book are by folio number, with column
specifications where appropriate. Relevant abbreviations are as follows:

Abing	*Charters of Abingdon Abbey*, ed. S. E. Kelly, AS Charters vii–viii (Oxford, 2000–1)
ANS	*Anglo-Norman Studies*
AntJ	*The Antiquaries' Journal*
ASC	*Anglo-Saxon Chronicle*
AS Charters	Anglo-Saxon Charters
ASE	*Anglo-Saxon England*
ASNC	Anglo-Saxon, Norse and Celtic
ASWrits	F. E. Harmer, *Anglo-Saxon Writs* (Manchester, 1952)
BAFacs	*Facsimiles of Anglo-Saxon Charters*, ed. S. Keynes, AS Charters, Supplementary Series 1 (Oxford, 1991)
BAR	British Archaeological Reports
BCS	W. de G. Birch, *Cartularium Saxonicum*, 3 vols. (London, 1885–93)
BL	British Library
BNJ	*British Numismatic Journal*
Burt	*Charters of Burton Abbey*, ed. P. H. Sawyer, AS Charters ii (Oxford, 1979)
CantCC	*Charters of Christ Church, Canterbury*, ed. N. P. Brooks and S. E. Kelly, AS Charters 17–18, 2 parts (Oxford, 2013)

CantStA	*Charters of St Augustine's Abbey, Canterbury, and Minster-in-Thanet*, ed. S. E. Kelly, AS Charters iv (Oxford, 1995)
CC	Codex Carolinus
CCCC	Cambridge, Corpus Christi College
CCCM	Corpus Christianorum, Continuatio Mediaevalis
CCSL	Corpus Christianorum, Series Latina (Turnhout)
cf.	compare
CMCS	*Cambridge Medieval Celtic Studies* (1981–93)/*Cambrian Medieval Celtic Studies* (1993–)
CrawCh	*The Crawford Collection of Early Charters and Documents Now in the Bodleian Library*, ed. A. S. Napier and W. H. Stevenson (Oxford, 1895)
CSASE	Cambridge Studies in Anglo-Saxon England
DB	Domesday Book: *Domesday Book*, ed. J. Morris et al., 35 vols. (Chichester, 1973–86); and *Domesday Book: A Complete Translation*, trans. A. Williams and G. H. Martin (London, 2002)
GDB	Great Domesday Book: *Great Domesday Book: Library Edition*, ed. R. W. H. Erskine, 6 vols. (London, 1986–92)
LDB	Little Domesday Book: *Little Domesday Book: Library Edition*, ed. A. Williams and G. H. Martin, 6 vols. (London, 2000)
EconHR	*Economic History Review*
EEMF	Early English Manuscripts in Facsimile
EETS	Early English Text Society
EHD	*English Historical Documents c. 500–1042*, ed. D. Whitelock, English Historical Documents I, 2nd edn (London, 1979)
EHR	*English Historical Review*
EME	*Early Medieval Europe*
Glast	*Charters of Glastonbury Abbey*, ed. S. E. Kelly, AS Charters 15 (Oxford, 2012)
Gn-L, *ASMss*	H. Gneuss and M. Lapidge, *Anglo-Saxon Manuscripts: a Bibliographical Handlist of Manuscripts and Manuscript Fragments Written or Owned in England up to 1100* (Toronto, 2014)
HBS	Henry Bradshaw Society
HE	Bede, *Historia ecclesiastica gentis Anglorum*

HE Comm.	J. M. Wallace-Hadrill, *Bede's Ecclesiastical History of the English People: A Historical Commentary* (Oxford, 1988)
Iud. Dei	*Iudicia Dei*
HSJ	*Haskins Society Journal*
JEH	*Journal of Ecclesiastical History*
KCD	J. M. Kemble, *Codex Diplomaticus Aevi Saxonici*, 6 vols. (London, 1839–48)
MÆ	*Medium Ævum*
Malm	*Charters of Malmesbury Abbey*, ed. S. E. Kelly, AS Charters xi (Oxford, 2005)
MGH	Monumenta Germaniae Historica
D	Diplomata
K	*Die Urkunden Konrads III und seines Sohnes Heinrich*, ed. F. Hausmann, MGH Diplomata regum et imperatorum Germaniae 9 (Vienna, 1969)
SSRG	Scriptores rerum Germanicarum
NChron	*Numismatic Chronicle*
NCirc	*Numismatic Circular*
NH	*Northern History*
North	*Charters of Northern Houses*, ed. D. A. Woodman, AS Charters 16 (Oxford, 2012)
N&Q	*Notes and Queries*
n. s.	New Series
ODNB	H. C. G. Mattews and B. Harrison (eds.), *Oxford Dictionary of National Biography, from the Earliest Times to the Year 2000*, 61 vols. (Oxford, 2004)
OEN	*Old English Newsletter*
OSFacs	W. B. Sanders, *Facsimiles of Anglo-Saxon Manuscripts*, 3 vols. (Southampton, 1878–84)
PBA	*Proceedings of the British Academy*
Pet	*Charters of Peterborough Abbey*, ed. S. E. Kelly, AS Charters 14 (Oxford, 2009)
PL	*Patrologiae cursus completus. Series (latina) prima*, ed. J. P. Migne, 221 vols. (Paris, 1844–64)
RS	Rolls Series
S	P. H. Sawyer, *Anglo-Saxon Charters: An Annotated List and Bibliography*, Royal Historical Society Guides and Handbooks viii (London, 1968) (and see also www.esawyer.org.uk)

StAlb	*Charters of St Albans*, ed. J. Crick, AS Charters xii (Oxford, 2007)
Shaft	*Charters of Shaftesbury Abbey*, ed. S. E. Kelly, AS Charters v (Oxford, 1996)
Sherb	*Charters of Sherborne*, ed. M. A. O'Donovan, AS Charters iii (Oxford, 1988)
TLS	*The Times Literary Supplement*
TRE	*tempore regis Edwardi* ('in the time of King Edward'; used with reference to Domesday Book)
TRHS	*Transactions of the Royal Historical Society*
VCA	*Vita sancti Cuthberti auctore anonymo*
VCH	*Victoria History of the Counties of England*
VM	Sulpicius Severus, *Vita sancti Martini*
VW	Stephen of Ripon, *Vita Wilfridi*
WBEASE	M. Lapidge, J. Blair, S. Keynes and D. Scragg (eds.), *The Wiley Blackwell Encyclopedia of Anglo-Saxon England*, 2nd edn (Chichester, 2014)
Wells	*Charters of Bath and Wells*, ed. S. E. Kelly, AS Charters 13 (Oxford, 2007)
WinchNM	*Charters of the New Minster, Winchester*, ed. S. Miller, AS Charters ix *Winchester* (Oxford, 2001)

Publications by Simon Keynes

The list presented here, prepared in consultation between Simon and the editors, covers publications to summer 2016. It does not include work in progress. Abbreviations for names of journals and series are as used in the list of abbreviations earlier in this book (see preceding section). It should also be noted that Simon has served as a member of the editorial board of *ASE* since 1979 and as an executive editor since 1982, contributed to the annual bibliographies between vols. 6 (1977) and 13 (1984), and was co-ordinating editor of the bibliographies in vols. 11 (1983) to 40 (2011) (with Paul Remley from vol. 31 (2002)).

Monographs

1980

The Diplomas of King Æthelred 'the Unready' 978–1016: A Study in their Use as Historical Evidence, Cambridge Studies in Medieval Life and Thought, 3rd Series 13 (Cambridge, 1980)

1983

[with M. Lapidge] *Alfred the Great: Asser's 'Life of King Alfred' and Other Contemporary Sources* (Harmondsworth, 1983)

1991

Facsimiles of Anglo-Saxon Charters, AS Charters, Supplementary Series 1 (Oxford, 1991)

1996

The 'Liber Vitae' of the New Minster and Hyde Abbey, Winchester, EEMF 26 (Copenhagen, 1996)

Edited Books

1999

[with M. Lapidge, J. Blair and D. Scragg] *The Blackwell Encyclopaedia of Anglo-Saxon England* (Oxford, 1999), reprinted with corrections in paperback (Oxford, 2000); 2nd edn as *The Wiley-Blackwell Encyclopedia of Anglo-Saxon England* (Chichester, 2014)

2004

Quentin Keynes 1921–2003: Explorer, Film-Maker, Lecturer, and Book-Collector (Cambridge, 2004)

2006

[with A. P. Smyth] *Anglo-Saxons: Studies Presented to Cyril Roy Hart* (Dublin, 2006)

2007

Ethiopian Encounters: Sir William Cornwallis Harris and the British Mission to the Kingdom of Shewa (1841–3) (Cambridge, 2007)

Other Books

1981

[with J. Fellows] *Domesday Book 18: Cambridgeshire* (Chichester, 1981)

1987

Anglo-Saxon History: A Select Bibliography, OEN Subsidia 13 (Binghamton, NY, 1987); 2nd edn, OEN Subsidia 13 (Binghamton, NY, 1993); 3rd edn, OEN Subsidia 13 (Kalamazoo, MI, 1998)

1992

Anglo-Saxon Manuscripts and Other Items of Related Interest in the Library of Trinity College, Cambridge, OEN Subsidia 18 (Binghamton, NY, 1991 for 1992)

2000

Anglo-Saxon England: A Bibliographical Handbook for Students of Anglo-Saxon History, ASNC Guides, Texts and Studies 1 (Cambridge, 2000), 2nd edn (2001), 3rd edn (2002); 4th edn (2003); 5th edn (2004), 6th edn (2005), 7th edn (2006)

2002

An Atlas of Attestations in Anglo-Saxon Charters, c. 670–1066, I: *Tables*, ASNC Guides, Texts and Studies 5 (Cambridge, 2002); published online in 2012

Articles and Contributions to Edited Volumes

1978

'The Declining Reputation of King Æthelred the Unready', in *Ethelred the Unready: Papers from the Millenary Conference*, ed. D. Hill, BAR British Series 59 (Oxford, 1978), pp. 227–53; reprinted (with revised and updated footnotes) in *Anglo-Saxon History: Basic Readings*, ed. D. A. E. Pelteret, Basic Readings in Anglo-Saxon England 6 (New York, 2000), pp. 157–90
'An Interpretation of the *Pacx, Pax* and *Paxs* Pennies', *ASE* 7 (1978), 165–73

1984

'Introduction', in *The Golden Age of Anglo-Saxon Art 966–1066*, ed. J. Backhouse, D. Turner and L. Webster (London, 1984), pp. 11–16

1985

'Anglo-Saxon Architecture and the Historian', *ASE* 14 (1985), 293–302
'Anglo-Saxon Kingship', *History Today* 35 (January 1985), 38–43
'The Crowland Psalter and the Sons of King Edmund Ironside', *Bodleian Library Record* 11 (1985), 359–70
'Introduction' and 'Anglo-Saxon Coinage and the Historian', in *Anglo-Saxon Coins*, ed. T. R. Volk (Cambridge, 1985), pp. 6–14
'King Athelstan's Books', in *Learning and Literature in Anglo-Saxon England: Studies Presented to Peter Clemoes*, ed. M. Lapidge and H. Gneuss (Cambridge, 1985), pp. 143–201

1986

'The Additions in Old English', in *The York Gospels*, ed. N. Barker (London, 1986), pp. 81–99

'Episcopal Succession in Anglo-Saxon England' and 'Anglo-Saxon Church Councils', in *Handbook of British Chronology*, ed. E. B. Fryde, D. E. Greenway, S. Porter and I. Roy, Royal Historical Society Guides and Handbooks 2, 3rd edn (London, 1986), pp. 209–24 and 583–9

'A Tale of Two Kings: Alfred the Great and Æthelred the Unready', *TRHS*, 5th series, 36 (1986), 195–217

1988

'Regenbald the Chancellor (*sic*)', *ANS* 10 (1988), 185–222

1989

'The Lost Cartulary of Abbotsbury', *ASE* 18 (1989), 207–43

1990

'Royal Government and the Written Word in Late Anglo-Saxon England', in *The Uses of Literacy in Early Mediaeval Europe*, ed. R. McKitterick (Cambridge, 1990), pp. 226–57

1991

'The Æthelings in Normandy', *ANS* 13 (1991), 172–204

'Crime and Punishment in the Reign of Æthelred the Unready', in *People and Places in Northern Europe 500–1600*, ed. I. Wood and N. Lund (Woodbridge, 1991), pp. 67–81

'The Developing State', 'The Mercian Supremacy' and 'The Age of Alfred', in *The Making of England: Anglo-Saxon Art and Culture AD 600–900*, ed. L. Webster and J. Backhouse (London, 1991), pp. 38–9, 193–4 and 254–6

'The Historical Context of the Battle of Maldon', in *The Battle of Maldon A.D. 991*, ed. D. G. Scragg (Oxford, 1991), pp. 81–113

1992

'The Comet in the Eadwine Psalter', in *The Eadwine Psalter: Text, Image, and Monastic Culture in Twelfth-Century Canterbury*, ed. M. Gibson, T. A. Heslop and R. Pfaff (London and University Park, PA, 1992), pp. 157–64

'The Fonthill Letter', in *Words, Texts and Manuscripts: Anglo-Saxon Studies Presented to Helmut Gneuss*, ed. M. Korhammer (Cambridge, 1992), pp. 53–97

'Rædwald the Bretwalda', in *Voyage to the Other World: The Legacy of Sutton Hoo*, ed. C. B. Kendall and P. S. Wells, Medieval Studies at Minnesota 4 (Minneapolis, 1992), pp. 103–23

1993

'Andover 994', *Lookback at Andover: Journal of the Andover History and Archaeology Society* 1(4) (1993), 58–61

'A Charter of King Edward the Elder for Islington', *Historical Research* 66 (1993), 303–16

'The Control of Kent in the Ninth Century', *EME* 2 (1993), 111–31

'The Discovery and First Publication of the Alfred Jewel', *Somerset Archaeology and Natural History* 136 (1993 for 1992), 1–8

'George Harbin's Transcript of the Lost Cartulary of Athelney Abbey', *Somerset Archaeology and Natural History* 136 (1993 for 1992), 149–59

'A Lost Cartulary of St Albans Abbey', *ASE* 22 (1993), 253–79

'The Will of Wulf', *OEN* 26(3) (1993), 16–21

1994

'Anglo-Saxon History after *Anglo-Saxon England*', in *Stenton's 'Anglo-Saxon England' Fifty Years On*, ed. D. Matthew, Reading Historical Studies 1 (Reading, 1994), pp. 83–110

'Cnut's Earls', in *The Reign of Cnut, King of England, Denmark and Norway*, ed. A. R. Rumble (London, 1994), pp. 43–88

The Councils of Clofesho, University of Leicester Vaughan Paper 38 (Leicester, 1994)

'The "Dunstan B" Charters', *ASE* 23 (1994), 165–93

'The West Saxon Charters of King Æthelwulf and His Sons', *EHR* 109 (1994), 1109–49

1995

'England, 700–900', in *The New Cambridge Medieval History II: c. 700– c. 900*, ed. R. McKitterick (Cambridge, 1995), pp. 18–42

1996

'On the Authenticity of Asser's *Life of King Alfred*', *JEH* 47 (1996), 529–51

1997

'Anglo-Saxon Entries in the "Liber Vitae" of Brescia', in *Alfred the Wise: Studies in Honour of Janet Bately*, ed. J. Roberts and J. L. Nelson (Woodbridge, 1997), pp. 99–119

'Giso, bishop of Wells (1061–88)', *ANS* 19 (1997), 203–71

'Introduction', in P. Hunter Blair, *Anglo-Saxon England*, new edn (London, 1997), pp. xv–xxix

'The Reconstruction of a Burnt Cottonian Manuscript: The Case of Cotton MS. Otho A. I', *British Library Journal* 22 (1997 for 1996), 113–60

'The Vikings in England, *c.* 780–1016', in *The Oxford Illustrated History of the Vikings*, ed. P. H. Sawyer (Oxford, 1997), pp. 48–82

Entries on King Athelstan and King Edgar and minor corrections passim, in *The Oxford Dictionary of the Christian Church*, ed. E. A. Livingstone, 3rd edn (Oxford, 1997), pp. 122 and 533

1998

[with M. Blackburn] 'A Corpus of the *Cross-and-Lozenge* and Related Coinages of Alfred, Ceolwulf II and Archbishop Æthelred', in *Kings, Currency, and Alliances: The History and Coinage of Southern England in the Ninth Century*, ed. M. A. S. Blackburn and D. N. Dumville, Studies in Anglo-Saxon History 9 (Woodbridge, 1998), pp. 125–50

'King Alfred and the Mercians', in *Kings, Currency, and Alliances: The History and Coinage of Southern England in the Ninth Century*, ed. M. A. S. Blackburn and D. N. Dumville, Studies in Anglo-Saxon History 9 (Woodbridge, 1998), pp. 1–45

'Queen Emma and the *Encomium Emmae Reginae*', in *Encomium Emmae Reginae*, ed. A. Campbell, Camden third series 72 (London, 1949), Camden Classic Reprints 4 (Cambridge, 1998), pp. xiii–lxxx

1999

'Appendix I: Rulers of the English, *c.* 450–1066', in *The Blackwell Encyclopaedia of Anglo-Saxon England*, ed. M. Lapidge with J. Blair, S. Keynes and D. Scragg (Oxford, 1999), pp. 500–516 + Maps 9–12; 2nd edn as *The Wiley-Blackwell Encyclopedia of Anglo-Saxon England* (Chichester, 2014), pp. 521–38 + Maps 9–12

'The Cult of King Alfred the Great', *ASE* 28 (1999), 225–356

'England, 900-1016', in *The New Cambridge Medieval History III: c. 900–c. 1024*, ed. T. Reuter (Cambridge, 1999), pp. 456–84

Entries in *The Blackwell Encyclopaedia of Anglo-Saxon England*, ed. M. Lapidge with J. Blair, S. Keynes and D. Scragg (Oxford, 1999), reprinted with corrections in paperback (Oxford, 2000); 2nd edn as *The Wiley-Blackwell Encyclopedia of Anglo-Saxon England* (Chichester, 2014). Longer entries: Æthelbald, king of the Mercians; *Anglo-Saxon Chronicle;* Anglo-Saxonism; Asser; chancery, royal; charters and writs; Cnut; Coenwulf, king of the Mercians; episcopal lists; Koenwald, bishop of Worcester; Mercia; Offa, king of the Mercians; papacy; thegn; Wulfstan I of York. Shorter entries: *Adventus Saxonum*; Ælfheah II; Æthelred, Lord of the Mercians, and Æthelflæd; Æthelstan ætheling; alms; Anglo-Saxons, kingdom of; *bretwalda*; Burghal Hidage; Ceolnoth; County Hidage; Cynethryth; Eadric Streona; Edmund Ironside; Ely; *Encomium Emmae*; Florence of Worcester; Giso; Harold Harefoot; Harthacnut;

Hemming; heptarchy; *heregeld*; Hickes, George; Jænberht; Jews; Kemble, J. M.; Kingston-upon-Thames; Lindsey; liturgical commemoration; Middle Angles; Nothhelm; Penda; Plegmund; shire; Swein Forkbeard; Vikings; Wanley, H.; Wulfhere.

'King Alfred the Great and Shaftesbury Abbey', in *Studies in the Early History of Shaftesbury*, ed. L. Keen (Dorchester, 1999), pp. 17–72

2000

'Apocalypse Then (AD 1000)', in *Not Angels, but Anglicans: A History of Christianity in the British Isles*, ed. H. Chadwick and A. Ward (Norwich, 2000), pp. 41–7

'Diocese and Cathedral before 1056', in *Hereford Cathedral: A History*, ed. G. Aylmer and J. Tiller (London, 2000), pp. 3–20

2001

'The Age of Unification', in *The Penguin Atlas of British & Irish History*, ed. B. Cunliffe et al. (London, 2001), pp. 68–71

'Apocalypse Then: England A.D. 1000', in *Europe around the Year 1000*, ed. P. Urbanczyk (Warsaw, 2001), pp. 247–70

'Edward, King of the Anglo-Saxons', in *Edward the Elder 899–924*, ed. N. J. Higham and D. H. Hill (London, 2001), pp. 40–66

'Mercia and Wessex in the Ninth Century', in *Mercia: An Anglo-Saxon Kingdom in Europe*, ed. M. P. Brown and C. A. Farr (London, 2001), pp. 310–28

2003

'Changing Perceptions of Anglo-Saxon History' and 'Select Bibliography', in *An Introduction to Anglo-Saxon England*, ed. P. Hunter Blair, 3rd edn (Cambridge, 2003), pp. xvii–xxxv, 364–74

'Ely Abbey 672–1109' and 'The Discovery of the Bones of the Saxon "Confessors"', in *A History of Ely Cathedral*, ed. P. Meadows and N. Ramsay (Woodbridge, 2003), pp. 3–58, 401–4

'The Power of the Written Word: Alfredian England 871–899', in *Alfred the Great: Papers from the Eleventh-Centenary Conferences*, ed. T. Reuter (Aldershot, 2003), pp. 175–97

'A Tribute to Helmut Gneuss from Cambridge', in *Bookmarks from the Past: Studies in Early English Language and Literature in Honour of Helmut Gneuss*, ed. L. Kornexl and U. Lenker, Münchener Universitätsschriften: Texte und Untersuchungen zur Englischen Philologie 30 (Frankfurt, 2003), pp. xi–xv

2004

Entries in *Oxford Dictionary of National Biography*, ed. H. C. G. Matthew and
  B. Harrison, 60 vols. (Oxford, 2004), vol. I, 409–19 (King Æthelred the
  Unready) and 429 (Æthelstan the ætheling); vol. XVII, 535–8 (Eadric Streona)
  and 539–42 (King Eadwig); vol. XVIII, 412–14 (Queen Emma); and vol. LVIII,
  692–4 (Dorothy Whitelock)
'The *Liber Vitae* of the New Minster, Winchester', in *The Durham 'Liber Vitae'*,
  ed. L. Rollason, D. Rollason, A. Piper and M. Harvey (Woodbridge, 2004), pp.
  149–63

2005

'Between Bede and the *Chronicle*: BL Cotton Vespasian B. vi, fols. 104–9', in *Latin
  Learning and English Lore: Studies in Anglo-Saxon Literature for Michael Lapidge*,
  ed. A. P. M. Orchard and K. O'B. O'Keeffe, 2 vols. (Toronto, 2005), vol. I,
  47–67
'King Æthelred's Charter for Sherborne Abbey, 998', in *Sherborne Abbey
  Millennium*, ed. K. Barker (Oxford, 2005), pp. 10–14
'The Kingdom of the Mercians in the Eighth Century', in *Æthelbald and Offa:
  Two Eighth-Century Kings of Mercia*, ed. D. Hill and M. Worthington, BAR
  British Series 383 (Oxford, 2005), pp. 1–26
'A Note on Anglo-Saxon Personal Names' and 'Wulfsige, Monk of Glastonbury,
  Abbot of Westminster (*c.* 990–3), and Bishop of Sherborne (993–1002)', in *St
  Wulfsige and Sherborne: Essays to Commemorate the Millennium of the
  Benedictine Abbey 998–1998*, ed. K. Barker et al. (Oxford, 2005), pp. 20–3 and
  53–94

2006

'Angelsächsische Urkunden (7–9 Jahrhundert)/Anglo-Saxon Charters (7th–9th
  Century)', in *Mensch und Schrift im frühen Mittelalter*, ed. P. Erhart and
  L. Hollenstein (St Gallen, 2006), pp. 97–108
'Re-Reading King Æthelred the Unready', in *Writing Medieval Biography
  750–1250: Essays in Honour of Professor Frank Barlow*, ed. D. Bates, J. Crick
  and S. Hamilton (Woodbridge, 2006), pp. 77–97

2007

'An Abbot, an Archbishop, and the Viking Raids of 1006–7 and 1009–12', *ASE* 36
  (2007), 151–220

2008

'Anglo-Saxon Charters: Lost and Found', in *Myth, Rulership, Church, and Charters: Essays in Honour of Nicholas Brooks*, ed. J. Barrow and A. Wareham (Aldershot, 2008), pp. 45–66

'A Conspectus of the Charters of King Edgar (957–75)', in *Edgar, King of the English 959–975: New Interpretations*, ed. D. Scragg, Publications of the Manchester Centre for Anglo-Saxon Studies 8 (Woodbridge, 2008), pp. 60–80

'Edgar, *rex admirabilis*', in *Edgar, King of the English 959–975: New Interpretations*, ed. D. Scragg, Publications of the Manchester Centre for Anglo-Saxon Studies 8 (Woodbridge, 2008), pp. 3–59

[Introduction], in H. Foxhall Forbes et al., 'Anglo-Saxon and Related Entries in the *Oxford Dictionary of National Biography* (2004)', *ASE* 37 (2008), 183–232, at 183–7

'The Massacre of St Brice's Day (13 November 1002)', in *Beretning fra seksogtyvende tværfaglige vikingesymposium*, ed. N. Lund (Moesgaard, 2008), pp. 32–66

2009

[with R. Love] 'Earl Godwine's Ship', *ASE* 38 (2010 for 2009), 185–223

'Edward the Ætheling (*c.* 1005–16)', in *Edward the Confessor: The Man and the Legend*, ed. R. Mortimer (Woodbridge, 2009), pp. 41–62

'King Æthelred's Charter for Eynsham Abbey (1005)', in *Early Medieval Studies in Memory of Patrick Wormald*, ed. S. Baxter, C. Karkov, J. L. Nelson and D. Pelteret (Aldershot, 2009), pp. 451–73

2010

'Introductory Note on A. J. Robertson's *Anglo-Saxon Charters*', in *Anglo-Saxon Charters*, ed. A. J. Robertson, 2nd edn (Cambridge, 1956), reprinted (Cambridge, 2010), pp. i–iii

2011

'Introduction', in *Anglo-Saxon Charters*, ed. A. J. Robertson, 2nd edn (Cambridge, 1959), reprinted (Cambridge, 2011), pp. i–xii

'Introduction', in *Anglo-Saxon Wills*, ed. Dorothy Whitelock (Cambridge, 1930), reprinted (Cambridge, 2011), pp. i–viii

'Introduction', in *Select English Historical Documents of the Ninth and Tenth Centuries*, ed. F. E. Harmer (Cambridge, 1914), reprinted (Cambridge, 2011), pp. i–vi

'J. M. Kemble and His *Codex Diplomaticus Ævi Saxonici*', in *Codex Diplomaticus Ævi Saxonici*, ed. J. M. Kemble, 6 vols. (London, 1839–48), reprinted (Cambridge, 2011), vol. I, pp. v–xxv

2012

[with R. Naismith] 'The *Agnus Dei* Pennies of King Æthelred the Unready', *ASE* 40 (2012 for 2011), 175–223

'The Burial of King Æthelred the Unready at St Paul's', in *The English and Their Legacy 900–1200: Essays in Honour of Ann Williams*, ed. D. Roffe (Woodbridge, 2012), pp. 129–48

'The Cult of King Edward the Martyr during the Reign of King Æthelred the Unready', in *Gender and Historiography: Studies in the Earlier Middle Ages in Honour of Pauline Stafford*, ed. J. L. Nelson, S. Reynolds and S. M. Johns (London, 2012), pp. 115–25

'Manuscripts of the *Anglo-Saxon Chronicle*', in *The Cambridge History of the Book in Britain, I: c. 400–1100*, ed. R. Gameson (Cambridge, 2012), pp. 537–52

2013

'Church Councils, Royal Assemblies and Anglo-Saxon Royal Diplomas', in *Kingship, Legislation and Power in Anglo-Saxon England*, ed. G. R. Owen-Croker and B. W. Schneider (Woodbridge, 2013), pp. 17–182

2014

'Appendix II: Archbishops and Bishops, 597–1066', in *The Wiley Blackwell Encyclopedia of Anglo-Saxon England*, ed. M. Lapidge, J. Blair, S. Keynes and D. Scragg, 2nd edn. (Chichester, 2014), pp. 539–66

Entries in *The Wiley Blackwell Encyclopedia of Anglo-Saxon England*, ed. M. Lapidge, J. Blair, S. Keynes and D. Scragg, 2nd edn. (Chichester, 2014). In addition to entries from the first edition, new entries on Ælfhere, Ealdorman; Ælfric, Archbishop of Canterbury; Bamburgh; Byrhthelm, bishop and archbishop; Cuthbert, Archbishop of Canterbury; episcopal professions; guild regulations; Hereward; Regenbald; Sandwich; Seaxwulf, bishop; Sigeric, Archbishop of Canterbury; Stigand, Archbishop of Canterbury; Tostig, Earl; Waltham; Wight, Isle of.

'Mapping the Anglo-Saxon Past', in *Towns and Topography: Essays in Memory of David H. Hill*, ed. G. R. Owen-Crocker and S. B. Thompson (Oxford, 2014), pp. 147–70

2015

'Alfred the Great and the Kingdom of the Anglo-Saxons', *A Companion to Alfred the Great*, ed. N. Guenther Discenza and P. E. Szarmach (Leiden, 2015), pp. 13–46

'England and Spain during the Reign of King Æthelred the Unready', *SELIM: Journal of the Spanish Society for Medieval English Language and Literature* 20 (2015 for 2013–14), 121–66

'H. M. Chadwick and Anglo-Saxon England', *H. M. Chadwick and the Study of Anglo-Saxon, Norse and Celtic in Cambridge*, ed. M. Lapidge, *CMCS* 69/70 (Aberystwyth, 2015), pp. 111–41

'King Æthelred the Unready and the Church of Rochester', *Textus Roffensis: Law, Language, and Libraries in Early Medieval England*, ed. B. O'Brien and B. Bombi, Studies in the Early Middle Ages 30 (Turnhout, 2015), pp. 315–62

'Welsh Kings at Anglo-Saxon Royal Assemblies (928–55)', *Haskins Society Journal* 26 (2015), 69–122

2016

[with B. Crawford and J. L. Nelson] 'Nicholas Peter Brooks 1941–2014', *Biographical Memoirs of Fellows of the British Academy* XV (Oxford, 2016), pp. 25–43

[with R. Naismith] 'A New *Agnus Dei/Last Small Cross* Mule', *ASE* 44 (2016 for 2015), 307–8

Book Reviews

1975

H. P. R. Finberg, ed., *Scandinavian England: Collected Papers by F. T. Wainwright* (Chichester, 1975), in *Antiquity* 49 (1975), 319–20

P. Clemoes et al., eds., *ASE* 3 (1974), in *JEH* 26 (1975), 397–8

1976

H. Pálsson, ed. and trans., *The Confederates and Hen-Thorir: Two Icelandic Sagas* (Edinburgh, 1975), in *TLS*, 16 (April 1976), 464

P. Clemoes et al., ed., *ASE* 4 (1975), in *JEH* 27 (1976), 188–9

1977

D. Parsons, ed., *Tenth-Century Studies: Essays in Commemoration of the Millennium of the Council of Winchester and 'Regularis Concordia'* (Chichester, 1975), in *JEH* 28 (1977), 407–8

1978

W. J. P. Boyd, ed., *Aldred's Marginalia: Explanatory Comments in the Lindisfarne Gospels* (Exeter, 1975), in *JEH* 29 (1978), 241–2

1980

P. H. Sawyer, ed., *Charters of Burton Abbey*, AS Charters 2 (London, 1979), in *JEH* 31 (1980), 213–17

H. M. Taylor, *Anglo-Saxon Architecture III* (Cambridge, 1978), in *JEH* 31 (1980), 347–8

1982

J. Campbell, P. Wormald and E. John, *The Anglo-Saxons* (Oxford, 1982), in *TLS* 5 (November 1982), 1229

1983

D. Hill, *An Atlas of Anglo-Saxon England 700–1066* (Oxford, 1982), in *Antiquity* 57 (1983), 66–7

H. A. MacDougall, *Racial Myth in English History: Trojans, Teutons and Anglo-Saxons* (New York, 1982), in *TLS* 25 (March 1983), 16

D. Whitelock, *From Bede to Alfred: Studies in Early Anglo-Saxon Literature and History* (London, 1980), and *History, Law and Literature in 10th–11th Century England* (London, 1981), in *JEH* 34 (1983), 455–7

P. Wormald, ed., *Ideal and Reality in Frankish and Anglo-Saxon Society: Studies Presented to J. M. Wallace-Hadrill* (Oxford, 1983), in *EHR* 100 (1985), 826–8

1986

H. R. Loyn, *The Governance of Anglo-Saxon England 500–1087* (London, 1984), in *EHR* 101 (1986), 967–8

M. M. Archibald and C. E. Blunt, *British Museum: Anglo-Saxon Coins, Part 5. Athelstan to the Reform of Edgar, 924–c. 973*, SCBI 34 (London, 1986), in *AntJ* 66 (1986), 451–2

1987

P. Stafford, *The East Midlands in the Early Middle Ages* (Leicester, 1985), in *History & Archaeology Review* 2 (1987), 85–6

A. J. Frantzen, *King Alfred* (Boston, MA, 1986), and M. J. Whittock, *The Origins of England 410–600* (London, 1986), in *History Today* 37 (July 1987), 60–1

1988

J. Campbell, *Essays in Anglo-Saxon History* (London, 1986), in *JEH* 39 (1988), 296–7

1989

J. C. Holt, *Domesday Studies: Papers Read at the Novocentenary Conference of the Royal Historical Society and the Institute of British Geographers, Winchester, 1986* (Woodbridge, 1987), in *The Cambridge Review* 110 (1989), 36–7

R. P. Abels, *Lordship and Military Obligation in Anglo-Saxon England* (Berkeley and Los Angeles, CA, 1988), in *Albion* 21 (1989), 477–9

1991

D. Dales, *Dunstan: Saint and Statesman* (Cambridge, 1988), and B. Yorke, ed., *Bishop Æthelwold: His Career and Influence* (Woodbridge, 1988), in *EHR* 106 (1991), 970–2

1993

P. Stafford, *Unification and Conquest: A Political and Social History of England in the Tenth and Eleventh Centuries* (London, 1989), in *EHR* 108 (1993), 165–6

1994

P. A. Clarke, *The English Nobility under Edward the Confessor* (Oxford, 1994), in *TLS* 26 (August 1994), 24

1997

R. R. Darlington and P. McGurk, eds., *The Chronicle of John of Worcester,* vol. II: *The Annals from 450 to 1066* (Oxford, 1995), in *Speculum* 72 (1997), 177–9

1998

T. Berga, *Latvian Collections: Anglo-Saxon and Later British Coins*, SCBI 45 (Oxford, 1996), in *EME* 7 (1998), 126–7

2002

R. Fletcher, *Bloodfeud: Murder and Revenge in Anglo-Saxon England* (London, 2002), in *The Spectator* 2 (March 2002), 35

A. G. Rigg, *A Book of British Kings 1200 BC–1399 AD* (Toronto, 2000), in *N&Q* 247 (September 2002), 391–2

Other Publications

1985

'The Conception and Unification of Britain', *Times Higher Education Supplement* 22 (February 1985), 15

1987

'A Cambridge Hoax: The Post-Impressionist Exhibition of 1913', *Cambridge Review* 108 (1987), 116–24

1990

'Changing Faces: Offa, King of Mercia', *History Today* 40 (November 1990), 14–19

1992

'Replicas of the Alfred Jewel', *Museums Journal* (May 1992), 40–2

1995

'Note on the Re-Issue of the Second Edition' and 'Select Bibliography', in *An Introduction to Anglo-Saxon England*, ed. P. Hunter Blair, 2nd edn. (Cambridge, 1977; reissued 1995), pp. x and 364–70

'It Is Authentic' [short contribution to a debate on the authenticity of Asser's *Life of King Alfred*], *Times Higher Education Supplement* 8 (December 1995), 17

1999

'Apocalypse Then (AD 1000)', *Church Times* 29 (October 1999), 12–13

'Anglo-Saxon Charters', *British Academy Review July 1998–July 1999* (1999), 22–4

2000

'The Cult of King Alfred the Great', *Worcester College Record* (2000), 39–51

2001

'The Cartulary of Athelney Abbey Rediscovered', *Monastic Research Bulletin* 7 (2001), 2–5

2002

'Queen's Gambits', *BBC History Magazine* (December 2002), 18–20

2004

'The Illustrated Quentin Keynes', in *Quentin Keynes 1921–2003: Explorer, Film-Maker, Lecturer, and Book-Collector*, ed. S. Keynes (Cambridge, 2004), pp. 61–238

2008

'Lighting up the Dark Ages', *Folio Magazine* (Winter/Spring 2008), 3–8

2012

'Mark Blackburn (1953–2011) and the Sylloge of Coins of the British Isles', *British Academy Review* 19 (January 2012), 26–8

2016

'Æthelred the Unready', *History Today* 66 (May 2016), 38–45

Unpublished Dissertations

1976

'Studies on Anglo-Saxon Royal Diplomas', 2 vols., Fellowship dissertation for Trinity College, Cambridge (1976)

1977

'The Diplomas of King Æthelred II (978–1016)', Ph.D. dissertation, University of Cambridge (1977)

CHAPTER I

Introduction

Rory Naismith and David A. Woodman

Writing, Kingship and Power

Kings engaged with writing of one sort or another from the very earliest stages of recorded Anglo-Saxon history. Bede, in his *Historia ecclesiastica gentis Anglorum*, famously told of how Æthelberht I, king of Kent (d. 616/17), 'established with the advice of his counsellors a code of laws after the Roman manner . . . these are written in English and are still kept and observed by the people.'[1] Letters were also addressed to Æthelberht by Pope Gregory I and to Edwin of Northumbria (616–33) by Pope Boniface V and Pope Honorius I,[2] while Æthelberht's son, Eadbald (616/17–40), issued the first known coins inscribed with the name of an English king,[3] and later in the seventh century the earliest charters were produced in the names of Anglo-Saxon kings.[4] What seems to have been the first literary text directly addressed to a king was the *Epistola ad Acircium*, a sprawling assortment of grammatical and related texts put together by Aldhelm of Malmesbury (d. 709/10) for his old friend 'who rules over the northern lands': Aldfrith, king of the Northumbrians (685–704).[5] Bede's *Historia* was also of course dedicated to a king of the Northumbrians (Ceolwulf (729–37)) and had much more to say on kings and kingship than Aldhelm's learned treatise. But it was to be some

---

[1] 'Decreta illi iudiciorum iuxta exempla Romanorum cum consilio sapientium constituit; quae conscripta Anglorum sermone hactenus habentur et obseruantur ab ea': Bede, *Historia ecclesiastica* [hereafter *HE*] ii. 5, in *Bede's Ecclesiastical History of the English People*, ed. B. Colgrave and R. A. B. Mynors (Oxford, 1969), pp. 150–1.

[2] Bede, *HE* i. 32, ii. 10 and 17 (ed. Colgrave and Mynors, pp. 110–15, 166–71 and 194–7).

[3] M. Blackburn, 'Two New Types of Anglo-Saxon Gold Shillings', in *Coinage and History in the North Sea World, c. AD 500–1250: Essays in Honour of Marion Archibald*, ed. B. Cook and G. Williams (Leiden, 2006), pp. 127–40, at 127–35.

[4] S 7–8 (*CantStA* 6, *CantCC* 2). For context, see P. Wormald, 'Bede and the Conversion of England: The Charter Evidence', in his *The Times of Bede: Studies* in *Early English Christian Society and Its Historian*, ed. S. Baxter (Oxford, 2006), pp. 135–66.

[5] 'Aquilonalis imperii sceptra gubernanti': Aldhelm, *Epistola ad Acircium*, in *Aldhelmi Opera*, ed. R. Ehwald, MGH Auct. antiq. 15 (Berlin, 1919), p. 61. On the relationship between Aldfrith and Aldhelm, see M. Lapidge, 'The Career of Aldhelm', *ASE* 36 (2007), 15–69, at 22–6.

time before texts at least ostensibly produced by a king appeared in Anglo-Saxon England. Alfred the Great (871–99) certainly played a major part in a series of Old English adaptations of Latin texts, though the nature and extent of his involvement remain contentious.[6] And even if writings by kings were to remain exceptional, England in the tenth and eleventh centuries saw the bond between writing and power go from strength to strength.

All of this is to say that writing and kingship enjoyed a long and successful partnership in Anglo-Saxon England. There were many ways in which writing, kingship and power came together, leading to just as many ways in which one might write about kingship and power. This parallel is not solely a modern contrivance, and neither of course is it one restricted to Anglo-Saxon England.[7] Kings themselves could use the written word for their own ends; equally, others could employ writing to interact with kings or think about various kinds of authority. The results of these two processes can be difficult to distinguish, and that was often the point: expressing and invoking authority could look much the same in practice. Adopting the position of the king, or even the voice of the king, could lend strength to a document or historical narrative,[8] especially if written by an agency with close ties to the throne – or by one that sought to cultivate such ties.[9] This fluid use of writing is the central process which the contributors to this volume seek to examine from various angles. One way was simply by association. Written invocation of the king's name and his implied seal of approval carried weight, not least in the case of the Alfredian translations, which were, of course, the work of long-dead Latin authors, albeit carefully mediated. Yet even attachment of the name of a king or

---

[6] Malcolm Godden has challenged the authorship of Alfred the Great: see (*inter alia*) 'Did King Alfred Write Anything?', *MÆ* 76 (2007), 1–23. For the counter-argument, see D. Pratt, *The Political Thought of King Alfred the Great* (Cambridge, 2007); and D. Pratt, 'Problems of Authorship and Audience in the Writings of King Alfred the Great', in *Lay Intellectuals in the Carolingian World*, ed. P. Wormald and J. L. Nelson (Cambridge, 2007), pp. 162–91.

[7] Even sticking to the early Middle Ages, there is a great deal of literature (especially from the 1980s onwards) on the theme of writing and power elsewhere in Europe. For just a small selection of important scholarship, see P. H. Sawyer and I. N. Wood (eds.), *Early Medieval Kingship* (Leeds, 1977); R. McKitterick, *The Carolingians and the Written Word* (Cambridge, 1989); N. Everett, *Literacy in Lombard Italy, c. 568–774* (Cambridge, 2003); P. E. Schramm and F. Mütterich, *Denkmale der deutschen Könige und Kaiser*, 2 vols. (Munich, 1962–78); N. Staubach, *Rex christianus: Hofkultur und Herrschaftspropaganda im Reich Karls des Kahlen* (Cologne, 1993); and H. Hoffmann, *Buchkunst und Königtum im ottonischen und frühsalischen Reich*, 2 vols. (Stuttgart, 1986).

[8] L. Roach, 'Penitential Discourse in the Diplomas of King Æthelred "the Unready"', *JEH* 64 (2013), 258–76; and S. Keynes, 'Church Councils, Royal Assemblies, and Anglo-Saxon Royal Diplomas', in *Kingship, Legislation and Power in Anglo-Saxon England*, ed. G. R. Owen-Crocker and B. W. Schneider (Woodbridge, 2013), pp. 1–182, on conditions of charter production.

[9] For a recent case-study, see D. Pratt, 'The Voice of the King in "King Edgar's Establishment of Monasteries"', *ASE* 41 (2012), 145–204.

other powerful figure to a text begs the question of why the author turned to those individuals and how the endorsement might have been constitutive as well as reflective of power. This is just one of many questions raised by the central issue of the written word's relationship to power. How could it be harnessed to exert and conceptualise power in Anglo-Saxon England? What strengths did different forms of writing have, and in which contexts would they be employed? A charter did not do the same job as a chronicle, and a church dedication inscription did not do the same job as a praise poem. What did writers in all these contexts stand to gain from engaging with royal authority in particular? And how did that authority interface with divine power or the roles of the Church, bishops and other powerful laypeople?

Answers to some of these questions can be found in the chapters making up this volume, but it is first worth digging a little deeper on the nature of the sources at our disposal. The historian is of necessity bound to study what survives, and especially what survives in written form. Much therefore depends on how representative that surviving sample might be. Churches played a central role in both making and preserving documents and codices. Nothing beyond brief runic inscriptions survives from before Christianisation in the seventh century, and whatever still exists from then onwards had to pass through many filters in order to enter an ecclesiastical library or archive and survive to modern times. Naturally, materials produced by or relating to the Church loom large, and appropriately so, for bishops, monasteries and the rest of the ecclesiastical infrastructure were a major force in society and closely involved (sometimes to the point of blurring boundaries) with kings and secular authority.[10] But one always has to be on guard against the possibility that what the surviving record presents is shaped by its ecclesiastical context of production and preservation. It is only by good fortune, for instance, that the famous Fonthill Letter – crucial for knowledge of how local society might interface with royal authority in the decades around 900 – survives, bearing on its dorse the word *inutile* ('useless').[11] One must be wary in reading these texts too. Early medieval writers were informed by a rich literary and intellectual tradition, laden with symbolism. With regard to 'rituals', for example, it can and has been argued in recent scholarship that any coronation, council, speech, display of loyalty or other act might be manipulated in the telling

---

[10] This issue, with reference to charters, is explored in F. M. Stenton, *The Latin Charters of the Anglo-Saxon Period* (Oxford, 1955). For wider relations between the Church and the rest of society, see now H. Foxhall Forbes, *Heaven and Earth in Anglo-Saxon England: Theology and Society in an Age of Faith* (Farnham, 2013).

[11] S 1445 (*CantCC* 104).

to make a political point or as a literary nod to similar gestures in earlier literature. However, clerics clearly expected audiences to understand and react to comments on rituals, implying their prevalence and importance, while kings and other laypeople were as saturated in the same Christian culture as their friends, neighbours and brothers in the Church – so much so that their own acts might well have been very symbolically conscious too.[12] This is too large an area to discuss in any detail; all that need be stressed here is that extant sources reflect a symbiotic relationship between writing and power. The written record is our primary source for establishing what power consisted of; influence over that record, therefore, was a core component of power.

But writing arguably stops short of actually being power: it was reactions to writing that mattered. 'Power' is a loose concept, used here as shorthand for the capacity to exert one's will over others, whether directly or through the agency of others.[13] It was the ability to get things done. There are further dimensions which muddy the waters, however. Those who occupy a position of power are paradoxically not always able to act as they desire because of the expectations of those over whom they exert 'power', not least when that position took the form of an institution with a ready-made bundle of responsibilities, such as kingship. The responsibilities of kingship constrained individual holders of the position at the same time as it empowered them. King Heremod in *Beowulf* fell from his position when he stopped distributing gifts to win the support of his men, for example.[14] The message the poet apparently sought to convey with this parable was that when the king stopped behaving like a king, he stopped being a king. Power was a two-way process, created and maintained by people buying into it, existing in the imagination of ruled and ruler alike. It was fed by reactions as well as actions, and therein lies the disconnect between writing

[12] Very different views are taken of the interpretation of these acts by P. Buc, *The Dangers of Ritual: Between Early Medieval Texts and Social Scientific Theory* (Princeton, NJ, 2001); G. Althoff, *Family, Friends and Followers: Political and Social Bonds in Medieval Europe*, trans. C. Carroll (Cambridge, 2004); G. Koziol, *Begging Pardon and Favor: Ritual and Political Order in Early Medieval France* (Ithaca, NY, 1992); G. Koziol, *The Politics of Memory and Identity in Carolingian Royal Diplomas: The West Frankish Kingdom (840–987)* (Turnhout, 2012); also, for Anglo-Saxon context, see J. Barrow, 'Demonstrative Behaviour and Political Communication in Later Anglo-Saxon England', *ASE* 36 (2007), 127–50; L. Roach, *Kingship and Consent in Anglo-Saxon England, 871–978* (Cambridge, 2013), esp. pp. 161–211; and C. Insley, 'Charters, Ritual and Late Tenth-Century English Kingship', in *Gender and Historiography: Studies in the Earlier Middle Ages in Honour of Pauline Stafford*, ed. J. L. Nelson, S. Reynolds and S. M. Johns (London, 2012), pp. 75–89.
[13] This interpretation stems ultimately from M. Weber, *Economy and Society: An Outline of Interpretive Sociology*, trans. E. Fischoff, 2 vols. (Berkeley, CA, 1978–9).
[14] *Beowulf* 1709–22a, in *Klaeber's Beowulf and The Fight at Finnsburg*, ed. R. D. Fulk, R. E. Bjork and J. D. Niles (Toronto, 2008), p. 58.

and power. How could writing create or benefit from power in a world of highly restricted literacy?

It is an axiom of scholarship that literacy was very limited in the early Middle Ages.[15] Reading and especially writing were largely the preserve of the clergy, at least in England. These skills were not in themselves essential for appreciating the value of written documents, and in Anglo-Saxon England, widespread use of the vernacular made the written word still more accessible.[16] Nevertheless, there are precious few documents or literary texts likely to be the work of laypeople. Most examples relate to the highest elite. Alfred the Great was mentioned earlier, and one might add to the list two ealdormen: Ordlaf and Æthelweard, who are presented as authors of the Fonthill Letter and of a Latin chronicle, respectively.[17] There are also very many texts that openly proclaim royal patronage or a royal audience, among them the letters written to the recently converted Christian kings of the seventh century. The contents of these elegant Latin missives must have been mediated to Æthelberht and Edwin through translation. Writing, in short, generated discussion.

This aspect of the written word – the text beyond the text – was probably far more important than can be divined from the surviving written record alone. It is not unreasonable to suppose that most texts read or translated for the benefit of the king would be heard and discussed by some portion of his counsellors; similarly, directives emanating from the king would commonly be read aloud to gatherings of worthies and were not necessarily

---

[15] M. T. Clanchy, *From Memory to Written Record: England, 1066–1307*, 3rd edn (Chichester, 2013); and R. McKitterick (ed.), *The Uses of Literacy in Early Mediaeval Europe* (Cambridge, 1990).

[16] In addition to the works just cited, see also K. A. Lowe, 'Lay Literacy in Anglo-Saxon England and the Development of the Chirograph', in *Anglo-Saxon Manuscripts and Their Heritage*, ed. P. Pulsiano and E. Treharne (Aldershot, 1998), pp. 161–204. On English and Latin, see Chapter 14 in this volume.

[17] For Ordlaf and the Fonthill Letter (for which see further below), see S. D. Keynes, 'The Fonthill Letter', in *Words, Texts and Manuscripts: Studies in Anglo-Saxon Culture Presented to Helmut Gneuss on the Occasion of His Sixty-Fifth Birthday*, ed. M. Korhammer (Cambridge, 1992), pp. 53–97, at 55; also M. Boynton and S. Reynolds, 'The Author of the Fonthill Letter', *ASE* 25 (1997), 91–5; and N. P. Brooks, 'The Fonthill Letter, Ealdorman Ordlaf and Anglo-Saxon Law in Practice', in *Early Medieval Studies in Memory of Patrick Wormald*, ed. S. Baxter, C. E. Karkov, J. L. Nelson and D. A. E. Pelteret (Aldershot, 2009), pp. 301–18. For Æthelweard, see the edition of his *Chronicon* in, *The Chronicle of Æthelweard*, ed. A. Campbell (London, 1962); and also M. Gretsch, 'Historiography and Literary Patronage in Late Anglo-Saxon England: The Evidence of Æthelweard's Chronicon', *ASE* 41 (2012), 205–48. For royal patronage of books and writing, see (*inter alia*) D. Pratt, 'Kings and Books in Anglo-Saxon England', *ASE* 43 (2014), 297–377; and S. Keynes, 'King Athelstan's Books', in *Learning and Literature in Anglo-Saxon England*, ed. M. Lapidge and H. Gneuss (Cambridge, 1985), pp. 143–201.

accepted uncritically.[18] Writing, talk and action all informed one another. From meetings of the powerful it is very likely that knowledge of texts' contents would percolate out into the wider consciousness, perhaps spiced with gossip and speculation that accumulated in the telling.[19] Yet it remains true that the immediate, intended audience of many written texts was small and specific, dictated by the circumstances under which they were produced. Quality mattered much more than quantity: getting through to the king, bishop or ealdorman must often have mattered much more than the number of also-rans (or indeed later scholars) who might read or hear of the text. Just a tiny number of copies could have been made of some of the most fascinating early medieval texts such as Asser's *Life* of Alfred, the *Encomium Emmae reginae*, and most letters.

Writing, in other words, was a powerful tool when used in connection with kingship but could function in many different ways. Some of the most elaborate and ambitious texts were razor sharp in their nuance and highly targeted in their intended readership. Inscriptions on coins, conversely, boiled down the essentials of royal status into a brief, epigraphic form, rarely extending to more than the name and title of the king. Yet coin inscriptions were combined with visual and material invocations of power and probably had wider reach than any other written manifestation of royal authority. If extended texts were the rapier, coin inscriptions were the mace. Students, colleagues and friends of Simon Keynes will remember the trinity proclaimed by him in numerous lectures: that charters, law-codes and coins are central to an understanding of government and institutions in Anglo-Saxon England and can add much to the narratives presented by chronicles and histories. It is in this spirit that the contributions to this volume have been assembled, to showcase and explore the different media and techniques of writing with which Anglo-Saxons conceived kingship and power. They have been broken down into three loose sections. The first, 'The Formation of Power: The Early Anglo-Saxon Kingdoms', includes chapters that examine the pre-viking period of Anglo-Saxon history. It is a powerful reflection of the richness of early Northumbrian

---

[18] S. D. Keynes, 'Royal Government and the Written Word in Late Anglo-Saxon England', in *Uses of Literacy*, ed. McKitterick, pp. 226–57; D. Pratt, 'Written Law and the Communication of Authority in Tenth-Century England', in *England and the Continent in the Tenth Century*, ed. C. Leyser, D. W. Rollason and H. Williams (Turnhout, 2010), pp. 331–50; and L. Roach, 'Law Codes and Legal Norms in Later Anglo-Saxon England', *Historical Research* 86 (2013), 465–86.

[19] See, for select comparative perspectives, C. Wickham, 'Gossip and Resistance among the Medieval Peasantry', *Past & Present* 160 (1998), 3–24; T. Fenster and D. L. Smail (eds.), *Fama: The Politics of Talk & Reputation in Medieval Europe* (Ithaca, 2003); and C. West, 'Visions in a Ninth-Century Village: An Early Medieval Microhistory', *History Workshop Journal* 81 (2016), 1–16.

sources that two of the four contributions in this section focus on the northern kingdom: Sarah Foot addresses 'Bede's Kings', while David Woodman considers 'Hagiography and Charters in Early Northumbria'. In doing so, they call attention to the strengths and weaknesses of Northumbrian material, which is exceptionally strong in historical and hagiographical texts but more limited in its representation of charters and other administrative documents. The third chapter in this section, 'Origins of the Kingdom of the English', by David Dumville, takes a *longue durée* approach to the establishment of the components of royal government in England. Zooming in for a particular case-study, Jinty Nelson ('Losing the Plot? "Filthy Assertion" and "Unheard-of Deceit" in Codex Carolinus 92') considers a cluster of letters that illuminate the complex links between England, Francia and Rome in the late eighth century.

The second and third sections of this book both concern tenth- and eleventh-century England, a period that is overall richer and more balanced in its range of source material. Yet important challenges remain in deciding how to interpret and combine these texts and the best framework into which they should be set. For this reason, they are divided into a section on 'Authority and Its Articulation in Late Anglo-Saxon England', which consists of chapters on the political and institutional dimensions of kingship, power and writing in later Anglo-Saxon England, and a section on 'Books, Texts and Power', which assembles contributions approaching the theme from a more linguistic or literary point of view, often with specific reference to surviving manuscripts. Division into these sections should not be taken to suggest that there are no connections between their contents; on the contrary, the two depend closely on each other, with numerous parallels in methodology and subject matter. The second section contains five chapters. Pauline Stafford's 'Fathers and Daughters: The Case of Æthelred II' presents a case-study of female power and its exercise at the highest levels during the reign of Æthelred II (978–1016). Rory Naismith, in 'The Historian and Anglo-Saxon Coinage: The Case of Late Anglo-Saxon England', considers how the celebrated monetary system of the later tenth and eleventh centuries should be understood as part of an evolving governmental and political scene, while David Pratt looks at some of the other mechanics related to this, specifically those of the precocious *geld* taxation system, in 'Charters and Exemption from Geld in Anglo-Saxon England'. Katy Cubitt, in 'On Living in the Time of Tribulation: Archbishop Wulfstan's *Sermo Lupi ad Anglos* and Its Eschatological Context', examines Wulfstan's *Sermo Lupi* within the broader context of his apocalyptic writings, while Levi Roach, in 'A Tale of Two Charters:

Diploma Production and Political Performance in Æthelredian England',
focuses on charters from the reign of Æthelred II as snapshots of key
turning points in his reign.

The third and final group of chapters approaches the writing of kingship
and power from a slightly different perspective, driven by literary and
manuscript considerations. Helen Foxhall Forbes and Julia Crick move
the discussion to how religion intersected with society, specifically in the
forms (respectively) of a re-evaluation of judicial ordeals in late Anglo-
Saxon England ('Making Manifest God's Judgement: Interpreting Ordeals
in Late Anglo-Saxon England') and an analysis of an unusual prayerbook
showing signs of female use ('An Eleventh-Century PrayerBook for
Women? The Origins and History of the Galba PrayerBook'). Finally,
Francesca Tinti brings in the well-known linguistic dynamic of writing and
authority in Anglo-Saxon England in a study of the numerous bilingual
(Latin and Old English) leases from Worcester ('Writing Latin and Old
English in Tenth-Century England: Patterns, Formulae and Language
Choice in the Leases of Oswald of Worcester').

As a group, these chapters touch on a broad range of topics. Recurring
themes include the multi-faceted roles of charters and the centrality of the
reign of Æthelred II as a time when crisis drove experimentation. Related
to both topics is the influence of the Church and religious devotion in
power relations, creating an arena in which earthly and heavenly authority
could interact in complex fashion. All combine to present a well-rounded
and innovative view of how power (especially royal power) and writing
intermeshed in England; in addition, all reflect very well the incisive and
diverse scholarship of Simon Keynes and the profound impact he has had
on the contributors to this volume and on the field as a whole. It is to
Simon and his particular contribution to the field that we now turn.

Simon Keynes and Anglo-Saxon Charter Scholarship

In the Preface to his groundbreaking 1980 book,[20] Simon Keynes discussed
the importance of the new edition – begun under the joint auspices of the
British Academy and the Royal Historical Society – of every single surviving Anglo-Saxon charter. At that stage, only two such volumes had
appeared in print, one by Professor A. Campbell and the other by

---

[20] S. Keynes, *The Diplomas of King Æthelred 'the Unready': A Study in Their Use as Historical Evidence* (Cambridge, 1980).

Professor P. H. Sawyer.[21] Even if the first of these volumes did not quite do justice to the material,[22] they nevertheless collectively demonstrated the 'intrinsic interest' of the enterprise and the possibilities offered in the study of Anglo-Saxon charters.[23] Of all scholars, Keynes understood the necessity of studying Anglo-Saxon charters first and foremost in the context of the archive in which they had been preserved. It was only against this background that the authenticity of these documents, so often hotly debated, could be properly gauged. If the idiosyncrasies of a particular archive as a whole were known, one could begin to build a picture of the likelihood of any individual document being genuine. So while one might be naturally suspicious of charters surviving at Malmesbury,[24] one could be more accepting of the few northern charters preserved in York Minster.[25]

The questions that demand to be asked of any one archive are numerous and complicated. For an archive to be properly understood, an editor has to be intimately acquainted with the relevant manuscripts. If confronted by a cartulary, an editor has to form an opinion of the copying practices of the scribe(s) in question. Were the texts of Anglo-Saxon charters faithfully preserved, or were elements changed during the copying process? Can the tenurial patterns shown in Domesday Book help in an assessment of the shape an archive might be expected to take? In some cases, as with the Abingdon or Malmesbury archives, the charters themselves are inextricably linked (and literally incorporated) with narrative material, making their assessment all the more difficult.[26] In fact, every archive offers its own issues of interpretation. Nothing can be taken for granted, and it is only after gaining familiarity with the material that one can begin to form opinions about the individual documents. With the archival context in mind, an editor can then start to criticise each charter on its own merits, comparing it with charters of similar date, to see what details of diplomatic or history it preserves and how it can be used in

---

[21] *Charters of Rochester*, ed. A. Campbell, AS Charters I (London, 1973), and *Charters of Burton Abbey*, ed. P. H. Sawyer, AS Charters II (Oxford, 1979). Once finished, there will be some forty volumes in the series. For Keynes' own role at the forefront of this project, making sure that it has remained funded and viable, see further below.

[22] N. P. Brooks, 'Review of *Charters of Rochester*', *EHR* 90 (1975), 626–7.

[23] The phrase is borrowed from Keynes, *Diplomas*, p. xiii.

[24] See *Charters of Malmesbury Abbey*, ed. S. E. Kelly, AS Charters XI (Oxford, 2005), pp. 51–64, with discussion of the group known as the 'Decimation' charters at 65–91.

[25] *Charters of Northern Houses*, ed. D. A. Woodman, AS Charters 16 (Oxford, 2012), pp. 9–18.

[26] *Charters of Abingdon Abbey*, Part I, ed. S. E. Kelly, AS Charters VII (Oxford, 2000); with *Historia Ecclesie Abbendonensis; The History of the Church of Abingdon*, vol. I, ed. J. Hudson (Oxford, 2007); and Kelly, *Charters of Malmesbury*.

conjunction with a wider array of sources. Such judgements are of a palaeographical, linguistic, historical and diplomatic kind.

Given the very large amount of endeavour and wide array of skills needed to master such material, it may have seemed premature in 1980, with only two British Academy editions published, for Keynes to embark on a study of diplomas outside of their archival context for the reign of a particular king (and looking back to the reigns of previous Anglo-Saxon kings). Keynes himself recognised this problem, saying, 'It may seem a rash venture to produce a study of Anglo-Saxon royal diplomas at the outset of the new edition, when the texts collectively are still in the process of being securely established and properly criticized for the first time.'[27] But what followed was a book that truly opened up new ways for charters to be appreciated and exploited by Anglo-Saxonists. As recently as 1970, Professor F. Barlow, in writing his biography of Edward the Confessor, had expressed his disquiet in trusting the 'scrappy and recalcitrant ... governmental records' surviving from the Confessor's reign. His disquiet rested on two counts: that such documents were drawn up by the beneficiaries of the grants and that they were therefore second-hand accounts of royal action, divorced from the realities of court life.[28] These were very serious methodological problems.[29] Students and scholars of Anglo-Saxon kingship were left unsure of the exact status of the Anglo-Saxon charter. Ostensibly records issued by kings, they were being considered as accounts that did not originate at the centre of royal government but rather as summaries written by those who often had vested interests in the transactions described. The problem was compounded by the nature of the survival of charters, the vast majority of which are preserved only as later copies in cartularies and always in the archives of a religious house. This meant that in combination with some of the clearly religious elements of the documents themselves (especially the proem and sanction), charters had a distinctly ecclesiastical aspect, taking them further and further away from the royal court in which they purported to belong.

---

[27] Keynes, *Diplomas*, p. xiii.   [28] F. Barlow, *Edward the Confessor* (London, 1970), pp. xxi–xxii.
[29] In making these points, Barlow cites especially the work of P. Chaplais, who wrote a series of important articles concerning the production of Anglo-Saxon charters: P. Chaplais, 'The Origin and Authenticity of the Royal Anglo-Saxon Diploma', *Journal of the Society of Archivists* iii(2) (1965), 48–61; and P. Chaplais, 'The Anglo-Saxon Chancery: From the Diploma to the Writ', *Journal of the Society of Archivists* iii(4) (1966), 160–76, both reprinted in *Prisca Munimenta: Studies in Archival and Administrative History Presented to Dr A. E. J. Hollaender*, ed. F. Ranger (London, 1973).

Keynes tackled these issues head-on. Drawing on the work of earlier scholars,[30] he demonstrated in various ways how charters at least of the tenth century onwards could be shown, on numerous occasions, to be the products of some kind of centralised agency under the control of the king, invested with the authority to draw up documents in his name and on his behalf. This involved detailed analysis of the diplomatic of Anglo-Saxon charters, critically compared across all ecclesiastical archives. If a charter of, say, the 910s, preserved in the Barking archive, was possessed of a rather unusual diplomatic element that could be found in a charter of similar date but in, perhaps, the Abingdon archive, then one could begin to have greater faith in its genuineness. Such judgements will always involve a degree of subjectivity, and scholars remain divided on such issues. Given that the British Academy editions had only begun to appear when he was writing, it was all the more important that Keynes was already demonstrating such diplomatic connections between archives. It was also his examination of a most difficult kind of evidence that helped to unravel the true nature of the charters concerned. In his handling of the witness-lists of these documents, Keynes brought to life the realities of court politics, what it meant to be attendant on an Anglo-Saxon king and a member of the king's witan. The year 956, with its uniquely large number of diplomas issued in the name of King Eadwig, brought a special opportunity here for comparison. By dividing these diplomas into four groups, linked above all by their similar witness-lists and further by their diplomatic, Keynes showed how these diplomas really were true records of meetings of the king and his councillors at particular moments throughout the year.[31] Because they were preserved in archives across the country, there could be no other explanation for their detailed and minute similarities. Keynes' work on diplomatic analysis and the composition of witness-lists meant that scholars could now have renewed faith that Anglo-Saxon diplomas of a certain date and type could be taken as documents issued at the centre of Anglo-Saxon royal government.[32] They could thus be utilised for all of the

---

[30] W. H. Stevenson, 'An Old English Charter of William the Conqueror in Favour of St Martin's-Le-Grand, London, A.D. 1068', *EHR* 11 (1896), 731–44; H. W. C. Davis, *Regesta Regum Anglo-Normannorum I* (Oxford, 1913); and R. Drögereit, 'Gab es eine Angelsächsische Königskanzlei?', *Archiv für Urkundenforschung* 13 (1935), 335–436.

[31] Keynes, *Diplomas*, pp. 48–69.

[32] The techniques involved in his analysis of witness-lists resulted in the later publication of S. Keynes, *An Atlas of Attestations in Anglo-Saxon Charters, c. 670–1066*, Department of Anglo-Saxon, Norse and Celtic, University of Cambridge (2002), where the potential of witness-lists can be fully realised. And for recent analysis, see Roach, *Kingship and Consent*.

details they contain about the workings of Anglo-Saxon kingship and the implementation of royal power, the dual themes of this book.

At the core of Keynes' work lay a deep familiarity with each archive of charters. That this was achieved before the advent of a more plentiful supply of the British Academy editions is remarkable.[33] In 1981, Keynes became a member of the British Academy's Joint Committee on Anglo-Saxon Charters, entrusted with oversight of the major research project designed to overcome the famous lament in 1895 of W. H. Stevenson that 'it cannot be said that the Old English charters have yet been edited.'[34] In 1982–3 Keynes became honorary secretary to the committee, and in conjunction with various committee members and chairmen, he has consistently worked to ensure that the project could be completed. The so-called Kemble website, managed by Keynes and hosted on a server at Trinity College, Cambridge, acts as a kind of portal to all things relating to Anglo-Saxon charters and the Anglo-Saxon charters project.[35] To date, nineteen volumes have been produced for the series, and one of Keynes' former PhD students, Dr S. E. Kelly, is responsible for an extraordinary twelve of these in her own right. She has co-edited a further two volumes in conjunction with the late Professor N. P. Brooks,[36] who likewise did so much for Anglo-Saxon charter scholarship and who was chairman of the Anglo-Saxon charters committee from 1991 until 2013.[37] Throughout Keynes' academic career and since the publication of his 1980 book, charters have remained at the forefront of his work and thought. While certain groups of diplomas can be thought of as products of some kind of centralised agency, Keynes has shown that the system was flexible and open to other forms of production away from the diplomatic mainstream, and the wider implications for Anglo-Saxon kingship have

---

[33] At the beginning of his 1978 PhD thesis, Keynes explains the importance of analysing each archive individually: S. D. Keynes, 'The Diplomas of King Æðelred II (978–1016)', Department of Anglo-Saxon, Norse and Celtic, University of Cambridge.

[34] *The Crawford Collection of Early Charters and Documents*, ed. A. S. Napier and W. H. Stevenson (Oxford, 1895), p. viii.

[35] See www.kemble.asnc.cam.ac.uk. On this website can be found very useful summaries of the contents and character of each ecclesiastical archive containing Anglo-Saxon charters, together with a section giving details of the key characteristics of an Anglo-Saxon diploma, written by Keynes.

[36] N. P. Brooks and S. E. Kelly, *Charters of Christ Church Canterbury*, AS Charters 17–18 (Oxford, 2013).

[37] See, for example, Brooks' summary of the state of Anglo-Saxon charter scholarship: N. P. Brooks, 'Anglo-Saxon Charters: A Review of Work 1953–73; with a Postscript on the Period 1973–98', in *Anglo-Saxon Myths: State and Church 400–1066*, ed. N. P. Brooks (London and Rio Grande, 2000), pp. 181–215.

always been examined.[38] Such assessments have been vital for those working in the field.[39]

Charters of course constitute just one genre of source and only one way to access the world of Anglo-Saxon kingship and politics. In his publications, just as in his teaching, Keynes stresses the wider applications to which these documents can be put, the information they can yield about the nature of Anglo-Saxon government and the ways in which they have to be combined with the evidence of Anglo-Saxon coins,[40] material artefacts more broadly and the whole range of narrative and textual sources preserved from the pre-Conquest (and early Anglo-Norman) period. Here Keynes' approach is always one involving close reading, working outwards from the minute detail necessary to gain control of a particular source or artifact towards the wider conclusions that can be drawn about different issues. Any graduate student taught by Keynes will have heard his maxim, 'Be your own harshest critic', and this comes through clearly in his own work. While unafraid to challenge scholarly orthodoxy, this is never done simply for its own sake. Instead, the Anglo-Saxon historical record is allowed to speak on its own terms as Keynes draws out the significance of the material being assessed.

Keynes' examination of the famous Fonthill Letter is a case in point.[41] Here an Old English letter about the history of an estate at Fonthill is dissected in minute detail, each turn of phrase scrutinised and explicated.[42] But this is done with much wider issues in view as Keynes directs the reader

[38] This was clearly demonstrated, for example, in Keynes' treatment of the 'Dunstan B' charters produced while King Eadred was unwell: S. Keynes, 'The "Dunstan B" Charters', *ASE* 23 (2008), 165–93. For his most recent assessment of such matters, and for some exceptionally useful discussion of the relationship between charters and royal assemblies, see Keynes, 'Church Councils'. Needless to say, these are issues widely discussed by other scholars.

[39] In various published pieces, Keynes includes a categorisation of different diplomas into groups on the basis of their authenticity or type (for example, in his *Atlas of Attestations*, table no. XXVII, Keynes identifies all diplomas produced by 'Æthelstan A', while, for his work on Edgar, he has published 'A Conspectus of the Charters of King Edgar, 957–975', in *Edgar, King of the English, 959–975*, ed. D. Scragg (Woodbridge, 2008), pp. 60–80). There is a danger in taking such lists for granted, but in reality, they should be noted for the very difficult diplomatic judgements involved and for their ability to guide students of Anglo-Saxon charters through the minefield of documents confronting them.

[40] Keynes has constantly stressed the importance of Anglo-Saxon coins for the historian, as shown by one of his first published articles: S. Keynes, 'An Interpretation of the Pacx, Pax and Paxs Pennies', *ASE* 7 (1978), 165–73. See also Chapter 8 in this volume.

[41] Keynes, 'The Fonthill Letter'.

[42] For the most recent edition and further commentary, see Brooks and Kelly, *Charters of Canterbury*, pp. 852–62. For a similar treatment of Old English additions to the York Gospels, see S. Keynes, 'The Additions in Old English', in *The York Gospels: A Facsimile with Introductory Essays by Jonathan Alexander, Patrick McGurk, Simon Keynes and Bernard Barr*, ed. N. Barker (London, 1986), pp. 81–99.

to the importance of this document for what it can reveal about the operation of Anglo-Saxon law and the use of written documentation in that same process.[43] Needless to say, it is of fundamental importance for modern scholars to understand as best they can how Anglo-Saxon government functioned. In his analysis of charters, vernacular records and narrative texts, Keynes has been at the forefront of this drive for understanding.

Few themes in Anglo-Saxon historiography have been more discussed than the emergence in the late ninth century of a 'kingdom of the Anglo-Saxons', which became, in turn, the 'kingdom of the English' from the early tenth century onwards.[44] Scholars have been fascinated by the processes that drove this formation of an embryonic England, the mechanisms by which it was achieved and the extent to which it may be deemed a reality at any given moment in the Anglo-Saxon period and in different parts of the country.[45] Keynes' work on these grand historical themes has significantly helped in guiding modern historians. Sir Frank Stenton, in his seminal *Anglo-Saxon England*,[46] found the great Mercian kings, Æthelbald and Offa, to be statesman-like figures who themselves had grand visions for what could be achieved during their time on the throne. Keynes, in conjunction with the work of others,[47] offers a more balanced view which, while it acknowledges the power of the Mercian kings, also demonstrates the limits of their kingship and the realities of Mercia's interactions with other early Anglo-Saxon kingdoms, in particular, Kent.[48] This work – underpinned by close readings of charters and analysis of witness-lists – reflects the realities of eighth-century politics and the ruthless self-aggrandisement carried out in particular by Offa.[49] By the late ninth century, the stakes had never been higher.

---

[43] These are themes Keynes explores elsewhere, with a particularly useful discussion of the nature of Æthelstan's law-codes: Keynes, 'Royal Government'.

[44] See, for example, P. Stafford, *Unification and Conquest: A Political and Social History of England in the Tenth and Eleventh Centuries* (London and New York, 1989); and J. Campbell, *The Anglo-Saxon State* (London, 2000).

[45] G. Molyneaux, *The Formation of the English Kingdom in the Tenth Century* (Oxford, 2015); D. A. Woodman, 'Charters, Northumbria and the Unification of England in the Tenth and Eleventh Centuries', *NH* 52 (2015), 35–51, and Chapter 5 in this volume.

[46] F. M. Stenton, *Anglo-Saxon England*, 3rd edn (Oxford, 1971).

[47] See, for example, P. Wormald, 'The Age of Offa and Alcuin', in *The Anglo-Saxons*, ed. J. Campbell, E. John and P. Wormald (London, 1991), pp. 101–28; and M. P. Brown and C. A. Farr (eds.), *Mercia: An Anglo-Saxon Kingdom in Europe* (Leicester, 2001).

[48] S. Keynes, 'The Control of Kent in the Ninth Century', *EME* 2 (1993), 111–31. See also S. Keynes, 'The Reconstruction of a Burnt Cottonian Manuscript: The Case of Cotton MS Otho A I', *British Library Journal* 22 (1996), 113–60.

[49] See further R. Naismith, '"An Offa You Can't Refuse", Eighth-Century Mercian Titulature on Coins and in Charters', *Quæstio Insularis* 7 (2006), 71–100; and R. Naismith, *Money and Power in Anglo-Saxon England: The Southern English Kingdoms, 757–865* (Cambridge, 2012).

Threatened by continued viking attack and settlement, King Alfred looked beyond his West Saxon horizons and encouraged the formation of a more unified polity that might be better able to repel external attacks. Born in uncertain circumstances, and against the background of extreme political turmoil, it would have been wholly unclear to a late-ninth-century Anglo-Saxon that this 'kingdom of the Anglo-Saxons' could evolve into a wider political entity still, and it would be for Alfred's successors, in particular, his grandson, King Æthelstan, to drive this possibility forward.[50]

In his examinations of such issues, Keynes has of course had occasion to consider in detail the reigns of various kings, with a focus on their policies and on the sources that have a direct bearing on the tenor of their rule. Two kings in particular have occupied his interests, King Alfred the Great and King Æthelred 'the Unready'. In conjunction with Professor Michael Lapidge, Keynes produced a Penguin translation of Asser's *Life of Alfred* in which a case for a specifically Welsh audience was forcefully and persuasively put, as was the importance of reading the *Life* in conjunction with the contemporary production of the *Anglo-Saxon Chronicle*, a work that Keynes sees as appearing for the first time in 892, just as vikings returned to England and posed a renewed threat to Alfred's kingdom.[51] The years 892 and 893 (when Asser's work was published) were therefore a time of significant scholarly output, and Keynes' analysis of these texts shows how important it is to judge them against this specific political background. But, as in other areas of his scholarship, Keynes' interest is by no means confined to the Anglo-Saxon period, and his article about the cult of King Alfred does much to unravel the fascination that we have long held about this most famous of Anglo-Saxon kings.[52]

While Alfred's positive reputation as a king interested in religion, politics and learning was secured from the Anglo-Saxon period onwards,

---

[50] S. Keynes, 'King Alfred and the Mercians', in *Kings, Currency and Alliances: History and Coinage of Southern England in the Ninth Century*, ed. M. A. S. Blackburn and D. N. Dumville (Woodbridge, 1998), pp. 1–45; S. Keynes, 'Edward, King of the Anglo-Saxons', in *Edward the Elder, 899–924*, ed. N. J. Higham and D. H. Hill (London, 2001), pp. 40–66; and S. Keynes, 'England, *c.* 900–1016', in *New Cambridge Medieval History III: c. 900–c. 1024*, ed. T. Reuter (Cambridge, 1999), pp. 456–84. For Wessex throughout this period, see D. N. Dumville, *Wessex and England from Alfred to Edgar: Six Essays in Political, Cultural and Ecclesiastical Revival* (Woodbridge, 1992).

[51] S. Keynes and M. Lapidge, *Alfred the Great: Asser's 'Life of Alfred' and Other Contemporary Sources* (Harmondsworth, 1983). On the *Chronicle*, see S. Keynes, 'Manuscripts of the *Anglo-Saxon Chronicle*', in *The Cambridge History of the Book in Britain*, vol. I: *c. 400–1100*, ed. R. Gameson (Cambridge, 2011), pp. 537–52; and cf. N. P. Brooks, 'Why Is the *Anglo-Saxon Chronicle* about Kings?', *ASE* 39 (2010), 43–70.

[52] S. Keynes, 'The Cult of King Alfred the Great', *ASE* 28 (1999), 225–356.

Æthelred II, however, has suffered a rather negative press. Keynes, never-theless, has done much to redress this. In a direct comparison between Alfred and Æthelred, Keynes focused on the accounts of their reigns given in the *Anglo-Saxon Chronicle*. When one appreciates the very particular political contexts within which the relevant sections of the *Chronicle* were written, it emerges that the author(s) responsible for the account of Æthelred's reign had every reason to denigrate that Anglo-Saxon king, thereby trying to explain and justify the beginning of Scandinavian rule in the country.[53] Indeed, the reign of Æthelred has proved a lasting fascina-tion for Keynes who – in particular in his analysis of Æthelred's diplomas and coins – showed how Æthelred's actions and policies not only changed from the early stages of his career when he was (mis)guided by a powerful faction at court but also were often enacted on the basis of good practical sense and with sound royal precedent in mind.[54]

It is impossible in a short introduction adequately to convey the broad scope of Keynes' scholarly interests or to highlight the full range of scholarly disciplines his work embraces. No mention has been made, for example, of his work on King Æthelstan's own scholarly interests,[55] or his outlining of the careers of Cnut's earls,[56] nor of his explanations of the æthelings Alfred and Edward and their time in exile in Normandy,[57] or of Regenbald *cancellarius* or Giso, bishop of Wells,[58] which do so much to highlight the workings of late Anglo-Saxon government. Nor has account been taken of his spectacular edition of the *Liber Vitae* of the New Minster, Winchester, produced for the series 'Early English Manuscripts in Facsimile', in which his scholarly expertise in Anglo-Saxon history,

[53] S. Keynes, 'A Tale of Two Kings: Alfred the Great and Æthelred the Unready', *TRHS*, 5th series, 36 (1986), 195–217.
[54] Keynes, *The Diplomas*; S. Keynes, 'Crime and Punishment in the Reign of Æthelred the Unready', in *People and Places in Northern Europe 500–1600: Essays in Honour of Peter Hayes Sawyer*, ed. I. N. Wood and N. Lund (Woodbridge, 1991), pp. 67–81; S. Keynes, 'Re-Reading King Æthelred the Unready', in *Writing Medieval Biography*, ed. D. Bates, J. Crick and S. Hamilton (Woodbridge, 2006), pp. 77–97; S. Keynes and R. Naismith, 'The *Agnus Dei* Pennies of King Æthelred the Unready', *ASE* 40 (2011), 175–223; and S. Keynes, 'King Æthelred the Unready and the Church of Rochester', in *Textus Roffensis: Law, Language, and Libraries in Early Medieval England*, ed. B. O'Brien and B. Bombi (Turnhout, 2015), pp. 315–62.
[55] Keynes, 'King Athelstan's Books'.
[56] S. Keynes, 'Cnut's Earls', in *The Reign of King Cnut: King of England, Denmark and Norway*, ed. A. R. Rumble (London, 1994), pp. 43–88.
[57] S. Keynes, 'The Aethelings in Normandy', *ANS* 13 (1991), 173–205.
[58] S. Keynes, 'Regenbald the Chancellor (*sic*)', *ANS* 10 (1988), 185–222; and S. Keynes, 'Giso, Bishop of Wells (1061–88)', *ANS* 19 (1997), 203–71.

diplomatic, iconography and palaeography are deployed to masterful effect.[59] But if this Introduction at least points in the direction of his own wide interests and the breadth of his achievements, then it has fulfilled its purpose. Anyone who opts for the Anglo-Saxon history course in the Department of Anglo-Saxon, Norse and Celtic at the University of Cambridge has the rare privilege of being exposed to Keynes' thoughts on Anglo-Saxon charters, Anglo-Saxon history and Anglo-Saxon kingship more broadly, as they evolve during his own research and on a weekly basis. His teaching and the palpable fascination he brings to the study of Anglo-Saxon history are nothing short of inspiring, and many of his students have continued to postgraduate work and beyond in an attempt to emulate his formidable example. The thirteen essays collected here – written by Keynes' former students, colleagues past and present and friends – reflect his own interests but also the very great influence he has had on all of our thinking about the Anglo-Saxon period.[60] We offer them to him even if they fall short of his own exacting standards.

---

[59] *The Liber Vitae of the New Minster and Hyde Abbey Winchester. British Library Stowe 944 together with Leaves from British Library Cotton Vespasian A. viii and British Library Cotton Titus D. xxvii*, EEMF 26, ed. S. Keynes (Copenhagen, 1996).

[60] There are of course many other friends, colleagues and former students who are not represented here because of the constraints of space and time and the need to construct an internally coherent volume. It should be noted in particular that Professor Nicholas Brooks was invited to contribute, and in the spirit of his and Simon's shared interest in charters, he offered a chapter on 'Kings, Nobles and Church: The Control of Land at "Barham" (Kent) in the Early Ninth Century'. Nicholas passed away just a few days after communicating his intentions to the editors at the end of January 2014.

CHAPTER 2

Simon Keynes:
The Man and the Scholar

Oliver Padel

An appreciation of Simon's contribution to scholarship appears elsewhere in this volume, so my pleasant role here is to give an account of him as a person. Among academics, it is hard to distinguish a person from their work because our work constitutes such a major aspect of our lives, and this is especially true of Simon. Those who have known him closely, as colleague or teacher, would probably agree that among his chief attributes are modesty, courtesy, idealism, integrity and humour. These qualities do not always lead in the same direction and may indeed conflict at times, but they are ever-present in his dealings with close friends and colleagues.

Simon has the unusual distinction of having actually been born in Trinity College, since his mother's own parents were living in the Master's Lodge in 1952 (Simon's grandfather, Lord Adrian, being Master of Trinity from 1951 to 1965), and it has been his home for most of his life. At the Leys School, he had an exceptional history teacher, John Harding, to whom Simon's enthusiasm for history can partly be attributed, but for his particular choice of direction within that discipline, I suggest three possible influences, though he might himself cite others additionally or instead. First, for his A-level Simon did a project on the history of the Keynes family, developing work done by his great uncle Maynard (whom Simon never met, having been born six years after Maynard's death). After he had investigated a line that can be traced back to the Norman conquest, it would have been natural for Simon to become interested in that defining period of English history and hence in the Anglo-Saxon background which is essential for understanding the Conquest itself. Second, growing up in Cambridge, he gained and has retained a particular interest in his home town and county. For Simon, history is grounded in topography, both the natural and the human-made environment, and he is always especially pleased to learn that a student has visited significant sites around the country. Since East Anglia is one of the most deeply Anglo-Saxon parts of England, it would be natural for him to focus on this period which constitutes the earliest recorded history of his native region. Third and more specifically, holidays on the coast of Norfolk formed a particularly important part of Simon's childhood. These provided the opportunity for sailing a small boat from an early age with Roger, the youngest of his three elder brothers. (In their attitude to letting children loose in their own sailing-boat, his parents presumably followed the line articulated telegrammatically in Ransome's *Swallows and Amazons*: 'Better drowned than duffers if not duffers wont drown.') As a result of these childhood experiences, one of Simon's favourite novels is *The Riddle of the Sands* (1903), the patriotic spy-thriller by Erskine Childers based around the danger to England of a potential German invasion across the North Sea. In this novel, Childers (who was himself executed by firing squad for treason in 1922) used his own detailed topographical knowledge of the Frisian coast as an essential component of the plot. It can be surmised that venturing onto the North Sea in a small sailing-dinghy may have enhanced Simon's own enthusiasm to learn more about those who defined England, linguistically and culturally, by doing the same a millennium and a half earlier.

Whatever the influences, Simon was already intending to concentrate on Anglo-Saxon history before he came up to read the Anglo-Saxon, Norse and Celtic Tripos. Like many taking the Tripos, he was particularly impressed by Old Norse literature, and (again perhaps also because of his own East Anglian background) a love of Scandinavian history and literature is thus another essential component in his personal make-up. After graduating, Simon stayed on to do his doctoral thesis on the evidence of charters, and it was during this period particularly that he came under the influence of Dorothy Whitelock. She had retired as professor in 1969, a year before Simon came up as an undergraduate, but she was still active in Cambridge and served as his doctoral supervisor. It has been said of Whitelock that she was 'always appreciative of real scholarship . . . shrewd in her assessment of people . . . did not suffer fools gladly'.[1] She will have recognised a true intellectual heir in this young man, and accordingly, she eventually made him her literary executor. Her benign but rigorous influence has remained a crucial component of Simon's approach. At this time, too, he formed his collection of Anglo-Saxon coins (with which he would later impress his undergraduates by passing specimens round casually in his

---

[1] H. Loyn, 'Dorothy Whitelock, 1901–1982' (1984), reprinted in *Interpreters of Early Medieval Britain*, ed. M. Lapidge (Oxford, 2002), pp. 427–37, at 428; in the first of these phrases, Loyn was, in turn, quoting Mrs Kathleen Ede (née Bond), an undergraduate contemporary of Whitelock's.

lectures): a broad approach to evidence of all kinds, material as well as textual, has been another notable feature of his scholarship.

Having proceeded to a research fellowship at Trinity College and to his PhD, which it gave him pleasure to take on the thousandth anniversary (to the very day) of King Æthelred's accession to the throne of England, Simon was appointed to a lectureship in the Department of Anglo-Saxon, Norse and Celtic in 1978, one of the four wonderfully perceptive appointments made by Peter Clemoes which determined the intellectual vigour of Anglo-Saxon, Norse and Celtic during the 1970s and 1980s and beyond. Simon became one of the 'Gang of Four', the group of young, toweringly able scholars who moved the various disciplines forward so significantly, particularly through their close collaboration with one another in all aspects of the work covered by the Tripos – first under Clemoes, subsequently (and somewhat less harmoniously) under Ray Page, professor in 1984–91, and then (1991–8) under Michael Lapidge, the eldest member of the group itself. (The other two members were David Dumville and Patrick Sims-Williams; those who were students during that period will testify to the air of excitement that percolated throughout the Department from these four outstanding young scholars collaborating so closely.)[2]

Simon's own approach to teaching was a major component in that atmosphere. His teaching made undergraduates feel not only that they were being led to the cutting edge of fresh research but also how they might contribute to it. It is remembered particularly, too, for the clarity with which complex problems were explained. All these characteristics arise from the care that he takes in preparing teaching materials for undergraduates, as well as his celebrated and elegant handouts; one obvious example of this care is the well-known *Bibliographical Handbook* of Anglo-Saxon England, reissued regularly until 2006, which grew from a pamphlet to a major book and is an important resource for scholars as well as for undergraduates. Among the latter, this bibliography, in its larger manifestations, must be exhilarating for stronger students but perhaps somewhat daunting for some, despite the carefully worded disclaimer at the start. ('No-one would be expected, able, or inclined to read more than a small selection of the items listed.') The distinctive maps included latterly at the end of this book and the tail-piece, an apt quotation from *Alice Through the Looking Glass* (accompanied by equally apt illustrations of 'Anglo-Saxon attitudes'), are typical of his detailed care and

---

[2] Details of the appointments made during this period are now readily available in 'The Institutional Growth of Anglo-Saxon, Norse and Celtic Studies in Cambridge: A Timeline', Appendix VIII in *H. M. Chadwick and the Study of Anglo-Saxon, Norse and Celtic in Cambridge*, ed. M. Lapidge, *CMCS* 69–70 (2015), pp. 272–8.

his humour. Simon's teaching has given generations of undergraduates, within the scholarly profession and elsewhere, an enduring grasp of the problems and the excitement of Anglo-Saxon history. Similarly, his public lectures are meticulously prepared and scrupulously worded; the humour is never far away, though sometimes sufficiently subtle to be overlooked on casual hearing or reading. One example fondly remembered by colleagues was a dummy question which appeared repeatedly in a draft examination paper, occupying the slots for questions on Celtic history to be inserted by a colleague, and using a genuine question which had once caused anguished discussion when set in a draft paper: 'Is the Celtic Church a dead duck?'

In 1992 Simon was made Reader in Anglo-Saxon History, and in 1999 he was himself appointed to the Elrington and Bosworth Chair in Anglo-Saxon, as successor to Michael Lapidge. Simon enjoys the fact that this position has an actual chair that goes with it, handsomely complete with brass plaque. (On the night when he learnt of the appointment, two of us took him out to celebrate at Efes Turkish restaurant, which he had never been to. On emerging from it afterwards onto King Street, he asked us, with characteristic self-deprecation, the way back to Trinity College.)

An awareness of family has always been an important component of Simon's personality, unsurprisingly in view of the number of illustrious names incorporated within it. He was amused once on going to give a lecture at the University of Kent at Canterbury and being told on arrival, 'We thought you might prefer not to speak in the Keynes Lecture Theatre, so we have put you in the Darwin Theatre instead' (overlooking the fact that Simon's grandmother was a granddaughter of Charles Darwin). His integrity and meticulous care are well illustrated by his being chosen by his Keynes uncles as an executor of their estates, no small task in the case of men who had themselves amassed significant collections of art, artefacts and documents. But many who have passed through the Department of Anglo-Saxon, Norse and Celtic over the years and many colleagues in the wider world of early medieval history may feel that they too have an almost familial connection with Simon and will wish to join in celebrating his completion of forty years as a member of staff in the Department (now approaching fifty years since he first entered it as an undergraduate), at the same time as wishing him many happy returns on his sixty-fifth birthday.

PART I

The Formation of Power
The Early Anglo-Saxon Kingdoms

CHAPTER 3

Bede's Kings*

Sarah Foot

Anglo-Saxon kings and kingship have always lain at the heart of Simon Keynes' academic interests. Several of his publications have assessed the activities of individual monarchs ranging from Rædwald 'the bretwalda' to Cnut; others explored aspects of royal government, particularly as revealed through charters, most notably his study of the diplomas of Æthelred 'the Unready'.[1] Simon communicates his enthusiasm to great effect in his undergraduate lectures and used to open (and perhaps still does open) his annual Cambridge lecture series on the history of pre-Conquest England with a bravura performance debunking popular mythology about Anglo-Saxon kings. As I now recall it, the account that he gave in my first undergraduate year ranged from the obvious (Alfred and the cakes, Cnut and the waves, Harold with the arrow in his eye) to some rather more obscure figures. The whole lecture offered unexpected insights into the memorialisation of the Anglo-Saxon past across a range of cultural media from architecture to opera. An accompanying hand-out was a masterpiece of the genre, reproducing at its centre a poem published in *The Times* in November 1977: Christopher Logue's 'An Archaic Jingle' with its refrain 'Ethelred! Ethelred! / Spent his royal life in bed / one shoe off and one shoe on / greatly loved by everyone', together with Bert Kitchen's illustration of the prone king, one foot duly unshod, his crown slung over the bed-post.[2]

---

* An earlier version of this chapter was given as the Richard Rawlinson Lecture at the 50th International Congress on Medieval Studies at Kalamazoo, Michigan, in May 2015. I am grateful to the delegates who contributed to the discussion that followed, particularly to Steven Harris and Rosalind Love, and also to Conor O'Brien, Richard Sowerby and the editors of this volume for commenting helpfully on the paper in draft. None of these bears any responsibility for such errors or infelicities that remain.

[1] S. Keynes, *The Diplomas of King Æthelred 'The Unready' (978–1016): A Study in Their Use as Historical Evidence* (Cambridge, 1980).

[2] C. Logue, *Abecedary*, illustrated by B. Kitchen (London, 1977) (unpaginated); the poem was reproduced in *The Times* (Issue 60163) on the day of the book's publication: 17 November 1977, p. 14.

I can trace my own interest in the history of the Anglo-Saxons and their kings back to that lecture, but also to the stimulus of weekly supervisions with Simon over my first two terms in Cambridge, his direction of my final-year dissertation on King Æthelstan and the many later conversations I enjoyed as a graduate student and as my own career has developed. Since first writing an essay for him on Bede's merits as an historian, I have frequently discussed Bede's writings with Simon. In many ways I thus owe it to him that I now find myself beginning work on a major intellectual biography of the Venerable Bede, for which this chapter on Bede's ideas about kingship represents a preliminary study.[3]

Bede's *Ecclesiastical History*, completed *c.* 731, has unparalleled significance as the most informative source for the study of kings and kingship in early Anglo-Saxon England. Dedicated to a king (Ceolwulf of Northumbria), the *History* can be seen at least in part as a mirror for princes, explicitly providing examples of kingly behaviour to be emulated or avoided.[4] Yet, as James Campbell observed, for all its outward trappings of comprehensiveness and objectivity, it supplies a highly selective account of royal behaviour and of the nature of monarchy, one tailored to Bede's own wider purposes in writing an ecclesiastical history, which did not include the definition or description of secular institutions.[5] Simon Keynes has noted that 'it is difficult for all of those who have followed him, from the compilers of the *Anglo-Saxon Chronicle* in the late 9th century onwards, to break free from his influence.'[6] That problem relates as much to the silences in Bede's account – particularly, for example, over the early history of Mercia – as to those passages in which he offered notably strong opinions of his own. Already in his own day Bede's writings were in great demand among ecclesiastics on the continent, as well as readers in his own land.[7] One of the most frequently copied books

---

[3] *The Venerable Bede: A Located Life* has been commissioned by Princeton University Press.

[4] Bede, *Historia ecclesiastica* [hereafter *HE*] Preface, in *Bede's Ecclesiastical History of the English People*, ed. B. Colgrave and R. A. B. Mynors (Oxford, 1969), pp. 2–3. Ceolwulf ruled Northumbria from 729 until 737, when he abdicated to become a monk at Lindisfarne; he died at that monastery in 764. D. Kirby, 'King Ceolwulf of Northumbria and the *Historia Ecclesiastica*', *Studia Celtica* 14–15, for 1979–1980 (1981), 168–73.

[5] J. Campbell, *Essays in Anglo-Saxon History* (London and Ronceverte, 1986), p. 85; and H. R. Loyn, 'Bede's Kings: A Comment on the Attitude of Bede to the Nature of Secular Kingship', in *Eternal Values in Medieval Life*, ed. N. Crossley-Holland (Lampeter, 1991), pp. 54–64, at 56.

[6] S. Keynes, 'The Staffordshire Hoard and Mercian Power', Staffordshire Hoard Symposium, British Museum, March 2010; https://finds.org.uk/staffshoardsymposium/papers/simonkeynes (accessed 19 July 2015).

[7] R. H. C. Davis, 'Bede after Bede', in *Studies in Medieval History Presented to R. Allen Brown*, ed. C. Harper-Bill, C. J. Holdsworth and J. L. Nelson (Woodbridge, 1989), pp. 103–16, at 103–4.

written in pre-Conquest England, the *Historia* was translated into Old
English in the late ninth century, albeit in an abridged form, omitting
many of the documents Bede had faithfully transcribed as well as passages
about chronology, doctrinal dispute and natural phenomena.[8] Those
omissions, by narrowing the focus of the text as a whole, served to
accentuate further the stories of the individuals whose example Bede
intended his readers to imitate or to condemn, among them the saints
but also, of course, kings.[9] Kings and the formation (and destruction) of
kingdoms dominated the writings of twelfth-century Anglo-Norman
historians who used Bede (together with other sources such as the
Anglo-Saxon Chronicle, royal genealogies and king-lists and legends of
the saints) to construct their own visions of the pre-Conquest past.[10]

Modern scholars have devoted considerable attention to Bede's conception of kingship, and it is not my intention to reprise all that literature here;
rather, I wish to reconsider the question of whether Bede promoted a
particular ideal of kingship. Charles Plummer's edition of Bede's historical
works, with its detailed commentary, is still the starting-point for all
modern study, shedding light on numerous aspects of Bede's thought as
well as on the sources on which he drew.[11] Among more recent literature,
Michael Wallace-Hadrill's Ford Lectures of 1970 on the nature of early
Germanic kingship together with his article comparing Bede's views of
royal behaviour with those of Gregory of Tours and his own commentary
on Bede's *Historia ecclesiastica* remain essential,[12] as do the essays by Judith
McClure, Clare Stancliffe and Alan Thacker in Wallace-Hadrill's own
Festschrift.[13] Equally important are Campbell's Jarrow Lecture, a volume
of essays on Saint Oswald and the contributions of Patrick Wormald,
Stephen Fanning, Simon Keynes and Barbara Yorke on the vexed problems

---

[8] D. Whitelock, 'The Old English Bede', *PBA* 48 (1962), 57–90; and G. Molyneaux, 'The *Old English Bede*: English Ideology or Christian Instruction?', *EHR* 124 (2009), 1289–1323.
[9] Molyneaux, '*Old English Bede*', pp. 1310–12, 1316.   [10] Keynes, 'Staffordshire Hoard'.
[11] C. Plummer, *Bedae opera historica*, 2 vols. (Oxford, 1896).
[12] J. M. Wallace-Hadrill, *Early Germanic Kingship in England and on the Continent: The Ford Lectures Delivered in the University of Oxford in Hilary Term 1970* (Oxford, 1971); J. M. Wallace-Hadrill, 'Gregory of Tours and Bede: Their Views of the Personal Qualities of Kings', *Frühmittelalterliche Studien* 2 (1968), 31–44; reprinted in his *Early Medieval History* (Oxford, 1975), pp. 96–14; and J. M. Wallace-Hadrill, *Bede's Ecclesiastical History of the English People: A Historical Commentary* [hereafter *HE Comm.*] (Oxford, 1988).
[13] J. McClure, 'Bede's Old Testament Kings', in *Ideal and Reality in Frankish and Anglo-Saxon Society: Studies Presented to J. M. Wallace-Hadrill*, ed. P. Wormald et al. (Oxford, 1983), pp. 76–98; C. Stancliffe, 'Kings Who Opted Out', *ibid.*, pp. 154–76; and A. Thacker, 'Bede's Ideal of Reform', *ibid.*, pp. 130–53.

of the kings whom Bede described as holding *imperium*, termed 'bretwaldas' in the ninth-century *Anglo-Saxon Chronicle*.[14]

Wallace-Hadrill argued that, like Gregory the Great (who probably more than any single patristic writer had the most influence on Bede's understanding of kingship), Bede did not have a developed doctrine of kingship; he did, however, consider that Bede was 'feeling his way towards one'.[15] Clare Stancliffe went further than this. Her own reading of the *Historia* led her to the view that Bede did not articulate a single stereotyped ideal of a Christian king to which he believed that each individual should conform in some fashion; rather, she has suggested that Bede took account of the different personalities and actions of the kings about whom he wrote and used them as a basis on which to draw a series of portraits, which in each case emphasised the different qualities of the individuals concerned.[16] In her opinion, among the various kings included in the *Historia*, Bede presented only Oswald unambiguously as a saint, even while he served as a successful king; most other saint-kings owed their sanctity to lives lived after giving up their throne or to their death as martyrs in battle,[17] with the exception perhaps of Oswine, who evinced saintly characteristics also in life.[18] Although Stancliffe has indeed shown, to considerable effect, how Bede presented portraits of different kings in various idealised terms, I should like to reconsider her proposition that these reflect his lack of a single ideal model.[19] Here I shall adopt a self-consciously biographical perspective, looking at the effect that Bede's own personality and

---

[14] J. Campbell, *Bede's reges and principes*, Jarrow Lecture 1979, reprinted in his *Essays*, pp. 85–98; C. Stancliffe and E. Cambridge (eds.), *Oswald: Northumbrian King to European Saint* (Stamford, 1995); P. Wormald, 'Bede, the Bretwaldas and the Origin of the *Gens Anglorum*', in *Ideal and Reality*, ed. Wormald et al., pp. 99–129; S. Fanning, 'Bede, *Imperium*, and the Bretwaldas', *Speculum* 66 (1991), 1–26; S. Keynes, 'Rædwald the Bretwalda', in *Voyage to the Other World: The Legacy of Sutton Hoo*, ed. C. B. Kendall and P. S. Wells (Minneapolis, 1992), pp. 103–23; and B. Yorke, 'The Bretwaldas and the Origins of Overlordship in Anglo-Saxon England', in *Early Medieval Studies in Memory of Patrick Wormald*, ed. S. Baxter, C. E. Karkov, J. L. Nelson and D. Pelteret (Farnham, 2009), pp. 81–95.

[15] Wallace-Hadrill, *Early Germanic Kingship*, p. 74.

[16] Stancliffe, 'Oswald, "Most Holy and Most Victorious King of the Northumbrians"', in *Oswald*, ed. Stancliffe and Cambridge, pp. 33–83, at 62. See also S. Ridyard, 'Monk-Kings and the Anglo-Saxon Hagiographic Tradition', *HSJ* 6, for 1994 (1995), 13–27, at 21–2.

[17] Stancliffe, 'Oswald', p. 41.   [18] Bede, *HE* iii. 14 (ed. Colgrave and Mynors, pp. 256–60).

[19] Bede does seem to have had a relatively fixed model of sanctity; although he recounted the miraculous deeds that saints had effected (or that were done in their name) in ways that frequently reflected something of individual saint's own interests or characteristics, he tended to describe the virtues that denoted their sanctity in remarkably uniform terms. Compare, for example, his accounts of Aidan (Bede, *HE* iii. 17 (ed. Colgrave and Mynors, p. 266)), Chad (Bede, *HE* iv. 3 (ed. Colgrave and Mynors, p. 342)) and Cuthbert (Bede, *HE* iv. 28 (ed. Colgrave and Mynors, p. 438)) with the language that he used of Oswald: Bede, *HE* iii. 6 (ed. Colgrave and Mynors, p. 230). I discuss this further in my 'Bede's Northern Saints', in *Saints of North-East England, 600–1500*, ed. M. Coombe, A. Mouron and C. Whitehead (Turnhout, 2017).

experience might have had on the ideas he articulated about kingship in his own day and considering how his views of earthly power cohered with his broader theological understanding of human existence. What was the role of kings in Bede's wider narrative about God's plan for humanity; where did Bede place kings in his economy of salvation; and how did Bede reconcile the tensions found inevitably in this newly Christianised society between a religious ideal that promoted peace and love (love of Christ, love of neighbour) and the brutal realities of the exercise of kingship in a Germanic warrior society?

Several passages in Bede's *Historia* illustrate those tensions, perhaps most memorably his description of the battle of Chester at which (sometime between 613 and 616) the pagan Northumbrian king, Æthelfrith, defeated a great army of Britons. When the king 'was about to give battle and saw [the Britons'] priests, who had assembled to pray to God on behalf of the soldiers taking part in the fight standing apart in a safer place, he asked who they were and for what purpose they had gathered there'. Told that they were from the Welsh monastery of Bangor Is-coed, the king reportedly said, 'If they are praying to their God against us, then, even if they do not bear arms, they are fighting against us, assailing us as they do with prayers for our defeat'. So he ordered the clergy to be attacked first, before going on to destroy the rest of the British host, albeit with heavy losses on the Northumbrian side. Bede reported that about twelve hundred men who had come to pray were killed on that day, only fifty managing to escape by flight, the force that had been meant to protect them from the enemy having 'turned their backs on them, leaving them unarmed and helpless before the swords of their foes'.[20]

Bede said nothing about what these defenceless monks carried with them to aid their intercession for their enemies' downfall. They might have brought one or more precious manuscripts from their monastery's collection, a prayer-book or a volume of scripture. Or perhaps they held more immediately obvious Christian symbols up before them, including either small altar crosses, capable of being held in the hand, or processional crosses, raised high aloft above the battle on long shafts. Bede's account of King Oswald's behaviour before the battle of Heavenfield (634) refers directly to the erection of a cross at the site of a battle. In a passage that depicts Oswald as a quasi-second Constantine, Bede recounted how Oswald himself had supposedly held the shaft of a hastily made wooden standing cross as it was positioned in a hole dug in the ground, while his

---

[20] Bede, *HE* ii. 2 (ed. Colgrave and Mynors, p. 140).

men poured earth round it, to fix it into position. The king then called out
to the whole army to kneel together and pray to the almighty and ever-
living God to defend them in his mercy from the proud and fierce enemy;
'for He knows', Oswald asserted, 'that we are fighting in a just cause for the
preservation of our whole race'.[21]

One item discovered among the Staffordshire Hoard (the 'bling for
warrior companions of the king',[22] datable to *c.* 700 that was found in a
field at Hammerwich, near Lichfield in Staffordshire in 2009) supports the
suggestion that the members of early English Christian armies could have
expected prayers to be said on the battlefield itself for the victory of their
king and the defeat of his enemies. A small strip of gold alloy, perhaps torn
from the crosspiece of a decorated cross, bears an inscription taken from a
verse from the Old Testament book of Numbers: 'When he had lifted up
the ark, Moses said "Rise up, Lord, and may your enemies be dispersed and
those who hate you flee from your face."'[23] The designer of the inscription
may also have had in mind the similar verse from Psalm 67: 'Let God arise
and his enemies be dispersed and those who hate him flee from his face.'[24]
The familiarity of both verses is shown by their quotation in Felix's *Life of
St Guthlac*, written between 730 and 740.[25] On one occasion the saint used
the psalm text to vanquish devils who had appeared to him in a vision, and
on another he prophesied to the future King Æthelbald, using words from
Numbers: 'those who fear you shall flee from before your face.'[26] The 3,500

---

[21] Bede, *HE* iii. 2 (ed. Colgrave and Mynors, pp. 214–5); Stancliffe, 'Oswald', p. 63; for the suggestion
that the elevation of such crosses may have been influenced by crosses in the Holy Land, see I. Wood,
'Constantinian Crosses in Northumbria', in *The Place of the Cross in Anglo-Saxon England*, ed. C. E.
Karkov et al. (Woodbridge, 2006), pp. 3–13, at 11–13.

[22] This memorable description of the Hoard was coined by N. Brooks, 'The Staffordshire Hoard and
the Mercian Royal Court', paper read at the Staffordshire Hoard Symposium, 2010; https://finds
.org.uk/staffshoardsymposium/papers/nicholasbrooks (accessed 19 July 2015).

[23] The text, divided into words and with the abbreviations expanded and likely letters assumed, reads:
'[s]URGE DOMINE DISEPENTUR INIMICI TUI ET [f]UGENT QUI ODERUNT TE A FACIE TUA'. It comes
from Numbers 10: 35: 'cumque elevaretur arca dicebat Moses surge Domine et dissipentur inimici tui et
fugiant qui oderunt te a facie tua'. The reverse of the strip bears a very similar text, inscribed less expertly,
which may represent a trial for the final version. See E. Okasha, 'The Staffordshire Hoard Inscription',
https://finds.org.uk/staffshoardsymposium/papers/elisabethokasha (accessed 19 July 2015).

[24] Psalm 67: 2: 'exsurgat Deus et dissipentur inimici eius et fugiant qui oderunt eum a facie eius'.
Muirchú put the same verse into the mouth of St Patrick in the course of a dispute he had with
pagan druids: *Vita sancti Patricii confessoris*, I. 18, in *The Patrician Texts in The Book of Armagh*, ed.
and trans. L. Bieler and F. Kelly (Dublin, 1979), p. 90; I owe this reference to Conor O'Brien.

[25] B. Colgrave, *Felix's Life of Saint Guthlac* (Cambridge, 1956; 1985 edn), p. 19.

[26] Felix, *Life of St Guthlac*, chaps. 33 and 49 (ed. and trans. Colgrave, pp. 108 and 148); Okasha,
'The Staffordshire Hoard Inscription'; D. Ganz, 'The Text of the Inscription', https://finds.org
.uk/staffshoardsymposium/papers/davidganz (accessed 19 July 2015). For a similar juxtaposition
of images of kingship with those of religious judgement, compare the Repton Stone, one side
of which bears a mounted warrior (probably King Æthelbald) and the other a serpent

silver and gold pieces of broken and twisted war gear that make up the Staffordshire Hoard include not only a remarkable number of sword ornaments but also one complete cross (now twisted and folded) and various cross fragments, among them the inscribed strip.[27]

Whether the items in the hoard had been torn from the bodies of the dead lying on a battlefield, gathered together in haste to pay a king's ransom or collected from diverse sources over time to make up a king's treasure chest remains unknown. Yet this assemblage of war gear does seem to point to the presence of Christian priests or monks at or near the sites of battle, just as Bede described them at the battle of Chester and as we might assume they attended Oswald's successful engagement at Heavenfield, especially if we imagine that Oswald might have brought clergy with him from Dal Riata on his return to Northumbria from exile. In both those episodes we can readily envisage the use of the war-gear found in the Staffordshire Hoard, especially on those portions of the battlefield closest to the warring kings and their immediate retinues. But as well as imagining those swords, helmets and shields, we can also see the use to which the inscription on the now-folded piece of gold alloy would have been put and the place of prayer to the Almighty in invoking divine assistance in what the Christian protagonists believed to be just conflicts.[28] It clearly fell to these clerics to ask God to scatter his enemies and make those that hate him flee from before his face, taking on themselves the responsibility for divine intercession that the king could not perform himself in the heat of battle. I have chosen to begin this discussion of Bede's views about kingship with the question of warfare because one could make the case that for most of the chronological period covered by Bede in his *Historia*, a key (if not the central defining) feature of good kingship lay in success in war. In many ways, the finding of the Staffordshire Hoard has served, at least in popular imagination, only to confirm such a view.

Bede's narrative frequently mapped the rivalries between (and often within) the separate English kingdoms, explaining how those disputes often worked themselves out on the field of battle. In his *Historia*, the two kings mentioned so far – Æthelfrith and Oswald – both stood out for

swallowing the damned into hell: M. Biddle and B. Kjølbye-Biddle, 'The Repton Stone', *ASE* 14 (1985), 233–92; for the iconography of the serpent, see particularly pp. 277–9 and 285–6.

[27] D. Symons, *The Staffordshire Hoard* (Birmingham, 2014), pp. 36–7; the crosses in the Hoard include StH 655 (an altar or processional cross), StH 303 (a pendant cross) and two cross-shaped mounts, StH 820 and StH 920. The inscribed strip is StH 550; K. Leahy, 'The Contents of the Hoard', paper read at the Staffordshire Hoard Symposium, 2010; https://finds.org.uk/staffshoardsymposium/papers/kevinleahy (accessed 19 July 2015).

[28] Stancliffe, 'Oswald', pp. 44–5.

their military achievements, building successful realms (and extending their borders) on the back of martial victories. But there was also a sharp contrast between them, illustrated by the two vignettes that we have already considered: Æthelfrith's reign predated the conversion of Northumbria to Christianity, and the pagan king's willingness to slaughter 1,200 monks may stand as an index of his lack of respect for the religion of others.[29] Oswald, however, arguably came closest to Bede's ideal of kingship, for Bede famously described him not just as 'most holy and most victorious king of the Northumbrians' and 'most Christian king' but also gave him the epithet conventionally reserved for monks and other religious: 'soldier of Christ.'[30] Manifestly for Bede, the institution of kingship involved much more than military prowess; as the Christian faith took root among the English people, he judged rulers increasingly according to the extent of their commitment to the new religion and their generosity in its support; he also frequently emphasised the moral imperatives underpinning secular rulership.[31]

Although the *Historia ecclesiastica* provides some of the most detailed available information relating to the exercise of kingship among the early Anglo-Saxon peoples and identifies and dates the rules of many individual kings, we should recall that Bede did not compose his history with the primary purpose of explaining the institution of kingship.[32] Those details merely provided the chronological framework for the wider narrative of the conversion of the English and the spread of the 'catholic peace and truth of the universal Church' among most of the other inhabitants of Britain,[33] which Bede depicted as the fulfilment of Christ's injunction to his apostles to be his witnesses 'in Jerusalem, and in all Judea, and Samaria, and even to the uttermost part of the earth'.[34] Even so, as Bede traced the spread of

[29] Bede, of course, memorably likened Æthelfrith to the Old Testament King Saul: Bede, *HE* i. 34 (ed. Colgrave and Mynors, p. 116).

[30] Bede, *HE* iii. 7 (ed. Colgrave and Mynors, p. 232): 'sanctissimus ac victoriosissimus rex Nordanhymbrorum'; *HE* iii. 9 (p. 240): 'Christianissimus rex Nordanhymbrorum'; *HE* iv. 14 (p. 380): 'rex ac miles Christi' (cf. 2 Timothy 2: 3). Loyn, 'Bede's Kings', pp. 57–8; and Stancliffe, 'Oswald', p. 41.

[31] Wallace-Hadrill, *Early Germanic Kingship*, p. 74.   [32] Loyn, 'Bede's Kings', pp. 54–5.

[33] Bede, *HE* v. 23 (ed. Colgrave and Mynors, p. 560); in the idyllic picture of the state of Britain that Bede painted at the end of the *Historia*, only the Britons remained mired in their evil customs, including the incorrect celebration of Easter; see C. Stancliffe, *Bede and the Britons*, Whithorn Lecture 14 (Whithorn, 2007).

[34] Acts 1: 8. The structure of Bede's *HE* deliberately mirrored that of the Acts of the Apostles: R. Ray, 'What Do We Know about Bede's Commentaries?', *Recherches de théologie ancienne et médiévale* 49 (1982), 5–20, at 19–20. For the importance of Bede's *Historia* as salvation history, see R. W. Hanning, *The Vision of History in Early Britain: From Gildas to Geoffrey of Monmouth* (New York and London, 1966), pp. 83–90.

missionary activity to the island of Britain (a place far from 'the first part of the world', 'an island in the ocean')[35] and recounted the creation of structures of ecclesiastical governance, he set the representatives of religious authority firmly within a framework of earthly power. Thus, at the midpoint of history when drawing attention to the importance of the archiepiscopate of Theodore of Tarsus, 'the first archbishop whom the whole English church consented to obey', Bede drew a direct relationship between success in the faith and wellbeing of the nation.[36] Similarly, when summarising the state of Britain at the end of book V, Bede listed the names of the bishops of each diocese, noting that all those south of the Humber (together with their various kings) were subject to Æthelbald, king of the Mercians, whilst the four Northumbrian bishops answered to King Ceolwulf.[37] For Bede, there was a clear connection between the material prosperity of a nation (which often depended upon its leaders' martial prowess) and its standing in the eyes of the Almighty.[38] Oswald's cause, which we have already considered, was just in Bede's eyes because he was fighting for the protection of his people, not only for the faith; it was his willingness to work for the greater good of the whole nation that incurred divine favour. Other factors besides military ones, however, contributed to Bede's broader visions of ideal kingly rule.

One could explore Bede's view of the role and function of kings by looking at the qualities that he presented as typical of good kings – courage, wisdom, generosity, devotion and piety, learning, humility – and then contrasting them with those that would characterise bad rulers – cowardice, greed, jealousy, cruelty, injustice, faithlessness and apostasy, sinfulness, and so on. Alternatively, one might look at kings as ideal types: the warrior, the law-giver, the peacekeeper, the dynastic founder, the missionary, the church-builder, the benefactor or the pilgrim. Organising the kings about whom Bede wrote under either their functions or their attributes could be revealing. It would, however, have the major methodological disadvantage of starkly dividing Bede's pantheon of champions

[35] Bede, *In Cantica Canticorum*, prol. lines 509–10; *Bedae Venerabilis Opera, pars II: Opera exegetica 2b*, ed. D. Hurst, CCSL 119B (Turnhout, 1983), 180; and *On the Song of Songs and Selected Writings*, trans. A. Holder (New York, 2011), pp. 28–9. Compare also Bede's description of Britain as 'an island of the ocean that lies to the north west' located at a considerable distance from 'the greater part of Europe': Bede, *HE* i. 1 (ed. Colgrave and Mynors, p. 14); see N. Howe, 'An Angle on This Earth: Sense of Place in Anglo-Saxon England', *Bulletin of the John Rylands University Library of Manchester* 82 (2002), 3–27, at 4–10.

[36] Bede, *HE* iv. 2 (ed. Colgrave and Mynors, p. 334).

[37] Bede, *HE* v. 23 (ed. Colgrave and Mynors, p. 558).

[38] Compare, for example, the contrast he drew between good and bad kings of past eras in his commentary *In Ezram et Neemiam*, ii. 6: 6–7, ed. D. Hurst, CCSL 119A (Turnhout, 1969), p. 294; and *Bede: On Ezra and Nehemiah*, trans. S. DeGregorio (Liverpool, 2006), p. 88.

into those whom he held up for emulation and imitation (almost exclusively the strong advocates for the Christian faith) and the 'smaller retinue of demonized villains',[39] those whose behaviour brought them the misfortune that Bede believed they deserved. This would not contribute significantly to our understanding of his views of kingship as an institution. More profitably, we might think about how Bede depicted kings under three rubrics, which traverse the chronology of their lives and careers and so neatly sum up the life cycle of a king from his first acquisition of the throne, through his behaviour while holding it, to his death. First, we shall consider kings in the contexts of their families, before moving onto the kingly *ministerium*, the exercise of royal rule over a king's own subjects and in expansion of his realm;[40] finally, we shall touch on the ends of kings, looking at how their reigns concluded and at Bede's understanding of the ultimate fate of their souls.

Dynastic Kings

Re-reading the *Historia ecclesiastica* in preparation for writing this chapter, I felt afresh the importance that Bede placed on locating rulers within their wider family contexts. In part, of course, this reflects the nature of Bede's sources; others have commented on the way that Bede incorporated material from early annalistic sources and from king-lists or genealogies and on his skill in rationalising these diverse (and often contradictory) pieces of information into a coherent and seemingly sequential narrative.[41] On most occasions when Bede introduced the name of a new king into his narrative, as well as fixing that man's rule on the arrow of chronological time elapsed since the Incarnation, he also located him in his immediate family context. So, for example, he noted that on the death of Cynegisl of the West Saxons in 643, his son Cenwealh came to the throne and that Sigeberht acceded to the East Anglian throne in 630 or 631, after the death of his brother Eorpwold, who had succeeded Raedwald.[42] This represented most obviously a means of demonstrating a king's legitimacy, tacitly drawing attention to rulers who had usurped thrones from their rightful

---

[39] A. H. Merrills, *History and Geography in Late Antiquity* (Cambridge, 2005), p. 239.

[40] G. Tugene, 'Rois moines et rois pasteurs dans l'*Histoire Ecclésiastique* de Bède', *Romanobarbarica* 8 (1984–5), 111–147, at 118.

[41] For example, D. N. Dumville, 'Kingship, Genealogies and Regnal Lists', in *Early Medieval Kingship*, ed. P. H. Sawyer and I. Wood (Leeds, 1977), pp. 72–104, at 74 and 77–81; McClure, 'Bede's Old Testament Kings', p. 86; and more recently, C. Behr, 'The Origins of Kingship in Early Medieval Kent', *EME* 9 (2000), 25–52, at 27–31.

[42] Bede, *HE* iii. 7; iii. 18 (ed. Colgrave and Mynors, pp. 232 and 266).

holders. Bede's concern that only those of the right lineage should be elevated to the rank of king came across vividly when he recounted how Wulfhere, son of Penda, obtained sufficient support to oust from his kingdom those ealdormen who were not of the proper stock (*eiectis principibus regis non proprii*), who had been ruling Mercia since Penda's defeat at the battle of *Winwæd*.[43] Yet one might go further and argue that Bede's interest in the families of kings and in dynastic stability related to more than merely the issue of their entitlement to power and their suitability to perform the royal office.

Let us consider the short passage in the fourth book of his *Historia ecclesiastica* in which Bede recounted the death of Hlothhere, one of the few portions that in Wallace-Hadrill's opinion had no bearing whatever on ecclesiastical history.[44] Bede reported that, on 6 February 685:[45]

> Hlothhere, king of Kent, died after a reign of twelve years, having succeeded his brother Ecgberht, who had reigned nine years. He was wounded in battle with South Saxons, whom Eadric, son of Ecgberht, had raised against him. He died while his wounds were being attended to. Eadric ruled for a year and a half after Hlothhere and, when Eadric died, various usurpers or foreign kings plundered the kingdom for a certain space of time until the rightful king [*legitimus rex*], Wihtred, son of Ecgberht, established himself on the throne and freed the nation from foreign invasion by his devotion and zeal.

Readers of the *Historia* had, of course, already encountered Ecgberht, Hlothhere's predecessor as king of Kent (the figure to whom all these individuals were related) before they reached this chapter.[46] Oswiu of Northumbria had consulted with Ecgberht about the state of the English Church before sending the unfortunate Wighard to Rome to be consecrated as archbishop (his death in the Holy City leading to the decision to send the Greek-born Theodore to Canterbury instead).[47] Ecgberht and Hlothhere were the sons of Eorcenberht of Kent, the first king to order the destruction of pagan idols in his realm, who had also tried to enforce the

---

[43] Bede, *HE* iii. 24 (ed. Colgrave and Mynors, p. 294); and Loyn, 'Bede's Kings', p. 60. Commenting on this passage, Georges Tugene has noted that it was the fact of having their own king (namely, one from the right *stirps regia*) that brought freedom to the Mercians; Bede thus seemed to approve of the Mercian rebellion against their Northumbria overlords: 'Reflections on "Ethnic" Kingship in Bede's *Ecclesiastical History*', *Romanobarbarica* 17 (2000–2), 309–31, at 315.

[44] *HE Comm.*, p. 170. S. E. Kelly, 'Hlothhere (d. 685)', *ODNB*, vol. XXVII, pp. 339–40; www.oxforddnb.com/view/article/39262 (accessed 26 July 2015).

[45] Bede, *HE* iv. 26 (ed. Colgrave and Mynors, pp. 430–1).

[46] For Ecgberht I (d. 673), see S. E. Kelly, 'Eorcenberht (d. 664)', *ODNB*, vol. XVIII, p. 473.

[47] Bede, *HE* iii. 29; iv. 1 (ed. Colgrave and Mynors, pp. 318 and 328).

keeping of the Lenten fast.[48] Eorcenberht's wife, Ecgberht's mother, was
Seaxburg, daughter of Anna of the East Angles, who in widowhood became
abbess of the monastery at Ely founded by her sister Æthelthryth.[49] While
Wallace-Hadrill noted correctly that this passage about the confused
succession in Kent following Hlothhere's death makes no direct reference
to Church matters, the connection (and close involvement) of this royal
family with the initial establishment and later flourishing of the Church in
both Kent and East Anglia is unquestionable.

Bede's careful recitation of the familial relationships between Hlothhere,
his brother Ecgberht and Ecgberht's sons – Eadric and Wihtred – reinforced in his readers' minds a fundamental point about the stability of the
Kentish royal family. All of these claimants were close members of the *stirps
regia*; all descended directly from Æthelberht, whose son and successor,
Eadbald, was the father of Eorcenberht. Each in his turn sought to follow
the advice Pope Gregory had given to their ancestor, Æthelberht, to
promote the faith among all those subject to them.[50] This passage thus
concerns more than the legitimate claim of any single man, or even a
succession of men, to rule; it draws attention to the role of kings as fathers,
both begetters of sons to succeed them and simultaneously fathers to their
own people. In a celebrated passage, Bede characterised Æthelberht as 'the
third English king who ruled over the southern kingdoms, which are
divided from the north by the river Humber and the surrounding territory,
but he was the first to enter the kingdom of heaven'.[51] Æthelberht's own
lineage gave him the right to rule, but in not just accepting but promoting
the Christian faith, he created a model for a sort of rulership previously
unknown among the Anglo-Saxons, one based securely on biblical teachings. Bede quoted a letter from Pope Gregory in which the pope wrote to
Æthelberht, 'Almighty God raises up certain good men to be rulers over
nations in order that he may by their means bestow the gifts of his right-
eousness upon all those over whom they are set. We realize that this has
happened to the English race over whom your Majesty is placed, so that, by
means of the blessings granted to you, heavenly benefits may also be

---

[48] Bede, *HE* iii. 8 (ed. Colgrave and Mynors, p. 236); Kelly 'Eorcenberht'; and B. Yorke, *Kings and Kingdoms of Early Anglo-Saxon England* (London, 1990), pp. 32–6.
[49] Bede, *HE* iii. 8; iv. 19 (ed. Colgrave and Mynors, pp. 236 and 392–4); on Seaxburg's career, see S. J. Ridyard, *The Royal Saints of Anglo-Saxon England* (Cambridge, 1988), pp. 56–8, 89–92; and D. Rollason, 'Seaxburh (b. in or before 655, d. *c.* 700)', *ODNB*, vol. XIX, p. 616.
[50] Bede, *HE* i. 32 (ed. Colgrave and Mynors, p. 112).
[51] Bede, *HE* ii. 5 (ed. Colgrave and Mynors, pp. 148); Wormald, 'Bede, the bretwaldas', pp. 105–6; Fanning, 'Bede', pp. 3–4, 15–17; and Yorke, 'The *Bretwaldas*', pp. 82–7.

bestowed on your subjects.'[52] Gregory may have called Æthelberht his son, but he also gave him a clearly defined role as father over his own people.[53] And the ultimate role model for the kingship that he exercised on Earth was of course God the Father, the king of kings.

Some support for the suggestion that Bede placed particular weight on the paternal role of kings may be found in his treatment of kings whose bad behaviour he described as a warning to his readers. Among these were several who subverted the stability of their own families either by rejecting their father's religious choices or by acts of rebellion. For example, after the death of Æthelberht in 616, his son Eadbald took over the realm and there followed what Bede described as 'a severe setback to the tender growth of the church'. The 'apostate king' received an appropriate reward, however, being punished by frequent fits of madness and an unclean spirit.[54] Similarly, the three sons of Sæberht of the East Saxons had also all remained heathen during their father's lifetime; after his death in 616 or 617, they openly worshipped idols, a decision which in Bede's narrative led to their military defeat at the hands of the *Gewisse* (the people of Wessex).[55] More famously, following the death of Edwin, when Edwin's cousin Osric (son of his uncle Ælfric) became king of Deira and Æthelfrith's son Eanfrith ruled in Bernicia, both kings abandoned their Christian faith and, in Bede's words, 'returned to the filth of their former idolatry'. Therefore, Cædwalla of the Britons 'executed a just vengeance on them by killing them, although with unrighteous violence. And so those who compute the dates of kings have decided to abolish the memory of these perfidious kings and to assign this year to their successor, Oswald, a man beloved of God'.[56] On each of these occasions Bede made his moral point explicit: the stubbornly pagan rulers all suffered for their failure to embrace Christianity. While we must assume that Bede disapproved as strongly of

---

[52] Bede, *HE* i. 32 (ed. Colgrave and Mynors, pp. 110–12).

[53] Gregory drew on familial language in the advice he gave to leaders in his *Regula pastoralis*, iii. 4, ed. and trans. B. Judic, F. Rommel and C. Morel, Sources chrétiennes 381–2, 2 vols. (Paris, 1992), iii. 276, quoting Ephesians 6: 1 (cf. Colossians 3: 22).

[54] Bede, *HE* ii. 5 (ed. Colgrave and Mynors, p. 150). We might note here, however, as Richard Sowerby has pointed out to me, that Eadbald's other crime was to take his father's wife as his own, yet Bede seemingly made less of that familial sin than he did of the king's religious crimes.

[55] Bede, *HE* ii. 5 (ed. Colgrave and Mynors, pp. 152–4). For discussion of royal sons who apostacised (or, more plausibly, never fully converted but reverted publicly to paganism on their fathers' deaths), see H. Mayr-Harting, *The Coming of Christianity to Anglo-Saxon England* (London, 1972; 3rd edn, 1991), pp. 75–6; and B. Yorke, 'The Adaptation of the Anglo-Saxon Royal Courts to Christianity', in *The Cross Goes North: Processes of Conversion in Northern Europe 300–1300*, ed. M. Carver (Woodbridge, 2003), pp. 243–57, at 244–5.

[56] Bede, *HE* iii. 1 (ed. Colgrave and Mynors, pp. 212–14); and Loyn, 'Bede's Kings', p. 58.

royal princes who rebelled against legitimate kings – for example, the two Deiran kings Alhfrith, son of Oswiu, and Oethelwald, son of Oswald, both of whom rebelled against Oswiu of Bernicia[57] – he remained silent about the fate of Alhfrith, who disappeared from his narrative after the Synod of Whitby, presumably having lost power.[58] Less clear-cut is the position of Ecgfrith, son of Oswiu, and king of Northumbria after his father's death in 670 until 685. Bede described him in his *Historia abbatum* as 'a venerable and most pious king' because of his friendship with Benedict Biscop and his generosity to Wearmouth and Jarrow as well as his support of Cuthbert's ministry.[59] But Bede represented the same king in the *Historia ecclesiastica* in more muted tones.[60] As he noted, Ecgfrith's first wife, Æthelthryth (daughter of Anna, king of the East Angles, and widow of Tondberht, *princeps* of the South Gyrwe), had always lived as a virgin and refused to consummate her marriage to Ecgfrith; in the end she retired to live as a nun at Coldingham before returning to her native East Anglia to become abbess of Ely.[61] Bede so admired Æthelthryth that he composed a poem in honour of her virginity that he included in the *Historia*.[62] Yet her insistence on remaining chaste through twelve years of marriage to Ecgfrith prevented him from fulfilling his proper duty of fathering princes to rule after him; no issue is recorded from Ecgfrith's second marriage (to Iurminburg) either, and he was succeeded by his (half-) brother, Aldfrith, who, according to Bede, was illegitimate (although also noted for his learning).[63]

Bede consistently advocated the importance of stability and unity throughout his *Historia*; indeed, various modern scholars have argued that he did much to exaggerate the historical unity of Northumbria – originally two separate kingdoms – in order to promote an ideal of a single Northumbrian realm. He showed particular approval for the period between the accession of Oswald in 634 and the early eighth century, the time when the two kingdoms together were ruled by the same line of Northumbrian

[57] Bede, *HE* iii. 14 (ed. Colgrave and Mynors, p. 254).
[58] Mayr Harting, *Coming of Christianity*, pp. 105–13; and R. Abels, 'The Council of Whitby: A Study in Early Anglo-Saxon Politics', *Journal of British Studies* 23 (1983), 1–25, at 6–9.
[59] Bede, *Historia Abbatum*, [hereafter *HA*], chap. 1, in *Abbots of Wearmouth and Jarrow*, ed. and trans. C. Grocock and I. N. Wood (Oxford, 2013), p. 22.
[60] See N. J. Higham, *Ecgfrith, King of the Northumbrians, High-King of Britain* (Donnington, 2015).
[61] Bede, *HE* iv. 19 (ed. Colgrave and Mynors, p. 392).   [62] *Ibid.*, pp. 396–400.
[63] Bede, *Vita S. Cuthberti*, chap. 24, in *Two Lives of Saint Cuthbert*, ed. B. Colgrave (Cambridge, 1940), p. 238. On Aldfrith's family background, see B. Yorke, *Rex doctissimus: Bede and King Aldfrith of Northumbria* (Jarrow, 2009), pp. 7–11.

royal family to which Oswald belonged.[64] Equally, he observed with regret that the political dominance once enjoyed by the Northumbrian realm began to diminish because of the rash military ventures undertaken by Ecgfrith in 685, culminating in his death in battle with the Picts at Nechtansmere.[65] Despite his positive attributes (notably his generosity to the Church), Ecgfrith did not ultimately live up to Bede's ideals in the public sphere any more than he had done in the domestic. Various factors can explain why Bede laid such importance on political stability, among them obviously his familiarity with biblical narratives about the fate of the people of Israel and his awareness of how closely their well-being related to the quality of their kings.[66] Bede had no doubt that the history of the chosen people in both spiritual and political terms depended, under God, on the influence, ability and military strength of its leaders. His own reading and reflection, including his commentary on the first book of Samuel, revealed all too clearly how the disputes between kings and feuds within the families of Saul and David affected the fate of Israel; they also offered direct parallels for the royal families of Bernicia and Deira of Bede's own day.[67] When Bede wrote in his account of the reign of Oswald, 'By the efforts of this king, the kingdoms of Deira and Bernicia which had up to this time been at strife with one another, were peacefully united and became one people', he intended his readers to hear a moral message, one that commended unity.[68]

Similar promotion of the advantages to a secular realm of having a single strong ruler occurs more surprisingly in a passage in Bede's *Historia abbatum* about the succession to the abbacy of the joint monasteries of Wearmouth and Jarrow:

> Benedict [Biscop] thought it would be very salutary in every way for maintaining the peace, unity, and harmony of the two places if they had one father-abbot and ruler in perpetuity, often calling to mind the example of the kingdom of Israel, which always remained undamaged and unconquerable by foreign nations so long as it was ruled by a single leader, and he from that same people; but after it was split apart in a hateful internal

---

[64] D. Rollason, 'Hagiography and Politics in Early Northumbria', in *Holy Men and Holy Women: Old English Prose Saints' Lives and their Contexts*, ed. P. Szarmach (Albany, NY, 1996), pp. 95–114, at 105–6.

[65] Bede, *HE* iv. 26 (ed. Colgrave and Mynors, pp. 426–8); N. J. Higham, 'Bede's Agenda in Book IV of the *Ecclesiastical History of the English People*: A Tricky Matter of Advising the King', *JEH* 64 (2013), 476–493, at 491–3; compare Higham, *Ecgfrith*, pp. 170–29.

[66] See S. Zacher, *Rewriting the Old Testament in Anglo-Saxon Verse: Becoming the Chosen People* (London, 2013), pp. 26–8 and 103–4.

[67] Wallace-Hadrill, *Early Germanic Kingship*, pp. 76–8; and Higham, 'Bede's Agenda', pp. 483–6.

[68] Bede, *HE* iii. 6 (ed. Colgrave and Mynors, pp. 230–2); and Loyn, 'Bede's Kings', p. 57.

struggle because its sins overtook it, it perished little by little, and struck down from its position of security it became extinct.[69]

Bede clearly intended to draw a parallel between the familial model of a monastery – a community of brothers in Christ gathered together under a father, the abbot, to whom they owed obedience – and a kingdom, specifically, it seems, the united kingdom of Northumbria (for the abbey of Wearmouth-Jarrow enjoyed good connections with both Deira and Bernicia). Let us move our conspectus out more widely and look in more general terms at the ways in which Bede depicted the rule of kings. Does our understanding of his views change if we focus our gaze through the lens of fatherhood?

Kingly *Ministerium*

One of the primary obligations owed by a king to his own people directly reflected the role that a father should perform for his own blood family. It fell to a king to provide for the needs of his people, to bring them peace and prosperity in the form of freedom from danger and external threat and to secure sufficient resources to shelter and provide materially for his people and their own households. The military side of that role – the achieving of peace by victory in war – we have already considered, and I will offer just one further example here, that of Æthelfrith, father of Oswald and Oswiu, whom we encountered earlier.[70] He clearly met with Bede's approval despite his adherence to paganism. Bede described Æthelfrith as 'a very brave king and most eager for glory', asserting that no other king or ruler subjected more land to the English race or settled it. Thus he could be likened to the character of Saul and the words used of Benjamin (to whose tribe Saul belonged) in the Old Testament: 'Benjamin shall ravin as a wolf; in the morning he shall devour his prey and at night shall divide the spoil.'[71] As Tugene has explained, this allusion rests upon an understanding that it might also be applied to the apostle Paul (called Saul before his conversion): the wolf that devours in the morning by persecuting Christians distributes his prey in the evening by preaching the gospel to the gentiles.[72] The whole chapter does more than celebrate Æthelfrith's

---

[69] Bede, *HA* chap. 13 (ed. and trans. Grocock and Wood, pp. 52–3).   [70] *Ibid.*

[71] Bede, *HE* i. 34 (ed. Colgrave and Mynors, p. 116), quoting Gen 49: 27. On the importance of Saul as a model for kingship to Bede, see Wallace-Hadrill, *Early Germanic Kingship*, pp. 76–8; and McClure, 'Bede's Old Testament Kings', pp. 89–92.

[72] G. Tugene, 'L'histoire "ecclésiastique" du peuple anglais: réflexions sur le particularisme et l'universalisme chez Bède', *Recherches augustiniennes* 17 (1982) 129–172, at 163–4; and *HE Comm.*, p. 48.

military power and his role in punishing the Britons; it also prepares the reader for the future missionary role of the English and the fulfilment of Augustine's prophecy to the British that if they would not accept their duty of preaching the gospel to the English, then they should anticipate the vengeance of death at their hands, as Æthelfrith duly delivered at the battle of Chester.[73]

The capacity of a king to provide in this way for his people depended significantly upon the nature of his relationship with God. Thus, as we have already seen, Oswald prayed with his army at Heavenfield, and before the battle of *Winwæd*, Oswiu made a bargain with God that if he were successful in the fight, he would dedicate his young daughter to God.[74] St Augustine may have warned against worshipping the Christian God merely in hope of obtaining good fortune (making specific comparison with the prosperity, happiness and military success enjoyed by the emperor Constantine as a direct result of his favour in God's eyes), stating that 'every man should be a Christian only for the sake of eternal life.'[75] Yet it is hard not to agree with Wallace-Hadrill's reading that Bede attached a rather higher value than did Augustine to the prosperity and victory that were the material consequences of good rule.[76] The celebrated passage in which Bede described the proverbial peace of Northumbria in King Edwin's day, when it was said that a woman might safely carry a babe in her arms from shore to shore without harm, touches both on the king's paternal care for his people (setting up stakes with bronze drinking cups on them near wayside springs so that thirsty travellers could refresh themselves) and on the splendour of his own majesty, marked out by the standards that he had carried before him wherever he went.[77] The peace of Edwin's realm paralleled that of the Old Testament King Solomon, son of David, who enjoyed dominion over a huge area, and over all its kings, and had peace on all his frontiers.[78] In a homily on the Incarnation, Bede also laid great stress on the peace achieved in the time of the Emperor

---

[73] Bede, *HE* ii. 2 (ed. Colgrave and Mynors, pp. 140–1); Plummer, *Bedae opera*, vol. II, pp. 76–7; Yorke, 'The *Bretwaldas*', p. 89.

[74] Bede, *HE* iii. 2; iii. 24 (ed. Colgrave and Mynors, pp. 214 and 290).

[75] *Augustine: The City of God against the Pagans*, vol. 25, ed. and trans. R. W. Dyson (Cambridge, 1998), p. 233.

[76] Wallace-Hadrill, *Early Germanic Kingship*, p. 73.

[77] Bede, *HE* ii. 16 (ed. Colgrave and Mynors, p. 192); and Loyn, 'Bede's Kings', p. 57.

[78] 1 Kings 4: 24–5; and McClure, 'Bede's Old Testament Kings', p. 88. For discussion of how Bede wove his image of Edwin from scriptural typologies and the imagery and ceremony of the later Roman empire, melding the idea of *pax* with that of *imperium*, see P. J. E. Kershaw, *Peaceful Kings: Peace, Power, and the Early Medieval Political Imagination* (Oxford, 2011), pp. 31–9.

Augustus (in whose day Christ was born, at the time when the emperor had sent out an edict 'that the whole world should be enrolled')[79]: '[W]hat could be a greater indication of peace in this life than for the entire world to be enrolled by one man and to be included in a single coinage.'[80]

King Edwin's capacity to provide such a safe and prosperous environment for his people to flourish resulted obviously from his military capacity to ensure the peace of his borders for the brief duration of his reign but more in Bede's eyes because of his decision to bring his people to the true faith and to support the work of Christian missionaries in his realm.[81] In that same Christmas sermon, Bede reminded his hearers that 'we must not pass over the fact that the serenity of that earthly peace at the time when the Heavenly King was born, not only offered testimony to his grace, but it provided a service, since it bestowed on the preachers of his word the capability of travelling over the world and spreading abroad the grace of the gospel.'[82] Bede also quoted a letter of Pope Vitalian to Oswiu of Northumbria: '[T]hat race is indeed blessed which has been found worthy to have so wise a king and one who is a worshipper of God'; quoting Isaiah, the pope compared Oswiu to a root of Jesse 'which shall stand for an ensign of the people, to which the Gentiles shall seek'.[83] Manifestly, a range of factors was at play here, but paternal imagery does not seem inappropriate. Here we have examples of kings treating their subjects as extended family, taking upon themselves a role for their material and also their spiritual wellbeing that extended beyond their immediate locality to the very bounds of their shores. Like bishops, kings were fathers and shepherds with responsibilities not only to their own households but also over the larger flock entrusted to their care.[84]

A variety of models was available to Bede in his search for definitions of good kingship in addition to the Old Testament exemplars already mentioned, including both Roman and early Christian statements of political

---

[79] Luke 2: 1.

[80] Bede, *Homelia*, i. 6, in *Bedae Venerabilis Opera Pars III/IV*, ed. D. Hurst, CCSL 122 (Turnhout, 1955), p. 37; and *Bede the Venerable, Homilies on the Gospels: Book One, Advent to Lent*, trans. L. T. Martin and D. Hurst (Kalamazoo, MI, 1991), p. 52,

[81] Bede, *HE* II. 14 (ed. Colgrave and Mynors, pp. 186–8).

[82] Bede, *Homelia* i. 6, in *Bedae Venerabilis Opera Pars III/IV*, ed. Hurst, p. 38; in *Bede the Venerable, Homilies on the Gospels: Book One, Advent to Lent*, trans. Martin and Hurst, p. 53.

[83] Bede, *HE* iii. 29 (ed. Colgrave and Mynors, p. 318).

[84] These same motifs recur interestingly in the reign of King Edgar, who was described as *Christi vicarius* in the New Minster foundation charter (S 745, chap. vii); some of the central players in the religious reform movement of Edgar's reign, especially Æthelwold, bishop of Winchester, looked back to Bede for inspiration: A. Gransden, 'Traditionalism and Continuity during the Last Century of Anglo-Saxon Monasticism', *JEH* 40 (1989), 159–207.

theory as well as the traditions of leadership in Germanic society. Whatever conceptions of rulership the various Anglo-Saxon peoples had brought with them from their native homelands in Europe, these will have undergone considerable adaptation during the migration process and after the settlement and formation of the first English kingdoms. While warfare remained a central kingly duty (indeed, the Old English word for a lord or ruler, *dryhten*, meant 'warband leader', as Wormald noted),[85] other obligations attached themselves to the role, including those of judge and law-giver, even before the more significant adaptations that followed from conversion to Christianity.[86] Fundamentally, Bede considered secular rule to have a firm moral basis and clearly defined Christian objectives.[87] The decrees of God's law specified the manner in which kings ought to live and taught them what they should do. As Bede wrote to Nothhelm in his *Thirty Questions on the Book of Kings*, '[H]e who sees himself as exalted to rule over the people must remember that he himself is to be ruled and subject to divine laws.'[88] Here he echoed the sentiments expressed in Isidore's *Etymologies*, where kings are said to be 'so called from governing ... But he does not govern who does not correct. Therefore the name of king is held by one behaving rightly (*recte*) and lost by one doing wrong ... The royal virtues are these two especially: justice and mercy, but mercy is more praised in kings because justice in itself is harsh.'[89] In Isidore's thought, P. D. King has argued, the king was 'the predestined appointee of God, set at the summit of society in the same way that the head is set over the body, and for the same purpose, to rule the "subject members"'. The king was God's minister, the agent through whom God worked; the most useful tool at his disposal for ensuring wellbeing of society was the law.[90] All of these principles also find expression in Bede's representations of kingship.

---

[85] P. Wormald, 'Kings and Kingship', in *The New Cambridge Medieval History*, vol. I: *c. 500–c. 700*, ed. P. Fouracre (Cambridge, 2005), pp. 571–604, at 595–6.

[86] P. Wormald, '*Lex scripta* and *verbum regis*: Legislation and Germanic Kingship, from Euric to Cnut', in *Early Medieval Kingship*, ed. P. H. Sawyer and I. N. Wood (Leeds, 1977), pp. 105–138; and Loyn, 'Bede's Kings', pp. 59–60.

[87] Wallace-Hadrill, *Early Germanic Kingship*, p. 74.

[88] Bede, *In regum librum xxx quaestiones* xix, in *Bedae venerabilis opera, pars II: Opera exegetica 2*, ed. D. Hurst, CCSL 119 (Turnhout, 1962), p. 314; *Bede: A Biblical Miscellany*, trans. W. Trent Foley (Liverpool, 1999), p. 123; and see McClure, 'Bede's Old Testament Kings', p. 92.

[89] *Isidori Hispalensis Episcopi Etymologiarum sive originum libri XX, IX. iii. 4*, ed. W. M. Lindsay, 2 vols. (Oxford, 1911); *The Etymologies of Isidore of Seville*, trans. S. A. Barney, W. J. Lewis, J. A. Beach and O. Berghof (Cambridge, 2006), p. 200.

[90] P. D. King, 'The Barbarian Kingdoms', in *The Cambridge History of Medieval Political Thought c. 350–c. 1450*, ed. J. H. Burns (Cambridge, 1988; 2nd edn, 1991), pp. 123–53, at 144.

Like Isidore, Bede had an essentially ministerial conception of kingship, as Tugene has shown; in his eyes, kings had obligations to render service to God, the Church and to the Christian people. They performed that role most obviously when they took it upon themselves to promote the Christian faith, not just by encouraging missionaries and promoting conversion but also by providing for the material support of the Church by endowing cathedrals and monasteries with lands and moveable wealth.[91] Bede acquired much of the underpinning of this understanding from the writings of Gregory the Great, whose political vocabulary tended to merge the secular and ecclesiastical worlds into one, making secular governance as much a *ministerium* as was ecclesiastical rule.[92] Some of Gregory's notions concerning authority reflected Benedict of Nursia's image of the abbot, which provides a deeply paternalistic view of authority.[93] Gregory also observed, however, that those who were placed in authority needed to deserve their position by merit and to remember the fundamental equality of humans while performing their ministry. Pope Gregory spelt out these obligations in a letter to King Æthelberht that Bede quoted in full: '[S]o my illustrious son, watch carefully over the grace you have received from God and hasten to extend the Christian faith among the people who are subject to you. Increase your righteous zeal for their conversion, suppress the worship of idols, overthrow their buildings and shrines, strengthen the morals of your subjects by outstanding purity of life, by exhorting them, terrifying, enticing and correcting them, and by showing them an example of good works.'[94] Thus Bede's ideal kings were those who most closely embodied those virtues, who could unite their own personal Christian attributes of faith and humility with a concern for the wellbeing of others, just as a father would do for his children.[95]

Humility might seem an unlikely virtue for a king, especially if we continue to hold in mind the imagery of the warrior kings suggested by the Staffordshire Hoard. But in Bede's account this was one of King Oswald's key attributes, a mark of the strength of his kingship and of his claim to sanctity.[96] He declared that Oswald was always wonderfully humble, kind and generous,[97] and the young Deiran king, Oswine, also

[91] Tugene 'Rois moines', pp. 117–18.
[92] R. A. Markus, 'The Latin Fathers', in *Cambridge History of Medieval Political Thought*, ed. Burns, pp. 83–122, at 120.
[93] *Ibid.*; cf. Wallace-Hadrill, *Early Germanic Kingship*, p. 74.
[94] Bede, *HE* i. 32 (ed. Colgrave and Mynors, p. 112).   [95] Stancliffe, 'Oswald', p. 64.
[96] Wallace-Hadrill, *Early Germanic Kingship*, p. 83.
[97] Bede, *HE* iii. 6 (ed. Colgrave and Mynors, p. 230); and Stancliffe 'Oswald', p. 61.

stood out for his humility. Bishop Aidan declared of the latter that he had never seen such a humble king, yet this led him to prophesy that the king would not live long 'for this nation does not deserve to have such a ruler'.[98] That humility – and obedience – were kingly virtues Bede made clear in his commentary on the First Book of Samuel. He commented on Saul's humility after he had been anointed by Samuel[99] and commended his humility in adhering to God's teachings, listening to his voice and walking in the ways in which the Lord had sent him.[100] But he was also highly critical when Saul's pride and independence of mind got the better of him so that he ceased to listen to God's word.[101] Gregory had advised those who rule of the need for humility, also drawing attention to Saul and pointing to the dangers of pride, but he was equally clear that while a ruler should be humble in his heart, in governing he should not fear to use discipline when necessary.[102] Oswald (and Oswine) stood in stark contrast to Edwin, whose pride baulked at the humility of the Christian cross; Bishop Paulinus recognised how hard it would be for King Edwin's 'proud mind to turn humbly to the way of salvation'.[103] The humility that so characterised Oswald found its strongest articulation in his obedience to the Church, something of which Pope Gregory would certainly have approved.[104]

The paternal role of a king to bring his own people to faith takes on a different perspective when kings made use of alliances with the rulers of other realms to advance the Christian religion. Consider, for example, the spiritual relationship that Oswald supposedly had with Cynegils of Wessex, a complicated arrangement involving his standing as godfather to the West Saxon king at the font but also marrying his daughter. The two kings together are credited with having helped Birinus to establish an episcopal see at Dorchester (the site of a former Roman fort).[105] One might express some doubts about the extent of the political realities that underpin this story – particularly its implication that the land at Dorchester could have been in Oswald's gift – but what is relevant here

---

[98] Bede, *HE* iii. 14 (ed. Colgrave and Mynors, p. 258); and Loyn, 'Bede's Kings', p. 56.

[99] Bede, *In primam partem Samuhelis libri IIII* [hereafter *In I Sam.*], II. xiii. 1, in *Bedae venerabilis opera, pars II: Opera exegetica 2*, ed. D. Hurst, CCSL 119 (Turnhout, 1962), p. 102; Wallace-Hadrill, *Early Germanic Kingship*, pp. 85–6; Wallace-Hadrill, *Early Medieval History*, p. 108; and McClure, 'Bede's Old Testament Kings', p. 92.

[100] *In I Sam.* II. xv. 20 (ed. Hurst, pp. 132–3).   [101] *In I Sam.* II. xv. 16 (ed. Hurst, p. 132).

[102] Gregory, *Regula pastoralis*, ii. 6, trans. H. Davis, in *St Gregory the Great, Pastoral Care* (New York, 1950), p. 62.

[103] Bede, *HE* ii. 12 (ed. Colgrave and Mynors, p. 176); and Stancliffe, 'Oswald', p. 62.

[104] Wallace-Hadrill, *Early Germanic Kingship*, p. 86.

[105] Bede, *HE* iii. 7 (ed. Colgrave and Mynors, p. 232); and J. Blair, *The Church in Anglo-Saxon Society* (Oxford, 2005), p. 188.

is the significance of the extension of an understanding of family to include parents and children bound through the sacrament of baptism as spiritual kin. Bede portrayed Oswald as extending his own family by marriage and taking an active evangelising role with his in-laws.[106] Aldfrith, son of Oswiu, did the same for his brother-in-law Peada, son of Penda, king of the Middle Angles.[107] No family connection linked Oswiu and Sigeberht of the East Saxons; rather, Oswiu appears to have been the East Saxon king's overlord, yet Bede showed how the Northumbrian king used religious arguments about the nature of the Almighty and his promises of eternal reward to teach Sigeberht about the Christian religion, until the pagan king came to believe. He was baptised by Bishop Finan on a Northumbrian royal estate near Hadrian's Wall.[108] Despite the apparent evidence of this last anecdote that Oswiu had enough grasp of the principles of the Christian faith to be able to use some theological understanding and biblical knowledge in his efforts to persuade the East Saxon king, few of the kings found in the pages of Bede's history receive praise for their learning.[109] A reputation for learning would not have conflicted with the paternalistic role of kings that we have been describing, but neither was it self-evidently a major part of Bede's conception of ideal kingship.

The Ends of Kings' Reigns

Bede's accounts of the deaths of kings often reveal his views about the institution of kingship most clearly, demonstrating which individuals had best conformed to an ideal that saw the king as the predestined appointee of God, set over the body to rule its members. Kingship was certainly inheritable, but Bede obviously also believed that kings were appointed by God and that God could – and did – determine when to take the rulership away from a king who did not meet his standards. We have already encountered the sons of the earliest Christian kings in the south of England whose reversion to paganism incurred divine displeasure.[110] Ecgfrith of Northumbria similarly provoked the Almighty's wrath by

[106] J Lynch, *Christianizing Kinship: Ritual Sponsorship in Anglo-Saxon England* (Ithaca, NY, and London, 1998), pp. 66, 83–5 and 210.

[107] Bede, *HE* iii. 21 (ed. Colgrave and Mynors, p. 278); and Lynch, *Christianizing Kinship*, p. 209.

[108] Bede, *HE* iii. 22 (ed. Colgrave and Mynors, pp. 280–2).

[109] One notable exception was Aldfrith, Ecgfrith's half-brother and his successor as king of Northumbria, who was described by Bede as a man 'most learned in the scriptures' and 'most learned in all respects': Bede, *HE* iv. 26 and v. 12 (ed. Colgrave and Mynors, pp. 430 and 496); cf. also Bede, *HA*, chap. 15 (ed. and trans. Grocock and Wood, pp. 58–9); and see Yorke, *Rex doctissimus*.

[110] Bede, *HE* ii. 5 (ed. Colgrave and Mynors, pp. 150–4). See above.

undertaking a military expedition against the blameless Irish and the following year 'rashly took an army to ravage the kingdom of the Picts, against the urgent advice of his friends' and especially that of Bishop Cuthbert. He died in that battle, and Bede remarked that having failed to heed the guidance he had been given not to attack the Irish who had done him no harm, 'the punishment for his sin was that he would not now listen to those who sought to save him from his own destruction.' It was from this time on, Bede believed, that the 'hopes and strength of the English kingdom began to "ebb and fall away"'.[111]

Death in battle or in violent circumstances did not have to serve as a mark of God's lasting disfavour, however; quite the contrary. In a short chapter describing the spread of Christianity to the last area of English occupation to receive missionaries – the Isle of Wight – Bede recounted the execution of two newly baptised princes on the island, who, in dying, were assured that they would pass to the eternal life of the soul. Their death reflected the West Saxon king Cædwalla's determination to wipe out the local population and replace it with his own followers. Although not technically martyrs for their faith (for it was their identity as sons of the island's king that necessitated the princes' death in Cædwalla's eyes, not their religious affiliation), the neophytes were able to receive the grace of baptism as the first fruits of the conversion of the island and so were specially crowned with God's grace.[112] Edwin, Oswald and the unfortunate Oswine (who was murdered on the orders of Oswiu) could all be shown to have fulfilled Bede's image of ideal Christian kings, and yet all three met violent deaths in circumstances that could give them a claim to sanctity in martyrdom.[113] Cults of all three did indeed ensue, even if Bede did not choose to reveal in his *Historia* anything about the cult of Edwin at Whitby or that of Oswine, just across the river from Jarrow at Tynemouth.[114] Even in death these kings continued to act for the protection and support of the living by interceding on their behalf with the Almighty. Bede argued that 'it is not to be wondered at that the prayers of this king [Oswald] who is now reigning with the Lord should greatly prevail, for while he was ruling over his temporal kingdom, he was always accustomed to work and pray most diligently for the kingdom which is eternal.'[115] And it was not only for

---

[111] Bede, *HE* iv. 26 (ed. Colgrave and Mynors, p. 428).
[112] Bede, *HE* iv. 16 (ed. Colgrave and Mynors, p. 382).   [113] Loyn, 'Bede's Kings', p. 56.
[114] Wallace-Hadrill, *Early Germanic Kingship*, pp. 86–7; and I. N. Wood, 'Bede's Jarrow', in *A Place to Believe in: Locating Medieval Landscapes*, ed. C. A. Lees and G. R. Overing (University Park, PA, 2006), pp. 67–84, at 81–2.
[115] Bede, *HE* iii. 12 (ed. Colgrave and Mynors, p. 250).

his own flock that Oswald apparently prayed in heaven. Bede narrated an
episode about an outbreak of plague at the South Saxon monastery of
Selsey from which the majority of the monks were apparently saved by the
intercession of King Oswald, 'who prayed to the Lord for them as if of his
own race though [they were] strangers'.[116]

Bede revealed himself to be more ambivalent about kings' behaviour and
the fate due to them in the circumstances in which, to use Clare Stancliffe's
phrase, they 'opted out'. His hesitations related to those kings whose
commitment to the new religion conflicted with their duties to rule and
guide their people, including that of leading them in battle. Sigeberht, king
of the East Angles, was the first of six Anglo-Saxon kings who abdicated their
thrones in order to enter monasteries; he was dragged out by his people and
forced to face an invading Mercian army; refusing to bear arms, he was killed
and his army defeated.[117] Five others resigned to go to Rome on pilgrimage,
and others such as Oswiu wanted to do so but died before they could. The
first to make the journey was, somewhat ironically given the tale I just told
about the princes of the Isle of Wight, the West Saxon Cædwalla, who went
to Rome in 689 with the intention of receiving baptism there but died soon
after.[118] Bede seemed to approve the decision of Cenred of Mercia, who had
'reigned very nobly but renounced his kingdom with still greater nobility'.[119]
But he expressed distinctly more ambivalence about the decision of Offa, son
of a king of the East Saxons, 'a youth so lovable and handsome that the whole
race longed for him to have and to hold the sceptre of the kingdom' to travel
with Cenred to Rome; he left his wife, lands, kinsmen and fatherland for the
gospel to inherit one-hundred-fold in the life to come.[120] It is hard not to feel
that Bede had some hesitations about the virtue of such behaviour, however
admirable it might have seemed on religious terms. If he shared with Pope
Gregory a vision of rulership as a *ministerium*, as a form of service, he will
also have subscribed to the pope's belief that religious leaders needed to
sacrifice their own desire for peace and contemplation in order to serve the
needs of others.[121] Kings who opted out of the task placed on them by God
were not fulfilling the divine will. Their path to salvation, as Gregory spelt
out clearly in the advice he gave to Anglo-Saxon kings, was in ensuring the
salvation of their own flock.[122] This represents another respect in which
kings exercised a paternal role. Those who failed to bring that responsibility

[116] Bede, *HE* iv. 14 (ed. Colgrave and Mynors, p. 378).
[117] Bede, *HE* iii. 18 (ed. Colgrave and Mynors, p. 162); and Stancliffe, 'Kings Who Opted Out', p. 154.
[118] Bede, *HE* v. 7 (ed. Colgrave and Mynors, p. 292).
[119] Bede, *HE* v. 19 (ed. Colgrave and Mynors, p. 516).   [120] *Ibid.*
[121] Stancliffe, 'Kings Who Opted Out', p. 176.   [122] Tugene, 'Rois moines', pp. 142–3.

to completion – by persisting in it until the end of their natural lives – not only left their realms potentially leaderless, but they also contrived to make orphans of their subjects.

Conclusion

These reflections on Bede's attitudes towards the kings about whom he wrote in his *Historia* form part of a wider project of mine to write an intellectual biography of Bede; in that endeavour I shall seek connections between the ideas that Bede articulated in different contexts and attempt to identify some of the coherent themes that underpinned his wider worldview. It is not coincidental, therefore, that I found myself focusing particularly on the responsibilities of kings to act as fathers to their people, because I think that this spoke particularly to Bede's personal circumstances.

Commenting on a verse in Proverbs – which warns against removing the boundary stones of little ones or entering into the lands of orphans because their kinsmen are powerful and can argue their case against one – Bede pointed out that God can be considered the near kin of little ones and orphans and the protector of all who call upon him.[123] Given what we know about Bede's own background – that he was given by his *propinqui* (by which he might have meant his mother and father but could equally have referred to some more distant relatives or kinsmen) to the care of the monastery at Wearmouth at the age of seven – one might wonder whether he were in fact an orphan.[124] Clearly, this is a speculative idea, but let me push the speculation a little further by drawing attention to the close relationship that Bede appears to have made with Ceolfrith, abbot of the monastery of Jarrow.[125] Might that closeness have arisen because Bede had never known his own father, with the result that Ceolfrith came to fulfil that emotional need in the young oblate's life? If so, this would put into better context Bede's apparent complete emotional collapse when Ceolfrith left for Rome in 716, a collapse that he movingly described in the Prologue he wrote to the fourth book of his commentary on Samuel:

---

[123] Bede, *In proverbia Salomonis*, II. xxiii. 10/11, in *Bedae Venerabilis Opera, pars II: Opera exegetica* 2B, ed. D. Hurst, CCSL 119B (Turnhout, 1983), 118 (Proverbs 23: 10–11).

[124] Bede, *HE* v. 24 (ed. Colgrave and Mynors, p. 566).

[125] He described Ceolfrith as 'noster parens': *HA*, chap. 23 (ed. and trans. Grocock and Wood, p. 74). See also M. Brown, 'Bede's Life in Context', in *The Cambridge Companion to Bede*, ed. S. DeGregorio (Cambridge, 2010), pp. 3–24, at 5–9. Compare the way in which Stephen portrayed Wilfrid as a father in the life of that saint; see W. Trent Foley, *Images of Sanctity in Eddius Stephanus' Life of Bishop Wilfrid* (Lewiston, Queenston, Lampeter, 1992), pp. 53–70.

'Having completed the third book of the commentary I thought that I would rest a while, and, after recovering that way my delight in study and writing proceed to take in hand the fourth. But that rest – if sudden anguish of mind can be called rest – has turned out much longer than I intended owing to the sudden change of circumstances brought by the departure of my most reverend abbot.'[126] Clearly Bede's mental distress caused him to be unable to work for some while; only with the return of quieter times did he regain both the leisure and the delight for searching out the wondrous things of Holy Scripture carefully and with his whole soul.[127] Others have commented on the seemingly disproportionate nature of this response to Ceolfrith's departure and Bede's articulation of a level of emotional distress that one would not necessarily have anticipated.[128] But if Ceolfrith had effectively been the only father Bede had ever known, it might be more explicable. Would it stretch imagination too far to wonder whether Bede's particular view of the paternal role of kings might also have owed something to his own insecure early childhood and his search for a father?

Bede manifestly valued uniformity and unity of observance not only in the Church but also in the secular realm. He approved of stability within individual royal houses and believed that Northumbria functioned better when united into a single kingdom. Further, he looked for opportunities to point out how much the separate English kingdoms shared through language, culture, social organisation, history and above all their common faith. Ultimately, it was that faith in the gospel and in the saving power of Christ that seems to me to underpin Bede's worldview. As Wallace-Hadrill argued in a memorable passage, Bede saw kings on Earth essentially as reflections of the majesty of the heavenly king. Kings exercised their temporal power 'by God's authority and for his purposes, namely the furthering of religion by protecting his priests and monks, encouraging their work, exhorting the faithful by personal example, and by carrying the Gospel, by fire and sword if necessary, into neighbouring territories where it was unknown or misunderstood. It is this that binds together a people into a *Populus Dei* after the manner of the Israelites.'[129] While Bede may indeed have attached himself emotionally to the fathers who served as abbots of his monastery, he knew of course that his real father was the

---

[126] *In I Sam.*, iv. prol (ed. Hurst, p. 212; trans. Plummer, *Bedae Opera*, vol. I, pp. xv–xvi).

[127] Plummer pointed out (*ibid.*) that when Bede wrote this, it would seem that news of Ceolfrith's death had not yet reached Jarrow.

[128] I. N. Wood, *The Most Holy Abbot Ceolfrid* (Jarrow 1995), p. 18; and Brown, 'Bede's Life', p. 9.

[129] Wallace-Hadrill, *Early Germanic Kingship*, p. 97.

father he would ultimately meet in heaven. While acknowledging him as god of gods and king of kings, the righteous judge, Bede also saw him as the loving father who, when humanity, like the prodigal son, was still far off, met his children in his son and brought them home.[130] It seems reasonable to suggest that Bede himself had only the most limited personal experience of how effective familial relationships worked themselves out on a daily basis in a secular household; his whole experience of father/son and brotherly relations was forged in the quite different context of the cloister. In making his ideal kings into perfect fathers, Bede consciously echoed a well-defined line of patristic thought. He may also unconsciously have been answering a more personal, unspoken desire to be fathered himself. As his own end drew near – on the eve of the feast of the Ascension of the risen Christ to heaven – the monk Cuthbert who witnessed his death said that Bede apparently struggled to say the words of the antiphon: 'Leave us not comfortless' (literally, 'orphaned': *ne derelinquas nos orphanos*). But once he knew that it was time to be released from his body and return to his creator, Bede could say confidently, '[M]y soul longs to see Christ my King in all his beauty.' He therefore asked to be held as he sat where he had always been wont to pray, in order that he might call upon his Father. And so upon the floor of his cell, singing the words of the *Gloria patri*, 'he breathed his last.'[131]

---

[130] Luke 15: 20. Cf. Bede, *In Lucae euangelium expositio*, IV. xv. 20, in *Bedae venerabilis opera, pars II: Opera exegetica* 3, ed. Q. Hurst, CCSL 120 (Turnhout, 1960), p. 290.

[131] Cuthbert's letter on the death of Bede, ed. Colgrave and Mynors, pp. 582–6.

CHAPTER 4

Hagiography and Charters in Early Northumbria*

David A. Woodman

If you walk into St Paul's church in Jarrow today, you will see a late-seventh-century Northumbrian inscription recording the dedication of the church on 23 April, 685 (see Figure 4.1). It has been incised on two stones, and, with the abbreviations expanded and word divisions inserted, the upper stone reads:

[chi-rho] DEDICATIO BASILICAE
SANCTI PAVLI VIIII KALENDAS MAIAS
ANNO XV ECFRIDI REGIS

and the lower stone reads:

CEOLFRIDI ABBATIS EIVSDEMQVE ECCLESIAE DEO AUCTORE CONDITORIS
ANNO IIII[1]

Higgitt has shown how these inscriptions demonstrate Jarrow's *romanitas* at this early stage in its history: the language of the inscriptions may find inspiration from documents of the papal chancery,[2] while the way in which the letters are formed can be closely compared with capitals in the *Codex Amiatinus*.[3] These similarities demonstrate collaboration between those at

---

* It is not possible adequately to express my gratitude to Simon Keynes, both professionally and personally. From the moment I was interviewed in December 1998 for an undergraduate place to read Anglo-Saxon, Norse and Celtic at Trinity College, Cambridge, he has shown the greatest generosity, and latterly friendship, to me. Were it not for his inspirational example as a teacher and scholar, I would not be attempting to pursue an academic path. In this chapter I am drawing on research done and ideas formulated during the writing of my MPhil and PhD dissertations, the first of which was examined by Simon Keynes and the second of which was supervised by him. It therefore seems a particularly appropriate offering for the honorand of this volume.

[1] 'The dedication of the church of St Paul [was] on 23 April in the fifteenth year of King Ecgfrith and the fourth year of Ceolfrith the abbot and, under God's guidance, founder of this same church.' E. Okasha, *Hand-List of Anglo-Saxon Non-Runic Inscriptions* (Cambridge, 1971), pp. 85–6 (no. 61); cf. R. Cramp, *Wearmouth and Jarrow Monastic Sites*, 2 vols. (Swindon, 2005), esp. vol. I, pp. 365–6.

[2] J. Higgitt, 'The Dedication Inscription at Jarrow and Its Context', *AntJ* 59 (1979), 343–74, at 350 and 364.

[3] *Ibid.*, pp. 358–9 and 362–3.

Figure 4.1 Jarrow dedication stone. (By Bob Naismith.)

Jarrow responsible for the writing of texts and those tasked with the composition of a dedication inscription. But it is also worth noting that the chi-rho used, although typical of early Italian models,[4] is also employed as a pictorial invocation at the beginning of various Anglo-Saxon diplomas.[5] And the use of the regnal year in the dating of the inscription can likewise be paralleled in Anglo-Saxon diplomatic.[6] Similar evidence of cross-fertilisation or generic 'mixing' can be seen in the case of Anglo-Saxon charters.

In the seventh century, Anglo-Saxon ecclesiastics saw the value in having a form of written proof of ownership so that lands could be held free from

---

[4] *Ibid.*, p. 349.

[5] Higgitt compares the Jarrow chi-rho to that found in two late-eighth-century Mercian diplomas: *ibid.*, p. 349.

[6] One should compare here the chapter of the *Life of Ceolfrith* that records the beginning of the building of the Wearmouth church using a dating-clause that employs an indiction, a regnal year and an *anno Domini* date. The same chapter states that this church was given fifty hides of land by King Ecgfrith. Both the dating-clause and the grant of land are written in terms reminiscent of charter diplomatic. See the *Vita Ceolfridi*, chap. 7, in *Abbots of Wearmouth and Jarrow*, ed. and trans. C. Grocock and I. N. Wood (Oxford, 2013), pp. 84–6.

certain financial obligations and could be passed from generation to generation. These were some of the reasons that charters were first introduced
in England, as instruments of the Church.[7] S 8 (*CantCC* 2), issued in 679
by King Hlothhere of Kent and celebrated as the earliest extant original
Anglo-Saxon diploma, opens with a divine invocation ('In nomine
Domini nostri saluatoris Iesu Christi'). It is therefore interesting that the
words with which Stephen opens his account of St Wilfrid's life, the *Vita
Wilfrithi* (hereafter *VW*), are 'In nomine Domini nostri Christi Iesu' ('In
the name of our Lord Christ Jesus').[8] Did Stephen have in mind the
wording of a diploma? At the outset of his work, was he trying to suggest
that his *vita* aspired to the formal status of a legal document? The question
is worth asking in the light of the circumstances in which the *VW* was
composed.

Lindisfarne and the Anonymous *Vita sancti Cuthberti*

Anglo-Saxon Northumbria was the kingdom where many of the most
celebrated early religious houses were situated. Some of these institutions
enjoyed fame across contemporary Europe and maintained links with
other European houses. But, despite the political and ecclesiastical reputation of Northumbria, there were signs of discord and internal divisions.[9] In
664, the Council of Whitby had shown this very publicly, and it was here
that Wilfrid, in Bede's *Historia ecclesiastica*, was celebrated as the champion
of the Roman method of calculating the date of Easter.[10] The departure of
Wilfrid's principal opponent at the Council of Whitby, Colman, indicated
the kind of discontent that remained for those at Lindisfarne who still

[7] For the introduction of the Anglo-Saxon charter, see P. Chaplais, 'Who Introduced Charters into
England? The Case for Augustine', *Journal of the Society of Archivists* 3. 10 (1969), 526–42, reprinted
in *Prisca Munimenta*, ed. F. Ranger (London, 1973), pp. 88–107; S. Kelly, 'Anglo-Saxon Lay Society
and the Written Word', in *The Uses of Literacy in Early Mediaeval Europe*, ed. R. McKitterick
(Cambridge, 1990), pp. 37–62, at 40–2; S. Keynes, 'Church Councils, Royal Assemblies and Anglo-
Saxon Royal Diplomas', in *Kingship, Legislation and Power in Anglo-Saxon England*, ed. G. R.
Owen-Crocker and B. W. Schneider (Woodbridge, 2013), pp. 17–139, at 19–20; and B. Snook, 'Who
Introduced Charters into England? The Case for Theodore and Hadrian', in *Textus Roffensis: Law,
Language, and Libraries in Early Medieval England*, ed. B. R. O'Brien and B. Bombi (Turnhout,
2015), pp. 257–90.
[8] *VW* preface, in *The Life of Bishop Wilfrid by Eddius Stephanus*, ed. and trans. B. Colgrave
(Cambridge, 1927), pp. 2–3.
[9] C. Cubitt, 'Wilfrid's "Usurping Bishops": Episcopal Election in Anglo-Saxon England, *c.* 600–
c. 800', *NH* 25 (1989), 18–38.
[10] Bede, *Historia ecclesiastica* [hereafter *HE*] iii. 25, in *Bede's Ecclesiastical History of the English People*,
ed. B. Colgrave and R. A. B. Mynors (Oxford, 1969), pp. 294–309.

favoured Irish modes of religious observance.[11] Although Bede in his *Historia ecclesiastica* attempts to depict a scene of relative religious unity, his private letter to Bishop (and later Archbishop) Ecgberht indicates that the reality was far from harmonious, as nobles abused charters to found fake monasteries as an early kind of tax evasion and ecclesiastics everywhere failed to uphold their religious duties.[12] One reason that Bede provided a picture of a unified Church in his *Historia ecclesiastica* is that he hoped to present a model for his contemporaries so that Christianity could thrive. But there were any number of potential obstacles to such a plan as political structures fragmented or religious communities had different modes of worship and found themselves in competition with one another for limited amounts of land, resources and patronage. Any breakdown in political or religious authority also afforded the opportunity for a reshuffling of personnel, and at various moments in this early period of Northumbrian history different ecclesiastics were moved from (control of) one ecclesiastical house to another or removed entirely depending on whether or not they (or their patrons) were in favour. Wilfrid's ecclesiastical career arguably typifies this pattern more than any other, for he found himself both in and out of favour and sought to impose himself over various ecclesiastical communities. By the time of his death in 710, his life had involved many controversial episodes.[13]

It is against this background that an early sequence of Northumbrian *vitae* emerges into view in the late seventh and early eighth centuries, some championing Cuthbert of Lindisfarne and one championing Wilfrid of Ripon.[14] These texts are very significant: not only are they some of the

---

[11] For the different 'factions' in the aftermath of the Council of Whitby, see C. Stancliffe, *Bede, Wilfrid, and the Irish*, Jarrow Lecture 2003 (Jarrow, 2004), pp. 10–11.

[12] Bede, *Epistola ad Ecgbertum*, in *Abbots*, ed. Grocock and Wood, pp. 124–61. For Bede's concerns (and proposed solutions), see A. Thacker, 'Bede's Ideal of Reform', in *Ideal and Reality in Frankish and Anglo-Saxon Society*, ed. P. Wormald, with D. Bullough and R. Collins (Oxford, 1983), pp. 130–53, at 132–3.

[13] For an important collection of work about Wilfrid, see N. J. Higham (ed.), *Wilfrid: Abbot, Bishop, Saint; Papers from the 1300th Anniversary Conferences* (Donington, 2013); for the dating of significant events in Wilfrid's life, see C. Cubitt, 'St Wilfrid: A Man for his Times', *ibid.*, pp. 311–47, at 342–7.

[14] An anonymous Lindisfarne prose *vita* of Cuthbert [hereafter *VCA*] was composed some time between 699 and 705 (see B. Colgrave, *Two Lives of Saint Cuthbert* (Cambridge, 1940), p. 13). About ten years after publication of the *VCA*, Stephen produced the *VW*: B. Colgrave, *The Life of Bishop Wilfrid by Eddius Stephanus* (Cambridge, 1927); for recent comments about the date at which this *vita* was written, see C. Stancliffe, 'Dating Wilfrid's Death and Stephen's *Life*', in *Wilfrid: Abbot, Bishop, Saint*, ed. Higham, pp. 17–26, where a date of *c.* 713 is suggested; see also D. P. Kirby, 'Bede, Eddius Stephanus and the "Life of Wilfrid"', *EHR* 98 (1983), 101–14. The *VCA* was later supplemented by a metrical version of the *vita* written by Bede, which was finished in the period 704 × 716 but probably nearer 704 and possibly revised at a later stage (see M. Lapidge, 'Bede's Metrical *Vita S. Cuthberti*', in *St Cuthbert: His Cult and Community to A.D. 1200*, ed.

earliest examples of Anglo-Saxon hagiography, but they were written by members of religious communities that were at times in competition with each other.[15] It would be incorrect to imagine that the early Northumbrian Church was divided simply between the followers of Cuthbert and Wilfrid, since there were manifold influences on early Northumbria, from those of the native British to those of the Franks.[16] But it was these two communities, Lindisfarne and Ripon, that pursued their differences by means of texts. It is important to understand why and how they did so and to demonstrate the ways in which they describe and depict their subjects, Cuthbert and Wilfrid, for two very different characters emerge from any such reading. These differences are all the more interesting given that these early *vitae* have long been known to be responding to one another in a kind of 'hagiographic feud'. This chapter does not differ from established scholarly orthodoxy about the interactions of these Northumbrian *vitae* but seeks instead in a small way to supplement it, by offering a close reading of the *VCA* and *VW* in particular and highlighting some of the ways in which they were responding to one another.[17]

In the atmosphere of competition between Northumbrian religious houses,[18] one of Lindisfarne's reactions was to commission the writing by one of its community of a prose *vita* in honour of Cuthbert, the *VCA*. In

---

G. Bonner, D. W. Rollason and C. Stancliffe (Woodbridge, 1989), pp. 77–94). Finally, at some point *c.* 721, to accompany his recently finished metrical version, Bede produced a new prose *vita* that based itself on the *VCA* but also added new material (D. P. Kirby, 'The Genesis of a Cult: Cuthbert of Farne and Ecclesiastical Politics in Northumbria in the Late Seventh and Early Eighth Centuries', *JEH* 46 (1995), 383–97, at 385–6; in this new prose *vita*, Bede states that he gained this new material from conversations with the priest Herefrith).

[15] For very useful comments about the nature of the relationships between these early Northumbrian communities, see I. N. Wood, 'Monasteries and the Geography of Power in the Age of Bede', *NH* 45 (2008), 11–25.

[16] For an overview of such influences, see D. Rollason, *Northumbria, 500–1100: Creation and Destruction of a Kingdom* (Cambridge, 2003), pp. 110–70. See also I. N. Wood, 'Northumbrians and Franks in the Age of Wilfrid', *NH* 31 (1995), 10–21.

[17] Nothing is said about the later *vitae* written by Bede, which have recently been discussed by C. Stancliffe, 'Disputed Episcopacy: Bede, Acca, and the Relationship between Stephen's *Life of St Wilfrid* and the Early Prose Lives of St Cuthbert', *ASE* 41 (2012), 7–39. See also W. Goffart, *The Narrators of Barbarian History (A.D. 550–800): Jordanes, Gregory of Tours, Bede, and Paul the Deacon* (Princeton, NJ, 1988), pp. 235–328 (at 262–3 for useful comments about the Cuthbertine and Wilfridian factions); and A. Thacker, 'Lindisfarne and the Origins of the Cult of St Cuthbert', in *St Cuthbert*, ed. Bonner et al., pp. 103–24. For discussion of some of the changes effected by Bede in his rewriting of the *vita* of Cuthbert, with a particular focus on place-names, see A. Joseph McMullen, 'Rewriting the Ecclesiastical Landscape of Early Medieval Northumbria in the Lives of Cuthbert', *ASE* 43 (2014), 57–98.

[18] For the effects of this competition on the burial practices with regard to Northumbrian kings, see B. Yorke, 'The Burial of Kings in Anglo-Saxon England', in *Kingship, Legislation and Power*, ed. Owen-Crocker and Schneider, pp. 237–57, at 248–9.

any reading of the *VCA*, it is important to remember that this was composed with the 'ghost of Wilfrid' in the background.[19] Some scholars have judged the *VCA* in rather negative terms, particularly when compared with the later prose *vita* written by Bede, suggesting that it possesses a kind of chronicle-like simplicity in which accounts of miracles are heaped up without any narrative development.[20] Actually, however, there is greater sophistication than first appears in terms of the *VCA*'s content and structure. It opens with a prologue that demonstrates a programmatic fondness for a very similar kind of inter-textual relationship to that mentioned earlier. The prologue borrows from different sources, including the Evagrian *Vita Antonii*, the *Vita Martini* by Sulpicius Severus, the *Actus Silvestri* and a letter drawn up *c.* 450 introducing the paschal cycle by Victorius of Aquitaine and addressed to Hilarus, who was elected pope in 461.[21]

Of these sources, the *Vita Martini* seems to have had an important influence on the *VCA*, whose first two chapters in effect constitute a double preface of the sort initiated by Sulpicius Severus.[22] Two chapters of the *VCA* borrow from the *Vita Martini*, and many other episodes, as Thacker has shown, have their counterpart in Sulpicius' account.[23] Sulpicius had

---

[19] This phrase is borrowed from Goffart, *The Narrators*.

[20] See, for example, Colgrave, *Two Lives*, p. 16; and C. E. Newlands, 'Bede and Images of Saint Cuthbert', *Traditio* 52 (1997), 73–109, at 83–4.

[21] For this opening passage, see B. Colgrave, 'The Earliest Saints' Lives Written in England', *PBA* 44 (1958), 35–60, at 42–4; and B. Colgrave, *Two Lives*, pp. 60–5 and 310–11. For the motivations of the Lindisfarne author in borrowing from such earlier *Vitae*, see M. Lapidge, 'The Saintly Life in Anglo-Saxon England', in *The Cambridge Companion to Old English Literature*, ed. M. Godden and M. Lapidge, 2nd edn (Cambridge, 2013), pp. 251–72, at 262. For more about this prologue, where new sources are identified, see Stancliffe, 'Disputed Episcopacy', pp. 12–14, where it is shown that the *VCA*, by certain borrowings, 'reveals itself as standing in the same tradition as saints' Lives written by Irish adherents of the Roman Easter' (at 14).

[22] For the particular influence of Sulpicius' writing on the author of the *VCA*, see Thacker, 'Bede's Ideal', pp. 136–7; and Thacker, 'Lindisfarne', pp. 110–12. The *Vita Antonii* by Athanasius formed a significant model for Sulpicius Severus when he was writing his *Vita Martini*. Sulpicius observed in Athanasius' work what appeared to him to be a double preface (in fact, the second part of the preface was added as a kind of translator's note when Evagrius made his translation into Latin), so the presence of a 'double preface' in an Insular *Vita* suggests that the *Vita* in question was modeling itself on the *Vita Martini*. See further, J.-M. Picard, 'Structural Patterns in Early Hiberno-Latin Hagiography', *Peritia* 4 (1985), 67–82; C. Stancliffe, *St Martin and His Hagiographer. History and Miracle in Sulpicius Severus* (Oxford, 1983), pp. 73–4; and S. Coates, 'The Bishop as Pastor and Solitary: Bede and the Spiritual Authority of the Monk-Bishop', *JEH* 47 (1996), 601–19.

[23] *VCA* i. 2 and iv. 1 (ed. Colgrave, pp. 62–4 and 110–12) borrow from the *Vita Martini*. Thacker, 'Lindisfarne', pp. 109–15, discusses the range of different influences on the *VCA* (at pp. 110–11, Thacker describes the *VCA* as 'distinctly innovatory in structure' and suggests that this structure derives from the pattern established by Sulpicius). For further comments on the *VCA*'s use of sources in general, not just the *Vita Martini*, see also C. Stancliffe, 'Cuthbert and the Polarity between Pastor and Solitary', in *St Cuthbert*, ed. Bonner et al., pp. 21–42, at 25–7.

dedicated his work to Desiderius, an Aquitanian in the same ascetic circles
as Sulpicius, and at the end, Sulpicius closes by hoping that his book will
bring pleasure to *omnibus sanctis*.[24] Published just before Martin's death,
the *Vita Martini* was launched at a time of great ecclesiastical dissension,[25]
when the Gallo-Roman episcopate displayed particular hostility to the
ascetic movement. As part of his response to this threat, Sulpicius,
throughout his *vita*, promotes and defends the ascetic life that Martin
had led, even as a bishop.[26] What is continually stressed is that Martin is a
true monk and a true bishop and that neither role is exclusive of the
other.[27] Martin may use his ascetic virtue to win him favours from God,
but these favours are invariably used to help people and to fulfil his pastoral
duty. In championing the ideal of a 'monk-bishop',[28] Sulpicius was producing a kind of ascetic propaganda and thus an indirect attack on the
worldly bishops of Gaul.

It seems very likely that, by alluding to the work of Sulpicius, the author
of the *VCA* was attempting to characterise Cuthbert in the same manner as
Martin and hence to confirm that Cuthbert could also be a kind of 'monk-
bishop'.[29] And it is further probable that this was a response to the
character of one of the Lindisfarne community's principal opponents,
Wilfrid, who at times seemed more akin to a secular lord than a devout

---

[24] *VM*, chap. 27.6, in *Vie de Saint Martin*, ed. and trans. J. Fontaine, Sources chrétiennes 133–5, 3 vols.
(Paris, 1967–9), vol. I, pp. 316–17. Sulpicius' prologue evokes the opening words of Sallust's *Bellum
Catilinae*, perhaps in an attempt to address and appeal to all readers, not just ascetics. The part of
Sallust to which Sulpicius refers stresses man's transience in the world and suggests that, to
overcome this, a man has to strive to attain everlasting fame, founded on *virtus*, by deeds or
words. However, Sulpicius proceeds to undermine Sallust and to assert instead the Christian
ideal, 'For what use to them was the acclaim, which will vanish with this world, accorded to their
writings?' ('Quid enim aut ipsis occasura cum saeculo scriptorum suorum gloria profuit?') (*VM* 1.3,
ed. and trans. Fontaine I, 250–1). The reader is to realise that eternal life, achieved through living
religiously rather than as a pagan, was preferable to eternal fame. Sulpicius was correcting his
classical models and refashioning them to suit his aim: an account of a Christian soldier attempting
to win eternal life. For the influence of classical biography on the *Vita Martini*, see Stancliffe,
St Martin, pp. 58–61, 71–80 and 86–102, esp. 89–90; Picard, 'Structural Patterns', pp. 70–1; and
G. B. Townend, 'Suetonius and His Influence', in *Latin Biography*, ed. T. A. Dorey (London, 1967),
pp. 79–111.

[25] Stancliffe, *St Martin*, p. 86.   [26] *Ibid.*, pp. 71–80.

[27] For Martin's continued monastic way of life while bishop, see Thacker, 'Bede's Ideal', pp. 136–7;
and Stancliffe, 'Cuthbert', p. 38.

[28] Stancliffe, *St Martin*, p. 95.

[29] For Thacker, 'Bede's Ideal', p. 148, 'the parallels with Martin of Tours, for example, suggest that
Cuthbert was already being promoted as the Northumbrian equivalent of the Gaulish
Reichsheiliger'. Coates, 'The Bishop', pp. 613–14, demonstrates that the *VCA*'s reliance on
Martinian models resembled contemporary Irish interests and that 'since Iona was the mother
church of Lindisfarne the anonymous *Life* displayed close links with Adomnán's *Life of Columba*' (at
613). See also Thacker, 'Lindisfarne', pp. 112–13; and Stancliffe, 'Cuthbert', pp. 22–3.

cleric.[30] The structure of the *VCA* is carefully arranged in order to help create this image of Cuthbert. It is divided into four books,[31] of which the first three deal, respectively, with Cuthbert's childhood, his time as pastor and prior and his life as a hermit on Inner Farne, while the fourth, the longest of all the books, talks of Cuthbert's time as a bishop and a little about his posthumous cult. They are arranged in such an order that they highlight Cuthbert's achievement in combining the ascetic lifestyle with his episcopal office, in the true Martinian sense. As would be expected, the words employed to describe Cuthbert underline this structure of the work as a whole, since he moves from being described as *homo Dei* or *seruus Christi* in books two and three until he finally becomes *sanctus episcopus* in book four.

Although Cuthbert is ultimately depicted as being reluctant to take up episcopal office, his elevation to the rank of bishop was a principal issue around which the anonymous author constructed his account; this is made clear at several points in the *vita*. In the preface he announces that he 'will therefore undertake to write the life of St Cuthbert and how he lived both before and after he became bishop'.[32] The very first chapter after the preface continues this theme. A young boy, scarcely three years old, finds Cuthbert indulging in idle play with other children and frantically urges Cuthbert to stop. Being able to stand it no longer, the boy exhorts Cuthbert, 'O holy Bishop and priest Cuthbert [*O sancte episcope et presbiter Cuðberhte*], these unnatural tricks done to show off your agility are not befitting to you or your high office'.[33] Here, in our first encounter with Cuthbert, he is described as *episcope*, a term that is not used again until book four. The Lindisfarne author, at the very beginning of his work, is highlighting a major theme he wishes to develop, that Cuthbert was simultaneously *sanctus* and *episcopus* even early in life.[34] Two chapters

---

[30] For the *VCA*'s depiction of Cuthbert as a bishop who did not abandon a monastic way of life, see Thacker, 'Lindisfarne', p. 111; and Stancliffe, 'Cuthbert', pp. 35–6 (and further pp. 36–42 for the image (and its models) of Cuthbert as both 'pastor and solitary' in accounts of his life).

[31] Thacker, 'Lindisfarne', p. 111, suggests that this division into four books 'harks back to Martinian exempla'.

[32] *VCA* i. 2 (ed. and trans. Colgrave, pp. 62–3). Incidentally, it is noticeable that at this very moment when the Lindisfarne author wishes to place an emphasis on the importance of Cuthbert as bishop, he borrows a passage from Sulpicius; see Colgrave, *Two Lives*, p. 62.

[33] *VCA* i. 3 (ed. and trans. Colgrave, pp. 64–5). For discussion of this passage, see Thacker, 'Lindisfarne', p. 111; Stancliffe, 'Disputed Episcopacy', pp. 20–1.

[34] And, as Stancliffe has shown, this passage is likewise designed to demonstrate 'Cuthbert's predestination as one of God's elect from infancy': Stancliffe, 'Disputed Episcopacy', p. 20. For comments about the nature of ecclesiastical life at this time, see J. Campbell, 'Elements in the Background to the Life of St Cuthbert and his Early Cult', in *St Cuthbert*, ed. Bonner et al., pp. 3–19.

later, Cuthbert is given encouragement to pursue his destiny when he is overjoyed by witnessing 'the soul of a most holy bishop or of some other great person' being borne to heaven by angels.[35] Later he realises that this bishop was none other than Aidan himself. Subsequent events in the first three books demonstrate Cuthbert's ability as a miracle-worker. These not only guarantee Cuthbert's status as *sanctus* but depict him as the ideal pastor and *episcopus*. For example, Cuthbert was invited by the nun Æbbe to visit the monastery of Coldingham. He agrees to go but 'did not relax his habitual way of life'. He continues his ascetic lifestyle and endures a period of penitence in the ice-cold sea. When he returns from the water, he has his feet washed by 'two little sea animals, humbly prostrating themselves on the earth … wiping them [his feet] with their skins and warming them with their breath',[36] demonstrating that through his extreme asceticism he has been granted the respect and reverence even of animals. But at this very moment, when Cuthbert's individual sanctity is stressed, we learn that 'the man of God, returning home at cockcrow, came to the church of God to join in public prayer with the brethren' (*Ille iam homo Dei in galli cantu reuertens ad orationem communem cum fratribus ad aecclesiam Dei*). Cuthbert, both *sanctus* and *episcopus*, always has a mind for his brethren and *familia*.

A major event in Cuthbert's life occurs at the very beginning of book four when he becomes bishop. At this crucial stage in the work, Cuthbert 'graduates' from being a *homo Dei* or a *seruus Christi* to *sanctus episcopus noster*. Thus the very first words that had been used to describe Cuthbert have eventually come full circle and fulfilled the young boy's prophecy at the beginning of the *vita* that he would become *episcopus*. And this transition is further underlined by the Lindisfarne author. At the end of the first and fourth books, the Lindisfarne author uses carefully selected verbs, *sanauit* ('he healed') and *sanatus sit* ('[he] was healed'). These verbs connect the first and last books by means of ring composition and frame the two middle books which describe Cuthbert's journey towards becoming bishop. The ring composition is further underlined by the etymology involved: *sanctus* ('holy') is the past participle of *sancire* ('to confirm'), which was thought to be etymologically connected (through their common derivation from *sanguis*) with *sanus* ('healthy').[37]

---

[35] 'Animam … sanctissimi episcopi, aut alterius magne persone' (*VCA* i. 5 (ed. and trans. Colgrave, pp. 68–9)). His destiny had been made explicit by the anonymous author in i. 3: 'Behold, brethren, how even before he is recognised by the performance of his works, he is shown by the providence of God to be elect' ('videte fratres quomodo iste antequam per laborem operum suorum agnoscatur, per prouidentiam Dei electus ostenditur').

[36] *VCA* ii. 3 (ed. and trans. Colgrave, pp. 80–1).

[37] R. Maltby, *A Lexicon of Ancient Latin Etymologies* (Leeds, 1991), pp. 542–3.

The Lindisfarne author has taken pains to emphasise Cuthbert's development from the first book to the last, where he attains the bishopric.[38] In the uncertain religious-political context of the late seventh and early eighth centuries, where religious houses were jostling for episcopal status and an immensely powerful individual such as Wilfrid could emerge as bishop, it was especially important for Lindisfarne to depict its community as being worthy of its see; the portrait of Cuthbert as a holy 'monk-bishop' was an astute response to decidedly turbulent times.[39]

Ripon and the *Vita sancti Wilfrithi*

Some ten years after the composition of the *VCA*, the priest Stephen produced his *VW*.[40] Even a superficial reading of the *VW* demonstrates just how different its form and content are to the *VCA*; in fact, the two appear to have wholly disparate concerns.[41] The *VW* minimises the miraculous (while the *VCA* describes thirty miracles of Cuthbert, the *VW* has only ten) and depicts Wilfrid as a wealthy, powerful and almost secular-like figure (features noticeably absent from the *VCA*).[42] Stephen's text also

---

[38] For more about the structure of the *VCA*, see J. C. Eby, 'Bringing the *Vita* to Life: Bede's Symbolic Structure of the Life of St Cuthbert', *American Benedictine Review* 48 (1997), 316–38, at 323.

[39] For recent comments placing all these early Northumbrian *vitae* in their appropriate religious-political setting, see Stancliffe, 'Disputed Episcopacy'. Coates, 'The Bishop', pp. 601–19, considers in detail the characterisation of bishops by Bede, demonstrating the importance of 'continued attachment to ascetic traditions once they had been elevated to the episcopate ... He [Bede] presented bishops as ascetic giants' (at p. 602). For the importance of the work by Sulpicius Severus in championing Martin as someone who successfully combined asceticism with his episcopal responsibilities, see *ibid.*, pp. 606–7, and for the depiction of Cuthbert in the *VCA*, see *ibid.*, pp. 612–15, where Coates argues that the anonymous author has a rather 'negative view of episcopal office' (at p. 613).

[40] For the date of composition of the *VW*, see the work by Stancliffe, cited earlier, n. 14.

[41] For the biblical imagery and typology in Stephen's *VW*, see W. T. Foley, *Images of Sanctity in Eddius Stephanus' 'Life of Saint Wilfrid', an Early English Saint's Life* (Lewiston, 1992); and M. D. Laynesmith, 'Stephen of Ripon and the Bible: Allegorical and Typological Interpretations of the *Life of St Wilfrid*', *EME* 9 (2000), 163–82.

[42] Note the explicit reference to Wilfrid's wealth and power in *VW* chap. 24 (ed. and trans. Colgrave, pp. 48–9), in which Queen Iurminburh describes 'the temporal glories of St Wilfrid, his riches, the number of his monasteries, the greatness of his buildings, his countless army of followers arrayed in royal vestments and arms' ('sancti Wilfrithi episcopi omnem gloriam eius secularem et divitias necnon coenobiorum multitudinem et aedificiorum magnitudinem innumerumque exercitum sodalium regalibus vestimentis et armis ornatum'). In the context of this chapter, Iurminburh is warning her husband, Ecgfrith, that Wilfrid was a potential threat; Wilfrid, here, embodies the opposite of the 'holy-monk' bishop ideal as highlighted by Cuthbert. For the network of monasteries associated with Wilfrid, see S. Foot, 'Wilfrid's Monastic Empire', in *Wilfrid: Abbot, Bishop, Saint*, ed. Higham, pp. 27–39, at 33–4. For comments about various secular characteristics found in the *VW*, see also Goffart, *The Narrators*, p. 281; and A. Thacker, 'Wilfrid, His Cult and His Biographer', in *Wilfrid: Abbot, Bishop, Saint*, ed. Higham, pp. 1–16. D. Pelteret, 'Saint Wilfrid: Tribal Bishop, Civic Bishop of Germanic Lord?', in *The Community, the Family and the Saint:*

contains much that is defensive in tone, which is suggestive of the challenges to his authority and position that Wilfrid had to endure.[43]

Despite these different concerns and depictions of their respective heroes, and despite the fact that the *VW* was written roughly ten years after the *VCA* had first appeared, Stancliffe has recently emphasised that Stephen's *vita* was indeed a response to the earlier version by the anonymous Lindisfarne author. This is made particularly apparent by another example of textual engagement: Stephen borrows three passages of text verbatim from the earlier Lindisfarne hagiography.[44] The first of these borrowings occurs as early as Stephen's preface, enabling the author to conjure the absent presence of Cuthbert into the reader's mind and thereby also to demonstrate that the present *vita* is a response to the *VCA*.[45] Another passage to exhibit borrowing is the account of Wilfrid's election to the bishopric (in 664) in chapter 11.[46] It is surely no coincidence that one principal issue upon which the *VCA* had structured its account (that of Cuthbert as the perfect example of a bishop) is one of the three occasions where Stephen refers directly to the earlier *Life*.[47] It is in itself interesting that just when Stephen wants to prove Wilfrid's readiness and suitability for the episcopal see, he inserts passages taken almost entirely from the earlier *VCA*. Such borrowing was no doubt intended to guarantee that Wilfrid was just as worthy as Cuthbert of episcopal rank despite his different character and way of life.[48] Yet there are also subtle differences in terms of the structure and content of these two chapters. The following table sets out in summary form the main elements of the respective chapters in *VCA* and *VW* in the order in which they occur in the original texts (the italicised text shows in these instances where the *VW* borrows directly from the *VCA*):

Patterns of Power in Early Medieval Europe, ed. J. Hill and M. Swan (Turnhout, 1998), pp. 159–80, esp. 179–80, stresses that Wilfrid had the outlook of a Germanic lord.

[43] The *VW* depicts Wilfrid as going to Rome three times as a result of accusations made against him. See also D. P. Kirby, 'Northumbria in the Time of Wilfrid', in *Saint Wilfrid at Hexham*, ed. Kirby, pp. 1–34.

[44] There are three occasions where the *VW* borrows from the *VCA*, which are all discussed and explored by Stancliffe, 'Disputed Episcopacy', who says (at p. 19). 'Without ever naming Cuthbert, it is tantamount to declaring that it is Wilfrid, not Cuthbert, who is the model of the perfect bishop.'

[45] The extent of the borrowing is clearly visible in the edition by Colgrave, who has italicised the relevant passages. See also Goffart, *The Narrators*, pp. 283–4; and Stancliffe, 'Disputed Episcopacy', pp. 14–15.

[46] Again, the extent of borrowing from the *VCA* is visible in Colgrave's italics. See also Goffart, *The Narrators*, pp. 283–4.

[47] See also Stancliffe, 'Disputed Episcopacy', pp. 15–16.

[48] See similarly Thacker, 'Lindisfarne', p. 117.

Structure of *VCA* iv. 1	Structure of *VW* chap. 11
1a. Postquam igitur ab Egfrido rege et episcopis Saxorum omnique senatu deposcenti, ad episcopatum nostrae aecclesiae Lindisfarnensium electus est.	1b. Reges deinde consilium cum sapientibus suae gentis post spatium inierunt, quem eligerent in sedem vacantem … responderunt omnes uno consensu: 'Neminem habemus meliorem et digniorem nostrae gentis quam Wilfrithum presbiterum et abbatem'.
2a. invitus et coactus lacrimans et flens, abstractus est expectante etiam adhuc senatu, cum archiepiscopo Theodoro.	2b. … quia in omnibus rebus sapientem agnovimus et talem esse, qualem Paulus apostolus ad Titum scribens docuit.
3a. Iam vero post spatium sumpto episcopatu …	3b. Tunc quoque consenserunt reges et omnis populus huic electioni, et sancto Wilfritho presbitero omnis conventus in nomine Domini accipere gradum episcopalem praecepit. Ille autem primo abnuens, non esse se dignum excusavit; postremo tamen oboediens factus est, noluitque benedictionem Dei effugere.
4a. Idem enim constantissime perseverabat, qui prius fuerat.	4b. Qualem ergo illi tunc eum intellexerunt, talem et nos adhuc viventes novimus.
5a. In omnibus iam observans Pauli apostolici doctrinam, ad Titum dicentem recordatus est.	5b. *Fuit* enim *sermo eius purus et apertus, plenus gravitatis et honestatis … cum Domino nostro Iesu Christo accipere mereatur.*
6a. Ideo namque *purus fuit eius sermo, et apertus plenus gravitatis et honestatis, … cum Domino nostro Iesu Christo accipere mereatur.*	

Both chapters begin with the statement that the appropriate authorities all agreed to the election of the relevant holy man; this forms the basis of each. However, the statement in the *VCA* that Cuthbert was elected 'at the request of King Ecgfrith and the bishops of the Saxons and all the council' (item 1a in the table) seems to act merely as preparation for the emphasis on Cuthbert's humility (item 2a), for one is then told (in part of the chapter not quoted in the table) that Cuthbert had to be persuaded by various select men (including King Ecgfrith, Bishop Tumma and 'chosen men from our community') to accept the position. When eventually Cuthbert does accept, he is led away *invitus, coactus, lacrimans* and *flens*, terms that heighten the realism and drama. Most significantly, the reader is informed that Cuthbert 'maintained the dignity of a bishop without abandoning the ideal of the monk or the virtue of the hermit' (*implebat episcopi dignitatem non tamen ut propositum monachi et anachoritae uirtutem desereret*).

Although Stephen has deliberately modelled his chapter on that found in the *VCA*, he nonetheless has engineered a certain 'tweaking' of his text that does not advance Wilfrid as a Cuthbert-like figure, as might have been expected in a case of allusion, but which demonstrates the difference in Wilfrid's character.[49] The emphasis the anonymous author had placed on Cuthbert's election to illustrate that he was humble is absent from this chapter in Stephen; Stephen's aim is partly to stress that Wilfrid's accession to the episcopal see had been legitimate.[50] Though both accounts begin similarly, the *VW*, careful to stress Wilfrid's legitimacy, adds a phrase that is absent from the *VCA*, that the kings and counsellors consented (*responderunt omnes uno consensu*): 'We consider that none of our fellow-country-men is better and more worthy than Wilfrid, priest and abbot' (item 1b). Stephen further emphasises that Wilfrid was the proper choice by inserting the letter of the Apostle Paul to Titus in a more advanced position than in the *VCA* (item 2b, and cf. item 5a). Again, the reader is informed that the king and all the people agreed to the election of Wilfrid (item 3b). Then, imitating the style of the *VCA*, which had so dramatically portrayed Cuthbert's initial refusal of the bishopric on account of his humility, Wilfrid is described as, at first, excusing himself (*abnuens*) from the role of bishop. But his refusal is described in terms noticeably brief when compared to those applied to Cuthbert; it is not long before Wilfrid is *oboediens* (item 3b). These terms are abrupt, as Stephen's focus is not on depicting Wilfrid as a humble 'monk-bishop' but rather on justifying his election and position as bishop and, as Stancliffe has shown, on demon-strating Wilfrid's 'readiness to undertake a public role'.[51]

The pivotal part that this chapter played in the earlier *VCA* influenced Stephen to imitate it and, with subtle changes, to try to undermine it.[52] And Stephen, in an attempt to eradicate the ambiguous reputation of Wilfrid and to justify his position and status, resorts to claims for Wilfrid's defence. This becomes clear in another instance in this chapter where Stephen again can be seen as borrowing. It seems to have been particularly important to the anonymous author that Cuthbert was *electus Dei*.[53] In the very first chapter

---

[49] Stancliffe, 'Disputed Episcopacy', pp. 16–17, shows how 'in his subtle adaptation of the Lindisfarne account, Stephen both presents a different conception of episcopal office as a blessing and as an office that is quite separate from the monastic vocation' (at 17).

[50] Wilfrid's position was of course not straightforward. After he had been elected to the bishopric for the first time, he departed to Gaul to be consecrated; in his absence, King Oswiu had Chad consecrated in his place (*VW* chap. 14). It is little wonder, then, that Stephen took every opportunity to defend Wilfrid's position and appointment as bishop.

[51] Stancliffe, 'Disputed Episcopacy', p. 17.   [52] *Ibid.*

[53] See the comments of Stancliffe, 'Cuthbert', p. 25.

after the two prefaces, the reader meets the phrases *Dei electionem* and *Dei electus*.[54] Now, in the chapter concerning Cuthbert's election to the bishopric, one finds, close together, the two expressions,

> ad episcopatum nostrae aecclesiae Lindisfarnensium **electus est**. Tunc enim supradicto rege et episcopo sanctae memoriae Tumma, et de familia nostra **electissimis viris** venientibus ad eum.[55]

As discussed earlier, this statement regarding Cuthbert's election forms the basis for the *VCA*'s attempt to stress its hero's humility. But, for Stephen, the importance in this repetition resided in the fact that it emphasised Cuthbert's legitimacy, not in the statements of his humility that followed. Thus, when making use of this chapter, Stephen reproduces a form of the repetition of *electus* but puts it to a different purpose:

> Erat autem ita homo ille **electus**, sicut Iohannes praecursor Domini et Ezechiel propheta, xxx annorum aetatis. Tunc quoque consenserunt reges et omnis populus huic **electioni**.[56]

Both men are described as being *electus*, but Cuthbert is so holy, the perfect monk, that he wishes to avoid the wealth and honour associated with being bishop; therefore, it is only through the persuasion of those *electissimis viris* that he accepts the position; the anonymous author has emphasised Cuthbert's humility and that Cuthbert was truly the right man to be *electus*.[57] Despite following the Lindisfarne author in style and content, this allusion in the *VW* does nothing to further Wilfrid as a Cuthbert-like character; it is merely a method to prove that Wilfrid had indeed been chosen.

Strikingly, the sentence that stands out most, in those lines which Stephen himself wrote and did not borrow, is the one that introduces the passage that concludes the chapter.[58] This sentence reads, 'Qualem ergo illi tunc eum intellexerunt, talem et nos adhuc viventes novimus' (item

---

[54] *VCA* i. 3 (ed. and trans. Colgrave, pp. 64–6).

[55] 'He was elected to the bishopric of our church at Lindisfarne. For at that time the above-mentioned king [Ecgfrith] and Bishop Tumma of holy memory, and chosen men of our community came to him' (*VCA* iv. 1 (ed. and trans. Colgrave, pp. 110–11)).

[56] 'Now this man was elected, like John the forerunner of the Lord and the prophet Ezekial, when thirty years of age. The kings and all the people agreed to this election' (*VW*, chap. 11 (ed. and trans. Colgrave, pp. 24–5)).

[57] That Cuthbert had been 'chosen' (*electus*) by the 'chosen men' (*electissimis viris*) recalls the classical proverb, *laudari a laudato viro* ('To be praised by a man who himself had received praise'), an expression that itself was used to indicate that the praise received was genuine and could not be bettered. See, for example, Cicero, *Letters to Friends* 5.12.7; and in general, R. Tosi, *Dizionario delle sentenze latine e greche* (Milan, 1991), p. 600 §1333.

[58] Stephen's concluding passage is borrowed verbatim from the Lindisfarne *VCA*.

4b), which is translated by Colgrave: 'Their opinion of him in those days did not differ from that of us who are still alive'. A look at the context of this chapter within the *vita* perhaps helps to explain this remark. The immediately preceding chapter in the *VW* (chapter 10) describes the conflict (*conflictu*) that had raged at the Council of Whitby, where Wilfrid had succeeded in his pleas for the Roman party; this chapter ends on a particularly bitter note with Colman, a Lindisfarne man, being forced to retire 'and leave his see to be taken by another and a better man'. It was in this confused aftermath of one of the most heated incidents of the seventh century,[59] that Alhfrith managed to foster Wilfrid's promotion.[60] If Wilfrid had been thrust upon the Northumbrian Church, he would have embittered many religious men, especially those he had defeated at Whitby (the Irish party) and then also their close supporters at Lindisfarne. Thus this peculiar sentence provides significant witness to the feelings surrounding Wilfrid. It demonstrates Stephen's realisation that, following his role at Whitby, Wilfrid was by no means universally well received.[61] Here Stephen wishes to eradicate this low regard for Wilfrid; he emphasises that just as he, the author, can testify that Wilfrid is loved in the present (i.e. at the time Stephen is writing and after Wilfrid has died), he also can prove that Wilfrid had been loved even in the immediate post-Whitby era. In doing so, Stephen makes use of the recent hagiography of one of the celebrated bishops of the time, Cuthbert. And, concerning the very point on which Wilfrid had been controversial (namely, the kind of man that could be a bishop), Stephen borrowed from the earlier *vita* while making changes that allowed him to demonstrate both how Wilfrid was suited for episcopal office and how his position was legitimate.

The Power of Writing in Early Northumbria

One of the most controversial episodes in Wilfrid's career is recounted by Stephen in chapters 46 and 47 of the *VW*, when Wilfrid was summoned to a council at *Ouestraefelda* in the presence of King Aldfrith of Northumbria and Archbishop Berhtwald and 'the bishops of nearly all Britain' (*totius*

---

[59] For the issues debated at Whitby, see Stancliffe, *Bede, Wilfrid, and the Irish*.

[60] It is noticeable that Stephen ignores the fact that Tuda was the first to be elected bishop in Colman's place after Whitby, preferring instead to imply that Wilfrid immediately took over. Bede supplies this information about Tuda; *HE* iii. 26. See also Colgrave, *The Life of Bishop Wilfrid*, p. 158.

[61] For comments about anti-Wilfridian feeling and the defensive tone of the *VW*, see Thacker, 'Lindisfarne', pp. 119–20.

paene Brittanniae episcopis).[62] Stephen describes a meeting in which those present argued with Wilfrid and attempted to deprive him of his possessions and status. In a passage of dramatic prose, Stephen describes how a thegn who was devoted to Wilfrid escaped from Aldfrith's tent and attempted to warn Wilfrid of the plan by those at the council to deceive the bishop. The thegn is made to say:

> They are attempting by this treachery to deceive you utterly, in order that at the outset you may confirm by your own signature their sole judgment, so as to support whatever they may settle and decide: so that after you have been bound by this chain of constraint, for the rest you will never able to make a change afterwards in any way. This will be the upshot of their judgment, that you shall surrender all which you were seen to possess in the land of Northumbria, whether bishopric or monasteries or aught else; and whatever you have gained in Mercia under King Aethilred, you will surrender it all by force to the archbishop that he may give it to whom he wishes; and finally, by condemning yourself you will degrade yourself, by your own signature, from your holy office.[63]

This passage is one of many in the *VW* in which the importance of written documentation for the justification of land ownership or status is explicitly stated or implicitly stressed. On this occasion, those presiding at the council are attempting to trick Wilfrid into signing something that would later be binding and disadvantageous to him. In other words, by the time Stephen was writing in the early eighth century, written documents such as diplomas and papal privileges were becoming ever more important. Elsewhere in the *VW* we learn of written judgements that are sent to Rome and there heard by the pope and indeed of papal privileges that are brought back to England as proof of possessions or status and that have been signed and then sealed.[64] Towards the end of the *VW*, in chapter 60, we are told of another council, presided over by King Osred of Northumbria, in which both Archbishop Berhtwald and Bishop Wilfrid

---

[62] For the historical context of this council, see *ibid.*, pp. 116–17. For the views that these chapters contain about the Irish, see Stancliffe, *Bede, Wilfrid, and the Irish*.

[63] 'Hac omnino fraude te moliuntur decipere, ut primitus per scriptionem propriae manus confirmes eorum tantummodo iudicium, quodcunque constituentes diffinient succumbere, ut, postquam isto alligatus fueris districtionis vinculo, de caetero in posterum permutare nullatenus queas. Ista siquidem erit illorum iudicii apertio, ut, quicquid in Ultrahumbrensium aliquando terra possidere visus fuisti vel in episcopatu vel in monasteriis vel in qualibet re, cuncta dimittas; et si quid in Myrciorum regno subsecutus eras sub Aethelredo rege, omnia reddendo archiepiscopo coacte relinquas, ipso donando cui vult; et ad postremum temetipsum dampnando, de tuo te sanctitatis honore cum subscriptione degraderis' (*VW* chap. 47 (ed. and trans. Colgrave, pp. 94–7)).

[64] See, for example, *VW* chap. 34. For the importance of canon law in proving Wilfrid's position, see Stancliffe, 'Disputed Episcopacy', pp. 17–18.

had brought 'writings from the Apostolic See' (*scripta apostolicae sedis*) so that they could be read out to those assembled. The importance of these documents was not lost on Berhtfrith, a high-ranking secular official there that day, who requested that a translation of the papal documents be provided.

Given that Stephen felt that documentary evidence was crucial for justifying status and landed possessions, and given that on various occasions he inserts extracts from documents such as papal letters and privileges, it is no surprise to find that in chapter 17 of the *VW*, describing the dedication day of the Ripon church, a large proportion of the second half evokes the language of a diploma. It begins with a reference to the status of those present on the day, which is set out hierarchically and therefore reminiscent of a diploma's witness-list. Stephen also recounts a ceremony whereby Wilfrid, from in front of an altar, read out a list of lands being granted that is at once suggestive of a ceremony of conveyance and the contents of a boundary clause.[65] Perhaps most tellingly, the reader is informed that the chief men and bishops present gave their signatures to the document, *cum consensu et subscriptione*, thereby using a formula very similar to a common kind of attestation, *consensi et subscripsi*. It seems clear that, in this chapter, Stephen inserted language and detail that, if not relying on an actual charter, deliberately recalled the style of such a document.[66] Stephen intended this legalistic language to prove that the building and endowment of the church for the Wilfridian community were above suspicion. Such formulaic language is unusual in a saint's *vita* (it is never found in the *VCA*): that Stephen felt it necessary to resort to it may suggest that he was under pressure to defend and prove what he was saying about Wilfrid.

One can imagine that, in the early days of the Northumbrian Church, ecclesiastical communities would have encountered a degree of competition as each one strove not only to secure its existence (in terms of property, privileges and power) but also to enhance its position. In order to do so, it was natural that these institutions sought to publicise the deeds of their most famous saints, for to be able to boast of a powerful saint helped to guarantee the position of that church in the locality.[67] This 'hagiographic feud' therefore represents a very early attempt to assert power and status

---

[65] For the ritual involved in such ceremonies, see D. A. E. Pelteret, 'The Religious Elements in the *Textus Roffensis* Charters', in *Textus Roffensis*, ed. O'Brien and Bombi, pp. 291–311.

[66] For biblical imagery in this same passage, see Laynesmith, 'Stephen of Ripon', pp. 172–3.

[67] Thacker, 'Lindisfarne'.

through the medium of writing in the Northumbrian kingdom. The individual *vitae* are crucial witnesses to the ways in which the respective communities sought to place themselves in the wider ecclesio-political world of the late seventh and early eighth centuries. That they do respond to one another may suggest that the authors of these *vitae* envisaged them having a wider audience than just the ecclesiastical cloister.[68] Designed to trumpet the saintly credentials of their subjects, the authors may have hoped that these texts could influence powerful secular contemporaries as well as those in the religious hierarchy.

The Lindisfarne community had at various moments been placed in a difficult position by Wilfrid and subsequently by his followers who promoted the memory of Wilfrid. Wilfrid himself had been renowned as an individual intent on building up his network of ecclesiastical houses, and increasing his own wealth and status. He seems also to have taken a keen interest in the evolution of the diplomatic used in Anglo-Saxon charters.[69] This concern was in some ways only to be expected, for these newly introduced legal documents offered unprecedented levels of security to the holder, in terms of financial and hereditary rights, and any bishop with the kind of portfolio belonging to Wilfrid would have had a vested interest in acquiring that sort of legal documentation. The inclusion of charter language in the *VW* may suggest that a charter was somehow used as a source of information when describing the foundation of Wilfrid's church at Ripon. But it may also reveal that, in Stephen's mind, it was particularly appropriate to invoke such charter language when describing how Wilfrid built and dedicated his own church at Ripon. The emergence of the *VW* caused Lindisfarne to have the *Vita Cuthberti* rewritten by Bede.[70] But the very particular form of threat posed by Wilfrid and his followers embraced also the use of charters in order to soak up Northumbrian lands and privileges. It is therefore worth considering whether Lindisfarne took precautionary measures other than the publication of a sequence of *vitae*. Unfortunately, no Northumbrian charters survive from this early period. But when Northumbrian charters do emerge from the tenth century

---

[68] Thacker, 'Wilfrid, His Cult and His Biographer', pp. 13–14, has some useful comments about Stephen's intended audience being Wilfridian communities, in particular, Ripon and the Mercian houses.

[69] P. Sims-Williams, 'St Wilfrid and Two Charters Dated A.D. 676 and 680', *JEH* 39 (1988), 163–83. For Wilfrid's landed possessions, see M. Roper, 'Wilfrid's Landholdings in Northumbria', in *Saint Wilfrid at Hexham*, ed. D. P. Kirby (Newcastle upon Tyne, 1975), pp. 61–79; and G. R. J. Jones, 'Some Donations to Bishop Wilfrid in Northern England', *NH* 31 (1995), 22–38.

[70] Stancliffe, 'Disputed Episcopacy'.

onwards, those associated with St Cuthbert's community have a form that is strikingly, and surely pointedly, different from those in use elsewhere in Northumbria. Gone are the formal Latin diplomatic elements and in their stead are brief summaries in Old English of land transactions made directly to St Cuthbert's church and inserted into that community's precious manuscripts.[71] It is just possible that Lindisfarne, as an off-shoot of the Ionan mission, had encountered such a practice in the Celtic world.[72] It is also possible that, faced with an acquisitive bishop such as Wilfrid, the Lindisfarne community sought, already in the early eighth century, to distance itself from the use of documents which could be harnessed by that figure to exert pressure and influence over his rivals. In doing so the Cuthbertines would have at once invalidated the documents used by Wilfrid and simultaneously also allowed themselves the ability to operate according to terms dictated by them. Of course, without the survival of early Northumbrian charters, this must remain a hypothesis, but it would have constituted another method of writing power, alongside the use of hagiography, in this formative period of the early Northumbrian Church.

[71] For an account of this practice, see D. A. Woodman, *Charters of Northern Houses*, AS Charters 16 (Oxford, 2012), pp. 9–16, 316–35. For the use of charters and diplomas in early Northumbria, see P. Wormald, *Bede and the Conversion of England: The Charter Evidence*, Jarrow Lecture 1984 (Jarrow, 1985); and I. N. Wood, 'The Gifts of Wearmouth and Jarrow', in *The Languages of Gift in the Early Middle Ages*, ed. W. Davies and P. Fouracre (Cambridge, 2010), pp. 89–115.

[72] See, for example, W. Davies, 'The Latin Charter-Tradition in Western Britain, Brittany and Ireland in the Early Mediaeval Period', in *Ireland in Early Mediaeval Europe: Studies in Memory of Kathleen Hughes*, ed. D. Whitelock, R. McKitterick and D. N. Dumville (Cambridge, 1982), pp. 258–80.

CHAPTER 5

Origins of the Kingdom of the English

David N. Dumville

England is arguably the oldest European national kingdom: it has had a continuous institutional history since its creation (in 927).[1] English ethnicity no doubt originated in early mediaeval Britain but it nonetheless acknowledged aspects of identity derived from contributory Germanic ethnicities. The context was settlement by migration from Continental *Germania* in a post-colonial environment after *Brittaniae* (the Roman provinces of Britain) ceased to be an effective diocese of the Roman empire.[2] How was this new society created and organised? How was it affected by its neighbours? Bede wrote of genocide (*exterminium gentis*) of the Britons by the English. What were the institutions of English leadership, power and consent? The kingdom provided one important long-term organising framework. But what were kingdoms and kings? How many were there? Multiple kingship was a given not only among the English but

---

[1] It is, however, a radical curiosity that King Æthelstan's démarche in 927 has only recently been acknowledged by scholars as the moment of the creation of the kingdom and of Æthelstan himself as its first king. Cf. n. 7, below.

[2] This context has been a subject of endless discussion. Reliance on Gildas's account of Romano-British history has proved disastrous: his ignorance of the period before the mid-fifth century seems profound. In the two concluding paragraphs of E. A. Thompson, *Saint Germanus of Auxerre and the End of Roman Britain* (Woodbridge, 1984), pp. 114–15, we are (quite rightly) presented with a penetratingly bleak picture: 'Fortunately, it has been given to few writers to draw as dark a picture as that which Gildas sketches of the Britain of his day – or of that limited part of Britain about which he had information ... As far as we can discover, Gildas knew nothing whatever, apart from this handful of facts, about the Roman empire as a whole or about the past history of the entire world. The most frightening feature in the picture drawn by Gildas is not the destruction of city-life in Britain or the break-up of the Imperial system with its guarantee of peaceful life, but rather the destruction of knowledge itself. Knowledge of the outside world and knowledge of the past had been wiped out of men's minds.' Cf. E. A. Thompson, 'Gildas and the History of Britain', *Britannia* 10 (1979), 203–26 and 11 (1980), 344. There are very various material-culture approaches to the subject – cf. K. Dark, *Britain and the End of the Roman Empire* (Stroud, 2000), pp. 10–26 – but archaeologists have also allowed themselves to be mesmerised by the year 410, to no evident profit: F. K. Haarer et al. (eds.), *A.D. 410: The History and Archaeology of Late and Post-Roman Britain* (London, 2014); and S. Moorhead and D. Stuttard, *A.D. 410: The Year that Shook Rome* (London, 2010).

also among their neighbours in Britain. 'International' relations occurred not only within Britain (between Britons, English, Gaels and Picts) but also among kingdoms describable as English.

The received political narrative of early mediaeval English history is of a progressive reduction of the number of English kingdoms to an eventual seven (heptarchy), then to four (tetrarchy) and then (assisted by vikings) to one which, by eventually conquering intrusive Scandinavian polities, created a kingdom and a monarchy of the English. Such historiography is not sustainable. It seems teleological: England's long-term success as a political unit has encouraged a patriotic view that its creation was inevitable – even that the English nation's success in Britain was fore-ordained, as Bede, the father of English historiography, argued in 731. Relieving ourselves of that mediaeval and modern burden, while at the same time paying close attention to the dynamics of the Anglo-Saxon centuries, offers the prospect of a thoroughgoing creative re-conceptualisation of origins of the kingdom of the English.

We can be precise about the date of creation of the kingdom of the English and about the identity of its creator. In 927, Æthelstan, (over)king of the Anglo-Saxons, had conquered the Scandinavian kingdom of the Northumbrians centred on York and, at a meeting on 12 July at Eamontbridge, by Penrith on the Cumberland-Westmorland border (the south-western frontier-point between the kingdoms of Strathclyde and England), had agreed a political relationship with the principal non-English kings ruling in Britain, most notably since 900 *Cosstantin*, the king of Alba, the other non-English bordering power to the north.[3] Æthelstan had also received the submission of the English king of the northern Northumbrians, whose realm was centred on Bamburgh (Co. Northumberland) and whose dynastic line we henceforth find neither attracting nor bearing royal title.[4] In 927×939, Æthelstan's charters and coins asserted grand styles, *rex Anglorum* ('king of the English'), imperial styles (notably the hellenising *basileus*) and styles claiming Britain-wide rule: REX TOT: BRIT: = *rex totius Britanniae* ('the king of the whole of Britain').[5] The

---

[3] For contextualised discussion of the origins of Scotland, see D. Broun, *Scottish Independence and the Idea of Britain, from the Picts to Alexander III* (Edinburgh, 2013). Further to Broun's work, see on this subject A. Woolf, *From Pictland to Alba, 789–1070* (Edinburgh, 2007).

[4] On the end of independent English rule in the north-east of England and south east of Scotland, see D. Whitelock, *History, Law and Literature in 10th–11th Century England* (London, 1981), essay III; cf. W. E. Kapelle, *The Norman Conquest of the North. The Region and Its Transformation, 1000–1135* (Chapel Hill, NC 1979).

[5] On royal styles, see R. Drögereit, *Sachsen, Angelsachsen, Niedersachsen. Ausgewählte Aufsätze*, 3 vols. (Hamburg, 1978), vol. I, pp. 11–125; H. Kleinschmidt, *Untersuchungen über das englische Königtum*

completion of an English project was announced in a letter-poem (imitating one in Charlemagne's name) to the queen-mother and the prince at court, sent from the royal army in the north-west.[6] Whatever previous perceptions there may have been, England (*Englaland*) and the kingdom of the English certainly now existed. Yet it is striking that the first scholarly biography of the kingdom's founder is of recent date.[7]

The Passage of Dominion

The English had inhabited part of Britain for about a half-millennium in 927. To be sure, a great variety of Germanic ethnicities could be met in the founding era of English history, as place-names and Bede's evidence amply attest.[8] Collectively, they could be seen by their native British neighbours as *Saxones* (a Late-Latin name for a major alliance of Germanic-speaking peoples), as *Garmani* (Classical Latin *Germani*)[9] – a larger such ethnic identity (now defined linguistically), but also sometimes (on the evidence of Old-Welsh poetry) as *Eingl* (Latin *Angli*, Old-English *Engle*),[10] another Germanic people, who would eventually provide the name 'English' (*englisc*) for both people and language. It is clear already from seventh-century evidence that the most prominent peoples of early Anglo-Saxon

im 10. Jahrhundert (Göttingen, 1979), pp. 33–105; and S. Keynes, *The Diplomas of King Æthelred 'the Unready', 978–1016. A Study in Their Use as Historical Evidence* (Cambridge, 1980), pp. 1–83. On coins, see C. E. Blunt et al., *Coinage in Tenth-Century England, from Edward the Elder to Edgar's Reform* (Oxford, 1989) and C. E. Blunt, 'The Coinage of Athelstan, King of England 924–939', *BNJ* 42 (1974), 35–160 + plates.

6 This was edited and translated by M. Lapidge, 'Some Latin Poems as Evidence for the Reign of Athelstan', *ASE* 9 (1981), 61–98, reprinted in his *Anglo-Latin Literature, 900–1066* (London, 1993), pp. 49–86. Cf. D. N. Dumville, *The Mediaeval Foundations of England?* (Aberdeen, 2006), pp. 11–15, reprinted in his *Anglo-Saxon Essays, 2001–2007* (Aberdeen, 2007), pp. 266–310, at 274–7.

7 S. Foot, *Æthelstan, the First King of England* (New Haven, CT, 2011). This book gives Æthelstan a place in historians' purview – which he had not enjoyed since the sixteenth century – but there is much still to be done. On the ways in which Æthelstan was overtaken and marginalised in early modern historical writing, in favour of his grandfather, Alfred 'the Great', see S. Keynes, 'The Cult of King Alfred the Great', *ASE* 28 (1999), 225–356, which deserves re-issue by Cambridge University Press as a book.

8 E. Ekwall, 'Some Notes on English Place-Names Containing Tribal Names', *Namn och bygd* 24 (1936), 178–83; and E. Ekwall, 'Tribal Names in English Place-Names', *Namn och bygd* 41 (1953), 129–77. For a larger context, see W. Piroth, *Ortsnamenstudien zur angelsächsischen Wanderung. Ein Vergleich von -ingas, -inga- Namen in England mit ihren Entsprechungen auf dem europäischen Festland* (Wiesbaden, 1979).

9 On the British pronunciation, see Bede, *Historia ecclesiastica gentis Anglorum* [hereafter HE], v.9, in *Bede's Ecclesiastical History of the English People*, ed. B. Colgrave and R. A. B. Mynors (Oxford, 1969; rev. imp., 1990), pp. 476–7.

10 *The Poems of Taliesin*, ed. I. Williams (Dublin, 1968), pp. 3–4 (no. III, line 20, *Eigyl*; commentary on p. 48) and 7–9 (no. VII, line 28, *Eigyl*; summary commentary on p. 87).

England were *Engle* (Angles) and *Seaxas* (Saxons), whose origins Bede in 731 sought to pinpoint in what are now northern Germany and the Jutlandic peninsula of Denmark.[11] From the evidence of material culture, it is apparent that the immigrants came from a yet broader North Sea zone extending from southern Norway to the Netherlands.[12]

The circumstances which brought significant immigration from Continental *Germania* to Britain over a period of perhaps 150 years – I discount immobilist theories of the last generation, which crudely sought to deny such migration – had a shattering effect on the post-colonial polities and culture of the native British. It is, and will remain, a matter of vigorous dispute what happened to the indigenes in the new settler-colonial environment. There are some certainties. There was southward emigration which created new Britains in western Gaul (Brittany, 'Little/Lesser Britain') and in northern Iberia (Britoña in Galicia). (Less certainly, on one interpretation of toponymic evidence, there were widespread individual British settlements in post-Roman Gaul, especially along the North Sea/Atlantic coast; and the British migrations from southern Britain to Brittany may have continued for centuries.)[13] The British language disappeared from large areas of the southern half of Britain,[14] to be replaced by Germanic speech in dialects which eventually came to be known collectively as English. The material and social culture of those areas became that associable with speakers of Germanic languages.

In 731, Bede was in no doubt what had happened to the British. By a conventional Christian interpretation, the Britons' criminal immorality had driven their God to bring them to the brink of extinction, by using the Germanic-speaking heathen invaders as agents of *exterminium gentis*, genocide.[15] For Bede, God's new chosen people in Britain were the English.[16]

---

[11] Bede, *HE* i. 15 (ed. Colgrave and Mynors, pp. 48–53). For a partially self-defeating attempt to shift this focus southwards on toponymic evidence, see J. Udolph, 'The Colonisation of England by Germanic Tribes on the Basis of Place-Names', in *Language Contact and Development around the North Sea*, ed. M. Stenroos et al. (Philadelphia, 2012), pp. 23–51.

[12] S. C. Hawkes and M. Pollard, 'The Gold Bracteates from Sixth-Century Anglo-Saxon Graves in Kent, in the Light of a New Find from Finglesham', *Frühmittelalterliche Studien* 15 (1981), 316–70; and J. Hines, *The Scandinavian Character of Anglian England in the Pre-Viking Period* (Oxford, 1984).

[13] D. Fahy, 'When Did Britons Become Bretons?', *Welsh History Review* 2 (1964–5), 111–24; Thompson, *Saint Germanus*, pp. 78–90; T. M. Charles-Edwards, *Wales and the Britons, 350–1064* (Oxford, 2012), pp. 21–6, 44–74; and L. Fleuriot, *Les Origines de la Bretagne. L'émigration* (Paris, 1980), esp. pp. 39–109.

[14] K. Jackson, *Language and History in Early Britain. A Chronological Survey of the Brittonic Languages, First to Twelfth Century A.D.* (Edinburgh, 1953), pp. 3–30; and T. Charles-Edwards, 'Language and Society among the Insular Celts, 400–1000', in *The Celtic World*, ed. M. J. Green (London, 1995), pp. 703–36, at 729–36.

[15] Bede, *HE* i. 14, *capitulum* (ed. Colgrave and Mynors, pp. 8–9).

[16] *Ibid.*, i. 22 (ed. Colgrave and Mynors, pp. 66–9).

In justification, Bede referred to the sixth-century British author Gildas, whose massive letter of admonition, *De excidio Britanniae* ('The Ruin of Britain'), was a call for moral re-armament by a people whom he presented as God's 'latter-day Israel' being divinely tested in its faith.[17] While a British elite remained convinced of its civilised superiority to the invaders, its members' only satisfaction can have been that their culture had not been entirely eradicated. Roman Britain, still visible within the emerging English landscape, was already a distant memory in Gildas's world, even though he himself was living testimony to a continuing *romanitas* in British Britain.[18]

It is a long time since literal genocide was a preferred explanation of how a large part of Britain became England. A favoured theory – which could be heard enunciated over and over again during the last generation – was that a few Germanic-speakers who happened to be in late Roman or post-Roman Britain proved to be such superior and therefore powerful role-models that over the course of the immediately succeeding centuries the Britons hurried to shed their inherited culture and to adopt that which by the end of the sixth century we can recognise as English. Although this remarkable hypothesis was advanced with moral self-righteousness, we can see it to have been in all its essentials misleading (to put the matter no more strongly). If we were to set (an imaginary ancient-history committee of) the United Nations to investigate what happened to the native Britons in the fifth, sixth, and seventh centuries in terms of its Convention on Genocide (1948), it is difficult to imagine that the result would be other than a judgement that genocide took place. Part of that process would have been literal, involving a significant amount of bloodshed. Part might have involved an apartheid system restricting the indigenes' access to resources and status.[19] Part would have been the creation of an environment in which the only hope of personal survival or advancement would have been assimilation to the mores of Germanic-speakers or to flee the Island, never to return. The overall verdict: cultural genocide following resisted invasion and colonisation.[20]

[17] Gildas, *Epistola de excidio Britanniae*, I. 25–6, in *Gildas*, ed. H. Williams (London, 1899–1901), pp. 56–65; and *Gildas: The Ruin of Britain and Other Works*, ed. and trans. M. Winterbottom (Chichester, 1978), pp. 98–9 and 27–9. Cf. T. O'Loughlin, *Gildas and the Christian Scriptures. Observing the World through a Biblical Lens* (Turnhout, 2012).

[18] D. N. Dumville, 'Post-Colonial Gildas: A First Essay', *Quaestio insularis* 7 (2006), 1–21, reprinted in his *Celtic Essays, 2001–2007*, 2 vols. (Aberdeen, 2007), vol. I, pp. 1–15.

[19] Cf. A. Woolf, 'Apartheid and Economics in Anglo-Saxon England', in *Britons in Anglo-Saxon England*, ed. N. Higham (Woodbridge, 2007), pp. 115–29.

[20] For general issues, see *Genocide: Conceptual and Historical Dimensions*, ed. G. J. Andreopoulos (Philadelphia, 1994); for text of the 'Convention on Genocide', see pp. 229–33. For larger contexts, see *The Oxford Handbook of Genocide Studies*, ed. D. Bloxham and A. D. Moses (Oxford, 2010).

Even so, there remain many questions about the British conditions in which Germanic settlement began and to which the incomers had to adapt. Here I shall sketch out a dramatic scenario of systemic collapse which seems to me to provide a helpful interpretative context. The antiquated junior-school textbook image of the end of Roman Britain defined by Roman legionary field armies marching out in 409/10 to support their embattled colleagues in Gaul and Italy has nothing to recommend it, but scholars' language continues to be defined by such a perception, which, in our sources, begins with Gildas.[21] There are two certain essential points. The first is that there were repeated rebellions by Imperial forces in Britain in 406/7, the last of which led to a usurping emperor, Constantine III (407–11), taking forces from Britain to campaign in Gaul (and subsequently in Iberia).[22] Second, at some point (perhaps around 410) in the lengthy reign of the legitimate emperor of the West, Honorius (395–423), the regular flow of coinage to support the army in Britain abruptly ceased.[23] These two matters may be closely linked. It is likely that the sudden shock to the Romano-British economy produced dramatic results.

Less closely datable, but certainly within a couple of decades of the latter events, we see a collapse of mass production of goods in Britain and a loss of distributive networks. It is not certain which came first, but it is unimaginable that these changes are independent. No new money receipts and no new pottery (with its many functions) would have been severe developments. How cities and towns now fed themselves may have come into question. Certainly, archaeology has provided evidence to suggest the ending of some Roman social norms in urban Britain.[24] We have evidence (as likewise in later-fifth-century Gaul) for the inability of owners of elite property to have their central-heating systems maintained adequately or at all. As urban life slipped from its predictable rhythms, an increasing uncertainty about

[21] Gildas, *Epistola de excidio Britanniae*, I (ed. Williams, pp. 2–11, 14–39, 44–65; ed. and trans. Winterbottom, pp. 87–99 and 13–29).

[22] C. E. Stevens, 'Marcus, Gratian, Constantine', *Athenaeum* (Pavia) 45 (n. s. 35) (1957), 316–47; and E. A. Thompson, *Romans and Barbarians. The Decline of the Western Empire* (Madison, WI 1982), pp. 137–229, 289–307. On the textbook image, see Dumville, 'Post-Colonial Gildas', pp. 5–6, 14–16, reprinted in *Celtic Essays, 2001–2007*, vol. I, pp. 4, 10–12. The crucial source is Orosius, *Historiarum aduersus paganos libri septem* [Seven Books of Histories against the Stupid], in which this alleged Iberian showed an unusual interest in Insular affairs. The standard edition remains *Pauli Orosii Historiarum adversum Paganos Libri VII*, ed. C. Zangemeister (Wien, 1882). The most recent discussion is that of P. van Nuffelen, *Orosius and the Rhetoric of History* (Oxford, 2012). The modern translators seem not to have understood Orosius's argument.

[23] S. Archer, 'Late Roman Gold and Silver Coin Hoards in Britain: A Gazetteer', in *The End of Roman Britain*, ed. P. J. Casey (Oxford, 1979), pp. 29–64.

[24] See K. R. Dark, *Civitas to Kingdom: British Political Continuity, 300–800* (London, 1994), pp. 55–64, 68–70, for a discussion.

survival in such contexts may have provoked an urban exodus. In those circumstances, governance is likely to have been exerted from different centres and over more restricted areas.

Barbarian military adventures are attested for this period of British history, both in 410 and in the early 440s.[25] If we accept the testimony of the late-fifth-century hagiography of St Germanus of Auxerre, they were an issue in 429/30 also.[26] A Marxist reading of the socio-religious history of early-fifth-century Britain, as partly seen through the eyes of an unreliable mid-sixth-century Byzantine historian, has produced a hypothesis of a root-and-branch revolt against Imperial authority structures and the ejection of Constantine III's administrators in 409/10.[27] As we leave contemporary evidence, circumstances necessarily become more difficult to evaluate, as this example shows. Nevertheless, we know that *bacaudae* – peasant rebels – were active and effective in western Gaul in precisely this period.[28]

A sudden decline in normality, prosperity and order in early-fifth-century Roman Britain would have created its own social, economic and political momentum. We do not need the very uncertainly attested suspension for Britain of *Lex Iulia de ui publica* (the ban on civilians bearing arms in the Roman commonwealth) by Honorius in 410 as an indicator of crisis. There are other indicators aplenty.

However, my earlier point about a growing localism – indeed, one could say 'autonomy' – in governance should exercise restraint over any temptation to generalise too eagerly. Considerations of place and time will always point to complexity. We should expect to see in all these circumstances both parallel and consecutive development of different perceptions of present and future and of different patterns of behaviour. Whether Britons saw Britain crashing out of the Roman empire at a particular moment or

---

[25] For characterisation of Germanic military activity in Britain in the fifth century, using as a comparandum the *Suebi /Sueui* active in Iberia in the same period, see Thompson, *Romans and Barbarians*, pp. 212–17 (and cf. pp. 239–40, 251–7). Cf. also H. Kleinschmidt, 'Swabians in Early Medieval England', *Alemannisches Jahrbuch* (1994), 9–32.

[26] Constantius, *Vita Sancti Germani*, is the source for any detail: *Passiones vitaeque sanctorum aevi merovingici*, VII, ed. B. Krusch and W. Levison (Hannover, 1919–20), pp. 247–83. But the fact of Germanus' visit to Britain beginning in 429 is due to the contemporary chronicler Prosper of Aquitaine, §1301, in *Chronica minora saec. IV.V.VI.VII*, ed. T. Mommsen, 3 vols. (Berlin 1891–8), vol. I, p. 472. Cf. Thompson, *Saint Germanus*, pp. 7–14 (and p. 126, *s.v.* 'Saxons').

[27] Thompson, *Saint Germanus*, pp. 33–7. See further E. A. Thompson, 'Zosimus 6.10.2, and the Letters of Honorius', *Classical Quarterly* 76 (n. s. 32) (1982), 445–62.

[28] Thompson, *Saint Germanus*, pp. 34, 62–3, 104. More generally, see B. Czúth, *Die Quellen der Geschichte der Bagauden* (Szeged, 1965); and L. Montecchio, *I bacaudae. Tensioni sociali tra tardoantico e alto medioevo* (Rome, 2012). For an interesting Bacaudic episode in north-western Iberia in the reign of Rechiarius, king of Sueves (448–56), see Thompson, *Romans and Barbarians*, pp. 211–12.

imagined that they were constitutionally or legally still part of it, even after
the middle of the fifth century, or had very various simultaneous views at any
moment, must remain a moot point in the absence of specific evidence.

A thought should be spared for an issue which has received all too little
attention in the scholarly literature. What was the effect, beyond the
frontier, of the collapse – whether sudden or progressive – of the Roman
imperial diocese of Britain? It was Roman policy to manage the politics of
frontier zones, which required good intelligence and (where possible)
reliable local allies. Payment of subsidy, sometimes lavish, was an essential
option in the maintenance of alliance. So too was forward military patrol-
ling. When these ceased, the political landscape changed at once.[29] Over
the past two generations there has been a growing recognition that there
was significant change in the mid-fifth century in the landscape of power in
what is now southern and central Scotland. The Britons and (farther
north) the Picts of these areas can be seen to have developed new types
of fortified centres, often replacing larger hill-forts.[30] New enemies
emerged. New opportunities and alliances might be perceived. But in the
deep frontier zone which the Roman army had once sought to manage, the
money had dried up, just as in the early-fifth-century Roman diocese
itself – and for the same reason: the Imperial fiscal tap had been turned
off. In different ways, in a different society (or two: northern Britons and
southern Picts), the consequences nonetheless must have been severe and
the adaptation painful. And when, after the mid-sixth century, the English
came calling, the pain was no doubt greater still.[31]

We cannot avoid the question how it was that English, ultimately
Germanic, language, social customs (including law and religion) and
institutions came to prevail in a large part of Britain. Part of the answer
is likely to lie in the circumstances in which Roman rule – or, perhaps even

[29] On Traprain Law, perhaps the central place of the Uotadini, see A. O. Curle, *The Treasure of
Traprain. A Scottish Hoard of Roman Silver Plate* (Glasgow, 1923); and Dark, *Britain and the End*,
p. 205; and F. Hunter and K. Painter (eds.), *Late Roman Silver. The Traprain Treasure in Context*
(Edinburgh, 2013). The contrast with Burnswark (Dumfriesshire), *caput* of the Damnonii, is
striking and instructive.
[30] R. B. K. Stevenson, 'The Nuclear Fort at Dalmahoy, Midlothian, and Other Dark Age Capitals',
Proceedings of the Society of Antiquaries of Scotland 83 (1948–9), 186–98; L. Alcock, 'Early Historic
Fortifications in Scotland', in *Hill-Fort Studies. Essays for A. H. A. Hogg*, ed. G. Guilbert (Leicester,
1981), pp. 150–80; and Alcock's detailed reports on excavations of a number of early mediaeval
fortified sites in northern Britain, as well as his summation of his Scottish work in *Kings and
Warriors, Craftsmen and Priests in Northern Britain, A.D. 550–850* (Edinburgh, 2003).
[31] On this period of (pre-Scottish) history in North Britain, see J. E. Fraser, *From Caledonia to Pictland.
Scotland to 795* (Edinburgh, 2009). For the English arrival and expansion, the papers by P. Hunter
Blair, *Anglo-Saxon Northumbria* (London, 1984), still have much to offer. See also P. Clack and J. Ivy
(eds.), *The Borders* (Durham, 1983).

more, the Roman imperial economy – ceased in Britain. Our written sources for that period are poor, and what are sometimes taken as certainties are far from such. But we have seen that the evidence of material culture may be held to be decisive. The economy collapsed. Cash flow into the Roman diocese ended; industry and mass production ceased; communications (freedom of movement) and distribution broke down. Management of technology gradually became impossible as manpower and skills were lost; starvation became a problem, particularly in urban communities; civil violence became a significant issue; the cities and towns began to empty as normal life became impossible; population decline, probably severe, became inevitable. New governmental forces made themselves felt, ad hoc; barbarian raiding increasingly gave way to immigration.[32]

If we turn to Gildas, writing in the mid-sixth century in fear of further disasters, we find that cities were now empty; that the barbarian presence, which had provoked a *diuortium* in *Britannia*, was heavily felt; that civil war was endemic in British Britain; that Britons had emigrated. We do not have to accept Gildas's historiography or his religious position: we must merely note what he took for granted in relation to his own time. The Roman era was a dim and distant memory, however prompted by the remains of the built environment of the Empire. Trade no longer flowed along the principal riverine arteries of southern Britain. There had been wars until relatively recently, which had drawn to a close around the time of Gildas's birth, and he at least feared their resumption with newly catastrophic consequences.[33]

As we contemplate systems collapse, the end (in Britain at least) of an Imperial mode whose ways had dominated British life for four centuries (and yet no certainty that 'Rome' would not or could not return), we can suppose that the most heavily Romanised (and therefore the most urbanised and populous) parts of the diocese would have suffered disproportionately. In other words, we do not have to imagine that immigrant (or even indigenous) barbarians pushed Roman Britain over: whatever the merits of such an argument might be in relation to other parts of the western Empire, it is not necessary in Britain. One could even argue that systems collapse would have made *Britannia* a less attractive target for raiding and

---

[32] R. Fleming, *Britain after Rome. The Fall and Rise, 400–1070* (London, 2010), has recently produced a lively and colourful history largely from material-culture evidence: the evidence has often been pressed too hard, but the result is nonetheless important and deserves respect.

[33] Dumville, 'Post-Colonial Gildas', pp. 15–21, and Dumville, *Celtic Essays, 2001–2007*, vol. I, pp. 11–15.

immigration. But we know that from the 360s to the 440s, for which we do have relevant contemporary evidence, Germanic barbarians were attacking Britain.[34]

Yet what is certain is, to take a long view, that the British-speaking Britons were not wholly conquered militarily from England until the thirteenth century and that they were not confined to Dumnonia (understood as Devon and Cornwall), Wales and what is now south-western Scotland until the mid-seventh century. As has long been acknowledged in modern scholarship, if we see English expansionism in Britain as a process, perhaps still on-going or perhaps having just passed its high-water mark in the later seventh century, then the first major stage took some two hundred years to be completed.[35]

In any event, 'the passage of dominion' from Britons to English, as it has been conceptualised since the time of Bede and thoroughly developed since 1100, was a lengthy process. In the eyes of twelfth-century writers it was brought to a close by the reign of Æthelstan as first monarch of England and tidied up by Norman domination of Wales and Scotland from 1093 in what has recently and rather unfortunately been called 'The First English Empire' (presumably because the writer thought that Saxons became English by Normanisation after 1066).[36]

Nomenclature

The terminology of historical peoples and their territories is often, perhaps always, fraught with difficulty, and this is certainly true in relation to ancient and mediaeval Britain. There are scholars for whom the word 'English' remains difficult to use in relation to the six centuries before 1066: for them, 'Anglo-Saxon' is a favoured term of art, while for most students of the first millennium AD it is simply a period designation, 'Anglo-Saxon England' meaning England before the Norman conquest. It is as if there were in some minds a rule 'Anglo-Saxon + French = English'! At the other end of the historical scale, there is a problem of knowing what

---

[34] I. N. Wood, 'The Channel from the Fourth to the Seventh Centuries A.D.', in *Maritime Celts, Frisians and Saxons*, ed. S. McGrail (London, 1990), pp. 93–7.

[35] E. A. Thompson, 'Britain, A.D. 406–410', *Britannia* 8 (1977), 303–18; and Thompson, *Romans and Barbarians*, pp. 137–248, *passim*.

[36] R. William Leckie, Jr., *The Passage of Dominion: Geoffrey of Monmouth and the Periodization of Insular History in the Twelfth Century* (Toronto, 1981), produced the outstanding account of the literary development of this idea. For the 'English' empire from 1093, see R. R. Davies, *The First English Empire. Power and Identities in the British Isles, 1093–1343* (Oxford, 2000).

to do about the opposition of meaning of *Engle* ('Angle') and *Seaxe* ('Saxon') when Latin *Angli* and *Saxones* could be used to mean one and the same thing (most easily translated 'English') but when in a document of 736 *Suuthengle* might be taken to mean 'the Southern Angles' (viz. the Mercians) or 'the Southern English'.[37] *Angelcynn* seems likely to have meant 'the English people' and, by extension, 'England' but in principle might also have meant 'Angles'. The changing territory of Anglo-Saxon England can be held to be problematic in terms of nomenclature, and it is striking that modern Scottish historians (and some linguists of like mind) are still unwilling to allow that the English-speakers who were absorbed into 'Scotland' in the tenth and eleventh centuries might be called 'English' rather than 'Angles' or 'Anglians'. This is rendered even more absurd by the circumstance that fifteenth-century native speakers of Scots called their language *Inglis*. But by that stage Scots was no more mainstream English than is twenty-first-century American.

It remains a fact that the land and the people came to be known as 'England' (*Englaland*, 'land of the Angles') and 'English' (Angle-ish). The implied defining role of the Angles in this process has yet to find convincing explanation. Are we to suppose that such ethnogenesis crystallised during the dominance of Southumbrian England by Anglian over-kingdoms from the time of Rædwald of the East Angles (?610s×627) to that of Æthelbald of the Mercians (716–57), perhaps even in one of the brief periods when the whole of England was in the hegemony of Northumbrian kings, Edwin (616×627–33) to Oswiu (651–8)?[38] Yet *Englaland* itself seems to be a relative latecomer to the territorial vocabulary of Old English – and it should be stressed that Latin *Anglia* was not naturally used in England until after the Norman conquest.

In this context, the phrases *rex Anglorum* and *rex Saxonum* (which could mean either 'a king of the English' or 'the king of the English') need careful thought and sensitive interpretation. By extension, *regnum Anglorum*, 'a/the kingdom of the English', requires yet more cautious treatment. It has famously been pointed out that Pope Gregory I (590–604), the father of English Christianity, initiated a papal diplomatic usage of *rex Anglorum*

---

[37] P. H. Sawyer, *Anglo-Saxon Charters. An Annotated List and Bibliography* (London, 1968), p. 94, S 89 (BCS 154). This survives as an original single sheet: see E. A. Lowe, *English Uncial* (Oxford, 1960), p. 21; and *Chartae Latinae Antiquiores*, vol. III, ed. A. Bruckner and R. Marichal (Olten, 1963), no. 183.

[38] On that period, see E. B. Fryde et al. (eds.), *Handbook of British Chronology*, 3rd edn (London, 1986), pp. 4–6.

for any English king; and that Pope has on this basis been heralded, however improbably, as the father of Englishness itself, the very author of an ethnogenesis.[39]

England, then, at its fullest extent in the mid-ninth century, was bounded on the south by the English Channel, in the west by the Cornish and Welsh borders, in the north-west by the ethnically British kingdoms of what is now south-western Scotland and in particular by the kingdom of Dumbarton (the precise boundaries and all the British players are uncertain), and in the north by the upland massif of *Bannog* (as in Modern Scots Bannockburn, the site of a famous battle in 1314), which provided the southern boundary of the over-kingdom of the Picts.[40] The resemblance of this English territory to the effective dimensions of the Roman province, later diocese, of Britain (*Brittaniae*, 'the Britains', viz, 'the Imperial provinces of Britain', in Classical Latin) is very striking, and it is arguable that in this respect the Roman heritage was of great importance in the Middle Ages in respect of the formation of kingdoms, ethnic identities and imperial aspirations. Latin *Brittania* (Classical)/*Britannia* (mediaeval) was therefore either Great Britain (the island as a whole) or the territory dominated by the Romans: it is worth remembering that up to one third of the British landmass, what is now northern Scotland, was never incorporated into the Roman empire.

It is necessary always to grasp that in the earlier Middle Ages Britain was a place of considerable ethnic complexity and even greater political diversity. That said, we must equally remember that the very idea of Britain was a driver and moulder of political thought and action, a name for a contested world of its own. The Britons held it to be their own sphere (although mediaeval Welsh literature allows that the name Britain may exclude the Pictish north, above the Antonine Wall or above *Bannog*).[41] We find, however, the Britons of the earlier Middle Ages able to refer to any of Britoña, Brittany, Cornwall, Wales, or British-speaking northern Britain (of which the kingdom of Dumbarton would have been the northernmost) as *Britannia* without qualification. For them it was an affirmation

---

[39] P. Wormald, 'The Venerable Bede and the "Church of the English"', in *The English Religious Tradition and the Genius of Anglicanism*, ed. G. Rowell (Wantage, 1992), pp. 13–32; cf. Dumville, *The Mediaeval Foundations*, p. 12.

[40] On Bannog, see *The Gododdin. The Oldest Scottish Poem*, trans. K. H. Jackson (Edinburgh, 1969), pp. 4–6, 78–9.

[41] *Trioedd Ynys Prydein, The Welsh Triads*, ed. and trans. R. Bromwich, 1st edn (Cardiff, 1961), p. 483, *s.n. Pabo post Prydein*, and, supplementarily, 2nd edn (1978), p. 561. But, since there seems to be no sign of a locution *Ynys Prydyn*, the force of *Ynys Prydein*, 'The Island of Britain', remains uncertain. That last issue hangs awkwardly over Bromwich's book.

of inherited culture, an unwillingness to release that, but also a pointed reminder of what had been lost.[42] At the end of the ninth century, as the inhabitants of what is now north-eastern Scotland started to shake off the unwelcome embrace of the vikings of Dublin, we begin to meet kings of *Alba*, an Old-Gaelic name meaning 'Great Britain/the island of Britain'.[43] Again, we must recognise the note of aspiration – and in its rulers we see the lineal ancestors of the later kings of Scots.[44] All these contested Britain with Germanic speakers, first the English and then Viking-Age Scandinavians. Over the course of early Anglo-Saxon history, English regional over-kings, inspired by stimuli which historians still dispute, enjoyed a developing rhetoric of rule of Britain in their competition for dominance. In a document of the year 736, already mentioned, Æthelbald, (over)king of the Mercians, has the styles *rex Britanniae* ('king of Britain') and *rex . . . omnium prouinciarum quae Sutangli dicuntur* ('the king of all the kingdoms which are called Southern English'), a formula which can be connected directly with what the recently deceased Bede had to say in his *Historia ecclesiastica gentis Anglorum* ('Ecclesiastical History of the English People') about seven over-kings who intermittently dominated the Midlands and south of England from Anglo-Saxon proto-history to the time when he wrote.[45] A century and a half later, the *Anglo-Saxon Chronicle* (published in 892) gives us in a crudely augmented version of Bede's list the vernacular equivalent of Æthelbald's *rex Britanniae* – *brytenwealda* ('ruler of Britain').[46] In Bede's terms, the West-Saxon kings who received the submission of their East-Anglian and Mercian counterparts, making themselves over-kings of the English Midlands and south, would have joined this list of exceptionally powerful rulers: Ecgberht (829/30), Edward the Elder (899–924), Ælfweard (924) and Æthelstan (924/5–927). In as much as kings from 927 to 1066 continued (albeit with occasional viking-induced disruption) to dominate this Southumbrian area, they might also have rejoiced in such a title. However, it is from 927 that we have explicit evidence of the deployment (in Latin) of royal styles of entitlement to rule Britain.

---

[42] A. W. Wade-Evans et al., *The Historical Basis of Welsh Nationalism* (Cardiff, 1950); and Charles-Edwards, *Wales and the Britons*, pp. 519–35, has analysed the tenth-century poem *Armes Prydein Vawr*, where the continuing sense of loss – of rights, territory, and power – is palpable.

[43] C. Downham, *Viking Kings of Britain and Ireland. The Dynasty of Ívarr to A.D. 1014* (Edinburgh, 2007; 2nd edn, 2008), pp. 137–75; and D. N. Dumville, 'Ireland and Britain in *Táin bó Fraích*', *Études celtiques* 32 (1996), 175–87.

[44] Broun, *Scottish Independence*, pp. 71–97.

[45] Bede, *HE* v. 23 (ed. Colgrave and Mynors, pp. 558–9).

[46] *ASC* MS A, 827, in *The Anglo-Saxon Chronicle MS. A*, ed. J. M. Bately, AS Chronicle: A Collaborative Edition, III (Cambridge, 1986), p. 42.

An English claimant to be a ruler or king or emperor of Britain must have his outlook examined closely. Given the variety of meanings, in that period, of words translatable as 'Britain' – any one of the British-speaking territories, the Roman imperial diocese at its fullest extent, the island of Britain – a premature, insufficiently contextualised interpretation could be very misleading.[47] Another dimension is provided by parallel usage in Ireland in the earlier Middle Ages: from 642 (an obituary notice) we encounter from time to time persons given the title *rex Hiberniae /rí Érenn* ('the king of Ireland'), who show no sign of having dominated an area any larger than (at best) the northern half of that island.[48] We see in Gaelic literature in Latin the transfer of this kind of ideology to Britain when Northumbrian over-kings were dominant in England.[49]

In sum, political theory and practice could cross borders between ethnicities as well as between polities of shared ethnicity. Christian evangelising missions and political exile provided two conduits for such transfer. Even negative views about neighbours did not offer a defence against reception of new ideas. The language of ethnic and religious differences does, however, present a reminder of the points at which lines might be drawn.

Within Britain, the English had three sets of ethnically differentiable neighbours in the early Middle Ages – Picts (Old-English *Pehtas*), Gaels (Old-English *Scottas*) and Britons (*Brettas*), joined by a fourth in the Viking Age, Scandinavians (*Dene*).[50] Attitudes to these neighbours would vary with time, place and political circumstance, and these attitudes might have been variously different between seculars and ecclesiastics. What is clear is that in Anglo-Latin political discourse any one of them might be called *barbari* ('barbarians'). In late Roman terms, any one of them (save

[47] See, for example, the classic essay by N. Wright, 'Gildas's Geographical Perspective: Some Problems', *Gildas: New Approaches*, ed. Lapidge and Dumville, pp. 85–105.

[48] On King Domnall mac Aedo, who died at the end of January 642, see the brief account of F. J. Byrne, *Irish Kings and High-Kings* (London, 1973), p. 114, whose point about the distribution of chronicle evidence is crucial. Cf. T. M. Charles-Edwards, *Early Christian Ireland* (Cambridge, 2000), esp. pp. 481–7, on 'Tara and the Kingship of Ireland', relying on a mix of sources of various dates; his very important, indeed unprecedented, study, chap. 13, 'The Powers of Kings', pp. 522–85, is indispensable reading.

[49] Adomnán, *Vita Sancti Columbae*, i. 1, in *Adomnán's Life of Columba*, ed. and trans. A. O. Anderson and M. O. Anderson, 2nd edn (Oxford, 1991), pp. 12–19.

[50] D. N. Dumville, 'Old Dubliners and New Dubliners in Ireland and Britain: A Viking-Age Story', *Medieval Dublin* 6 (2004), 79–94, reprinted in his *Celtic Essays, 2001–2007*, vol. I, pp. 103–22; and C. Downham, '"Hiberno-Norwegians" and "Anglo-Danes": Anachronistic Ethnicities and Viking-Age England', *Mediaeval Scandinavia* 19 (2009), 139–69, reprinted in her *No Horns on Their Helmets? Essays on the Insular Viking-Age* (Aberdeen, 2013), pp. 41–71.

those Britons counted as Roman provincials, therefore *ciues*, '[Roman] citizens') might be accounted thus, including any one of the Germanic peoples who contributed to the post-Roman population of Britain. It is striking that this language could be adopted and applied to their Insular neighbours by the (newly) Christian English, whose heathen forefathers their Italian evangelists would certainly have regarded as *barbari*. It is no surprise that the Britons called the English barbarians, and it is striking to find Gaelic writers also able to use it of the English.[51] We should perhaps (except in the case of the grim Anglo-British relationship) not read too much meaning into the word, perhaps regarding it simply as a way of affirming the user's sense of his own civility over against his neighbour.

However, one exception to this must be recorded, also in the context of Anglo-British interaction. Much effort has been expended in recent years on lightening the dark picture of mutual racial hatred between the two peoples, and there has been significant gain in the quality of our understanding of the existence of a complex interrelationship.[52] But, if we are to have a generalisation, it remains the case that the default position on either side was characterised by contempt and racial hatred. The word which has become 'Welsh' in Modern English, and therefore both a straightforward ethnic label for the inhabitants of a precisely defined geographical and constitutional space and for the indigenes' original language, had, however, a darker earlier history. Old-English *wealh* (plural *wealas*, adjective *welhisc*) was a word which denoted a foreigner, particularly one of Roman heritage and Romance speech, who was worthy only to be a slave – indeed, it became a standard word for 'slave'. This is part of a much larger Germanic picture and can be seen (for example) on the Germanic-Romance linguistic

---

[51] For Bede's usage, see P. F. Jones, *A Concordance to the Historia Ecclesiastica of Bede* (Cambridge, MA, 1929), pp. 53–4 (*s.vv. barbaricus, barbarus*). In the letters of St Patrick, we meet the word once – *Epistola contra Coroticum*, §1: K. Devine, *A Computer-Generated Concordance to the Libri Epistolarum of Saint Patrick* (Dublin, 1989), p. 23. For an Italian view, probably shared in Gaul/Francia, see Bede, *HE* i. 23–5 (ed. Colgrave and Mynors, pp. 68–77). For the long-term history, see J. Gillingham, 'The Foundations of a Disunited Kingdom', in *Uniting the Kingdom? The Making of British History*, ed. A. Grant and K. J. Stringer (London, 1995), pp. 48–64, whose opening pages are of capital importance. On the Celtic side of the relationship, see Gildas, *Epistola de excidio Britanniae*, esp. i. 3–26 (ed. Williams, pp. 14–65; and ed. and trans. Winterbottom, pp. 89–99 and 16–29) and (later and in Ireland) the late seventh-century lives of St Patrick, where *barbarus* was a heathen Gael: *The Patrician Texts in The Book of Armagh*, ed. and trans. L. Bieler and F. Kelly (Dublin, 1979), pp. 74–5 (Muirchú, I.10), 136–9 (Tírechán, §17), 150–1 (§35) and 164–5 (§52) where *barbarae gentes* are foreign peoples.

[52] See especially P. Sims-Williams, *Religion and Literature in Western England, 600–800* (Cambridge, 1990).

frontier in Belgium.[53] What is striking is that in the conversion of this word into an ethnic label in Britain (as *Wealh, Wealas*, therefore), it became specialised into a description of Britons who inhabited what is now consequently Wales, with the Bretons (*Suðbryttas, Lidwiccas*) and the North Britons (*Cumbras*) receiving different names of a non-negative character and the Cornish (*Westwealas*, but in time *Cornwealas* from which developed Modern-English Cornwall) having their 'Welshness' qualified.[54]

New Societies, New Polities

In sum, the English polity or polities, once established in Britain, must be regarded as intrusive on a previous sub-Roman order, the immigrant presence in the context of system collapse inevitably provoking severe tensions, indeed interethnic hostilities, and leading to a radical political reordering in an ethnogenetic (not to mention ethnonemetic) context. One of the long-standing problems of general interpretation of this process has been whether or not to insist on comparability with the better-documented history of other regions of the western Roman empire which were conquered and settled by Germanic-speaking groups, in Gaul, Iberia, North Africa and Italy. Here I take the view that, while the insights gained by comparison are to be welcomed and developed, there is no merit in insisting that the course of history in Britain and any other sub-Roman region must have been essentially similar.[55] Indeed, it is apparent from the outcome – in terms of language, political and social culture and material culture – that British history has many important differences from that of the other Roman regions in which Germanic-speaking peoples established themselves in the fifth and sixth centuries. There are many reasons for these differences, extending from the circumstances of late-fourth- and earlier-fifth-century Britain to the nature of

---

[53] M. L. Faull, 'The Semantic Development of Old English *wealh*', *Leeds Studies in English*, n.s. 8 (1975), 20–44. G. Kurth, *La Frontière linguistique en Belgique et dans le nord de la France*, I (Bruxelles, 1896); C. Verlinden, *Les Origines de la frontière linguistique en Belgique et la colonisation franque* (Bruxelles, 1955); and J. Stengers, *La Formation de la frontière linguistique en Belgique ou de la légitimité de l'hypothèse historique* (Bruxelles, 1959).

[54] For Old-English names of peoples, the brief study by F. Mezger, *Angelsächsische Völker- und Ländernamen* (Berlin, 1921), is seminal.

[55] This has proved to be a rather powerful vein of thought over the past generation. For example, it clearly influenced the idea that Gildas's life-span should be given an earlier start: M. Lapidge, in 'Gildas's Education and the Latin Culture of Sub-Roman Britain', *Gildas: New Approaches*, ed. Lapidge and Dumville, pp. 27–50. More generally, see I. N. Wood, *The Merovingian North Sea* (Alingsås, 1983); and (in the context of 'Late-Antiquity theory') Dark, *Britain and the End*.

the immigrant population which had by the mid-seventh century defined a very new cultural map of Britain.[56]

The ways in which the new polities and societies were established in Britain, and their interactions with and effects on the indigenes, remain very uncertain; interpretation has been, and has continuing potential to be, acutely controversial.

From such a base we begin the history of Anglo-Saxon England. As we gain contemporary evidence of its society – evidence which is very thin for the first seventy to one hundred years from the despatch in 596 of the first evangelising mission from Rome – two features of governance may be observed. We see aggressive regional over-kings locking horns with one another, and in these the historian may be tempted to see the heirs of leaders who commanded significant barbarian forces in fifth-century Britain.[57] But, second, at the same time we see dependent royalty operating at a much more local level, and, as we see more of early Anglo-Saxon England, that evidence increases and diversifies variously. These more local rulers have usually been less interesting (indeed, all too often invisible) to historians, especially in the twentieth century, and it is only in the last twenty-five years that there have been some attempts to write their histories.[58] Nevertheless, historians' focus has remained resolutely on their transience as the English marched their inevitable way to national identity, a monarchy and a nation-state.

---

[56] For a discussion of the development of Germanic socio-politics in early mediaeval England, see P. Wormald, 'Germanic Power Structures: The Early English Experience', in *Power and the Nation in European History*, ed. L. Scales and O. Zimmer (Cambridge, 2005), pp. 105–24; and S. Foot, 'The Historiography of the Anglo-Saxon "Nation-State"', *ibid.*, pp. 125–42. Three important introductions to the foundational role of the Germanic contribution in the making of Anglo-Saxon culture are M. McC. Gatch, *Loyalties and Traditions. Man and His World in Old English Literature* (New York, 1971); J. M. Wallace-Hadrill, *Early Germanic Kingship in England and on the Continent* (Oxford, 1971); and M. J. Swanton, *Crisis and Development in Germanic Society, 700–800: Beowulf and the Burden of Kingship* (Göppingen, 1982).

[57] H. M. Chadwick, *The Origin of the English Nation* (Cambridge, 1907), pp. 144–5 and 153–91 (2nd edn, 1924, pp. 135–6, 144–80), seems to have come to the conclusion that royal leadership of Germanic migration into Britain in the *Völkerwanderungszeit* was a given. Confounded by the realities of very local kingship which he himself had described in his ground-breaking book, *Studies on Anglo-Saxon Institutions* (Cambridge, 1905), he declared that 'the [English] Invasion' was followed in the new colony by 'a period of disintegration' (p. 416, *ad* 291, line 9), which he needed in order to avoid any implication that he thought 'that the number of English kingdoms in Britain was originally very large'(!). Cf. *The Origin* (1st edn), pp. 182–3, at greater length.

[58] The way was led by J. Campbell, *Bede's Reges and Principes* (Jarrow, [1980]), and by the contributors to S. Bassett (ed.), *The Origins of Anglo-Saxon Kingdoms* (London, 1989). For full-length works, see B. Yorke, *Kings and Kingdoms of Early Anglo-Saxon England* (London, 1990); and D. P. Kirby, *The Earliest English Kings* (London, 1991; 2nd edn, 2000); while these latter books have been welcome, they have nevertheless done little more than scratch the surface of the historiographical problem.

In 1974, a hypothesis was advanced that parts of early Anglo-Saxon England might not have been ruled thus.[59] This is a useful reminder that Germanic-speaking peoples can be seen in chequered relations with king-ship.[60] The Germanic word which gave English 'king' (Old-English *cyning*, later *cyng*) was not one whose etymology conveyed such a notion or had great time depth, unlike Welsh *rhi* (a word now long since abandoned) or Old-Gaelic *rí*, cognate with kingly words in very various Indo-European languages.[61] Furthermore, comparative study suggests that the 'free Germanic peasant', much derided in recent generations, deserves further and positive consideration.[62] How the Germanic-speaking immigrants were led in their migration to Britain – if they were – is not known, and very different hypotheses have been advanced over the last century. Indeed, the effects of migration on political organisation have received too little attention both in general and in particular relation to this period.[63]

Two moments at which this focus might have changed proved illusory. In 1905, Hector Munro Chadwick, Germanic philologist and all-round Anglo-Saxonist (to say nothing of his other remarkable achievements),[64] published a variously groundbreaking book, *Studies on Anglo-Saxon Institutions*. It contained the first detailed study of English local kingship. The book was damned by Frank Merry Stenton in an extraordinary and immediate review:[65] historians of Anglo-Saxon England thereafter largely

[59] W. Davies and H. Vierck, 'The Contexts of Tribal Hidage', *Frühmittelalterliche Studien* 8 (1974), 223–93, at 240–1.
[60] This is a theme which runs through the works of E. A. Thompson: *The Early Germans* (Oxford, 1965; rev. imp., 1968) (not helped by his adoption of the dismal scheme of chief, chieftainship, clan [kindred] and clan-chieftainship, tribe [*pagus*], to say nothing of Germans and Germany); *The Visigoths in the Time of Ulfila* (Oxford, 1966); and *Romans and Barbarians*. The 'anthropological' usage is that canonised by P. Vinogradoff, *The Growth of the Manor* (London, 1905; 2nd edn, 1911); P. Vinogradoff, *Outlines of Historical Jurisprudence*, 2 vols. (Oxford 1920–2), vol. I and Vinogradoff, *Tribal Law*, pp. 163–372.
[61] D. E. Evans, *Gaulish Personal Names. A Study of Some Continental Celtic Formations* (Oxford, 1967), pp. 243–9 (and p. 492, *s.v. reg-*); cf. D. H. Green, *Language and History in the Early Germanic World* (Cambridge, 1998), pp. 102–40.
[62] The new work has considerable implications in this area. In general, while being grateful for and stimulated by the publications of Rosamond Faith – in particular, *The English Peasantry and the Growth of Lordship* (London, 1997); and D. Banham and R. Faith, *Anglo-Saxon Farms and Farming* (Oxford, 2014) – I feel a strong need to reconnect with where the great nineteenth-century works on Germanic law and society left the subject and to begin a reconsideration of the evidence at that point.
[63] Chadwick, *The Origin*, provided the inspiration for the remarkable work of B. S. Phillpotts, *Kindred and Clan in the Middle Ages and After* (Cambridge, 1913), which was particularly focused on migration.
[64] M. Lapidge (ed.), *H. M. Chadwick and the Study of Anglo-Saxon, Norse and Celtic in Cambridge* (Aberystwyth, 2015).
[65] Chadwick, *Studies on Anglo-Saxon Institutions*; F. M. Stenton, *Folklore* 16 (1905), 122–6. For my earlier remarks on this subject, see D. N. Dumville, 'The Terminology of Overkingship in Early

avoided it until the 1960s, thus perpetuating the traditions which serious engagement with Chadwick's work would have disrupted.[66] One of the few references (and even fewer positive references) to Chadwick's *Institutions* in the intervening half-century was made in 1937 by J. E. A. Jolliffe (1891–1964), whose historical interests were especially devoted to the study of English local institutions, their origins in what he called 'the era of the folk' and their development in English constitutional history.[67] No English historian was better placed than Jolliffe to appreciate and develop Chadwick's insight. Yet he was unable to find a consistent place for the petty kingdom when seeking to articulate England's 'constitutional history': he faced the constant distraction of feeling the need to raise his eyes to higher levels of rule, and he repeatedly stressed the alleged appointed nature of local kingship.[68] Only in the last generation has a more sympathetic attitude been taken to local, sub-regional and regional kingdoms and their various interactions. Even so, that interest has remained more descriptive than structural, concerned less with their function in the governance of Germanic-speaking Britain than with a few of their individual histories within a predetermined movement of political history towards a known destination.

Our contemporary written sources begin to thicken – that would not be difficult! – from the late seventh century with the advent of royal diplomas, 'The Tribal Hidage', further correspondence, chronicles and (in 731) Bede's 'Ecclesiastical History'. The list does not, of course, end with Bede. In these sources taken as a whole, numerous kingdoms can be seen. But historians have tended not to be curious about this phenomenon and therefore not to see much of what is on the surface, let alone what might lie just beneath it. Comparative approaches have not been exploited. The reason is again that a long-term, overarching structure of interpretation has inhibited free thought and critical enquiry. In short, the idea of the nation—which underpinned the English (and subsequently the British)

Anglo-Saxon England', in *The Anglo-Saxons from the Migration Period to the Eighth Century. An Ethnographic Perspective*, ed. J. Hines (San Marino, 1997), pp. 345–73, esp. 345–6.

[66] The return to Chadwick was perhaps encouraged by the outstanding social and economic history textbook by H. R. Loyn, *Anglo-Saxon England and the Norman Conquest* (London, 1962), pp. 289–314, 390–1 (cf. 2nd edn, Harlow, 1991, pp. 301, 305), a volume which marked the culmination of Loyn's major scholarly output. Another fine survey produced in that period (but without specific reference to Chadwick) was the work of D. P. Kirby, *The Making of Early England* (London, 1967).

[67] J. E. A. Jolliffe, *The Constitutional History of Medieval England*, 1st edn (London, 1937), pp. 5, n. 1 (with a spectacular confusion of Chadwick with Frederic Seebohm) and 32, n. 2; cf. his article, 'The Era of the Folk in English History', in *Oxford Essays in Medieval History Presented to Herbert Edward Salter* (Oxford, 1934), pp. 1–32.

[68] See Jolliffe, *The Constitutional History*, p. 58, for example.

nation-state – has long rendered irrelevant deeper probing of the origins and early history of English political organisation.

A crucial early witness is provided by a royal diploma of the 670s, preserved in the archives of Chertsey Abbey through the Middle Ages, augmented and at length incorporated in the abbey's cartulary-chronicle in the second half of the thirteenth century.[69] Although both the royal style of the donor and a confirmatory subscription acknowledge the importance of a regional over-king – Wulfhere, over-king of the Mercians (658–75) – this is a charter peopled by local kings (*subreguli*), perhaps themselves of various grades of royalty. This donor was one Frithuwald of the kingdom of the men of *Suthrige* (the Southern District, now [Co.] Surrey), *Fritheuualdus prouincie Surrianorum*: his grant was to enhance the endowment of the minster (*monasterium*) which had first been built under King Ecgberht (presumably Ecgberht I, [over]king of the Cantware, 664–73). Frithuwald's grant was massive – a substantial slice of northern Surrey, constituting much of the *prouincia* ('kingdom') of the Woccingas, as far north-westwards as the boundary of the kingdom of the Sunningas. The size of Surrey at this date is a matter for dispute, but the formation in *-gē* (cf. German *Gau*, 'district') is characteristic of south-eastern England before about 700: Kent, for example, has a number of such units which seem to have been kingdoms.[70] Names in *–ingas* ('followers/dependants/descendants of'), with the leader's name preceding, likewise seem to have been early kingdoms (but the date range of their creation remains controversial). Within Surrey, we meet a number of *-ingas* units: with the aid of this document, we can see the frontier between Surrey and Berkshire (where the territory of the Sunningas began), as well as within Surrey at the *Fullingadic*, the boundary of the Fullingas. It has been well remarked that, from study of local political organisation, 'What emerges most strongly … is the stability of the early' units of such sort.[71] It has sometimes been argued

[69] Sawyer, *Anglo-Saxon Charters*, pp. 343–4, S 1165. See M. Gelling, *The Early Charters of the Thames Valley* (Leicester, 1979); and J. Blair, *Early Medieval Surrey* (Guildford, 1991). Most recently, this diploma has been re-edited by S. Kelly, *Charters of Chertsey Abbey*, AS Charters 19 (Oxford, 2015), pp. 89–104 (no. 1): its text and (above all) its contexts have been treated in that book as essentially unproblematic. I have therefore prepared a new text, translation, and study of this document.

[70] A. H. Smith, *English Place-Name Elements*, 2 vols. (Cambridge, 1956), vol. I, pp. 196–7 (under **gē*): 'found chiefly in the SE in p.ns. of great antiquity'. For comment, see W. H. Stevenson, *EHR* 4 (1889), 359–63, reviewing J. Earle, *A Hand-Book to the Land-Charters, and Other Saxonic Documents* (Oxford, 1888). Such units are later found as hundreds: O. S. Anderson, *The English Hundred-Names*, 3 vols. (Lund 1934–9), vol. III, p. 196.

[71] Blair, *Early Medieval Surrey*, p. 102.

that Frithuwald was a representative of a type of early Mercian regional deputy of royal status – in other words, probably not a native of Surrey, which had only recently come under Mercian hegemony.[72] King Wulfhere would on this argument have represented the next grade on an ascending scale of Anglo-Saxon royalty. One of the various striking features of this diploma is found in the witness-list, of which a section is explicitly devoted to *subreguli*: there are four, of whom Frithuwald is the first, followed by Osric, Wigheard and Æthilwald. It would be possible to argue that these royals were equivalents of Frithuwald in other districts of Wulfhere's over-kingdom, were other local kings in 'the kingdom of the men of *Suthrige*' and/or were other local rulers of neighbouring minor kingdoms (such as the *Sunningas*). This diploma reveals a world of lesser kings and of petty kingdoms: the word which the author of this diploma used for such a kingdom was *prouincia*.[73] For Bede, that word was characteristically (but by no means exclusively) restricted to the (over) kingdom of a regional over-king – of the Bernicians, the Deirans, the East Angles, the East Saxons, the Mercians and suchlike: he usually employed *regio* to describe a more local kingly unit.[74] Here, as in other charters, *prouincia* is used of a broader range of kingdom types. But the crucial point is that these words describe kingdoms and that the minor kingdoms were the building blocks of larger regional over-kingdoms, themselves of very varying degrees of size and importance.

We can recognise such units across the length and breadth of early Anglo-Saxon England, although our sources are unevenly distributed across time and space.[75] Toponymic evidence is of particular importance,

---

[72] P. Wormald, 'Bede, the *Bretwaldas* and the Origins of the *gens Anglorum*', in *Ideal and Reality in Frankish and Anglo-Saxon Society. Studies Presented to J. M. Wallace-Hadrill*, ed. P. Wormald et al. (Oxford, 1983), pp. 99–129, at 112.

[73] It is necessary to restrain any instinct to deduce from this word that a division of a larger polity is intended: the usage comes from Isidore of Seville, *Etymologiae seu origines*, written in the first third of the seventh century, where it is explicitly associated with kingship. For texts and commentaries, see *Isidori Hispalensis Episcopi Etymologiarum sive Originum Libri XX*, ed. W. M. Lindsay, 2 vols. (Oxford, 1911); and A.-I. Magallón García, *Concordantia in Isidori Hispaliensis Etymologias* (Hildesheim, 1995). A multi-volume edition and translation, by many hands, is in course of publication in the series 'Auteurs Latins du Moyen Âge': *Isidore de Séville, Étymologies*, 20 vols. (Paris and Besançon, 1983–). For an English translation, see *The Etymologies of Isidore of Seville*, trans. S. A. Barney et al. (Cambridge, 2006).

[74] For specific references to Bede's use of these words, see Jones, *A Concordance*, pp. 429–31 (*s. vv. prouincia* and *prouincialis*) and 448 (*s.v. regio*).

[75] The pioneering attempt to draw up a list of such units was that of J. M. Kemble, *The Saxons in England. A History of the English Commonwealth till the Period of the Norman Conquest*, 2 vols. (London, 1849), vol. I, pp. 449–86 (2nd edn, rev. W. de G. Birch (London, 1876)). For his pains, Kemble attracted a dismissive and misleading footnote from F. M. Stenton, *Anglo-Saxon England* (Oxford, 1943), p. 314, n. 1 (3rd edn [1971], p. 318, n. 1).

as have been local studies of patterns of rights and dues, of relationships within and between estates.[76] It is clear that England in the early Middle Ages had a culture of plural, multiple kingdoms. By extrapolating from the size of local territories described in early Anglo-Saxon texts as *regio* and/or *prouincia* and/or having names in -*gē* or -*ingas*, we could start to draw a map of the local polities of England before the Viking Age and provide a very different, fresh analysis of the culture of the early English polity as a whole: we might find that even a partial map would show kingdoms numbered in three figures. Such an exercise would help us to enhance our appreciation of a middle-ranking tier of over-kingdoms which are at present poorly understood.[77] Comparison with neighbouring or related societies would help us to grasp something of the factors tending to stability and instability in such polities. A model has been offered, generated from the history of the Mediterranean (and particularly the Hellenic) world in Antiquity, of 'peer-polity interaction' which could be very usefully tested, with some of its manifest inadequacies probed, against the evidence of the Insular (and Scandinavian) societies of the earlier Middle Ages.[78]

An obvious point of comparison, crossing an evident linguistic and cultural divide but into a neighbouring society with which the early

---

[76] The almost innumerable studies by G. R. J. Jones should be mentioned here: see P. S. Barnwell and B. K. Roberts (eds.), *Britons, Saxons, and Scandinavians. The Historical Geographer Glanville R. J. Jones* (Turnhout, 2011). For some searching questions about Jones's methods, see N. Gregson, 'The Multiple Estate Model: An Adequate Framework for the Analysis of Early Territorial Organisation?', in *The Borders*, ed. Clack and Ivy, pp. 49–81; for further iteration and debate, cf. N. Gregson, 'The Multiple Estate Model: Some Critical Questions', *Journal of Historical Geography* 11 (1985), 339–51, with reply by Jones, 'Multiple Estates Perceived', *ibid.* 11 (1985), 352–63. Worthy of mention here too is the work of a scholar whose contribution (still very worthy of scrutiny) ended exactly a century earlier, in 1911 – Frederic Seebohm, whose remarkable (and profoundly controversial) trilogy of books deserves continuing attention: *The English Village Community Examined in its Relations to the Manorial and Tribal Systems and to the Common or Open Field System of Husbandry. An Essay in Economic History* (London, 1883, and subsequent editions); *The Tribal System in Wales, Being Part of an Inquiry into the Structure and Methods of Tribal Society* (1st edn, London, 1895; 2nd edn, 1904); and *Tribal Custom in Anglo-Saxon Law, Being an Essay Supplemental to (1) 'The English Village Community', (2) 'The Tribal System in Wales'* (London, 1911).

[77] I have begun the process by writing a series of short papers, indicating the methods needed and providing a detailed example: (1) 'The Kings and Kingdoms of Early Anglo-Saxon England: A Study of Hierarchy and Scale'; (2) 'Bede, Place-Names, and the Constitutional History of Early Anglo-Saxon England'; (3) 'The Kingdom of Oundle'; (4) 'Bede's Use of *antiquitus* in his *Historia ecclesiastica gentis Anglorum*'; and (5) 'Criteria for the Establishment of Bishoprics in Early Anglo-Saxon England'.

[78] C. Renfrew and J. F. Cherry (eds.), *Peer Polity Interaction and Socio-Political Change* (Cambridge, 1986). See also C. Renfrew and S. Sherman (eds.), *Ranking, Resource and Exchange. Aspects of the Archaeology of Early European Society* (Cambridge, 1982).

English interacted, is provided by Gaeldom – Ireland and Gaelic (north-western) Britain – in the early and central Middle Ages.[79] A recent analysis of the evidence of one major class of written evidence has revealed that throughout that period Ireland (by far the greater part of Gaeldom in the early Middle Ages) had a minimum of 600 to 650 kingdoms.[80] It has been well observed that '[e]arly medieval kingship was naturally small-scale' and, if somewhat less happily for England at least, that 'In Ireland ... dynasties expanded only to segment, whereas the rulers of expanding English king-doms were careful to deny the royal aspirations of their fellow kinsmen', that 'Irish royal dynasties could expand as much as any Anglo-Saxon counterpart, but that their need to maintain the [royal] status of as many as possible of their branches ensured that the primary kingdoms remained small.'[81]

A recurrent joint difficulty in analysis of such developments is the question of what is primary and where to start the story. For these purposes, the advantage of study of the English polity is that it did not exist before the fifth century. What happened in the fifth and sixth centuries will have been of literally fundamental importance. At the time of the appearance of written evidence, in the generation from the mid-590s to the mid-620s, we can see a regional over-kingdom based in East Kent and a glimpse of a subordinate (and ethnically different – Saxon) kingdom (over-kingdom?) in West Kent, which was judged worthy of its own bishopric at Rochester.[82] If Bede's testimony about this generation, written

---

[79] The classic studies are those of D. A. Binchy, 'The Fair of Tailtiu and the Feast of Tara', *Ériu* 18 (1958), 113–38; and D. A. Binchy, 'The Passing of the Old Order', in *Proceedings of the [First] International Congress of Celtic Studies, Held in Dublin, 6–10 July, 1959*, ed. B. Ó Cuív (Dublin, 1962), pp. 119–32, as well as his edition of a law-tract on status, *Críth Gablach* (Dublin, 1941). Also seminal was the work of Binchy's predecessor in this subject: E. MacNeill, *Celtic Ireland* (Dublin, 1921; rev. imp. by D. Ó Corráin, 1981); and E. MacNeill, *Early Irish Laws and Institutions* (Dublin, [1935]). The most important recent account of early mediaeval Ireland is that of Charles-Edwards, *Early Christian Ireland* (cf. n. 48, above), with much which is useful and illuminating about local polities, but it is at the same time an attempt to argue the supposed merits of big government in that unlikely quarter. See also the shorter account (but more exclusively focused on kingship) by B. Jaski, *Early Irish Kingship and Succession* (Dublin, 2000).

[80] K. M. McGowan, 'Political Geography and Political Structures in Earlier Mediaeval Ireland: A Chronicle-Based Approach' (unpublished PhD dissertation, University of Cambridge, 2002), and accompanying database. On rulership in early mediaeval Gaeldom in Britain, see D. N. Dumville, 'Political Organisation in Dál Riata', in *TOME. Studies in Medieval Celtic History and Law in Honour of Thomas Charles-Edwards*, ed. F. Edmonds and P. Russell (Woodbridge, 2011), pp. 41–52.

[81] T. M. Charles-Edwards, 'Early Medieval Kingships in the British Isles', in *The Origins of Anglo-Saxon Kingdoms*, ed. Bassett, pp. 28–39 and 245–8, at 37 and (two quotations at) 36.

[82] Bede, *HE* ii. 8 (ed. Colgrave and Mynors, pp. 158–61), quoting a letter from Pope Boniface V to Iustus, bishop of Canterbury; cf. P. Hunter Blair, 'The Letters of Pope Boniface V and the Mission of Paulinus to Northumbria', in *England before the Conquest. Studies in Primary Sources Presented to Dorothy Whitelock*, ed. P. Clemoes and K. Hughes (Cambridge, 1971), pp. 5–13, at 7–8, referring to papal correspondence in the early seventh century.

more than a century later, has aught to commend it, then the East
Kentish over-king also dominated the East Saxons and East Angles and
indeed as far as the River Humber, as well as having diplomatic influence
of an unspecified character which reached as far west as the southern
boundary of the Hwicce in the south-western Midlands (presumably
Gloucestershire).[83] Soon afterwards, papal correspondence tells us of the
major kingship of Edwin, king of the Deire, and similarly of Eadbald
(*Audubaldus*) of Kent *gentibusque ei subpositis*, 'with the peoples subject
to him', still an over-king though not in his father's league.[84] In other
words, on the earliest available evidence, major over-kingships had come
into existence not later (but perhaps also not earlier) than the late sixth
century.

   Whether such over-kingships had existed from English origins in
Britain or had grown as the English polity had developed is a question
that has divided scholars. This issue returns us to uncertainties about the
effects of migration and of the impact of whatever British polities were
encountered by the settlers. One could imagine small communities of
free peasants making a crossing to Britain or groups characterised by
having a clear leader or both in parallel.[85] Whichever of these three
options one chooses, the fact remains that in our earliest written sources
we can see structural gradations of kingly power. If the toponymists'
current arguments in historical interpretation of -*ingas* place-names have
merit, they (and therefore the local kingdoms bearing such names) were
not created in the primary phase(s) of Germanic migration into Britain.[86]
But that does not of itself dispose of the possibility that comparable units
were already in existence, characterised for example by place-names
in -*gē*.

   When English regional (over)kingdoms come into view, some have an
origin reported as an act of creation by a more powerful over-king. The
over-kingdom of the Middle Angles is a case in point, constituted

---

[83] For the eastern kingdoms, see Bede, *HE* ii. 3, ii. 5, i. 25, and ii. 5 (the Humber); for the Hwicce, see ii.
   2 (ed. Colgrave and Mynors, pp. 142–5, 148–55, 72–7, and 134–43).
[84] *Ibid.*, ll. 10, pp. 166–71   [85] On royal leaders, held by Chadwick to be a given, see n. 57, above.
[86] J. McN. Dodgson, 'The Significance of the Distribution of the English Place-Names in -*ingas*,
   -*inga*- in South-East England', *Medieval Archaeology* 10 (1966), 1–29, reprinted in *Place-Name
   Evidence for the Anglo-Saxon Invasion and Scandinavian Settlements*, ed. K. Cameron
   (Nottingham, 1975), pp. 27–54. It is very doubtful that all his conclusions and (above all) those of
   the scholars who extended them (and heralded them as the beginning of a toponymic revolution)
   can still be sustained. In many ways, the 'gold standard' remains the first edition of E. Ekwall,
   English Place-Names in -ing (Lund, 1923); his second edition (1962) seems to represent a mistaken
   turn.

(according to Bede) by Penda, king of the Mercians (*ob.* 655), for his son Peada.[87] This has led to rather adventurous suggestions that all such units in the Greater Mercian over-kingdom created by Penda derived from over-kingly acts of will. On that argument, King Frithuwald's subkingdom in Surrey would be another such, if smaller and less complex than the subkingdom of the Middle Angles, which was itself a substantial over-kingdom. The kingdom, perhaps over-kingdom, of the *Magonsætan* (in what is now Herefordshire) within the Mercian over-kingdom is another case in point, but its rulers and their mode of rule are not well documented; it did, however, acquire a bishopric (at Hereford) in 676, with a pontiff translated from Rochester.[88] Much better reported is the neighbouring kingdom (probably over-kingdom) to the east, that of the Hwicce, which came in 680 to have a bishopric at Worcester. In its charters, the kingdom of the Hwicce is classically represented as having up to three kings at any one time. It is not known whether each had responsibility for a particular area or constituency within the kingdom or whether the kings ruled as a committee concerned with the whole. The origins of this kingdom are quite unknown but may have occurred in a context of dispute between (West) Saxons and Angles with different ethnic components belonging to this unit. Within it, *-ingas* units are visible.[89]

A superficially similar case is the kingdom of the East Saxons, for long a core part of the Mercian hegemony, but with an older and a more complex

[87] Bede, *HE* iii. 21, 24, and v. 24 (annals 653, 655) (ed. Colgrave and Mynors, pp. 278–81, 288–95, 564–5). Cf. D. N. Dumville, *Britons and Anglo-Saxons in the Early Middle Ages* (Aldershot, 1993), essay IX, pp. 15–16.

[88] K. Pretty, 'Defining the Magonsæte', *The Origins*, ed. Bassett, pp. 171–83, 277–9, provided a thoughtful survey; however, M. Gelling, 'The Early History of Western Mercia', *ibid.*, pp. 184–201, 279–80, is full of improbable assertions offered without justification. See further *Cartularium Saxonicum*, ed. W. de Gray Birch, 4 vols. (London, 1885–99), vol. III, pp. 242–4 (no. 1040), on a royal diploma issued in 958; H. P. R. Finberg, *The Early Charters of the West Midlands*, 2nd edn (Leicester, 1972), pp. 197–224, 136–46, and H. P. R. Finberg, *Lucerna. Studies of Some Problems in the Early History of England* (London, 1964), pp. 66–82. Apart from the terminology *in pago Magesætna* in the mid-tenth-century diploma, we read of a royal dynasty belonging to the seventh century. For more substantial (if contextual) eighth-century evidence, see M. Lapidge, *Anglo-Latin Literature, 600–899* (London, 1996), pp. 357–79, 510–12; P. Sims-Williams, *Religion and Literature*, pp. 328–59; and P. Sims-Williams, *Britain and Early Christian Europe* (Aldershot, 1995), essays IX and X.

[89] The Hwicce have received much (and increasing) attention in the last half-century: linguistically, from A. H. Smith, 'The Hwicce', in *[Franciplegius.] Medieval and Linguistic Studies in Honour of Francis Peabody Magoun, Jr*, ed. J. B. Bessinger Jr and R. P. Creed (New York and London, 1965), pp. 56–65; and R. Coates, 'The Name of the Hwicce: A Discussion', *ASE* 42 (2013), 51–61; variously, S. Bassett, and others, in *The Origins*, ed. Bassett, p. 294 (some twenty references); and by D. Hooke in numerous publications, especially *The Anglo-Saxon Landscape. The Kingdom of the Hwicce* (Manchester, 1985) and *Worcestershire Anglo-Saxon Charter-bounds* (Woodbridge, 1990).

organisation. It lost the territory dependent on London, whose people came to be known as 'the Middle Saxons', annexed to the Greater Mercian over-kingdom in the early eighth century;[90] Surrey may have been the East Saxon kingdom's 'Southern District' if it existed with that name before a Mercian takeover in the third quarter of the seventh century.[91] West Kent, which was an object of interest to East Saxon dynasts in the later seventh and eighth centuries, may have been an earlier example of the same. *-ingas* units are visible across the kingdom of the East Saxons and have been an element in the assignment of a chronology of the type. Its three rulers as seen in the early seventh century may have exercised authority as a committee but may equally have been responsible for three parts: the core, Middlesex and Surrey, and West Kent. It cannot by that date have been the creation of a Mercian over-king.[92]

Here our focus is on different sizes and types of kingdom (or over-kingdom). What they all have in common is domination by a powerful regional over-kingship, but their origins have been differently explained. Their internal constitution suggests the existence of subkingdoms as a routine part of their structure. Although some subkingdoms had relative longevity, it may be the case that 'the early *regiones* [were] organic entities combined and recombined like building bricks to form more transient territories'.[93]

If we look to a yet larger level of political organisation, we meet those over-kingdoms – of the Northumbrians, the Mercians and (eventually) the West Saxons – which intermittently (but seemingly in turn) dominated first the English as a whole (from the 620s) and then (from the late 650s) the Southumbrian political scene.

The Northumbrian over-kingdom we can see under construction, from the kingdoms (probably over-kingdoms) of the Bernicians and Deirans, from the late sixth century to 679; these players are given extra life by being

---

[90] Bede, *HE* iv. 6 (ed. Colgrave and Mynors, pp. 354–7), referred to Surrey as a kingdom (*regio Sudergeona*) in the 670s.

[91] For some vigorous discussion of this point, see Hines (ed.), *The Anglo-Saxons,* pp. 348, 370–1.

[92] On all this, see D. N. Dumville, *Wessex and England from Alfred to Edgar. Six Essays on Political, Cultural, and Ecclesiastical Revival* (Woodbridge, 1992), chap. I (esp. pp. 3–4); Yorke, *Kings and Kingdoms,* pp. 13, 25–57, 109, 113; and Dodgson, 'The Significance'. It ought to be a question whether Bede's evidence on early East Saxon history is consistent or contradictory. The over-kingdom of the Hwicce seems to have had similar arrangements, with three kings exercising authority. According to Bede, *HE* ii. 3 (ed. Colgrave and Mynors, pp. 142–3), London was, when he wrote, in the kingdom of the East Saxons (*quorum metropolis Lundonia ciuitas est*). Unless this was a slip, or resulted from ignorance of change in southern English politics, it runs against our other evidence.

[93] Blair, *Early Medieval Surrey,* p. 102.

at the core of Bede's historical narrative.[94] That construction was not solely northern or English but involved continuing conquests of Britons and ferocious struggle with the growing over-kingdom of the Mercians. In the process, a 'Transhumbrian' political formation was probably destroyed. There has been relatively little discussion of the building blocks from which the Deiran and Bernician over-kingdoms were previously constructed, and indeed the frontiers of both peoples remain in part uncertain.[95]

A Mercian over-kingdom has seemed to be the work almost of one man, King Penda (*ob.* 655), who emerges from Midland proto-history in league with Britons as an implacable opponent of Bernician and Deiran expansionism and a voracious conqueror of England between the Thames-Severn line and the Northumbrian frontier. 'Greater Mercia', as his construction has come to be known, continued to grow after his death, reaching deep into south-eastern England. The fate of the political elites of the peoples, large and small, drawn into this hegemony is a subject which deserves a great deal more scrutiny, not least in its possible implications for Mercian governance in the ninth century.[96] As we have already seen, some of the middle-size kingdoms within 'Greater Mercia' have been held, if controversially, to be creations of the uppermost level of Mercian over-kingship: that is almost certainly true of the over-kingdom of the Middle Angles, which had longevity in defining a bishopric with its seat at Leicester from 737, but is largely invisible to us as a political entity within a few years of its creation by Penda in the mid-650s.[97] It is here that the remarkable but enigmatic document, untitled but known to twentieth-century scholarship by the desperately unhappy

---

[94] M. Miller, 'The Dates of Deira', *ASE* 8 (1979), 35–61; Dumville, *Britons and Anglo-Saxons*, essay III (reprinted from *The Origins*, ed. Bassett, pp. 213–22, 284–6); and H. Geake and J. Kenny (eds.), *Early Deira. Archaeological Studies of the East Riding in the Fourth to Ninth Centuries A.D.* (Oxford, 2000). The major recent regional study is that of D. Rollason, *Northumbria, 500–1100. Creation and Destruction of a Kingdom* (Cambridge, 2003), but he has ploughed very traditional furrows. There is much of relevance in D. Petts and S. Turner (eds.), *Early Medieval Northumbria. Kingdoms and Communities, A.D. 450–1100* (Turnhout, 2011).

[95] Hunter Blair, *Anglo-Saxon Northumbria*, essays III–V and VIII, were the 'gold standard' but now require thorough reconsideration; J. N. L. Myres, 'The Teutonic Settlement of Northern England', *History*, n.s. 20 (1935–6), 250–62; and Dumville, 'The Origins of Northumbria', in his *Britons and Anglo-Saxons*, essay III. Cf. T. Green, *Britons and Anglo-Saxons. Lincolnshire, A.D. 400–650* (Lincoln, 2012); and N. Higham, *The Northern Counties to A.D. 1000* (London, 1986).

[96] Dumville, *Britons and Anglo-Saxons*, essay IX; and S. Keynes, 'Mercia and Wessex in the Ninth Century', in *Mercia. An Anglo-Saxon Kingdom in Europe*, ed. M. P. Brown and C. A. Farr (London, 2001), pp. 310–28.

[97] Dumville, *Britons and Anglo-Saxons*, essay IX; Kirby, *The Earliest English Kings* (2nd edn), pp. 6–12, 74–82 (and 190, n. 42); and Yorke, *Kings and Kingdoms*, pp. 62–6 and 106–13. For the bishops, see Fryde et al. (eds.), *Handbook* (3rd edn), p. 218 (by S. Keynes); and M. Lapidge et al. (eds.), *The Wiley-Blackwell Encyclopedia of Anglo-Saxon England* (Chichester, 2014), pp. 539–66.

name of 'The Tribal Hidage', is a capital witness.[98] It begins by stating an original Mercian territory (presumptively in Staffordshire)[99] but is in its essentials an assessment list of the Middle-Anglian peoples, up to twenty-three often tiny political units stretching in an arc from southern Lincolnshire to eastern Oxfordshire, whose allegiance must have been contested in the east with the East Angles and in the south with the West Saxons in the seventh century.[100] When Wulfhere, over-king of the Mercians 658–75, led an army with thirty *duces regii* into the North, most of those 'royal ealdormen' (or 'kingly war-leaders') may have come from 'the Middle Angles'.[101]

The West-Saxon over-kingdom seems to pose some rather different problems. There are two of great importance. In 731, Bede wrote of the Christianisation of the West Saxons as occurring in synchrony with that of the Northumbrians through the efforts of the over-king of the latter, Oswald (634–42), whose hegemony extended over the West Saxons:[102] introducing the West Saxons for the first time in an extended narrative, Bede wrote *gens Occidentalium Saxonum qui antiquitus Geuissae uocabantur* ('the West Saxon *gens*, who were of old/originally called Geuissae') – Bede elsewhere always employed a Latin masculine form *Geuissi*: one is bound to wonder if this is a vernacular formation doubly analogous to *Lindissi, Lindissae* (Lindsey). Where Bede used the name suggests that he considered it current from the 610s to the 680s.[103] If this is correct, the renaming occurred in

98 D. N. Dumville, 'The Tribal Hidage: An Introduction to Its Texts and Their History', in *The Origins*, ed. Bassett, pp. 225–30, 286–7. For the text's name, see F. W. Maitland, *Domesday Book and Beyond. Three Essays in the Early History of England* (Cambridge, 1897), pp. 455–520. Cf. D. Hill and A. R. Rumble (eds.), *The Defence of Wessex. The Burghal Hidage and Anglo-Saxon Fortifications* (Manchester, 1996), pp. 18–23 and 253; for a remarkable and innovative recent study focusing on the Viking Age, see J. Baker and S. Brookes, *Beyond the Burghal Hidage. Anglo-Saxon Civil Defence in the Viking Age* (Leiden, 2013).

99 On this, see E. P. Hamp, '*Lloegr*: The Welsh Name for England', *Cambridge Medieval Celtic Studies* 4 (1982), 83–5.

100 Dumville, *Britons and Anglo-Saxons*, essay IX.

101 Bede, *HE* iii. 24 (ed. Colgrave and Mynors, pp. 288–95, at 290–1). For the same locution in relation to Sussex, see *ibid.*, iv. 15 (pp. 380–1). Cf. F. M. Stenton, *Preparatory to 'Anglo-Saxon England'* (Oxford, 1970), pp. 48–66, at 49–50, reprinting a paper first published in 1918.

102 Bede, *HE* iii. 7 (ed. Colgrave and Mynors, pp. 232–7, at 232–3).

103 *Ibid.* ii. 5, iii. 7, iv. 15, iv. 16 (14), v. 19 (ed. Colgrave and Mynors, pp. 152–5, 232–7 [three mentions], 380/1 [three mentions], 382–5 [three mentions], 516–31 at 522–3). On *Lindissae* (*Lindissi*, see M. Gelling, 'The Name Lindsey', *ASE* 18 (1989), 31–2. H. Kleinschmidt, 'The Geuissae, the West Saxons, the Angles and the English: The Widening Horizon of Bede's Gentile Terminology', *North-Western European Language Evolution* 30 (1997), 51–91; and H. Kleinschmidt, 'The Geuissae and Bede: On the Innovativeness of Bede's Concept of the *gens*', in *The Community, the Family and the Saint*, ed. J. M. Hill and M. Swan (Turnhout, 1998), pp. 77–102, are of outstanding interest on this subject. More generally, we owe to Professor Kleinschmidt both an outpouring of individual papers about the Anglo-Saxons over the past quarter-century and an extraordinary range of books of the very highest interest and remarkable intellectual range.

Bede's lifetime and is an interesting historical example of ethnogenesis, perhaps attributable to the long reign of King Ini (688/9–725/6).[104]

There may be a connexion with the second problem needing consideration here, for which once more Bede's 'History' provides the starting point. Ini's predecessor, Ceadwalla (685–8/9), is represented as a bloodthirsty warlord who was responsible in his brief reign for some major political upheavals across the deep south of England. According to Bede, 'When [King] Cenwealh [642–72] had died ... *subreguli* took the government (*regnum*) of the *gens* ('people'/'nation'); having divided it among themselves, they held it for about ten years'.[105] There have been two rival interpretations of these events: either the kingdom, normally 'united', 'fragmented'; or we have here an explicit glimpse of normality, a body of local rulers, usually acknowledging an over-king, dispensing with that practice for a decade or so.[106] There is much other evidence for petty kingship among the West Saxons in the seventh century. This period ended when Ceadwalla stormed to power. Bede continued the story: 'the *subreguli* having been defeated (*deuictis*) and removed (*amotis*), Ceadwalla received the over-kingdom (*imperium*)'. While sub-kings are certainly known from eighth-century Wessex, Ceadwalla's reign may have marked a moment of transition in their constitutional status.

When, in 825–8, Ecgberht, king of the West Saxons, relieved the Mercian over-kings of their south-eastern subkingdoms – Surrey, South Saxons, Kent, East Saxons – and ended such local royal rule, intrusive Mercian in Kent but native kingship of the East Saxons, he seems to have terminated the tradition of English (or, at any rate, southern) petty kingship.[107] There would be some appointed sub-kings until the end of the century, and there would be dominance of one king(dom) by another; on the face of it, however, petty kings were now creatures of the past.

It is certain that the idea of empire (*imperium*) played significant and varied roles in Anglo-Saxon political life. If an emperor was a king of kings, there was empire aplenty in that period. Charles Plummer usefully expounded Bede's understanding of the contrasting pair of kingship

---

[104] Or to the short, sharp shock represented by the reign of King Ceadwalla.
[105] Bede, *HE* iv. 12 (ed. Colgrave and Mynors, pp. 368–71, at 368–9).
[106] Charles-Edwards, 'Early Medieval Kingships', p. 37; and Campbell, *Bede's Reges*, re-issued in his *Essays in Anglo-Saxon History* (London, 1986), pp. 85–98, on the absence of West Saxon over-kingship, 672–*c.* 682. See further Dumville, 'The Terminology'; and Chadwick, *Studies on Anglo-Saxon Institutions*, p. 366.
[107] Dumville, *Wessex and England*, chap. I.

(*regnum*) and empire/over-kingship (*imperium*).[108] Bede's employment of *imperium* (the power exercised by one king[dom] over another or others) bears particular examination, for he could use it of the internal constitution of kingdoms (as here, concerning Ceadwalla) as well as the relationship of one (over)kingdom with another or others.[109]

An ad hoc relationship of one over-king with another (and so on) may be conveniently and clearly illustrated by Bede's treatment (for reasons of Church history) of the affairs of the South Saxon kingdom in the 670s. The over-king of the South Saxons, Æthelwealh, was subject to Wulfhere, over-king of the Mercians (658–75) and *brytenw(e)alda*, at whose instance Æthelwealh was converted to Christianity. His Christian wife, Eafe, was of the royal line of the (over)kingdom of the Hwicce. In token of Æthelwealh's baptism, Wulfhere gave him (*donauit illi*) two kingdoms (*prouincias*), namely, those of the Wihtware and Meonware, according to Bede Jutish kingdoms in which the Gewissi/West Saxons had an interest. Eventually, Æthelwealh was killed by Ceadwalla in 680×685, but the latter was driven out by two of Æthelwealh's subordinate kings (*duces regii*), Berhthun and Andhun, who then took power. Eventually, Ceadwalla returned as king of the Gewissi (685–8/9) and reduced the South Saxons to tribute, a relationship which remained stable under Ceadwalla's successor, Ini (688/9–725/6), thus providing a forty-year 'interruption' of Mercian dominance of the South Saxons and an end to Mercian/South Saxon dominance of the *Iutae* of Hampshire.[110]

On the evidence of their diplomas, some kings' administrations were more prone to use imperial language than others. But it is clear that the contextual strands of thought were various. The place of the English in a larger Christian polity, with its Roman roots, was one such. An idea of Britain (and its islands) as another world, a potential empire of its own, was another.[111] The relationship of English kingdoms to non-English peoples of Britain (and, later, Ireland), and in particular to an imagined polity of *Britannia*, was a third. But the simplest underpinning of the idea of

[108] *Venerabilis Baedae Opera Historica*, ed. C. Plummer, 2 vols. (Oxford, 1896), vol. II, pp. 43 and 86. Cf. Jones, *A Concordance*, pp. 449–51 (*regnum*) and 252 (*imperium*).
[109] Jones, *A Concordance*, p. 252.
[110] Bede, *HE* iv. 13–15 (ed. Colgrave and Mynors, pp. 370–81). For exposition, see Campbell, *Bede's Reges* (*Essays*, pp. 85–98). On Wulfhere's status, see F. M. Stenton, 'The Supremacy of the Mercian Kings', *EHR* 33 (1918), 433–52, reprinted in his *Preparatory to 'Anglo-Saxon England'*, pp. 48–66, at 49–50. On Bede's account of the Jutes in *HE* i. 15 (ed. Colgrave and Mynors, pp. 48–53, at 50–1), see H. Kleinschmidt, 'Bede and the Jutes', *North-western European Language Evolution* 24 (1994), 21–46.
[111] C. Erdmann, *Forschungen zur politischen Ideenwelt des Frühmittelalters* (Berlin, 1951), pp. 1–51; and E. John, *Orbis Britanniae and Other Studies* (Leicester, 1966), pp. 11–13.

imperium was provided by Bede or his source(s) of inspiration: kings who wielded power over other kings held *imperium*; that might be the power of one major supra-regional over-king over another, or it might be of kings who stood at the head of complex polities which encompassed numerous petty kingdoms (and perhaps also intermediate over-kingdoms) in a relatively stable constitutional framework. It might indeed (if Bede had written more about petty kings) have been used for the dominance of one petty king over two others.

'International' relations therefore operated at a variety of levels within the Anglo-Saxon polity as well as between English, Britons, Gaels, Picts and (in the Viking Age) Scandinavians. This was made absolutely explicit in a classic paper by Molly Miller.[112] A long-used and very crude English translation of Bede's political terminology of power, office, status and territory – only very slowly (and often reluctantly) given up since the 1950s – has left a language of provinces and ealdormen (or indeed dukes), for example, providing the conceptual framework for historians' reading of the early Anglo-Saxon polity. The failure to engage with H. M. Chadwick's work in the half-century after 1905 left the writing of the *Verfassungsgeschichte* of England in 'big government' mode. Where kingship and government might have been recognised as having their roots at local level, a top-down reading of the polity has almost universally prevailed. F. M. Stenton's classic and contemptuous treatment in 1943 of the kings of the Hwicce sums up that approach;[113] yet he was merely the most distinguished inheritor and purveyor of this long-standing outlook.

Twelfth-century historians provided an interpretative framework for early Anglo-Saxon political history in the concept of The Heptarchy.[114] Duly tweaked and republished in early modern England, this concept prevailed until challenged in the 1970s and 1980s.[115] Even those who have

---

[112] M. Miller, 'Eanfrith's Pictish Son', *NH* 14 (1978), 47–66. Cf. Dumville, *Anglo-Saxon Essays, 2001–2007*, pp. 47–54.

[113] Stenton, *Anglo-Saxon England*, pp. 45–6 (3rd edn, 1971, p. 46); cf. Dumville, 'The Terminology', esp. pp. 345–6.

[114] Various writers of the first half of the twelfth century, whether anonymous or named, whether from Durham, Huntingdon or Worcester, have been credited with creating this organisational myth. For the first clear signs of its rejection in modern scholarship, see the commentary by Kirby, *The Earliest English Kings*, 2nd edn, pp. 1–9.

[115] C. R. Hart, 'The Tribal Hidage', *TRHS*, 5th series, 21 (1971), 133–57; cf. Dumville, *Britons and Anglo-Saxons*, chap. IX. It should be noted, however, that it was denounced in 1831 by the estimable F. Palgrave in his *History of England*, I, *Anglo-Saxon Period* (London, 1831) – reprinted as *History of the Anglo-Saxons* (London, 1837), with identical pagination – , p. 46: 'In this manner were formed the states of the so-called *Heptarchy*, an erroneous term, but one which has become so familiar by usage, that there is some difficulty in discarding it from history. It must, however, be rejected, because an idea is conveyed thereby, which is substantially wrong. At no period of our history were

since then given precise and detailed treatment of polities more local than those of the Northumbrians, Mercians and West Saxons have barely looked beneath the 'Heptarchic' surface. Scholars have also treated the major (over)kingdoms as territorially defined (East Anglia, Mercia, Northumbria, Wessex) despite the language of peoples being the universal Anglo-Saxon discourse. It has mostly been in very local studies, with landscapes and their functions at the centre of enquiry, that a more grounded, realistic assessment has begun hesitantly to emerge,[116] though again with an inadequate conceptual vocabulary, as (for example) the reappearance of the woeful discourse of 'tribe' and 'tribal' has indicated.[117] The tetrarchy in which the Anglo-Saxon polity was organised in the middle quarters of the ninth century and in which condition it was destroyed in the years 865–78 may have been four unitary kingdoms or monarchies (although it has recently become clear that our appreciation of Mercian governmental forms has long been inadequate).[118] However, behind those four kingdoms which comprised mid-ninth-century England lay a political history of significant complexity whose dynamic has, we can now say, never been well understood. Furthermore, as one marked trend in the subject is to argue for ever bigger, more intrusive, government at ever earlier dates,[119] it is arguable that understanding continues to be postponed. That there was a dynamic to the political system of England in the early Middle Ages, capable of delivering executive authority to kings and phases of reduction of kingly status and therefore of competition for royal power, seems clear, but that we yet understand structures and processes seems much more doubtful.

Received Narrative and Teleology

The received narrative of early Anglo-Saxon political history, of a *gens Anglorum* or English people developing in a pattern of successive dominant

---

there ever *seven* kingdoms independent of each other. And if we include those kingdoms which were subservient to larger states, the number must be increased.' However, the inertia of convention prevailed.

[116] J. Blair, 'Frithuwold's Kingdom and the Origins of Surrey', in *The Origins*, ed. Bassett, pp. 97–107, 261–5; Blair, *Early Medieval Surrey*; and J. Blair, *Anglo-Saxon Oxfordshire* (Stroud, 1994).

[117] See, for example, the index of Bassett (ed.), *The Origins*, p. 298, *s.v.* 'tribe *see* extended family', for at least a decent show of embarrassment: under that phrase, at p. 293, are a good many more 'tribes'.

[118] Keynes, 'Mercia', n. 96, above.

[119] A. Reynolds, *The Emergence of Anglo-Saxon Judicial Practice: The Message of the Gallows* (Aberdeen, 2009), and A. Reynolds, *Anglo-Saxon Deviant Burial Customs* (Oxford, 2009), carry a vigorous big-government message in an anthropological discourse.

over-kingdoms, is essentially Bede's, as augmented for the ninth century in the *Anglo-Saxon Chronicle*. A division of north and south was also in this way part of Bede's political heritage.[120] Whether Bede expected or desired that a monarchy of the English should be the eventual outcome of successive supra-regional over-kingships is far from certain, but he might nonetheless reasonably be described as an English nationalist in his political outlook.

A common feature in the writing of European national histories has been the power of a modern identity to determine the nature of historiography[121] – which continues apace in the cause of 'the European project' – and this has been manifest in the writing of English history. Everywhere in nineteenth- and twentieth-century English historiography is a sense of the inevitability, and indeed the desirability, of union of all the English. Given that the monarchy was achieved in 927 (although there has been a marked reluctance from the later sixteenth century until recently to acknowledge King Æthelstan's place in that history),[122] it is inevitable that all the effort in this direction should have been concentrated in Anglo-Saxon history. One of the games which historians have played in that cause has been to identify crucial antecedents to union, including major conceptual steps forward.

To this cause has been recruited the unlikely figure of Offa, over-king of Mercians in 757/8–96.[123] Various forged diplomas in his name have given him an uncompromising title of *rex Anglorum*.[124] When the facts of forgery had eventually been digested by scholarship, a legend of Offa had already grown deep and resilient roots. The textbooks of the 1930s and 1940s, still current in the 1960s, reflected this legend: for Jolliffe, 'Offa was clearly driving towards a lasting kingdom of the English ... The death of Offa stopped that normal development of a general English crown and title in which enlightened contemporaries had placed their faith.'[125] '"England" as a political fact was now emerging under the direction of a king whose

---

[120] Bede, *HE* ii. 5 and v. 23 (ed. Colgrave and Mynors, pp. 148–55 at 148–51, and 556–61).

[121] Jón Viðar Sigurðsson, 'Tendencies in the Historiography on the Medieval Nordic States (to 1350)', in *Public Power in Europe. Studies in Historical Transformations*, ed. J. S. Amelang and S. Beer (Pisa, 2006), pp. 1–15. See also D. N. Dumville, 'Did Ireland exist in the Twelfth Century?', in *Clerics, Kings and Vikings. Essays on Medieval Ireland in Honour of Donnchadh Ó Corráin*, ed. E. Purcell et al. (Dublin, 2015), pp. 115–26.

[122] But cf. Dumville, *Wessex and England*, chap. 4. See also above, pp. 72–3.

[123] On the date 757/8, see Kirby, *The Earliest English Kings*, p. 134, who has adopted 758 as the year of Offa's accession.

[124] Wormald, 'Bede, the *Bretwaldas*', pp. 109–11.

[125] Jolliffe, *The Constitutional History* (4th edn, 1961), pp. 48, 49; it is well worth hesitating over his word 'normal'.

political vision far transcended provincial limits and local interests and revealed a remarkable conception of the duties and potentialities of kingship', wrote G. O. Sayles; and with more than a nod in what would be the direction of the next generation's increasing identification of interaction with Continental powers as indices of virtue and importance, 'It was his drive towards the south-east of England, towards that part of the English Channel [coast] which came closest to the Continent, that reveals his vision and proves his ability to achieve his ambitions.'[126] Another generation later, this general approach to Offa, in its thoroughgoing improbability, has not changed in any essential. There is not space here for the necessary reappraisal, but one may advertise instead a view that almost every recorded action of Offa is testimony to his failure to hold or usefully develop what Æthelbald, his long-term predecessor, had built and points the way to the ultimately terminal decline of the Mercian hegemony.[127]

The most important over-kings of early Anglo-Saxon England can in the eighth century be seen expressing their power in terms of a relationship with *Britannia, Brytene*. It might be said that to be (or to think oneself) the most important king in Britain did not logically require him to hold every constituent part of England or to separate any number of sub-kings from their royal status. The absence of straightforward evidence for routinely continuing kingship of the East Angles from the mid-eighth to the mid-ninth century might be held to indicate a radical move in that direction; however, Offa's murder of Æthelberht, king (perhaps over-king) of the East Angles, in 794 provides a strong negative indication.[128]

A more direct, and variedly attested, pointer to major change in approach is provided by the politics of 829/30. According to the *Anglo-Saxon Chronicle* (829), 'And that year King Ecgberht conquered [both] the kingdom of the Mercians and everything south of the Humber, and he was the eighth king who was *brytenwealda*', and (830), 'In this year Wiglaf again obtained the kingdom of the Mercians.'[129] A temptation to read the East Angles too into the geographical statement of conquest should probably be resisted. If Wiglaf was driven out and his kingdom annexed to that of the West Saxons, that must indeed have been a remarkable development. The *Chronicle* is not merely a propagandist organ here, for we have a Mercian regnal list and a charter of Wiglaf himself – issued 'in the second year of my

---

[126] G. O. Sayles, *The Medieval Foundations of England* (London, 1948), pp. 69 and 68.

[127] Æthelbald, a remarkably powerful over-king with a 41-year reign, has not had his due of attention from historians. In D. Hill and M. Worthington (eds.), *Æthelbald and Offa, Two Eighth-Century Kings of Mercia* (Oxford, 2005), however, there is some redress.

[128] Fryde (ed.), *Handbook*, p. 9.   [129] *EHD*, ed. Whitelock (2nd ed.), p. 186.

second reign', 831 – which carry the same message.[130] (What occurred in 829 recurred ninety years later, in 918/19, but with a very different outcome.[131]) The only alternative interpretation would be that Wiglaf was replaced as king in 829 by a deputy who could not stay the course – but of such a royal there is now no trace. The conquest of the Mercians, followed by pre-emptive submission of the Northumbrians and (830) successful aggression against the Welsh (whatever one makes of this last), has been quite sufficient to gain Ecgberht an elevated place in histories of England[132] – although it must be said that it was his role as progenitor of a remarkable dynasty which is his principal legacy.

The end of petty kingship in England is often cited as a major constitutional achievement of Offa. In fact, it was not in his power to achieve that among the West Saxons and Northumbrians, if local kingship still survived in these two kingdoms. The kingship (once an over-kingship) of the East Saxons, the Mercians' most loyal long-term allies, outlived Offa by some thirty years. But once it was gone (following West Saxon conquest), we have (as yet, at least) no evidence for sub-kingship in the tetrarchic kingdoms of the mid-ninth century, save as a training ground and an apanage for the heir to the West Saxon throne.[133] Over the course of early Anglo-Saxon history, there were clearly periods in which succession or access to royal title came to be restricted in one over-kingdom or another. Only the last of those (in Offa's reign) has received any sustained analysis, but premature conclusions have been drawn.[134]

An English monarchy was achieved in the tenth century. The knowledge, and the millennium-long celebration, of that constitutional fact has had an all-pervasive impact on the writing of Anglo-Saxon history. Since the mid-sixteenth century, modern scholars on the whole have had neither taste nor time for local or lesser grades of royalty in English history; indeed, most historians have probably not even noticed that they were there. Where they have, the meaningless but pejorative adjective 'tribal' makes

---

[130] D. N. Dumville, 'The Anglian Collection of Royal Genealogies and Regnal Lists', *ASE* 5 (1976), 23–50, at 29–31 n. 3, for the regnal-list (preserved in a Worcester cathedral cartulary); the article is reprinted in his *Histories and Pseudo-Histories of the Insular Middle Ages* (Aldershot, 1990), essay V; S 188 (*CantCC* 60).

[131] *EHD*, ed. Whitelock, pp. 186–217; and F. T. Wainwright, *Scandinavian England* (Chichester, 1975), pp. 63–161 and 305–44.

[132] When I was invited in the 1980s at the instance of J. M. Wallace-Hadrill to take on the early mediaeval volume of *The New Oxford History of England* under the editorship of Vice-Chancellor John M. Roberts, the closing date was to be 802, which I refused – arguing instead for 927.

[133] The process began already in Ecgberht's reign, it seems.

[134] For some remarks on that context, see Dumville, 'The Terminology'.

a rapid appearance.[135] Yet it was the sixteenth and seventeenth centuries which gave us our conceptual tools for dealing with them, derived not least from colonial experience in Ireland and the New World: that the scholar today can speak of 'petty king(s)' and 'petty kingship' (*Kleinkönig[e]*, *Kleinkönigtum* in the German historiographical tradition) and of 'mesne (over)kings' and 'superior (over)kings' is due to encountering in a colonial context a phenomenon analogous to that seen in early mediaeval Europe.[136] As we have noted, when H. M. Chadwick attempted to initiate a twentieth-century discussion of grades of early English kingship, his work was belittled and frozen out of mainstream historiography. After all, the direction and destination of England were well known: why worry over distracting constitutional complications? Had not John Milton spoken truly of 'battles of kites and crows' which signified nothing?[137] Even though the study of Anglo-Saxon history is a business very different from fifty years ago, there are few students of history or archaeology who are interested in asking penetrating questions about early governance. The inevitability of English union (and then of British union) as a historiographical concept is a derivative of much later political desires or necessities; it has derailed

[135] Jolliffe, *The Constitutional History*, 1st edn, pp. 41–55; Yorke, *Kings and Kingdoms*, p. 13 *et passim*; and see above, n. 117. Stenton, *Anglo-Saxon England*, 1st edn, p. 37, insisted at the outset that 'Unlike Gaul, Spain, and Italy, Britain was invaded, not by tribes under tribal kings, but by bodies of adventurers.' In this, Stenton was determinedly criticising H. M. Chadwick: see above, n. 57.

[136] In modern historical writing, this usage was in English employed most in relation to Ireland, notably by D. A. Binchy. The early modern context has been explored by N. Canny, *Kingdom and Colony. Ireland in the Atlantic World, 1560–1800* (Baltimore, 1988), and in a number of subsequent works: 'mainstream' European cultures interacted with 'exotic' discovered cultures and had to develop terminology for describing their mores and institutions. See further N. Canny and A. Low (eds.), *The Oxford History of the British Empire*, I, *The Origins of Empire* (Oxford, 1998).

[137] J. Milton, 'The History of Britain', in *The Works of John Milton*, gen. ed. F. A. Patterson (18 vols. in 20, New York, 1931–8), vol. X (1932), ed. G. P. Krapp, p. 191 (lines 20–2). What is striking is that the quotation usually associated with Milton is not that derivable from his *History of Britain*, Book IV, where we read (p. 191, lines 20–2), 'such bickering to recount, met oft'n in these our Writers, what more worth is it than to Chronicle the Wars of Kites, or Crows, flocking and fighting in the Air?'. For commentary, see C. Nicholas, *Introduction and Notes to Milton's History of Britain* (Urbana, IL 1957), p. 113, who cross-referred to Milton's verbal assault on the monastic sources for the period, at X. 179, lines 14–22. W. Stubbs, *Lectures on Early English History* (London, 1906), p. 4, remarked that 'I have heard it observed that history has been written on the assumption that all Anglo-Saxons were alive at the same time: ... all clubbed together as kites and crows; for as such John Milton, a great poet but an execrable historian, is pleased to designate the heroes of the Heptarchy. We will guard ourselves at the outset from this silly blunder.' We should also note Milton's use of 'petty King', explicitly referring to Bede's account of West Saxon kingship in the years in which the word *subreguli* occurs uniquely in his *Historia* (see above, n. 105): 'After whom several petty Kings, as *Beda* calls them, for ten years space divided the West-Saxons; others name two, *Escwin* the Nephew of *Kinigils*, and *Kentwin* the Son, not petty by their deeds' (*The Works of John Milton*, X. 170, lines 16–19).

scholarly interaction with the evidence for pre-union, pre-monarchical political organisation among the English.

Two more modern tendencies may be observed. From the 1980s, British archaeologists began to speak, in imitation of neo-evolutionist American anthropologists of the 1960s and 1970s, of a succession of stages of increasingly complex human political organisation. There are internal variations, such that one group might speak (unfortunately) of a 'tribal' phase, while another rejects that category.[138] One might think that it could be helpful to have Anglo-Saxon archaeologists writing of chiefdoms in this context; but, in common with their peers in Scandinavia, they seem to have succumbed to a desire to find precocious 'states' at every turn, both an unhappy use of language and almost certainly an over-egging of the evolutionary pudding.[139] And it seems that, in this

[138] It will be useful to begin with C. Seymour-Smith, *Macmillan Dictionary of Anthropology* (London, 1986), p. 281, *s.v.* 'tribe': 'This term has been widely used in anthropology, but there is no general consensus as to its precise definition or appropriate application.' Some of this is conveniently on display in two volumes: (1) J. Helm (ed.), *Essays on the Problem of Tribe. Proceedings of the 1967 Annual Spring Meeting of The American Ethnological Society* (Seattle, WA, 1968), opening with a paper by M. H. Fried; and (2) M. H. Fried, *The Notion of Tribe* (Menlo Park, CA, 1975), which begins with a statement that Fried 'assaults the generally held concept of "tribe" by attacking the notion of highly discrete political units in pre-state society'. See also E. R. Service, *Primitive Social Organisation. An Evolutionary Perspective* (New York, 1962; 2nd edn 1971); A. Bard Schmookler, *The Parable of the Tribes The Problem of Power in Social Evolution* (Berkeley, CA, 1984); M. H. Fried, *The Evolution of Political Society An Essay in Political Anthropology* (New York, 1967); and M. Gluckman, *Politics, Law and Ritual in Tribal Society* (Oxford, 1965). A neo-evolutionist anthropologist at the centre of the last half-century's discussions of these issues is the redoubtable M. D. Sahlins, whose early essay, 'The Segmentary Lineage: An Organisation of Predatory Expansion', *American Anthropologist* 63 (1961), 322–45, has had a major effect on the writing of early mediaeval history (*inter alia permulta*); for his incisive treatment of the troubled concept, see *Tribesmen* (Englewood Cliffs, NJ, 1968). It was the varieties of often warring 'neo-evolutionists' who profoundly influenced the development of British archaeological theory in the 1980s; all too often such theorising (in one form or another) was taken as gospel and/or misunderstood but was recognised as trendy. It needs to be met with vigorous informed criticism by any historian(s) thinking of joining the resulting party.

[139] The problem can be carried back to Marx and Engels. Cf. M. Bloch (ed.), *Marxist Analysis and Social Anthropology* (London, 1975). Ancient Greek history played a large role: H. E. Seebohm, *On the Structure of Greek Tribal Society. An Essay* (London, 1895), sought to follow the work of his father (see n. 76, above: a scholar well known to students of Insular history) 'into the structure and methods of the Tribal System'. This is a subject which greatly concerned those who sought to understand the early development of English society. Some further complications may be observed in, for example, J. Middleton and D. Tait (eds.), *Tribes without Rulers. Studies in African Segmentary Systems* (London, 1958). Another popular topos has been the concept of the 'chief' (an epistemological cop-out) and the attendant 'chiefdom': see T. Earle, *How Chiefs Come to Power The Political Economy in Prehistory* (Stanford, CA, 1997), which has attracted much attention. A notable, but unhappy, result in adjoining territory is B. Arnold and D. B. Gibson (eds.), *Celtic Chiefdom, Celtic State The Evolution of Complex Social Systems in Prehistoric Europe* (Cambridge, 1995). Cf. E. R. Service, *Origins of the State and Civilization. The Process of Cultural Evolution* (New York, 1975). But most historians are likely to recoil from such anthropologists' use of the word 'state'. For an interesting book resulting from bringing together anthropologists and historians, see I. M. Lewis (ed.), *History*

context, kingship is being frozen out of anthropological discourse, a grave error.[140]

Second, one may observe such desire for universals in a discourse of comparative history, particularly of European societies, which has increasingly come to be associated with the European project. The result is that the lesser grades of kingship are in such schemes rapidly assimilated to aristocratic status. This has led to a writing-out of the royal dimension of sub-national government, a dimension which has its own particular importance as a cultural, religious, social and political phenomenon.[141]

Writing England: Bede, Alfred, the *Anglo-Saxon Chronicle*, Peter

It has long been recognised that Bede's 'Ecclesiastical History of the English People' (*Historia ecclesiastica gentis Anglorum*), published in 731, was written in national mode and had a profound impact in the development of an English Church, which, in turn, probably affected political development. It is not easy to produce a wholly satisfying answer to a question about what inspired Bede thus. It was probably study of the encyclopaedia of Isidore of Seville, *Etymologiae seu origines* ('Origins'), which enabled Bede to find a consistent descriptive language to adapt to the politics and social organisation of Germanic Britain.[142] While an interest in

---

and Social Anthropology (London, 1968). For the statist tendency among Scandinavian and English archaeologists, see, for example, M. Axboe, 'Danish Kings and Dendrochronology: Archaeological Insights into the Early History of the Danish State', in *After Empire. Towards an Ethnology of Europe's Barbarians*, ed. G. Ausenda (San Marino, 1995), pp. 217–51; A. Reynolds (n. 119, above); and S. Brookes and A. Reynolds, 'The Origins of Political Order and the Anglo-Saxon State', *Archaeology International* 13–14 (2009–11), 84–93.

[140] What has happened since the heady early years of anthropology – as captured by J. Frazer, *The Golden Bough*, 1st edn, 2 vols. (London, 1890; 2nd edn, 3 vols., 1900; 3rd edn, 12 vols, 1906–15; a supplement was issued in 1937) – is the discipline's detachment from or rejection of the concepts of 'king' and 'kingship'. For some works worth considering in that context, see G. Widengren et al. (eds.), *La Regalità Sacra. The Sacral Kingship* (Leiden, 1959); *Succession to High Office*, ed. J. Goody (Cambridge, 1966); and F. Oakley, *Kingship. The Politics of Enchantment* (Malden, MA, 2006).

[141] Cf. J. Crick, 'Nobility', in *A Companion to the Early Middle Ages. Britain and Ireland, c. 500–c. 1100*, ed. P. Stafford (Chichester, 2009), pp. 414–31, which opens the reader's eyes to some of this.

[142] The authoritative and inspirational quality of Isidore's encyclopaedia provided numerous and repeated stimuli throughout the early Middle Ages. See also n. 73, above. There are important studies by J. Y. duQ. Adams, 'The Political Grammar of Isidore of Seville', in *Arts libéraux et philosophie au moyen âge. Actes du quatrième congrès international de philosophie médiévale* (Montréal, 1969), pp. 763–75; and J. Y. duQ. Adams, 'The Political Grammar of Julian of Toledo', in *Minorities and Barbarians in Medieval Life and Thought*, ed. S. J. Ridyard and R. G. Benson (Sewanee, TN, 1996), pp. 179–95. In 1996, I presented to the San Marino conference (n. 65, above) a supplementary paper (not then intended for publication) discussing the history and rationale of this English application of Isidorian terminology. A remnant of the discussion of it may be found in *The Anglo-Saxons*, ed. Hines, p. 369 (P. Lendinara).

Britannia as a politico-geographical concept manifested itself intermittently in Anglo-Saxon history, occasionally with greater force and point, a concept of the English and subsequently of England was what at length proved more continuously compelling.[143]

We do not know when the dynasty founded by Ecgberht, king of the West Saxons (802–39), began to think of the creation of a kingdom of England; but we seem to find its most audible representative, King Alfred (871–99), sponsoring an adaptation of Bede's 'History' in Old English, and the king himself was content to write of England as a whole, using the phrase *geond Angelcynn* ('throughout England') quite naturally and of *Englisc* as his language.[144] It has even been argued that he declared himself king of all the English, whether those not in subjection to Scandinavian conquerors or to all ethnic English regardless of their political situation.[145] And it is to Alfred that we owe a political and/or ethnic formulation of the nature of his (over)kingdom from the mid-880s, when he began to style himself king of the *Angolsaxones* or *Angulsaxones* (we also find *rex Anglorum et Saxonum* and *Anglorum Saxonum rex*), presumably in general 'king of the Angles and Saxons', although finer shades of interpretation are possible.[146] The term 'Anglo-Saxons' is first found in Frankish Latin about a century earlier to distinguish the Saxons of England from those of Saxony, but that was hardly its purpose in Alfredian usage.[147]

---

[143] However, it is worth noting the Gregorian plan for, and the eventual (eighth-century) institutionalisation of, two archiepiscopal provinces within the English Church. Whether that would have happened in the 730s but for the Gregorian blueprint should be a moot point. Did everyone in the polity acknowledge that (as also in Ireland) the north and south were two very different worlds? On the two halves of Ireland, see Byrne, *Irish Kings*, chap. 10. G. Molyneaux, 'Why Were Some Tenth-Century English Kings Presented as Rulers of Britain?', *TRHS*, 6th series, 21 (2011) 59–91, has offered an interesting but conflicted analysis: for, if the matter had depended on the ability or potential to project power across all England (as in the seventh century), the result would have been very different.

[144] For the Alfredian Anglian adaptation of Bede's History, see *The Old English Version of Bede's Ecclesiastical History of the English People*, ed. and trans. T. Miller, 2 vols. (London, 1890–8); and, for discussion, see most recently G. Waite, 'The Preface to the Old English Bede: Author, Transmission, and Connection with the *West Saxon Genealogical Regnal List*', *ASE* 44 (2016), 31–93; and G. Molyneaux, 'The *Old English Bede*: English Ideology or Christian Instruction?', *EHR* 124 (2009), 1289–323. On *Angelcynn*, see S. Foot, 'The Making of *Angelcynn*: English Identity before the Norman Conquest', *TRHS*, 6th series, 6 (1996), 25–49. On Alfred's political thought, see the outstandingly penetrating study by D. Pratt, *The Political Thought of King Alfred the Great* (Cambridge, 2007). For the best general introduction to Alfred through the literature associated with him, see A. J. Frantzen, *King Alfred* (Boston, 1986).

[145] Cf. *Asser's Life of King Alfred*, ed. W. H. Stevenson (Oxford, 1904; rev. imp. by D. Whitelock, 1959), pp. 148–9.

[146] It is worth noting that the *Angol- /Angul-* spellings might be held to refer back to Angeln.

[147] W. Levison, *England and the Continent in the Eighth Century* (Oxford, 1946), pp. 92–3, although his views on the Angles seem to be misperceptions; *Alfred the Great*, trans. S. Keynes and M. Lapidge (Harmondsworth, 1983), pp. 227–8; cf. *Asser's Life of King Alfred*, ed. Stevenson, pp. 148–52.

The *Anglo-Saxon Chronicle* is in its earliest recoverable form a text written and published in the West Saxon over-kingdom in 892, therefore in Alfred's reign.[148] At various times it has been regarded as Alfred's own work or sponsored as his political mouthpiece or as a product of his court; but another view, never successfully refuted, is that it was written elsewhere in his kingdom, albeit with knowledge of and from the royal court.[149] In the *Chronicle* of 892, neither *Englaland* nor *Englisc /englisc* is to be found (*Engle* are in annal 473), but *Angelcynn* and *Angelcynneslond* were both used to convey the sense of 'England'.[150] However, overall it might be said that the *Chronicle* is focused most thoroughly on what has been called 'Greater Wessex' (the Saxon polity achieved in 825×828: southernmost England, including Essex) – not surprisingly, given the context of frequent and existential conflict with vikings in that region.

The national territory comes very sharply into focus almost on the day of the national kingdom's creation. King Æthelstan, at Eamontbridge on the frontier between the Northumbrians and the British (but Scandinavian-dominated) kingdom of Strathclyde for a council of northern kings on 12 July, 927, had in his entourage (like his great-grandfather Æthelwulf) a

---

[148] *Two of the Saxon Chronicles Parallel*, ed. C. Plummer, 2 vols. (Oxford, 1892–9; rev. imp. by D. Whitelock, 1952), vol. II, p. cxvii (§III), and cf. pp. cxiv–cxvii (§IIO); P. H. Sawyer, *The Age of the Vikings* (London, 1962), pp. 13–21; Dumville, *Wessex and England*, pp. 55–140; and C. Downham, 'Annals, Armies, and Artistry: "The Anglo-Saxon Chronicle", 865–96', reprinted in her book *No Horns*, pp. 9–37.

[149] C. Plummer, *The Life and Times of Alfred the Great* (Oxford, 1902), pp. 11 and 146, saw Alfred as the mind and force behind the creation of the *Anglo-Saxon Chronicle* but not as its author. For various views on Alfred's possible involvement, see first the studies by A. Scharer, 'König Alfreds Hof und die Geschichtsschreibung. Einige Überlegungen zur Angelsachsenchronik und zu Assers De rebus gestis Aelfredi', in *Historiographie im frühen Mittelalter*, ed. A. Scharer and G. Scheibelreiter (Wien, 1994), pp. 443–58; A. Scharer, 'Zu drei Themen in der Geschichtsschreibung der Zeit König Alfreds (871–899)', in *Ethnogenese und Überlieferung*, ed. K. Brunner and B. Merta (Wien, 1994), pp. 200–8; A. Scharer, 'The Writing of History at King Alfred's Court', *EME* 5 (1996), 177–206; and A. Scharer, *Herrschaft und Repräsentation. Studien zur Hofkultur König Alfreds des Grossen* (Wien, 2000). See further T. A. Shippey, 'A Missing Army: Some Doubts about the Alfredian Chronicle', *Anglo-Saxon* 1 (2007), 319–38; F. M. Stenton, 'The South-Western Element in the Old English Chronicle', in *Essays in Medieval History Presented to Thomas Frederick Tout*, ed. A. G. Little and F. M. Powicke (Manchester, 1925), pp. 15–24, reprinted in his book *Preparatory*, pp. 106–15; and N. P. Brooks, 'Why Is the *Anglo-Saxon Chronicle* about Kings?', *ASE* 39 (2011), 43–70.

[150] *Two of the Saxon Chronicles Parallel*, ed. Plummer, vol. II, pp. 375–7, 333. Cf. H. Sweet, 'Some of the Sources of The Anglo-Saxon Chronicle', *Englische Studien* 2 (1879), 310–12, on annal 473. It should be noted that in King Alfred's will we read of two estates which King Alfred owned *on Wealcynne*, whether in the territory of a neighbouring British polity or in British-speaking enclaves in Wessex: *Select English Historical Documents of the Ninth and Tenth Centuries*, ed. and trans. F. E. Harmer (Cambridge, 1914), pp. 15–19, 49–53 and 91–103, at lines 28–34; and *Alfred the Great*, trans. Keynes and Lapidge, pp. 173–8, at 175 (especially nn. 18 and 56), and pp. 313–26, at 317, n. 18, and 321, n. 56.

Continental secretary, one Peter.[151] We have a short letter-poem written by him in Æthelstan's name, directed to the Queen Mother and the prince (Latin *cliton*, representing Old English *æðeling*) at the royal court in the south. It is unambiguous in its announcement of Æthelstan's creation of England, *Saxonia*, 'now made whole' (*iam ... perfecta*), with himself as monarch.[152]

The Viking Age

Vikings' activities in England, which might have seemed a mere irritant or an urgent God-sent warning in the 790s, finally blew away the early Anglo-Saxon polity, now a tetrarchy, in the years from 865 to 878.[153] There was a brief period, in the first half of 878, when all England lay in Scandinavian hands, the royal family of Dublin being the most identifiable and perhaps most prominent of the conquerors.[154] In spite of the iconically English story of King Alfred and the cakes – set in a period when the defeated Alfred, his kingdom taken from him, planned and waged a guerrilla war from the marshes of Somerset to recover his inheritance and perhaps turn the tide – modern English historians have never acknowledged what the *Anglo-Saxon Chronicle* in its annal for that year says bluntly:[155]

> In this year in midwinter after Twelfth Night [6 January] the enemy-army (*here*) came stealthily to Chippenham [Wiltshire] and conquered (*geridon*) the land of the West Saxons and settled there (*gesæton*) and drove a great part of the people (*folc*) overseas and conquered (*geridon*) most of the others; and the people, except King Alfred, subjected themselves to them.

---

[151] On Felix, Æthelwulf's secretary, see *Asser's Life*, ed. Stevenson, pp. 203 n. 1, 225–6, 306; and S. Keynes, 'The West Saxon Charters of King Æthelwulf and His Sons', *EHR* 109 (1994), 1109–49. Peter's origin was deduced by Lapidge, 'Some Latin Poems', pp. 83–93 and 98 (and *Anglo-Latin Literature, 900–1066*, pp. 71–81 and 86) from his name (this particular type of biblical usage was not English at the time) and from his use of *Saxonia* (although that, taken by itself, could have pointed to a Celtic origin).

[152] Lapidge, 'Some Latin Poems', pp. 87 and 89: stanza 3 (*Anglo-Latin Literature, 900–1066*, pp. 75, 77). Cf. Dumville, *The Mediaeval Foundations*, pp. 13–14, reprinted in his *Anglo-Saxon Essays, 2001–2007*, pp. 266–310, at 275–7.

[153] Cf. Kirby, *The Earliest English Kings*, pp. 210–20. For an approach from the other end of the equation, see S. McLeod, *The Beginning of Scandinavian Settlement in England. The Viking 'Great Army' and Early Settlers, c. 865–900* (Turnhout, 2014).

[154] Dumville, 'Old Dubliners'; and Downham, *Viking Kings*, pp. 141–5 (North Britain) and 63–71 (England).

[155] *EHD*, trans. Whitelock, pp. 195–6.

Bishop Asser, translating the text soon after and adding to it (as long as we do not think of him as a forger of *c.* 1000),[156] softened this very slightly but added to it some further elaboration of the reality of guerrilla warfare:[157]

> [T]he heathen army left Exeter and went to Chippenham, a royal estate in northern Wiltshire . . . and spent the winter there. By strength of arms they forced many men of that people to sail overseas, through both poverty and fear, and very nearly all the inhabitants of that kingdom submitted to their authority. At the same time King Alfred, with his small band . . . was leading a restless life in great distress amid the woody and marshy places of Somerset. He had nothing to live on except what he could forage by frequent raids, either secretly or openly, from the heathens as well as from the christians who had submitted to the heathens' authority.

The West Saxons had at last been conquered. Historians have excused Alfred's earlier payment of tribute as buying time to build an effective defence. If there was such a policy, it failed. The brutal statement by the Chronicler has been refused acknowledgement by English historians who have preferred to accentuate the king's guerrilla warfare as a token of continuity. But January 878 was indeed a moment of fracture. After 878, the West Saxon kingdom could never be the same again. Conquest and settlement by heathen vikings, and exile at their hands, had formerly been the fate meted out to the Northumbrians, East Angles and Mercians. The West Saxons were not to be exempt. This was part of a process of radical political and social change – including movement of population – which was occurring across Britain. Ireland had received viking settlement earlier than Britain, and its Scandinavian invaders – while not devoid of great ambition – could adapt easily from their own background to the local culture of petty kingdoms in the host country.[158] The one viking entity which would acquire greatest prominence in Insular politics, sinking its teeth deeply into Britain, was the kingdom of Dublin.[159] The coalitions of raiding armies which bit into Pictland, Strathclyde and England were, while potentially fissiparous, capable of great achievements. And the kings of Dublin maintained a contest for England into the era of Danish

---

[156] *The Medieval Life of King Alfred the Great*, trans. A. P. Smyth (Basingstoke, 2002), whose arguments deserve very close continuing consideration.
[157] Asser, *De rebus gestis Ælfredi*, chaps. 52–3 (ed. Stevenson, pp. 40–1; and trans. Keynes and Lapidge, p. 83 (modified here)).
[158] P. H. Sawyer, 'The Vikings and Ireland', in *Ireland in Early Mediaeval Europe. Studies in Memory of Kathleen Hughes*, ed. D. Whitelock et al. (Cambridge, 1982), pp. 345–61.
[159] Downham, *Viking Kings*.

conquest under Swegen (Sveinn) and Cnut (Knútr) at the beginning of the eleventh century.[160]

There was, however, another side to the story: small-scale, local settlement, powerful enough to dominate an area but not having the strength in numbers and depth successfully to defy the approach of a determined leader of a substantial territorial kingdom. Whether in relation to the Hebrides or to eastern England, we can deduce the ninth-century establishment of small political units. Those in the Hebrides (and, later, Mann) – *Suðreyjar*, 'The Southern Isles', in Old Scandinavian – were knitted together into a fractious, unstable (over)kingdom called in Middle Gaelic *Inse Gall*, 'The Islands of the Foreigners'. In the 'Danelaw' of eastern England, we find two substantial kingdoms (then still known to Anglo-Saxon observers as the East Angles and the Northumbrians), a possible league of small polities ('The Five Boroughs'),[161] and a variety of minor polities (usually described as an army [*here, folc*]) focused on a fortified central place (*burg/burh*; the inhabitants were *burgware*). The process of settlement and land-taking can only occasionally be seen, however.

Much obloquy has attached to Lucien Musset's bracketing together of the late Antique Migration Age (*Völkerwanderungszeit*) and the Viking Age.[162] An implication of the subtitle of his second volume, *Le second assaut contre l'Europe chrétienne*, was of a religiously inspired age of Germanic heathen warfare against Christendom, which is perhaps farfetched but deserves calm analysis. There is a serious point of a different order, however. The migration of Germanic speakers into sub-Roman Britain derived from what are now Denmark and southern Norway, as well as from areas farther south.[163] In the Viking Age, just the same Scandinavian regions were the source of settlers in Britain. It is striking that Viking Age migration, unlike its late Antique counterpart, has not been denied, although there have been attempts to downplay its scale. What seems to have been delivered into England, after it had lost its complex native polity of layered kingships, was some Scandinavian petty kingdoms in Middle Anglian territory. Furthermore, if the received analysis of the social structure of the Scandinavian settlements is correct, the relationship of kings or earls and their farmer-soldiery was more akin to that of the English *ceorl* with his

---

[160] *Ibid.*, pp. 232–3.

[161] Stenton, *Anglo-Saxon England*, 3rd edn, pp. 385, 388–9, 502–25; K. Cameron, *Scandinavian Settlement in the Territory of the Five Boroughs* (Nottingham, [1965]); P. H. Sawyer, *Anglo-Saxon Lincolnshire* (Lincoln, 1998), pp. 4, 122, 128–9, 151; and C. Hart, *The Danelaw* (London, 1992), p. 685.

[162] L. Musset, *Les invasions*, 2 vols. (Paris 1965; 2nd edn, 1969–71).

[163] Hines, *The Scandinavian Character*.

royal lord as we first meet him in the seventh century.[164] On this basis, it is not difficult to see why the Scandinavians of Bedford, Hertford, Luton, Northampton, Leicester, Huntingdon, Cambridge, Stamford and Nottingham,[165] though occasionally combining in pairs, lacked the ability effectively to resist the determined efforts of King Edward the Elder to reduce them to his authority. It had proved impossible in this context for the more powerful viking armies of the period 865–78 (or occasional major campaigns thereafter) to be re-created to help to defend the settlements and minor polities of the northern Home Counties and the East Midlands.

The Scandinavian kingdom of East Anglia and the minor polities of the rest of the southern 'Danelaw' were overthrown in campaigns lasting for nine consecutive years (912–20). Something of the same sort had to be done again, though in face of the Dubliners and Northumbrians, in the reign of King Edmund I, 939–46: in 942, all the historical territory of the Mercians was seized for the English crown, including 'five boroughs' (*burga fife*) – Leicester, Lincoln, Nottingham, Stamford and Derby, of which Lincoln and Derby had not been specifically mentioned in reporting the campaigns of the 910s.[166]

Although the matter has proved controversial, the first major English responses to viking activity seem to have been initiated by Æthelwulf, king of the West Saxons (839–58). The religious response involved visits to Rome and royal decimation-offerings to God.[167] The political reply was to write a royal will which commanded a narrowing of eligibility to succeed to the kingship of the West Saxons, leaving Æthelwulf's last-standing son to control transmission of the throne to the next genera-tion.[168] That son was Alfred, well groomed for the role by his parents but perhaps not expected to be the one who would be left standing. Unification

---

[164] F. M. Stenton, 'The Thriving of the Anglo-Saxon Ceorl', in his *Preparatory*, pp. 383–93; R. H. C. Davis, 'East Anglia and the Danelaw', *TRHS*, 5th series, 5 (1955), 23–37 (a justly famous article), reprinted with additions in his *From Alfred the Great to Stephen* (London, 1991), pp. 15–32; and D. Hadley, *The Northern Danelaw, Its Social Structure, c. 800–1100* (London, 2000).

[165] The *ASC*, annals 912–20, provides the narrative basics for the events of these years, including these nine settlement-names.

[166] *ASC* MSS ABCD, 942, in *The Anglo-Saxon Chronicle According to the Several Original Authorities*, ed. and trans. B, Thorpe, 2 vols. (London, 1861), vol. I, pp. 208–9; C. Downham, 'The Chronology of the Last Scandinavian Kings of York', *NH* 40 (2003), 25–51; Sawyer, *Anglo-Saxon Lincolnshire*; and R. A. Hall, 'The Five Boroughs of the Danelaw: A Review of Current Knowledge', *ASE* 18 (1989), 149–206.

[167] S. Kelly, 'King Æthelwulf's Decimations', *Anglo-Saxon* 1 (2007), 285–317.

[168] Asser, *De rebus gestis Ælfredi*, chap. 16 (ed. Stevenson, pp. 14–16); J. B. Gillingham, *The Kingdom of Germany in the High Middle Ages (900–1200)* (London, 1971), p. 18; D. N. Dumville, 'The Ætheling: A Study in Anglo-Saxon Constitutional History', *ASE* 8 (1979), 1–33, at 21–4; P. Wormald, 'The Ninth Century', in *The Anglo-Saxons*, apud J. Campbell et al. (Oxford, 1982), pp. 132–57, at 140; and *Alfred the Great*, trans. Keynes and Lapidge, pp. 72–3 (§16 and pp. 236–7, nn. 33–7).

of the English was an essential aspect of policy, leading to Alfred's promotion of his '(over)kingdom of the Anglo-Saxons'. Alfred's military reforms created a network of fortresses, a standing field-army and a primitive navy. A series of other governmental reforms was designed to create a much enhanced kingship and royal administration. Finally, the crucial response, in the reign of Edward the Elder (899–924), was to secure the future by invasion and conquest of Scandinavian England.[169]

Three dimensions of the historiography of the First Viking Age in particular deserve exploration.[170] There has been some reluctance in principle among historians to accept the case for a long-term developing strategy on the part of the West Saxon royal dynasty from the mid-ninth century.[171] The focus on Alfred has been inevitable and entirely justified, even where it seems overly pious. But his father, in particular, is not to be overlooked.

The other two historiographical responses fall into the familiar categories of error. The invasion and conquest of the 'Danelaw', led by Edward the Elder, was for a long time described as 'the reconquest of Scandinavian England'.[172] A mild observation of the absurdity of this formulation, made a generation ago,[173] quickly and quietly led to its abandonment by most historians. The underlying thinking had been hopelessly anachronistic, based on the modern nation, supposing that the West Saxons could present themselves as if they were the natural heirs to the previous rulers of the conquered territories. In fact, West Saxon armies now embarked on the conquest, *de nouo*, of formerly Mercian regions, drawing them into 'the (over)kingdom of the Anglo-Saxons' which Alfred had created thirty years earlier.

In an identically nationalist vein has been the treatment of the incoming Scandinavians. There has been a century-long obsession with divining whether particular viking groups were Danish or Norwegian (the Swedes

---

[169] See N. J. Higham and D. H. Hill (eds.), *Edward the Elder, 899–924* (London, 2001), for a very varied discussion.

[170] For the terminology, see P. H. Sawyer et al., 'The Two Viking Ages of Britain. A Discussion', *Mediaeval Scandinavia* 2 (1969), 163–207; see further D. N. Dumville, *Vikings in Britain and Ireland: A Question of Sources*, 3rd edn (Aberdeen, 2014).

[171] For a discussion of one aspect of the case, see Dumville, *Wessex and England*, chap. VI.

[172] Wainwright, *Scandinavian England*, for example, p. 324, 'Edward's conquest of the Danish midlands [of England!]', and p. 328, 'the recovery of those areas which the Danish armies had occupied in the reign of Alfred the Great'. Loyn, *Anglo-Saxon England*, 1st edn, p. 51, offered a classic specimen of his thinking: 'English kings did not so much reconquer Scandinavianized England as absorb it.'

[173] In academic oral tradition, this is held to have been said in the context of the preparation of Campbell et al., *The Anglo-Saxons*.

never being allowed a significant role). It has been known since the seventeenth century that Latin *Dani* and *Nordmanni* were interchangeable in ninth- and tenth-century discourse. Likewise, the Old-Scandinavian words *Danr* and *dönsk*, applied whether to persons or to language, meant 'Scandinavian' rather than 'Dane'/'Danish'.[174] This was also reflected in Classical Latin usage. However, the pressure for nationalistic interpretation has produced a skewed treatment of a potentially important question by requiring a reductionist approach. We can see that outlook developing particularly as Norwegian nationality became an issue in the run-up to independence in 1905.[175]

927: The Kingdom of the English and the Struggle to Hold It

The kingdom of the English was created by King Æthelstan in the summer of 927 through direct military action against the one remaining Scandinavian polity in England, the kingdom of the Northumbrians. It is part of the unsatisfactory oddity of the apparently original record in the *Anglo-Saxon Chronicle* for Æthelstan's reign that it has no primary account of that year's events. It is only in two much later texts, Versions D and E, each with a Northern dimension, that such appears, but in two apparently contradictory narratives. King Sihtric, Æthelstan's brother-in-law since January 926, died, to be succeeded by King Guthfrith (Guðrøðr) II, who was then expelled by King Æthelstan. Version D is interesting in implying that Æthelstan's control of the Northumbrian kingdom was endorsed by a treaty with Northern kings, among whom is numbered Aldred Eadwulfing of Bamburgh, the ruler of English 'Bernicia', whose line now probably had to renounce its royal status.[176]

We can see a conscious foreign policy developing in Æthelstan's reign: the cultivation of relationships with Continental royal courts by successive

---

[174] Downham, *No Horns*, pp. 41–71, and references given therein, especially F. Amory, 'The dönsk tunga in Early Medieval Normandy: A Note', in *American Indian and Indoeuropean Studies: Papers in Honor of Madison S. Beeler*, ed. K. Klar et al. (Den Haag, 1980), pp. 279–89. Cf. Dumville, 'Old Dubliners', reprinted in his *Celtic Essays, 2001–2007*, vol. I, pp. 103–22. See also M. Schönfeld, *Wörterbuch der altgermanischen Personen- und Völkernamen nach der Überlieferung des klassischen Altertums bearbeitet* (Heidelberg, 1911), pp. 70–1, *s.n.* 'Dani'. For the easy interchange between 'Danish' and 'Norse' for one language, see J. L. Campbell, 'The Norse Language in Orkney in 1725', *Scottish Historical Review* 33 (1954), 175.

[175] Downham, '"Hiberno-Norwegians" and "Anglo-Danes"', pp. 152–7 (cf. her *No Horns*, pp. 54–9).

[176] The most attractive introduction to Æthelstan remains that of J. A. Robinson, *The Times of Saint Dunstan* (Oxford, 1923), pp. 25–80; cf. Dumville, *Wessex and England*, chap. IV. For Versions D and E, see *The Anglo-Saxon Chronicle. A Collaborative Edition*, gen. ed. Dumville and Keynes, vols. 6 and 7 (Cambridge, 1996, 2004); cf. *EHD*, ed. Whitelock, pp. 218–20.

marriages of his sisters; implacable opposition to the claims of kings of (Scandinavian) Dublin to rule at York, and military intervention in Scotland and France, thereby establishing – within a decade of the making of England – a practice which would last for 800 and 1,000 years respectively.[177]

The interested parties, against whom the new kingdom had to be held, were the Dubliners and the Northern powers: the kingdom of Strathclyde had since 871 been a satellite of the viking kingdom of Dublin; the kingdom of Alba (formerly of the Southern Picts) had a history of bitter hostility to the vikings of Dublin but was now in the hands of a ruler, Cosstantín/Constantine, who had become unfriendly to the approaching kingdom of the English and entered an alliance with the Dubliners;[178] and the more remote polities (as seen from England) of the Hebrides and Mann (known in Middle Gaelic as *Insi Gall*, 'The Islands of the Foreigners'), Muréb (Moray), formerly of the Northern Picts, and the Scandinavian earldom of Orkney and Shetland (including, on the mainland, Caithness and part of Sutherland). Mutual invasion, punctuated by treaty arrangements, seems to have become the norm of international relationships in northern Britain.[179]

Dublin remained a significant factor in this relationship until at least about 980. There were reverses when England was invaded by a coalition led from Dublin at the end of 939, immediately after the death of Æthelstan: 'Northumbria' and the Mercian/Midland 'Danelaw' were lost to the Dubliners for two to three years, in circumstances of which the campaigns of 1745/6 seem eerily reminiscent, and the Northumbrian kingdom proved difficult to hold for the next fifteen years.[180]

The historiography of that struggle to keep England intact by holding 'Northumbria' has produced some interesting twists and turns of interpretation. The role of Dublin has declined from a high point and then risen in importance again.[181] There have been some (but only some) significant

---

[177] Dumville, *Wessex and England*, chap. IV. [178] *Ibid.*, pp. 146–9.

[179] Downham, *Viking Kings*, chap. 5. There is a new account of Scottish history of this period: Woolf, *From Pictland*, chaps. 3 and 4.

[180] On 1745/6, see, for example, J. Black, *Culloden and the '45* (Stroud, 2000). Cf. the off-the-cuff remark of Thompson, *Romans and Barbarians*, p. 7: 'The German[ic] kindreds could no more have overthrown the Roman empire of Augustus or Marcus Aurelius or Constantine the Great than the Scottish clansmen of 1745 could have overwhelmed the England of King George II.' However true all that may be, it is nonetheless worth remembering that in 1746 the Scottish insurgents seized Derby, with the result that London began to empty as the capital panicked.

[181] A magnificent account of Viking Age Dublin was provided by C. Haliday, *The Scandinavian Kingdom of Dublin* (Dublin, 1881; 2nd edn, 1884; rev. imp. 1969); and (earlier) in the superb editorial introduction and notes to *Cogadh Gaedhel re Gallaibh, The War of the Gael and the Gaill*, ed. and trans. J. H. Todd (London, 1867). See further Downham, *No Horns*, chap. 8; M. Murphy et al., *The*

developments in understanding the history of the kingdom of Strathclyde,[182] which had – invisibly in surviving written record – pushed southwards to the middle of what is now Cumbria between 871 and 927. The relations of Alba and Strathclyde (and England) were and are difficult to follow, and remain so until the last recorded appearance of a king of Strathclyde, at the battle of Carham-on-Tweed in ?1014.[183]

The English foreign policy was on the whole successful, but a militarily more sensible definition of 'Northumbria' in early Anglo-Norman England led to the first establishment of something like the present Anglo-Scottish border in the 1090s, with northward advance in the west and a willingness to hold an eastern border on the River Tweed.[184] The struggle over the body of the much larger pre-Viking-Age territory of the kingdom of the Northumbrians and the difficulties which King William I faced in Yorkshire have encouraged observers of a 'north-south divide' in England to argue that the West Saxon and then Danish/Anglo-Danish kings who held the kingdom of the English from 927 to 1042 never succeeded in depriving the English north of its separate identity and incorporating it fully into their England.[185]

This arguable proposition can usefully be yoked to another. Some English historians have, over the past three-quarters of a century, found reason to downplay the success of the 'English project' of the dynasty of Ecgberht of Wessex. One very remarkable and high-profile manifestation of this was in F. M. Stenton's treatment of the later tenth century in his classic *Anglo-Saxon England*, first published in 1943. He announced Edgar's reign (959–75), seen by contemporaries and by twelfth-century historians as a high point of English governance and military power, as the beginning

Dublin Region in the Middle Ages. Settlement, Land-Use and Economy (Dublin, 2010); J. Bradley et al. (eds.), *Dublin in the Medieval World. Studies in Honour of Howard B. Clarke* (Dublin, 2009); and the splendid array of scholarship on view in the annual journal *Medieval Dublin*.

[182]   Downham, *Viking Kings*, chap. 5 and p. 337, *s.n.* Strathclyde; Woolf, *From Pictland*, has devoted the whole of a very interesting book to the transformation of North Britain in the Viking Age; cf. Dumville, *The Mediaeval Foundations* (reprinted in his *Anglo-Saxon Essays, 2001–2007*, pp. 266–310), for comment on various aspects of the period.

[183]   The scholarship on the contexts of this battle is very unsatisfactory. I have prepared an article offering a new analysis of the sources 'The Date and Context of the Battle of Carham-on-Tweed'.

[184]   G. W. S. Barrow, *The Kingdom of the Scots. Government, Church and Society from the Eleventh to the Fourteenth Century* (London, 1973), pp. 139–61 (2nd edn, Edinburgh, 2003), pp. 112–29. This essay has been repeatedly updated and augmented since its first appearance in 1966 as an Inaugural Lecture and an article, 'The Anglo-Scottish Border', *NH*, 1 (1966), 21–42.

[185]   H. M. Jewell, *The North-South Divide. The Origins of Northern Consciousness in England* (Manchester, 1994); N. J. Higham, *The Kingdom of Northumbria, 350–1100* (Stroud, 1993); and Rollason, *Northumbria*.

of a period of decline.[186] More generally, one is bound to wonder whether modern historians most committed to the existence and promotion of an idea of an English nation from at least the time of Bede and those who had come to regard King Alfred as its father found the role of Æthelstan and his successors a tiresome distraction from and complication of a subject held to be already closed by 900. Indeed, even relatively moderate opinion has been doubtful about admitting the kingdom's existence until it was uncontested.[187] This rather bizarre approach must mean that the kingdom did not exist until William I secured it – but that was certainly not King William's opinion!

Uí Ímair ('The Descendants of Ívarr'), the rulers of Dublin, were formidable and tenacious opponents of the first seven kings of England. But what struck most foreign observers of the kingdom of the English before 1066 was its power and wealth.[188] Historians may debate whether or not pre-Conquest England was a state (archaeologists, on a quite different trajectory, seem to be thinking of the state as a useful description of eighth-century English over-kingdoms) or a pre-state society. It had a governmental apparatus which functioned predictably; but royal government had noticeable limitations in the face of entrenched local power, whether in Kent or in Durham. Nevertheless, its kings had the military might (and the supporting wealth) to deliver a substantial military punch when and where they wished to land it. It is hard to imagine that in those circumstances the Dubliners – however seriously they might be taken in England (whether by tenth-century kings claiming the right to rule Dublin or indeed Ireland or by an eleventh-century queen who was fluent in Irish)[189] – could so disrupt the English polity (as they had in the later ninth century) as to call its new kingdom into question.

The origins of the kingdom of the English were of course various and reflected the travails of a long-developing body politic. Founded by settler-colonists on the wreckage of Roman Britain, Germanic Britain had at least 150 years' development before it began to leave records which speak to us with relative clarity. I see nothing in the history of early Anglo-Saxon

---

[186] Stenton, *Anglo-Saxon England*, 1st edn, pp. 359–67.

[187] It is rather curious that this seems not to have been a major issue debated by modern historians of the Norman conquest of England. If one searches their indexes, one does not find entries for 'England', 'kingdom of England', or the like.

[188] P. H. Sawyer, 'The Wealth of England in the Eleventh Century', *TRHS*, 4th series, 15 (1965), 145–64, and his Ford Lectures, *The Wealth of Anglo-Saxon England* (Oxford, 2013).

[189] The encomium of Queen Edith, in *Vita Ædwardi regis* i. 2, *in The Life of King Edward Who Rests at Westminster, Attributed to a Monk of Saint-Bertin*, ed. and trans. F. Barlow, 2nd edn (Oxford, 1992), pp. 22–5; cf. C. Downham, 'England and the Irish Sea Zone in the Eleventh Century', *ANS* 26 (2003), 55–73, esp. 65.

England which implies a nation in active search of a national kingdom or indicates an inevitable progression towards such an outcome. It was the long experience of a kingdom of the English, indeed of England, that in early modern times allowed the growth of such teleological thought. Perversely, perhaps, the effective creation of a British kingdom as the Tudors' contribution to the island's history convinced English historians of their nation's God-given inheritance. In a climate of increasing nationalism, modern historians saw no reason to rethink this fundamental proposition. Only now, perhaps, in the aftermath of Empire (and indeed of 'the European Project'), can the lengthy processes of the creation of both the kingdom of the English and the land of the English, England, be subjected to thorough analysis.[190]

Summation

I close by offering seven summary propositions.

1. England began in the fifth century amid the wreckage of what had been Roman Britain; control of increasing amounts of territory was wrested from the British indigenes in a process which (in the language of the 'Convention on Genocide' of the United Nations Organisation) may be called 'cultural genocide'.

2. The ethnic and linguistic variety of Britain in the earlier Middle Ages was great (and included racial hatred between English and Britons) but was as nothing in comparison with the political complexity: Britain (a lively concept associated with imperial pretension) was a theatre of inter-kingdom as well as international politics.

3. Early English kingship needs to be wholly problematised: at base, it was an intensely local institution (probably with hundreds of petty kings across England), but with rising layers of sub-regional, regional and quasi-national over-kingship; such a polity probably provided considerable local stability while allowing a significant dynamic at higher levels.

---

[190] I must acknowledge two great debts. A first version of this chapter was written in response to a very welcome invitation from Professor David S. Bachrach to contribute a 5,000-word article on the subject to *History Compass*, one of the liveliest academic journals in the discipline. The original result was much too long. To Dr Clare Downham, as at that time the willing friend at hand, I owe great thanks for her efforts and ingenuity in service of attempts to cut the article down. That it was in the end still much too big for the original purpose allowed me to offer it (with further revision and updating) when I was invited to contribute to this volume in honour of Simon Keynes, my friend and colleague of very many years, who is of course no stranger to discussion of fundamental questions about Anglo-Saxon England.

4. The central but unacknowledged problem of interpretation has been that the received narrative of Anglo-Saxon political development has depended on a teleology, that the creation of an English monarchy (after however many centuries of polyarchy) was both desirable and inevitable, given the existence of the *gens /natio Anglorum* already recognised and defined by Bede in 731.

5. Where between 802 and 927 the West-Saxon royal dynasty began to think of its members as potential kings of all the English we do not yet know. But we do have a letter-poem of 12 July, 927 (built on one from Charlemagne's reign), formally and royally proclaiming the creation of the kingdom of the English.

6. The years 865–78 marked a major turning point in the history of the English polity: Scandinavian conquest of all England (as of North Britain too) was in 878 briefly a reality, and the new Scandinavian-dominated polity incorporated some very old elements of socio-political organisation – notably the petty kingdom. It was the West Saxons' recovery from conquest which eventually allowed their own conquest of England.

7. When King Æthelstan created the kingdom of the English, this constituted a challenge to the kingdom of Dublin, whose power and influence in northern Britain were at once called fundamentally into question; the resulting contest was pursued vigorously through the tenth century but never succeeded in creating an existential crisis for the kingdom of the English, which proved resilient. The limits of England were defined by the relative strength and resolve not only of its own ruling elite but also by those of its neighbours, particularly in 'the kingdom of Alba [Britain]' (founded at much the same time as Alfred's 'kingdom of the Anglo-Saxons') on which Scotland was built.

CHAPTER 6

Losing the Plot? 'Filthy Assertions' and 'Unheard-of Deceit' in Codex Carolinus 92

Jinty Nelson

The Codex Carolinus (hereafter CC), a collection of eighth-century papal letters sent to Frankish potentates, almost all of them kings, made at Charlemagne's behest in 791 (no additions, hence none later) is a godsend for early medieval historians.[1] This is not just because these letters throw so much light on dark places but also because they expose so many problems – and few problems in the CC are as seriously problematic as those in no. 92.[2] Its date remains uncertain, 784×791, and that in itself ensures lively debate, vigorously stirred by young German scholars unafraid to plumb the intricacies of papal diplomatic.[3] In the context of this chapter, though, the best of the good news is that the debate has not been confined to specialists in papal or Frankish history but also engaged the attention of Anglo-Saxonist historians, not least Simon Keynes, whose attitudes, never confined to Anglo-Saxon England, have made him open to all kinds of Channel crossings and to whom this chapter is offered in gratitude and affection.

It was no coincidence that scholarly references to CC 92, though typically brief and low key, appeared just before and during the Second World War. The Channel was moat yet also corridor, and Channel crossers had been welcomed before England stood alone and Europe was in everyone's thoughts. Wilhelm Levison, who escaped from Nazi Germany,

---

[1] *MGH Epp. III*, ed. W. Gundlach (Berlin, 1892). See now A. T. Hack, *Codex Carolinus. Päpstliche Epistolographie im 8. Jahrhundert*, 2 vols., Päpste und Päpsttum 35, 1 and 2 (Stuttgart, 2006), with excellent introductory pages (pp. 39–90) on the collection, its context and the unique manuscript. T. F. X. Noble's review, *EME* 18 (2010), 233–6, does justice to Hack's achievement.

[2] CC 92 (ed. Gundlach, pp. 629–30). There is a good translation by the late John Percival in H. Loyn and J. Percival, *The Reign of Charlemagne* (London, 1975), pp. 132–4; and a partial translation by P. D. King, *Charlemagne. Translated Sources* (Kendal, 1987), pp. 305–6 (45 in King's numbering).

[3] F. Hartmann, *Hadrian I. (772–795)*, Päpste und Päpsttum 34 (Stuttgart, 2006); and also T. F. X. Noble, *The Republic of St Peter. The Birth of the Papal State, 680–825* (Philadelphia, 1984), still invaluable.

adorned the land of his exile, and in one of his Ford Lectures on *England and the Continent in the Eighth Century* delivered in Oxford in 1943 noted that between Charles and Offa,

> there was some co-operation in ecclesiastical politics. The strange rumour arose that Offa had suggested to Charles the deposition of Pope Hadrian, and the Frankish king, at Offa's request informed the Pope that the report was unfounded.[4]

Also in 1943, Frank Stenton published (after 'many years' of toil) *Anglo-Saxon England*, where he observed that

> between 784 and 796, Offa was the only ruler in western Europe who could attempt to deal on equal terms with Charlemagne ... Even at Rome Offa seemed a real, though inscrutable, force in the international world. In a deferential letter to Charlemagne, Pope Hadrian I at great length disclaimed belief in a rumour that his deposition and the election of a Frankish pope had been proposed to Charlemagne by Offa. Nothing is known of the origin of this story, but the language in which the pope expressed his confidence in Offa's devotion does not conceal his past anxiety.[5]

J. M. Wallace-Hadrill's deftly connective and comparative Ford Lectures delivered in 1970 included 'Charlemagne and Offa', in which the fact that 'Offa was in touch with Rome' was duly noted:

> Three or four years later [i.e. after 781], Pope Hadrian writes to Charlemagne about a rumour that Charlemagne himself had reported to him, to the effect that Offa had approached Charlemagne with a proposal that the pope should be deposed and replaced by a Frankish candidate. It was, of course, the pope added, *incredibilis*, but still he was alarmed ... [A] possible solution lay in [Offa's] bad relations with Archbishop Jænberht of Canterbury and in his plan to anoint his only son Ecgfrith ... It is guess where only a guess will do.[6]

This solution had in fact been sketched by Wallace-Hadrill at a large conference celebrating Charlemagne in Aachen in 1965. Here he had suggested that Offa in 784/5 'had been in touch with the big men of

---

[4] W. Levison, *England and the Continent in the Eighth Century. The Ford Lectures delivered in the University of Oxford in the Hilary Term, 1943* (Oxford, 1946), p. 112. Levison does not mention the source for the 'strange rumour'.

[5] F. M. Stenton, *Anglo-Saxon England*, 1st edn (Oxford, 1943), pp. 213–14 (3rd edn, p. 215). Stenton refers to A. W. Haddan and W. Stubbs, *Councils and Ecclesiastical Documents Relating to Great Britain and Ireland*, 3 vols. (London, 1871), vol. III, pp. 440–2, rather than to the MGH edition of *MGH Epp. III*, ed. Gundlach.

[6] J. M. Wallace-Hadrill, *Early Germanic Kingship in England and on the Continent* (Oxford, 1971), p. 114.

Europe', and his 'influence' had made Hadrian 'frightened'.[7] As it happens, the next crucial contribution came from the young Simon Keynes, for it was he who pointed out to Nicholas Brooks that the word *emuli* in CC no. 92 meant 'in its basic sense "rivals", "opponents"', where Wallace-Hadrill had seemed to understand 'friends' or 'envoys'.[8] When this vital contribution was made, only Simon can tell (around 1978 when he completed his PhD perhaps?). But the fact that it *was* vital makes the subject of this chapter in Simon's honour serendipitously apt. Nicholas, in his discussion of CC 92, rightly called the letter 'remarkable' and confessed to finding its meaning 'difficult'. Nevertheless he concluded thus:

> [I]t seems likely that Archbishop Jænberht and his Kentish kinsmen were the 'enemies' who were attempting to sow discord between the kings and pope in order to protect the archbishop and his see from Offa's assaults. Alternatively there may have been those in the Mercian and Frankish courts who wished to threaten a pope who seemed to be protecting the awkwardly independent archbishop.[9]

Jo Story has followed a similar interpretation of who the enemies were, and when the 'dastardly rumour' arose and reached him, namely, 784/5, but offered three comments of her own:

> The letter is illustrative of the very close bond which had developed between Charlemagne and Hadrian [and] demonstrates the respect which Offa's messengers could expect at Charlemagne's court and Rome . . . the messengers were received in Rome by the Pope 'with a joyful countenance out of respect for [Charles'] distinguished excellence' [and] it may have been this incident which prompted Hadrian to send his legates to England in 786 with a brief to 'uproot anything harmful' and 'to renew the faith and friendship which St Gregory sent'.[10]

One more Anglo-Saxonist voice deserves to be heard: that of Donald Bullough in his posthumously published *Alcuin: Achievement & Reputation*. Of CC 92, he says

[7] Wallace-Hadrill, 'Charlemagne and England', in *Karl der Grosse I*, ed. W. Braunfels (Düsseldorf, 1965), pp. 683–98, reprinted in his *Early Medieval History* (Oxford, 1975), pp. 155–80, at 157.

[8] N. Brooks, *The Early History of the Church of Canterbury* (Leicester, 1984), p. 350, n. 29. I am not sure that Wallace-Hadrill did think *emuli* meant 'friends', but it would be fair to say that he did not clarify that in this context the word could not mean anything other than 'enemies'. See D. A. Bullough, *Alcuin: Achievement & Reputation* (Leiden, 2004), pp. 337–8, n. 20, where a further and especially apt biblical example of *emulus*, 1 Reg. 28.16, could be added to the two cited. For other appearances of *emuli* in the CC, see below, n. 22, for CC 29, p. 535, and n. 26, for CC 49, p. 568.

[9] Brooks, *Early History*, p. 117.

[10] J. Story, *Carolingian Connections: Anglo-Saxon England and Carolingian Francia 750–870* (Aldershot, 2003), pp. 198–9.

[D]etractors or opponents of the kings of English Mercia and of Francia were reported to be taking false and mischievous accusations against Offa to the Papal Court, which had led to the dispatch of messengers from both monarchs energetically denying their stories, to the Pope's full satisfaction. (Hadrian had long and painful experience of false accusations against him which might or did reach the Frankish king).[11]

Bullough's footnote to these observations mentions the lengthy lemma (head note) to CC 92 in the unique manuscript, which he does not quote but is worth citing here:

> Item: the copy of the letter of this same pope that was sent to the lord king Charles in which was contained [information] about the *missi* of Offa king of the English, who together with the *missi* of the above-mentioned king Charles had hastened to Rome and how the above-mentioned pope had received those *missi* of the English honourably to the extent that the above-mentioned Charles, through his envoys, had told him [Hadrian] to do.[12]

In the same footnote Bullough adds: 'A dating [of CC 92] to 784 or 785 is possible, *but it could well be later* [italics added]'.[13] This is a possibility to be revisited.

The forty-nine letters in the CC sent to Charlemagne by Hadrian were dictated by the pope and written by scribes, some of whom were 'humbler men (writing-office hacks)' and others 'men of high standing'.[14] Many of Hadrian's letters were responses to letters received from Charles that have not survived in full but were quoted from liberally in the papal replies. Achim Hack has expertly reconstructed twenty-seven of these lost letters (*deperdita*).[15] An unusual feature of CC 92 is that it responded to a letter of Offa's to Charlemagne, who had forwarded Offa's letter to Hadrian along with one of his own. Offa's 'assertions' – Hadrian never actually used the

---

[11] Bullough, *Alcuin*, p. 337.

[12] 'Item exemplar epistolae eiusdem papae ad domnum carolum regem directa, in qua continetur de missis offae regis anglorum, qui simul cum missis praefati regis caroli roma properarent, et qualiter praedictus papa ipsos missos anglorum honorabiliter suscepisset quemadmodum ei praedictus rex Carolus per suos legatos mandaverat': CC 92 (ed. Gundlach, p. 629, app., 'a) Lemma'). On lemmata, see Hack, *Codex Carolinus*, vol. I, pp. 69–71, agreeing with Gundlach's view that these 'head-notes' were produced at the time of the collection, not added later when the unique manuscript was copied.

[13] Bullough, *Alcuin*, pp. 337–8, with n. 20, where other examples of 'rumoured accusations against Hadrian' are given as CC 51 (775) and CC 94, usually dated to 790/1.

[14] D. Bullough, '*Aula renovata*: The Carolingian Court before the Aachen Palace', *PBA* 71 (1985), 267–301, reprinted in his *Carolingian Renewal. Sources and Heritage* (Manchester, 1991), pp. 123–60, at 129–30. Hack quotes this in *Codex Carolinus*, vol. II, at p. 957, n. 12.

[15] Hack, *Codex Carolinus*, vol. II, 'Anhang B, Regesten der königlichen Briefe', pp. 957–74.

word 'rumour', *rumor*, or *fama*, because he needed something less ano-dyne, less like 'gossip' – were thought by the pope to be 'filthy' and 'unheard of' and by Charlemagne to be 'most wicked, hostile, and quite certainly false'. Strong or highly emotive language is frequently encoun-tered in the CC, but in CC 92 the language is exceptional for several reasons. The bearers of the letters to which CC 92 responded were not just Charlemagne's envoys but those of Offa as well. Hadrian said he had received both sets of envoys 'with a willing heart' and 'looked on them with a joyful face'. Hack has spotted that although the pope frequently asked for his own envoys to be received kindly by Charlemagne, in only two cases, of which CC 92 is one, did Hadrian give assurances that he had received Charlemagne's envoys kindly.

The other instance is CC 94, dated 790×791, which also expressed Hadrian's acute concern about 'iniqui ac procaces . . . qui adversus matrem vestram, sanctam Romanan ecclesiam, perverse moliebantur perpetrari', though he immediately affirmed that these onslaughts had been demol-ished and brought to nothing by 'vestra [Charlemagne's] laboriosa certa-mina'.[16] Further on in the letter were strong hints that the pope's most dangerous detractors were *Raviniani et Pentapolenses* who had apparently been 'turning to' Charlemagne rather than to the pope. Where these people were concerned, Hadrian did not trust Charlemagne to concert action with him.[17]

Other exceptional features, stylistic and structural, can be observed in CC 92. It begins with a long, florid paragraph of gratitude for Charles' letter (Dep. 49) to which it responds: 'Sagacissimos nectareosque a vestra praecipua regali in triumphis potentia directos suos suscepimus liquidos affatos [We have received from your royal power outstanding in triumphs the most wise, sweet as nectar and clear-flowing words you sent]'. The letter continues: 'Opening with more than usual love the letter we con-tinually awaited, we had first grasped what we wished to know, which is about your excellent health and well-being and also that of our spiritual daughter, your lady queen, and that of your most outstanding offspring as well as all their most faithful household.' After repeating these sentiments, Hadrian assures the king of his unceasing intercessionary prayers at the tomb of St Peter. 'This was the practice of your father too. Following it as

---

[16] CC 94 (ed. Gundlach, pp. 632–6 – an unusually long letter – at p. 633).
[17] CC 94 (ed. Gundlach, p. 635). For this and other instances of papal concerns over such unreliability, see J. Nelson, 'Charlemagne and Ravenna', in *Ravenna: Its Role in Earlier Medieval Change and Exchange*, ed. J. Herrin and J. Nelson (London, 2016), pp. 239–52.

he did, your royal power has likewise grown higher through our assiduous prayers.'

The preceding passage was more than usually effusive boilerplate. Now, unexpectedly, comes a resounding *Porro*: 'But. . . .'.[18] This next passage was the real heart of the letter: Offa's message to Charles, Charles' reaction and the messages of both kings brought now by their *missi* to the pope, as already detailed earlier, conveyed the raison d'être of CC 92. Hadrian, having spilled the beans, immediately assured Charles, '[W]e rely on your royal power, and we trust completely that your indestructible and orthodox loyalty (*fides*) towards our apostolic paternity will remain surpassing.' His use of the term *paternitas* in relation to Charles was exceptional. It occurs only in two CC letters, twice in CC 92 and once in CC 94.[19] Hadrian returned briefly to the 'filthy assertions (*inluvies assertiones*) proffered by King Offa' and repeated his own complete incredulity as to such 'unheard-of deceit (*inaudita versucia*)'.

The next section shifted into a quite different register: within only seventeen lines came no fewer than nine biblical citations. There were two themes: first, do not be afraid!; and second, believe that the pope has been chosen by God not man! The letter ended with assurances about how well Charles' and Offa's envoys had been received at Rome: a point observed by Hack, as noted earlier. David King's 'there is more than a touch of anxious defiance' caught the tone of paradoxical uncertainty.[20] Wallace-Hadrill's descriptions of Hadrian as 'frightened' and 'alarmed' were unequivocal, and justifiably so. CC 92 registered a moment on the pope's pathological graph: a 'high' of papal fear that sprang from the perception of a plot – one potentially more lethal than ever before, not just to Hadrian but to the papacy itself.

At this point it is worth stressing that plots, or rumours of plots, in themselves were not unheard-of in the already long history of the papacy. Even in the papacy's glory days popes had been violently removed at the hands of such Christian Roman emperors as Justinian and Constans II.[21]

---

[18] The English translations of King, *Charlemagne*, p. 305, and Loyn and Percival, *Reign of Charlemagne*, p. 133, both have 'Now' where 'But' seems to me to be needed.

[19] Hack, *Codex Carolinus*, vol. I, pp. 376–8, noting that only nine abstract nouns of 'self-labelling' occur, and nearly all the others express humility. Only *paternitas* and *apostolatus* (in CC 82 (ed. Gundlach, p. 615)) assert a concept not just positive but (I suggest – I hope, following Hack's line of thought) authoritative.

[20] King, *Charlemagne*, p. 305.

[21] *Liber Pontificalis*, in *Le liber pontificalis*, ed. L. Duchesne, 3 vols. (Paris, 1886–1957), vol. I, *Vita Vigilii*, pp. 297–8 and *Vita Martini*, pp. 337–8. Among the 'papal archives' that preserved knowledge of these events was, from the sixth century, the *Liber Pontificalis*: cf. W. Ullmann, *The Growth of Papal Government in the Middle Ages*, 2nd edn (London, 1962), p. 262: 'the [papacy's] unparalleled advantage . . . [was] its own storehouse of ideological memory'. For shrewd comment on the *Liber Pontificalis*, inter-textuality therein and the question of audience, see P. Buc, 'Nach 754', in *Die Macht der Königs*, ed. B. Jussen (Munich, 2005), pp. 27–37, at 31–3, with notes at 371–2.

Comparable moments can be identified in the eighth century well before Hadrian's pontificate. In the early 720s, a group of officials in Rome conspired to kill Gregory II (715–31), and when that misfired, two further attempts were made, led by a patrician sent first from Constantinople and then another from Ravenna, both of which also failed.[22] Pope Paul (757–67) in CC 29 (764) wrote to King Pippin about factions in Ravenna, one consisting of those faithful to God's holy Church and to us, whose warnings the pope transmitted to Pippin, the other consisting of 'emuli sanctae Dei ecclesiae et nostri atque vestrae excellentiae [qui] die noctuque non desinant pertractandum qualiter nos, sibi Deo contrario, praevalere ac superare possint' ('enemies of the holy Church of God and of us and of Your Excellency [who] do not stop plotting day and night, with God opposing them, to defeat and overcome us').[23] Whoever drafted CC 94 had surely seen CC 29 and diagnosed a recurrence of old problems. To believe you have good evidence that certain people 'are continually studying closely day and night how to prevail over you' is to suspect a plot. Single spies can become battalions.

After CC 29, there is no datable letter from Paul until 767, his last. Then there is a gap in the sequence, and the *Life of Stephen III* in effect opens with an alarming event:

> [Pope Paul] had not yet expired when, then and there, Duke Toto, who had long lived in the city of Nepi, together with his brothers Constantine, Passibus and Paschal gathered from Nepi and other Tuscan cities a large army and a band of peasants. They entered this city of Rome through the St Pancras gate and stayed under arms in the house of Toto, and there, all of a sudden they elected Constantine, Toto's brother, still a layman. Many of them were armed and wearing breastplates, like brigands, and they brought him to the Lateran patriarchate. They came with him up to the residence of the *vicedominus*, and immediately they forced George, the

[22] *Liber Pontificalis, Vita Gregorii II*, chaps. 14–16 (ed. Duchesne, vol. I, p. 403). These arose from papally led rebellions against imperial taxation: see C. Gantner, 'The Label "Greeks" in the Papal Diplomatic Repertoire in the Eighth Century', in *Strategies of Identification*, ed. W. Pohl and G. Heydemann (Turnhout, 2013), pp. 303–49, at 310–11. Writing of the 860s, C. Wickham, 'Byzantium through Western Eyes', in *Byzantium in the Ninth Century: Dead or Alive?*, ed. L. Brubaker (Aldershot, 1998), pp. 245–56, at 253, comments, 'the only people who seem to have hated the Greeks were the Romans.'
[23] The context is sketched by Davis, *Lives of the Eighth-Century Popes*, p. 77, in his introduction to the (very brief) *Life of Paul*, whose 'single-minded selectivity' (*sic*, Davis) indicates an editing-out of papal tribulations in the 760s. See also Noble, *Republic*, pp. 104–21, esp. 109, for a (very brief) mention of CC 29, not noting Paul's specific worries about factions in Ravenna.

bishop they had sent for, to bestow on Constantine the prayer to make him a cleric.[24]

Even the briefest of cold-eyed glances at the papacy's situation between the middle and the end of the eighth century reveals a pattern of conflict and violence in Rome itself and in northern and central Italy.[25] The anxieties expressed in CC 29 (764) and the unprecedented strife of 767–8 during and after the eleven-month pontificate of the intruder Constantine, intensified by the extreme violence of Stephen III's short reign (768–72), were indeed 'wicked novelty'.[26]

Hadrian (772–95) faced recurrent faithlessness from Ravenna. In 774, he informed Charles in a letter that began without ceremony: 'News has reached us that the insolent and most arrogant Archbishop Leo spreads lies to oppose us ... and behold, something we never expected, now in your times there exist wicked and perverse men, your enemies and ours (*impii atque perversi, qui vestri nostrique existunt emuli*), attempting to remove from our power what we were seen to rule and govern in Lombard times'.[27] In 775, Hadrian was alarmed to find there were 'most abominable tricksters (*stropharii*) in this very city of Rome itself who dared to perform such deeds as have never been heard of since the beginning of the world: I am amazed that you hold in high favour men who say such words about us – such unheard-of words ... such hostile, stupid words ... We beg you to punish them on our behalf'.[28] These speakers of evil sound

---

[24] 'At vero nondum adhuc spiritum [Paulus] exalaverat. Ilico Toto quidam dux, cum suis germanis Constantino, Passibo et Paschale aggregantes tam ex eadem Nepesina quamque ex aliis Tusciae civitatibus multitudinem exercitus atque catervam rusticorum ingredientesque per portam beati Pancratii in hanc Romanam urbem, adque in domo antedicti Totoni armati adsistentes elegerunt ibidem subito Constantinum, fratrem eiusdem Totonis, laicum existentem, quem cum armis plurimi eorum loricis induti latrocinanter in Lateranensem patriarchium introduxerunt Et ascendentes cum eo in vicedominio, continuo accersito Georgio episcopo conpulerunt eum orationem clericatus eidem Constantino tribui': *Liber Pontificalis, Vita Stephani III*, chap. 3 (ed. Duchesne, vol. I, p. 468).

[25] Cf. J. Nelson, 'Carolingian Contacts', in *Mercia. An Anglo-Saxon Kingdom in Europe*, ed. M. Brown and C. Farr (London, 2001), pp. 126–43, at 136–7, à propos Offa's 'allegations': 'It was not as if the papal position had been secure previously.' There I had in mind the 'lurid light' thrown by the writer of the *Vita Stephani III*, chaps. 1–15 (ed. Duchesne, vol. I, pp. 468–70), on Roman politics in the late 760s and early 770s and the 'potential military importance' of the 'permanently manned *scholae*' (certainly not mere eighth-century versions of youth hostels) housing 'Saxons, Franks, Lombards and Frisians, right next-door to St Peter's', as well as the 'whole militia': *Vita Leonis III* (correcting my 2001 typo, 'Leo IV'), chap. 19 (ed. Duchesne, vol. II, pp. 6–7; *The Lives of the Eighth-Century Popes (Liber Pontificalis)*, trans. R. Davis (Liverpool, 2007), pp. 185–6). It would be interesting to know, in the light of chapters 11 and 12, what was the part played by the inmates of the 'Greek' monasteries of SS Stephen and Silvester and St Erasmus in these events.

[26] CC 98 and 99 (ed. Gundlach, pp. 649–50 and 650–3). *Vita Stephani III*, chaps. 3–16 and 25–32, and chap. 18 (ed. Duchesne, vol. I, pp. 468–73, 475 and 477–80; trans. Davis, pp. 88–9, 90–6, 101–6, and 98 (for 'unholy novelty')).

[27] CC 49 (ed. Gundlach, p. 568). See further Nelson, 'Charlemagne and Ravenna', p. 243.

[28] CC 51 (775) (ed. Gundlach, p. 573).

more like influential Romans than mere 'scoundrels', such was the anxiety aroused in Hadrian by the words they uttered at Charles' court.

Later that year Hadrian wrote to tell Charles that *missi* of dukes Arichis of Benevento, Rodgaud of Friuli and Reginbald of Chiusi were in Spoleto with Duke Hildebrand

> laying a pernicious plot (*perniciosum consilium*) against us, and how this coming March [776] they would join forces with a band of Greeks and with Adelchis son of Desiderius and rush upon us by land and sea to fight us, and intended to invade this our city of Rome and to strip bare all the churches of God and steal the chalice of St Peter, your patron, and take us away – may the Divinity forbid! – as their captive, and restore a king of the Lombards and oppose your royal power.[29]

An invasion of Rome with such consequences was a nightmare the letter's sender wanted to share with its receiver. Not long after Hadrian sent off this letter, Rotgaud of Friuli rebelled against Charles, who crushed the revolt in a lightning midwinter campaign – and the nightmare faded. Already late in 775, the year of Constantine V's death, Hadrian had begun to issue his own coins and charters, adopting imperial privileges and signs of honour to signal his withdrawal from imperial authority, in effect a declaration of independence from Constantinople.[30] Desperation is not easily squared with hard-headed acts of political pragmatism. Did Hadrian choose (surely not delegating to a 'writing-office hack') this histrionic tone because he was 'essentially trying to *incite* panic' (italics added)?[31] Or had he been gripped by 'almost irrational phobia of the Greeks'?[32] Perhaps both impressions are 'right' in the sense of 'plausible'. Papal rhetoric had – and for modern historians still has – a lot to answer for. Perhaps it was a case of oscillating moods. In December 775, on a bad day, a plot seemed real enough to Hadrian.

Looking back from the 780s, then, Hadrian saw more than one plot, and Anglo-Saxon high-born and not-so-high-born visitors to Rome – *missi*, pilgrims, relic seekers, retirees – picked up rumours of plots. In explaining CC 92, Anglo-Saxonist historians had and have good reasons to link two

---

[29] 'Adibentes adversus nos perniciosum consilium: qualiter … proximo Martio mensae adveniente utrosque se in unum conglobent cum caterva Graecorum et Athalgihs Desiderii filium et terrae marique ad dimicandum super nos irruant, cupientes hanc nostram Romanam invadere civitatem et cunctas Dei ecclesias denudare atque ciborium fautoris vestri, beati Petri, abstollere vel nosmet ipsos, quod avertat divinitas, captivos deducere nec non Langobardorum regem redintegrare et vestrae regali potentiae resistere': CC 57, (ed. Gundlach, p. 582).

[30] See further CC 63 (776×780) (ed. Gundlach, p. 590), reports the blinding of Bishop Maurice of Istria by *nefandissimi Greci*. CC 64 (779×780) reports 'nefandissimi Neapolitani una cum Deo odibiles Grecos' invading Terracina on the advice of Duke Arichis and the patrician of Sicily.

[31] Gantner, 'The Label "Greeks"', pp. 331–2.   [32] Hartmann, *Hadrian*, p. 172. Cf. n. 22, above.

apparently rather distant things: Offa's frustration at papal delay in settling ecclesiastical/political affairs in Kent and in Mercia and Offa's thoughts of unsettling Hadrian in Rome to the extent of deposing him. Such thoughts were evidently not unthinkable. But the Anglo-Saxon connexion could be regarded as an unusual or eccentric instance – because emanating from England – of something *not* unusual, namely, enemies of the pope nearer home. Similarly, looking back from the early 790s to the 780s, the pope and his advisers could recall serious threats, from Beneventans and assorted city dwellers in Campania and in the north-east from Ravenna and its environs, as well as rumbles from Byzantium.

In 781, Charlemagne, with Hadrian's very active co-operation, re-created a kingdom of Italy. By 787–8, they were struggling to establish its southern limits in circumstances that turned very dangerous, especially as cracks in their apparently united front began to appear.[33] Alarm bells rang again in CC 94, 790/1, when Hadrian's nectar-sweet assurances thinly smeared over acute anxiety about enemies in Ravenna.[34] Only after Hadrian's death did there occur another outbreak of horrific disruption in Rome: the attempted assassination, which turned into a botched mutilation, of Hadrian's successor Leo III in broad daylight in the public street in the course of a great procession.[35] The date was 25 April 799. No wonder the king had bad dreams about it.[36] No wonder that the backlash took Charlemagne two years and his own imperial coronation to settle.[37] The factional politics that lay behind this and the appalling violence involved were familiar in great cities across the Mediterranean world.[38] What shocked contemporaries in Rome and far beyond Rome was the realisation

---

[33] See Hartmann, *Hadrian*, pp. 248–9. Cf. Nelson, 'The Mission of Meginar', forthcoming.

[34] See above, with n. 16.

[35] *Liber Pontificalis, Vita Leonis III*, chaps. 11 and 12 (ed. Duchesne, vol. II, pp. 4–5).

[36] Anon., *Karolus Magnus et Leo Papa* (also known as 'The Paderborn Epic'), in *MGH Poetae Latinae I*, ed. E. Dümmler (Berlin, 1881), pp. 366–84, at lines 326–34 and lines 344–99; see J. Nelson, 'England and the Continent in the Ninth Century, IV, Bodies and Minds', *TRHS*, 6th series, 15 (2005), 1–28, at 7–10.

[37] J. L. Nelson, 'Um 801', in *Die Macht der Königs*, ed. Jussen, pp. 38–54, with nn. 372–3. (an English version of this paper can be found in J. L. Nelson, *Courts, Elites and Gendered Power* (Aldershot, 2008), chap. XII).

[38] For other instances in Rome, see *Annales regni Francorum* s. a. 823, p. 161, where Church officials were blinded and beheaded, and in the same year, at Hadrianople, where Thomas the Slav suffered amputation of both hands, Theophanes Continuatus 2, 19, ed. C. de Boor (Bonn, 1883–5), vol. I, pp. 11–16 and 69. See M. McCormick, *Eternal Victory. Triumphal Rulership in Late Antiquity, Byzantium and the Early Medieval West* (Cambridge, 1986), pp. 144–6; and also, for a characteristically sharp sense of the role of rumour and rumoured violence and constructions of east-west difference, see C. Wickham, 'Ninth-Century Byzantium through Western Eyes', in *Byzantium in the Ninth Century*, ed. Brubaker, pp. 245–56, though not dealing with the specifics of ritual violence and humiliation, perhaps because those no longer differentiated the two cultures. For thoughtful comments on blinding, see G. Bührer-Thierry, '"Just Anger" or "Vengeful Anger"? The Punishment of Blinding in the Early Medieval West', in *Anger's Past*, ed. B. Rosenwein (Ithaca, NY, 1998), pp. 75–91.

that the deposition of a pope was not merely thinkable but practicable. Behind this lay more than an urban riot. There was a plot, and the plotters, that is, the would-be assassins, included two of Hadrian's nephews.[39]

In light of these symptoms of endemic political violence and instability in the second half of the eighth century, I want finally to return to CC 92. Basic questions of date and intent are easier to deal with in the context of the *longue durée* – twenty-three years – during which Charlemagne and Hadrian co-existed in what Florian Hartmann called 'Kooperation im Konflikt', or what Karl Leyser (metaphorically speaking and in another context) called 'an uneasy side-by-side'.[40] As noted earlier in this chapter, Bullough thought (and Brooks accepted) that CC 92 might well be dated a bit later than 784/5, which could fit with Story's suggestion that it was behind the mission of the legates Bishop George of Ostia and Amiens and Bishop Theophylact of Todi (near Spoleto) to England in 786.[41] Charlemagne's decision in that same year to make a third visit to Rome was put into effect in 787. This was a critical year even for a reign full of 'one goddamn crisis after another'.[42] Relations between Charlemagne and the Empress Eirene had been harmonious since 781 when Charlemagne's daughter was betrothed to Eirene's son. In 787, the agreement went sour: Eirene held a great council in Nicaea to which papal legates had been invited (and were eventually sent) but no Franks – a mighty snub; Charlemagne arrived at Rome (?in January); then he went to Capua wielding a big stick in the direction of Byzantine envoys and broke off the betrothal plan; then he went to Benevento, took Beneventan hostages and returned with them to Rome, where Bavarian envoys had been busy over the winter trying, unsuccessfully, to get Hadrian to mediate between Duke Tassilo and Charlemagne. Charlemagne had demonstrated his power to the pope, and the pope had disappointed the king on all fronts. Sights now firmly set on a Bavarian showdown, the king left Rome soon after Easter (8 April) and headed for home – via Ravenna, a place he had never previously visited.[43]

---

[39] CC 61 (ed. Gundlach, p. 589); see Hack, *Codex Carolinus*, vol. I, pp. 540–2, 646; *Vita Leonis III*, chap. 11 (ed. Duchesne, vol. II, p. 4). For Greek monasteries in Rome, see Gantner, 'The Label "Greeks"', pp. 317–18. Could these communities have escaped political involvement?

[40] Hartmann, *Hadrian*, pp. 197–265; K. Leyser, *Rule and Conflict in an Early Medieval Society* (London 1979), p. 98, writing about the relationship between 'royal sacrosanctity and the kings' year-in, year-out dealings with the aristocracy'.

[41] Story, *Carolingian Connections*, p. 57, notes that both these bishops had Greek names and that 786 was the year in which Charlemagne decided to make a third visit to Rome.

[42] Nelson, 'Making a Difference in Eighth-Century Politics: The Daughters of Desiderius', in *After Rome's Fall: Narrators and Sources of Early Medieval History. Essays presented to Walter Goffart*, ed. A. C. Murray (Toronto, 1998), pp. 171–90, at 172.

[43] In two previous papers on CC 81, cited in n. 46, below, I failed to spot the significance of Charlemagne's stay at Ravenna and its timing – *mea culpa*.

It is impossible to visit Ravenna without feeling inspired. From Ravenna Charlemagne sent a letter with contents inferable from CC 81 and classed by Hack as Deperditum 43.[44] He 'requested' authorisation from Hadrian to remove marbles and columns and other artistic materials from Ravenna (perhaps from Theoderic's palace itself), and it looks very much as if he had had the idea of installing them at the new palace he now planned at Aachen.[45] With the letter went gifts to the pope: two horses. What might have looked like a perfect gift exchange on close inspection turns out to be something quite different. In CC 81, Hadrian complained that one of the horses had died before getting to Rome, and the other was no more than 'usable'. What the pope had expected, naturally, were 'very famous horses', the best of their kind, which would have been an appropriate gift. What Charlemagne had sent was a calculated insult to show his displeasure.[46] He surely never doubted that he would get his marbles and columns. Relations between Charles and Hadrian were difficult in 787–8 and only improved after careful repair work chiefly on the pope's part.

If that one-horse gift meant what it said and was understood as the donor intended, for it could hardly have been 'read' otherwise, it seems to me a plausible context for another crack of the whip from Charlemagne. This was a threat. It was the plot described and vehemently disclaimed and denied in Deperditum 49, as retrieved from CC 92, and datable to 787. Every court is a forcing house for rumour–or filthy assertions. In 787, Charlemagne and Offa each had their own reasons for applying concerted judicious pressure where the pope was concerned. Was there a plot – or unheard-of deceit? The very *rumour* of such a plot, with the added oxygen of vociferous denial, as another form of insult, was enough to contribute helpfully to bringing Hadrian into a more co-operative and realistic frame of mind.[47]

---

[44] Hack, *Codex Carolinus*, vol. II, Deperditum 43, p. 970; see further, pp. 840–3, 853–6.

[45] R. Schieffer, 'Karl der Große laßt sich in Aachen nieder', in *Karl der Grosse und sein Nachwirken*, ed. P. Butzer, M. Kerner and W. Oberschelp (Turnhout, 1997), pp. 3–22, at 13–14; and see now H. Müller et al., 'Pfalz und *vicus*. Aachen in karolingischer Zeit', in *Aachen. Von den Anfängen bis zur Gegenwart*, 2, *Karolinger, Ottonen, Salier, 765–1137* ed. T. R. Kraus (Aachen, 2013), pp. 1–408, at 144.

[46] J. L. Nelson, 'The Setting of the Gift', in *The Languages of Gift in the Early Middle Ages*, ed. W. Davies and P. Fouracre (Cambridge, 2010), pp. 116–48, at 134–8; see further J. L. Nelson, 'The Role of the Gift in Early Medieval Diplomatic Relations', *Le Relazioni Internazionali nell'alto medioevo. Settimane di Studio della Fondazione Centro Italiano di Studi sull'alto medioevo* LVIII (2011), 225–53, at 244–8. By the time I wrote this, I had (a) remedied my ignorance of Hack's work (another *mea culpa* is in order), (b) been surprised to find that other scholars had not picked up Hack's perception (or indeed mine) of the deliberate insult entailed in Charlemagne's gift, and (c) thought more about why Charlemagne had been cross in 787.

[47] This change of mind in 788 is evident in the comments (though without direct mention of CC 84) of Hartmann, *Hadrian*, pp. 248–9: a realistic reassessment impelled Hadrian to accept what Hartmann nicely judges the more or less contemporaneous 'double snub' of Charlemagne's strategic treatment of Grimoald (sending him back to rule Benevento directly

This dating hypothesis is, to be sure, not the only possible one. CC 92 could fit earlier – and it could also fit later, in the early 790s, for instance. By then, though, the relationship between Charlemagne and Hadrian had grown more distant. By then, Charlemagne was preoccupied with planning and staging the integration of Bavaria into his much-expanded realm, a process that caused more difficulty than he might well have expected, and was rethinking priorities that now included dealing with Adoptionist heresy.[48] The *Libri Carolini* were written and safely put to bed for a long sleep.[49] A start had been made on the building of Aachen.[50] The CC was compiled, and also the first part of the *Annales regni Francorum.*[51]

But, in 787–8, what Charlemagne had got a firm hold on was a new ruling style. He was on the way to establishing a new kind of understanding with Hadrian: a new entente, not warm, but based on a cool appraisal by both parties of a relationship that would always be difficult. A rose-tinted story of cordiality and closeness between pope and king is now being given an overdue review.[52] In the early 790s, an edgy co-operation had become workable because both these men understood their own and each other's intentions – and limits. In Italy, Charlemagne and Hadrian had each recognised how far they could go. Plots had not ceased; indeed, the most dangerous for Charlemagne was yet to come, in the shape of his eldest son's revolt in Bavaria and, after Hadrian's death, so was the most dangerous for the eighth-century papacy, in the shape of the attack on Hadrian's successor in Rome. Where the Anglo-Saxons were concerned, entries in the *Liber Vitae* of Brescia as well as in the *Liber Pontificalis* can be seen, thanks not

---

against Hadrian's wishes) and his ruthless treatment of Tassilo's son (and Hadrian's godson) Theodo (consigned to a monastic prison for good).

[48] See J. Nelson, 'Staging the Integration of Bavaria', in *Neue Wege der Frühmittelalterforschung. FS Herwig Wolfram*, ed. M. Diesenberger and B. Zeller (Vienna, forthcoming).

[49] The *Libri Carolini*, also known as the *Opus Caroli regis contra synodum*, was a massive treatise largely written by Theodulf of Orleans against what was regarded at Charlemagne's court as the Greeks' errors over the veneration of icons. See the fine edition by Ann Freeman in *MGH Concilia II, Supplementum I* (Hannover, 1998). The eighty-eight-page German introduction to the edition is now published in English: A Freeman, *Theodulf of Orléans: Charlemagne's Spokesman against the Second Council of Nicaea* (Aldershot, 2003), chap. I.

[50] Müller, in *Aachen*, ed. Kraus (as above, n. 45), pp. 50–65.

[51] On the *Codex Carolinus*, see Hack, *Codex Carolinus*, vol. I, pp. 78–82; for the *Annales regni Francorum*, see M. Becher, *Eid und Herrschaft* (Sigmaringen, 1993), pp. 74–7; R. McKitterick, *Charlemagne. The Formation of a European Identity* (Cambridge, 2008), pp. 31–8, 48; and Bullough, '*Aula renovata*', pp. 142–6, points out the conjuncture of these startling initiatives.

[52] The work of Hack and Hartmann, in particular, has entailed some reassessment of the views of Noble and others. The rhetoric of letters is matched by that of epitaphs (not least Hadrian's): these are codes to be appreciated as powerful ideological statements yet approached critically and with large pinches of salt.

least to Simon Keynes, to show Continental connections continuing and becoming more regular, though with timing contingent on political exigencies at home and abroad.[53] To return, finally, to my title as a homespun English colloquialism is to answer the question in it with a firm 'No!'. Charlemagne and Offa hadn't lost the plot, nor, *mutatis mutandis*, had Hadrian.

[53] S. Keynes, 'Anglo-Saxon Entries in the *Liber Vitae* of Brescia', in *Alfred the Wise: Studies in Honour of Janet Bately*, ed. J. Roberts and J. L. Nelson, with M. Godden (Cambridge, 1998), pp. 99–119; and see now R. Naismith and F. Tinti, *The Forum Hoard of Anglo-Saxon Coins* (Rome, 2016).

PART II

Authority and Its Articulation in Late Anglo-Saxon England

CHAPTER 7

Fathers and Daughters:
The Case of Æthelred II

Pauline Stafford

When Simon – and I – first began working on Æthelred, over forty years ago, study of the king's family, and its importance in politics, was, to say the least, thin. That situation is, thankfully, now long past, and Simon's own work has played its part in that change. In his account of Æthelred's reign, Simon saw family as a group to which the king could and did turn for support in the 990s.[1] More recently, he has studied the sons of the king, the æthelings Alfred and Edward, and Æthelred's older brother, Edward the Martyr.[2] This chapter aims to supplement that work by considering a group of family members long ignored: the daughters of Æthelred. Simon himself referred to them – or some of them – and, typically, made careful note of a reference to them we might easily overlook, in the negotiations between Richard I of Rouen/Normandy and Æthelred.[3] These are women about whom we know very little that is firm and certain. Yet daughters have recently been shown to be family members who repay more attention.[4] In offering this chapter to Simon, I hope to throw

---

[1] S. Keynes, *The Diplomas of King Æthelred 'the Unready': A Study in Their Use as Historical Evidence* (Cambridge, 1980), p. 187.

[2] S. Keynes, 'The Æthelings in Normandy', *ANS* 13 (1991), 173–205; S. Keynes, 'The Cult of King Edward the Martyr during the Reign of Æthelred the Unready', in *Gender and Historiography. Studies in the Earlier Middle Ages in Honour of Pauline Stafford*, ed. J. L. Nelson, S. Reynolds and S. M. Johns (London, 2012), pp. 115–25.

[3] Keynes, *Diplomas*, p. 186, n. 116.

[4] Thus J. L. Nelson, 'Making a Difference in Eighth-Century Politics: The Daughters of Desiderius', in *After Rome's Fall: Narrators and Sources of Early Medieval History. Essays Presented to Walter Goffart*, ed. A. Murray (Toronto, 1998), pp. 171–90, reprinted in her *Courts, Elites and Gendered Power in the Early Middle Ages* (Aldershot, 2007), chap. X; J. L. Nelson, 'Women at the Court of Charlemagne: A Case of Monstrous Regiment?', in *Medieval Queenship*, ed. J. C. Parsons (New York, 1993), pp. 43–61, reprinted in her *The Frankish World, 750–900* (London, 1996), pp. 223–42; E. van Houts, 'The Echo of the Conquest in the Latin Sources: Duchess Mathilda, Her Daughters and the Enigma of the Golden Child', in *The Bayeux Tapestry: Embroidering the Facts of History*, ed. P. Bouet, B. Levy and F. Neveux (Caen, 2004), pp. 135–53; E. van Houts, 'Edward and Normandy', in *Edward the Confessor. The Man and the Legend*, ed. R. Mortimer (Woodbridge, Boydell, 2009), pp. 63–76; and S. MacLean, 'Making a Difference in Tenth-Century Politics: King Athelstan's Sisters and Frankish Queenship', in *Frankland. The Franks and the World of the Early Middle Ages. Essays in Honour of Dame Jinty Nelson*, ed. P. Fouracre and D. Ganz (Manchester, 2008), pp. 167–90.

a little more light on the politics of the reign of Æthelred, a subject that Simon's own work has so magnificently illuminated.

Identifying the Daughters of Æthelred

The daughters of Æthelred are an extremely elusive group. Women in general are under-represented in early medieval sources. Even at the level of royal dynasties, daughters are difficult women to identify and follow.[5] Janet Nelson has characterised the methodology of research on the court where such women were active as looking for 'unconsidered trifles' and then snapping them up.[6] In the case of the daughters of Æthelred, this can seem more like 'clutching at straws' and then trying to build a house out of them. Even the most basic facts are disputable.

Æthelred appears to have had five daughters, with two, if not three, different women. We are on safest ground with Godgifu/Goda, probably the youngest of them. She was the king's daughter with Emma of Normandy, who was married consecutively to Drogo of Mantes (7 April 1024) and Eustace II of Boulogne (probably 1036).[7] Four others can be identified, with more or less certainty: Ælfgifu, who was married to Uhtred of Bamburgh, the semi-independent ruler of the North; Eadgyth/Edith, who married Eadric Streona, Æthelred's appointee as ealdorman of Mercia; a third, perhaps named Ælfthryth, who was abbess of Wherwell in the reign of Edward the Confessor; and, most shadowy of all, *perhaps* a fourth daughter, Wulfhild, who perhaps married Ulfcytel of East Anglia and possibly also Thorkell, his successor as local ruler of East Anglia under Cnut.

Ælfgifu and Eadgyth, if not Wulfhild and the abbess, were probably daughters of Æthelred's first or second unions, that is, those before his marriage to the Norman Emma.[8] The husbands identified for these three

---

[5] See R. Schieffer, 'Karolingische Töchter', in *Herrschaft, Kirche, Kultur. Beiträge zur Geschichte des Mittelalters. Festschrift für Friedrich Prinz*, ed. G. Jenal and S. Haarländer (Stuttgart, 1993), pp. 125–139, comments and figures at p. 138 and n. 101 – 229 men to 130 women have been identified by Werner among Charlemagne's descendants (K. Werner, 'Die Nachkommen Karls des Grossen bis um das Jahr 1000 (1.–8. Generation)', in *Karls des Grossen Lebenswerk und Nachleben*, IV, ed. W. Braunfels (Düsseldorf, 1967), pp. 403–82).

[6] J. L. Nelson, 'Gendering Courts in the Early Medieval West', in *Gender in the Early Medieval World, East and West, 300–900*, ed. L. Brubaker and J. M. H. Smith (Cambridge, 2004), pp. 185–97, at 196.

[7] E. van Houts' discussion, 'Edward and Normandy', especially at pp. 63–8, replaces all earlier ones.

[8] The argument here would depend on age at marriage – taking the minimum as twelve – and the dating of the marriage to Emma to (late?) 1002. A daughter of Æthelred and Emma could not have been of marriageable age before 1015. All three marriages *could* belong as late as 1014–16, the very last years of the reign. The abbess could be a daughter of Emma and Cnut (see below). *ASC* MS E calls her Edward's sister; *if* Ælfthryth was her name, she is perhaps more likely a daughter of Æthelred.

married women were dead by the end of 1016/7. Emma and Æthelred were married by 1002: Edward was born by 1005.[9] It is more or less a physical impossibility for Æthelred and Emma to have produced three daughters who would all have been of marriageable age – assuming a minimum age at marriage of twelve – before 1016. It is possible that the abbess of Wherwell was a daughter of Emma and Æthelred, though we cannot completely rule out the possibility that she was a daughter of Emma and Cnut.[10]

'Probably', 'possibly', 'perhaps': everything about these women is hedged with uncertainty. What little we know of them is largely from later sources, including some very debatable ones. Only two of these five women are known from more or less contemporary evidence, none of it from Æthelred's reign itself. The briefest comment in *Anglo-Saxon Chronicle* MSS D and E, in the annal for 1051, identifies an unnamed abbess of Wherwell as a sister of Edward.[11] The first English reference to Godgifu comes from Domesday Book, 1086.[12] The Durham tract *De Obsessione Dunelmi*, along with another certainly twelfth-century, possibly Durham, document,[13] gives the name of Ælfgifu and tells of her marriage.

---

[9] Keynes, 'Edward the Ætheling (*c*. 1005–16)', in *Edward the Confessor*, ed. Mortimer, pp. 41–62, at 41–4, for most recent consideration.

[10] At the time of the Wherwell charter granted in 1002, S 904, Heanflæd was abbess. There is no named abbess in Domesday Book. The next list of abbesses comes from the La Trinité, Caen mortuary roll for Mathilda, daughter of William I: L. Delisle, *Rouleaux des Morts du IXe au XVe siècle*, Société de l'histoire de France (Paris, 1866), p. 188. Three abbesses are named there – Ælstrita, Matilda and Alberada. The latter two are likely post-Conquest and were both dead by 1113, when the mortuary roll was put together. Ælstrita is very likely a version of Ælfthryth – with 's' as a misreading of 'f'. Both Ælfdrida and Alftred occur as Latin versions of this name; see E. Okasha, *Women's Names in Old English* (Farnham, 2011), p. 20. No other latinisations of Old English women's names approximate to this. Ælfthryth is thus a candidate for the name of the last pre-1066 abbess and, more tentatively, for the daughter of Æthelred who was abbess in 1051. The likelihood that they were one and the same is increased by the fact that this was the name of Æthelred's mother, foundress of Wherwell. The date of the Wherwell charter – granting substantial land to the abbey, including *Æthelingadene*, which is land onomastically connected to the royal children – is a likely date of her entry. This would make her a daughter of one of the king's first marriages. It is, however, possible that 1008, when more land was given and a note added to the charter, is the relevant date – which opens up wider possibilities for her as a daughter of Æthelred and Emma.

[11] When Edward's wife was sent to his sister (*ASC* MS E), the abbess (*ASC* MS D), 'at Wherwell'. Both references may be as early as mid-eleventh century, though the chronicles as we now have them are both later than this.

[12] GDB I, fol. 34r, 'Terra Æcclæ de Lanchei [Lambeth]. S Maria manerium est quod Lanchei vocatur. Goda \comitissa/ tenuit soror R[egis] E[dwardi]'.

[13] *De Obsessione Dunelmi*, in *Symeonis Monachi Opera Omnia*, ed. T Arnold, RS 51 and 75, 2 vols. (London, 1882–5), vol. I, p. 216 ('Ucthredo, proficiente magis et magis in re militari, rex Ethelredus filiam suam Elfgivam ei copulavit uxorem'). *De primo Saxonum Adventu* also has (less) detail of this marriage – Ealdred was a son of Uhtred 'ex filia Alduni episcopi antequam duceret filiam regis Eathelredi', in *ibid.*, vol. II, p. 383. The dating of *De Obsessione* is disputed. Morris places it either in the 1070s or, more likely, 1110–1120: thus C. Morris, *Marriage and Murder in Eleventh-Century Northumbria. A Study of De Obsessione Dunelmi*, Borthwick Papers 82 (York, 1992), pp. 9–10.

De Obsessione may be as early as the mid-1070s. Eadgyth, wife of Eadric, first appears in the early twelfth-century Anglo-Norman chronicle of John of Worcester.[14] For the fifth, the shadowy Wulfhild, we have to turn to what has been called the supplement to the notorious Jomsviking saga in Flateyjarbok.[15]

Tenth-Century English Royal Daughters

This evidentiary deficit is far from confined to the daughters of Æthelred; it is a general situation applying to daughters (and thus sisters) of early English kings. Surviving pre-1066 sources say virtually nothing about *any* female members of the tenth- and eleventh-century royal house. Were it not for the prologue to Æthelweard's Latin translation of an *Anglo-Saxon Chronicle*, we would know of only six tenth-century royal daughters or sisters from early English sources and the names of only four of them.[16]

B. Meehan, 'Outsiders, Insiders and Property at Durham around 1100', *Studies in Church History* 12 (1975), 47–52, argues for a late-eleventh-century date; and C. Morris, 'The Siege of Durham, the Battle of Carham and the Cession of Lothian', *Scottish Historical Review* 55 (1976), 1–19, at 19, narrows this to 1073–6. K.-U. Jäschke, 'Remarks on Datings in the *Libellus de exordio atque procursu istius hoc est Dunhelmensis ecclesie*', in *Symeon of Durham, Historian of Durham and the North*, ed. D. Rollason (Stamford, 1998), pp. 46–60, at 47 and n. 8, accepts Meehan's dating to the mid-1070s. Morris acknowledges that it may be using a later eleventh-century source. The comments of *De Primo Adventu Saxonum* about sons of another wife do not match simply with those in *De Obsessione*, and the one may not be straightforwardly a source of the other. The *Historia Regum*, heavily dependent on John of Worcester for some sections, has the marriage of Eadric (see next note), more or less as John, but nothing on Uhtred (*Symeonis Monachi*, ed. Arnold, vol. II, p. 141).

[14] 'Gener eius habuit enim in coniugio filiam eius Edgitham': John of Worcester, *Chronicon, s.a.* 1031 (*recte* 1009), in *The Chronicle of John of Worcester*, ed. R. R. Darlington and P. McGurk, 2 vols. (Oxford, 1995–8), vol. II, pp. 462–4.

[15] *Encomium Emmae Reginae*, ed. A. Campbell, Royal Historical Society, Camden Series 3, 72 (London, 1949), p. 93. Campbell (pp. 87–91) traces sources of this to what is perhaps the oldest saga of Olaf the Holy (Helgi), but he is very sceptical of the veracity of these 'unsupported' statements, including that on Wulfhild/Ulfhildr. The situation is confused by John of Worcester's identification, *s.a.* 1021/1043, of Thorkell's wife as Edith. This was the name of the widow of Eadric, although John does not identify her as such. It could be argued that both Northern and Worcester tradition identified the wife of Thorkell as one of Æthelred's daughters. The situation is complicated yet further by reference to the king's *aðum* in *ASC* MS CDE, 1010, who died in Cambridgeshire. *Aðum* usually translates as 'son-in-law': see, for example, Ælfric's grammar where it translates *gener* (*Ælfrics Grammatik und Glossar*, ed. J. Zupitza (Berlin, 1880), p. 300). In *ASC* MS E, 1091, it means 'brother-in-law'; and *EHD*, p. 243, n. 4, gives the alternative 'son-in-law'. If the reference is to a son-in-law of the king, then a daughter would have been married to a leading man involved in a local battle in East Anglia – also Ulfcytel's area of activity. Marriage to three consecutive local leaders in East Anglia is not impossible. See also S. Keynes, 'Cnut's Earls', in *The Reign of Cnut, King of England and Norway*, ed. A. Rumble (London, 1994), pp. 43–88, at 56, n. 67.

[16] (1) Eadgyth, daughter of Edward Elder, unnamed but referred to in *ASC* MS D, 924, and MS C, 982, again unnamed; (2) an unnamed sister of Æthelstan and thus very likely daughter of Edward, given to Sihtric *ASC* MS D, 925; (3) Eadgyth/Edith, named as 'sister of our king Æthelred' (*The Liber Vitae of the New Minster and Hyde Abbey, Winchester*, ed. S Keynes (Copenhagen, 1996), fol. 26r);

Three of these named ones are nuns or abbesses.[17] Only Ælfwyn, daughter of Æthelflæd and Æthelred of Mercia, and the two daughters of Edward/ sisters of Æthelstan who married Otto I and Sihtric of York, appear in the vernacular chronicles – all unnamed. Ælfwyn alone is recorded in the witness-lists of charters, though Eadburh, daughter of Edward the Elder, is a grantee of a charter of her brother Æthelstan.[18]

Æthelweard's prologue is our best source on tenth-century royal daughters.[19] He lists and names not only the daughter of Alfred married to Baldwin of Flanders – and her sons and daughters – but also gives details of four daughters of Edward the Elder who made continental European marriages, naming three of them. It is no coincidence that Æthelweard is also one of our very few lay aristocratic authors. He was writing, again unusually, to a kinswoman about their common ancestors. Abbess Mathilda of Essen, granddaughter of Eadgyth, one of Edward's daughters, was the recipient of Æthelweard's text. She may well have been his source for some of this detail.[20]

Both authorship and audience affected Æthelweard's content. So, too, did genre. The information about daughters/sisters is in his Latin prologue-cum-letter, *not* in his Latin translation of the vernacular chronicle. This is an interesting inversion of the situation in early English documents

(4) Eadgifu, abbess of Nunnaminster, 'the king's daughter' (S 1449 (BCS 1163; *Anglo-Saxon Charters*, ed. and trans. A. J. Robertson (Cambridge, 1939), pp. 102–5 (no. 49)), disputed as a daughter of Edgar by Robertson, p. 348; by A. Rumble in his new edition of this charter (A. R. Rumble, *Property and Piety in Early Medieval Winchester*, Winchester Studies 4. iii (Oxford, 2002), p. 142, n. 16); and by B. Yorke ('The Women in Edgar's Life', in *Edgar King of the English, 959–975: New Interpretations*, ed. D. Scragg (Woodbridge, 2008), pp. 143–57, at 145, n. 17); (5) Eadburga 'sister' is the named recipient of a charter of Æthelstan (S 446 (BCS 742)). (6) Ælfwyn, daughter of Æthelflæd and Æthelred of Mercia, should be included in this list. She is mentioned, unnamed, in *ASC* MSS BC in the 'Mercian Register' section, 919. For a royal daughter, she appears remarkably often in charters – S 1280 (BCS 608), where she is named in a three-life lease; S 225 (*Abing* 20), where the first witness to a charter of her mother is Ælfwyn 'episcopus' likely a later error in transmission; and S 367 (*CantCC* 101), where an 'Ælfwyn' without any title appears in the witness-list. Other witnesses without titles are her father and mother and an Æthelweard, most likely the youngest son of King Alfred, and Osferth – whose name recalls Osburh Alfred's mother and who is a candidate for a close grand-maternal relative.

[17] Arguably, Edith of Polesworth might be added, named in the list of saints' resting places (D. W. Rollason, 'Lists of Saints' Resting-Places in Anglo-Saxon England', *ASE* 7 (1978), 61–93, at 63 and 90), but she is not identified there as a royal daughter.

[18] S 446 (BCS 742); see MacLean, 'Making a Difference', esp. pp. 177–8, on the possible significance of this charter and this sister.

[19] Æthelweard, *Chronicon*, Prologue, in *The Chronicle of Æthelweard*, ed. A. Campbell (London and Edinburgh, 1962), p. 2.

[20] See more discussion in P. Stafford, 'Gender and the Gift of Women', in *Italy and Early Medieval Europe: Essays Presented to Chris Wickham*, ed. P. Skinner, J. Barrow and R. Balzaretti (Oxford, forthcoming).

concerning landholding, where Latin charters have very little on women
and family and vernacular documents far more. As this difference suggests,
the circumstances of production, purpose and use of documents affect the
details they preserve – as does later transmission and the editing that could
involve. Ælfwyn, one of the few women in the Latin charters, was so rare a
witness *qua* daughter that a later Abingdon cartularist transformed her into
a bishop! Unlike the vernacular wills and dispute records, the vernacular
chronicles, one of which Æthelweard was using, rarely mention women.
The generic traditions of these chronicles exercised a strong hold across the
two centuries or so of their development.[21] Genres and their traditions
exert their own power. Æthelweard included his family detail in his
prologue, which is cast partly in letter form; when translating and adapting
a vernacular chronicle, he followed his source, thus sharing the reticence on
women that characterises all the vernacular chronicles.

Much of what we know about Æthelred's daughters derives from post-
Conquest and later sources. After 1066, there was obviously an effort to
recover and preserve English history.[22] In that desire to capture and
chronicle the pre-1066 past, more women were included. But post-1066
chroniclers faced some of our evidence problems. They clearly found it
much easier to get information on nuns or abbesses; laywomen, daughters
who married, were already much harder to trace. It should be noted that
Worcester and Durham are our major sources of information on these
women. This is no surprise in one sense; both were great centres of
historical writing after 1066. But their information on these women may
be more than a mere reflex of their historical interests. The question of
which women were remembered, where and when, is one to which we
must return.

A review of the evidence reveals significant factors affecting remem-
brance and underlines its paucity. Much has likely been lost. We may lack a
full picture, even a full complement, especially of married daughters or
women other than nuns and saints. Even allowing for the fact that Kings
Æthelstan, Eadred and Edward the Martyr never apparently married and
that Edgar, if not also Edmund, died in their thirties, we cannot be sure
that there were not more royal daughters of whom we know nothing. This
affects all our analysis, but it is an especial concern when trying to establish

[21] See P. Stafford, 'Noting Relations and Tracking Relationships in English Vernacular Chronicles,
Late Ninth to Early Twelfth Century', *Medieval Chronicle* 10 (2016), 23–48.
[22] From a growing literature, H. Thomas, *The English and the Normans. Ethnic Hostility, Assimilation
and Identity 1066–c. 1220* (Oxford, 2003); and A. Williams, *The English and the Norman Conquest*
(Woodbridge, 1995), are now the essential starting points.

patterns and comparisons. What follows must thus be heavily caveated. But exploration of patterns and comparison is essential if we are to interpret Æthelred's daughters.

Æthelred appears unusual. Three (probably four) of his five identifiable daughters married, and one became a nun. In at least two, if not three, cases, decisions as to the daughters' fates were made by their father, Æthelred himself, before his death. Godgifu, as we shall see, was given in marriage after his death. Those two, if not three, decisions all involved gifts of his daughters to his own great nobles. This contrasts markedly with what we know of his ancestors since Alfred, if not before.[23]

Edward the Elder and Edgar both had daughters who entered convents, as did Alfred.[24] But only Edward and Alfred had daughters whom we know were given in marriage. Alfred gave a daughter to the count of Flanders.[25] Five daughters of Edward the Elder were given as brides – again, all outside the kingdom of the English; the short-lived union of one of them with the

---

[23] This chapter does not consider evidence from before the time of Alfred, but it should be noted that Alfred's only known sister, Æthelswith, was given by her father to the king of the Mercians, Burgred (*ASC* MS A, 853, named 888). However, the West Saxon royal family history of the ninth century had been heavily edited during Alfred's reign if not after – see P. Stafford, 'Succession and Inheritance: A Gendered Perspective on Alfred's Family History', in *Alfred the Great: Papers from the Eleventh-Centenary Conferences*, ed. T. Reuter (Aldershot, 2003), pp. 251–64, reprinted in P. Stafford, *Gender, Family and the Legitimation of Power. England from the Ninth to Early Twelfth Century* (Aldershot, 2006), chap. III.

[24] Three of Edward's – Eadburh, on whom see S. Ridyard, *The Royal Saints of Anglo-Saxon England: A Study of West Saxon and East Anglian Cults* (Cambridge, 1988), pp. 16–37 and 96–105; Eadflæd and Æthelhild, on whom see John of Worcester, *Chronicon, s.a.* 901 (ed. Darlington and McGurk, vol. II, pp. 632–3, the Bury St Edmund's B MS interpolations); and William of Malmesbury, *Gesta Regum*, ii.126, in *William of Malmesbury, Gesta regum Anglorum*, ed. and trans. R. A. B. Mynors, R. M. Thomson and M. Winterbottom, 2 vols. (Oxford, 1998–9), vol. I, pp. 198–201. The last two were daughters of his second union with Ælfflæd according to the Bury MS of John and William of Malmesbury. William has Ælfflæd buried at Wilton along with these two daughters. Were they placed there with, or by, their mother? Eadburh was the daughter of Edward and his third wife, Eadgifu: see John's own manuscript (ed. Darlington and McGurk, vol. II, p. 354, plus the Bury addition); and William. Edgar's daughter, Edith, was given by her father to be a nun at Wilton, according to Goscelin's *Vita*, in 'La légende de Ste Édith par le moine Goscelin', *Analecta Bollandiana* 56 (1938), 5–101 and 265–307, at 43. On the abbess of Nunnaminster, called 'king's daughter' in a document of Edgar's reign, see above n. 16. St Æthelflæd, abbess of Romsey, said in her later *Vita* to have been a daughter of the noble Æthelwold, was conceivably a step-daughter of Edgar's queen, Ælfthryth, which might help to explain the choice of Romsey as a resting place for Ælfthryth's son, Edmund, who died as a child (full references in S. Foot, *Veiled Women, Female Religious Communities in England, 871–1066*, 2 vols. (Aldershot, 2000), vol. I, pp. 150–2; and B. Yorke, *Nunneries and the Anglo-Saxon Royal Houses* (London, 2003), pp. 78 and 116). Alfred's daughter Æthelgifu became a nun at Shaftesbury, which her father founded (Asser, *De rebus gestis Ælfredi*, chaps. 75 and 98, in *Asser's Life of King Alfred*, ed. W. H. Stevenson (Oxford, 1904), pp. 58 ('Æthelgeofu monasticae vitae regulis, devota Deo virginitate, subiuncta et consecrate, divinum subiit servitium') and 85 ('in quo propriam filiam Æthelgeofu, devotam Deo virginem, abbatissam constituit').

[25] E. van Houts, 'Ælfthryth (*d.* 929)', *ODNB*, vol. I, p. 389.

viking king of York is not an internal 'English' marriage. In every case but
one – the marriage of Eadgifu to Charles the Straightforward – the
marriages of Edward the Elder's daughters were contracted after their
father's death, during the reign of their brother, Æthelstan.[26] By contrast,
Æthelred himself gave three of his daughters, all within his kingdom, to
leading nobles.[27] No earlier English king, from Alfred's time on, is known
to have given his daughters to his own nobles. The giving of Alfred's
daughter, Æthelflæd, to the Mercian 'noble', Æthelred, is the exception.
But Æthelred was not a West Saxon noble. And this apparently unusual
gift of a daughter may be one more reason to examine this marriage – and
the relationship between the West Saxon ruler Alfred and Æthelred 'Lord
of the Mercians' – very carefully.[28] Prima facie, King Æthelred and his
actions appear odd.

Any attempt to interpret this must be extremely cautious, first, because
of the source problems already flagged but, second, because families
themselves are so different. Facile comparisons can be very misleading.
Edward and Æthelred, for example, appear to have been the most philo-
progenitive kings of the late Old English period. In tenth- and eleventh-
century England, Æthelred appears to be as odd in *having* so many
daughters as in what he decided for them. Moreover, royal families – all
families – operate in very specific contexts; attempts to generalise from
these can be very dangerous.

Continental European Comparisons

A first possible pattern or generalisation underlines this danger. It could be
argued that in the early Middle Ages, rising – or new – families restricted
daughters' marriages, whilst established ones felt more secure and able to
consider this. So, for example, Jinty Nelson has remarked that the early
Carolingians kept their daughters unmarried – because, she suggests, they
were 'parvenus', an insecure new dynasty following a long period in which
an old one had been dominant. Keeping the family's blood in a narrow

---

[26] On all these women and their marriages, see Stafford, 'Gender and the Gift'. For the Continental
ones, cf. S. Foot, 'Dynastic Strategies: The West Saxon Royal Family in Europe', in *England and the
Continent in the Tenth Century. Studies in Honour of Wilhelm Levison (1876–1947)*, ed. D. Rollason,
C. Leyser and H. Williams (Turnhout, 2010), pp. 237–53.

[27] All three of their husbands were dead by 1017, only a year after their father, two of them (Uhtred and
Ulfcytel) already in 1016.

[28] For more discussion of this marriage and this relationship, see P. Stafford, 'Political Women in
Mercia, Eighth to Early Tenth Centuries', in *Mercia: An Anglo-Saxon Kingdom in Europe*, ed. M. P.
Brown and C. A. Farr (London, 2001), pp. 35–49, esp. 44–9.

stream was part of giving them 'a new kind of inviolability'. By contrast, the late eighth-century Lombard royal family of Desiderius was secure, marrying their daughters from a position of strength – which those marriages themselves underscore – and recalling an earlier Italian pattern under Theoderic. This was outward marriage in pursuit of the politics of hegemony, with daughters married to men to extend Lombard power and influence.[29] These contrasting decisions highlight the dangers involved in giving daughters – the threats to status, the spread of blood claims – but also the advantages, with, for example, out-marrying daughters as cultural emissaries.

However, this contrast and generalisation are seriously questioned if we extend the comparison to the tenth century – to, for example, the Ottonians and the Capetians. Both would count as 'rising families', yet the daughters of Henry I, the first Saxon/Ottonian king, were married, one at least by her father.[30] And at the end of the tenth century, Hugh Capet – or more likely his son Robert – gave all his daughters or sisters in marriage.[31] We could argue here that eighth-century politics differ from tenth-century ones; that pre- and post-Carolingian Western Europe are different; that, for example, tenth-century kings, especially in West Francia, were operating in a more territorial politics. So the Capetians look much more like other aristocratic operators as they manoeuvred in the politics of this world and used marriage to do so.

But we would need also to note that there is no simple 'tenth-century politics'. The Ottonians in the later tenth century differ again and have what appears to be a very distinctive pattern. Very few daughters were given in marriage after 950; most were placed in convents, often at a very young age. Two of Otto II's three daughters became canonesses then abbesses of the great family houses of Gandersheim and Quedlinburg; only one, Mathilda, was married – and that during the minority of her brother, Otto III.[32] This pattern seems to apply also to collateral lines and to any line that maintained its claim on the throne; indeed, such action could be interpreted as asserting 'Ottonian-ness'. Thus the only married daughter, Mathilda – the only fertile child of Otto II – had seven

---

[29] Nelson, 'Making a Difference'; and cf. Schieffer, 'Karolingische Töchter', for the Carolingian point.

[30] Gerberga and Hadwig were both married: Gerberga by her father to Gislebert of Lotharingia and Hadwig probably by her brother to Hugh the Great (two years or so after her father's death in 936, so perhaps planned by him?). Full details of all these women are in W. Glocker, *Die Verwandten der Ottonen und ihre Bedeutung in der Politik. Studien zur Familienpolitik und zur Genealogie des sächsischen Kaiserhauses* (Cologne and Vienna, 1989).

[31] Details of Capetian marriages also from Glocker, *Die Verwandten*; and from Werner, 'Die Nachkommen Karls des Grossen'.

[32] See K. Leyser, *Rule and Conflict in an Early Medieval Society* (London, 1979), pp. 27, 52 and 54.

daughters; five became abbesses, one a canoness and only one married – to
the king of Poland. Henry the Wrangler, Otto II's cousin, also followed
what we might like to call a late tenth-century Ottonian – and arguably
royal – pattern in his plans for his children: two sons became bishops/
archbishops, one daughter married a king of the Hungarians and the other
two were confined to convents. His other son went on to follow Otto III as
Henry II (and probably played some part in the pattern of his sisters' lives).
Mathilda and Henry both seem to be 'thinking royally' – or at least
'thinking later tenth-century Ottonian royally'.[33] In both cases, their
actions might indicate that plans for daughters send out signals of self-
perception. Both should remind us that we need to keep in mind the
expectations and interpretations of those who receive those signals, as well
as those who receive the daughters.[34]

The Ottonian pattern – if it should be seen as that – underlines the
danger of giving daughters in marriage, including the possibility of being
drawn into aristocratic feuds and politics via daughters' marriages, as Karl
Leyser has stressed,[35] but also the danger of spreading royal blood and thus
claims. It reminds us, too, of the problems for kings in giving daughters –
in particular, the problem of status and status matching.[36] Status is arguably of great concern for all kings, but especially for new dynasties; the
decisions of Hugh Capet and his son Robert are noteworthy. But it is a
warning, too, of the specificity of family situations. The later-tenth-century

---

[33] Leyser, *Rule and Conflict*, p. 150, n. 31, saw Ezzo taught to 'think and act regally' as a result of this
marriage – noting especially his choices concerning the fates of his daughters. On the politics of this
marriage and Ottonian marriage choices more generally, see L. Leleu, 'Une princesse gagnée aux dés.
Le marriage d'Ezzo avec Mathilda, soeur d'Otton III', in *Splendor Reginae. Passions, genre et famille.
Mélanges en l'honneur de Régine Le Jan*, ed. L. Jégou, S. Joye, T. Lienhard and J. Schneider
(Turnhout, 2015), pp. 69–78.

[34] I have discussed these questions of gift and its perception more fully in Stafford, 'Gender and the
Gift'.

[35] Leyser, *Rule and Conflict*, p. 27. Otto I, after his problems with his son-in-law Conrad, pursued a
deliberate restriction of his daughters' marriages – Mathilda was placed at Quedlinburg, where she
became abbess. All three of Otto II's daughters were still very young at the time of his death in 983.
But his decision to place Sophia at Gandersheim in 979 at the age of about four, may give some
indication of his intentions; see Leleu, 'Une princesse', for more discussion.

[36] Status seems to have been a question in the marriage of Mathilda and Ezzo, at least retrospectively.
Thietmar commented on the marriage of Mathilda and Ezzo, noting that it 'displeased many' ('hoc
multis displicuit') with the clear implication that it was seen as degrading. Her brother endured it
patiently, though 'he endowed her richly enough that the inborn honour she possessed by virtue of
her celebrated ancestors would not be degraded' ('dans ei quamplurima ne vilesceret innata sibi a
parentibus summis gloria'). Thietmar of Merseburg, *Chronicon*, iv. 60, in *Die Chronik des Bischofs
Thietmar von Merseburg*, ed. R. Holtzmann, MGH SSRG, n.s. 9 (Berlin, 1935), p. 201; and *Ottonian
Germany: the Chronicon of Thietmar of Merseburg*, trans. D. A. Warner (Manchester, 2001), p. 194.
This is probably only half the story: see, on Ezzo's status, Glocker, *Die Verwandten*, pp 212–13;
Leyser, *Rule and Conflict*; and especially now Leleu, 'Une princesse'.

Ottonians were rich in daughters; the need to answer the daughter question was especially pressing. And the availability and acceptability of answers to that question other than marriage were critical. The great family nunneries into which these Ottonian daughters were placed were an acceptable high-status alternative.

This brief overview of other early medieval dynasties certainly warns us to be wary of patterns, to be alert to contexts and specificities. But, as I have recently argued elsewhere, it should also alert us to the need to understand the basic language within which contemporaries – and we as historians – should read the giving of women.[37] There are ground rules and parameters, a basic structure to the language of this gift, which are then inflected within precise contexts and read against recent meanings. This is not a babble of meaningless actions but a language we need to learn to read and to interpret – and, as always, meaning is contextual.

The gift of a daughter – or a sister – was one of the greatest of gifts. Like all gifts, it was part of an ongoing social relationship, which it could both reinforce and destabilise. The reading and interpretation of it by contemporaries were embedded in their own politics and, in turn, affected those politics.

Interpreting Æthelred's Choices for His Daughters

Returning to the daughters of Æthelred with such comparisons in view, their likely political importance and the implications of their father's decisions for them are underscored. But our source problems now become doubly acute. There are no contemporary accounts of these gifts of daughters in which we can see how they were received at the time. Indeed, as their presence in later sources indicates, it is the longer-term political meanings of these marriages that are more readily available to us. What we can do, however, is examine in more detail the context of Æthelred's giving.

First, as in Ottonian Germany, there *were* significant royal nunneries in England in the early eleventh century. Æthelred, however, chose at most to place only one of his daughters in a nunnery, and not in one of those already connected with his ancestors. He preferred, if the choice was his, Wherwell, a house connected to his mother, if not founded by her.

Second, we are relatively well informed about the identity and careers of his daughters' husbands. All their husbands were men who rose to prominence no earlier than the 990s and who were especially significant after

---

[37] See Stafford, 'Gender and the Gift'.

1000, particularly in the last decade or so of the reign.[38] All were men prominent in the military activities of this last decade. Thus Eadric can be identified in the witness-lists of royal charters from *c*. 996/7 but really rises in witness rank, and thus arguably significance at the royal court, after 1000; by 1007, he was first among the royal thegns, and in the same year he was made ealdorman of Mercia.[39] Uhtred was a member of the great and largely independent family of Bamburgh. Unlike Eadric, his career was not formed gradually in the context of the royal court, but he also never appears as a thegn in witness-lists; his first appearance is as *dux* ('ealdorman') in 1009, after the extension of his power south over York.[40] He was promoted as ealdorman of all Northumbria after *c*. 1006, when his predecessor there disappeared.[41] Ulfcytel is, like Eadric, a more regular attender of the royal court. He first appears as a witness to a royal diploma in 1002. He heads the list of thegns in the last years of the reign, 1013–16. Before 1016, at least one vernacular chronicle account of the reign could be read as implying that he was 'ealdorman among the East Angles', but he is never given the title *dux* ('ealdorman') in charter witness-lists.[42]

Three of the daughters of Æthelred were given in marriage to nobles, but the choice of husbands was far from random. Uhtred was semi-independent ruler of the far North and given control after *c*. 1006 of York, too. From 1008, Eadric was ealdorman of a vast and re-created Mercian ealdormanry spread across midland England. Ulfcytel was military leader of East Anglia, an old kingdom too often forgotten in studies of tenth-century

[38] Eadric's witnesses probably begin in 997 (S 890 (*OSFacs* iii. 35)), and he is the likely beneficiary of a charter of 996 (S 887 (*Abing* 127)). He is a regular witness from 1001 onwards, by 1005 appearing third among the thegns (S 912 (*StAlb* 11)), and first in 1007/8 (S 916 (*StAlb* 12) and S 918 (*Abing* 135)). Ulfcytel is first identifiable as a witness in 1002 (S 900 (*StAlb* 10) and S 903 (*Gilbert Crispin, Abbot of Westminster*, ed. J. A. Robinson (Cambridge, 1911), pp. 167–8)) and remains a fairly regular witness from then on. In three charters of 1013 (S 931 (KCD 1308)), 1014 (S 933 (*Sherb* 15)) and 1016 (S 935 (KCD 723)), he heads the list of thegns. Uhtred never seems to appear as a *minister* ('thegn'). His first witness is as *dux* ('ealdorman') in 1009: S 921 (KCD 1306) and S 922 (*Burt* 32).

[39] Keynes, *Diplomas*, pp. 213–14.

[40] S 921 (KCD 1306) and S 922 (*Burt* 32). For the extension of his authority, see D. Whitelock, 'Dealings of the Kings of England with Northumbria', in *The Anglo-Saxons. Studies in Some Aspects of Their History and Culture Presented to Bruce Dickins*, ed. P. Clemoes (London, 1959), pp. 70–88, at 82.

[41] Cf. Keynes, *Diplomas*, p. 158, n. 11.

[42] *ASC* MS C, 1016, in *The Anglo-Saxon Chronicle MS. C*, ed. K. O'Brien O'Keeffe, AS Chronicle: A Collaborative Edition 5 (Cambridge, 2001), p. 103, reads, 'Godwine ealdormann on Lindesige 7 Ulfcytel on Eastenglum', implying his position as ealdorman. But D and E read, '7 Godwine ealdorman 7 Ulfcytel of Eastenglan' (*The Anglo-Saxon Chronicle MS D*, ed. G. P. Cubbin, AS Chronicle: A Collaborative Edition 6 (Cambridge, 1996), p. 62; *The Anglo-Saxon Chronicle MS E*, ed. S. Irvine, AS Chronicle: A Collaborative Edition 7 (Cambridge, 2004), p. 74), where no such implication need be read. C is usually taken as the 'better' text of these annals, but all versions are later copies. Cf. Keynes, *Diplomas*, p. 208, n 199.

England. None of these daughters were given in marriage to nobles from the old West Saxon heartland. All were gifted to husbands whose power, whether old established or newly boosted, lay in areas where a Wessex-based dynasty's control was more or less problematic. All were given to husbands whose prominence belongs especially to the last decade of the reign, when answers to mounting problems of external attack were foremost in royal concerns.

That same decade saw the growing significance of Æthelred's family more generally. Indeed, there is a marked coincidence between the growing prominence of these (future?) husbands and that of the king's sons. The sons of Æthelred also began to appear in charters of the 990s,[43] more so after AD 1000 and especially after 1007. Obviously, age is a factor here, affecting when sons become old enough to be politically active. But it is not simply a question of physical maturity. After AD 1000, sons appear as witnesses even in infancy, including Edward in 1005, for example, when he can have been at most a toddler.[44] The king's family had simply become more important. During the last years of the reign, in 1009 and 1012, it was especially the eldest three brothers, the ones of military age, who were to the fore. This prominence of the king's sons is almost as remarkable as the marriages of their sisters and a marked departure from Edgar's reign.[45] Royal sons do not always appear in the witness-lists of tenth- and eleventh-century English royal charters. Whether the marriages preceded the last decade or belong there, the political significance of the sons-in-law of Æthelred proceeded in tandem with that of his sons.

A crude linking of the marriages to the careers of husbands might point to 1006/9 for at least two of them, with one or more possibly in the very last stages of the reign. There is, however, a real danger of circularity. The marriages may have preceded the prominence of these men, not followed it, in effect, being the cause of their success rather than an effect of it. Our only firm clue to the chronology is the *De Obsessione*'s statement that Uhtred married three times. The union with Æthelred's daughter was the last, and subsequent to a marriage with Sigen, which on the evidence of this

---

[43] Their first appearance is in 993 (S 876 (*Abing* 124)), but then especially from 996/7 (S 878 (*Burt* 27)) and S 891 (KCD 698)). By 1005, seven sons witness, including the infant Edward (S 910 (*Sherb* 19), S 911 (KCD 714) and S 912 (*StAlb* 11)). From 1007 onwards, they appear very regularly in witness-lists, though in 1009 and 1012 only the eldest three. Alfred first appears in 1013; Eadred and Edgar disappear in 1012 and 1008, respectively.

[44] S 910 (*Sherb* 19), S 911 (KCD 714) and S 912 (*StAlb* 11).

[45] See, for example, their charter witnessing in S. Keynes, *An Atlas of Attestations in Anglo-Saxon Charters, c. 670–1066*, rev. edn (Cambridge, 2002), comparing tables XXXIc and LIX.

text took place in or after 1006.[46] The chronology of Uhtred's marriage need not apply to the other two. But the prominence of these husbands after *c*. 1006 shows how deeply these unions were implicated in the politics of the reign and especially those of its final decade. Those politics were dominated by a response – both secular and religious – to external threat and the pressing military situation. These years were characterised by penitential responses to attack, with which the gift of Æthelred's daughter to God at Wherwell would chime very well. Penance is already marked in the Wherwell charter of 1002.[47] The marriages and/or the prominence of sons-in-law belong with an emphasis on the king's family and an extension of that through affinal ties. They reflect the structure of the kingdom of the English; the marriages seem designed to bridge its potentially deepest fissures at a time of strain.

How would these – unusual – marriages have been interpreted by contemporaries? How should they be interpreted by us? We could note them as a sign and source of strength: a group of leading men knitted together by family ties. We could emphasise the king's astute use of the most traditional of family politics to bind key men and areas, enlisting the bonds of father-in-law and son-in-law to do this. We could envisage Æthelred appearing in his later years surrounded by a phalanx of sons and sons-in-law, a family group at the heart of royal meetings and councils and a patriarchal figure embodying the most traditional authority. The giving of daughters thus could be read as a sign of dynastic strength and its confident political exploitation. These would be marriages expressing a notion of the kingdom as a family enterprise, bound together, or emphasised as bound together, at this time of severe strain – traditional patriarchal authority invoked anew. Such interpretations would speak the most traditional scripts of marriage as gift and the ties it ideally produces. That script was placed in the mouth of Uhtred in late eleventh-century Durham, the son-in-law reciprocating the *gift* of a daughter: 'No reward could persuade me to do what I ought not to. I will keep faith with King Æthelred as long as he lives. For he is my lord and my father-in-law, by

---

[46] *De Obsessione* (ed. Arnold, vol. I, p. 216). Uhtred is said to have put aside his first wife after the king gave him York – undated in this text but datable to *c*. 1006 or after. His (third) marriage to the king's daughter thus would be subsequent to this.

[47] S 904 (KCD 707), with the phrase *Poenitentiam agite* in the proem. The penitential mood was marked across these years; see S. Keynes, 'An Abbot, an Archbishop, and the Viking Raids of 1006–7 and 1009–12', *ASE* 36 (2007), 151–220; more generally, see K. Cubitt, 'The Politics of Remorse: Penance and Royal Piety in the Age of Æthelred the Unready', *Historical Research* 85 (2012), 179–92. The gift of a daughter in 1008, associated with additional grants to Wherwell in that year, would still fit in this penitential context. See also Chapter 11 in this volume.

whose gift I have enough riches and honours.'[48] There can be no doubt that such meanings were potentially readable by contemporaries, as well as by us.

We could, alternatively, emphasise the dangers and the risks Æthelred took. If the king's actions in giving his daughters to nobles were as unusual as they appear, they could have been read as witness to weakness rather than as a sign of strength. Their reception within his family was not obviously straightforward: did they add up to a simple broadening of support, or did they pose a threat of new factionalism? Uhtred's is an ideal script – and even then only of the father-in-law/son-in-law relationship. Marriages were as likely to feed potential splits within the family as to hold it together. By 1006, Æthelred's family, with a stepmother and a new baby boy alongside adult sons from earlier marriages, had its own tensions. The marriages of, and choices for, daughters demand a family context as well as a political one. As with his clutch of daughters, Æthelred's quiverful of sons was itself unusual, unmatched since Edward the Elder's time. If Æthelred was unusual within his own recent dynastic history in his treatment of his daughters, his choices for his sons were arguably more traditional. None of them were married, even though three or more were adult men by the last decade of the reign. Did that create its own tensions within the family? Eadgyth, Eadric, Ælfgifu and Uhtred had children, discussed below. What impact did their birth have on unity among unmarried brothers and their sisters and brothers-in-law?

The reign ended in a 'rebellion' of the eldest surviving son, Edmund. That included his marriage, into a North Midlands family who can be seen as rivals to his brother-in-law, Eadric, for power in Mercia. Uhtred fought alongside his brother-in-law, Edmund, that same eldest surviving son, in 1016. Eadric was a less straightforwardly loyal ally of Edmund in 1016. Eadric's growing role as scapegoat in narratives of the reign means that we must be very wary of interpreting his attitudes and loyalties.[49] But he is a reminder that we should not assume a happy family group in these years. These marriages may have created or fed factions within the family. Did Æthelred's sons have a say in any of them? Equally, could any of these

---

[48] 'Nullius rei gratia ... hoc agere volo. Quia nec debeo; Ethelredo regi, quamdiu vixerit, fidem servabo. Est enim dominus meus et socer, cujus dono divitias et honores satis habeo': *De Obsessione* (ed. Arnold, vol. I, p. 218) (see n. 13, above, on the date of this tract).

[49] These last years are discussed in, for example, P. Stafford, 'The Reign of Æthelred II, a Study in the Limitations on Royal Policy and Action', in *Ethelred the Unready. Papers from the Millenary Conference*, ed. D. Hill, BAR British Series 59 (Oxford, 1978), pp. 15–46, at 35–7; and C. Insley, 'Politics, Conflict and Kinship in Early Eleventh-Century Mercia', *Midland History* 25 (2000), 28–42.

marriages have aimed to counterbalance the sons' influence? Did sons-in-law and sons stand together as a solid phalanx? Or did Æthelred turn to some family members but not others? Depending on time, place and circumstance, the happy family group may dissolve into snapshots of bitter rivals.

I have treated these marriages as a group, having implied common aims and strategies behind them. But each involved the gift of a woman, and gifts demand to be read in context. Broad similarities should not mask the specificity of each gift – even if their individual contexts are now irrecoverable. These marriages did not necessarily all take place together. Indeed, they may have responded in some ways to each other, as well as to (changing) political situations. And their family context includes decisions made about sons as well as daughters. Interpretation of them can range from a strategy forced on a reluctant king by circumstances – the more normal tenth-century English pattern of placing daughters in nunneries abandoned in dire straits – to the mature response of a king with a growing family using the political means at his disposal, the techniques of early medieval family-based rule. They may be seen as a betrayal of royal status or as an assured command of it. They can be viewed as a source of strength or a recipe for, even individual responses to, yet further division. If this range appears to frustrate our efforts at understanding, we would do well to remember that its gamut of meanings was available to contemporaries, too. The general context of these marriages was one of growing political difficulty. But these gifts of women likely evoked differing responses from various contemporary audiences in diverse circumstances.

Æthelred's Daughters: Identity and Politics

Looking at women always means 'making a difference', but so far the analysis has been within the now-familiar frame of 'marriage politics', albeit recast by attention to marriage as gift. There has been little consideration of the daughters themselves: of relations between fathers and daughters, of daughters' presence at court, of their identity and of the extent of its formation in a court context. These are questions important in themselves but also relevant to the more traditional ones. They take us beyond the point of transacted gift to raise the active role of women like these – alongside their husbands (and children) – after marriage. They require us to probe the upbringing, and identity formation of the daughters of Æthelred. How strong was that 'daughter-of-Æthelred' identity, and what did it mean to these women? They are questions pioneered by

Jinty Nelson, especially in her work on Charlemagne and the daughters of Desiderius.[50] But she has asked them on the basis of evidence, especially letters and court poetry, virtually non-existent for early eleventh-century England.

Did Æthelred's daughters spend much time at court, and, if so, what would they have imbibed and learnt there? The only surviving picture of an Anglo-Saxon royal court and its children is in Asser's *Life* of Alfred. At the time Asser wrote two of Alfred's daughters had already left court, destined for marriage and the convent: the eldest daughter and eldest child, Æthelflæd, was already married; the second daughter (and third child), Æthelgifu, had been committed to the religious life at Shaftesbury. The youngest child, Æthelweard, had been given into the care of *magistri*, along with many other noble and non-noble children. Asser may imply a contrast with the third daughter and fourth child, Ælfthryth, whom he specifically states was still at court,[51] raised alongside her eldest brother, the second child, Edward. Asser gives us a picture of their upbringing there. Edward and Ælfthryth learnt 'in subjection/submission' to their father; they learnt the psalms, Saxon books and songs 'and very frequently made use of books'; they studied liberal arts (*liberalis disciplina*) but also this present life, 'as befitted nobles'. Whether education 'befitting nobles' hides gendered difference it is difficult to tell. Einhard's Charlemagne had his sons taught to ride, use arms and hunt, his daughters to spin and weave.[52] For Asser, arts 'befitting nobles', which included hunting, required strength (*vires*) but were labelled 'human/humane' (*humanis artibus*) rather than simply gendered masculine. Asser stresses that both son and daughter learned not only letters, including Saxon, but also the courtly virtues and behaviours of 'humility to all the poor and to strangers, affability and gentleness/graciousness'.[53] Elsewhere he speaks of Alfred's court as a place where not only education in letters but also moral education took place.[54] All this seems to have extended to at least some daughters – whilst they were at court – as well as sons. But all this is a century or more before Æthelred and an idealised picture. We should be wary of using Asser for understanding Æthelred's practices whilst at the same time noting the possibility of women spending considerable time in a court environment

---

[50] See n. 4, above.
[51] Asser, *De rebus gestis Ælfredi*, chap. 75 (ed. Stevenson, p. 58), for all this: 'semper in curto regio nutriti'.
[52] Einhard, *Vita Karoli*, chap. 19, in *Einhardi Vita Karoli Magni*, ed. G Waitz, MGH SSRG 25 (Hanover, 1911), p. 23.
[53] 'Et ad omnes indigenas et alienigenas humilitate, affabilitate et etiam lenitate'.
[54] Asser, *De rebus gestis Ælfredi*, chap. 76 (ed. Stevenson, pp. 59–60).

where their royal nurturing – and their resulting royal sense of self – would parallel that of their brothers.

As Stuart Airlie has argued, the court is a state of mind as much as a physical place, though physical presence at or close to the court helps inculcate that mentality.[55] If the king committed his own daughter to Wherwell, it could have been at a very early age. Their much later saintly *Lives* make Eadburg, daughter of Edward the Elder, about three when she was given to Nunnaminster;[56] Edith, Edgar's daughter, two.[57] But such a commitment to religion did not necessarily isolate a daughter from her royal kin, from royal activities or from a sense of royal identity. Sophia of Gandersheim entered that nunnery aged about four in 979 but seventeen years later was accompanying her brother, Otto III, to Rome.[58] Both Eadburg and Edith were, according to their *Vitae*, visited by their fathers; both remained, as Barbara Yorke has pointed out, very much royal princesses in their nunneries.[59] Edith was allegedly visited by foreign ambassadors at Wilton and continued to exert influence over her father's actions, calling on him for justice and mercy. There is much hagiographical elaboration here, but Wilton has recently been highlighted both for its learning and for its close involvement in royal politics.[60] Both Wilton and Nunnaminster were in the very heartlands of West Saxon royal power, as was Wherwell itself. A daughter who was a nun at Wherwell was not geographically remote from court and would surely have retained a strong sense of royal identity.

If we are ill informed as to the date of Æthelred's daughters' marriages, we are in total darkness as far as their age at marriage is concerned. It is difficult to know how long they were even potentially at court or raised in a royal family setting. But if the marriages date to 1008 or even later, this leaves a considerable length of time for such raising. Æthelred's child-producing years probably began *c.* 985. Simon noted the reference to

---

[55] S. Airlie, 'The Palace of Memory: The Carolingian Court as Political Centre', in *Courts and Regions in Medieval Europe*, ed. S. R. Jones, R. Marks and A. J. Minnis (York, 2000), pp. 1–20; and S. Airlie, 'Bonds of Power and Bonds of Association in the Court Circle of Louis the Pious', in *Charlemagne's Heir, New Perspectives on the Reign of Louis the Pious*, ed. P. Godman and R. Collins (Oxford, 1990), pp. 191–204.

[56] Osbert of Clare, *Vita beate uirginis Ædburge*, chap. 2, in *The Royal Saints of Anglo-Saxon England: A Study of West Saxon and East Anglian Cults*, ed. S. J. Ridyard (Cambridge, 1988), p. 265.

[57] Goscelin, *Vita* ('La Légende de Ste Édith', ed. Wilmart, p. 44).

[58] Sophia has been seen as acting as a *consors imperii*, having a share in rule, by historians of Ottonian Germany: see Glocker, *Die Verwandten*, pp. 206–7.

[59] B. Yorke, 'The Legitimacy of St. Edith', *Haskins Society Journal* 11 (2003 for 1998), 97–113.

[60] E. Tyler, 'The *Vita Ædwardi*: The Politics of Poetry at Wilton Abbey', *ANS* 31 (2009), 135–56.

daughters in the early 990s,[61] albeit in a context that may make the reference notional. The king's daughters could well have been in their twenties when they married, though a much younger age is perfectly possible. But how much of that time was necessarily at court? The only thing we know for certain about the raising of Æthelred's children is that his eldest son was brought up by his grandmother, the dowager queen Ælfthryth, and that he had a foster mother, as did his half-brother Edward.[62] The sons *may* have spent some time in childhood geographically remote from their father, in Edward's case at Ely. Did the daughters, too? Or was there a gender difference here?

Once married, we can probably assume that the daughters left court. But did they return with their husbands? Was their contact with the court, their father and royal politics thus renewed? If so, there would be an important difference between Eadgyth, who married Eadric, and Ælfgifu, who married Uhtred. Eadric came regularly to court after 1008 and was perhaps the king's chief adviser in these years; Uhtred appears a much less frequent visitor. It is, of course, an intriguing possibility that Eadgyth herself was a factor in the closeness of Æthelred and Eadric. These women are the most shadowy of presences, but present in some sense they were in the last stages of Æthelred's reign and its politics. That presence was of women who would have had a strong sense of royal identity, whether or not acquired through many years at court, but that need not have extended to a strong sense of family unity.

Æthelred's Daughters and Later Eleventh-Century Politics

By the end of 1016, Æthelred was dead, as were the husbands to whom he had given three of these women. Of the women's personal fates we are entirely ignorant. Were the daughters of Æthelred like the daughters of Desiderius, manoeuvring politically after their father's downfall? Seeking vengeance? More united by his death than during his life? Were they a lost factor in the unknown politics of Cnut's reign and its aftermath?

Only one can be tracked in any detail: Godgifu, daughter of Æthelred and Emma. As Liesbeth van Houts has so forcefully reminded us, she remained a political actor to be reckoned with. Godgifu has featured little in this discussion. She was the exception among the known daughters of

---

[61] See n. 3, above.

[62] S 1503 (*CantCC* 142; *Anglo-Saxon Wills*, ed. and trans. D. Whitelock (Cambridge, 1930), pp. 56–63, no. 20); and S 1137 (*ASWrits* 93).

Æthelred; married, but not by her father. Godgifu was still a child at her father's death; her likely date of birth is *c.* 1007.[63] She had been taken, like her full brothers Edward and Alfred, to Normandy to the protection of her uncles. There she was given in marriage *c.* 1024 to Drogo of Mantes, perhaps with her brothers' permission, certainly as part of Norman politics. By *c.* 1035, her first marriage had ended, and she was married again, this time to Eustace of Boulogne. As a widow, she may have had more say in this marriage. It was certainly one that had immediate benefits for her brothers – if, that is, Alfred's fateful crossing to England in 1036 launched with her help can be said to have been a benefit.

Godgifu's religious benefactions in the Seine valley had already sup-ported her brothers, including ideologically. Godgifu's Northern French marriages enabled her to act, and gave her a capacity for action, in some respects denied her brothers. That action points to a continuing sense of herself as a sister of Edward, if not a daughter of Æthelred, an interesting sense of identity since, as probably the youngest of all the daughters, she would have had the least time to imbibe that identity at court but would have shared a strong sense of common experience in exile with her brothers in Normandy.

The abbess of Wherwell lived on into the reign of Edward the Confessor. Her sense of family identity with Edward was obviously suffi-ciently strong for him to use her as a semi-gaoler for his wife, Edith, in 1051. Edward turned to her, as to other members of his natal family, like Godgifu's son, Ralf, in these years. The visit of Godgifu's second husband, Eustace, to England in 1051 is usually remembered for its fateful impact on the crisis between Earl Godwine and King Edward. Its purpose was surely connected to his wife's death a few years before and the securing of any claims for his children with her. Godgifu herself held land in England during her brother's reign. The descendants of Godgifu continued to be a factor in English politics long after 1066. Her grandson with Drogo, Harold, Ralf's son, was a landholder in 1066, if a much diminished one. Another grandson, probably child of her daughter with Eustace, accom-panied his grandfather to England in 1067, where he was captured by William the Conqueror at Dover and disappeared.[64] The claims of this

---

[63] P. Stafford, *Queen Emma and Queen Edith: Queenship and Women's Power in Eleventh-Century England* (Oxford, 1997), p. 221.

[64] F. Barlow, *Edward the Confessor*, 2nd edn (New Haven, 1997), pp. 307–8 (Appendix C: the descendants of Eustace of Boulogne and Godgifu).

family, as a family and as descendants of Godgifu, specifically named as sister of Edward, were still recognised in Domesday Book in 1086.[65]

Godgifu had husbands and a position as a wife and mother to work from: the abbess of Wherwell, an official position. If they survived, the three married sisters in England all lost their husbands in the carnage of 1016–17. One – the shadowy Wulfhild – *may* have gone on to marry Thorkell. Was this arranged by Cnut? Thorkell certainly took over Wulfhild's previous husband's sphere of power in East Anglia. Or was this Thorkell's own initiative? He was a semi-independent operator in early-eleventh-century England. In either case, the marriage to an English royal daughter could have been a source of tension between Thorkell and Cnut. It may help to explain Thorkell's outlawry in 1021, taking his wife with him.[66] Wulfhild may have ended her life in Scandinavia. Did the other two sisters survive in England, to complicate Cnut's reign? We simply do not know. Godgifu's northern French connections and obvious closeness to Edward make her relatively easy to track after 1016. Paradoxically, her sisters, who had married in England, are much more obscure. But, as with Godgifu, we *can* trace their descendants, even into post-1066 politics.

We encounter those descendants at Barking, among the great English nobles who submitted after William's coronation; in the West Country, in Domesday Book and in a judicial plea; in the rule of Northumbria (Earl Cospatric); and perhaps especially significantly, we find them in Scotland by the early twelfth century – where so much English royal blood sought refuge after 1066.[67] Their ancestry was certainly not forgotten. Domesday

---

[65] The grouping and treatment of lands in the Surrey Domesday suggest this. GDB, fol. 34r, 'Terra Æcclae de Lanchei [Lambeth]. S. Maria manerium est quod Lanchei vocatur. Goda \comitissa/ tenuit soror R E.' The next tenant listed is Eustace holding Oxted, 'Gida \mater Heraldi/ tenuit'; the next tenant is *Comitissa bononiensis* (i.e. Ida of Boulogne), who holds Nutfield. Is the listing of this little group of lands brought together by their family connection? Lambeth is the last ecclesiastical landholder, Eustace the first lay one, but it is very odd to have a female landholder mentioned as early as this in the listing of lay tenants in any Domesday shire.

[66] E. A. Freeman, *A History of the Norman Conquest: Its Causes and Its Results*, 6 vols., 2nd edn (Oxford, 1867–79), vol. I, p. 656, on this as a possible source of tension – though he believed that Thorkell married Eadric's widow.

[67] Siward the rich/fat (*dives/grossus*) in the West Country, grandson (?) of Eadric and Eadgyth, was one of those who came to terms with William at Barking but who lost his substantial possessions nonetheless. His pre-1066 position was recognised when Bishop Wulfstan called him as a witness in the famous suit with Evesham, after 1077; see A. Williams, *The English and the Norman Conquest* (Woodbridge, 1995), pp. 93–5. He held eighty-eight hides TRE, which had been reduced to some nine or more by 1086, and these as a subtenant. All documents concerning the suit are printed in *Domesday Book: Worcestershire*, ed. F. and C. Thorn (Chichester, 1982), Appendix V. H. One of Siward's descendants may have been in Scotland by the early twelfth century: Orderic Vitalis, *Historia ecclesiastica*, viii. 22, in *The Ecclesiastical History of Orderic Vitalis*, ed. M. Chibnall, 7 vols.

Book itself gives Siward the Fat, probably the grandson of Eadgyth, the (relatively unusual) identifier *cognatus* of King Edward.[68] His son was given the royal name Edward and survived in Scotland as a constable of King David, himself a descendant of Æthelred, through a granddaughter of that Edmund who rebelled against his father in 1016. Is it coincidence that the last, enigmatic annal added to the *Anglo-Saxon Chronicle* MS D recorded the defeat of Angus of Moray in 1130 by that very same Edward, son of Siward?[69] The royal blood that flowed from the marriages of Æthelred's daughters was still remembered and was still a factor in politics a century or more after the king's death, a reminder perhaps of why so many kings restricted such marriages.

These great- and great-great-grandchildren of Æthelred return us to the sources with which I began. We know about the daughters of Æthelred from later sources: about Wulfhild from the Scandinavian North, where her second husband returned, and about Eadgyth and Ælfgifu from Worcester and from Durham/Northern England, respectively. This is at least in part because it was in these areas that the descendants of these women survived. It was also at Worcester and in the North that the only memories of Æthelred's first two wives survived. Doubts have been raised about the two marriages of Æthelred prior to his union with Emma, concerning the reality of two separate women.[70] The fact that they are recorded, quite distinctly and separately, in the two areas where descendants of the king's children long remained important is perhaps reason to accept the reality of two separate unions. Reason, too, to remind ourselves of the political significance of the daughters they produced.

The daughters of Æthelred raise as many questions as they provide answers, some of them questions to which we shall never know the answers. Much has to be argued from little – a little that itself is often debatable or speculative. The straws clutched at have built a house, but, as

---

(Oxford, 1968–80), vol. IV, pp. 276–7, where a rebellion in 1130 was put down by Edward, son of Siward, a kinsman and royal constable of David I; Williams, *The English*, p. 95, *contra* Barrow and others is surely right in making Edward – a significant name in itself – a descendant of this Siward, not of the Northumbrian earl. Orderic says that Siward *sub Eduardo rege tribunus Merciorum fuit*. Cospatric, son of Maldred, was the grandson of Ælfgifu and Uhtred; he paid a large sum to William for rule in the North but received the Danish fleet in the Humber in 1069, fell from grace and fled to Flanders, before he too found his way north, to become earl of Dunbar. If Williams is right, then descendants of these two daughters of Æthelred appear in Scotland after 1066, that significant refuge of pre-1066 claims on the English throne.

[68] Hollow, GDB, fol. 180v – Herefordshire; *terra regis* in 1086.
[69] *ASC* MS D, 1080, *recte* 1130 (ed. Cubbin, p. 89) – the annal does not mention Edward, but it is truncated. The annal follows an apparent gap in coverage after the annals for the 1070s.
[70] For example, Keynes, *Diplomas*, p. 187, n. 118.

proverbially, a huff and a puff might be felt easily to blow it down. Questions and speculation can be productive, however. We have lost so much family history of the Old English nobility, even of the royal family. That is in part at least because 1066 ruptured aristocratic memory, or rather the families that were conduits of it. By the early twelfth century, there were few Æthelweards to recall their Old English ancestors; Worcester and the North preserved something of that memory, but we shall never know all we would wish to about the daughters of Æthelred. But that little we know underlines their likely significance in eleventh-century politics. Questions and speculation about these women are justifiable, if not necessary. No picture of the reign is complete without them.

CHAPTER 8

The Historian and Anglo-Saxon Coinage:
The Case of Late Anglo-Saxon England

Rory Naismith

One of the great strengths of Anglo-Saxon historical scholarship has been a long-standing willingness to engage with diverse sources, including material culture. Coinage in particular has played a prominent role. Since the 1950s, when Michael Dolley (1925–83) and his colleagues started to forge links between a new generation of Anglo-Saxon numismatists and the historical establishment, later Anglo-Saxon coinage has gradually taken on a central role in the study of the administrative and institutional aspects of tenth- and eleventh-century England.[1] This is consequently a very fitting subject for inclusion in a volume in honour of Simon Keynes. Simon has served since 2003 as chairman of the British Academy's Sylloge of Coins of the British Isles project, with predecessors including his own PhD supervisor, Dorothy Whitelock (1901–82), and her mentor, Sir Frank Stenton (1880–1967). Even more so than most other Anglo-Saxon historians, Simon has taken full account of coinage in his research on rulers from Offa (757–96) and Alfred the Great (871–99) to Æthelred II (978–1016). His integration of numismatic sources, and critical engagement with them, stands as an example to all students and scholars who work on Anglo-Saxon history.

It is in this spirit that this chapter looks afresh at the segment of Anglo-Saxon coinage that has been at the heart of the modern *entente cordiale* of historians and numismatists: the late Anglo-Saxon currency. Dolley's view of the subject (sometimes encapsulated as the 'sexennial thesis') remains dominant. He enlarged upon the principle of successive type-changes (already reached in earlier scholarship)[2] by arranging these type-changes into an orchestrated sequence of national re-coinages, which took place at

---

[1] M. Blackburn, 'Stenton and Anglo-Saxon Numismatics', in *Anglo-Saxon England Fifty Years On*, ed. D. Matthew (Reading, 1994), pp. 61–81.

[2] P. W. P. Carlyon-Britton, 'Eadward the Confessor and his Coins', *NChron*, 4th series, 5 (1905), 179–205; and C. A. Nordman, *Anglo-Saxon Coins Found in Finland* (Helsingfors, 1921).

fixed and regular intervals beginning much earlier than had previously been thought. The first such re-coinage Dolley placed at Michaelmas 973, representing a major reform undertaken by King Edgar, and others followed every six years thereafter, with a slight wobble in the troubled last days of Æthelred II. Significant changes came after the death of Cnut in 1035, when his sons upped the frequency of re-coinages to every two years. Edward the Confessor adjusted this to every three years with his fifth type, introduced in the eventful year 1051.[3]

Challenges to any aspect of this scheme were met with such robust defence by Dolley that critique of his views was limited until after his death in 1983.[4] In subsequent years, Lord Stewartby noted the practical difficulties in sticking to so strict a scheme over such a long period,[5] and a much more caustic attack was made by John Brand, who had often been the victim of Dolley's sharp pen.[6]

The decades since about 1990 have provided the means for a fresh approach to the late Anglo-Saxon currency. There has been important work on the coinage in the period up to Edgar's reform, which was poorly understood in the mid-twentieth century.[7] Another crucial new resource is a much-enlarged body of find material from England, particularly single-finds, which shed significantly more light on the role of coinage in its home kingdom than was available to Dolley (who relied heavily on Scandinavian hoards).[8] Last but not least, the coinage now stands against a changed

---

[3] Important articles laying out the 'sexennial thesis' include R. H. M. Dolley and D. M. Metcalf, 'The Reform of the English Coinage under Eadgar', in *Anglo-Saxon Coins: Studies Presented to F. M. Stenton on the Occasion of His 80th Birthday, 17 May 1960*, ed. R. H. M. Dolley (London, 1961), pp. 136–68; and R. H. M. Dolley, 'An Introduction to the Coinage of Æthelræd II', in *Ethelred the Unready: Papers from the Millenary Conference*, ed. D. Hill, BAR British series 59 (Oxford, 1978), pp. 115–33.

[4] An exception is P. Grierson, 'Numismatics and the Historian', *NChron*, 7th series, 2 (1962), i–xiv (reprinted in his *Dark Age Numismatics* (London, 1979), no. XVIII).

[5] B. H. I. H. Stewart, 'Coinage and Recoinage after Edgar's Reform', in *Studies in Late Anglo-Saxon Coinage in Memory of Bror Emil Hildebrand*, ed. K. Jonsson, Svenska Numismatiska Meddelanden 35 (Stockholm, 1990), pp. 455–85; and 'The English and Norman Mints, *c.* 600–1158', in *A New History of the Royal Mint*, ed. C. E. Challis (Cambridge, 1992), pp. 49–68.

[6] J. D. Brand, *Periodic Change of Type in the Anglo-Saxon and Norman Periods* (Rochester, 1984).

[7] C. E. Blunt, B. H. I. H. Stewart and C. S. S. Lyon, *Coinage in Tenth-Century England, from Edward the Elder to Edgar's Reform* (Oxford, 1989); H. E. Pagan, 'The Pre-Reform Coinage of Edgar', in *Edgar, King of the English 959–975: New Interpretations*, ed. D. Scragg (Woodbridge, 2008), pp. 192–207; and R. Naismith, 'Prelude to Reform: Tenth-Century English Coinage in Perspective', in *Early Medieval Monetary History: Studies in Memory of Mark Blackburn*, ed. R. Naismith, M. R. Allen and E. Screen (Aldershot, 2014), pp. 39–83.

[8] The major resources are the Corpus of Early Medieval Coin Finds (EMC: www.fitzmuseum.cam .ac.uk/dept/coins/emc/) and the Portable Antiquities Scheme (PAS: https://finds.org.uk/). An important exploration of late Anglo-Saxon single-finds, written before the Internet repositories became available, is D. M. Metcalf, *An Atlas of Anglo-Saxon and Norman Coin Finds c. 973–1086* (London, 1998).

historical backdrop: views of late Anglo-Saxon government, in which coinage plays such a prominent role, have evolved significantly since the 1950s and 1960s (and indeed continue to do so).

The first of these new developments is important for views of the inception of the late Anglo-Saxon currency. In general, it is now more prudent to see the reform of Edgar's later years as one step in a process of evolution rather than a great leap forward that left behind all that had gone before. Edgar's reform was deeply rooted in earlier tenth-century practices.[9] The principle of recognising the current West Saxon king, and using only his coins, had held firm in English territory since the time of Alfred the Great. Æthelstan attempted – albeit without complete or lasting success – to establish a single common type including the mint-name as well as the moneyer's name across the expanding territory of the kingdom of the English.[10] Edgar replicated Æthelstan's Circumscription Cross and Bust Crowned types in the earlier part of his reign, before a more thoroughgoing reform near its end based on an adapted version of Æthelstan's Bust Crowned type. Other rare types from the early part of Edgar's reign resurrected designs from the preceding century, including the London monogram of Alfred and another rare cruciform inscription used by the same king.[11]

Edgar's last reform thus grew out of a time of experimentation and revival early in his reign and represented a more ambitious and firm imposition of what earlier English kings had tried. There is no indication that a repeat performance was envisaged at this stage. Dolley took the maintenance of the newly established design under Edgar's two sons, Edward the Martyr (975–8) and Æthelred II, as a signal that a full six-year cycle was being waited out.[12] This was the one occasion in the period of the late Anglo-Saxon coinage when he accepted a coinage as continuing on a substantive scale across multiple reigns. But persistence of coin-types across reigns was perfectly standard in the earlier tenth century, and moreover, there is considerable uncertainty about when Edgar's reform actually took place. Dolley's authority for dating it to 973 stemmed from Roger of Wendover's *Flores historiarum*.[13] This thirteenth-century text actually places

[9] Naismith, 'Prelude', pp. 80–3.
[10] C. E. Blunt, 'The Coinage of Athelstan, King of England 924–939', *BNJ* 42 (1974), 35–160, esp. 47–51.
[11] Blunt, Stewart and Lyon, *Coinage*, pp. 203–4; and R. Naismith, 'A New Pre-Reform Coin-Type of Edgar', *BNJ* 86 (2016), 232–4 (cf. EMC 2014.0296).
[12] Dolley and Metcalf, 'Reform', p. 152.
[13] R. H. M. Dolley, 'Roger of Wendover's Date for Eadgar's Coinage Reform', *BNJ* 49 (1979), 1–11.

the coin reform in 975 but associates it with events that other sources date to 973 or 974. This difference of a year or two is significant, for the sexennial system depended quite heavily upon a beginning in 973.[14]

The point of this is not to downplay Edgar's reform. Edgar succeeded in enforcing a single design at all mints in the kingdom, with universal imposition of mint names as well as moneyers' names. His reform was a major landmark, but it needs to be placed more fully into context. Above all, it should be seen as part of a longer story, looking back to earlier tenth-century coinage, as well as to its successors in the time of Æthelred II. It was during the latter's reign that the system of repeated re-coinages developed, in fits and starts, as part of a looser, more adaptive mechanism than was envisaged by Dolley. The first new coinage of Æthelred, the so-called Hand type, illustrates how flexible the early stages of this new system were.[15] According to Dolley's scheme, there were two major and quite discrete Hand types (First and Second Hand) (Figures 8.1 and 8.2).[16] A third and much rarer variant, Benediction Hand, seems to have emerged late in the duration of the coinage (Figure 8.3). As the name suggests, Benediction Hand was marked out by the hand on the reverse showing a blessing gesture and by minor differences in the design of the obverse. But the division between First and Second Hand is less immediately

(a)   (b)

Figure 8.1 Æthelred II (978–1016), First Hand type, Canterbury mint, moneyer Leofstan. (Image reproduced with the kind permission of the Fitzwilliam Museum, Cambridge: CM.YG.3195-R.)

[14] Naismith, 'Prelude', pp. 39–40.   [15] See Stewart, 'Coinage and Recoinage', pp. 471–4.
[16] E.g. Dolley, 'Introduction', pp. 121–2.

Figure 8.2 Æthelred II (978–1016), Second Hand type, London mint, moneyer Ásketill. (Image reproduced with the kind permission of the Fitzwilliam Museum, Cambridge: CM.5.62–1933.)

Figure 8.3 Æthelred II (978–1016), Benediction Hand type, Rochester mint, moneyer Siduwine. (Image reproduced with the kind permission of the Fitzwilliam Museum, Cambridge: CM.1.679–1990.)

obvious. On the Second Hand type, the king has a sceptre on the obverse, and additional pellets and curls are added on the reverse. These changes are small enough that users must have had difficulty in readily distinguishing one coinage from the other, a significant problem if the Second Hand type was meant to replace the first in general circulation. There are also oddities in the distribution of the Second Hand type. No specimens at all survive from Lincoln and only a handful from York, both of which normally served as some of the most productive mints in the kingdom. Other northern and western mints are also poorly represented in the type, and at Lincoln and York there is some evidence that production of First Hand pennies continued while Second Hand prevailed in the south. Yet there are also signs that point towards Second Hand being a major undertaking. Moneyers at Rochester adapted their First Hand dies to look like those of Second Hand, implying that there was some need to produce coins of this form,[17] and a small number of English and Scandinavian hoards consist solely or largely of Second Hand pennies. These indicate that at least some users actively sought out coins of the type and/or that they made up a dominant portion of the currency.

The best framework within which to interpret these coinages is one that allows for a degree of flexibility, one in which coin reforms were beginning to take place more frequently but not yet on a fixed model or timetable. The extensive but not universal coinages of Æthelstan are probably the best parallel. The Hand types give the strong impression of rulers and moneyers still making it up as they went along, which would accord well with a more qualified view of Edgar's reform. Second Hand probably represents an outgrowth rather than a replacement of First Hand, one that gained a significant amount of traction in some but not all parts of the kingdom. Between them, the three Hand types probably cover most or all of the 980s, with First Hand lasting somewhat longer than Second.

Subsequent coinages were for the most part more discrete, though there were still aberrations that reinforce the impression of what an optimist would call adaptation and a pessimist trial and error. Another large subtype representing an evolution of a preceding coinage in its design and weight was the so-called Helmet type, which has traditionally been seen as the penultimate coinage in Æthelred's reign.[18] Smaller groups are equally revealing, for they show that new designs could be essayed but not put into full production. The so-called Intermediate Small Cross type (Figure 8.4) appeared during the time of the much larger Crux type and survives in only a tiny number of specimens, mostly from mints in the southwest, though a larger number of places dotted around the kingdom used obverse dies of this design with reverses of the Crux type: in other words, the Intermediate Small Cross dies were made and distributed, but for whatever reason the design was

---

[17] R. H. M. Dolley, 'An Unpublished Link between the First and Second Hand Types of Æthelræd II', *BNJ* 35 (1966), 22–4.

[18] Brand, *Periodic Change*, pp. 30–1.

(a)   (b)

Figure 8.4 Æthelred II (978–1016), Intermediate Small Cross type, Wilton mint, moneyer Sæwine. (Image reproduced with the kind permission of the Fitzwilliam Museum, Cambridge: CM.1920–2003.)

discontinued quickly in favour of the pre-existing type, suggesting that there was no fixed timetable for coin reforms at that point.[19] Similar cases can be found as late as the final years of Edward the Confessor.[20] The late Anglo-Saxon coinage was thus the product of a significantly longer and bumpier developmental process than Dolley advocated. Several of its features had grown out of earlier tenth-century coinages, Edgar's reform added a higher level of unity, and the principle of repeated re-coinages was a product of the reign of Æthelred II, with significant changes thereafter (not least more frequent re-coinages in the period after Cnut's death).

Another central pillar of the 'sexennial thesis' was the regularity of re-coinages. No concrete evidence for an absolute date within any reign is given away by the coins themselves or any surviving text. Dolley therefore supported his chronology by associating hoards from England, Ireland and Scandinavia with specific viking raids, which (as was common in scholarship of the day) were thought of as the primary reason for the deposition and non-recovery of hoards. But there is rarely anything to suggest that hoards were indeed the result of violent action, let alone historically recorded violent

---

[19] Stewart, 'Coinage and Recoinage', p. 476; Dolley, 'Introduction', pp. 123–4; and R. H. M. Dolley and F. Elmore Jones, 'An Intermediate Small Cross Issue of Æthelræd II and Some Late Varieties of the Crux Type', *BNJ* 28 (1955–7), 75–87.

[20] B. H. I. H. Stewart and C. E. Blunt, 'The Droitwich Mint and *BMC* Type XIV of Edward the Confessor', *BNJ* 48 (1978), 52–7.

action, and these connections are best left to one side.[21] Other proposals for the chronology of the coinage depend on tying the pattern of minting to known military and political events. This, too, is a treacherous exercise. For example, one of the best cases for dating the coinage revolves around the relocation of a group of moneyers from Wilton to the nearby hill fort of Old Sarum, the location of Salisbury until the thirteenth century. This shift coincided with the change from the Long Cross to the Helmet type under Æthelred II. It was suggested in the 1950s that a viking attack on Wilton recorded by the C, D and E versions of the *Anglo-Saxon Chronicle* and other sources in the year 1003 was the occasion for the move from Wilton to Salisbury, seemingly fixing the date of one type-change.[22] This remains an attractive argument in some respects, although the *Chronicle* also says that the viking army in 1003 went to Salisbury immediately after Wilton, and John of Worcester adds that they sacked it (though this may have been his own inference from reading the *Chronicle* entry)[23]: in other words, the move is unlikely to have taken place in the immediate context of the viking attack, though it is entirely conceivable in the aftermath when the moneyers and others would have seen the attraction of a large hill fort. It is therefore only reasonable to use the sack of Wilton as a likely *terminus post quem*.

Two features of the coinage together form a more convincing case for dating another set of monetary changes to 1009. The first of these relates to the moneyers at Oxford and Wallingford. Coins of Æthelred II's last major type, Last Small Cross, are very rare for both mints, and all known specimens can, on stylistic and metrological grounds, be assigned to the beginning of the type. Stewart Lyon has plausibly suggested that the abrupt cessation of the type results from the destruction of Oxford by vikings around New Year 1010, implying that the type had been introduced towards the end of 1009.[24] The second piece of evidence relating to 1009 is the remarkable Agnus Dei coinage (Figure 8.5).[25] Abandoning the traditional bust and cross designs, this

---

[21] For a careful critique of this methodology, see S. Armstrong, 'Carolingian Coin-Hoards and the Impact of Viking Raids in the Ninth Century', *NChron* 158 (1998), 131–64.

[22] R. H. M. Dolley, 'The Sack of Wilton in 1003 and the Chronology of the "Long Cross" and "Helmet" Types of Æthelræd II', *Nordisk Numismatisk Unions Medlemsblad* 5 (May 1954), 152–6.

[23] John of Worcester, *Chronicon*, s.a. 1003 (*The Chronicle of John of Worcester*, vol. 2: *The Annals from 450 to 1066*, ed. and trans. J. Bray, R. R. Darlington and P. McGurk (Oxford, 1995), pp. 454–5).

[24] C. S. S. Lyon, 'The Significance of the Sack of Oxford in 1009/1010 for the Chronology of the Coinage of Æthelred II', *BNJ* 35 (1966), 34–7. Wallingford is not specifically said to have been laid waste, although the *Chronicle* does note that the viking army 'made their way then on both sides of the Thames' (*namon hit þa on twa healfe Temese*) (*ASC* MSS CDE, 1009 (*Two of the Saxon Chronicles Parallel*, ed. C. Plummer, 2 vols. (Oxford, 1892), vol. I, p. 139; *EHD*, trans. Whitelock, p. 243)).

[25] S. Keynes and R. Naismith, 'The Agnus Dei Pennies of King Æthelred the Unready', *ASE* 40 (2011), 175–223.

(a)   (b)

Figure 8.5 Æthelred II (978–1016), Agnus Dei type, Salisbury mint, moneyer
Sæwine. (Image reproduced with the kind permission of the Fitzwilliam Museum,
Cambridge: CM.1–2009.)

issue instead places the Lamb of God on the obverse and the Holy Dove (or,
just possibly, an eagle) on the reverse.[26] It is known from only twenty-two
surviving specimens, struck at nine small to middling mint-places in an arc
extending from the East Midlands through Mercia down into Wessex. In
relative chronological terms, it clearly falls between Helmet and Last Small
Cross. Several features of the Agnus Dei type had become characteristic of
Æthelredian re-coinages: it was noticeably heavier than the preceding
Helmet issue and introduced small yet influential variations in the legend.
These features, above all the obvious religious message of the exceptional
iconography, together suggest that the coinage was issued in connection with
the events of late summer and autumn 1009 recorded in the *Anglo-Saxon
Chronicle*. After infighting had led the English fleet to disperse, a great viking
raiding army appeared off the coast of Kent in August and proceeded to fight
and pillage its way across southeast England. Æthelred and his counsellors
gathered in the safety of Bath, where they issued a law-code, now known as
VII Æthelred, which called for prayers, alms and other acts of devotion from
the populace so that God might spare them the wrath of the vikings.[27] The
Agnus Dei coinage would fit very well into this context.

---

[26] For the interpretation of the bird as an eagle, see D. Woods, 'The Agnus Dei Penny of King
Æthelred II: A Call to Hope in the Lord (Isaiah XL)?', *ASE* 42 (2013), 299–309.
[27] *Die Gesetze der Angelsachsen*, ed. F. Liebermann, 3 vols. (Halle, 1903–16), vol. I, pp. 260–2. See S.
Keynes, 'An Abbot, an Archbishop, and the Viking Raids of 1006–7 and 1009–12', *ASE* 36 (2007),
151–220, at 179–89.

Other arguments can be made for the dates of various late Anglo-Saxon coin issues, but few can be made to stick with any force. Beyond regnal dates, it is quite simply impossible to assign absolute dates to most late Anglo-Saxon coinages. It is also, consequently, impossible to determine how regular new coinages were – though the complexities of the initial reform and Æthelred II's Hand types and sudden changes of type at the deaths of kings or (probably) with Agnus Dei imply a degree of variation. Single-finds may now provide additional support for the proposition that coinages did not enjoy equal periods of circulation. As of 2010, a total of some 1,300 single-finds were known of coins minted between Edgar's reform and the Norman conquest.[28] These probably represent individual, chance losses rather than deliberate concealments. More finds are, of course, coming to light all the time, but these tend to confirm rather than challenge the broad patterns of the existing corpus. Small variations between the numbers of finds of different types are of uncertain significance, but larger ones are less easily explained away. Probably the most dramatic imbalance is in the reign of Cnut (1016–35). His three principal types – known as Quatrefoil, Helmet and Short Cross – have traditionally been assigned a roughly equal share of his nineteen-year reign. But the third type is known from dramatically more single finds than the other two – 182 specimens (as of 2011), by far the most of any late Anglo-Saxon type – whereas the two preceding types are known from fifty-seven and fifty-three finds, respectively. Possible explanations for the burst of finds during Short Cross might include changes in patterns of trade and tribute payments that led to a higher proportion of output than usual being injected into domestic circulation,[29] but the most straightforward explanation is that Short Cross simply lasted longer.

Single finds are only of any help in assessing the duration of types, however, if it is possible to accept that all or most losses of a given type took place during its period of circulation. Were the frequent type changes of late Anglo-Saxon England re-coinages that replaced each other in circulation? Overall, it is likely that they were, albeit with some limitations. Michael Dolley and others have drawn attention to the large number of hoards deposited in England that consist of just one type.[30] These account for about 55 per cent of all English hoards of the period and range in date

[28] Based on the sample assessed in R. Naismith, 'The English Monetary Economy, *c.* 973–1100: The Contribution of Single-Finds', *EconHR* 66 (2013), 198–225.

[29] R. Naismith, 'London and Its Mint *c.* 880–1066: A Preliminary Survey', *BNJ* 83 (2013), 44–74, at 57–8 and 68–9.

[30] See in particular Dolley and Metcalf, 'Reform', pp. 156–8.

from the early days of Æthelred II's reign to a small hoard made up entirely of Edward the Confessor's last type found hidden in the armpit of an execution victim near Winchester.[31] On the whole, hoards from the time of Æthelred II and Cnut include more single-type deposits than the subsequent thirty years to the Norman conquest, but the latter period includes several large and complex hoards associated with the events of 1066 (one of the few cases where military upheaval genuinely does seem to have left a large impact on hoard deposition) and, moreover, covers a period of more frequent changes in type. Many of the multi-type hoards consist of just two contiguous types, but there is also an appreciable number that contain a broader spread of more than two types, sometimes spanning several reigns or decades. Again, these occur throughout the period. A hoard from Lincolnshire of pennies of Æthelred II covered three or four early types,[32] while the huge Lenborough hoard of over 5,000 coins consisted of a large parcel of Cnut's last type alongside a cluster of pennies of several types of Æthelred minted some twenty or thirty years earlier.[33] The mixed messages of late Anglo-Saxon hoards suggest two conclusions. On the one hand, there was always a general tendency towards use of the current type, most pronounced in small assemblages likely to reflect circulating currency. On the other, people clearly held savings that might go back decades. One way to account for these divergent tendencies would be to imagine a system in which the current type was needed for important but specific purposes, such as payments to the king or transactions that would be witnessed by others.[34] These were enough to keep the current type circulating in force such that it supported a large number of mints across England and made up the bulk of what people had in their purses at any one time. But the common retention of older coins indicates that people anticipated some use for them, perhaps in private transactions. Re-coinages were thus major undertakings. People of high and low status across the kingdom would have frequently needed to gather up much of their moveable wealth and have it re-struck with the new design.

   To a certain extent, this relates to another well-known feature of late-tenth- and eleventh-century English coinage: the existence of many mints.

---

[31] A full Checklist of Coin Hoards from the British Isles, c. 450–1180 is maintained at www.fitzmu seum.cam.ac.uk/dept/coins/projects/hoards/, with the Stockbridge Down (Hants.) hoard no. 251. See also M. Allen, *Mints and Money in Medieval England* (Cambridge, 2012), pp. 382–97.

[32] Welbourn, Lincs. (Checklist no. 189).

[33] Full publication of this find is forthcoming as of November 2016; for now, see G. Williams, 'A Hoard from the Reign of Cnut from Buckinghamshire: A Preliminary Report', *ASE* 44 (2016 for 2015), 287–305.

[34] Stewart, 'Coinage and Re-coinage', p. 468.

In total, about 113 locations are named on coins as mint-places between the 970s and 1066. Eighty-five of these can be identified with confidence, while twenty-eight remain un-located. Not all worked at once: the most active during any one coin type is seventy-two. Moreover, most mint-places seem to have been relatively small in scale and often operated briefly. Some are known from just one surviving coin. The bulk of production was in fact heavily concentrated in a much smaller number of locations – above all, the major towns of eastern and southern England, such as Lincoln, Stamford, York, Winchester and particularly London.[35] For most of the late Anglo-Saxon period, the top five mint-towns together account for between half and three-quarters of all single-finds discovered in England. It is important to note that all five of these mint-towns, together with virtually all others of any substantial size, were well established by the time of Edgar's reform. The fifty-two mint places named on coins from between Alfred's later years and Edgar's reform already cover roughly the same area as the later mints, stretching from Exeter and Dover to York and Chester. What the later period added was a multitude of smaller mint-places in the spaces between. They include a cluster in the southwest associated with the numerous towns of Somerset and neighbouring shires and an interesting group of so-called emergency mints such as Salisbury, set up as defended refuges during the periods of heaviest viking attacks under Æthelred II.

Put simply, the large network of late Anglo-Saxon mint-places was not a support system for re-coinages. Re-coinages of a dramatically larger English currency were carried out in the late twelfth and thirteenth centuries on the basis of about a dozen or fewer mints.[36] The numerous late Anglo-Saxon mints were also not concentrated in areas of particularly dense population or intense coin circulation; East Anglia, for example, was one of the richest areas according to Domesday Book, but Norfolk and Suffolk had only four mints between them. The roles of different mint-places varied dramatically. London and York, for example, were probably driven by the demands of bustling cities with extensive overseas trade connections and important administrative roles. But most small mints were a function of local power and institutional geography. There was a strong connection between towns, even small ones, and minting, and any of them with a local goldsmith might be named on a few coins every now and then.[37] In an important sense, late Anglo-Saxon mints were simply

---

[35] Naismith, 'London', pp. 56–8.
[36] Allen, *Mints and Money*, pp. 41–72; and N. J. Mayhew, 'From Regional to Central Minting, 1158–1464', in *A New History of the Royal Mint*, ed. C. E. Challis (Cambridge, 1992), pp. 83–178.
[37] Cf. Dolley and Metcalf, 'Reform', pp. 147–9.

towns where moneyers worked, usually each in a separate workshop.[38] A few hints also point to the influence of local elite patronage. One layman claimed the income from a moneyer at Stamford,[39] and some of the small mints that are not situated in known towns may have been the creation of local landowners, suggesting that there was sometimes a greater degree of flexibility than was permitted in the law-codes.[40] Small mints and their operators undoubtedly benefited from re-coinages, which is probably when they did much or all of their business, but it is unlikely that they were set up with the intention of facilitating them.

The motives behind late Anglo-Saxon England's many re-coinages also remain opaque. Broadly speaking, the extraction of revenue for the king has been the dominant theme in scholarship.[41] However, there is very little evidence for how much income was drawn from the coinage or in what way. Domesday Book refers to moneyers in 1066 who had to pay twenty shillings when a new coin-type came in, and they had to collect fresh dies from London, possibly with another payment of similar scale soon after.[42] There is no specific mention in any source of proportional income from output being taken.[43] Yet, on some level, it is likely that one of the most puzzling features of the late Anglo-Saxon coinage relates to the manipulation of minting for profit: the weight of the penny. Late Roman and Carolingian legislation had stipulated that consistent weight was an integral feature of the coinage, crucial for distinguishing reliable currency and keyed into larger systems of weights and measures.[44] Although modelled on Roman and Carolingian precedents in many respects, tenth- and eleventh-century English coinage departed from this principle. There was significant variation in weight both between and

---

[38] Brand, *Periodic Change*, pp. 45–50; and Allen, *Mints and Money*, pp. 1–8.

[39] *Charters of Peterborough Abbey*, ed. S. Kelly, AS Charters 14 (Oxford, 2009), no. 31 (xi).

[40] E.g. III Æthelred c. 8. 1, declares that 'nan mann ne age nænne mynetere buton cyng' ('no-one except the king shall have a moneyer') (ed. Liebermann, vol. I, p. 230). II Æthelstan c. 14 (ed. Liebermann, vol. I, pp. 158–9) stipulates that minting must take place in a town, while IV Æthelred c. 5. 4 (ed. Liebermann, vol. I, p. 234; a composite text of uncertain date) states that moneyers forfeit their lives for working in woods or other places (presumably outside towns) unless the king shows mercy. The latter are usually presumed to be forgers but could have been working for patrons based nearby. See further E. Screen, 'Anglo-Saxon Law and Numismatics: A Reassessment in the Light of Patrick Wormald's *The Making of English Law*', *BNJ* 77 (2007), 150–72.

[41] E.g. Stewart, 'English and Norman', pp. 55–8.

[42] References are collected in P. Grierson, 'Domesday Book, the *Geld de moneta* and *monetagium*: A Forgotten Minting Reform', *BNJ* 55 (1985), 84–94, at 85–7.

[43] R. Naismith, *Money and Power in Anglo-Saxon England: The Southern English Kingdoms 757–865* (Cambridge, 2012), p. 43, assembles references to proportional income from minting in early medieval Europe.

[44] M. F. Hendy, *Studies in the Byzantine Monetary Economy, c. 300–1450* (Cambridge, 1985), pp. 329–38; K. F. Morrison and H. Grunthal, *Carolingian Coinage* (New York, 1967), pp. 35–7; and W. Kula, *Measures and Men*, trans. R. Szreter (Princeton, 1986), pp. 161–4.

within coin-types. Generally, it seems that early coins within a type were heavier and that mints in the west tended to make heavier coins than those in the east.[45] Both factors probably relate to the interplay of supply and demand and beg the question: *cui bono?* Weight variation of similar form can be traced back to well before Edgar's reform, at least to the time of Æthelstan.[46] Then and later, centralised management was apparent in nationwide tendencies for some types to be heavier or lighter, but the high degree of regional fluctuation points away from this being very prescriptive.[47] Indeed, a lot of the responsibility for deciding how much silver to put into each coin fell to individual mints or even moneyers, which on the face of it suggests that the initiative lay at this level. Weight variation may have been the way in which moneyers profited from their work. In 1066, according to Domesday Book, the king's profit would have included the flat fees charged on moneyers at the time of re-coinage, and earls benefitted from these too by means of the third penny levied on urban dues.[48] In addition to this, the king may also have had the special privilege of commanding payment in forms other than simply counting out coins. This appears to have been how most of the population operated before 1066. Laws stipulated that one good penny had to be accepted for another,[49] and hoards do not seem to show evidence of users systematically extracting low-weight coins. But Domesday Book shows royal estates sometimes using different means of payment besides *ad numerum* ('by number/ account'): the king could demand payment by weight or by assay – that is, melted and purified. The latter meant, in 1066, a surcharge of 30 per cent in terms of the number of pennies needed.[50]

The king could, if he wished, probably use these means to bring in quite a substantial sum. But it is worth pausing to consider how the exercise of re-coinage was viewed. It was not necessarily a money-making scheme in the sense of profit, or at least not primarily. Datable re-coinages point in several directions. New types seem to have been the norm when new kings from Cnut onwards took the throne.[51] The case of the Agnus Dei coinage also suggests that the exercise could be undertaken at a time of dire and

---

[45] Metcalf, *Atlas*, pp. 66–9 and 133; and Keynes and Naismith, 'Agnus Dei', p. 189.

[46] Naismith, 'Prelude', pp. 68–70.

[47] Critical for assessment of weight standards are the tables in H. B. A. Petersson, 'Coins and Weights. Late Anglo-Saxon Pennies and Mints, *c.* 973–1066', in *Studies*, ed. Jonsson, pp. 207–433.

[48] For the following points, see now S. Harvey, *Domesday: Book of Judgement* (Oxford, 2014), pp. 133–60.

[49] Screen, 'Anglo-Saxon Law'.   [50] DB I, fol. 16r.

[51] It should be noted, however, that Edmund Ironside apparently never issued any coins in 1016, and small numbers of coins using the last type of the previous king were struck for Harold I and Edward the Confessor.

unforeseen need. What stands out is the coinage's capacity to adapt swiftly to changing circumstances, especially at the highest political level. Late Anglo-Saxon legislation and religious literature strongly support this view of a symbolically charged and highly responsive monetary system.[52] Re-coinage was hence on one level a practical exercise that could produce royal income, but on another it was an affirmation of the high expectations for society expressed in charters, religious tracts and other sources.[53] Forgery of the king's coinage was a deep concern, re-coinage being the best defence against it in the view of the ruling authorities. Works associated with Archbishop Wulfstan in particular refer a number of times to re-coinage with the term *feos bot* ('improvement of the coinage'). Wulfstan put *feos bot* alongside improvement of the peace, *friðes bot*, and avoidance of heinous crimes such as theft, treachery and adultery.[54] As is well known, Wulfstan was partly driven by a taste for alliteration as well as by zeal to improve English morals, but his discussion of the coinage placed it at the heart of general concern with the spiritual wellbeing of the kingdom.[55] How often kings actually patterned their actions on such teachings is a matter of debate – but Æthelred II is especially likely to have paid heed. It is probable that his coinage, and with it the idea of frequent re-coinage, was the product of moral and religious motives as well as financial ones, and of course all of these could combine in different ways under different circumstances.

It was this coinage that constituted one of the most impressive characteristics of the late Anglo-Saxon 'state', as described most famously by Sir Frank Stenton and James Campbell.[56] Both came to the subject in the wake of the phenomenal burst of activity by Dolley and his colleagues, at a time when the 'sexennial thesis' was generally accepted. They set the currency alongside Domesday Book and other aspects of late Anglo-Saxon infrastructure as evidence for the ambition and reach of royal

---

[52] Keynes and Naismith, 'Agnus Dei', pp. 197–9.

[53] A point developed in R. Naismith, 'The Coinage of Æthelred II: A New Evaluation', *English Studies* 97 (2016), 117–39, esp. 125–32.

[54] See V Æthelred, c. 26. 1; VI Æthelred, c. 31, 32. 1–2; II Cnut, c. 8 (ed. Liebermann, vol. I, pp. 242–3, 254–5 and 314–15); also *Wulfstan: Sammlung der ihm zugeschriebenen Homilien nebst Untersuchungen über ihre Echtheit*, ed. A. Napier (Berlin, 1883), pp. 171 a (no. L).

[55] D. Whitelock, 'Wulfstan, Homilist and Statesman', *TRHS*, 4th series, 24 (1942), 25–45, at 42–4; also P. Wormald, 'Archbishop Wulfstan: Eleventh-Century State-Builder', in *Wulfstan, Archbishop of York: The Proceedings of the Second Alcuin Conference*, ed. M. Townend (Turnhout, 2004), pp. 9–27, at 21–4.

[56] F. M. Stenton, *Anglo-Saxon England*, 3rd edn (Oxford, 1971), pp. 535–7; F. M. Stenton, *Preparatory to Anglo-Saxon England: Being the Collected Papers of Frank Merry Stenton*, ed. D. M. Stenton (Oxford, 1970), pp. 374–5; and J. Campbell, *Essays in Anglo-Saxon History* (London, 1986), pp. 155–89; and J. Campbell, *The Anglo-Saxon State* (London, 2000).

government, tantamount to a 'state'. The view of the coinage outlined earlier consequently has ramifications for interpretation of the later tenth- and eleventh-century kingdom of England as a whole.

It should first be stressed that the coinage still retains considerable force as a gauge for the scale and effectiveness of late Anglo-Saxon government. None of the points made here seriously shake or stir the estimation of the monetary system. The major qualification relates to how the coinage evolved and fitted into other aspects of thought and administration. The monetary system probably did not appear fully formed in one go but was the product of a long course of development in the tenth century and a generation of particularly intense elaboration under Edgar and in the early years of Æthelred II. The coinage project of this time fits comfortably into a concern for unity and an affirmation of the Christian responsibilities of kingship in a realm that was, in its current form, still quite newly established.[57] Probably the most prominent manifestation of this outlook comes in texts associated with the so-called Benedictine reform circle. The *Regularis concordia* celebrated the role of the king at the head of a network of reformed monastic houses, and the vernacular tract known as *Edgar's Establishment of Monasteries* praised Edgar for bringing the divided kingdom of 957–9 back together.[58] St Æthelwold, who probably drafted both of these texts, along with St Dunstan, enjoyed close contact with the royal household and influenced aspects of Edgar and the young Æthelred's rule. They had both the outlook and the position needed to help steer modification of the coinage over the course of several decades.[59]

The mature form of the late Anglo-Saxon monetary system, as it emerged by about the 990s, was a versatile entity. Despite severe viking attacks later in the reign of Æthelred II, royal strife in the mid-1030s and even the Norman conquest in 1066, the system persevered. The coinage provides an important example of an institution vested in local agents

[57] G. Molyneaux, *The Formation of the English Kingdom in the Tenth Century* (Oxford, 2015), pp. 182–99 and 216–30; and Naismith, 'Prelude', pp. 80–3.

[58] *Regularis concordia*, Prologue Chap. 4 (*Consuetudinum saeculi X/XI/XII monumenta non-Cluniacensia*, ed. T. Symons, rev. S. Spath, M. Wegener and K. Hallinger, Corpus Consuetudinum Monasticarum 7.3 (Siegburg, 1984), p. 71); and *Councils and Synods, with Other Documents Relating to the English Church 871–1204*, ed. D. Whitelock, C. Brooke and M. Brett, 2 vols. (Oxford, 1981), vol. I, pp. 146–7. For the latter text, see now D. Pratt, 'The Voice of the King in "King Edgar's Establishment of Monasteries"', *ASE* 41 (2013), 145–204.

[59] Molyneaux, *Formation*, pp. 189–93; B. A. E. Yorke, 'Æthelwold and the Politics of the Tenth Century', in *Bishop Æthelwold: His Career and Influence*, ed. B. A. E. Yorke (Woodbridge, 1988), pp. 65–88; N. P. Brooks, 'The Career of St Dunstan', in his *Anglo-Saxon Myths: State and Church 400–1066* (London, 2000), pp. 155–80; and M. Winterbottom and M. Lapidge, *The Early Lives of St Dunstan* (Oxford, 2012), pp. xx–xlii.

dispersed over a wide area that was at the same time highly responsive to the actions of the central authority.[60] The late Anglo-Saxon monetary system must have come into being because there was both a will and a way at several levels in society to keep the system on track. Campbell's point remains valid: if late Anglo-Saxon government was able to do this with the coinage, much the same could have been accomplished in other less well-evidenced arenas.[61] Timothy Reuter rightly noted the risk of inferring too much from a single sphere such as coinage,[62] but the benefit of the coinage is surely that while its relatively good level of survival (governed by forces quite separate from those which affected charters and manu- scripts) makes it an important source for modern historians, there is no sign that contemporaries thought of it as a uniquely well-managed aspect of life. If it really was so unrepresentative, it has left a faint footprint in a relatively large body of written material. When the monetary system does feature in Domesday Book or late Anglo-Saxon law-codes, it is in a relatively minor way, alongside a great deal else described in much the same vein. Hence there is good cause to wonder whether the evidently efficient methods of co-ordinating activity at over a hundred mint-places were similar to those used for the distribution of writs and collection of *heregeld*.[63]

In other words, the coinage is representative of a core cluster of functions and powers that later Anglo-Saxon kings could use to make their presence felt in a real and sometimes very forceful way across a large swathe of the kingdom, with looser forms of over-lordship beyond.[64] These functions and powers had developed in response to specific circumstances. The coinage is a very good example of this; so, too, is the *heregeld*, an annual tax to support viking mercenaries that appeared in 1012 during a time of crisis but persisted for generations to come.[65] Implementation of both the coinage and the *heregeld* involved brutal consequences for those who did not participate. Severe fines, even mutilation, were stipulated for those caught forging false coin and for those who refused good coin. The city of Worcester was ravaged when its inhabitants killed two tax collectors in

[60] Stenton, *Preparatory*, p. 374.   [61] F. g Campbell, *Anglo-Saxon State*, pp. 32–3.
[62] T. Reuter, *Medieval Politics & Modern Mentalities*, ed. J. L. Nelson (Cambridge, 2006), p. 290.
[63] For discussion of this, see Chapter 9 in this volume.
[64] G. Molyneaux, 'Why Were Some Tenth-Century English Kings Presented as Rulers of Britain?', *TRHS*, 6th series, 21 (2011), 59–91, at 80–91; and Molyneaux, *Formation*, pp. 2–9 and 15–47.
[65] C. Wickham, 'Lineages of Western European Taxation, 1000–1200', in *Actes. Colloqui Corona: municipis i fiscalitat a la baixa Edat Mitjana*, ed. M. Sánchez and A. Furió (Lleida, 1997), pp. 25–42, at 28–32; and L. Roach, *Kingship and Consent in Anglo-Saxon England, 871–978: Assemblies and the State in the Early Middle Ages* (Cambridge, 2013), pp. 216–17.

1041.[66] This dimension of royal power could leave an impressive footprint in silver and in ink, but also in blood. Effective authority came at a price.

The term 'state' carries a great deal of baggage, not least in a medieval context. Both the concept and the word need to be handled with care, as Sarah Foot, Susan Reynolds and others have stressed.[67] Anglo-Saxon England's royal government was robust and durable, weathering multiple invasions and changes of dynasty; it was thus not bound to any one king or family and so invites conceptualisation as a 'state' based on the specific circumstances of tenth- and eleventh-century England.[68] The 'nation-state' is just one possible dimension of the term, though it is the one that has been explicitly or implicitly central to consideration of late Anglo-Saxon England.[69] But there can also be a 'nanny state' or a 'welfare state', referring to a particular outlook or area of activity for the ruling authorities rather than a totalising definition for the polity as a whole.[70] This is, of course, to transplant yet more labels and ideas from one period to another but might be a helpful way to see late Anglo-Saxon kingship operating. In this sense, kingship itself comes close to being the state. The coinage, collection of *heregeld* and nationwide tribute payments and some aspects of legislation and documentation stand out as key means of the king implementing his will across the kingdom through the support of numerous local agents of different levels of prominence.[71] Oaths and pledges helped to cement a general allegiance to the crown.[72] No one group in society was charged with direct responsibility for all these areas. Rather, the burden of maintaining the king's prerogatives was spread quite widely. Ealdormen and earls seem to have had little to do

[66] *ASC* MSS CD, 1041.
[67] S. Foot, 'The Historiography of the Anglo-Saxon "Nation-State"', in *Power and the Nation in European History*, ed. L. E. Scales and O. Zimmer (Cambridge, 2005), pp. 125–42; and S. Reynolds, 'The Historiography of the Medieval State', in *The Routledge Companion to Historiography*, ed. M. Bentley (London, 1997), pp. 117–38.
[68] S. Baxter, 'The Limits of the Late Anglo-Saxon State', in *Der frühmittelalterliche Staat – europäische Perspektiven*, ed. W. Pohl (Vienna, 2009), pp. 503–14; and Reuter, *Medieval Polities*, p. 290.
[69] Foot, 'Historiography'.
[70] R. Davies, 'The Medieval State: The Tyranny of a Concept?', *Journal of Historical Sociology* 16 (2003), 280–300, esp. 283–93; with S. Reynolds, 'There Were States in Medieval Europe: A Response to Rees Davies', *Journal of Historical Sociology* 16 (2003), 550–5.
[71] Cf. Campbell, *Anglo-Saxon State*, pp. 201–25.
[72] M. Ammon, '"Ge mid wedde ge mid aðe": the Functions of Oath and Pledge in Anglo-Saxon Legal Culture', *Historical Research* 86 (2013), 515–35; Molyneaux, *Formation*, pp. 63–5; and P. Wormald, '*Papers Preparatory to the Making of English Law: King Alfred to the Twelfth Century. Volume II: From God's Law to Common Law*', ed. S. Baxter and J. G. H. Hudson (London, 2014), pp. 112–29.

with minting except a slice of the profits,[73] for example, while shire and other reeves had separate duties,[74] as did moneyers. Dispersal of responsibility for the machinery of royal government created mutually supporting pillars, each depending on the others. No hard and fast line should be drawn for where a 'nanny state', or perhaps better a 'schoolmaster state', version of the late Anglo-Saxon kingdom began and ended. There was evidently a great deal the royal regime could not do or did not want to do. Local agents supportive of the regime in one context could challenge it in others. Law-codes tend to foreground a relatively regularised vision of justice, whereas dispute settlements show that things were much more variable on the ground and engagement with the royal establishment very selective.[75] If there was an Anglo-Saxon state, it needs to be seen as one aspect and perspective of life in the kingdom; more than a glint in the eye of the kings and top-level counsellors who lay at its apex yet less than the totality of all that lay between the Channel and the debatable lands of the north.

[73] S. Baxter, *The Earls of Mercia: Lordship and Power in Late Anglo-Saxon England* (Oxford, 2007), pp. 74–124.
[74] C. Cubitt, '"As the Lawbook Teaches": Reeves, Lawbooks and Urban Life in the Anonymous Old English *Legend of the Seven Sleepers*', *EHR* 124 (2009), 1021–49, at 1034–43; and A. Williams, *Kingship and Government in Pre-Conquest England, c. 500–1066* (Basingstoke, 1999), pp. 108–13.
[75] P. Wormald, *The Making of English Law, King Alfred to the Twelfth Century,* vol. 1: *Legislation and Its Limits* (Oxford, 1999), pp. 430–65; Wormald, 'Papers Preparatory', pp. 8–11; and Roach, *Kingship*, pp. 122–46.

CHAPTER 9

Charters and Exemption from Geld in Anglo-Saxon England

David Pratt

This chapter brings together a subject central to Simon's interests – the role of charters in late Anglo-Saxon government – and a further subject on which he has offered sound guidance, the *heregeld*, or land tax, introduced in 1012 for the purpose of paying the Scandinavian mercenary fleet based in London.[1] In making connections, it pays homage to Simon's outstanding contributions not only with regard to Anglo-Saxon charters but also concerning so many other subjects. The geld itself is reasonably well understood as a component of the late Anglo-Saxon administrative system. It appears to have been levied in the period 1012–51; sums raised included £21,000 in 1014, £21,099 in 1040–1 and £11,048 in 1041 or 1042. The tax's operation has largely to be inferred from later evidence, leading to some debate on the overall scale of revenue, on exemptions from geld and on the question of its abolition in 1051. Elsewhere I have argued that the general exemption of demesne land from geld was a post-Conquest innovation.[2] There were pre-Conquest exemptions from geld, but these took the form of specific concessions or reductions in hidage; it follows that geld in the pre-Conquest period was ordinarily levied on larger hidages, which helps to make sense of the *Chronicle*'s figures. The report that the geld had been abolished in 1051 should be taken seriously.

Of this overall picture, however, one may ask the question that Simon always rightly urges: what about the charter record? The question of the relationship between the operation of the geld and the terms conceded in Latin diplomas has not been systematically explored, but this may reflect

---

[1] S. Keynes, 'The Historical Context of the Battle of Maldon', in *The Battle of Maldon AD 991*, ed. D. Scragg (Oxford, 1991), pp. 81–113, at 99–102.
[2] D. Pratt, 'Demesne Exemption from Royal Taxation in Anglo-Saxon and Anglo-Norman England', *EHR* 128 (2013), 1–34. See also A. Wareham, 'Fiscal Policies and the Institution of a Tax State in Anglo-Saxon England within a Comparative Context', *EconHR* 65 (2012), 910–31; S. Harvey, *Domesday: Book of Judgement* (Oxford, 2014), esp. pp. 210–38; and D. Roffe and K. S. B. Keats-Rohan (eds.), *Domesday Now: New Approaches to the Inquest and the Book* (Woodbridge, 2016).

the problems involved.[3] There is a lack of explicit references to geld in certainly authentic diplomas; one faces the difficulty of working backwards from Domesday and of relating Anglo-Saxon charter material to the Domesday record. Conceptually, nevertheless, important issues are raised by the levying of geld in an administrative system underpinned by the conveying of land by diploma and by the distinction between bookland and folkland, for from the eighth century in the case of Mercian diplomas and from the mid-ninth century in the case of diplomas issued by West Saxon kings, immunity clauses had regularly specified the conveying of land as exempt from all secular burdens, with the exception of the three 'common burdens' of military service, bridge-building and fortress work.[4] The formulation amounted to the standard terms for the conveying of bookland in later Anglo-Saxon England and remained typical during the period in which geld was levied.

Of particular importance is the general freeing of land from all burdens, save the common three. At the time of the emergence of more detailed immunity clauses, in eighth-century Mercia, the language is thought to have referred to forms of tribute, render and hospitality ordinarily due from all forms of land and levied by means of the hidage system.[5] Although such duties may have been in long-term decline, the enduring nature of the standard form of reservation clause suggests that they remained important. Yet geld too was a form of secular taxation levied per hide. An important question is whether geld also counted as a secular burden. Prima facie it would be unwise to judge the matter beyond reviewing the range of possible scenarios. It is conceivable that geld liability might have been treated as a secular burden, but if so, one would need to revise very significantly all understanding of the pre-Conquest geld, since this would imply that bookland had typically been exempt. Alternatively, it is conceivable that geld liability was regarded as falling within the burden of military service, in which case the possession of a diploma reserving the common burdens would be of no consequence for the levying of the tax. A further possibility is that geld liability was regarded as falling outside the

---

[3] For some relevant remarks, cf. P. Vinogradoff, *English Society in the Eleventh Century: Essays in English Mediaeval History* (Oxford, 1908), pp. 195–6 and 254–5; F. M. Stenton, *The Latin Charters of the Anglo-Saxon Period* (Oxford, 1955), pp. 56–9 and 72–4; and C. W. Hollister, *Anglo-Saxon Military Institutions on the Eve of the Norman Conquest* (Oxford, 1962), pp. 20–1, 49–50, 53–5 and 59–63.

[4] W. H. Stevenson, '*Trinoda Necessitas*', *EHR* 29 (1914), 689–703; and N. Brooks, 'The Development of Military Obligations in Eighth- and Ninth-Century England', in his *Communities and Warfare 700–1400* (London, 2000), pp. 32–47.

[5] Brooks, 'Development of Military Obligations', pp. 34–5; and A. Gautier, 'Hospitality in Pre-Viking Anglo-Saxon England', *EME* 17 (2009), 23–44.

usual terms of immunity and reservation clauses, in which case one might envisage wider administrative leeway in determining the tax's incidence.

Assessing these scenarios is a tricky task, which must rely on three categories of evidence. The first two are forms of exemption from geld as recorded in Domesday material: firstly, instances of exemption from geld specifically identified as having been conceded in the pre-Conquest period, which I have listed elsewhere, and, secondly, the broad category of estates or territory regarded as geld-free or as having never paid geld, examples of which are conveniently listed by Rosamond Faith.[6] The third category is the small group of pre-Conquest writs concerned with royal decisions relating to hidage and geld assessment.[7] To the various exemptions may be added one further perspective afforded by a small group of later Anglo-Saxon diplomas, namely, those which appear to concede outright exemption from the common burdens.[8] Although the diplomas in question are exceptional and variously problematic, they have special value for the unusual treatment of military service. The purpose of this chapter is to compare the three categories of evidence with the Anglo-Saxon charter record. The enquiry is inevitably limited by issues of survival: in each case there is only limited overlap with estates whose later Anglo-Saxon history can be even partially reconstructed from the charter record. Although the opportunities for comparison are modest, they yield a number of instructive examples.

Domesday Instances of Specific Exemption and the Evidence of Pre-Conquest Writs and Diplomas

Of the three categories, one may begin with the first: Domesday instances of specific pre-Conquest exemption from geld, which provide the best opportunity to reconstruct aspects of the geld regime.[9] Entries typically record a reduction in the assessment of an estate, either by treating a number of hides as exempt or by reducing the overall number of assessed hides. Eighteen instances are known, but they probably reflect more widespread practices. Two features of the corpus seem particularly significant. Firstly, concessions are universally represented as depending on the king's will, in most cases Edward, but Æthelred II and Cnut each have a single

---

[6] Pratt, 'Demesne Exemption', pp. 33–4, to which one should add the instance of Alverstoke, Hampshire: GDB, fol. 41c (Hampshire 3: 12). R. Faith, *The English Peasantry and the Growth of Lordship* (London, 1997), pp. 268–9.

[7] F. E. Harmer, *Anglo-Saxon Writs* (Manchester, 1952), pp. 19, 61 and 65.   [8] See below.

[9] Pratt, 'Demesne Exemption', pp. 33–4, cf. p. 19.

entry.[10] Secondly, four examples are recorded in terms implying that an exemption might be confirmed by royal writ. Two entries, for Lechlade, Gloucestershire, and Rockbourne, Hampshire, have been seen as referring to lost writs in the Confessor's name.[11] Two further entries, for Pyrford, Surrey, and Hartley Mauduitt, Hampshire, record purported exemptions that had come to be disputed after the Conquest.[12] In each case, the lack of a writ is regarded as undermining the claim, as if a writ would ordinarily be expected in such circumstances.

These Domesday entries are important because they lend support to what might be termed the 'maximum view' of the use of writs in the pre-Conquest period. Simon's observations remain compelling in the case made for the centrality of writs in communicating royal judgements and enactments to the shire court, their skewed survival reflecting the fact that writs would initially have reached the officials of the shire court and less commonly have been retrieved for preservation in ecclesiastical archives.[13] Another strand in his argument is also relevant, that while the vast majority of writs relate in some way to the conveying of land, the smaller number on other subjects provides an indication of the form's wider use.[14] The small sub-group of writs relating to hidage and geld assessment appears to confirm the Domesday picture. The classic Bury writ in the name of King Edward, either from the latter part of 1051 or conceivably from later in the 1050s, announcing the exemption of the house's inland from '*here-geld* and from every other render (*gaful*)' may be of the same type as those referred to in Domesday.[15] Two further writs, pertaining to Canterbury and Wells, each give royal confirmation of the rate at which an office-holder should discharge the obligations falling on his landholding.[16] The

---

[10] GDB, fol. 165d (Gloucestershire 12: 1) and fol. 252c (Shropshire 3C: 2).

[11] GDB, fol. 169a (Gloucestershire 59: 1) (= S 1869) and fol. 50b (Hampshire 69: 30) (= S 1864). Harmer, *Anglo-Saxon Writs*, pp. 543–4.

[12] GDB, fol. 32b (Surrey 6: 5) and fol. 47c (Hampshire 35: 2).

[13] S. Keynes, *The Diplomas of King Æthelred 'the Unready' 978–1016* (Cambridge, 1980), pp. 140–5; cf. also Harmer, *Anglo-Saxon Writs*, pp. 16–19 and 34–8; and R. Sharpe, 'The Use of Writs in the Eleventh Century', *ASE* 32 (2003), 247–91, esp. 283–9.

[14] Keynes, *Diplomas*, p. 141.

[15] S 1075 (*ASWrits* 15); for the dating, see Sharpe, 'The Use of Writs', p. 280. Cf. S 1131 (*ASWrits* 87), a writ of King Edward giving notice of his conveying of land at Shepperton, Middlesex, to Teinfrith, his 'churchwright', 'exempt from scot and tribute' (*scotfreo and gafulfreo*), which lacks reference to *heregeld*. See Harmer, *Anglo-Saxon Writs*, pp. 319–20; cf. other purported writs relating to Shepperton of questionable authority (S 1120, S 1130, S 1137 and S 1148).

[16] S 987 (*CantCC* 156); S 1113 (*Wells* 36). Cf. also S 1067 (*North* 13), a writ by which King Edward gave permission to Archbishop Ealdred to draw up a *priuilegium* for the lands of St John's minster at Beverley. The Domesday entry for Beverley reported that 'St John's carucate' had always been free from the king's geld: GDB, fol. 304a (Yorkshire 2: E1). It is unclear whether this arrangement was

formulaic nature of the terms points to a standard type of document in wider use.

These writs may be compared with two others that are problematic. Pride of place is taken by the much-discussed Chilcomb writ in the name of King Æthelred, which purportedly assessed the large Chilcomb estate of the Old Minster, Winchester, at one hide.[17] The document relates to a sequence of forged charters designed to demonstrate the long-standing nature of Chilcomb's assessment and may be best regarded as a further piece of wishful thinking, but it remains valuable in indicating, by inference from the claim that the document was intended to defend, a credible type of document.[18] Different problems are posed by the extraordinary writ of Gospatric, pertaining to Cumbria, the terms of which state that all who dwell there are to be 'exempt from geld (*geyldfreo*) as I am'.[19] Of great importance for the understanding of the northwest, the writ survives as a very late single-sheet, and many aspects of it remain obscure. Perhaps the most satisfactory interpretation would regard the writ as having been issued by Gospatric, son of Maldred, while earl of Northumbria (1067–8 and 1070–2), in which case the reference to geld would need to be seen in a post-Conquest context.[20] As David Woodman has pointed out, the fact that Cumbria had recently fallen under English rule 'may have made the requirement of tax an unlikely expectation'.[21] As I have argued, a strong case can be advanced that the Conqueror presided over a major reassessment of the kingdom, principally involving the general exemption of the demesne land of tenants-in-chief.[22] It is conceivable that Gospatric's concessions, along with the reference to his own freedom from tax, may have related to this broader reassessment, but the suggestion can only be speculative.

Taken together, the specific exemptions and the writs point away from the first scenario raised earlier, that geld might have been a secular burden. The specific exemptions, and at the very least the Bury writ, show the king reducing the assessment of particular estates and doing so without regard

---

among the rights conceded by S 1067; see D. A. Woodman, *Charters of Northern Houses*, AS Charters 16 (Oxford, 2012), p. 223.

[17] S 946 (*ASWrits* 107), with *Property and Piety in Early Medieval Winchester: Documents Relating to the Topography of the Anglo-Saxon and Norman City and Its Minsters*, ed. A. R. Rumble, Winchester Studies 4. iii: The Anglo-Saxon Minsters of Winchester, ed. M. Biddle (Oxford, 2002), pp. 223–5 (no. 30).

[18] See below.   [19] S 1243 (*North* 21), reproduced in *North*, plate 2.

[20] C. Phythian-Adams, *Land of the Cumbrians: A Study in British Provincial Origins, A.D. 400–1120* (Aldershot, 1996), pp. 174–81, cf. 152–5; and Woodman, *Charters of Northern Houses*, pp. 363–4.

[21] Woodman, *Charters of Northern Houses*, p. 365.   [22] Pratt, 'Demesne Exemption', pp. 10–16.

for the terms on which the land was held. If geld had been a secular burden, with the consequence that bookland had typically been exempt, any adjustments to the assessment of estates already held as bookland would not have been meaningful. This view may be strengthened by consideration of the different formulae used to record the assessment of estates in the various Domesday regional circuits. Common to several of the circuits was the concept of an estate's assessment 'TRE', in the time of King Edward, representing the number of hides (or carucates or sulungs) on which the estate had discharged obligations during the Confessor's reign. The TRE figure ordinarily included demesne hidages: this is shown by the formula of Circuit I, covering the southeast, which contrasted the TRE figure with the number of hides 'now' (*modo*), usually a lesser figure.[23] The south-eastern formula was a distinctive means of representing the Conqueror's major reassessment of the kingdom based on the general exemption of the demesne lands of tenants-in-chief.[24] The TRE figures for Circuit III, covering the central and east midlands, similarly included demesne hidages, but in this case the formula involved the separate recording of hides in demesne.[25] Throughout these formulae one should note the lack of interest in the tenure or terms on which estates had been held in the pre-Conquest period.[26] If one imagines a scenario in which bookland had typically enjoyed exemption from geld, then the TRE hidages would have been wildly inaccurate as a measure of the hides actually liable to the tax due to the scale of landholding held as bookland rather than folkland. Though one may debate the precise purpose of the TRE hidages, these considerations point away from geld having been a secular burden.

One may also compare the specific exemptions with the charter record, which is, unfortunately, not voluminous. Of eighteen instances of specific exemption, only three estates yield pre-Conquest diplomas of unimpeachable authenticity: the sparsity may relate to the relatively large number of estates in secular hands TRE, a notable feature of the corpus. Of considerable interest is the estate at Beedon, Berkshire, held TRE by a certain Northmann from the abbot of Abingdon.[27] According to Domesday,

---

[23] S. P. J. Harvey, 'Taxation and the Economy', in *Domesday Studies*, ed. J. C. Holt (Woodbridge, 1986), pp. 249–64, at 257–60.

[24] Pratt, 'Demesne Exemption', pp. 10–14 and 16.

[25] Harvey, 'Taxation and the Economy', pp. 260–1.

[26] D. Roffe, *Domesday: The Inquest and the Book* (Oxford, 2000), pp. 34–46, has suggested that the [x] *tenuit* formula was used within Domesday to identify pre-Conquest king's thegns holding bookland with sake and soke; for objections to this view, see the review by S. Baxter, available at www.history.ac.uk/reviews/review/216.

[27] GDB, fol. 58d (Berkshire 7: 15).

Beedon had been assessed at ten hides TRE but had properly comprised fifteen hides and had been subject to a concession by King Edward reducing the assessment to eleven hides. Part of the estate, comprising ten hides at Stanmore in Beedon, had been conveyed by King Eadred to the king's thegn Wulfric in a diploma dated 948 (possibly in error for 947), with freedom from all secular duties save the common burdens.[28] The diploma, universally regarded as authentic, is one of a substantial series preserved in the Abingdon archives in favour of laymen, relating to estates in which Abingdon had an interest.[29] Beedon is also referred to in a problematic diploma in the name of King Edgar, conveying five hides at Beedon to Abingdon in 965, with reservation of the common burdens only.[30] The diploma is one of a group with suspicious formulation and employing a witness list seemingly borrowed from a charter of 970: it probably represents a fabrication intended to provide documentation for interests that Abingdon had acquired in the Beedon estate.[31] In the case of the Eadred diploma, therefore, and probably the Edgarian one as well, Abingdon had diplomas freeing the Beedon estate from all duties save the common burdens, yet it was still necessary during the Confessor's reign to have the assessment reduced by the king's decision.

A second case is the estate at Pyrford, Surrey, held TRE by Harold from King Edward. The assessment appears to have been disputed after the Conquest: according to Domesday, Pyrford had been assessed at twenty-seven hides before Harold held it, but after he had it, at sixteen hides 'at Harold's pleasure', an assessment for which the men of the hundred could not remember seeing a writ.[32] In a diploma of 956, King Eadwig had conveyed sixteen hides at Pyrford to his *carus* Eadric, subject only to the common burdens.[33] The diploma is also among those in favour of laymen preserved in the Abingdon archives, in this case relating to land with no known connection to the abbey.[34] Although the tenure on which Harold

---

[28] S 542 (*Abing* 42).

[29] Keynes, *Diplomas*, p. 12; cf. also S. E. Kelly, *Charters of Abingdon Abbey*, AS Charters vii–viii, 2 parts (Oxford, 2000), pp. cxxxi–cxxxvi.

[30] S 732 (*Abing* 103).

[31] Keynes, *Diplomas*, p. 11, n. 16; cf. also Kelly, *Charters of Abingdon*, pp. 412–14; and S. Keynes, 'A Conspectus of the Charters of King Edgar, 957–75', in *Edgar, King of the English 957–975: New Interpretations*, ed. D. Scragg (Woodbridge, 2008), pp. 60–80, at 69 and 76. Abingdon may have acquired Beedon through a bequest by Ealdorman Eadwine of Sussex (*d.* 982): Kelly, *Charters of Abingdon*, p. 581 (app. 4. xi), cf. pp. clxii and 414.

[32] GDB, fol. 32b (Surrey 6: 5); and S. Baxter, *The Earls of Mercia: Lordship and Power in Late Anglo-Saxon England* (Oxford, 2007), p. 108. See also below.

[33] S 621 (*Abing* 63).

[34] Keynes, *Diplomas*, p. 12; cf. also Kelly, *Charters of Abingdon*, pp. cxxxvi–cliii.

had held Pyrford from King Edward is uncertain, it seems that the estate had become royal property in the intervening period. Interestingly, although Pyrford had previously been freed from all secular burdens save the common burdens by the charter of 956, during the Confessor's reign, it was clearly subject to geld. Although the estate might conceivably have reverted to folkland or have been otherwise reorganized by Edward's day, Harold's reduced assessment of sixteen hides may suggest memory of Pyrford's mid-tenth-century hidage.[35]

The third case is unexpectedly poignant: the estate at Maugersbury, Gloucestershire, eight hides of which were held in 1086 by St Mary's, Evesham.[36] According to Domesday, a ninth hide, pertaining to the church of St Edward, had been given by King Æthelred free from geld. The entry provides the earliest reference to the church dedicated to King Edward at Stow-on-the-Wold, on the nearby hill overlooking Maugersbury.[37] The record of Æthelred's favour supports the case for regarding the dedication as part of the early cult of Edward the Martyr. The bounds of an estate comprising seven hides at Maugersbury are included in an unimpeachable 'alliterative' charter of King Eadred dated 949, by which he conveyed twelve hides at Bourton-on-the Water to the king's thegn Wulfric.[38] Evesham's possession of both Maugersbury and Bourton in 1086 may explain the diploma's preservation in the abbey's archives. Unfortunately, the terms on which Maugersbury was held by Evesham before the Conquest are uncertain, but the near fit of the diploma's hidage figure for Maugersbury and the specificity of Æthelred's concession remain striking.

Domesday Geld-Free Areas and the Charter Record

A further angle of enquiry is provided by the broader category of estates and territory in Domesday that are regarded as geld-free or as having never paid geld: these, too, may be compared with the charter record. These

---

[35] For a discussion of the possibilities, see Kelly, *Charters of Abingdon*, p. 269, cf. pp. cxli–cxlii.

[36] GDB, fol. 165d (Gloucestershire 12: 1).

[37] *VCH Gloucestershire*, vol. VI, ed. C. Elrington (London, 1965), pp. 144 and 159; cf. S. Keynes, 'The Cult of King Edward the Martyr during the Reign of King Æthelred the Unready', in *Gender and Historiography: Studies in the Earlier Middle Ages in Honour of Pauline Stafford*, ed. J. L. Nelson, S. Reynolds and S. M. Johns (London, 2012), pp. 115–25.

[38] S 550 (KCD 426 and vol. III, pp. 429–30), reproduced in *BAFacs*, no. 43. On Maugersbury, see D. N. Dumville, *Wessex and England from Alfred to Edgar* (Woodbridge, 1992), pp. 41–2, n. 58. S 935 (KCD 723), a purported charter of King Æthelred restoring one hide at Maugersbury to Evesham, is unacceptable in its received form; Thomas of Marlborough, *Liber de gestis abbatum* III. 125, in *Thomas of Marlborough: History of the Abbey of Evesham*, ed. J. Sayers and L. Watkiss (Oxford, 2003), p. 135.

instances of exemption have uncertain origins but may in some cases reflect the favourable treatment of particular estates, especially those in ecclesiastical hands, in the pre-Conquest period. The charter record is only marginally more substantial for this category: of the eleven instances listed by Faith, four estates yield substantial charter material.[39] In general, these cases point to a significant role for 'beneficial hidation', namely, a favourable reduction in the assessment of an estate by royal decision.[40] This may be strongly suspected in the case of Sturminster Newton, Dorset, held by the church of St Mary of Glastonbury TRE when it was assessed at twenty-two hides but with an additional exemption: the Domesday entry records, besides the twenty-two hides, land for fourteen ploughs in demesne that has never paid geld.[41] Sturminster Newton had been the subject of an acceptable diploma of King Edgar in the Glastonbury cartulary, dated 968 and bearing 'Edgar A' formulation, by which the king conveyed thirty hides at Sturminster to Glastonbury.[42] The estate provides a particularly clear instance of an estate that had by diploma been freed from all secular service, save the common burdens, remaining liable to geld. It has been suggested that the TRE assessment of twenty-two hides might be reconciled with the Edgarian diploma by adding the eight hides that Glastonbury held at *Acford* (Okeford Fitzpaine), but, as Susan Kelly notes, the bounds of the diploma exclude Okeford.[43] The situation TRE seems most likely to be explained by 'beneficial hidation' in the intervening period: the implied reduction in hidage from thirty to twenty-two hides would account for a substantial proportion of the exempt land in demesne.

More complex is the case of Sherborne, Dorset, where the Domesday entry distinguishes between three different categories of land: firstly, land ordinarily held by the bishop and formerly held by Ælfweald as bishop of Sherborne, assessed at forty-three hides TRE (much of this land was in the hands of tenants in 1086); secondly, a further sixteen carucates held in demesne by the bishop, which was regarded as never having been hidated, nor having paid geld; thirdly, a further nine and a half carucates held by the

---

[39] Faith, *Growth of Lordship*, pp. 268–9.

[40] F. W. Maitland, *Domesday Book and Beyond: Three Essays in the Early History of England* (Cambridge, 1897), pp. 448–50.

[41] GDB, fol. 77c (Dorset 8: 1).

[42] S 764 (*Glast* 54); Keynes, 'Conspectus', p. 71; cf. S. E. Kelly, *Charters of Glastonbury Abbey*, AS Charters 15 (Oxford, 2012), pp. 496–7. On the disputed pre-Æthelredian Orthodoxorum charters, see also D Pratt, 'The Voice of the King in "King Edgar's Establishment of Monasteries"', *ASE* 41 (2013), 145–204, at 186, n. 221.

[43] L. Abrams, *Anglo-Saxon Glastonbury: Church and Endowment* (Woodbridge, 1996), pp. 225–8; and Kelly, *Charters of Glastonbury*, p. 497.

monks of Sherborne, also regarded as never having been hidated or having paid geld.[44] The difficult question concerns the relationship between this recorded situation and the Sherborne 'foundation' charter of 998.[45] As Simon has explained, by this compelling document, King Æthelred gave permission for the establishment of the Sherborne community as monastic, also confirming the endowment of the monastery in terms that have proved difficult to interpret, namely, 'in Sherborne itself, one hundred plots (*agelli*) in the place which is called Stockland, and the estate (*predium*) of the monastery, just as Bishop Wulfsige enclosed it with ditches and hedges', together with a further eleven estates amounting to ninety-five hides, in perpetual freedom subject only to the common burdens.[46] Taking her cue from a known later medieval distinction between the bishop's 'In-Hundred' and his 'Out-Hundred', Katherine Barker has equated the 'one hundred plots in the place which is called Stockland' with the forty-three hides held TRE by the bishop, identifying this as the 'Out-Hundred', whereas she views the estate of the monastery as comprising the sixteen carucates held in demesne by the bishop and nine and a half carucates held by the monks, equating this with the 'In-Hundred'.[47] Several of these identifications are problematic, however. The later terminology of the 'Out-Hundred' did not concern fiscal status but referred to tithings, lying outside the Sherborne hundred, which nevertheless owed suit of court to the hundred court in Sherborne.[48] Furthermore, 'Stockland' has been more convincingly interpreted as referring to 100 fields in a location to the east of Sherborne, near the site of the original British church.[49] The Sherborne diploma implies a concern to identify land specifically assigned to the monks: the most economical reading may be to regard the 'Stockland' and the 'estate (*predium*) of the monastery' as forming a single component within the Domesday entry, namely, the nine and a half

[44] GDB, fol. 77a (Dorset 2: 6 and 3: 1). Cf. also the relevant entry in the Geld Account: Exeter, Cathedral Library, 3500, fol. 23r; and *Libri Censualis Vocati Domesday Book Additamenta*, ed. H. Ellis (London, 1916), p. 25.

[45] S 895 (*Sherb* 11), with S. Keynes, 'King Æthelred's Charter for Sherborne Abbey, 998', in *St Wulfsige and Sherborne: Essays to Celebrate the Millennium of the Benedictine Abbey 998–1998*, ed. K. Barker, D. A. Hinton and A. Hunt (Oxford, 2005), pp. 1–14,

[46] S. Keynes, 'Wulfsige, Monk of Glastonbury, Abbot of Westminster (*c.* 990–3), and Bishop of Sherborne', *St Wulfsige*, ed. Barker et al., pp. 53–94, at 69–71.

[47] K. Barker, 'Sherborne in Dorset: An Early Ecclesiastical Settlement and Its Estate', *Anglo-Saxon Studies in Archaeology and History* 3 (1984), 1–33, at 10–11 and 21–7. Cf. Faith, *Growth of Lordship*, pp. 18–22.

[48] J. Fowler, *Mediaeval Sherborne* (Dorchester, 1951), p. 2, cf. pp. 73–85.

[49] L. Keen, 'The Towns of Dorset', in *Anglo-Saxon Towns in Southern England*, ed. J. Haslam (Chichester, 1984), pp. 203–47, at 211–12 and 217.

carucates held by the monks.[50] The arrangements would be of interest in suggesting a further means by which land came to be geld-exempt in the pre-Conquest period, namely, by the favourable apportioning of hidage assessments within a larger group of estates. When authorized from above, as it appears to have been in this case, the mechanism amounted to a form of 'beneficial hidation'.

Relating to two pertinent diplomas, the case of Littleton-on-Severn, Gloucestershire, held by Malmesbury abbey, is of special interest. The estate was assessed at five hides in 1086, of which two and a half hides paid geld, the remainder being exempt.[51] Littleton-on-Severn had been the subject of an authentic diploma of 986, by which King Æthelred conveyed an estate of five hides to the king's thegn Wenoth, with reservation of the common burdens only.[52] As a late example of 'Dunstan B' formulation, the diploma may have been issued in unusual circumstances; its preservation in the Malmesbury archive presumably reflects the abbey's subsequent interest in the estate.[53] The diplomatic circumstances are complicated by a problematic diploma in favour of Malmesbury in the name of King Edward, dated 1065, in which the king is represented as confirming the abbey's title to many of her estates, including the five hides at Littleton: the elaborate reservation clause concedes freedom from all secular service, unusually specifying outright exemption from geld: 'namely in shires and hundreds and pleas and suits and all gelds and customary dues (*omnibus geldis et consuetudinibus*)'.[54] Although the Edwardian diploma has generally been regarded as disreputable, it bears comparison with other documents confirming privileges from late in the Confessor's reign and should not be dismissed out of hand.[55] Nevertheless, in the treatment of geld, the terms of the privilege arouse strong suspicion. If the abbey had been in possession of such a privilege in 1086, one would expect to find evidence for its impact, yet there is no hint within the Domesday entry of its generous terms.[56] The

[50] See Fowler, *Mediaeval Sherborne*, pp. 80–1, who plausibly equates the *predium* with the site of the later 'Abbey Barton'.
[51] GDB, fol. 165b (Gloucestershire 9: 1).   [52] S 862 (*Malm* 32).
[53] Keynes, *Diplomas*, pp. 94–5; S. Keynes, 'The "Dunstan B"' Charters', *ASE* 23 (1994), 165–93, at 179; and S. E. Kelly, *Charters of Malmesbury Abbey*, AS Charters xi (Oxford, 2005), p. 97.
[54] S 1038 (*Malm* 33).
[55] S. Keynes, 'Regenbald the Chancellor (*sic*)', *ANS* 10 (1988), 185–222, at 214, n. 174; S. Keynes, 'Giso, Bishop of Wells (1061–88)', *ANS* 19 (1997), 203–71, at 234–5; and Kelly, *Charters of Malmesbury*, pp. 247–9.
[56] The Malmesbury diploma bears comparison with S 1036 (KCD 813), a problematic diploma in the name of King Edward for Waltham, dated 1062, confirming Harold's foundation of the minster and its endowment: the immunity clause similarly conveys exemption from shires and hundreds and from all gelds (Keynes, 'Regenbald', pp. 201–3; cf. Kelly, *Charters of Malmesbury*, p. 247). The

estates in question remained subject to geld, as did Littleton, though at the rate of two and a half hides: the reduction may be a further case of 'beneficial hidation'.

Two remaining instances relate to the outright forging of charter material. The Domesday entry for Ombersley, Worcestershire, offers the unique case of a seemingly pre-Conquest geld exemption in which reference is made to charter testimony.[57] The estate had been 'in early times (*antiquitatus*) free for 3 hides, as the charters of the church say (*sicut dicunt cartae de aecclesia*)', but TRE it was assessed at fifteen hides, 'and of these, 3 hides are free [from geld]'. This account correlates suggestively with a spurious diploma from the Evesham archives in the name of Æthelweard, *subregulus* of the Hwicce, purporting to record the conveying of twelve hides at Ombersley to Evesham in 706, with subsequent confirmations by eighth-century Mercian kings.[58] The diploma's assessment of the estate at twelve rather than fifteen hides, together with its outrageous conferring of exemption from the common burdens, might help to explain the Domesday account of its history. In other words, the diploma probably needs to be considered in an eleventh-century context as an attempt to support the beneficial rating of the estate at twelve hides. Whatever was meant by the statement that the Ombersley had originally been 'free for 3 hides', the later claim that the estate had three hides free from geld might have been defended by appeal to the spurious 706 document. Although the earliest manuscript witness dates from the twelfth century, and fabrication after Domesday remains a possibility, the forgery is a strong candidate for one of the charters proffered in 1086.[59]

The second case is that of Chilcomb, Hampshire, which, in addition to the problematic writ mentioned earlier, generated a series of notoriously problematic charters.[60] As Alexander Rumble has pointed out, it may be significant that Chilcomb was effectively a core territory of the Old Minster endowment, lying in the immediate vicinity of Winchester.[61]

Waltham privilege also warrants careful scrutiny but remains vulnerable to the same objection, that one would expect to find some impact of exemption within Domesday: cf., for example, LDB, fols. 15v–16r (Essex 7: 1 and 8: 1).

[57] GDB, fol. 175b (Worcestershire 10: 10); the entry might be added to Faith's list (*Growth of Lordship*, pp. 268–9). Cf. J. H. Round, 'Danegeld and the Finance of Domesday', in *Domesday Studies*, ed. P. E. Dove, 2 vols. (London, 1888 and 1891), vol. I, pp. 77–142, at 99.

[58] S 54 (BCS 116); and C. Cubitt, *Anglo-Saxon Church Councils c.650–c.850* (London, 1995), p. 262, with references.

[59] For the likely involvement of ecclesiastical institutions in the recording of their own fees within Domesday, see S. Baxter, 'The Representation of Lordship and Land Tenure in Domesday Book', in *Domesday Book*, ed. E. Hallam and D. Bates (Stroud, 2001), pp. 73–102 and 203–8, at 81–93.

[60] See above.   [61] Rumble, *Property and Piety*, pp. 224 and 226–8.

Identifying it as among those supporting the monks of the Old Minster, the Domesday entry bluntly recorded that this large estate with land for sixty-eight ploughs had been assessed at one hide TRE and now.[62] It is convenient to list what appear to be the earliest documents in the sequence, all preserved in the Codex Wintoniensis:

S 946 (*ASWrits* 107): writ in the name of King Æthelred declaring Chilcomb to be assessed at one hide.[63]

S 821 (BCS 1146), S 817 (BCS 1147 and 1148) and S 818 (BCS 1159): material relating to Chilcomb included within the composite document known as the *sinthama*, a dossier of purportedly Edgarian charters probably drawn up during Æthelred's reign, either under Æthelwold (*d.* 984) or by one of his pupils.[64] S 821: restoration by King Edgar to the Old Minster of 100 hides at Downton, Wiltshire, and thirty hides at *Drethecumb* (Calbourne), Isle of Wight, and confirmation of the privileged tenure of Chilcomb; S 817: confirmation by King Edgar of the privileged tenure and beneficial hidation of Chilcomb, and confirmation of the monastic status of the Old Minster, in Latin and Old English versions; S 818: confirmation by King Edgar of the endowment of the Old Minster and of certain named estates, with provision for the rendering of food from Chilcomb to the monks of the Old Minster.

S 376 (BCS 620): diploma in the name of King Edward, dated 909, in favour of Frithestan, bishop of Winchester, confirming the beneficial hidation of Chilcomb at one hide, in return for Frithestan's confirmation to the king of leases for 100 hides at Downton, Wiltshire, and seventy hides at Beddington, Surrey. This is a document presenting a number of suspicious features: the earliest manuscript is a single sheet of the late tenth or early eleventh century.[65]

The Chilcomb writ stands or falls by comparison with this wider body of material.[66] Although the text contains nothing fatal to its authority, it has

---

[62] GDB, fol. 41a (Hampshire 3: 1).   [63] Rumble, *Property and Piety*, pp. 223–5 (no. 30).

[64] *Ibid.*, pp. 98–135 (no. 5); for the dating and context, see *ibid.*, pp. 98–104.

[65] A facsimile is available on the 'Kemble' website (http://dk.usertest.mws3.csx.cam.ac.uk/). S. Keynes, 'The West Saxon Charters of King Æthelwulf and his Sons', *EHR* 109 (1994), 1109–49, at 1145; J. Crick, 'Script and the Sense of the Past in Anglo-Saxon England', in *Anglo-Saxon Traces*, ed. J. Roberts and L. Webster (Tempe, AZ, 2011), pp. 1–29, at 11 and 13–14; and P. A. Stokes, *English Vernacular Minuscule from Æthelred to Cnut c. 990 to c. 1035* (Cambridge, 2014), pp. 155 and 159–60, cf. pp. 64 and 84.

[66] Harmer, *Anglo-Saxon Writs*, pp. 373–80, with references; H. P. R. Finberg, *The Early Charters of Wessex* (Leicester, 1964), pp. 220, 226, 230–3, 237–41; Keynes, *Diplomas*, p. 143, n. 209; and Rumble, *Property and Piety*, p. 224.

verbal similarities with the Old English version of S 817 and supports a
claim for beneficial hidation for which the Old Minster demonstrably
produced other forgeries.[67] A further point against the writ is its appeal
to the consulting of a charter of King Alfred, which has not survived and
was seemingly not available to the compiler of the Codex Wintoniensis.[68]
Rumble has made the case for regarding the Chilcomb writ as earlier than
the *sinthama* on two grounds: firstly, that the writ does not mention Edgar,
whereas the *sinthama* presents Edgar as central to Chilcomb's status and,
secondly, that the writ refers to a charter of King Alfred, whereas the
sinthama appeals to charters in the name of Ecgberht, Æthelwulf, Alfred
and Edward.[69] It is possible, however, that the writ and the *sinthama* had
been constructed for different purposes: the documents are not mutually
reinforcing, but there is no need to assume that forgeries had to be so. One
may only speculate, but since the geld had been initiated under Æthelred
II, there may have been advantages in holding a document issued in his
name. Quite what prompted this energetic documentary output remains
uncertain, but, as landholding reserved for the monks, Chilcomb's status
was potentially sensitive, and as Rumble has shown, there are other signs
that the estate had been administratively anomalous in the pre-Conquest
period.[70] It is possible that the documents gave wishful support to an
existing practice or claim.

The Evidence of Diplomas Purporting to Concede Exemption from the Common Burdens

It may be helpful to summarize the findings that are so far permitted,
before moving to a final angle of enquiry. Exemption from geld in the
pre-Conquest period regularly depended on the king's will, and matters
relating to assessment could be communicated by writ. Geld liability
was probably not regarded as a secular burden because diplomas conveying freedom from secular service, with the reservation of the common burdens, offered no defence against the tax. There is also a general
lack of fit between geld-free areas and the charter record: in no case is an
exemption supported by the immunity clause of an authentic diploma.

---

[67] For the relationship to S 817, see Rumble, *Property and Piety*, pp. 102–3 and 224.
[68] The latter point casts doubt on the significance of S 1812, a now lost charter in the name of King
Alfred concerning Chilcomb reportedly at Winchester in 1643 (Rumble, *Property and Piety*, pp. 223–
4); see also S 325 (BCS 493), the spurious vernacular 'decimation' charter for Chilcomb in the name
of King Æthelwulf (cf. S 439 (BCS 713)).
[69] Rumble, *Property and Piety*, pp. 102–3 and 223–4.   [70] *Ibid.*, pp. 226–8.

There is some evidence for the use of forged documents to support specific claims of exemption or hidage concession in the post-Conquest period and, in the case of the Old Minster, Winchester, from as early as the late tenth or early eleventh century, but in respect of diplomas, the examples are too problematic to cast light on pre-Conquest forms of procedure.

If, then, geld liability was not treated as a secular burden, how did it stand in relation to immunity clauses? So far the analysis has left open the possibility that geld liability was regarded as falling within the burden of military service, since, as shown by several of the preceding cases, land appears to have remained liable to the tax even when a diploma had been issued reserving only the common burdens. It is on this question that one may add the perspective of the small group of Anglo-Saxon diplomas that appears to have conceded outright exemption from the common burdens.[71] Unfortunately, the corpus is troublesome to assess for two reasons. Firstly, one faces the difficulty of interpreting diplomas that refer to privileges or freedom in general terms but without explicitly mentioning the common burdens.[72] Secondly, the inclusion of an immunity clause conveying outright exemption from the common burdens is ordinarily regarded as grounds for suspicion, featuring in a number of known forgeries. One must therefore take a conservative approach, excluding diplomas that refer to general freedom or privilege only,[73] and excluding also diplomas conveying outright exemption whose authenticity is in doubt, or where there are grounds for suspecting that the immunity clause has been tampered with.[74] An interesting example of the latter is a Crediton charter in the name of King Æthelstan, dated 29 April 930, which appears to have been modelled on a

---

[71] For relevant discussion, see Stevenson, '*Trinoda Necessitas*', pp. 701–2; S. Keynes, *Facsimiles of Anglo-Saxon Charters*, AS Charters, Supplementary Series 1 (Oxford, 1991), pp. 8–9.

[72] Stevenson, '*Trinoda Necessitas*', pp. 697–8, n. 41; cf. Hollister, *Anglo-Saxon Military Institutions*, p. 60, n. 5; see also J. Crick, 'Pristina Libertas: Liberty and the Anglo-Saxons Revisited', *TRHS*, 6th series, 14 (2004), 47–71.

[73] Prominent examples are S 416 (BCS 677) and S 425 (*CantCC* 106), both diplomas of 'Æthelstan A' (facsimiles available on the 'Kemble' website: http://dk.usertest.mws3.csx.cam.ac.uk/); see also the early-ninth-century diplomas cited by Stevenson, S 41, S 165, S 173, S 187 and S 296; cf. S 1067 (*North* 13). One might compare the activities of the Anglo-Norman cartulist at Christ Church, Canterbury, who adopted a standard form of immunity clause, with reservation of the common burdens, adding this where necessary to his charter sources: N. Brooks and S. E. Kelly, *Charters of Christ Church, Canterbury*, AS Charters 17 and 18, 2 vols. (Oxford, 2013), pp. 61–2 and 70–1; cf. Stevenson, '*Trinoda Necessitas*', pp. 696–7, n. 37 and n. 40.

[74] For twelfth-century forgeries, see Keynes, *Facsimiles*, p. 8; and J. Crick, 'St Albans, Westminster and Some Twelfth-Century Views of the Anglo-Saxon Past', *ANS* 25 (2002), 65–83. Another problematic case is S 1408 (KCD 805). For S 1036 and S 1038, see above.

genuine diploma of 'Æthelstan A';[75] one may compare a diploma of King Æthelred in favour of St Albans from 1005, which has an authentic basis save for the lavishly comprehensive immunity clause, best regarded as a later interpolation.[76]

When such cases are stripped away, the outstanding candidate for an authentic diploma conveying exemption from the common burdens is one close to Simon's heart: the Confessor's diploma conveying ten hides at Wheathampstead, Hertfordshire, to Westminster abbey, dated 1060, included in Simon's British Academy edition of facsimiles.[77] This beautiful document survives as a single sheet in what appears to be its original form, from which it may be inferred that the exemptions amounted to a mark of special favour by King Edward to his abbey at Westminster.[78] It is therefore striking to compare the corresponding Domesday entry.[79] Since the monks of Westminster had in their possession an authentic diploma granting exemption from the common burdens and all secular service, one may assume that if geld liability had fallen within military service, they would have made use of the diploma to claim Wheathampstead's exemption from geld. On the contrary, however, the estate's current assessment was simply recorded at ten hides, with no special arrangements. Moreover, the entry included a record of five hides in demesne, thus indicating that the remaining portion of the estate had been liable to the geld in 1086. There is a certain irony in the Wheathampstead diploma's negative impact: whereas in the case of Ombersley, discussed earlier, the monks of Evesham had appealed to 'charters of the church', including in all like-lihood the surviving forgery S 54, to support a claim to reduced assessment, the monks of Westminster did not use their authentic and comprehensive immunity.[80] The hypothesis that geld liability did not lie within military service receives moderate support from Domesday, where, as Warren Hollister showed, there are some indications of geld liability and military service being treated as separate obligations in the pre-Conquest period.[81]

One further diploma deserving discussion is that of King Cnut, dated 1018, conveying *Hæselersc* (Lower Hazelhurst in Ticehurst), Sussex, to

[75] S 405 (*CrawCh* 4). A facsimile is available on the 'Kemble' website (http://dk.usertest.mws3.csx.cam .ac.uk/); Keynes, *Facsimiles*, pp. 8–9.

[76] S 912 (*StAlb* 11); Keynes, *Facsimiles*, p. 8. Cf. also S 888 (*StAlb* 9); Keynes, *Diplomas*, pp. 122–3; S. Keynes, 'A Lost Cartulary of St Albans Abbey', *ASE* 22 (1993), 253–79, at 273–4; and J. Crick, *Charters of St Albans Abbey*, AS Charters xii (Oxford, 2007), pp. 185–6, cf. pp. 69–74 and 171–3.

[77] S 1031 (F. Barlow, *Edward the Confessor* (London, 1970), pp. 334–5), reproduced in *BAFacs*, no. 22.

[78] Keynes, *Facsimiles*, p. 8.   [79] GDB, fol. 135a (Hertfordshire 9: 1).   [80] See above.

[81] Hollister, *Anglo-Saxon Military Institutions*, pp. 20–1, 49–50 and 53–5; cf. also Vinogradoff, *English Society*, p. 196.

Archbishop Ælfstan (Lyfing).[82] The diploma survives as an apparent original in the hand of Eadui Basan and has an immunity clause conferring freedom in general terms, 'absque omni seruitute terrena'. Nicholas Brooks and Susan Kelly have suggested that these words should be understood as implying exemption from the common burdens on the basis that the estate, consisting of swine pasture in the Weald, may not have been hidated.[83] This view depends on an acceptance of Faith's model of inland and warland; moreover, it is difficult to reconcile with the relevant sections of Domesday.[84] Upper Hazelhurst lay within Shoyswell hundred: although the hundred is identified in Domesday as never having paid geld, estates within Shoyswell are accorded assessments, and its unusual treatment may relate to the fact that the entire hundred lay in the hands of William, count of Eu.[85] Brooks and Kelly have suggested that Lower Hazelhurst may have been absorbed into the Canterbury manor of South Malling, but if so, this estate, which comprised the hundred of Malling, was also substantially hidated, with an assessment of eighty hides TRE.[86] It is hard to be certain that Eadui's immunity clause was understood as conferring exemption from the common burdens: the diploma was drafted at a time when it is more difficult to discern a diplomatic 'tradition' reliant on standardized formulation.[87] On balance, his words seem more likely to be a variation on the typical late Anglo-Saxon immunity clause, having no deeper implications for the estate's public obligations.[88]

The Geld and Late Anglo-Saxon Administrative Change

Overall, then, although the record is limited and fragmentary, it is difficult to build a case for diplomas having a significant bearing on geld liability. The tax was not treated as a secular burden, nor, as the Wheathampstead diploma shows, does it seem to have fallen within the burden of military

[82] S 950 (*CantCC* 144). A facsimile is available on the 'Kemble' website (http://dk.usertest.mws3 .csx.cam.ac.uk/).

[83] Brooks and Kelly, *Charters of Christ Church, Canterbury*, p. 1056.

[84] Cf. Faith, *Growth of Lordship*, pp. 55–6. For assessments in Sussex, see J. H. Round, 'Introduction to the Sussex Domesday', in *VCH Sussex: I*, ed. W. Page (London, 1905), pp. 351–85, esp. 354–60.

[85] GDB, fol. 19b (Sussex 9: 60).

[86] Brooks and Kelly, *Charters of Christ Church, Canterbury*, p. 1057; GDB, fol. 16b (Sussex 2: 1a).

[87] S. Keynes, 'Church Councils, Royal Assemblies, and Anglo-Saxon Royal Diplomas', in *Kingship, Legislation and Power in Anglo-Saxon England*, ed. G. R. Owen-Crocker and B. W. Schneider (Woodbridge, 2013), pp. 17–182, at 126–9.

[88] Cf. the immunity clauses in the 'Æthelstan A' diplomas S 416 and S 425: see above. The Anglo-Norman cartularist followed his standard practice of incorporating a full immunity clause, with reservation of the common burdens, in his summary version of the *Hæselersc* charter (*CantCC* 144A).

service. It is, additionally, difficult to postulate the regular use of diplomas in 'beneficial hidation': of the eight instances discussed earlier, only for Ombersley and Chilcomb can plausible connections be made with surviving charter material, both cases relying on fabricated rather than authentic documents.[89] Against these negative findings one may compare the positive evidence from Domesday for the use of writs in communicating royal decisions relating to geld assessment and the various pre-Conquest writs on this subject.[90] The relative lack of forged writs here is striking, but it should be remembered that only certain houses appear to have taken steps to retrieve writs from the shire court for archival purposes, so models may not have been so widespread.[91] In the post-Conquest period, moreover, the administration of the geld may have changed significantly in the light of the Conqueror's geld exemptions.[92]

It might seem counter-intuitive to find an administrative obligation that lay outside all elements of the diploma's immunity clause. It is possible that geld had been understood as an extraordinary tax justified by crisis conditions, falling outside the existing structures.[93] Yet one should note that other judicial and financial rights regularly conceded in pre-Conquest writs also seem to have lain outside the standard diploma immunity clause: sake and soke, for example, probably related to the right to a share in the profits of justice in respect of men held under a particular form of lordship; *hamsocn, griðbryce, mundbryce, foresteall* and other rights concerned forfeitures ordinarily due to the king but sometimes alienated to others;[94] *toll ond team* probably related to payments made on the sale of livestock and the witnessing of transactions; and the right to a moneyer may have related to fees ordinarily paid to the king.[95] The geld must be seen in the broader context of administrative developments in the final three generations of

---

[89] See above.
[90] For the similar use of writs in the post-Conquest period, see Sharpe, 'The Use of Writs', pp. 280–3; also see *Regesta Regum Anglo-Normannorum: The Acta of William I*, ed. D. Bates (Oxford, 1998), pp. 958–9 (no. 326), concerning eight hides at Pyrford (cf. above).
[91] Keynes, *Diplomas*, pp. 142–4.   [92] Pratt, 'Demesne Exemption', pp. 10–16.
[93] Vinogradoff, *English Society*, p. 196.
[94] S. Baxter, 'Lordship and Justice in Late Anglo-Saxon England: The Judicial Functions of Soke and Commendation Revisited', in *Early Medieval Studies in Memory of Patrick Wormald*, ed. S. Baxter, C. Karkov, J. L. Nelson and D. Pelteret (Farnham, 2009), pp. 383–419, esp. 391–5, 404–7, 410–17; and Harmer, *Anglo-Saxon Writs*, pp. 73–6. Cf. also T. B. Lambert, 'Royal Protections and Private Justice: A Reassessment of Cnut's "Reserved Pleas"', in *English Law before Magna Carta: Felix Liebermann and Die Gesetze der Angelsachsen*, ed. S. Jurasinski, L. Oliver and A. Rabin (Leiden, 2010), pp. 157–75, whose discussion has a tendency to elide the important distinction between a right to receive fines and outright jurisdiction, strongly indicated by certain aspects of the evidence: see Baxter, 'Lordship and Justice', pp. 404–7.
[95] Harmer, *Anglo-Saxon Writs*, pp. 76–82.

Anglo-Saxon England, in which the shire court became increasingly central not only to dispute settlement but also to the brokering of royal rights in financial form.[96] It must be remembered that the geld had been introduced in 1012, late in Æthelred II's reign, whereas the secular burdens referred to in diplomas were very long established. In the micro-politics of exemption and 'beneficial hidation', the geld actively contributed to the shire court's importance and to the use of written documentation, but there may also have been other reasons for the strident treatment of the tax. At a purely practical level, if geld had been understood as a secular burden, its yield would have been severely reduced, in view of the large numbers of diplomas in circulation dating from the eighth century onwards which conceded exemption from secular burdens.[97] However, treating geld liability as a form of military service may have risked compromising existing commitments at a time when military resources were under severe pressure. Such considerations offer an interesting perspective on the *Chronicle*'s words that the *heregeld* 'always came before other taxes (*oðrum gyldum*), which were variously paid': the statement was especially true for any holder of bookland.[98]

While the geld probably contributed to the rise of the writ, this was also a period in which attitudes towards the diploma may have been evolving under various pressures. As Simon himself has argued, although the diploma and the writ should be understood as forms that were fundamentally complementary, the lower numbers of diplomas from the reign of Cnut onwards probably reflects a genuine drop in the numbers issued.[99] Such a decline may be best explained by the continuing transfer of existing diplomas, issued in earlier reigns, and by the possibility that less land was available for booking afresh. A further development was the use of the diploma for purposes beyond the formal conveying of land, in the form of 'foundation' charters associated with the monastic reform movement, typically confirming a house's privileges as

---

[96] P. Wormald, 'Charters, Law and the Settlement of Disputes in Anglo-Saxon England', and 'Lordship and Justice in the Early English Kingdom: Oswaldslow Revisited', both in his *Legal Culture in the Early Medieval West* (London, 1999), pp. 289–311, at 298–310, and pp. 313–32, at 326–32; S. Keynes, 'Royal Government and the Written Word in Late Anglo-Saxon England', in *The Uses of Literacy in Early Medieval Europe*, ed. R. McKitterick (Cambridge, 1990), pp. 226–57, at 245–50; and J. A. Green, *English Sheriffs to 1154* (London, 1990), pp. 9–11.

[97] Vinogradoff, *English Society*, p. 196.

[98] *ASC* MS D, 1051, in *The Anglo-Saxon Chronicle, 6: MS. D*, ed. G. P. Cubbin (Cambridge, 1996), pp. 69–70.

[99] Keynes, *Diplomas*, pp. 140–2 and 144–5; cf. also C. Insley, 'Where Did All the Charters Go? Anglo-Saxon Charters and the New Politics of the Eleventh Century', *ANS* 24 (2002), 109–27.

well as elements of its endowment.[100] Such documents involved a degree of
innovation within the usually conservative diploma form, yet they were not
without difficulties. At Canterbury, early in Cnut's reign, Eadui Basan prepared a writ, of uncertain authority, reporting that Cnut had given permission
to Archbishop Lyfing (1013–1019/20) to draw up a 'new' charter of freedom
(*freols*) in Cnut's name.[101] Lyfing's oft-quoted response, that he had plenty of
freolsas 'if only they were good for anything', might be taken as an index of
some new realities relating to demands and pressures not reflected in the long-
established forms of documentation. Perhaps significantly, Lyfing's successor,
Æthelnoth (1020–38), secured some important privileges from Cnut early in
his archiepiscopate in the form of a royal writ granting him sake and soke
together with the full range of forfeitures (*griðbryce, hamsocn, foresteall, infan-
geneðeof* and *flymenafyrmð*) over his own men, over Christ Church and over
thegns assigned to him.[102] As part of an elaborate programme to assemble
documents supportive of Canterbury's privileges, the writ was duly copied in a
royal book of venerable origins, London, Lambeth Palace 1370 (*olim* 771), an
Irish 'pocket' gospel book that had been given to Christ Church by King
Æthelstan.[103] Under Æthelnoth, the volume acted as a repository for royal
writs relating to the archbishopric, including the writ relating to geld assessment, confirming the rate at which Æthelnoth should discharge the obligations on his landed property.[104] Issued towards the end of Cnut's reign, the
writ indicates some sort of tensions over Æthelnoth's assessment; its preservation would, one presumes, have assisted during the reign of Harthacnut,
where there are signs of especially heavy taxation.[105]

As Canterbury's practices indicate, diplomas were no longer the whole
story. Whereas elaborate diplomatic statements of privilege or freedom might
need robust defence, writs now mattered, and not just for their content but for
what they indicated about the rights, dues and taxes being administered in the
shire court. In providing title to land, diplomas remained central to landholding, but late Anglo-Saxon political and administrative developments

[100] S. Keynes, 'King Æthelred's Charter for Eynsham Abbey (1005)', in *Early Medieval Studies*, ed. Baxter et al., pp. 451–73, esp. 456–9; and S. Keynes, 'Church Councils, Royal Assemblies', pp. 108–16, 122–3 and 125–6, with references.
[101] S 985 (*CantCC* 145); and Keynes, 'Church Councils, Royal Assemblies', p. 127.
[102] S 986 (*CantCC* 150A); Brooks and Kelly, *Charters of Christ Church, Canterbury*, p. 1078; cf. Pratt, 'Demesne Exemption', p. 9, n. 53.
[103] D. Pratt, 'Kings and Books in Anglo-Saxon England', *ASE* 43 (2015), 297–377, at 355–61.
[104] Brooks and Kelly, *Charters of Christ Church, Canterbury*, pp. 86–7, cf. 53. S 987 (*CantCC* 156). See above.
[105] S. Keynes, 'Harthacnut', in *The Wiley Blackwell Encyclopedia of Anglo-Saxon England*, ed. M. Lapidge, J. Blair, S. Keynes and D. Scragg, 2nd edn (Chichester, 2014), p. 235.

appear to have encouraged a sense of distance between current circumstances and the deeper diplomatic tradition: one might think of a heightened awareness of temporal difference or historicity.[106] What is striking in the case of geld liability is the degree of disregard that its handling appears to have involved for the entire diplomatic tradition of immunity clauses, extending back to the eighth century: the sharp overlooking of all claims of freedom, while at the same time the expectation that, in military service, the raw provision of warriors by landholders was no longer enough. Such treatment was doubtless necessary for the geld's effectiveness and may not have been widely contested: that may, indeed, have been the point. Yet one is entitled to suspect that in addition to its direct impact, the geld may have had other important and hitherto unrecognized effects. In undermining the basic rationale of the Anglo-Saxon immunity clause, the tax indicated the limited privileges now enjoyed by any holder of bookland and in so doing established a new administrative basis for the fundamental historicity of the charter record.

---

[106] For relevant perspectives, see Keynes, *Diplomas*, pp. 141–2 and 144–5; Keynes, 'King Æthelred's Charter for Eynsham', pp. 456–70; C. Insley, 'Archives and Lay Documentary Practice in the Anglo-Saxon World', in *Documentary Culture and the Laity in the Early Middle Ages*, ed. W. C. Brown, M. Costambeys, M. Innes and A. J. Kosto (Cambridge, 2013), pp. 336–62; Crick, 'Script and the Sense of the Past'; and J. Crick, 'Insular History? Forgery and the English Past in the Tenth Century', in *England and the Continent in the Tenth Century: Studies in Honour of Wilhelm Levison (1876–1947)*, ed. D. Rollason, C. Leyser and H. Williams (Turnhout, 2010), pp. 515–44.

CHAPTER 10

On Living in the Time of Tribulation:
Archbishop Wulfstan's Sermo Lupi ad Anglos and Its Eschatological Context

Catherine Cubitt

The reign of Æthelred the Unready is one of unusual historical interest: the dramatic events of its last decades saw the conquest of the kingdom after years of decimating attacks and the elevation of a new foreign ruler to the throne. However, what perhaps gives the period a particular attraction for the early medieval historian is the variety of sources and of voices illuminating tumultuous events. From the rich diplomatic record to the homiletic writings of Ælfric and Wulfstan, Æthelred's reign is distinguished by interlocking and sometimes conflicting narratives that give a rare diversity of insights. Simon Keynes's seminal research on the reign is probably best known for his groundbreaking study of Æthelred's charters, but his work has always interpreted these in the widest historical frame, alongside the evidence from a broad range of sources: numismatic, archaeological and literary. *The Diplomas of Æthelred II 'the Unready'* ranged across Latin texts (both pre- and post-Conquest) and Old English and Old Norse writings and integrated them with evidence from coinage and excavations in Scandinavia. As a historian, Simon has been a model of the wide-ranging inter-disciplinary curiosity coupled with the sensitivity and rigour needed to work fruitfully on England before the Conquest.[1] This outlook has shaped not only his writing but also his teaching: he introduced me and many generations of other undergraduates to this approach. It was from Simon that I learnt of the historical importance and fascination of the study of place-names and of numismatics. I remember vividly how in

---

[1] S. Keynes, *The Diplomas of King Æthelred 'the Unready' 978–1016: A Study in Their Use as Historical Evidence* (Cambridge, 1980); see also S. Keynes, 'Re-reading King Æthelred the Unready', in *Writing Medieval Biography Essays in Honour of Frank Barlow*, ed. D. Bates, J. Crick and S. Hamilton (Woodbridge, 2006), pp. 77–97; and S. Keynes, 'Wulfsige, Monk of Glastonbury, Abbot of Westminster (c. 990–3), and Bishop of Sherborne', in *St Wulfsige and Sherborne Essays to Celebrate the Millennium of the Benedictine Abbey 998–1998*, ed. K. Barker, D. A. Hinton and A. Hunt (Oxford, 2005), pp. 53–94.

undergraduate lectures Simon used to pass around his audience a box of his own Anglo-Saxon coins to illustrate his discussion of minting and coinage. It was an unforgettable introduction to the importance of the physical remains of the pre-Conquest past.

Archbishop Wulfstan's *Sermo Lupi ad Anglos* has always been integral to Simon's interpretation of Æthelred's reign, for example, in emphasizing the authority of its testimony to the murder of Edward the Martyr and the burning of his corpse.[2] In 2007, he published a characteristically illuminating and erudite study of the final years of Æthelred's reign, bringing together the writings of Ælfric and Wulfstan, diplomatic evidence and the Agnus Dei coinage that emphasized the desperation and demoralization of England shortly before the 1016 conquest. This essay includes a major analysis of the thorny issue of the composition of the *Sermo Lupi ad Anglos* that places it in a new light by re-examining the authority of the 1014 dating for the sermon, opening up new possibilities for understanding the sermon within Wulfstan's oeuvre.[3] My chapter will offer a fresh look at Wulfstan's *Sermo Lupi*. It will consider the sermon as part of the archbishop's apocalyptic oeuvre and argue that it reflects his understanding of his own troubled era as the time of tribulation prophesied in the New Testament, which is described as immediately preceding the coming of Antichrist and characterized by the intensification of human evil. Building on recent scholarly work that has shown that the traditional early date of Wulfstan's interest in the end-time and of his major apocalyptic sermons is no longer acceptable, it puts forward a revised understanding of the chronology of his sermons.

Wulfstan's writings need to be set first in the context of biblical and patristic thought that shaped not only his attitudes but also those of his audience.

The New Testament and Patristic Background

The sequence of events at the end of the world is outlined in three of the Gospels – Matthew 24, Mark 13 and Luke 21. These three accounts, which differ only in details, report Jesus' prophecy about the end of the world and final judgement, given in response to the direct questions about the end-time from his disciples.[4] They describe three stages in the unfolding of the

---

[2] Keynes, *Diplomas*, p. 167.   [3] Keynes, 'An Abbot', pp. 203–13.
[4] For these accounts, see *The Oxford Bible Commentary*, ed. J. Barton and J. Muddiman (Oxford, 2001), pp. 876–79, 912–14 and 953–5.

final drama. First comes a period of tribulation characterized by the emergence of false prophets and teachers who will mislead the people with persecutions, natural disasters, wars, civil violence and social disharmony. This time would be followed by the advent of Antichrist, the 'abomination of desolation'. His reign will be the most terrifying of all times, as he leads the faithful into sin and error, persecuting those who resist. Such will be the misery of Antichrist's rule that God will pity the sufferings of the just and shorten it. Finally, the sun and the moon will darken, signalling Christ's second coming and the Last Judgement.[5]

The first of these three phases, the time of tribulation, is described as a time of great anguish but also as a time of lesser misery than Antichrist's reign. Christ describes this first stage as a time when many will go astray because of the increase of wickedness and cooling of men's love:

> Take heed that no one leads you astray. For many will come in my name, saying: 'I am the Christ', and they will lead many astray. And you will hear of wars and rumours of wars; see that you are not alarmed; for this must take place, but the end is not yet come. For nation will rise up against nation, and kingdom against kingdom, and there will be famines and earthquakes in various places: all this is but the beginning of the sufferings.
>
> Then they will deliver you up to tribulation, and put you to death; and you will be hated by all nations for my name's sake. And then many will fall away, and betray one another, and hate one another. And many false prophets will arise and lead many astray. And because wickedness is multiplied, most men's love will grow cold.[6]

The idea of the multiplication of evil was elaborated by St Paul in his second letter to Timothy in which he identified his own age as the last days and catalogued the endemic wickedness that characterized it. Here Paul describes the various sinners conspicuous at that time:

> But understand this, that in the last days there will come times of stress. For men will be lovers of self, lovers of money, proud, arrogant, abusive, disobedient to their parents, ungrateful, unholy, inhuman, implacable, slanderers, profligates, fierce, haters of good, treacherous, reckless, swollen,

[5] On biblical apocalypticism, see C. Rowland, *The Open Heaven* (London, 1982); B. McGinn, J. J. Collins and S. Stein (eds.), *The Continuum History of Apocalypticism* (New York and London, 2003), especially the essays by J. J. Collins, 'From Prophecy to Apocalypticism: The Expectation of the End', D. C. Allison Jr, 'The Eschatology of Jesus', M. C. de Boer, 'Paul and Apocalyptic Eschatology', and B. E. Daley, 'Apocalypticism in early Christian Theology', pp. 64–88, 139–165, 166–217, and 221–53.
[6] Matthew 24: 4–12.

with conceit, lovers of pleasure rather than lovers of God, holding the form of religion but denying the power of it. Avoid such people.[7]

These New Testament ideas about the multiplication of wickedness before the coming of Antichrist were complemented by ideas about the escalation of evil as the world ages. Gregory the Great described how as the world grew old it would be afflicted with many tribulations and by the increased savagery of the devil.[8] Bede's influential writings on time and the six ages of the world also widely disseminated this idea of moral and physical decline at the end of each age. He followed Augustine in dividing biblical history into six different eras, culminating with the sixth age, which was inaugurated by the birth of Christ. Bede described how the course of each age followed a sequence of deterioration, like that of a day, from morning to evening, and like the aging of man, from birth to old age.[9] Thus each age concluded in a descent into sin and decrepitude, and '[t]he evening of this [sixth] Age, darker than all the others, will come in Antichrist's persecution.'[10] The Earth's aging was manifest in the failure of its agricultural fertility and in the diminishing powers of its people. These ideas of the senescence of the world found a receptive audience amongst the Anglo-Saxons and were widely circulated by the tenth and eleventh centuries. They are expressed in a wide range of sources, from poetry to charter diplomatic, and were exploited by vernacular homilists such as Ælfric and Wulfstan.[11]

The English were therefore mindful in the tenth and eleventh centuries of the waning of the world and its inevitable movement towards the end-time.[12] They understood themselves as living at the end of the sixth and

---

[7] II Timothy 3: 1–5. On St Paul and apocalyptic eschatology, see M. C. de Boer, 'Paul and Apocalyptic Eschatology'; and Rowland, *The Open Heaven*, pp. 46–9. On the time of tribulation, see also M. Dubis, *Messianic Woes in First Peter: Suffering and Eschatology in I Peter 4: 12–19* (New York and Oxford, 2002).

[8] Gregory the Great, *Moralia in Iob*, ed. M. Adriaen, 3 vols., CCSL 143, 143A, 143B (Turnholt, 1979), 143B: c. 34: vol. I, pp. 1 and 1733.

[9] R. K. Emmerson, *Antichrist in the Middle Ages* (Seattle, 1981), pp. 16–19; and P. Darby, *Bede and the End of Time* (Farnham, 2012), pp. 21–4, 27–9.

[10] *Bede, The Reckoning of Time*, trans. F. Wallis (Liverpool, 1999), 10 (311), pp. 39–41, at 41.

[11] See J. E. Cross, 'Aspects of Microcosm and Macrocosm in Old English Literature', in *Studies in Old English Literature in Honor of Arthur G. Brodeur*, ed. S. Greenfield (University of Oregon, 1963), pp. 1–22; H. L. C. Tristram, *Sex aetates mundi Die Weltzeitalter bei den Angelsachsen und den Iren Untersuchungen und Text* (Heidelberg, 1985); and R. A. Bremmer, 'The Final Countdown: Apocalyptic Expectations in Anglo-Saxon Charters', in *Time and Eternity in the Medieval Discourse*, ed. G. Jaritz and G. Moreno-Riano (Turnhout, 2003), pp. 501–14, esp. 505–14, for the diplomatic references.

[12] M. McC. Gatch, *Preaching and Theology in Anglo-Saxon England: Ælfric and Wulfstan* (Toronto, 1977); C. Cubitt, 'Apocalyptic and Eschatological Thought in England around the year 1000', *TRHS* 25 (2015), 27–52; and L. Roach, 'Apocalypse and Atonement in the Politics of Æthelredian England', *English Studies* 7 (2014), 737–57.

final age. However, it was by no means clear how long this would last. In the Gospel, Christ does not indicate the duration of the time of tribulation, whether a short while or very much longer. Thus a writer and thinker such as Wulfstan could consider himself and his contemporaries as living in this last age, without an expectation that Antichrist's coming was immediately around the corner. They could live in a state of expectation and readiness, without constant disappointment that the end had been postponed. This point of view tallies with important thinking about end-time anxieties by Bernard McGinn, recently emphasized by James Palmer.[13] McGinn argued that the orthodox condemnation of speculation concerning the exact timing of the end led to a different type of apocalyptic preoccupation, termed 'non-predictive imminence'; the latter does not seek to discover the timing of the end but is rather a frame of mind 'in which life is lived under the shadow of the end'.[14] Opposition to predictive imminence (particularly in the authoritative writings of St Augustine) ultimately led, McGinn argues, to an emphasis on psychological imminence resulting in an awareness of the need for moral reform and also missionary activity in preparation for the Last Judgement.[15] His arguments certainly have deep resonances in the early medieval world, for example, with the thought of Wulfstan and his contemporaries, where repentance, personal reformation and the practice of penance were prominent issues and integrally linked to preparations for death and the Last Judgement.[16]

This preoccupation with sin and the need for reformation before Judgement constituted a long tradition reaching back to Gregory the Great and beyond. Gregory's writings, so influential in the early medieval church, vividly illustrate McGinn's psychological imminence. Gregory was very conscious that he was living the last times of the world, and he identified many of the calamities of his own age with the signs preceding the coming of Antichrist prophesied by Christ in the New Testament. However, Gregory's message was not a simple urgent anticipation of the time of the end. The signs of the end were for Gregory reminders of the frailty of the world and earthly life and served as a warning against earthly attachments and as a spur to renunciation rather than as part of an attentive countdown to Judgement Day.[17]

---

[13] J. T. Palmer, *The Apocalypse in the Early Middle Ages* (Cambridge, 2014), pp. 7–24; and B. McGinn, 'The End of the World and the Beginning of Christianity', in *Apocalypse Theory and the End of the World*, ed. M. Bull (Oxford, 1995), pp. 58–89.

[14] McGinn, 'The End of the World', p. 60.   [15] *Ibid.*, p. 63.   [16] See n. 13 above.

[17] R. Markus, 'Gregory and Bede: The Making of the Western Apocalyptic Tradition', in *Atti dei convegni Lincei* (Rome, 2004), 247–56; R. Markus, 'Living within Sight of the End', in *Time in the Medieval World*, ed. C. Humphrey and W. M. Ormrod (York, 2001), pp. 23–34; and C. Dagron, 'La Fin des Temps et église selon Saint Grégoire le Grand', *Recherches de sciences religeuses* 58 (1970), 273–88.

Gregory saw reminders of the last days not only in the natural calamities and earthly conflicts of his time but also in the operation of evil and in the actions of those who carried out the work of Antichrist before his coming:

> For how many have not beheld Antichrist, and yet are his testicles: because they corrupt the hearts of the innocent by the example of their doings! For whoever is exalted with pride, whoever is tortured by the longings of covetousness, whoever is relaxed with the pleasures of lust, whoever is kindled by the burnings of the unjust and immoderate anger, what else is he but a testicle of Antichrist?[18]

Gregory followed Augustine in seeing Antichrist as preceded by his disciples, ideas taken up by Isidore of Seville, whose very popular writings summarized their teaching:

> He is called the Antichrist, because he is to come against Christ ... But Antichrist is also one who denies that Christ is God, for he is the opposite of Christ. So all those who depart from the Church and are cut off from the unity of faith are themselves Antichrists.[19]

Isidore's definition of Antichrist was borrowed by Wulfstan in two of his apocalyptic homilies.[20] Wulfstan therefore saw himself as living in an aging world of physical and moral deterioration, one also afflicted by devilish attack. The faithful needed to be warned to be constantly vigilant against sin and to protect themselves against the deceits and deceptions of those whose wickedness presaged that of Antichrist himself. But Wulfstan's sense of urgency, of the imminence of the end, shifted over time.

---

[18] Gregory the Great, *Moralia*, ed. Adriaen, vol. 143B, 32: 16: 28, p. 1652: 'Quam multi enim antichristum non uiderunt, sed tamen testiculi eius sunt, quia corda innocentium actionis suae exemplo corrumpunt. Quisquis namque in superbia extollitur: quisquis auaritiae desideriis cruciatur; quisquis luxuriae uoluptatibus soluitur; quisquis iniustae atque immoderatae irae flagris ignitur, quid aliud quam antichristi testis est?'. Translation from *Morals on the Book of Job by S. Gregory the Great*, trans. J. Bliss, 3 vols. in 4 (London, 1844–50), vol. III, pp. 2, 534. And see K. L. Hughes, *Constructing Antichrist* (Washington, 2005), pp. 108–13; and H. Savon, 'L'antéchrist dans l'oeuvre de Grégoire le Grand', in *Grégoire le Grand*, ed. J. Fontaine, R. Grillet and S. Pellistrandi (Paris, 1986), pp. 389–405.

[19] 'Antichristus appellatur, quia contra Christum venturus est ... Sed et ille Antichristus est qui negat esse Deum Christum. Contrarius enim Christo est. Omnes enim, qui exeunt de Ecclesia, et ab unitate fidei praeciduntur, et ipsi Antichristi sunt'. Isidore, *Etymologiae* viii. 11.20–3, in *Isidori Hispalensis Episcopi Etymologiarum sive Originum Libri XX*, ed W. M. Lindsay, 2 vols. (Oxford, 1911), vol. I, p. 330; *The Etymologies of Isidore of Seville*, trans. S. A. Barney, W. J. Lewis, J. A. Beach and O. Berghof (Cambridge, 2006), pp. 184–5. See also D. Verhelst, 'La préhistoire des conceptions d'Adson concernant l'Antichrist', *Recherches de théologie ancienne et médiévale* 40 (1973), 52–103, at 81–2.

[20] See below.

Wulfstan's Apocalyptic Preaching

Wulfstan was a key player in the politics of Æthelred's reign. He was appointed bishop of London in 996 and was elevated to the archdiocese of York in 1002.[21] His role in the composition of law-codes is well known, and his homiletic works are much studied.[22] Scholarship has stressed the intimate connections between these two activities, and increasingly, the political significance and context of a number of the sermons have been explored.[23] Wulfstan is important in the study of eschatological thought because of his composition of five major sermons exclusively devoted to warnings about the coming end-time.[24] These are rich and complex works, replete with Wulfstan's characteristic rhetorical flair, rewarding to study in numerous ways, for example, in their stylistic and linguistic skill or in their use of the tenth-century continental tract, Adso's *De ortu et tempore Antichristi*.[25] For the historian, they are perhaps chiefly notable because one, *Secundam Lucam*, explicitly identifies the viking attacks with the Gospel prediction concerning strife between nations before the coming of Antichrist. Further, in his final apocalyptic sermon, *Secundum Marcum*, the Archbishop emphasizes the significance of the passing of the year 1000,

---

[21] For Wulfstan's biography, see P. Wormald, 'Wulfstan', *ODNB*, vol. LX, pp. 558–62; and the essays in the collection, M. Townend (ed.), *Wulfstan Archbishop of York* (Turnholt, 2004). On Wulfstan's probable family origins and possible training at Peterborough, see C. Cubitt, 'Personal Names, Identity and Family in Benedictine Reform England', in *Verwandtschaft, Name und Soziale Ordnung (300–1000)*, ed. S. Patzold and K. Ubl (Tübingen, 2010), pp. 223–42; on his career as bishop of London, see A. Rabin, 'Wulfstan at London: Episcopal Politics in the Reign of Æthelred', *English Studies* 97 (2016), 186–206.

[22] D. Whitelock, 'Archbishop Wulfstan, Homilist and Statesman', *TRHS*, 4th series, 24 (1942), 25–45; D. Whitelock, 'Wulfstan and the Laws of Cnut', *EHR* 63 (1948), 433–52; D. Whitelock, 'Wulfstan's Authorship of Cnut's Laws', *EHR* 70 (1970), 75–85; K. Jost, *Wulfstanstudien* (Bern, 1950); and K. Lawson, 'Archbishop Wulfstan and the Homiletic Element in the Laws of Æthelred II and Cnut', *EHR* 107 (1992), 565–86.

[23] See most recently A. Rabin (ed. and trans.), *The Political Writings of Archbishop Wulfstan of York* (Manchester, 2015); and Cubitt, 'Apocalyptic and Eschatological Thought', pp. 46–52.

[24] On Wulfstan's eschatological and apocalyptic thought, see M. McG. Gatch, *Preaching and Theology in Anglo-Saxon England: Ælfric and Wulfstan* (Toronto, 1977); M. Godden, 'Apocalypse and Invasion in Late Anglo-Saxon England', in *From Anglo-Saxon to Middle English: Studies Presented to E. G. Stanley*, ed. M. Godden, D. Gray, and T. Hoad (Oxford, 1994), pp. 130–62; M. Godden, 'The Millennium, Time and History for the Anglo-Saxons', in *The Apocalyptic Year 1000: Religious Expectation and Social Change, 950–1050*, ed. R. Landes, A. Gow and D. C. Van Meter (Oxford, 2003), pp. 155–80; J. Hill, 'Ælfric and Wulfstan: Two Views of the Millennium', in *Essays on Anglo-Saxon and Related Themes in Memory of Lynne Grundy*, ed. J. Roberts and J. Nelson (London, 2000), pp. 231–5; M. Richards, 'Wulfstan and the Millennium', in *The Year 1000 Religious and Social Response to the Turning of the First Millennium*, ed. M. Frassetto (New York, 2002), pp. 41–8; Cubitt, 'Apocalyptic and Eschatological Thought'; and Roach, 'Apocalypse'.

[25] On his style in these sermons, see Orchard, 'Crying Wolf'; and W. L. DeLeeuw, 'The Eschatological Homilies of Wulfstan: A Historical Introduction' (unpublished PhD dissertation, Auburn University, Alabama, 1972). I am most grateful to Andy Orchard for alerting me to this dissertation.

stating that '[a] thousand years and also more have now passed since Christ was among people in human form, and now Satan's bonds are very loose.'[26] These references have naturally aroused the interest of scholars concerned to explore and chart the significance of the year 1000 in contemporary consciousness.[27] This section provides a brief overview of Wulfstan's apocalyptic sermons in order to set the scene for the *Sermo Lupi*.[28]

The first two sermons printed in Bethurum's edition are a pair, a Latin sermon, *De antichristo*, with an Old English version of this, 'Antichrist' (Bethurum sermons 1a and 1b).[29] Wulfstan's main purpose in these is to admonish priests of their duty to preach concerning Antichrist and his times, to educate their flocks so that they are prepared for the terrible trials and persecutions of his reign. He opens both texts with statements that identify disobedient and negligent Christians with Antichrist himself – those who practice Christianity wrongly are opposed to God just like Antichrist, whom Wulfstan designates as 'contrarius Cristi' or 'Godes wiðersaca'.[30] Sinful Christians are therefore the members of Antichrist in their opposition to Christ and his teaching. So Wulfstan emphasizes both the evil of his own day, seen in the presence of the wicked – Antichrist's members – and impending terrors. Many, he says, may never see Antichrist but witness the evil doings of the antichrists of their own day. Both texts are indebted to Adso's *De ortu et tempore Antichristi*, but this is by no means the sole or even the dominant influence.[31] The opening sentences, for example, closely follow Isidore's *Sententiae*, echoing his comments that many who will not witness the times of Antichrist will be found to be his members and his discussion of the testing of the elect.[32]

The starting point for sermons printed by Bethurum as sermons 2, 3 and 5 is the Gospel prophecies, the so-called Little Apocalypse. *Secundum*

---

[26] 'Þusend geara 7 eac ma is nu agan syððan Crist wæs mid mannum on menniscan hiwe, 7 nu syndon Satanases bendas swyðe toslopene', in *The Homilies of Wulfstan*, ed. D. Bethurum (Oxford, 1957), no. 3, pp. 123–4, at 124, and no. 5, pp. 134–41, at 136–7 (lines 44–6).

[27] See, for example, Palmer, *The Apocalypse*, pp. 208–14.

[28] See also the perceptive account given by Godden, 'The Millennium', pp. 167–72.

[29] *Homilies*, ed. Bethurum, nos. 1 and 1a, pp. 113–15 and 116–18.

[30] *Homilies*, ed. Bethurum, no. 1a, pp. 113–15 (at line 6 for quotation), and no. 1b, pp. 116–18 (at line 8 for quotation).

[31] See below. See also the recent discussion of these sermons by Rabin, 'Wulfstan at London'.

[32] *Homilies*, ed. Bethurum, p. 283. 'Omnis qui secundum professionis suae normam aut non uiuit aut aliter docet, Antichristus est. – Plerique autem Antichristi tempora non uisuri sunt, et tamen in membris Antichristi inueniendi sunt. C. 3: Antequam ueniat Antichristus, multa eius membra praecesserunt,et prauae actionis merito caput proprium praeuenerunt secundum apostoli sententiam qui iam iniquitatis mysterium operare illum adfirmat, etiam antequam reueletur.' Isidore, *Sententiae* i. 25, in *Isidorus Hispalensis Sententiae*, ed. P. Cazier, CCSL 111 (Turnhout, 1998), p. 79.

Matheum (Bethurum sermon 2) provides a paraphrase and brief commentary on Matthew 24: 1–14, 42, which describes the times of tribulation preceding the coming of Antichrist and the appearance of false prophets in his time.[33] Wulfstan emphasizes the role of deception in the last days and that while the end is very close, the Gospel must be preached throughout the world first. Here, while wishing to impress his audience with the need for vigilance and Christian renewal, the archbishop's admonitions do not sound a note of imminent anxiety.

Secundum Lucam (Bethurum sermon 3) is marked by a notable shift in tone and by a sharper sense of urgency.[34] This is a commentary on Luke 21: 25 identifying Christ's prophecies concerning the time of tribulation with the misfortunes of Wulfstan's own day:

> And therefore it is always the longer the worse in the world, as we ourselves very well know. And it is also clear and to be seen within ourselves that we obey the Lord too weakly ... And therefore many evil events injure and afflict us harshly, and foreigners and strangers severely oppress us, just as Christ clearly said must happen in his Gospel. He said, 'Nation will rise up against nation.'[35]

Wulfstan also goes on to preach about the Christian meaning of famine and dearth:

> Heaven strives against us when it sternly sends us storms that greatly injure cattle and land. The earth strives against us when it withholds earthly fruits and sends us too many weeds.[36]

Wulfstan's words here are a striking reference to the dearths and famines that afflicted the English in the late tenth and early eleventh centuries, no doubt in part the result of viking-inflicted devastation. It could also be – as Dorothy Bethurum suspected – a reference to the devastating famine of 1005 that the *Anglo-Saxon Chronicle* describes as the worst in living memory.[37]

---

[33] *Homilies*, ed. Bethurum, no. 2, pp. 119–22.   [34] *Homilies*, ed. Bethurum, no. 3, pp. 123–7.
[35] 'And ðy hit is on worulde a swa leng swa wyrse, þæs þe we sylfe gecnawað ful georne. And eac is on us sylfum swytol 7 gesyne þæt we to wace hyrað urum Drihtne ... And ðy us deriað 7 ðearle dyrfað fela ungelimpa 7 ælþeodige men 7 utancumene swyðe us swencað, ealswa Crist on his godspelle swutollice sæde þæt scolde geweorðan. He cwæð: *Surget gens contra gentem.*' *Homilies*, ed. Bethurum, no. 3, pp. 123–4 (lines 14–23). Translations for all Wulfstan's apocalyptic sermons from those provided for Bethurum sermons 1–5 can be found on Lionarons' very useful website: http://webpages.ursinus.edu/jlionarons/wulfstan/wulfstan.html
[36] 'Seo heofone us wind wið þonne heo us sended styrnlice stormas 7 orf 7 æceras swyðe amyrred. Seo eorðe us wind wið þonne heo forwyrned eorðlices wæstmas 7 us unweoda to fela asended.' *Homilies*, ed. Bethurum, no. 3, p. 125 (lines 38–41).
[37] *Homilies*, ed. Bethurum, pp. 287–8.

Secundam Marcum (Bethurum sermon 5) rewrites and extends *De temporibus antichristi* (Bethurum sermon 4).[38] Both use Adso's tract and concentrate on the dangers of the reign of Antichrist. The purpose of the *De temporibus antichristi* is to warn the faithful of the dangers of the reign of Antichrist – the persecution and suffering and especially his deceits which will lead Christians to damnation. The faithful therefore need to understand the nature of Antichrist's deceptions and strengthen their faith and turn from sin so that they may gain God's protection. *Secundam Marcum* reuses *De temporibus* but has a different approach to the reign of Antichrist. Here Wulfstan's warnings about the duplicity of Antichrist and the severity of his rule are joined to a castigation of contemporary evils, which are identified by Wulfstan with those described by the Apostle Paul in II Timothy 3: 1–5 quoted earlier.

Chronology of the Apocalyptic Sermons

It is important now to turn to questions of chronology, starting first with the sequencing of these sermons. What is their order of composition? Bethurum, a literary scholar, saw Wulfstan's use of Adso in the sermons *De antichristo* and 'Antichrist' (1a and 1b), *De temporibus antichristi* and *Secundam Marcam* (Bethurum sermons 4 and 5) as diagnostic for the order of their composition. She argued tentatively that these four sermons must be later than the sermons *Secundum Matheum* and *Secundum Lucam* (Bethurum sermons 2 and 3) because neither of the latter two draws upon Adso.[39] However, this assumption is open to question. The *De antichristo* and 'Antichrist' are informed by a number of theological writings – those of Isidore, Gregory and Augustine, for example – of which Adso is by no means the major influence. Bethurum's source notes in fact make this clear: she cites parallels from Gregory the Great three times but Adso only twice.[40] The sermon's opening sentences in the Latin

---

[38] *Homilies*, ed. Bethurum, nos. 4 and 5, pp. 128–41. On Bethurum sermon 5's rewriting of Bethurum sermon 4, see J. Pope, *The Homilies of Ælfric*, pp. 584–5; Godden, 'The Millennium', pp. 170–1; and M. Godden, 'The Relations of Wulfstan and Ælfric', in *Archbishop Wulfstan*, ed. Townend, pp. 353–74, at 369–70.

[39] *Homilies*, ed. Bethurum, p. 282: 'It is possible that they were written in this order: II, III, Ia, Ib, IV, V, since the first two show no close use of Adso.' Bethurum's arguments were carefully phrased to express caution, but her tentative dating is widely followed. See, for example, Lionarons, *Homiletic Writings*, pp. 49–50; Wormald, 'Archbishop Wulfstan: Eleventh-Century Statebuilder', in *Archbishop Wulfstan*, ed. Townend, pp. 9–27, with a chronological table on pp. 26–7 that is largely adopted by S. Pons-Sanz, *Norse-Derived Vocabulary in Late Old English Texts: Wulfstan's Works, a Case Study*, North-Western European Language Evolution Supplement 22 (Odense, 2007), p. 25.

[40] *Homilies*, ed. Bethurum, pp. 282–6.

De Antichristo articulate an idea found in Adso but are taken from Isidore's *Sententiae*.[41] Neither of these two provides the kind of narrative detail and description for which Wulfstan used the *De ortu* in the *De temporibus antichristi* and *Secundum Marcam* (Bethurum sermons 4 and 5). Bethurum's confidence that Wulfstan's reading of Adso provided a watershed in his thinking on matters eschatological seems questionable. His exploitation of Adso may have depended on his present needs and anxieties rather than on his discovery of the text. It may be that it is only after the moment when Wulfstan saw in his own age the extraordinary events described in the Gospels as immediately preceding the coming of Antichrist that he felt the need to describe in detail the nature of his reign.

The question of when Wulfstan composed the Latin and Old English pair, *De antichristo* and 'Antichrist', is an important one because Bethurum's chronology flies in the face of the natural reading of Wulfstan's apocalyptic sermons.[42] As we have seen, these two envisage Antichrist's coming as an event that may happen after the lifetime of his audience. *Secundum Matheum* firmly states that the Gospel must be preached throughout the world before the end-time comes. However, *Secundum Lucam* (which Bethurum places chronologically before *De Antichristo* and 'Antichrist') is the real watershed, in which Wulfstan explicitly identifies events in his own day with the time of tribulation foretold by Christ: the urgency of *De temporibus antichristi* and *Secundum Marcam* follow on logically from this. The immediacy of these sermons, both with regard to the imminence of the coming of Antichrist and the moral position of the English, contrasts with the more relaxed and theoretical stance of *De antichristo* and 'Antichrist'.

These apocalyptic texts have been widely accepted as representing Wulfstan's earliest work, from about 996 to the early years of the eleventh century. Dorothy Whitelock even suggested that it was these fiery sermons that established Wulfstan's reputation and led to his promotion to the archiepiscopate of York.[43] But there are strong reasons for questioning this.[44] The issue of the dating of Wulfstan's apocalyptic sermons is

---

[41] 'Anticristus est, quia secundum interpretationem sui nominis apellatur. Anticristus enim contrarius Cristi dicitur. Multi ætiam tempora Anticristi non uidebunt, sed tamen in membris eius multi inueniuntur.' *Homilies*, ed. Bethurum, no. 1a, p. 113 (lines 4–7). These are translated in the Old English, 1b, *Homilies*, ed. Bethurum, and p. 116. See n. 30 above for the Isidore passage. And see http://fontes.english.ox.ac.uk (accessed 26 July 2016).

[42] See Godden's perceptive reading of these sermons in 'Apocalypse and Invasion', pp. 142–61, where he reads them in the order 1 to 5 without noting that this disagrees with Bethurum's argument.

[43] D. Whitelock, 'Archbishop Wulfstan, Homilist and Statesman', *TRHS*, 4th series, 24 (1942), 24–45, at 39, followed by *Homilies*, ed. Bethurum, p. 101.

[44] See the important critique by Rabin, 'Wulfstan at London'.

important for the interpretation of the *Sermo Lupi*. The traditional dating of all these sermons, placing the apocalyptic sermons early in Wulfstan's career and the *Sermo Lupi* relatively late (in 1014, possibly with later revisions), meant that it appeared that at least a decade separated their composition. But recent scholarship, particularly that of Malcolm Godden on the eschatological sermons and that of Keynes on the *Sermo Lupi*, has narrowed this gap very considerably. In fact, Wulfstan's articulation of apocalyptic fears continued into the second decade of the eleventh century and, it will be argued, overlapped with his composition of the *Sermo Lupi*.

Whitelock and Bethurum's dating of these sermons rested on two factors: firstly, the explicit statement in *Secundum Marcum* concerning the passing of 'a thousand years and also more' since Christ's incarnation[45] and, secondly, close textual analysis of the verbal parallels and interdependence of Wulfstan's writings. This suggested to Bethurum that the homilist completed his apocalyptic sermons and then subsequently drew upon them in other treatments of the end-time and related themes.[46] However, neither of these assumptions is secure. The statement in *Secundum Marcum* concerning the passing of the millennium is not a precise chronological marker: it could denote the years immediately after 1000 but need not do so. It could refer to five, ten or more years since the millennium. There are, in fact, strong textual reasons (which will be discussed later) that can be evinced for dating this sermon after 1005–6.[47]

The second linchpin of Bethurum's dating of Wulfstan's homilies – the possibility of constructing a kind of genealogy for his borrowings from one homily to another – was radically challenged by Andy Orchard's seminal article, 'Crying Wolf: Oral Style and the *Sermones Lupi*', published in 1992, in which Orchard analyzed three of Wulfstan's sermons, *Secundam Lucam, De fide catholica* and *De septiformi spiritu* (Bethurum sermons 3, 7 and 9) – all of which have apocalyptic content. Orchard argued that the relationship between them was

> not linear in the sense that no one passage is clearly the model for any other, and no development of ideas or phraseology can be discerned.[48] Each passage contains both additions and omissions (and variants) with respect to each of the other passages. Furthermore each passage occurs in the

---

[45] 'Þusend geara 7 eac ma is nu agan syððan Crist wæs mid mannum on menniscan hiwe.' *Homilies*, ed. Bethurum no. 5, p. 136 (lines 44–5).

[46] See the analysis in Bethurum, *Homilies*, pp. 101–3.

[47] Godden, 'The Relations', pp. 368–70; and P. Clemoes, 'Review of the Homilies of Wulfstan by Dorothy Bethurum', *Modern Languages Review* 54 (1959), 81–2.

[48] A. Orchard, 'Crying Wolf: Oral Style and the *Sermones Lupi*', *ASE* 21 (1992), 239–64, at 256.

context of three quite different sermons on . . . three quite different topics. I suggest that we can best consider this repetition as three quite separate treatments of the same theme.[49]

Orchard's conclusions suggest that Bethurum's model of Wulfstan's working method, a progressive reuse of phrases and passages from one sermon to another, is flawed and needs to be treated with caution.

A further assumption behind Bethurum and Whitelock's early dating of these sermons was that Wulfstan had a kind of schedule for his writings, starting with preaching about the Apocalypse and progressing through doctrinal and pastoral matters to political (rather like Picasso's famous 'Blue Period'). This also requires a sceptical approach.[50] While it is true that Ælfric had a programmatic sense of purpose in his main series of sermons, this idea may work less well for a busy bishop, producing sermons for particular occasions and in response to recent events.[51]

Further, as early as 1959, Peter Clemoes made significant criticisms of the early dating of two of Wulfstan's apocalyptic sermons, *De temporibus antichristi* and *Secundum Marcam*, based on his knowledge of the date of the Ælfrician texts to which these are indebted. His arguments were repeated and extended by Godden in an important article that argued that Wulfstan's use of Ælfric's sermons is very likely reliant upon a sermon collection put together after 1005 and that *De temporibus antichristi* and *Secundum Marcam* may date to the period 1006–12.[52] Questions of the end-time therefore continued to preoccupy the archbishop well into the first decade of the new millennium and beyond.[53]

Wulfstan's Continuing Engagement with Apocalypticism

Moreover, Wulfstan's engagement with apocalyptic matters was not limited to these five sermons, although these extensive treatments of the end-time have tended to hog all the attention. There are significant treatments

---

[49] *Ibid.*

[50] *Homilies*, ed. Bethurum, pp. 101–4. See, for example, her comparison of homilies *De temporibus antichristi* and *Secundum Marcam* (Bethurum sermons 4 and 5) and Bethurum sermon 6, where the verbal parallels she sets out between them are not exact repetitions but rather fit Orchard's description of 'separate treatments of the same theme'. And see her assumption on p. 103: 'What Wulfstan apparently did in the early years of his incumbency was to compose homilies on the fundamentals of the Christian faith.'

[51] For Ælfric's aims and working methods, see J. Hill, 'Ælfric: His Life and Works', in *A Companion to Ælfric*, ed. H. Magennis and M. Swan (Leiden, 2009), pp. 35–65; and P. Clemoes, 'The Chronology of Ælfric's Works', in *The Anglo-Saxons*, ed. P. Clemoes (London, 1959), pp. 212–47.

[52] See n. 47 above.

[53] See Cubitt, 'Eschatological Thought'; and Roach, 'Apocalypse', pp. 737–57.

of the end-time, the rule of Antichrist and the Last Judgement in four other sermons: Bethurum sermon 6, *De fide catholica* (Bethurum sermon 7) and *De septiformi spiritu* (Bethurum sermon 9) and Napier L.[54]

Bethurum sermon 6 presents an outline of Christian history, drawing upon Pirmin's *Scarapsus* and Ælfric's opening sermon on Creation from *Catholic Homilies* I, but is still a characteristically Wulfstanian creation.[55] It combines a linear account of Christian history, from Creation to Judgement, with an emphasis on the ancient cycle of the sin and divine punishment seen in the Old Testament and its relevance to the present. There is no mistaking the relevance for his audience of his comments on how the devil led the people away through deceit and illusions or how God punished the Israelites for their sins by allowing a heathen army to ravage the land.[56] While the Apocalypse and Last Judgement are the inevitable conclusion of a survey of Christian history, Wulfstan's account is not routine. He concludes by warning that the end-time is close because some of the signs foretold by Christ as preceding the coming of Antichrist have occurred.[57] This sermon has significant parallels in tone and subject matter to *Secundam Lucam, De temporibus antichristi* and *Secundum Marcam* and to his *Sermo Lupi*.[58]

The *De fide catholica* (Bethurum sermon 7) is an exposition of Christian faith, setting out Christ's life and resurrection, with a strong focus on penitence and the forgiveness of sins.[59] The second half is largely taken up with an account of the Last Judgement and the torments of hell whither sinners – enumerated in an alliterating list closely akin to the list of sinners in the *Sermo Lupi* – are condemned.[60] Like Bethurum sermon 6, it notes that the end is near because of the appearance of the signs prophesied by Christ.[61]

Antichrist also makes a significant appearance in a sermon, *De septiformi spiritu*, where Wulfstan has expanded upon a base text by Ælfric.[62]

[54] *Homilies*, ed. Bethurum, no. 6, pp. 142–56, no. 7, pp. 157–65, no. 9, pp. 185–91; and Napier L. On Napier L, see J. T. Lionarons, 'Napier L: Wulfstan's Eschatology at the Close of his Career', in *Archbishop Wulfstan*, ed. Townend, pp. 413–28; and Lionarons, *Homiletic Writings*, pp. 43–74.

[55] *Homilies*, ed. Bethurum, no. 6, pp. 142–56. On Wulfstan's reworking of Ælfric and his use of other sources in this sermon, see Bethurum's commentary, *Homilies*, pp. 293–8; Godden, 'The Relations', pp. 362–70; and Lionarons, *Homiletic Writings*, pp. 82–5.

[56] *Homilies*, ed. Bethurum, p. 150.   [57] *Ibid.*, p. 155.

[58] For these, see *ibid.*, p. 296, note on lines 77–95, and p. 298, notes on lines 193ff and 205–7.

[59] *Ibid.*, no. 7, pp. 157–65.   [60] See discussion below.

[61] *Homilies*, ed. Bethurum, no. 7, p. 161.

[62] *Ibid.*, no. 9, pp. 185–91. And see *Wulfstan Sammlung der ihm zugeschriebenen Homilien nebst Untersuchungen über ihre Echtheit*, ed. A. Napier (Zurich, 1883), no. VIII, pp. 56–60, for the original Ælfric sermon. See the close comparison and discussion by Orchard, 'Crying Wolf', pp. 251–7. For discussion of Wulfstan's use of his source, see *Homilies*, ed. Bethurum, pp. 304–6; Godden, 'The Relations', pp. 363–5; and Lionarons, *Homiletic Writings*, pp. 130–1.

Wulfstan's re-workings emphasize more keenly the idea that the evil qualities given by the devil appear under the guise of good ones and include fiendish deception. This leads the archbishop naturally on to Antichrist himself in a lengthy excursus going beyond Ælfric's text. Those in thrall to the devil and his evils deceive and mislead others, just as Antichrist will do. They are slaves of Antichrist and forerunners of his coming who prepare the way for him.[63]

Finally, Wulfstan composed Napier L, a composite sermon, with an excursus on the end of the world.[64] The sermon is addressed to the king and to an assembly, outlining the Christian duties and responsibilities of the king and each order of society – those charged with secular responsi-bilities, the men and women of the Church, and laying down Christian conduct. Finally, Wulfstan meditates on the aging and decay of the world and on the imminent coming of Antichrist. This sermon has parallels with Cnut's legislation of 1018 and must be dated late in Wulfstan's career. While Bethurum and Lionarons suggest a date after 1020, Wormald argues more convincingly for a date preceding Cnut's code, 1017–18.[65]

These four sermons demonstrate how Wulfstan's sense of the immi-nence of the end penetrated his wider thinking and permeated his under-standing of Christian history and doctrine. Taken with the six apocalyptic sermons (Bethurum sermons 1–5), they also plainly indicate that the archbishop's interest in the Apocalypse was not limited to his time as bishop of London (996–1002) and the early years of his archiepiscopate. It is necessary therefore to postulate a new, more feasible chronology and dating for Wulfstan's corpus of apocalyptic sermons. A provisional and tentative dating sequence would be that the *De antichristo* and 'Antichrist' and *Secundum Matheum* belong to an early period of Wulfstan's literary activity. *Secundum Lucam* perhaps then dates to after 1005, while *De temporibus antichristi* and *Secundum Marcam* are later, possibly even asso-ciated in some way with Æthelred's Enham code of 1008.[66] Bethurum

---

[63] *Homilies*, ed. Bethurum, pp. 189–90.

[64] *Wulfstan Sammlung*, ed. Napier, no. L, pp. 266–74; for discussion, see Jost, *Wulfstanstudien*, pp. 249–61; Lionarons, 'Napier Homily L: Wulfstan's Eschatology at the Close of His Career', pp. 413–28; Lionarons, *Homiletic Writings*, pp. 171–5; and see the valuable discussion and translation in Rabin, *The Political Writings of Archbishop Wulfstan*, pp. 143–53.

[65] On the dating, see Jost, *Wulfstanstudien*, pp. 249–61 (who does not attribute the sermon to Wulfstan); Kennedy, 'Cnut's Code of 1018', pp. 62–6; P. Wormald, *The Making of English Law, King Alfred to the Twelfth Century*, vol. 1: *Legislation and Its Limits* (Oxford, 1999), p. 335, n. 336; Lionarons, 'Napier Homily L', p. 416; Lionarons, *Homiletic Writings*, p. 175; and Rabin, *Political Writings*, p. 143.

[66] See my 'Apocalyptic and Eschatological Thought', pp. 48–9. And see below.

sermon 6 and *De septiformi spiritu* (Bethurum sermon 9) are both indebted to Ælfric's works and may therefore fall into the period 1006–12, hypothesized by Godden as the time when Wulfstan had access to a manuscript of Ælfric sermons. Napier L is reasonably securely dated to 1017–18.

Now it is time to turn to the question of the relationship of the *Sermo Lupi* to Wulfstan's apocalyptic interests. This discussion involves four key issues.

1. The development of the *Sermo* as evidenced in its three surviving versions.
2. The date of the first composition of the *Sermo* and its subsequent versions.
3. The verbal and linguistic parallels between the *Sermo* and Wulfstan's eschatological sermons.
4. The interpretation of the *Sermo* in the context of Wulfstan's eschatological thinking.

Development of the *Sermo Lupi* as Evidenced in Its Three Extant Versions

The transmission of Wulfstan's *Sermo Lupi ad Anglos* in three different versions has provoked considerable controversy over the development of the text. Simon Keynes's analysis in his 2007 article, 'An Abbot, an Archbishop, and the viking Raids of 1006–7 and 1009–12', not only provides an invaluably clear overview of the issues but also puts forward important new ways of considering the problem, which will inform the discussion in this chapter.[67] The three versions differ chiefly in their length, and debate has focused upon the question of whether Wulfstan initially composed the short version and subsequently expanded it or completed the longest text and then edited it down.[68] This question is important with regard to the *Sermo Lupi*'s eschatological purpose and apocalyptic content. Malcolm Godden has argued that not only does the short version represent the earliest of the three texts but also that this

---

[67] Keynes, 'An Abbot', pp. 203–14.

[68] Keynes conveniently dubbed these three versions the short, medium and long versions. All three are printed by Bethurum in her *Homilies* as no. 20. Short version: pp. 255–60; medium: pp. 261–6; long version: pp. 267–75. The manuscript transmission of these is as follows: the short text is preserved in CCCC MS 419 and Oxford, Bodleian Library MS 343 (N. Ker, *Catalogue of Manuscripts containing Anglo-Saxon* (Oxford, 1957), nos. 68 and 310); the medium in CCCC MS 201, pp. 82–6 (Ker, *Catalogue*, no. 49); and the long in London, BL, Nero A. I and Oxford, Bodleian Library, MS Hatton 113 (Ker, *Catalogue*, nos. 164 and 331).

purveyed a strong apocalyptic message that was revised and reappraised in the course of expansion of the homily into its two longer versions.[69] In his view, the short text of the *Sermo* explained the contemporary disasters and defeats of the English as signs of the imminence of the end. He noted the importance of Paul's descriptions of the intensification of evil in his Second Letter to Timothy and contextualizes the warnings of the sermon within an apocalyptic scenario of the evils prophesied before the coming of Antichrist.[70] The long version, however, contains passages reflecting on contemporary circumstances not present in the short.[71] These directly comment on abuses and horrors resulting from the viking raids, and the sermon finishes with a unique passage (derived ultimately from Gildas via Alcuin) on how the Saxon conquest of Britain was a divine punishment for the sins of the British.[72] God's wrath at the wickedness of the English may likewise lead them to forfeit their kingdom to the invaders. Godden sees these passages as additions that shift the explanatory framework of the sermon from the disasters attendant upon the end-time to divinely incurred punishments, conforming to an age-old pattern of sin and retribution. He concludes that Wulfstan's apocalyptic ardour had therefore cooled and that his historical understanding of the present had shifted from a linear view of history in which the events of today unfold on an eschatological trajectory moving towards the Last Judgement to a cyclic understanding of his own time, whose disasters belong to a cycle attested from biblical times onwards of human wrong-doing and divine punishment.[73]

Godden's interpretation countered that of Stephanie Hollis, who argued in two detailed articles for the priority of the longest version.[74] Hollis argued from her analysis of the thematic structure and verbal style of the *Sermo* that the additional passages in the long text were integral to its

---

[69] *Sermo Lupi*, ed. Whitelock, pp. 1–5; and Bethurum, *Homilies*, pp. 22–4.

[70] Godden, 'Apocalypse', p. 147; and Godden, 'The Millennium', p. 172.

[71] For a succinct summary of the differences between the three versions, see Keynes, 'An Abbot', pp. 206–7, focusing on four key passages: the discussion of the betrayal of Edward the Martyr and expulsion of Æthelred; the section that he dubs 'God's anger', which describes the disorder resulting from the viking raids; 'Sinners', the catalogue of sinners; and finally, the passage concerning Gildas and the conquest of the British.

[72] As noted by Keynes, 'An Abbot', p. 206 and n. 251, on Wulfstan's probable use of Alcuin's letter to Archbishop Æthelheard on Gildas and the Britons in the form copied into CCCC, MS 190. And see Bethurum in *Homilies*, pp. 363–4; and her 'Archbishop Wulfstan's Commonplace Book', *Proceedings of the Modern Languages Association of America* 57 (1942), 916–29, at 920–1.

[73] Godden, 'Apocalypse', pp. 152–6; and Godden, 'The Millennium', pp. 173–7.

[74] S. Hollis, 'The Thematic Structure of the *Sermo Lupi*', *ASE* 6 (1977), 175–95; and see S. Dien, '*Sermo Lupi ad Anglos*: the Order and Date of the Three Versions', *Neuphilologische Mitteilungen* 64 (1975), 561–70.

meaning and purpose and also that the sermon was both profoundly topical and eschatological. She highlights the significance of Wulfstan's emphasis on the increase of sin before the end of the world. The vikings, she suggests, were seen by Wulfstan as 'antichrists whose victory establishes the reign of the arch-enemy'.[75] While her analysis is powerful and perceptive, this interpretation of the vikings' position in the sermon is not convincing. Hollis argues from the fact that Wulfstan described disobedient Christians as opponents of God, and thus as antichrists, to suggest that Wulfstan therefore equated the vikings as heathens with antichrists. But her reasoning here is flawed. Not all enemies of God are antichrists: sinful Christians are false in their Christian vocation where heathens are not.[76] But many aspects of her analysis are persuasive: Wilcox has followed Hollis and also argued on independent grounds for the priority of the longest version and emphasized the eschatological nature of the sermon.[77]

Ultimately, the question of the evolution of the sermon may not be definitively resolvable. Simon Keynes suggests that the longest text represents the earliest version of those extant, noting that the omission of the most topical passages diminished its bite and apparently 'sanitized' it by the removal of painful reminders of recent events.[78] However, he also emphasizes the vital point that other versions of the text have been lost: the sermon's stemma postulates four lost versions.[79] Our understanding of its evolution is therefore incomplete.[80]

Keynes's hypothesis raises important questions about the time and context of the composition of the sermon. The rubric found in the Wulfstan manuscript (London, BL, Cotton Nero A. I) of the long version of the sermon has been thought to provide a secure date for its composition:

> The sermon of the Wolf to the English when the Danes persecuted them most, which was in the year 1014 from the incarnation of our Lord Jesus Christ.[81]

Further, all three versions derive from a text that cited the murder of Edward the Martyr and the expulsion of Æthelred as examples of the betrayal of lords (*hlafordswice*) amongst the English, thus dating this source

---

[75] Hollis, 'The Thematic Structure', pp. 175–95, esp. 185.
[76] See also Godden, 'Apocalypse', pp. 152–3, for further important objections to this identification.
[77] Wilcox, '*Sermo Lupi*', pp. 388–92.   [78] Keynes, 'An Abbot', p. 208.
[79] *Sermo Lupi*, ed. Whitelock, pp. 3–5; and *Homilies*, ed. Bethurum, pp. 22–3.
[80] Keynes, 'An Abbot', pp. 206–7, and see my discussion below.
[81] 'Sermo Lupi ad Anglos quando Dani maxime persecuti sunt eos, quod fuit anno millesimo.XIIII. ab incarnatione domini nostri Iesu Cristi.' *Homilies*, ed. Bethurum, no. 20, p. 266 (lines 1–6). See Godden, 'Apocalypse', p. 158, on the retrospective nature of the composition of this rubric. Translation from *EHD*, ed. Whitelock, p. 929.

text to after 1013 and Æthelred's flight.[82] This fact, together with the date of 1014 supplied in Cotton Nero A. I, has made a strong prima facie case for placing the original composition of the sermon at this date. Jon Wilcox has suggested that the sermon might first have been preached to the assembly meeting in York for the consecration of the new bishop of London on 16 February, 1014. He hypothesizes that it was this meeting, held in the aftermath of the death of the conqueror Swein thirteen days earlier, that made the decision to recall and restore Æthelred to the throne.[83] This provides an inviting scenario in which to locate the sermon, but Wilcox's argument falls short of definitive proof.[84]

However, this rubric is also found in variant versions in two other manuscripts, prefacing the long version in Oxford, Bodleian Library, Ms Hatton 113, where the date has been replaced by the more generic statement 'IN DIES AEÐELREDI REGIS', and in CCCC, Ms 201, where it precedes the short version and gives 1009 as the date instead of Nero A. I's 1014. This text also includes an addition stating that the sermon was preached four years before the king's death, that is, 1012. These conflicting dates were explained by Whitelock and Bethurum as scribal errors. However, in Keynes's view, they may preserve evidence of multiple iterations of the sermon. He offers a hypothesis in which a lost version may have been composed in 1009–12 at the time of the arrival of Thorkel's army, a date that fits more closely than 1014 with the statement that the sermon was preached when the Danes persecuted the English most. Wulfstan may have revised this in 1014, resulting in the surviving long version, which was subsequently reworked in a number of versions including the existing short one, which Keynes would date to 1020.[85] This new dating hypothesis places the composition and revisions of the *Sermo* nearer to the period when Wulfstan is now thought to have composed his later apocalyptic sermons, that is, to 1006–12, and when he was working on Bethurum sermon 6 and the *De septiformi spiritu* (Bethurum sermon 9), which also contains apocalyptic material.[86] Wulfstan returned to the theme of the Last Judgement in Napier L, a sermon that has strong affinities to the *Sermo Lupi* and that dates to 1018, when it is possible that Wulfstan was revising the *Sermo Lupi*.

---

[87] In the medium text in CCCC, MS 201 and the longest in Nero A. I and Hatton 113, Æthelred's expulsion is omitted, but the text must descend from a version in which both kings were named. See *Homilies*, ed. Bethurum, no. 20, p. 270 and p. 22 for the text and for discussion of this point. *Sermo Lupi*, ed. Whitelock, p. 3, note 79, and for the dating, see her discussion, *Sermo Lupi ad Anglos*, ed. D. Whitelock, rev. ed. (Exeter, 1976), p. 6.

[83] Wilcox, 'Wulfstan's *Sermo Lupi*', pp. 380–8.

[84] For some cautious caveats, see Keynes, 'An Abbot', pp. 204–5.   [85] *Ibid.*, pp. 209–11.

[86] Bethurum, sermons 6, 7 and 9, see above.

Sermo Lupi in Its Apocalyptic Context

My discussion here falls into two parts – firstly, an investigation of the verbal parallels between the *Sermo* and Wulfstan's eschatological writings.[87] These are important guides to Wulfstan's meaning. Orchard's 1992 analysis of Wulfstan's style emphasized the exceptionally high degree of verbal repetition in the preacher's work. Orchard describes him as 'constantly reus[ing] what one might call characteristic formulae'.[88] But Orchard also emphasizes that this is not mechanical repetition; he 'alters and adapts', he repeats, rephrases and reworks.[89] This is not routine cut and paste, but a deliberate use of characteristic formulae to express similar ideas, coupled with a strong stylistic sense of the importance of variation and variety within this repetition. Three examples of this kind of reworking of phrases and passages where the words of the *Sermo Lupi* overlap with Wulfstan's eschatological sermons can tell us much about the sermon's origins and context.

The first example concerns that familiar Wulfstan trope with which he opens the *Sermo*:

> Leofan men, gecnawað þæt soð is: ðeos worold is on ofste, 7 **hit nealæcð þam ende, 7 þy hit is on worolde aa swa leng swa wyrse**; 7 swa hit sceal nyde for folces synnan ær Antecristes tocyme yfelian swyþe, 7 huru hit wyrð þænne egeslice 7 grimlic wide on worolde.[90]

The phrases that make up this opening sentence can all be paralleled from other sermons, four of the apocalyptic sermons, as well as Bethurum sermon 6 and the *De fide catholica* (Bethurum sermon 7), where these phrases also refer to the imminent coming of Antichrist.

> *Secundum Lucam:* And gyt weorþeð mare, þæs ðe bec secgað, wracu 7 gedrecednes þonne æfre ær wære ahwar on worulde; þæt bið, þonne Antecrist wedeð 7 ealle woruld bregeð, **7 ðærto hit nealæcð nu swyðe georne. And ðy hit is on worulde a swa leng swa wyrse**, þæs þe we sylfe gecnawað ful georne.[91]

---

[87] *Sermo Lupi*, ed. Whitelock, p. 36.   [88] Orchard, 'Crying Wolf', p. 258.   [89] *Ibid.*, pp. 257–8.

[90] Long version: *Homilies*, ed. Bethurum, 20 (E, I), p. 267 (lines 7–9), translation from *EHD*, ed. Whitelock, p. 929. 'Beloved men, realise what is true: this world is in haste and the end approaches; and therefore in the world things go from bad to worse, and so it must of necessity deteriorate greatly on account of the people's sins before the coming of Antichrist'.

[91] 'And yet more evils and afflictions will come, as the book says, than ever happened before anywhere in the world; that is, when Antichrist rages and terrifies all the world, and that is now coming very quickly. And therefore it is always the longer the worse in the world, as we ourselves know very well.' *Homilies*, ed. Bethurum, no. 3, p. 123 (lines 10–15). Translation from http://webpages.ursinus.edu/jlionarons/wulfstan/wulfstan.html.

Secundum Matheum: And ðy man sceal wacigean 7 warnian symle þæt man geara weorðe huru to ðam dome, weald hwænne he us to cyme, we witan mid gewisse **þæt hit þæt hit þærto nealæcð georne**.[92]

Secundum Marcam: Anticristes tima is wel gehende, **7 ðy hit is on worulde a swa leng swa wacre**. Men syndon swicole, 7 woruld is þe wyrse, þæt us dereð eallum.[93]

'Antichrist': forðam þæt mæste yfel cymð to mannum þonne Antecrist sylf cymð, þe næfre ær on worulde ne geweard. And us þincð þæt hit sy þam timan swyðe gehende, **forþam þeos woruld is fram dæge to dæge a swa leng swa wyrse**.[94]

De temporibus antichristi: [The time of Antichrist approaches soon.] And þæt is gesyne, þy is **ðeos woruld fram dæge to dæge wyrse 7 wyrse**.[95]

These verbal parallels underline the apocalyptic nature of the statement with which Wulfstan opens this sermon.[96] He tells his audience that they are living in the period immediately preceding Antichrist's coming, when the world is degenerating into the worst depravity. His tirade against the sins of the English is therefore framed by the idea of the intensification of evil at the end of the world.

The second example is the catalogue of woes and wickednesses that Wulfstan provides to substantiate his generalized denunciation of English depravity:

Ne dohte hit nu lange inne ne ute, ac wæs **here 7 hunger, bryne 7 blodgyte**, on gewelhwylcan ende oft 7 gelome. And us stalu 7 cwalu, **stric 7 steorfa**, orfcwealm 7 uncoþu, **hol 7 hete 7 rypera reaflac** derede swyþe þearle . . . .[97]

---

[92] *Homilies*, ed. Bethurum, no. 2, p. 121 (lines 62–4).   [93] *Ibid.*, no. 5, p. 137 (lines 46–8).

[94] *Ibid.*, no. 1b, p. 117 (lines 20–4).   [95] *Ibid.*, no. 4, p. 132 (lines 77–9).

[96] As noted by Godden, 'Apocalypse', p. 146. Godden points to this as a clear announcement of the apocalyptic context of the sermon with regard to the short version of the *Sermo* in support of his argument about the diminishing apocalyptic meaning of the sermon but fails to emphasize that this opening was maintained in all three versions. See the discussion of Hollis, 'Thematic Structure', pp. 177–81.

[97] 'Things have not gone well now for a long time at home or abroad, but there has been devastation and famine, burning and bloodshed in every district again and again; and stealing and killing, sedition and pestilence, murrain and disease, malice and hate and spoliation by robbers have harmed us very grievously...'. *Homilies*, ed. Bethurum, no. 20, p. 269 (lines 55–67). Translation from *EHD*, ed. Whitelock, p. 930.

Similar catalogues occur in a handful of other Wulfstan sermons, but amongst these, the *Sermo* is verbally closest to *Secundum Marcam*, which has already been cited earlier in parallel to the *Sermo*. In *Secundum Marcam*, this set of miseries is part of a description of the last days.

> Eac sceal aspringan wide 7 side sacu 7 clacu, **hol 7 hete 7 rypera reaflac,** **here 7 hunger, bryne 7 blodgyte** 7 styrnlice styrunga, **stric 7 steorfa** 7 fela ungelimpa.[98]

Wulfstan's memorable catalogue of current ills may therefore deliberately be a reminder of the tribulations at the end of the world.

The third and final example of verbal overlap concerns Wulfstan's enumeration of the sinners prevalent in England (a catalogue that Simon Keynes suggested may echo Revelations 22: 15).[99] This passage is only found in the longest version of the *Sermo*:

> Her syndan **mannslagan** 7 mægslagan 7 mæsserbanan 7 mynsterha-tan; 7 her syndan **mansworan 7 morþorwyrhtan**; 7 her syndan myltestran 7 **bearnmyrðran 7 fule forlegene horingas** manege; 7 her syndan **wiccan** 7 wælcyrian; 7 her syndan **ryperas 7 reaferas 7** **woruldstruderas, 7 hrædest is to cweþenne,** mana 7 misdæda ungerim ealra.[100]

Similar lists of sinners can be found in *De fide catholica* (Bethurum sermon 7) and Bethurum sermon 13, where they describe not contemporary earthly sinners but also the inhabitants of hell.

> *De fide catholica*: Ðider sculan **mannslagan**, 7 ðider sculan manswican; ðider sculan æwbrecan 7 ða fulan forlegenan; ðider sculan **mansworan 7** **morðwyrhtan**; ðider sculan gitseras, **ryperas 7 reaferas 7 woruldstruderas**; ðider sculon þeofas 7 ðeodscaðan; ðyder sculon **wiccan** 7 wigleras, 7 **hrædest to secganne**, ealle þa manfullan þe ær yfel worhton 7 noldan geswican ne wið God þingian.[101]

---

[98] *Ibid.*, no. 5, p. 140 (lines 102–4). And see *ibid.*, no. 19, p. 253 lines (60–6): 'Þonne sceal eow sona weaxan to hearme wædl 7 wawa, sacu 7 wracu, **here 7 hunger** . . . And eow unwæstm þurh unweder gelome gelimpeð, 7 stalu 7 steorfa swyþe gehyneþ.' And see Godden, 'Apocalypse', p. 147, where he notes the parallel with Bethurum sermon 5 and comments that in Bethurum sermon 5 this passage is in the future tense, whereas in the *Sermo* it is in the present.

[99] Revelations 22: 15: '[D]ogs and sorcerors, and fornicators, and murderers, and idolators and everyone who loves and practices falsehood'. Keynes, 'An Abbot', p. 205, n. 248.

[100] *Homilies*, ed. Bethurum, no. 20, p. 273 (lines 161–6). Translation from *EHD*, ed. Whitelock, p. 933: 'Here there are manslayers and slayers of their kinsmen, and slayers of priests and persecutors of monasteries, and here there are perjurers and murderers, and here there are harlots and infanticides and many foul adulterous fornicators, and here there are wizards and sorceresses, and here there are plunderers and robbers and spoliators, and, in short, a countless number of all crimes and misdeeds.'

[101] *Homilies*, ed. Bethurum, no. 7, p. 163 (lines 128–34).

Bethurum sermon 13: Ðyder sculan **manslagan** ... ðider sculan **wiccan** 7 **bearnmyrðran**; ðider sculan þeofas 7 ðeodscaðan, **ryperas** 7 **reaferas**, 7 **hrædest to secganne**, ealle þa manfullan þe God gremiað.[102]

So here Wulfstan's reworking of this list could be seen as a very conscious echo of the *De fide catholica* and Bethurum sermon 13, reminding the English of the ultimate and eternal punishment of their crimes.[103] These verbal echoes in the *Sermo* relate not simply to style but also to content – they highlight its close kinship with Wulfstan's thinking about the last days and his own understanding of how his present age relates to the Gospel teaching concerning the Apocalypse.

Sermo Lupi and the Time of Tribulation

The *Sermo* therefore signals its position in earthly time in its opening words – the period immediately preceding the coming of Antichrist, a time of earthly disasters when nation will rise up against nation and families turn against each other. This is above all a dangerous time when wickedness and human vice flourish beyond measure, a time signalled by the Gospel prophecy concerning the multiplication of evil when men's love cools, which formed the starting point for St Paul's disquisition on sinners and wrongdoing in his Second Letter to Timothy, as discussed earlier. The Apostle's words are paraphrased by Wulfstan in *Secundum Marcam*, a sermon that, as noted previously, bears significant kinship with the *Sermo*:

> Indeed, it must of necessity become very evil in the world because of the people's sins, for now is the time that Paul the apostle foretold long ago. He said once to bishop Timothy that in the last days of this world it would be a dangerous time because of people's sins, and people would then love, he said, the deceitful world all too much and be overly greedy for worldly treasures, and too many would become too proud and entirely too arrogant and too boastful, and some would blaspheme horribly against God's divinity and despise the teachings of scripture and love injustice and some would become deceitful and very fickle and treacherous, guilty in their sins. And let him know it who can, now is the time that this world is involved with manifold crimes and with many evils, just as the gospel says: 'Because iniquity abounds, the love of many grows cold.' That is in English, because evil grows entirely too widespread, true love cools. No one loves God as a person should. No one remains faithful to anything, but injustice

---

[102] *Ibid.*, no. 13, p. 231 (lines 92–6).
[103] Hollis, 'Thematic Structure', p. 188. For a discussion of parallels to the *Sermo* list, see *Sermo Lupi*, ed. Whitelock, pp. 63–4, note to lines 166–73.

rules far and wide, and loyalty among people is uncertain, and that is seen in many ways, let him know it who can … Now it must of necessity become very evil because [Antichrist's] time is coming quickly … And thus it is in the world always the longer the weaker.[104]

The catalogue of sinners in Wulfstan's paraphrase lists the greedy, the proud and arrogant, blasphemers, lovers of injustice, the deceitful and the fickle and treacherous, and he glosses this by denouncing the infidelity, injustice and disloyalty of his own day. These three vices are the dominant notes of his denunciation of the sins of the English in the *Sermo*. Wulfstan's *Sermo Lupi* looks like an extended meditation on this theme of the New Testament discourses about the intensification of evil at the end of the world.

The *Sermo* is a long and discursive text, not exactly rambling but fluid in its movement. It is underpinned by Wulfstan's strong belief that Christian conduct and the godly state of the kingdom are held in place by the rule of law.[105] The long version of Wulfstan's sermon alternates between castigations of English depravity and the sections foregrounding the inevitable divine punishment that this brings. So the first part describes Anglo-Saxon lawlessness – the withholding of church dues and the abuse of vulnerable groups such as widows and orphans who should have been afforded the protection of the law. These passages are then followed by the account of disasters quoted earlier.

Wulfstan then returns to the sins of the English, whom he excoriates for their disloyalty. English wickedness is characterized by deceit, treachery and infidelity, highlighted by his well-known citations of the murder of Edward the Martyr and the expulsion of Æthelred. His description of the social and sexual humiliation of the Anglo-Saxons by the vikings illustrates the consequence of such failures. These misfortunes are the result of the sins of the English:

[104] 'La, nyde hit sceal eac on worulde for folces synnan yfelian swyðe, forþam nu is se tima þe Paulus se apostol gefyrn foresæde. He sæde hwilum þam biscope Tymothee þæt on ðam endenyhstan dagum þissere worulde beoð frecenlice tida for manna synnum, 7 men þonne lufiað, he cwæð, ealles to swyðe þas swicolan woruld 7 beoð ofergrædige woruldgestreona, 7 to manege weorðaþ to wlance 7 ealles to rance 7 to gylpgeorne, 7 sume weorþað egeslic godcundnessa hyrwende 7 boclare leande 7 unriht lufiende 7 sume weorðað swicole 7 swæslice ficole 7 butan getrywðum forscyldgode on synnan. And gecnawe se ðe cunne, nu is se tima þæt ðeos woruld is gemæncged mid mænigfealdan mane 7 mid felafealdan facne, 7 ðæs hit is þe wyrse wide on worulde, ealswa þæt godspel cwæð: *Quoniam abundabit iniquitas refrigescet caritas multorum.* Ðæt is on Englisc, forðam þe unriht weaxeð ealles to wide, soð lufu colað. Ne man God ne lufað swa swa man scolde, ne manna getrywða to ahte ne standað, ac unriht ricsað wide 7 side, 7 tealte getrywða syndon mid mannum 7 þæt is gesyne on mænigfealde wisan, gecnawe se ðe cunne.… Nu sceal hit nyde yfelian swyðe, forðam þe hit nealæcð georne his timan.…7 hit is on worulde a swa leng a swa wacre.' *Homilies*, ed. Bethurum, no. 5, pp. 134–5 (lines 14–32).

[105] Wormald, 'Holiness of Society'; and on the importance of law in the *Sermo*, see Hollis, 'Thematic Structure', p. 181.

It is no wonder that things go wrong for us, for we know full well that now for many years men have too often not cared what they did by word or deed; but this people ... have become very corrupt through manifold sins and many misdeeds: through murders and crimes, through avarice and through greed, through theft and robbery, through selling of men and through heathen vices.[106]

His rehearsal of the depravity into which the English have fallen during the viking incursions and of their betrayal of each other and their sexual excesses graphically demonstrates the terrifying increase in England's wickedness and its degeneration.

These are not the only apocalyptic echoes in the *Sermo*. His bitter accusation that 'Now too often a kinsman does not protect a kinsman any more than a stranger, neither a father his son, nor sometimes a son his own father, nor one brother another' recalls the Gospel prophecies of the end in the Gospels of Mark and Luke: 'Now the brother shall betray the brother to death and the father the son; and children shall rise up against their parents.'[107] Wulfstan's tirade against men who club together to purchase a woman for sexual abuse may also contain an apocalyptic allusion, since this depravity also features in the description of the last days in Pseudo-Methodius.[108] Wulfstan also makes the telling observation that

[a]nd also there are here in the country degenerate apostates and fierce persecutors of the Church and cruel tyrants all too many, and widespread scorners of divine laws and Christian virtues ...[109]

---

[106] *EHD*, ed. Whitelock, p. 932. *Homilies*, ed. Bethurum, no. 20, pp. 266–75, at p. 272 (lines 129–35): 'Nis eac nan wundor þeah us mislimpe, forþam we witan ful georne þæt nu fela geara men na ne rohtan foroft hwæt hy worhtan wordes oððe dæde, ac wearð þes þeodscipe ... swyþe forsyngod þurh mænigfealde synna 7 þurh fela misdæda: þurh morþdæda 7 þurh mandæda, þurh gitsunga 7 þurh gifernessa, þurh stala 7 þurh strudunga, þurh mannsylena 7 þurh hæþene unsida.'

[107] 'Ne bearh nu foroft gesib gesibban þe ma ðe fremdan, ne fæder his bearne, ne hwilum bearn his agenum fæder, ne broðor oðrum.' *Homilies*, ed. Bethurum, no. 20, p. 263 (lines 69–71); translation from *EHD*, ed. Whitelock, p. 931. Mark 13: 12 and Luke 21: 16. For a different interpretation, see Godden, 'The Millennium', pp. 174–5. *Sermo Lupi*, ed. Whitelock, p. 36, says that these remarks are drawn from Antichrist, Bethurum 1b. This Gospel reference is also found in *Homilies*, ed. Bethurum, no. 3, *Secundum Lucam*, p. 125.

[108] Pseudo-Methodius, *Apocalypse*, chap 11, in *Apocalypse, Pseudo-Methodius An Alexandrian World Chronicle*, ed. and trans. B. Garstad, Dumbarton Oaks Medieval Library (Cambridge, MA, 2012), pp. 112–13. It is unclear if Pseudo-Methodius was known in England before the Conquest; the earliest surviving manuscripts date from the late eleventh century. See the important discussion by S. Pelle, 'The *Revelationes* of Pseudo-Methodius and "Concerning the Coming of Antichrist" in British Library Ms Cotton Vespasian D XIV', *N&Q* 53(3) (2009), 324–30.

[109] 'And eac her syn on earde apostatan abroðene 7 cyrichatan hetole 7 leodhatan grimme ealles to manege 7 oferhogan wide godcundra rihtlaga 7 cristenra þeawa.' *Homilies*, ed. Bethurum, no. 20, p. 272 (lines 141–2); translation from *EHD*, ed. Whitelock, pp. 932–3.

Here Wulfstan's denunciation resembles descriptions of the reign of Antichrist, which will result in apostasy and persecution of the Church. Moreover, the phrase 'degenerate apostates' is linked to or replaced in some manuscripts with the phrase 'God's adversaries' (*Godes wiðersacan*), one of the main designations of Antichrist in *Antichrist* (Bethurum sermon 1b).[110]

Wulfstan's *Sermo Lupi* is framed by warnings of the end – it opens with an un-ambivalent warning of the imminence of the coming of Antichrist signalled by the escalation of evil amongst the English. Its description of Anglo-Saxon depravity is an illustration of the intensification of evil in the end-time. The identification of Wulfstan's time with that of the time of tribulation conditions his understanding not only of his own time but also of political action too.

Homiletic Exhortation and Legislation

The *Sermo Lupi* displays numerous thematic parallels with Æthelred's great law code issued at Enham in 1008 (V Æthelred). The Enham council was convened on the feast of Pentecost, when the Church celebrates the Holy Spirit, who gives wisdom and purges away sin.[111] This is the first code known to have been composed by Wulfstan and initiates his great series of programmatic legislation designed to secure the Christian and moral reform of his nation.[112] It is a lengthy and comprehensive piece of law, with another thirty clauses covering a huge range of topics from personal belief and individual Christian conduct, to protection of the Church and its ministers, to provisions of ships for military defence. Its aim was to establish the correct conduct for every order of society. There is an essential complementarity between the code and Wulfstan's teaching in the sermon, since the exhortations of the latter are predicated upon the need, as we have seen, to return to obedience to God's law if the kingdom is to be saved from divine ire. The opening of the code itself underlines the importance of law: the assembly pledged itself to 'hold one Christian faith under the rule of one king' and further declared that 'just practices be established and all

---

[110] 'And eac her synd on earde Godes wiðersacan 7 cirichatan hetole.' *Homilies*, ed. Bethurum, no. 20, p. 259 (lines 98–9), from CCCC 419, and Bodley 343 (both the short version) and no. 20, p. 265 (lines 139–41): 'And eac her synd on earde a Godes wiðersacan apostatan abroðene 7 cirichatan hetole.' from CCCC 201 (the medium version). Hollis, 'Thematic Structure', p. 192, notes this and argues that here *Godes wiðersacan* may represent the original text. And see *Homilies*, ed. Bethurum, p. 363 (note to line 142). See also *Sermo Lupi*, ed. Whitelock, p. 62, note to line 147.

[111] On the close overlap between Wulfstan's sermons and his law codes, see Lawson, 'Archbishop Wulfstan', pp. 565–86.

[112] Wormald, *The Making*, pp. 330–45.

illegal practices abolished, and that every man is to be permitted the benefit of law'.[113] The second great theme of the *Sermo*, the pressing necessity for repentance, atonement and penance for the endemic sins of the English also finds a counterpart in the code in the rulings that require individual Christians to regularly make confession to a priest.[114] The closing clauses of the code neatly parallel the agenda of the *Sermo Lupi*:

> For [only] as a result of suppressing wrong and loving righteousness shall there be improvement at all in the country in religious and secular concerns.[115]

These rather generalized correspondences between the *Sermo Lupi* and the code can be matched by more specific links. Perhaps the most striking of the precise parallels are those concerning the sale of Christian slaves to foreigners, a practice denounced in the sermon and prohibited in the code.[116] Similarly, the sermon's outrage at the ill treatment and forced marriage of widows and the cruelty of the law in severely punishing children for minor offences is matched by rulings concerning these abuses at Enham.[117] Its opening clause, which guarantees that every man should be allowed the benefit of the law, may address Wulfstan's perception expressed in the sermon that the rights of freemen and slaves had been violated.[118] Many more parallels can be cited: Enham's requirement that both laity and the religious live according to their order:

> And it is the decree of our lord and his councillors that men of every order are each to submit willingly to that duty which befits them both in religious and secular concerns.[119]

---

[113] Text and translations from *Councils and Synods with Other Documents Relating to the English Church*, ed. D. Whitelock, M. Brett and C. N. L. Brooke, 2 vols. (Oxford, 1981), vol. I, pp. 338–73, at 344–5: (1) '[U]nder anum cynedome ænne Cristendom healdan willað' and (1.1) 'þæt man rihte laga up arære 7 ælce unlaga georne afylle, 7 þæt man læte beon æghwylcne man rihtes wyrþe'. The text is transmitted in a number of different versions; for discussion, see *Councils*, ed. Whitelock et al., vol. I, pp. 338–43; and Wormald, *The Making*, pp. 330–5.

[114] V Æthelred, chap. 22, in *Councils*, ed. Whitelock et al., vol. I, p. 355.

[115] 'Forþam þurh þæt hit sceal on earde godian to ahte, þe man unriht alecge 7 rihtwisnesse lufie for Gode 7 for worulde.' V Æthelred, chap. 33.1, in *ibid.*, vol. I, p. 361.

[116] *Homilies*, ed. Bethurum, no. 20, p. 256 (lines 40–1); V Æthelred, chap. 2, in *Councils*, ed. Whitelock et al., vol. I, p. 348, with a possible verbal reminiscence noted by Whitelock in her edition, *Sermo Lupi*, pp. 51–2, n. 44.

[117] *Homilies*, ed. Bethurum, no. 20, p. 256 (lines 37, 42–3, 46); and V Æthelred, chaps. 3.1, 21 and 21.1, in *Councils*, ed. Whitelock et al., vol. I, pp. 346, 355.

[118] V Æthelred, chap. 1.1, in *Councils*, ed. Whitelock et al., vol. I, p. 345; and *Homilies*, ed. Bethurum, p. 256 (lines 43–4).

[119] '7 ures hlafordes gerædnes 7 his witena is, þæt ælces hades menn georne gebugan for Gode 7 for worulde, ælc to þam rihte þe him to gebyrige.' V Æthelred, chap. 4, in *Councils*, ed. Whitelock et al., vol. I, p. 347.

This seems to answer the homiletic complaint that 'nor has any one of us ordered his life as he should, neither ecclesiastics according to rule nor laymen according to law. But we have made desire a law unto us all too often, and have kept neither the precepts nor laws of God or man as we should'.[120] Other Enham clauses prohibit unlawful sexual practices, perjury and the breaking of oaths, sins condemned in more colourful detail in the sermon. The complaints of the sermon that the sanctity of the Church and its personnel has not been respected and Church dues have been withheld find their counterpart in clauses protecting the peace of the Church and its members and in detailed listing of the dues to be paid. Breakers of Church fasts and feasts are enumerated in one of Wulfstan's catalogues of sinners – their activities are declared unlawful in the more detailed prescriptions of the Enham code.

These specific and thematic correspondences between the two texts are rendered all the more striking when the *Sermo Lupi* is compared to Æthelred's eighth code, promulgated in 1014 when the King returned from Normandy.[121] It is very likely that what survives is the ecclesiastical half of the original code transmitted by Wulfstan, which probably addressed the grievances of the English arising out of the king's earlier rule.[122] The comparison with 1008 Enham is therefore only partial because we lack the secular counterpart. Nevertheless, the absence of the dominant themes of the *Sermo* is significant. Some issues, for instance, Wulfstan's regular preoccupations with Church dues and Church feasts and fasts, are certainly found in both codes, but other important matters, such as the concern with penance and confession or with correct Christian conduct, for example, are notably absent. The 1014 code reflects the very special circumstances of its production and seems designed to impose upon the king his duty as upholder of Christian faith rather than providing a programme for the renewal of society.[123]

The *Sermo Lupi* and Enham laws of 1008 share therefore a moral agenda and emerged from the same set of spiritual and religious concerns.[124]

---

[120] 'Ne ure ænig his lif ne fadode swa swa he sceolde, ne gehadode regollice, ne læwede lahlice; ne ænig wið oðerne getreowlice ne þohte swa rihte swa he sceolde.' *Homilies*, ed. Bethurum, p. 257 (lines 59–60); translation from *EHD*, ed. Whitelock, p. 931.

[121] *Councils*, ed. Whitelock et al., vol. I, pp. 386–402.

[122] *Ibid.*, pp. 386–7; and Wormald, *The Making*, p. 336. And see Wormald, 'Æthelred the Lawmaker', in *Ethelred the Unready, Papers from the Millenary Conference*, ed. D. Hill, BAR British Series 59 (Oxford, 1978), pp. 59–60.

[123] *Councils*, ed. Whitelock et al., vol. I, opening clause. And see the remarks of Wormald, *The Making*, pp. 335 and 341–2, on the differences between the two codes.

[124] It is possible, as Whitelock in *Sermo*, pp. 36–7 and n. 6 considered, that Æthelred's fifth code may have been a source for the *Sermo*, but the verbal parallels she cites are not convincing. Rather, as befits two texts with the same author, their correspondences seem to be the result of Wulfstan's moral agenda and his perception of contemporary wrongs and woes.

Patrick Wormald described the Enham code as throbbing with millennial fever, and its kinship with the *Sermo Lupi* underlines the truth of this observation.[125] Wulfstan's sermon and his 1008 code address the degenerate state of his kingdom as he perceived it, where sin was rampant and penitence absent. His homiletic exhortations were designed to make his audience understand the terrible situation of their country, plunged into the extremities of sin and disastrously unprepared for the coming of Antichrist, and to spur them to contrition and repentance. Æthelred's law-code laid out unambiguously the principles of what a Christian society needed to do to regain God's favour. The two texts emerged from the same religio-political environment. Whitelock considered it possible that the *Sermo* used material from the Enham code, but in fact, the textual evidence is slight. One might rather hypothesize that the *Sermo* aimed to reinforce the programme laid out in 1008. If an earlier version of the sermon was composed as early as 1009, it might even have been part of the call to penitence laid down by Æthelred's 1009 edict: the three texts might then possibly form a sequence. In 1008, king and archbishop laid out the conditions for moral reform in an attempt to win divine favour. The arrival of Thorkel's army in 1009 proved incontrovertibly that the kingdom had failed. The enforced penance was the follow-up to the failure to put into action the programme mapped out in 1008; the *Sermo Lupi* underlined the extent of the failure of the English to follow God's law as laid down in previous year and acted as an exhortation to penance.[126]

The iconography of the Agnus Dei coinage, almost certainly issued in the autumn of 1009, brings together the themes of apocalypse, repentance and divine mercy.[127] The coins feature a depiction of the Agnus Dei on the obverse and of the Holy Spirit on their reverse. The lamb is shown with its front feet on or close to a tablet, which on some coins bears the inscription alpha and omega. Close study of the surviving specimens suggests that this was the inscription on the original model.[128] The descending dove on the

[125] P. Wormald, 'Archbishop Wulfstan and the Holiness of Society', in his *Legal Culture in the Early Medieval West* (London, 1999), pp. 225–51, at 244.
[126] A. Cowen, '*Byrstas* and *Bysmeras*: The Wounds of Sin in the *Sermo Lupi ad Anglos*', in *Wulfstan*, ed. Townend, pp. 397–411.
[127] M. Dolley, 'The Nummular Brooch from Sulgrave', in *England before the Conquest*, ed. P. Clemoes and K. Hughes (Cambridge, 1971), pp. 333–49; Keynes, 'An Abbot', pp. 190–201, 215–20, 195 for dating; and S. Keynes and R. Naismith, 'The Agnus Dei Pennies of King Æthelred the Unready', *ASE* 40 (2011), 175–223, at 179–80, 187–8 for the dating.
[128] Keynes and Naismith, 'Agnus Dei Pennies', p. 145. For an alternative but unpersuasive interpretation of the bird as an eagle, see D. Woods, 'The Agnus Dei Penny of King Æthelred II: A Call to Hope in the Lord (Isaiah XL)', *ASE* 42 (2013), 299–309.

reverse represents the events of Pentecost and may have been a reminder of the legislation of Whitsunday 1008. The Agnus Dei represents Christ both as the paschal lamb whose sacrifice wipes away human sin, whose mercy is petitioned in the liturgical invocation, and as the triumphant lamb of the Apocalypse. The depiction of the tablet or book with its alpha and omega inscription confirms the lamb's apocalyptic meaning, alluding to passages in Revelations.[129] Leslie Webster has argued cogently on the basis of other contemporary English depictions of the Agnus Dei that the image here has strong apocalyptic resonances.[130]

The coinage is extraordinary. The lamb on the obverse, for example, takes the place of the usual representation of the king. While it may have been intended as a standard issue, it survives in a tiny quantity compared to other issues, and its function is unclear.[131] Moreover, a high proportion of the surviving coins have been pierced for suspension, suggesting that it was used for devotional purposes.[132] The coinage represents a material embodiment of the English political ideology and belief in 1008–9, an invocation for divine mercy grounded in a sense of sin and penitence and framed by an eschatological understanding of the national predicament. The Agnus Dei coinage, like perhaps the *Sermo Lupi*, represents a bridge between the Pentecost code of 1008 and the penitential regulations of 1009.[133]

The principles established at Enham informed the legislation drafted at the Council of Oxford in 1018 when Cnut was accepted as ruler. As Wormald comments, '[T]he 1018 code represents a provisional statement of the aspects of the previous regime which the archbishop considered fundamental.'[134] Shared items include the protection of the Church; the observance of their order by monks, clergy and other religious; prohibition of the sale of English as slaves abroad and of the death penalty for trivial offence, plus other regulars such as the enforcement of Church dues, feasts and fasts.[135] But the strictures of the *Sermo Lupi* harking back to past evil

---

[129] Revelations 5–6, 12: 11, 13, 8: 1, 13: 8–9, 14: 1–5, 10–11, 15: 3, 21: 9, 14, 24, 22: 4, 6. For the alpha and omega, see Revelations 21: 6, 22: 13.

[130] L. Webster, 'Apocalypse Then: Anglo-Saxon Ivory Carving in the Tenth and Eleventh Centuries', in *Aedificia Nova Studies in Honor of Rosemary Cramp*, ed. C. E. Karkov and H. Damico (Kalamazoo, 2008), pp. 226–53, at 240–53; and Lawson, 'Archbishop Wulfstan', p. 153, suggested that the coinage was issued in association with the 1008 council, but the numismatic dating points to 1009 (but see n. 122 above).

[131] Keynes and Naismith, 'Agnus Dei Pennies', pp. 196–200.

[132] Keynes, 'An Abbot', pp. 200–1; and Dolley, 'The Nummular Brooch'.

[133] Webster, 'Apocalypse Then', p. 253, also makes the connection between the coinage and the *Sermo Lupi*, anticipating in some ways Keynes's arguments for a 1009 dating.

[134] Wormald, *The Making*, p. 346; A. G. Kennedy, 'Cnut's Law Code of 1018', *ASE* 11 (1983), 57–81.

[135] Kennedy, 'Cnut's Law Code', chaps. 13, 13.1–13.7, 14, 14.1–14.7, pp. 76–7.

were less appropriate for this forward-looking piece of legislation, and Wulfstan seems to have composed a new sermon, 'On Justice, Virtue and the Law' (Napier L).[136]

The correspondences between this sermon and the 1018 code were noted by Kennedy and Wormald.[137] The text itself contains statements indicative of its composition at a time of regime change, which thus suggests of this date.[138] It is a composite sermon composed by the archbishop out of texts such as the *Institutes of Polity* and draws upon not only the *Sermo Lupi* but also his apocalyptic sermons.[139] But where the *Sermo Lupi* looks back at English behaviour to castigate their sins, 'On Justice, Virtue and the Law' seeks to provide – like the law codes – a blueprint for righteous Christian conduct for each order of society, dealing with the king, the Church and the lay elite in turn. It is less a call to repentance than a statement of how to go forward, but it frames its exhortations with a reminder of the coming end and imminence of Antichrist:

> Furthermore, let us recall that it is near this world's end, believe it who will, and the time of the devil Antichrist; however, the devil deceives men's thoughts so that they remember it too rarely. And believe it who will, we truly know that it inexorably approaches, for this world is full of sorrow and from day to day it grows ever worse.[140]

Conclusion

Wulfstan's apocalypticism was not a passing phase but a way of viewing the world that influenced his whole career. In *De antichristo* and 'Antichrist', he urged churchmen to prepare the faithful with correct doctrine to withstand the deceit of Antichrist but also exploits the powerful sense of evil invoked by Antichrist to admonish his fellows for their sinful behaviour by identifying them as his forerunners. He returned to this idea in a later sermon, *De septiformi spiritu*, where his denunciation of contemporary

---

[136] *Wulfstan Sammlung*, ed. Napier, no. L, pp. 266–74; trans. in *The Political Writings of Archbishop Wulfstan*, ed. and trans. Rabin, pp. 143–53.
[137] Kennedy, 'Cnut's Law Code', pp. 57–81; and Wormald, *The Making*, p. 335.
[138] Lionarons, *Homiletic Writings*, pp. 174–5.
[139] See Rabin, *The Political Writings of Archbishop Wulfstan*, pp. 143–53, which highlights particularly the relation to Bethurum sermons 4 and 1b.
[140] 'And utan geþencean, þæt hit is nyr þisse worulde ende, þonne hwa gelyfan wylle, and þæs deofles timan Antecristes. Ac deofol dwelað manna geþohtas, þæt hig to lyt þærymbe þenceað. And, gelyfe se, þe wylle, we witan to soðe, þæt hit þærto georne genealæcð, forþam þeos woruld is sorhful and from dæge to dæge a swa leng, swa wyrse.' *Wulfstan, Sammlung*, ed. Napier, no. L, pp. 272–3; trans. in *The Political Writings of Archbishop Wulfstan*, ed. and trans. Rabin, p. 152.

antichrists is embittered and urgent: those who dissemble and deceive are antichrists who prepare the way for him.[141] The disasters and defeats of the early eleventh century had intensified Wulfstan's sense of the dangers of his own time: the increase in evil required immediate remedy lest the faithful perish either through the deceits of Antichrist and his disciples or through lack of repentance at Judgement Day. His reading of his own times as a moment of the greatest evil shaped his agenda for Christian renewal in his law codes, which were framed to recall the English to Christian obedience. The coming Judgement could not be held off, but the English could through obedience to God and his laws mitigate the divine anger and prepare for the Judgement to come.[142]

---

[141] *Homilies*, ed. Bethurum, no. 9, pp. 185–91; and see Lionarons, *Homiletic Writings*, pp. 130–1.

[142] I am very grateful to the editors for their careful help, as well as to Andy Orchard, Andrew Rabin, Chris Wickham, Mark Whittow and other members of the Medieval History Seminar at All Souls, Oxford, for their comments on earlier versions of this chapter.

A Tale of Two Charters:
Diploma Production and Political Performance in Æthelredian England

Levi Roach

King Æthelred II of England (978–1016) – better known to posterity as 'the Unready' – has, it would be fair to say, received something of a bad press.[1] As Simon Keynes has shown, the only contemporaneous narrative of his reign, provided by the C, D and E versions of the *Anglo-Saxon Chronicle*, was composed after the king's death, probably in or around London. Its perspective is teleological and its account tendentious: it seeks to present the Danish conquest of 1016 as the inevitable result of national incompetence.[2] As an historical account, it must therefore be handled with great care: although it includes much informative detail, it is an unreliable guide to the realities of Æthelredian politics. The only option available to the historian wishing to understand this period, as Keynes notes, is to prioritize the reports of strictly contemporary sources – to study the charters, royal decrees and coinage of these years. Keynes himself has undertaken this endeavour on a number of occasions, and the results are most instructive.[3]

---

[1] It is a privilege and an honour to be able to present this chapter to the scholar who has done more than any other to enrich our understanding of Æthelred's reign. I offer it in fond memory, in particular, of an electrifying undergraduate supervision offered in Lent Term 2005, in which he laid out the lineaments of his forthcoming work on Wulfstan and the *Sermo Lupi*; I have not looked back since, nor have I ceased to be inspired by his example. Provisional versions of the following were presented at the British Academy Anglo-Saxon Charters Symposium and the Manchester Centre for Anglo-Saxon Studies. I am grateful to both audiences (as well as to the editors of this volume) for comments, questions and occasional good-humoured disagreement.

[2] S. Keynes, 'The Declining Reputation of Æthelred the Unready', in *Ethelred the Unready: Papers from the Millenary Conference*, ed. D. H. Hill (London, 1978), pp. 227–53, revised and reprinted in *Anglo-Saxon History: Basic Readings*, ed. D. Pelteret (New York, 2000), pp. 157–90; and S. Keynes, 'A Tale of Two Kings: Alfred the Great and Æthelred the Unready', *TRHS*, 5th series, 36 (1986), 195–217, at 201–3. See also now C. Konshuh, '*Anraed* in Their *Unraed*: The Æthelredian Annals (983–1016) and Their Presentation of King and Advisors', *English Studies* 97 (2016), 140–62.

[3] S. Keynes, *The Diplomas of King Æthelred 'the Unready', 978–1016: A Study in Their Use as Historical Evidence* (Cambridge, 1980), pp. 154–231; S. Keynes, 'Æthelred II ("the Unready"), King of the English (c. 966×968–1016)', *ODNB*, vol. I, pp. 409–19; and S. Keynes, 'Re-Reading King Æthelred

This chapter is conceived of as a contribution to this ongoing project, discussing two of the longest and most important diplomas of Æthelred's reign.

The documents in question are S 876 (*Abing* 124), the Æthelred Orthodoxorum charter, and S 911 (KCD 714), the Eynsham foundation charter. These documents are well known, but their similarities have only been noted in passing, and much of what follows seeks to demonstrate that they must be understood as a pair.[4] Thus conceived, they reveal a great deal about the politics of Æthelred's reign.

The first of these documents, the Æthelred Orthodoxorum charter, has received a great deal of attention. Its context is provided by the king's early experiences of rule. Æthelred first acceded in 978 as a boy of somewhere between nine and twelve; and in his earliest years, a de facto regency, led by Æthelred's mother, Ælfthryth, Bishop Æthelwold of Winchester and Ealdorman Ælfhere of Mercia, seems to have run the affairs of the realm on his behalf. In 984, however, this came to an abrupt end. It was in this year that Æthelwold, one of the key figures in the regency and a close associate of Queen Ælfthryth, passed away, and his death precipitated a sudden change in political climate. Thereafter, Ælfthryth disappears from diploma witness-lists – whether she was banned from court or simply chose to keep her distance is unknown – and new figures rose to prominence.[5] In the following years, the king despoiled a number of religious houses, granting lands and rights belonging to them to his new favourites. Centres associated with Æthelwold suffered particularly heavily, including Abingdon (the prelate's first monastic foundation), the Old Minster in

the Unready', in *Writing Medieval Biography, 750–1250: Essays in Honour of Professor Frank Barlow*, ed. D. Bates, J. Crick and S. Hamilton (Woodbridge, 2006), pp. 77–97.

[4] On S 876 (*Abing* 124), see Keynes, *Diplomas*, pp. 98–101 and 176–8; Keynes, 'Re-Reading', pp. 91–3; P. Stafford 'Political Ideas in Late Tenth-Century England: Charters as Evidence', in *Law, Laity and Solidarities: Essays in Honour of Susan Reynolds*, ed. P. Stafford, J. L. Nelson and J. Martindale (Manchester, 2001), pp. 68–82, reprinted in and cited from her *Gender, Family and the Legitimation of Power: England from the Ninth to the Early Twelfth Century* (Aldershot, 2006), no. VII; C. Cubitt, 'The Politics of Remorse: Penance and Royal Piety in the Reign of Æthelred the Unready', *Historical Research* 85 (2012), 179–92; and L. Roach, 'Penitential Discourse in the Diplomas of King Æthelred "the Unready"', *JEH* 64 (2013), 258–76. On S 911 (KCD 714), see S. Keynes, 'An Abbot, an Archbishop, and the Viking Raids of 1006–7 and 1009–12', *ASE* 36 (2007), 151–220, at 160; S. Keynes, 'King Æthelred's Charter for Eynsham Abbey (1005)', in *Early Medieval Studies in Memory of Patrick Wormald*, ed. S. Baxter et al. (Farnham, 2009), pp. 451–73; and S. Wood, *The Proprietary Church in the Medieval West* (Oxford, 2006), pp. 408–12. The only of these to note the similarities between the two (in both cases in passing) are Keynes, 'Æthelred's Charter', pp. 459 and 469; and Roach, 'Penitential Discourse', p. 274.

[5] Keynes, *Diplomas*, pp. 163–86. For Ælfthryth's attestations, see S. Keynes, *An Atlas of Attestations in Anglo-Saxon Charters, c. 670–1066*, rev. edn (Cambridge, 2002), table LIX.

Winchester (his bishopric) and Glastonbury (where he had received his training in monastic life). However, these years also witnessed a number of calamities: in 986, England experienced a bout of murrain, and the later 980s witnessed the return of the vikings, culminating in the defeat of a major English force at Maldon in 991 and further reverses in the following years. This occasioned something of a crisis: no diplomas are known to have been issued for 991 or 992, and when the stream resumes, it is in striking fashion.

It is in this context, at Pentecost 993, that the king called together a council at Winchester at which he promised to amend his youthful wrong-doing, starting by restoring liberty to Abingdon. The charter recording this act is the diploma in question, issued some six weeks later at Gillingham (probably in Dorset).[6] It would seem that the grant itself was enacted at the first event, but for various reasons – not least the length of the resulting charter – it was deemed preferable to hold off the production of the written documentation for a later gathering.[7] In restoring Abingdon's liberty, Æthelred was taking the first steps towards turning his back on his so-called youthful indiscretions; he was re-embracing the legacy of Æthelwold and the monastic reform, and doing so in emphatic fashion. The charter's enactment was carefully choreographed to create maximum effect: the original council took place at Pentecost, one of the three great Church festivals; it was held at Winchester, Æthelwold's old see; and it witnessed the restitution of liberty to Abingdon, Æthelwold's most important foundation. This was clearly a programmatic act: it marks the return of Æthelwoldian circles to royal favour, and the resulting diploma is the first attested by Ælfthryth since the prelate's death. The charter's text is unusually long (it is the second longest authentic document in the king's name), including many revealing details. It opens with a lengthy proem meditating upon the Fall and Redemption of Man, particularly poignant themes in the light of Æthelred's recent actions. This is followed by a narrative section (or *narratio*) explaining how the king and his nation have suffered various afflictions (*angustiae*) ever since Æthelwold's death (i.e. the moment he first struck out on his own!). These, so the document continues, inspired Æthelred to reflect upon his actions, coming to the conclusion that these misfortunes (*infortunia*) had come to pass partly because

---

[6] S 876 (*Abing* 124). Gillingham in Kent is also a possibility, though less likely.

[7] The distinction here is between what diplomatists sometimes call *actum* and *data*: H. Bresslau, *Handbuch der Urkundenlehre für Deutschland und Italien*, 2 vols., 2nd edn (Berlin, 1912–31), vol. II, pp. 446–78.

of his youth and partly because of the detestable love of money (*philargiria*) of others, who ought to have advised him better. Here the king singles out Bishop Wulfgar of Ramsbury and Ealdorman Ælfric as those who had offered him money to infringe upon Abingdon's liberty, selling the post of abbot to Eadwine, the latter's brother. However, wishing now to be freed from the 'terrible anathema' (*exhorrendo anathemate*) he had thus incurred,[8] the king explains how he called together a council at Winchester, at which he admitted to wrongdoing, promising to reject the money he had previously received and to restore Abingdon's liberty in exchange for masses and psalms freely performed by the monks (and also in the hope of being able to enjoy his own share in eternal liberty). Finally, Æthelred praises the present abbot, Wulfgar, before detailing the history of the centre's liberty, stretching back to the time of the ninth-century Mercian ruler Coenwulf. The main text then comes to a close with a sanction threatening eternal damnation on anyone who, for love of money (*philargiria*), breaches its terms.

The tenor of this document suggests a heightened degree of royal interest: it speaks of the king's innermost thoughts and feelings and singles out individual magnates (including Ealdorman Ælfric, who was still alive and in office) for censure.[9] The manner in which these thoughts are expressed suggests that the king was motivated by church teachings about sin and repentance: he (or rather the draftsman, acting in his name) presents recent misfortunes as a consequence of youthful error, expressing the hope that by making amends he will be able to restore order to the realm. The language employed confirms the repentant nature of the act. The Fall of Man, with which the proem opens, is a penitential commonplace, frequently alluded to in continental rites for public penance (and mentioned in Wulfstan of York's Ash Wednesday and Maundy Thursday sermons).[10] This was also a favoured metaphor within the circles of reform, whose leaders framed their efforts as an attempt to restore England's monasteries to a pre-lapsarian

---

[8] On the importance of such maledictions, see C. Cubitt, 'Archbishop Dunstan: A Prophet in Politics', in *Myth, Rulership, Church and Charters: Essays in Honour of Nicholas Brooks*, ed. J. Barrow and A. Wareham (Aldershot, 2008), pp. 145–66, at 163–4.

[9] Since the diploma stipulates that the ealdorman 'is still alive' (*qui adhuc superest*), there can be little doubt that Ælfric of Hampshire and not Ælfric *Cild* is intended (the latter had been exiled in 985, after only two years in office): Keynes, *Diplomas*, p. 177, n. 91. Cf. *Charters of Abingdon Abbey*, ed. S. E. Kelly, 2 pts, AS Charters vii–viii (Oxford, 2000–1), pp. cxc–cxci.

[10] S. Hamilton, *The Practice of Penance, 900–1050* (Woodbridge, 2001), pp. 18, 34, 36 and 114; M. Mansfield, *The Humiliation of Sinners: Public Penance in Thirteenth-Century France* (Ithaca, NY, 1995), p. 173; and *The Homilies of Archbishop Wulfstan*, ed. D. Bethurum (Oxford, 1957), pp. 233–8.

state.[11] The manner in which the king's reflections are described is similarly suggestive: he is said to be 'pricked by conscience through the grace of the Lord' (*Domini conpuctus gratia*), *compunctio* being associated with penitential contrition in these years.[12] The issuing of this document was therefore a demonstrative act: it not only restored Abingdon's liberty, but also signalled the king's remorse, laying the foundations for his actions in future years, which saw a series of restitutions to houses that had suffered in the 980s. The core message is hard to miss: the depredations of previous years are over, as is the dominance of those who lay behind them. This charter provides a context for the otherwise enigmatic *Chronicle* report that 'in this year [i.e. 993] the king ordered Ælfgar, the son of Ealdorman Ælfric, to be blinded.'[13] As we have seen, Ælfric was one of those who had infringed upon Abingdon's liberty in 984, and his son had also been involved in usurping monastic lands in previous years; the latter's blinding is therefore symptomatic of the family's fall from grace.[14]

This message is reinforced by two sets of textual allusions to the *Regularis concordia* within the charter. The first is in the proem, which describes Æthelred's recollections in the following terms: 'I recalled to memory this misfortune, in part on account of the ignorance of my youth – which is accustomed to employ various pursuits (*diversis solet uti moribus*) – and in part, moreover, on account of the detestable love of money of certain others, who ought to have counselled for my benefit.' This is a clear calque on the preface to the *Concordia*, which describes Edgar's youth as follows: 'from the start of his boyhood, as is customary of that age (*uti ipsa solet aetas*), he engaged in various pursuits (*diversis uteretur moribus*), but was also touched by divine regard; diligently admonished and shown the royal way of orthodox faith by a certain abbot, he began to fear, love and venerate God greatly.'[15] This verbal link creates a subtle but unmistakable

---

[11] J. Barrow, 'The Ideology of the Tenth-Century English Benedictine "Reform"', in *Challenging the Boundaries of Medieval History: The Legacy of Timothy Reuter*, ed. P. Skinner (Turnhout, 2009), pp. 141–54.

[12] H. Foxhall Forbes, 'The Development of the Notions of Penance, Purgatory and the Afterlife in Anglo-Saxon England' (unpublished PhD dissertation, Cambridge University, 2008), pp. 193–7

[13] 'On þyssum geare het se cyning ablendan Ælfgar, Ælfrices sunu ealdormannes.' *ASC* MSS CDE, 993 in *The Anglo-Saxon Chronicle; MS C*, ed. K. O'Brien O'Keeffe, The Anglo-Saxon Chronicle: A Collaborative Edition 5 (Cambridge, 2001), pp. 86–7.

[14] See S 861 (KCD 655), S 891 (KCD 698), S 918 (*Abing* 135); with L. Roach, *Æthelred the Unready* (New Haven, CT, 2016), pp. 107–8, 140 and 146.

[15] S 876 (*Abing* 124): 'Ad memoriam reduxi. partim hec infortunia pro meae iuuentutis ignorantia **que diuersis solet uti moribus**. partim etiam pro quorundam illorum detestand[a] philargiria qui meae utilitati consulere debebant accid[isse].' *Regularis concordia*, chap.i, ed. T. Symons and S. Spath, Corpus Consuetudinum Monasticarum 7. iii (Siegburg, 1984), p. 69: '[A]b ineunte suae pueritiae aetate, **licet uti ipsa solet aetas diuersis utereetur moribus**, attamen respectu diuino attactus abate

contrast: whilst, despite the various distractions of youth, Edgar heeded the advice of 'a certain abbot' (almost certainly Æthelwold himself) and was filled with fear and love of God, Æthelred fell victim to these, indulging in various misdemeanours. In echoing this phrase, the drafts-man casts Æthelred's actions in the 980s in the worst possible light, but presents the restoration of Abingdon's liberty as a return to the pious ways of his forbears. The *Regularis concordia* itself had been drafted by Æthelwold, and the king's reconciliation with his erstwhile regents thus even takes on a textual guise; he expresses his renewed support for Æthelwoldian reform in the prelate's own words.[16] That this charter is indeed meant to represent a return to the politics of Edgar, Ælfthryth and Æthelwold is indicated by a second, lengthier set of borrowings from the *Concordia*: the entire first dating clause is modelled on that of this work, and the 'synodal council of Winchester' (*synodale concilium Wintoniae*) of 993 is thus presented as the direct equivalent to the original 'synodal council of Winchester' convoked at Edgar's request (indeed, one wonders if the draftsman chose to call the former event a 'synodal council' to underline this parallel).[17] Such allusions would not have fallen on deaf ears: the original Council of Winchester (*c.* 970) was still within living memory, and many of those present at Winchester and Gillingham must have known the *Concordia* well.[18]

This charter can thus be read as something of a political manifesto, a statement of the new direction of the 990s. Its physical appearance is commensurate with its political importance: it is one of the grandest Anglo-Saxon charters to survive in single-sheet format (see Figure 11.1). And even at a visual level it embraces the best traditions of Æthelwoldian reform: written throughout in a clear Anglo-Caroline hand – making it the first royal diploma to be entirely produced in a fully Caroline script – of what has been identified as Style I, it is in the very style of writing

---

quodam assiduo monente ac regiam catholicae fidei uiam demonstrante cepit magnopere deum timere, diligere ac uernarari' (emphasis added).

[16] On Æthelwold's draftsmanship of the *Concordia*, see M. Lapidge, 'Æthelwold as Scholar and Teacher', in *Bishop Æthelwold: His Career and Influence*, ed. B. Yorke (Woodbridge, 1988), pp. 89–117, reprinted in and cited from his *Anglo-Latin Literature 900–1066* (London, 1993), pp. 183–211, at 192–4.

[17] H. Vollrath, *Die Synoden Englands bis 1066* (Paderborn, 1986), pp. 309–10, esp. 309, n. 70.

[18] It has been suggested that the *Concordia* was issued in the mid-960s, but a later date still seems preferable. See J. Barrow, 'The Chronology of the Benedictine "Reform"', in *Edgar, King of the English, 959–975: New Interpretations*, ed. D. Scragg (Woodbridge, 2008), pp. 211–23; and D. Pratt, 'The Voice of the King in "King Edgar's Establishment of Monasteries"', *ASE* 41 (2013), 145–204, at 170–2.

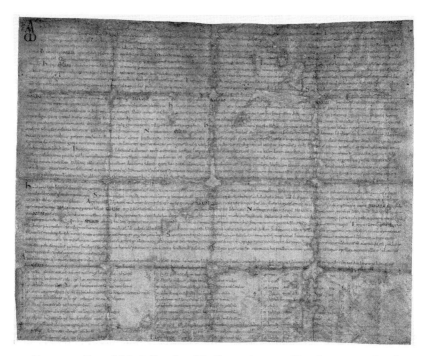

Figure 11.1 Face of S 876. (London, BL, Cotton Augustus II.38; Image reproduced with the kind permission of the British Library and the Anglo-Saxon Charters Project.)

Æthelwold and his students had promoted.[19] One further anomaly deserves comment: the witness-list. Most of the crosses next to the names of those attesting the charter are different in shape and aspect, making them the only securely identified autographs in a pre-Conquest diploma.[20] Close inspection reveals that at least two types of ink were used to produce these: the crosses of the first eight bishops are in a lighter ink similar to that of the main text (as is that of Ealdulf of Worcester, at the very end of the first column of attestations), whilst those of Bishops

[19] T. A. M. Bishop, *English Caroline Minuscule* (Oxford, 1971), pp. xxi–xxii and 13. Though doubts have been raised about this hand, which shows certain 'advanced symptoms', these are not sufficient to discard it as a later copy. Cf. D. N. Dumville, *English Caroline Script and Monastic History: Studies in Benedictinism, A.D. 950–1030* (Woodbridge, 1993), p. 135, n. 110.

[20] London, BL, Cotton Augustus ii. 38. A facsimile can be found in E. A. Bond et al. (eds.), *Facsimiles of Ancient Charters in the British Museum*, 4 vols. (London, 1873–8), vol. III, no. 36. What follows builds on the excellent analysis in S. Keynes, 'Church Councils, Royal Assemblies, and Anglo-Saxon Royal Diplomas', in *Kingship, Legislation and Power in Anglo-Saxon England*, ed. G. R. Owen-Crocker and B. W. Schneider (Woodbridge, 2013), pp. 17–182, at 112–16.

Figure 11.2 Detail of S 876. (Image reproduced with the kind permission of the British Library and the Anglo-Saxon Charters Project.)

Ordbriht of Selsey and Wulfsige of Sherborne, in ninth and tenth positions (immediately before Ealdulf), are darker (see Figure 11.2). This darker ink is also found at a few other places in the witness-list: in Wulfsige's name itself, which has been added into a blank space left for this purpose; in the autograph crosses next to the names of five of the abbots (Ælfsige of the New Minster, Lyfing of Chertsey, Ælfric of Malmesbury, Ælfhun of Milton and Ælfwine of Westminster); and in Ælfwine's own name, which, like Wulfsige's, is a later insertion (this time at the start of two blank columns on the far right of the charter, left to facilitate such additions). This darker ink also seems to have been used for the names of the main actors within the body of the charter, which were added after the rest of the text in rustic capitals (spaces had also been left for this purpose). It stands to reason that most, if not all, of these additions were made at the same time. That crosses are not found beside the names of all the witnesses strengthens the case for treating those present as bona fide autographs: evidently not all of those in attendance at the Winchester Council were present at Gillingham and in a position to sign it.

This diploma was clearly produced in two or three stages, and this rather complicated process of gestation explains the otherwise unusual presence of two dating clauses within it: the first, relating to the Council of Winchester, states that the act of restitution took place on this occasion; meanwhile, the second, relating to the Gillingham gathering, presents this event in terms of confirmation: it notes that the *auctoritas* of the diploma had then been granted and corroborated (*concessa et corroborata*) and that, following a mass in the oratory, the charter had been confirmed (*confirmata*) by those present. It is hard to know what exactly is meant here by 'granting and corroborating' and 'confirmation', but one possible scenario is that the charter was first presented to the recipients before the mass, some of whom signed it then (in lighter ink), then after the service those who had not already done so confirmed the document by appending their own crosses (in darker ink). It would presumably have been at this second stage that the names of those marked for distinguished treatment in the main text were added in majuscule. This final act was certainly anticipated, since the draftsman left spaces for this purpose. As we have seen, he also left space for additional names to be included at the end of the witness-list. As Simon Keynes notes, all indications are that he was working from a memorandum recording attendance of the original Winchester Council, but thought it prudent to allow space for figures not present there but now in attendance at Gillingham.[21] It is for this reason that Wulfsige appears both as abbot of Westminster (in lighter ink, without an autograph cross) and bishop of Sherborne (in darker ink, this time with a plausibly autograph cross): he seems to have been appointed bishop between the two gatherings (or perhaps at the start of the latter) and chose to sign in his new, more elevated post. The same is presumably true of Ælfwig, who replaced Wulfsige as abbot of Westminster and whose name is also added in darker ink. That both these figures are amongst those who signed the document reinforces the impression that the crosses in question stem from the Gillingham gathering, rather than being added in a series of later stages, as Susan Kelly proposes.[22] When the first round of episcopal attestations (in lighter ink) took place is hard to establish, but Ockham's razor suggests that this happened earlier on during the same event, perhaps soon after production of the original charter (whose main text is written in similar ink). It may be no more than a wishful thought, but one wonders whether these two rounds of subscriptions are not what the draftsman had in mind when he described the document undergoing two distinct stages of confirmation: a first before the mass (in lighter ink) and a second thereafter (in darker ink). If so, he must have written these words in anticipation of the latter act, but this is by no means inconceivable – as we have seen, he had already left spaces for this purpose. In any case, only the lighter crosses besides the names of Wulfric of St Augustine's and Byrhtnoth of Ely seem to stem from the main scribal hand, and here we are probably dealing with a slip (these names stand on their own in a space between the second and third columns of attestations, and the scribe may have absent-mindedly reverted to

---

[21] Keynes, 'Church Councils', pp. 112–13. [22] Kelly, *Charters of Abingdon*, pp. cxiii–cxiv.

his usual practice here).[23] Unfortunately, we cannot be certain whether the laymen in attendance signed the charter, since the relevant section of the parchment is heavily damaged. Space would have been tight, but there are traces of what may have been an autograph cross next to the name of Abbot Leofric of St Ablans at the start of this column, so the possibility cannot be entirely dismissed. Nevertheless, no such traces can be found next to the names of ealdormen Ælfric and Ælfhelm or the first two thegns who follow them, where the parchment is somewhat better preserved, which seems to militate against the proposition. Indeed, there is a surprisingly small number of lay witnesses. This might reflect the ecclesiastical nature of the gathering (the Winchester assembly is, after all, described as a Church council), but it is equally possible that the scribe of the original memorandum simply ran out of space – he had already included an unusually high number of ecclesiastical attestors, and the blank columns left on the far right of the final witness-list (where the thegns would normally attest) suggest that the inclusion of additional laymen was foreseen. In any case, the signing of this document must have been a demonstrative act, much like the signing and sealing of charters elsewhere in Europe: it publicly enacted the consent of the kingdom's leading churchmen to this most extraordinary of grants.[24]

This is not the place to go into the complex links between this document and the earlier Orthodoxorum charters in favour of Abingdon; suffice to say that while these other documents are unlikely to be authentic in the full sense of the term, this does not materially affect the arguments presented here: were the Æthelred Orthodoxorum charter to be modelled on genuine diplomas in the names of Eadwig and Edgar, this too would have suited the king's needs – like the reminiscences to the *Regularis concordia*, it would have aligned his actions with those of his father and the earlier reformers. Still if, as seems likely, this is indeed the only authentic charter of this type,[25] then it becomes all the more poignant a statement of the king's

---

[23] As Keynes, 'Church Councils', p. 114, suggests.

[24] See, for example, B. Bedos-Rezak, 'Ritual in the Royal Chancery: Text, Image and the Representation of Kingship in Medieval French Diplomas (700–1200)', in *European Monarchy: Its Evolution and Practice from Roman Antiquity to Modern Times*, ed. H. Duchhardt, R. Jackson and D. Sturdy (Stuttgart, 1992), pp. 27–40; B.-M. Tock, 'La mise en scène des actes en France au Haut Moyen Âge', *FS* 38 (2004), 287–96; and H. Keller and S. Ast, '*Ostensio cartae*. Italienische Gerichtsurkunden des 10. Jahrhunderts zwischen Schriftlichkeit und Performanz', *Archiv für Diplomatik* 53 (2007), 99–121, esp. 120.

[25] See L. Roach, 'The Privilege of Liberty in Later Anglo-Saxon England', in *Magna Carta: New Approaches*, ed. S. T. Ambler and N. C. Vincent (Woodbridge, forthcoming), arguing that the Orthodoxorum charters in favour of Abingdon and Pershore (and possibly also Romsey) are forgeries of the 990s.

regret at this point. Before leaving the document, however, it is worth emphasizing once more that it stands at the start of a series: it initiated a number of restitutions and pious donations in the 990s, all of which were intended to court divine favour and many of which were specifically designed to rehabilitate the legacy of Æthelwold and the reform.[26]

We must now turn to the second document, the Eynsham foundation charter (S 911). This was issued in 1005 at another key moment in Æthelred's reign. Although it only survives in later copies (most notably in the late-twelfth-century Eynsham Cartulary), there is no reason to doubt its authenticity: its formulation finds close parallels in authentic documents of the period, and its lengthy witness-list shows no signs of anachronism.[27] The background to the privilege is provided by the politics of the late 990s and early 1000s. As we have seen, the period from 993 on witnessed a concerted effort to propitiate God through pious acts. By the latter years of the decade, however, it must have become increasingly clear that these initial efforts had failed. There are signs of growing concern: the tone of the king's diplomas becomes darker, and it was in these years that Wulfstan of London (latterly of York) began to write sermons warning his listeners of the coming apocalypse. The clearest sign of tension is the Massacre of St Brice's Day (1002), which saw the king and his counsellors order the execution of 'all the Danish men' within his realm (apparently recent arrivals, above all mercenaries).[28] Thereafter, things went from bad to worse. In 1003–4, the Danish ruler, Swein Forkbeard, devastated much of the eastern coast of the kingdom, and though he departed in 1005, this brought little respite: the year saw severe famine throughout western Europe, including the British Isles (it was this which presumably occasioned the withdrawal of the Danish force).[29] It must have been painfully clear that a new direction was needed. Æthelred's response is telling: as he had twelve years earlier, he issued a diploma of unusual length and narrative detail – the Eynsham charter. This is a worthy successor to the Abingdon privilege of 993. Although the original does not survive, it must have been on a similar scale, if not larger: whereas S 876 boasts some 1,300

---

[26] Cubitt, 'Politics of Remorse'; L. Roach, 'Apocalypse and Atonement in Later Anglo-Saxon England', *English Studies* 95 (2014), 733–57, at 734–43.

[27] S 911 (KCD 714); with Keynes, 'Æthelred's Charter', esp. pp. 462–4.

[28] S. Keynes, 'The Massacre of St Brice's Day (13 November 1002)', in *Beretning fra seksogtyvende tværfaglige vikingesymposium*, ed. N. Lund (Aarhus, 2007), pp. 32–67.

[29] *ASC* MSS CDE, 1005 (ed. O'Brien O'Keeffe, p. 91). See F. Curschmann, *Hungersnöte im Mittelalter. Ein Beitrag zur deutschen Wirtschaftsgeschichte des 8. bis 13. Jahrhunderts* (Leipzig, 1900), pp. 108–10, assembling the continental evidence.

words of text followed by fifty attestations, the Eynsham charter runs to roughly 1,600 words with eighty-six names entered into the witness-list.[30]

What the size of this document already suggests is confirmed by its wording: like S 876, the text of S 911 is in a number of respects extraordinary, bearing witness to the charged atmosphere in which it was produced. It opens with a proem meditating on the ills that the English are enduring and the decisions taken by Æthelred and his counsellors to avert them. The king explains how he decreed that God's wrath, which has come upon the nation 'more than is usual' (*plus quam solito*), should now be assuaged 'by the continuous display of good works' (*continua bonorum operum exhibitione*). He notes specifically how 'since in our times we suffer the fires of wars and the pillaging of our wealth, and also from the cruellest plundering of the ravaging barbarian host, the manifold tribulation of pagan peoples, and of those reducing us almost to destruction, we discern that we are living in dangerous times'.[31] It is most unusual for diplomas to refer to contemporary events in this manner, and the Eynsham charter goes considerably further than the Abingdon privilege in this respect. While the latter refers vaguely to the *angustiae* and *infortunia* of the later 980s and early 990s, here the problems of the kingdom are spelled out: the ravages and plundering of the 'barbarian host'.[32] This section echoes the proem of the so-called First Decimation charters purportedly issued by King Æthelwulf in 844; however, as Keynes has shown, the latter documents were almost certainly modelled on the Eynsham privilege, which not only gives the more grammatically correct version of the relevant passage, but also was issued in a context in which such sentiments make good historical sense (the scattered Scandinavian raids of the 830s and early 840s could scarcely be said to have brought the English 'almost to destruction').[33]

The ideas expressed in this opening section chime well with other texts of Æthelred's reign. In particular, the last line of the quoted passage, explaining that recent attacks are signs that the English are living in 'dangerous times' (II Timothy III.1), finds close parallels in the letter sent to Bishop Wulfsige of Sherborne by an unnamed metropolitan (probably Ælfric of Canterbury (995–1005)), which employs the phrase to describe to

---

[30] Keynes, 'Æthelred's Charter', p. 459.
[31] 'Et quia in nostris temporibus bellorum incendia direptionesque opum nostrarum patimur, necnon ex uastantium crudelissima depraedatione hostium barbarorum, paganarumque gentium multiplici tribulatione, affligentiumque nos usque ad internecionem tempora cernimus incumbere periculosa'. S 911 (KCD 714).
[32] Cf. F. M. Stenton, *The Latin Charters of the Anglo-Saxon Period* (Oxford, 1955), pp. 27–8.
[33] Keynes, 'Æthelred's Charter', pp. 464–8. Cf. *Charters of Malmesbury Abbey*, ed. S. E. Kelly, AS Charters xi (Oxford, 2005), pp. 80–7.

the present state of affairs.[34] Ælfric of Eynsham also had recourse to this line in a piece about the duties of a preacher that he wrote as an addition to his First Series of Catholic Homilies (perhaps 1002×1006),[35] whilst Wulfstan quoted it in his sermon on Mark (1002×1008).[36] Any one or two of these instances might be deemed coincidence (this was a very popular biblical line); cumulatively, they suggest that it was something of a 'catch phrase' in these years. It may, moreover, be significant that this had been a favoured line of Alcuin of York, whose letters were the subject of intense scrutiny at this juncture: a number are excerpted in Wulfstanian manuscripts, and the letter to Wulfsige itself is largely lifted from one sent by Alcuin to Eanbald of York.[37] Of particular interest from our present standpoint is the fact that Ælfric employs the line in a passage that Robert Upchurch argues was intended as a critique of Æthelred and his closest advisors; since the homilist was to become abbot of the new foundation at Eynsham (indeed, he had probably already been appointed to this role), one wonders if there might not be a closer connection here.[38] Perhaps Ælfric influenced the draftsman's choice of words; alternatively (and perhaps more likely), the homilist himself may have been inspired by the charter's sentiments (which he also quotes elsewhere). In any case, there may be a deeper connection between II Timothy III, whence the phrase is drawn, and the context of the diploma's production: at this point the apostle speaks not only of the faithlessness that will precede the end of time, but also of how God saved him from persecution – the draftsman may well have wished the same for the English.

This eschatological tone is maintained as the proem continues. Æthelred goes on to state that it is most fitting that those 'on whom the ends of the ages are come' (*in quos fines saeculorum deuenerunt*) (I Cor. X.11) should

[34] *Councils and Synods with Other Documents Relating to the English Church*, I, *A.D. 871–1204*, ed. D. Whitelock, M. Brett and C. N. L. Brooke (Oxford, 1981), no. 41, pp. 227–9.

[35] *Ælfric's Catholic Homilies: The First Series Text*, ed. P. Clemoes, EETS s.s. 17 (Oxford, 1997), pp. 535–42, at 536. On the dating, see R. K. Upchurch, 'A Big Dog Barks: Ælfric of Eynsham's Indictment of the English Pastorate and *Witan*', *Speculum* 85 (2010), 505–33, at 506–8; and cf. *Councils*, ed. Whitelock et al., pp. 259–60, noting that Fehr's dating of Ælfric's homily on the Nativity of the Virgin (on which Upchurch indirectly relies) is not above question; a slightly later date is thus conceivable.

[36] *Homilies of Wulfstan*, ed. Bethurum, pp. 134–41, at 134–5. On the dating, see S. Pons-Sanz, *Norse-Derived Vocabulary in Late Old English Texts: Wulfstan's Works, a Case Study* (Odense, 2007), pp. 19–20 and 25.

[37] G. Mann, 'The Development of Wulfstan's Alcuin Manuscript', in *Wulfstan, Archbishop of York: The Proceedings of the Second Alcuin Conference*, ed. M. Townend (Turnhout, 2004), pp. 235–78, esp. 245–6; and *Councils*, ed. Whitelock, pp. 226–7. Cf. M. Garrison, 'The Bible and Alcuin's Interpretation of Current Events', *Peritia* 16 (2002), 68–84, on Alcuin's eschatology.

[38] Upchurch, 'A Big Dog Barks'.

examine themselves, thinking about how their souls are destined to live not only in this world but also the next. This line had been used earlier in a diploma issued upon the reform of Sherborne by Bishop Wulfsige (998); as with the phrase from II Timothy, it was very much 'in the air' in these years.[39] However, it is not just the proximity of the end that is emphasized here; the second half of the passage goes on to offer the English instruction in how they should respond to earthly transience: since they are come unto the ends of the ages, they must consider the fate of their immortal souls. The draftsman develops these thoughts further, citing the assertion in Hebrews XIII.14 that humans do not have a permanent abode in this world and so must look to the next. He then emphasizes the fleeting nature of earthly riches, before quoting Boethius' *Consolation of Philosophy* to the effect that all human action is dependent on two factors, the will and the power, in the absence of which it is impossible to perform any task.[40] The *Consolation* was a common source of solace in the Middle Ages, and the line in question had been cited in earlier royal diplomas. However, the borrowing here is longer than those previously witnessed, and it is tempting to suggest that Æthelred and his advisors had direct recourse to Boethius' wisdom at this point.[41] The proposition is not so outlandish as it may sound: the *Consolation* was extremely popular in later Anglo-Saxon England and, thanks to the 'Alfredian' translation, might even have been available in the vernacular.[42] In fact, Ealdorman Æthelweard, father of the man responsible for founding Eynsham at this point (Æthelmær), praises this work in his Latin *Chronicon*; it is, one imagines, exactly the sort of text on which he would have raised his son.[43] In any case, the proem comes to a close by emphasizing the importance of striving to do good so that despite worldly concerns (*temporalia . . . negotia*) one might secure eternal benefits.

Thereafter follows the dispositive section (or *dispositio*), covering the concrete details of the foundation. This maintains the Boethian theme, stating that since Æthelred has both the will and the power, he has seen fit

---

[39] S 895 (*Sherb* 11).

[40] Boethius, *Philosophiae consolatio* iv. 2. 5–7, ed. L. Bieler, CCSL 94 (Turnhout, 1957), p. 67.

[41] S 429 (*Shaft* 9), S 438 (BCS 714), S 470 (*WinchNM* 12); with Keynes, 'Æthelred's Diploma', p. 460.

[42] M. Lapidge, *The Anglo-Saxon Library* (Oxford, 2006), pp. 125, 127–8, 139–40, 173, 240, 243, 269 and 293; and *The Old English Boethius: An Edition of the Old English Versions of Boethius's De consolatione philosophiae*, ed. M. R. Godden and S. Irvine, 2 vols. (Oxford, 2009). More generally, see R. Love, 'Latin Commentaries on Boethius's *Consolation of Philosophy*', in *The Brill Companion to Alfred the Great*, ed. P. Szarmach and N. G. Discenza (Leiden, 2015), pp. 83–110, esp. 94–8 and 107–10.

[43] Æthelweard, *Chronicon* iv. 3, in *The Chronicle of Æthelweard*, ed. A. Campbell (London, 1962), p. 51. On Æthelweard, see most recently M. Gretsch, 'Historiography and Literary Patronage in Late Anglo-Saxon England: The Evidence of Æthelweard's *Chronicon*', *ASE* 41 (2012), 205–48; cf. M. R. Godden, 'Did King Alfred Write Anything?', *MÆ* 76 (2007), 1–23, at 5–6.

to have the transaction recorded for future generations. He explains how, at Æthelmær's request, he conceded the following privilege to Eynsham. The endowment is described as comprising thirty hides which the thegn had received from his son-in-law (*gener*) in exchange for lands elsewhere.[44] Stipulations are then set for the future of the foundation: the monks are to live in accordance with the Rule, whilst Æthelmær is to remain amongst them 'in the role of a father' (*patris uice*). Æthelred notes that the latter has appointed an abbot (apparently Ælfric, though he is not named) after whom successors are to be chosen by the monks by free election in consultation with the monarch. Finally, Æthelred charges himself with protecting the centre to the exclusion of (any other) secular authority. Such details are mostly what one might expect from the foundation charter of a reformed monastic house, and the lines in question echo the regulations of the Rule and the *Regularis concordia*. As we shall see, the final phrase about secular interference was also later quoted by Ælfric in his *Letter to the Monks at Eynsham*, further suggesting an association between the centre's future abbot and the privilege.[45] The rest of the dispositive section then gives a potted history of the abbey's estates, ending with a statement to the effect that Eynsham should remain free of all burdens save the three expected of all lands (bridgework, fortress work and military service). Finally, there comes a joint blessing/sanction, after which the bounds of the endowment are given.

It is here, immediately after the boundary clauses, that the most striking feature of the diploma is to be found: a first-person address in the vernacular by Æthelmær to Æthelred and his counsellors (*witon*). The thegn announces that he has given Eynsham to God and St Mary, and also to all of the saints and St Benedict, so that those who observe the Rule there can enjoy it for all time. He notes that he plans to remain leader (*ealdor*) of the community during his lifetime, but thereafter the monks are to choose a successor in accordance with the Rule. There follows a blessing on those who obey these stipulations and a curse on those who breach them, after which Æthelmær states his intention to live at the foundation for the rest of his days. Quite what we are to make of this is a good question. The West

---

[44] Wood, *Proprietary Church*, pp. 408–12; and B. Yorke, 'Aethelmaer: The Foundation of the Abbey at Cerne and the Politics of the Tenth Century', in *Cerne Abbey Millennium Lectures*, ed. K. Barker (Cerne Abbas, 1988), pp. 15–26, at 19–20.

[45] *Regula Benedicti*, chap. 64. 1–2, ed. J. Neufville, with notes and an introduction by A. de Vogüé, 2 pts, Sources Chrétiennes 181–2 (Paris, 1972), p. 648; *Regularis concordia*, chaps. 9–10 (ed. Symons and Spath, pp. 74–6); and *Ælfric's Letter to the Monks at Eynsham*, chap. 63, ed. C. A. Jones, CSASE (Cambridge, 1999), p. 140.

Country thegn is clearly trying to reserve a degree of control over his foundation, and this section adds further detail to the rather allusive earlier statement to the effect that he will oversee affairs there 'in the role of a father'.[46] Such a first-person address to the king and *witan* is unique within the corpus of Anglo-Saxon royal diplomas and finds its closest parallels in contemporary wills, which sometimes include statements to the effect that they are to be read before the king and his counsellors (generally in cases in which royal consent could not be obtained before the document had to be drawn up); it also echoes the language of vernacular letters and royal writs, which emerged out of a common epistolary tradition (in the latter case, perhaps in these years).[47] This section's wording suggests that it is a record of an oral declaration, presumably made by Æthelmær before the assembly that witnessed the abbey's foundation. Indeed, comparable texts, such as wills, writs and boundary clauses, were in the vernacular because they were meant to be read aloud, and the same is presumably true here.[48] There are also similarities with the oath sworn by the king at his consecration; it is unclear whether this was made in Latin or Old English (versions survive in both languages), but either way the text was apparently placed on the altar as a part of the proceedings. It would seem that such statements were written on schedules of parchment to facilitate public declamation, and this may provide the context for the integration of these details into the charter; presumably the draftsman had the text to hand and thought it worth including.[49] Whether Æthelmær did anything with this (hypothetical) schedule on the occasion of the foundation is, of course, impossible to say, but it is a pleasant thought that he might have placed it on an altar, Gospel book or even the provisional text of the diploma itself in order to solemnize the transaction.[50] In any case, there is every reason to believe that

[46] Wood, *Proprietary Church*, pp. 408–12 (cf. *ibid.*, pp. 312–412, for the bigger picture).

[47] L. Tollerton, *Wills and Will-Making in Anglo-Saxon England* (Woodbridge, 2011), pp. 67–70; *Anglo-Saxon Writs*, ed. F. E. Harmer (Manchester, 1952), pp. 1–38; and Keynes, *Diplomas*, pp. 140–5.

[48] P. J. Geary, 'Land, Language and Memory in Europe 700–1100', *TRHS*, 6th ser., 9 (1999), 169–84. Cf. B. Danet and B. Bogoch, '"Whoever Alters This, May God Turn His Face from Him on the Day of Judgement": Curses in Anglo-Saxon Legal Documents', *Journal of American Folklore* 105 (1992), 132–65.

[49] M. Clayton, 'The Old English *Promissio regis*', *ASE* 37 (2008), 90–150, at 107–8 and 112–13. See also P. J. Geary, 'Oathtaking and Conflict Management in the Ninth Century', in *Rechtsverständnis und Konfliktbewältigung. Gerichtliche und außergerichtliche Strategien im Mittelalter*, ed. S. Esders (Cologne, 2007), pp. 239–54, for continental comparanda.

[50] One thinks of the tradition of copying property transactions into Gospel books and other precious volumes (often of a liturgical nature): *Charters of Northern Houses*, ed. D. A. Woodman, AS Charters 16 (Oxford, 2012), pp. 316–23; and *Charters of Christ Church Canterbury*, ed. N. P. Brooks and S. E. Kelly, 2 pts., AS Charters 17–18 (Oxford, 2013), pp. 143–7. Cf. M. Rangow, 'Ritual before the Altar: Legal Satisfaction and Spiritual Reconciliation in Eleventh-Century Anjou', in *Medieval*

it, like the autograph crosses appended to the Abingdon privilege, takes us right into the ritualized world of the assembly. That this is the only declaration of this nature to survive may not be entirely coincidental; the charter in question was associated with important political developments, in which Æthelmær himself was deeply implicated.

To appreciate the significance of this document, we must return to its context. As noted earlier, it was issued at a moment of crisis: after years spent seeking a solution to the viking problem, in the early 1000s those in power seem to have started losing faith in previous policies. If the Massacre of St Brice's Day is a first sign of desperation, the 'Palace Revolution' of 1005–6, in which almost all of Æthelred's senior courtiers fell from grace, provides clearer evidence of this. Just as the Eynsham charter bears similarities to the Abingdon privilege of 993, so too this act, which shortly followed the issuing of the charter, bears comparison to the events of the early 990s: in 1005 as in 993, the king decided that a change of course was required, and this decision was announced by issuing an unusually impressive diploma; moreover, as at the Council of Winchester, this change went hand in hand with a change in court factions – one group fell from favour, and another rose to take its place.[51] However, there are important differences: whilst the years following 993 witnessed a gentle change of course (Ælfgar was blinded, but he was alone in this fate), the 'palace revolution' saw a spate of violent reprisals: Ealdorman Ælfhelm was slain, his sons Wulfheah and Ufegeat were blinded and Wulfgeat was deprived of his property. Only shortly before this, Ordulf and Æthelmær, the two most senior thegns at court, had left the scene: the former's attestations stop in 1005, and since he receives bequests in the will of Bishop Ælfwold of Crediton (1008×1012), it is presumed that he retired to his foundation at Tavistock; the latter, moreover, departed at the moment of Eynsham's foundation. The importance of the Eynsham diploma lies in the fact that it was an essential part of this process: it is the document that paved the way for Æthelmær's (and possibly also Ordulf's) retirement from political life, preparing the ground for the more dramatic events of the following year. Like the Abingdon privilege, it casts recent events as divine punishment, suggesting that the king and his

---

and Early Modern Ritual: Formalized Behavior in Europe, China and Japan, ed. J. Rollo-Koster (Leiden, 2002), pp. 57–79.

[51] The best account remains Keynes, *Diplomas*, pp. 209–14. See also Keynes, 'Tale of Two Kings', pp. 211–14; C. Insley, 'Politics, Conflict and Kinship in Early Eleventh-Century Mercia', *Midland History* 25 (2000), 28–43; A. Williams, *Æthelred: The Ill-Counselled King* (London, 2003), pp. 69–80; and E. Boyle, 'A Welsh Record of an Anglo-Saxon Political Mutilation', *ASE* 35 (2006), 245–9.

counsellors continued to see the Scandinavian threat primarily in moral terms. However, unlike the Abingdon diploma, it witnessed a move against many leading patrons of reform, including individuals who had risen to prominence since 993.

Given these similarities, we must ask why it is that Æthelred turned his back on so many erstwhile associates at this point. We can only speculate, but the answer would seem to lie in the very ideals of repentance and reform embraced since the 990s.[52] At the heart of these lay the belief that present ills were the wages of sin; only the eradication of this could lead to lasting peace. Initial efforts may have focused on the king and his 'bad' counsellors, but it would not be long before others were implicated: the aim was to cleanse society at large, and the language of purity and pollution abounds in the sources of these years. Even the Massacre of St Brice's Day seems to have been conceived of in such terms: the St Frideswide's charter of 1004, our earliest account of this event, presents the Danish settlers as polluting elements, as the cockle amongst the English wheat (cf. Matt. XIII: 24–30).[53] As the situation got progressively worse, Æthelred and his advisors seem to have scaled up this programme. The events of 1005–6 were thus in a sense a natural continuation of the politics of the 990s; it was the same policy writ large. This is not to say that the mercurial magnate Eadric Streona, who suddenly rose to prominence at this point, was not the architect behind this, as Simon Keynes has argued; it is merely to note that the rationale Eadric used to persuade the king is likely to have drawn on existing political discourse. That these events should indeed be understood in terms of moral purification is suggested by the actions of Ordulf and Æthelmær at this point: monastic retirement was a well-established practice elsewhere in Europe, where it frequently carried penitential undertones.[54] The punishment of blinding, meted out on Ælfhelm's sons, could also be understood in such terms: bodily mutilation was considered an act of kindness, since it allowed the criminal the opportunity to atone for his wrongdoing before death.[55] These thus represent further attempts to

---

[52] See Roach, *Æthelred*, pp. 200–16.

[53] S 909, in *The Cartulary of the Monastery of St Frideswide at Oxford*, vol. I, ed. S. R. Wigram (Oxford, 1895), pp. 2–7; with Keynes, 'Massacre', pp. 33–6; and J. Wilcox, 'The St. Brice's Day Massacre and Archbishop Wulfstan', in *Peace and Negotiation: Strategies for Co-Existence in the Middle Ages and the Renaissance*, ed. D. Wolfthal (Turnhout, 2000), pp. 79–91, at 84.

[54] M. de Jong, 'What Was Public about Public Penance? *Paenitentia publica* and Justice in the Carolingian World', *Settimane Spoleto* 44 (1997), 863–904, esp. 877–87.

[55] K. O'Brien O'Keeffe, 'Body and Law in Late Anglo-Saxon England', *ASE* 27 (1998), 209–32; and N. Marafioti, 'Punishing Bodies and Saving Souls: Capital and Corporal Punishment in Late Anglo-Saxon England', *HSJ* 20 (2008), 39–57.

cleanse society ('good works', in the language of the Eynsham charter); desperate times called for desperate measures, and Æthelred clearly felt that earlier undertakings had stopped too short. That such ideas about sin and society should now be used against those who had first promoted them in the 990s is ironic but by no means surprising. As Mayke de Jong and Courtney Booker have shown, penitential ideas were a double-edged sword in medieval politics; they might inspire reforming zeal when the going was good, but risked encouraging infighting and back-stabbing when things took a turn for the worse. The situation faced by Æthelred in his final decades is in certain respects comparable to that of Louis the Pious in the later 820s and early 830s, as described by de Jong and Booker: having bought into a penitential understanding of contemporary events, the only option available to him when the situation failed to improve was to up the ante, leading to ever more drastic culls of his leading magnates.[56] The punishments of 1006 are signs that Æthelred's regime had reached this critical tipping point: what had once been productive efforts to improve society through repentance, reform and moral purification were spiralling out into a cycle of mutual recrimination. That such sinister undertones lurk behind the Eynsham charter, which on the surface is a ringing endorsement of Æthelmær's reforming efforts, is suggested by a distinctive clause regarding secular interference. This reserves the king's right to involvement in the centre, but in doing so emphasizes that this prerogative is to be used 'not for the exercise of tyranny, but for the protection and benefit of the place' (*non ad tyrannidem sed ad munimen loci et augmentum*), sentiments that find no precedent in the equivalent sections of the Rule and *Regularis concordia*; evidently a strained relationship between monarch and monastery was foreseen, and it is surely no coincidence that Ælfric was later to take up this line in his *Letter to the Monks at Eynsham*.[57]

Reading the Abingdon and Eynsham charters in the manner proposed offers a number of new insights into the politics of the 990s and 1000s. That the two most decisive turning points in Æthelred's reign should have witnessed the production of his two longest diplomas is surely no coincidence. Though similar documents may have been produced and not survived, there cannot have been many: these charters stand out from the other diplomas of the era and were clearly intended to do something different, something out of the ordinary. They find few, if any, precedents

---

[56] M. de Jong, *The Penitential State: Authority and Atonement in the Age of Louis the Pious, 814–40* (Cambridge, 2009); and C. Booker, *Past Convictions: The Penance of Louis the Pious and the Decline of the Carolingians* (Philadelphia, PA, 2009).

[57] S 911 (KCD 714). For discussion, see Jones, *Ælfric's Letter*, pp. 44–6 and 213.

in this regard. The diplomas of Æthelred's predecessors are for the most part streamlined affairs, and even the bombastic charters produced by the extraordinary draftsman-scribe known as 'Æthelstan A' in the later 920s and early 930s do not approach them in size, length and narrative detail.[58] In fact, the only earlier document that is even vaguely comparable in scale and ambition is the New Minster re-foundation charter: produced by the monks at the New Minster and presented as a codex rather than a single sheet of parchment, it was the first document to reveal the potential for longer, more politically charged privileges.[59] Still, as a recipient product drawn up some time after the event – and quite possibly never seen beyond cloister walls – this is a rather different kettle of fish; it was an important further step to producing and presenting single-sheet diplomas on this scale at royal assemblies. Why this should happen in Æthelred's reign takes us back to the political shifts discussed earlier: these documents were clearly part and parcel of how the king announced and enacted new programmes. As such, they are 'performative acts' in the sense outlined by Geoffrey Koziol, documents that not only record a change in political climate but also were actively involved in creating this change.[60]

Æthelred and his advisors were thus doing something new. Although Anglo-Saxon diplomas had always possessed a performative aspect, in length, complexity and sheer size these charters far exceed anything that had hitherto been produced in single-sheet format.[61] The inspiration seems to have come at least in part from within the circles of monastic reform: as noted, the first diploma produced on this sort of scale was the New Minster charter, a document drawn up by the local brothers and probably drafted by Æthelwold himself; the second, the Æthelred Orthodoxorum charter, was issued in favour of Abingdon and makes allusions to the *Regularis concordia* (another Æthelwoldian text); and the third witnessed the foundation of Eynsham by Æthelmær, whose father may have been educated at Winchester and who entrusted control over the abbey to Æthelwold's most renowned student, Ælfric the homilist. Indeed, it

---

[58] D. A. Woodman, '"Æthelstan A" and the Rhetoric of Rule', *ASE* 42 (2013), 217–48; and B. Snook, *The Anglo-Saxon Chancery: The History, Language and Production of Anglo-Saxon Charters from Alfred to Edgar* (Woodbridge, 2015), pp. 86–124.

[59] S 745 (*WinchNM* 25).

[60] G. Koziol, *The Politics of Memory and Identity in Carolingian Royal Diplomas: The West Frankish Kingdom (840–987)* (Turnhout, 2012), esp. pp. 40–62.

[61] For earlier comparanda, see J. L. Nelson, 'England and the Continent in the Ninth Century: III, Rights and Rituals', *TRHS*, 6th series, 14 (2004), 1–24, at 14–24; and L. Roach, *Kingship and Consent in Anglo-Saxon England, 871–978: Assemblies and the State in the Early Middle Ages* (Cambridge, 2013), pp. 91–3.

would seem that Æthelwold in some sense set the tone for all these documents: he was not only the first to experiment with longer, more politically charged diplomas, but it was his death and Æthelred's subsequent indiscretions that made this approach to charter drafting both appealing and expedient to a court trying to reaffirm its support for the prelate's legacy. And where Æthelwold was to be found, Ælfthryth was rarely far from sight; though she did not live to see the Eynsham charter, the queen mother appears prominently amongst the witnesses to the Abingdon privilege, and it was her brother, Ordulf, who retired alongside Æthelmær in 1005, making his last attestation in this document.

How the finer details of such documents were communicated to those present is a good question. In part, one imagines that the act of granting served this purpose: the simple fact that Abingdon and Eynsham received grand privileges of liberty at these points must have spoken volumes. The surviving single sheet of the Abingdon diploma reveals the care that went into such texts: the writing is generously spaced, and the use of different ink and script to highlight the most important operative details makes it as much a piece of visual artistry as legal reality. The complex Latinity of these grants may have made them harder for some to comprehend, but presumes an audience of its own: one scarcely imagines that such care would have been expended in drafting documents that were meant to gather dust in a dry muniments chest.[62] While such flourishes may have been primarily intended for the ecclesiastics in attendance, some laymen were probably also in a position to appreciate them. Indeed, Æthelweard's *Chronicon* is a testament to the ability of noblemen to command the complex 'hermeneutic' Latin preferred by the reformers, and one imagines that his son would also have been capable of doing so. Byrhtferth of Ramsey's somewhat fanciful description of the production of a diploma in favour of Evesham in the eighth century may give us a sense for what these events were like: he reports that a papal privilege was first read out before those assembled; then the diploma itself was approved, drawn up and presented, before finally the document was taken back to the locality where it was solemnly placed upon the altar.[63] It would seem to follow that these documents were subject to a solemn public ritual of presentation. It may be that a vernacular précis accompanied such acts: a charter of Æthelred's later German counterpart, Conrad III, alludes to the text being translated

[62] Woodman, 'Rhetoric of Rule'; and Snook, *Anglo-Saxon Chancery*.

[63] Byrhtferth of Ramsey, *Vita S. Ecgwini* iii. 4–6, in *Byrhtferth of Ramsey: The Lives of St Oswald and St Ecgwine*, ed. M. Lapidge (Oxford, 2010), pp. 260–4. On which, see C. Cubitt, 'The Tenth-Century Benedictine Reform in England', *EME* 6 (1997), 77–94, at 91–2.

into the vernacular and read out to those present, and it is possible that similar practices were prevalent in England – in fact, Æthelmær's vernacular address in the Eynsham charter may represent elements of such a convention.[64] That such practices were known in England is suggested by an anecdote in the later eleventh-century *Vita S. Kenelmi*, in which a group of Anglo-Saxon pilgrims in Rome translate an Old English document miraculously dropped on the altar of St Peter's during the mass; evidently such linguistic difficulties were well known, and more educated figures were accustomed to bridging the gap for their less fortunate counterparts.[65] Finally, one imagines that the discussions and negotiations that lay behind these transactions also served to make their contents known. One might draw an analogy here with the negotiations that preceded the promulgation of Magna Carta in June 1215: though not all the rebel barons assembled at Runnymede could read the resulting charter, they were certainly well informed as to its contents.[66] The cases discussed above are somewhat simpler, but a similar principle applies. Indeed, Æthelmær and Ordulf are both mentioned as having played a role in the issuing of the Abingdon privilege, and one imagines that they were similarly involved behind the scenes at Eynsham; whether or not they could read the resulting charters themselves, they must have understood their gist.

Diplomas were thus an essential part of political communication in these years. Though the most important and exalted examples of this, the documents under discussion stand alongside many other diplomas that contributed to these programmes; they are but the most prominent tip of a large iceberg, giving us a sense for what lurks beneath the calm surface of developments as presented in the *Chronicle*. This is not to say that Æthelredian politics were expressed exclusively through diplomas, but it is to suggest that these documents were more intimately associated with Æthelred's regime than anyone save perhaps Keynes has realized. They need to be mined not only for what they tell us about the court factions, but also for what they say about prevailing attitudes and ideas.[67] When

[64] D K III 251, in *Die Urkunden Konrads III. und seines Sohnes Heinrich*, ed. F. Hausmann, MGH: Diplomata regum et imperatorum Germaniae 9 (Vienna, 1969), pp. 435–8. See H. Fichtenau, 'Bemerkungen zur rezitativischen Prosa des Hochmittelalters', in *Festschrift Karl Pivec. Zum 60. Geburtstag gewidmet von Kollegen, Freunden und Schülern*, ed. A. Haidacher and H. E. Mayer (Innsbruck, 1966), pp. 21–31, reprinted in and cited from his *Beiträge zur Mediävistik. Ausgewählte Aufsätze*, 3 vols. (Stuttgart, 1975–86), vol. I, pp. 145–62, at 145–6.
[65] *Vita et miracula S. Kenelmi*, chaps. 10–11, in *Three Eleventh-Century Anglo-Latin Saints' Lives*, ed. R. C. Love (Oxford, 1996), pp. 64–6.
[66] D. Carpenter, *Magna Carta* (London, 2015), pp. 339–72.
[67] For a pioneering effort, see Stafford, 'Political Ideas'.

from 1008 onwards royal decrees start to become longer and more self-reflective ('loquacious', 'vague' and 'futile', in the infamous judgement of Richardson and Sayles[68]), we can perhaps discern a subtle shift of tone, one away from communicating with diplomas and towards doing so with royal ordinances – a shift in which Archbishop Wulfstan must have been intimately involved. Still, charters continue to furnish precious insights throughout Æthelred's later years, and decrees themselves were subject to solemn public pronouncement, as Patrick Wormald has emphasized.[69] Moreover, if the medium changed, the message remained the same: to repent and reform before it is too late. Thus, whilst Æthelredian politics were certainly a politics of family and faction, as Pauline Stafford argues, they were also a politics of performance in which diplomas took on more than supporting roles; these were the message as well as the medium. As Simon Keynes first demonstrated almost four decades ago, to understand Æthelred's charters is therefore to understand his regime.

---

[68] H. G. Richardson and G. O. Sayles, *Law and Legislation from Æthelberht to Magna Carta* (Edinburgh, 1966), p. 27.

[69] P. Wormald, '*Lex scripta* and *verbum regis:* Legislation and Germanic Kingship from Euric to Cnut', in *Early Medieval Kingship*, ed. P. H. Sawyer and I. N. Wood (Leeds, 1977), pp. 105–38, reprinted in and cited from his *Legal Culture in the Early Medieval West: Law as Text, Image and Experience* (London, 1999), pp. 1–43.

PART III

Books, Texts and Power

CHAPTER 12

Making Manifest God's Judgement:
Interpreting Ordeals in Late Anglo-Saxon England

Helen Foxhall Forbes

> And let [the proband's] deed be made manifest in you [the iron], through the invocation of the name of Christ, that which he wants (by the persuading and the encouragement of the devil) to remain hidden to us.[1]

In late Anglo-Saxon England, a priest called to perform the liturgical ritual of the ordeal of hot iron would address the iron directly, adjuring it by God, by the angels and saints and by the holy catholic Church to reveal the truth of a hidden matter, the guilt or innocence of the suspected offender being thereby put to the test. But when a proband was subjected to this kind of ordeal or to the ordeal of hot water for which liturgical rituals also survive in late Anglo-Saxon books, how exactly would God's judgement be made manifest? In the light of modern scholarship on ordeals, this might seem like a daft question: according to Robert Bartlett, who has offered the most extended analysis of medieval judicial ordeals, if the range of evidence surviving from the tenth century to the twelfth is combined, 'it is possible to reconstruct a reasonably well-modelled picture of the ordeal in England in this period.'[2] Other scholars have argued that judicial ordeals held a particular function in small communities where it was important to come to consensus and where individuals' characters were well known to all, or that they were not so peculiar as they might seem to modern scholars because they were rational within the particular intellectual and social contexts in which they originated and were used.[3] This premise itself is questionable:

---

[1] 'Manifestumque fiat per inuocationem nominis christi in te eius commissum, quod diabolo suadente et cogente nobis esse uoluit occultum'. CCCC 391, p. 568, in *The Portiforium of St Wulstan: Corpus Christi College, Cambridge, Ms. 391*, ed. A. Hughes, 2 vols., HBS 89–90 (Leighton Buzzard, 1958–60), vol. II, p. 168.

[2] R. Bartlett, *Trial by Fire and Water: The Medieval Judicial Ordeal* (Oxford, 1986), p. 25.

[3] R. V. Colman, 'Reason and Unreason in Early Medieval Law', *Journal of Interdisciplinary History* 4 (1974), 571–91; P. Brown, 'Society and the Supernatural: A Medieval Change', *Daedalus* 104 (1975), 133–51; and P. R. Hyams, 'Trial by Ordeal: The Key to Proof in the Early Common Law', in *On the*

anthropological studies suggest that what looks strange to Us often looks strange to Them too, and that these events or moments that look strange demand attention in the communities or contexts in which they occur or are recorded precisely because they are considered to be fascinating, alarming or unsettling by contemporary observers.[4]

Perhaps more importantly, the surviving evidence for ordeals in tenth- and eleventh-century England, especially those of hot iron and hot water, is most puzzling for the fact that as a body of material it is so inconsistent – especially with regard to essential details such as how to interpret the outcome – that it seems likely that late Anglo-Saxon law-makers, ecclesiastics, judges or reeves were themselves not at all certain of what they expected to see, or how they expected God's judgement to be made manifest in the result of an ordeal. Given this complexity, it is perhaps unsurprising that even works of scholarship which suggest that it is possible to understand the workings of the ordeal are often themselves contradictory about what they suggest that interpreters of judicial ordeals expected to see or thought they were looking for. This chapter reconsiders the extent to which it is possible to understand the workings and practicalities of judicial ordeals in late Anglo-Saxon England, in part by setting the evidence alongside contemporary theological ideas about the miraculous. It is with great pleasure that I offer this chapter to Simon Keynes, who taught me the importance of pulling ideas apart in order to put them back together again, and especially to pay attention to details.

Evidence

The evidence for ordeals in late Anglo-Saxon England is fragmentary, sparse and often incidental to the main purposes of the texts in which it is found.[5] The most explicit outline of the process is found in tenth-century legal texts, particularly those issued in the name of King Æthelstan (924–39) or associated with him, such as a text now known as *Ordal*, probably dating from the first part of the tenth century, which has been described as a vernacular

---

Laws and Customs of England. Essays in Honor of Samuel E. Thorne, ed. M. S. Arnold et al. (Chapel Hill, NC, 1981), pp. 90–126.

[4] P. Boyer, *The Naturalness of Religious Ideas: A Cognitive Theory of Religion* (Berkeley, 1994), pp. 33–5.

[5] The earliest mention appears in the law-code of Ine, king of the West Saxons, which was probably produced between 688 and 694, but it is difficult to understand how they were supposed to work in this context, since there are simply two brief references to a *ceac* ('cauldron'), which suggest the use of an ordeal of hot water perhaps (though not necessarily) similar to those found in later texts. Ine 37, 62 in *Die Gesetze Der Angelsachsen*, ed. F. Liebermann, 3 vols. (Halle, 1903–1916), vol. I, pp. 104–5 and 116–17.

version of the rubrics that accompanied ordeal rituals.[6] Other than a few scattered references in law-codes, the next detailed legal information about ordeals comes from the early legislation of King Æthelred II (978–1013),[7] while a couple of late tenth-century hagiographical accounts offer other insights.[8] In the eleventh century, almost all the evidence is associated with Archbishop Wulfstan of York (d. 1023): he mentions ordeals in the legal texts that he authored, such as the later laws of Æthelred and the laws of King Cnut, as well as the compilation known as the *Canons of Edgar*, while he also seems to have influenced other texts that mention ordeals such as the *Northumbrian Priests' Law*.[9] However, it is really only the earlier tenth-century material that gives information about the process of ordeals: later texts primarily provide information about what should happen to those who failed ordeals, but do not discuss the process itself in significant detail.

One point worth noting at the outset is that legal texts show significant regional and chronological variations in how those who failed ordeals were treated, and this warns against the normalised picture that modern scholars have sometimes presented based on the surviving scraps of evidence.[10] The legislation of Æthelstan's reign includes local versions as well as the king's version, and illustrates that failing an ordeal was not considered in exactly the same way across the whole of Æthelstan's kingdom. For example, the supplement to Æthelstan's laws issued at London (V Æthelstan) demands fiercer penalties for those who failed ordeals than Æthelstan's decrees drawn up at Grately (II Æthelstan) had required, suggesting that we should

---

[6] II, IV, V, VI Æthelstan; *Ordal* (ed. Liebermann, vol. I, pp. 150–69, 171–83 and 386–7); and P. Wormald, *The Making of English Law: King Alfred to the Twelfth Century, I: Legislation and Its Limits* (Oxford, 1999), pp. 373–4.

[7] I, III, IV Æthelred (ed. Liebermann, vol. I, pp. 216–21 and 228–37).

[8] These are found in the material associated with the cult of St Swithun: *The Cult of St Swithun*, ed. M. Lapidge (Oxford, 2003); and Wulfstan of Winchester, *Life of Æthelwold*, in *Wulfstan of Winchester, the Life of St Æthelwold*, ed. M. Lapidge and M. Winterbottom (Oxford, 1991); see further below.

[9] Wormald, *Making of English Law*, pp. 208, 396–7.

[10] For example, Dorothy Whitelock describes the 'Anglo-Saxon' legal system based on evidence from several hundred years, but her synthesis presents a unified picture that can never have existed across the whole of England and in the precise details may not have existed anywhere during the period (D. Whitelock, *English Historical Documents*, 2nd edn (London, 1979), pp. 335–7); John. D. Niles gives an account of the 'Anglo-Saxon' ordeal based entirely on evidence from the early tenth century without querying how far period or place might have affected the details (J. D. Niles, 'True Stories and Other Lies', in *Myth in Early Northwest Europe*, ed. S. O. Glosecki (Tempe, 2007), pp. 1–30, at 3–6); Sarah Keefer assumes that statements of the eleventh century, such as Wulfstan's prohibition of ordeals on fast or feast days, are relevant also in the tenth (S. L. Keefer, '*Ut in Omnibus Honorificetur Deus:* The Corsnaed Ordeal in Anglo-Saxon England', in *The Community, the Family and the Saint: Patterns of Power in Early Medieval Europe: Selected Proceedings of the International Medieval Congress, University of Leeds, 4–7 July 1994, 10–13 July 1995*, ed. J. Hill and M. Swan (Turnhout, 1998), pp. 237–64; and S. L. Keefer, 'Ðonne Se Cirlisca Man Ordales Weddigeð: The Anglo-Saxon Lay Ordeal', in *Early Medieval Studies in Memory of Patrick Wormald*, ed. S. D. Baxter et al. (Farnham, 2009), pp. 353–67). See further below.

not imagine any sort of uniform legal process across the entire kingdom.[11] This remains true later in the tenth century, as in two of Æthelred's law-codes which seem to represent parallel versions for different areas, I Æthelred (perhaps dating from the 990s) for the English parts of Æthelred's kingdom, and III Æthelred for the Danish areas.[12] Here too there are significant differences in how ordeals were prescribed to be used and how those who failed them were treated: III Æthelred offers people of bad reputation the possibility of evading ordeals by paying fourfold, which is not apparently an option according to I Æthelred, but III Æthelred does not allow the choice between oath and ordeal that was available to those of good reputation in I Æthelred.[13] Moreover, while I Æthelred demands a fine from someone who fails an ordeal once and the death penalty on a second (and so last) occasion, III Æthelred requires the death penalty for those who fail ordeals.[14] There are contrasts too with a composite text of legal statements now known as IV Æthelred: this contains sections dealing with coinage and punishments for falsifying it which may be relatively early, perhaps predating I and III Æthelred.[15] IV Æthelred also specifies that those who are accused of false coining should go to ordeal and, if they fail, lose a hand, a provision that echoes the legislation of Æthelstan's Grately code.[16] By comparison, the punishment in III Æthelred for moneyers who fail an ordeal following an accusation of false coining is death.[17] Finally, Æthelred's later laws, written by Archbishop Wulfstan, as well as the laws that Wulfstan wrote for Cnut, rework judicial process concerning ordeals significantly so that the number of people sent to ordeals should in theory have been drastically reduced.[18] It is clear, therefore, that regional and chronological variations mean that there never was one process that applied to the whole of England.

---

[11] II Æthelstan 4–6. 2, 21; V Æthelstan 1. 4 (ed. Liebermann, vol. I, pp. 152–5, 162–3 and 168–9).

[12] P. Wormald, 'Æthelred the Lawmaker', in *Ethelred the Unready: Papers from the Millenary Conference*, ed. D. Hill (Oxford, 1978), pp. 47–80, at 61–3.

[13] I Æthelred 1. 1–2; III Æthelred 3. 4 (ed. Liebermann, vol. I, pp. 216–17 and 228–9).

[14] I Æthelred 1. 5–6, III Æthelred 4. 1 (ed. Liebermann, vol. I, pp. 218–19 and 230–1).

[15] Wormald, 'Æthelred the Lawmaker', pp. 62–3; though cf. also D. Keene, 'Text, Visualisation and Politics: London, 1150–1250', *TRHS*, 6th series, 18 (2008), 69–99, at 93–4, who argues (without much detail) that some elements at least may date from the twelfth century.

[16] II Æthelstan 14. 1; IV Æthelred 5. 2 (ed. Liebermann, vol. I, pp. 158–9 and 234–5).

[17] III Æthelred 8 (ed. Liebermann, vol. I, pp. 230–1).

[18] Compare the outlines in I Æthelred 1–2. 1 and III Æthelred 1–8 (ed. Liebermann, vol. I, pp. 218–21 and 228–31), with the prescriptions in II Cnut 22–22. 1, 30–30. 9 (ed. Liebermann, vol. I, pp. 324–5 and 330–5); for further discussion, see H. Foxhall Forbes, *Heaven and Earth in Anglo-Saxon England: Theology and Society in an Age of Faith* (Farnham, 2013), pp. 184–92.

In addition to the legal material, there is a complex body of liturgical texts connected with ordeals, edited in the early twentieth century by Felix Liebermann in his magisterial study of Anglo-Saxon law, though not always presented in a way that allows easy understanding of how these texts appear in the relevant manuscripts.[19] Both legal and liturgical texts mention ordeals of cold water, hot water and iron most frequently, though ordeal by bread and cheese also appears fairly regularly. It is useful to set out here how the liturgical texts are preserved because there is some variety in the surviving manuscripts. Some books contain only adjurations and blessings without mass liturgies and may attest to an earlier phase of the development of the rituals for ordeals: although the legal texts from Æthelstan's reign refer to a Mass in the context of the ordeal process, it is not clear whether this was a specific Mass for ordeals such as those found in the later pontificals, or whether the appropriate ferial liturgy could have been used.[20] The earliest liturgical material for ordeals appears in a book that may be roughly contemporary with Æthelstan's legislation: this is a prayerbook that was written in southern England probably in the late ninth or early tenth century and taken north later in the tenth century, where it was heavily glossed in Old English and augmented (in Old English and Latin) at the community of St Cuthbert (which eventually settled in Durham, where the book remains, as Durham, Cathedral Library, A. IV.19).[21] This book contains a blessing and an adjuration for hot water, as well as prayers asking God to reveal the truth (some of which reappear in the more developed rituals found in the later pontificals);[22] it also contains a blessing for the iron and an adjuration to it as well as an Old English adjuration to the proband, instructing him not to go to communion or to ordeal if he has any knowledge of the truth of the matter.[23] The material for ordeals is interspersed within a larger section of prayers and blessings, such as those for various kinds of food, for rooms and houses, for water and for veiling or consecrating virgins.[24] In contrast, the Ecgberht Pontifical, dating from *c.* 1000 (and of unknown provenance), includes one of the blessings for the hot iron or hot water found in other

---

[19] *Iud. Dei* (ed. Liebermann, vol. I, pp. 401–29).

[20] II Æthelstan 23 (ed. Liebermann, vol. I, pp. 162–3).

[21] A. Corrêa, *The Durham Collectar* (London, 1992), pp. 76–88; A. Corrêa, 'Daily Office Books: Collectars and Breviaries', in *The Liturgical Books of Anglo-Saxon England*, ed. R. W. Pfaff (Kalamazoo, 1995), pp. 45–60, at 48–9; and Keefer, 'Ðonne Se Cirlisca Man', pp. 362–3.

[22] Durham, Cathedral Library, A. IV. 19, fols. 48r–v; *Iud. Dei* IV (ed. Liebermann, vol. I, pp. 409–11).

[23] A. IV. 19, fols. 54r–55r; *Iud. Dei* V (ed. Liebermann, vol. I, pp. 411–12).

[24] A. IV. 19, fols. 45r–61r, in *The Durham Collectar*, ed. Corrêa, pp. 210–35.

books,[25] but it is squeezed into the bottom half of a page in the middle of the
rituals for Maundy Thursday: it was probably written by the scribe who wrote
the rest of this quire, but he has not respected the margins or kept to the line
rulings, and the writing is much smaller than elsewhere in the manuscript.[26]

For the most part, later books present a fuller treatment of ordeal
liturgies. The most detailed comprise a trio of rituals found in the
same sequence in seven late-tenth- and eleventh-century Anglo-Saxon
books, and again often in the context of other kinds of blessings.
These rituals are for cold water (including adjurations, a Mass and
instructions),[27] hot iron or hot water (adjurations and instructions)[28]
and then bread and cheese (adjurations and minimal instructions).[29]
Six of these books are pontificals,[30] and two of these also contain
adjurations to the proband in Latin and Old English.[31] The final book
containing this more detailed outline of ordeal rituals is now
Cambridge, Corpus Christi College, 422, a service-book that includes
a collectar, Mass liturgies and rituals for a number of occasional
offices such as baptism and the anointing of the sick.[32] Although in
some ways it looks closer to a book for 'ordinary' use than do the
pontificals, it is possible that it was written at the New Minster,

[25] *Iud. Dei* II, 3 (ed. Liebermann, vol. I, pp. 406–7).
[26] Paris, Bibliothèque nationale de France, lat. 10575, fol. 188v, in *Two Anglo-Saxon Pontificals (the Egbert and Sidney Sussex Pontificals)*, ed. H. M. J. Banting, HBS (London, 1989), p. 147. For discussion of the book, see J. L. Nelson and R. W. Pfaff, 'Pontificals and Benedictionals', in *Liturgical Books*, ed. Pfaff, pp. 87–98; and D. N. Dumville, 'On the Dating of Some Late Anglo-Saxon Liturgical Manuscripts', *Transactions of the Cambridge Bibliographical Society* 10 (1991), 40–57, at 51.
[27] *Iud. Dei* I (ed. Liebermann, vol. I, pp. 401–5).   [28] *Ibid.* II (ed. Liebermann, vol. I, pp. 406–7).
[29] *Ibid.* III (ed. Liebermann, vol. I, pp. 408–9).
[30] CCCC 146 ('Samson Pontifical'; s. x^ex; Old Minster, Winchester/Canterbury); CCCC 44 (s. xi^med; Christ Church, Canterbury); London, BL, Add. 57337 ('Anderson Pontifical'; *c.* AD 1000, Christ Church Canterbury); London, BL, Cotton Vitellius A. vii (fols. 1–112); ?Ramsey/?Exeter (the book seems to have belonged to Leofric, bishop of Crediton (1046) and Exeter (1050)); Paris, Bibliothèque nationale, 943 (Dunstan Pontifical' or 'Sherborne Pontifical'; AD 960 × ?973; probably Christ Church, Canterbury); and Rouen, Bibliothèque municipale, 368 ('Lanalet Pontifical'; s. xi^in; St Germans/Wells). For discussion, see Nelson and Pfaff, 'Pontificals'; and D. N. Dumville, *Liturgy and the Ecclesiastical History of Late Anglo-Saxon England: Four Studies* (Woodbridge, 1992), pp. 66–87.
[31] CCCC 146; London, BL, Cotton Vitellius A. vii.
[32] Corrêa, 'Daily Office Books', pp. 56–7; S. L. Keefer, 'Manuals', in *Liturgical Books*, ed. Pfaff, pp. 99–109; H. Gittos, 'Is There Any Evidence for the Liturgy of Parish Churches in Late Anglo-Saxon England? The Red Book of Darley and the Status of Old English', in *Pastoral Care in Late Anglo-Saxon England*, ed. F. Tinti (Woodbridge, 2005), pp. 63–82; R. Rushforth, *Saints in English Kalendars before AD 1100* (Woodbridge, 2008), pp. 41–2; and S. Keynes, 'Wulfsige, Monk of Glastonbury, Abbot of Westminster (*c.* 990–3) and Bishop of Sherborne (*c.* 993–1002)', in *St. Wulfsige and Sherborne: Essays to Celebrate the Millenium of the Benedictine Abbey, 998–1998*, ed. K. Barker et al. (Oxford, 2005), pp. 53–94, at 75–6.

Winchester, and intended for use at Sherborne.[33] Roughly contemporary with these books is the late-eleventh-century prayerbook (now Cambridge, Corpus Christi College, 391) associated with St Wulfstan, bishop of Worcester (d. 1095), which contains adjurations to the iron for ordeals found in other books but with no explicatory rubrics,[34] as well as a Mass that is more or less the same as that given for cold water in other books.[35] These are followed by blessings and adjurations for the ordeal of bread and cheese, the first of which are the same as those found in other books but including additional prayers over the elements and an adjuration to the person undergoing the ordeal.[36] As in many of the other books, these ordeal texts are sandwiched between other kinds of blessings.[37]

Interpretation

Understanding from the surviving texts how exactly ordeals were supposed to work is more difficult for some types of ordeals than for others. Legal texts mention ordeals of cold water without explaining exactly how they were understood to work,[38] but liturgical rituals for ordeal by cold water state that the interpretation depended on how the blessed water appeared to 'react' to the accused, since the water was instructed to behave in particular ways depending on the status of the accused: a proband who sank was understood to have been 'received' by the water and was therefore cleared, while the water was believed to have 'rejected' someone who floated, indicating that the ordeal had been failed.[39] Adjurations in Latin and Old English also warn the

[33] R. Rushforth, Saints in English Kalendars, pp. 41–2.
[34] CCCC 391, pp. 565–9 (ed. Hughes, vol. II, pp. 166–8); Iud. Dei II, 2–4; Iud. Dei V, 2 (ed. Liebermann, vol. I, pp. 406–7 and 411–12).
[35] CCCC 391, pp. 569–71 (ed. Hughes, vol. II, pp. 168–9); Iud. Dei I, 4–6, 8–14 and 17–18 (ed. Liebermann, vol. I, pp. 402–4).
[36] CCCC 391, pp. 571–6 (ed. Hughes, vol. II, pp. 169–72); Iud. Dei III, 1–3 (ed. Liebermann, vol. I, pp. 408–9). There are four prayers, a statement to the proband and an adjuration in CCCC 391 that are not included by Liebermann in his edition.
[37] CCCC 391, pp. 560–80 (ed. Hughes, vol. II, pp. 163–75).
[38] II Æthelstan 23. 1 (ed. Liebermann, vol. I, pp. 162–3).
[39] See, for example, Iud. Dei I, 21.3–5 (ed. Liebermann, vol. I, pp. 404–5): 'Adiuro te per nomen sanctum et indiuiduae Diuinitatis, cuius uoluntate aquarum elementum diuisum est, et populs Israel siccis pedibus statim transiuit, ad cuius etiam inuocationem Heliseus ferrum, quod de manubrio exierat, super aquam natare fecerat, ut nullo modo suscipias hos homines illos, si in aliquo sunt culpabiles de hoc quod illis obicitur, scilicet aut per opera aut per consensum uel per conscientiam seu per ullum ingenium; sed fac eos super te natare' or the instructions at the end of the ritual, Iud. Dei I, 23. 3 (ed. Liebermann, vol. I, p. 405): 'Et si submersi fuerint, inculpabiles reputentur; si supernatauerint, rei esse iudicentur.'

proband that if he knows the truth of the matter, the water will not receive him.[40] Identifying whether or not someone was sinking or floating might in reality be more difficult than the liturgical texts suggest, particularly if the proband could not actually swim and simply thrashed around; no requirements are stated for where cold water ordeals should take place.[41] However, regulations about depth for cold water ordeals, as in the laws issued by Æthelstan at an assembly at Grately (probably between 926 and 930) which state that the accused should sink one and a half ells (probably about a metre and a half) 'on a rope', suggest that the proband was tied to a rope before being thrown into the water and that the distance may have been marked on the rope itself.[42] This is not to say that interpreting the outcome of a cold water ordeal was necessarily straightforward even so,[43] but it seems likely that it was less ambiguous and problematic than for the 'hot' ordeals, that is, those of hot water and hot iron.

The most detailed outline about what was actually supposed to happen in an ordeal of hot water or hot iron is found in *Ordal*, which states that the proband should retrieve a stone from hot (boiling) water as deep as the wrist for a single ordeal or as deep as the elbow for a three-fold ordeal;[44] it also mentions for an ordeal of iron the number of paces that the proband was required to walk while carrying a piece of heated iron and how long the iron should stay in the fire.[45] Similar instructions are given in a rubric following the ritual for ordeals of hot water and hot iron found in the pontificals and in CCCC 422; this rubric also includes a statement about the differences between single and three-fold ordeals.[46] This rubric and *Ordal* agree too that the hand of the proband should be wrapped up and placed under a seal, to be opened for inspection on the third day (or after

---

[40] Latin and Old English adjurations with statements to this effect are found in CCCC 146, pp. 37–8; *Iud. Dei* VII, 23 and 23A (ed. Liebermann, vol. I, p. 414). A different Old English adjuration with a similar statement is in CCCC 422, pp. 330–2; *Iud. Dei* VIII, 2 (ed. Liebermann, vol. I, p. 415).

[41] One might think of Stevie Smith's poem, 'Not Waving but Drowning', in *The Collected Poems of Stevie Smith*, ed. S. Smith and J. MacGibbon (London, 1975), p. 303.

[42] II Æthelstan 23. 1 (ed. Liebermann, vol. I, pp. 162–3).

[43] There are no recorded cases of ordeal by cold water from Anglo-Saxon England, though there is a charter (S 1377 (*Pet* 17); AD 963 × 975) that records that the land being granted was forfeited by a widow and her son after they were accused of sticking pins into a doll; the woman drowned at London Bridge, and it is possible that this might be the result of mob 'justice' or ordeal by cold water.

[44] *Ordal*, 1b–2 (ed. Liebermann, vol. I, p. 386).

[45] *Ordal*, 1a, 4.2 and 5.1 (ed. Liebermann, vol. I, pp. 386–7).

[46] *Iud. Dei* II, 6 (ed. Liebermann, vol. I, p. 407); see also I Edgar 9 (ed. Liebermann, vol. I, pp. 194–5); and Wormald, *Making of English Law*, pp. 373–4.

three nights), a provision found also in Æthelstan's Grately code, though with reference to iron only.[47] While there is some clarity and consistency on the process outlined here, the interpretation of ordeals of hot iron and hot water, of course, hinged entirely on what was visible when the hand was unwrapped. However, the possible options described are not consistent either in the tenth- and eleventh-century texts or in modern scholarship.

Ordal clearly states that the hand should be identified as either *clæne* or *ful* ('clean' or 'foul') and refers to an inspection 'within the seal', that is, under the wrappings.[48] The rubric likewise refers to the assessment of success or failure using the words *mundus* and *insanies*, which broadly equate to the Old English terms *clæne* and *ful*:[49] it states that when the hand is unwrapped, 'if clean [*mundus*], thanks should be to God; if however *insanies* is found increasing in the trace of the iron, he should be reckoned blameworthy and unclean [*inmundus*].'[50] This is more complicated than it seems at first sight, however. In contrast to the instructions in *Ordal*, what is found clean according to the liturgical rubric should be the *person* not the hand, since *manus* is feminine and the masculine *mundus* should therefore refer to the proband. Moreover, *insanies* is an extremely rare word that appears scarcely at all before the twelfth century, ordeal rituals being one of only two contexts in which I can find it used.[51] It seems to be related to two other Latin words, *insania* ('madness', 'unsoundness of mind') and *sanies* ('bloody matter', 'diseased blood'), and is defined in the *Dictionary of Medieval Latin from British Sources* as 'ichorous matter issued from a wound; by metonymy, a wound'.[52] In addition, it is not clear either (1) whether a person who is *mundus* also shows the 'trace of the iron' in his hand or whether what is anticipated in the

---

[47] *Iud. Dei* II, 5 (ed. Liebermann, vol. I, p. 407); *Ordal* 5.2 (ed. Liebermann, vol. I, p. 387); II Æthelstan 23.1 (ed. Liebermann, vol. I, pp. 162–3). See also J. Roberts, 'What Did Anglo-Saxon Seals Seal When?', in *The Power of Words: Essays in Lexicography, Lexicology and Semantics in Honour of Christian J. Kay*, ed. G. D. Caie, C. Hough and I. Wotherspoon (Amsterdam and New York, 2006), pp. 131–58, esp. 131 and 150.

[48] *Ordal* 5.2 (ed. Liebermann, vol. I, p. 387): 'swa hwæðer swa heo béo ful swa clæne binnan þam insegle.'

[49] *Iud. Dei* II, 5 (ed. Liebermann, vol. I, p. 407).

[50] 'Si mundus est deo gratuletur si autem insanies crudescens in uestigio ferri inueniatur culpabilis et inmundus reputetur'. *Ibid.*

[51] This is from searching the Brepolis Cross Database Search Tool (www.brepolis.net); before the twelfth century, the word otherwise only appears in the works of Paschasius Radbertus, who seems to think of it as meaning 'insanity': see *Vita Walae abbatis Corbeiensis*, in *MGH Scriptores Rerum Sangallensium. Annales, Chronica et Historiae Aevi Carolini*, ed. G. H. Pertz (Hannover, 1829), pp. 533–69, at 556, l. 54; and *Expositio in lamentationes Hieremiae*, lib. II, l. 1382, in *Paschasius Radbertus: Expositio in Lamentationes Hieremiae Libri Quinque*, ed. B. Paulus, CCCM 85 (Turnhout, 1988), p. 124.

[52] D. R. Howlett et al., *Dictionary of Medieval Latin from British Sources* (London, 1975).

first case is miraculous preservation from burning or (2) whether we
should understand *insanies* here as a wound, an injury, festering skin or
something else. Royal legislation uses the vernacular *clæne* and *ful* to refer
to the *person* rather than to the hand, like the liturgical rubric and unlike
Ordal. In general, the laws refer to someone who failed an ordeal as *ful*,
with no mention of possible success, but in the one instance where it is
anticipated that the proband might pass an ordeal the decree states what
should happen if the proband is found *clæne*.[53] Moreover, it is possible to
read both literal and extended meanings from the terminology: *clæne* can
mean literally 'clean' but can also mean sinless or innocent, just as *mundus*
can refer to either physical or spiritual cleanliness and so by extension can
mean innocence.[54] In the same way, *ful* can mean literally 'dirty' but can
also indicate sinfulness, and given the probable relationship of *insanies* to
insania, it may be that we should consider the possibility of a spiritual or
mental stain in addition to physical damage.[55] It is also worth noting that
we are told that if *insanies* is found, the person should be reckoned
inmundus, highlighting the spiritual difference between this state and
the *mundus* ('person') who passes the ordeal.

More problematically, the liturgical rituals proper (as opposed to the
rubrics) are usually much less ambiguous in terms of what they request,
and this complicates our – and presumably also contemporaries' – understanding of what was expected from ordeals. Sometimes prayers simply ask
God to reveal the truth or to make manifest his judgement in the proband's
hand, but adjurations over the elements frequently demand miracles from
the heated iron and water, asking God to ensure that the proband who is
telling the truth does not get burned or scalded and likening the sought-for
miracle to biblical occasions where victims remained unharmed. A blessing
over the elements which begins by asking God to sanctify the burning iron
or boiling water explicitly requests that an innocent proband be left
undamaged: 'Almighty Lord and Father, you who through your holy
angel most kindly saved the three youths Sidrac, Misac and Abednego,
thrown into the furnace by order of the king of Babylon, grant that if the
one who, innocent of this theft (or murder or adultery or wickedness) puts
his hand on this burning iron or into this boiling water, may he remain

---

[53] See, for example, II Æthelstan 4–5; III Æthelred 7.1–8 (ed. Liebermann, vol. I, pp. 152–3 and 230–1);
the verb *clænsian* is also used with the meaning 'prove innocent', in, for example, III Æthelred 7 (ed.
Liebermann, vol. I, pp. 230–1).
[54] See Cameron, Angus, Ashley Crandell Amos and Antonette DiPaolo Healey, *Dictionary of Old
English: A to G online* (2007), 'clæne', definitions 1, 6, 6.d.
[55] *Ibid.*, 'ful', definitions 1, 2, 4, 4.c.

unharmed with you our Lord bestowing this; and just as you freed the three abovementioned youths from the furnace of burning fire, and delivered Susanna from a false accusation, in the same way, God Almighty, deign to keep the hand of the innocent one unharmed by any injury.'[56] The same prayer is much less clear on the fate of the hand of a guilty person, asking only – perhaps not without a hint of irony – that God's right hand deign to declare the guilt.[57] Other passages refer to what should happen to those who had committed offences, such as the adjuration that asks God to distinguish the faithful and unfaithful through this fire by the burning of the hands (or feet),[58] but, puzzlingly, another adjuration asks that the hand or feet of the innocent 'appear' unharmed, so it is not clear quite what is expected and whether the innocent person only appears unharmed or genuinely remains so.[59] Liturgical rituals are notoriously conservative and therefore do not tend to be updated or adapted rapidly, but even so, it is striking that ordeal liturgies – unlike, say, rituals for baptism or ordination – are so inconsistent in what they request.

This is particularly significant given that the sole narrative account of an ordeal from late Anglo-Saxon England reflects the ambiguity inherent in ordeals, turning on the way in which the proband's hand was perceived and thus how the result was interpreted by two different groups of people. This account appears in the *Translatio S. Swithuni*, written probably between 972 and 974, by Lantfred, a monk at the Old Minster, Winchester; if it refers to a genuine occurrence of an ordeal, this probably took place in late

---

[56] See, for example, the blessing from CCCC 391, pp. 565–6 (ed. Hughes, vol. II, p. 166): 'Qui tres pueros sidrac, misac, et abdenago iussu regis babylonae in camino ignis accensa forance saluasti illesos, per angelum sanctum tuum tu clementissime pater dominator omnipotens, presta ut si quis innocens de furto hoc. uel hoicidio. aut adulterio. seu maleficio. in hoc ferrum feruens aut in aquam feruentem miserit manum suam, illesus te domino nostro prestante permaneat, et sicut tres pueros supradictos de camino ignis ardentis liberasti, et susannam de falso crimine eripuisti, sic manum innocentis omnipotens deus ab omni lesionis insanae saluare digneris'. Cf. Also *Iud. Dei* II. 3 and IV. 4 (ed. Liebermann, vol. I, pp. 406–7 and 410–11).

[57] CCCC 391, p. 566 (ed. Hughes, vol. II, p. 166): 'Et si ille nocens uel culpabilis sit . . . et peccatum quod fecit confieri noluerit, tua dextera [for MS *dextram*] quesumus domine hoc declarare dignetur'. Cf. Also *Iud. Dei* II, 3 and IV, 4 (ed. Liebermann, vol. I, pp. 406–7 and 410–11).

[58] Durham A. IV. 19, f. 54; *Iud. Dei* IV, 1.4–6 (ed. Liebermann, vol. I, p. 411): 'Deus, qui ante aduentum sancti spiritus tui inlustratione ignis fideles tuos ab infidelibus decreuisti, ostende nobis in hoc paruitatis nostrae examine uirtutem eisdem Spiritus sancti et per huius ignis feruorem discerne fideles et infideles, ut tactu eius furti – criminis uel alterius – cuius inquisitio agitur, conscii et arescant manus eorum (aut pedes) conburantur aliquatenus; inm[u]n[e]s uero ab eiusmodi crimine liberentur penitus et inlesi permaneant'.

[59] *Iud. Dei* II, 4. 1 (ed. Liebermann, vol. I, pp. 406–7): '[S]i innocens de hoc furto – uel homicidio uel adulterio uel maleficio – unde purgatio quaerenda est, in hoc ignitum et tua benedictione sanctificatum ferrum (uel in hanc aquam feruidam et tua benedictione sanctificatam) manus – uel pedes – inmiserit, tua benignissima miseratione inlesus appareat'.

971 or 972.[60] Lantfred records that Flodoald, a merchant, owned a slave who was detained by the king's reeve on account of some small offence; the reeve insisted that the slave should undergo ordeal by hot iron. Flodoald attempted to negotiate with the reeve, offering him the slave and a pound of silver if he would allow the slave to avoid the ordeal.[61] This was rejected, so the slave went to the ordeal, described by Lantfred in some detail, including the searing burn that covered the slave's hand, and the fact that the hand was sealed up in the usual way for three days.[62] In the event, however, the slave was saved after Flodoald prayed for St Swithun's help and promised the slave to the saint in exchange for the slave's life being spared: as a result, while the slave's hand was clearly blistered and burned in the eyes of Flodoald and the slave's kinsmen, it appeared to the reeve and his men that the slave had a 'whole hand, almost as if he had never touched the hot iron', and so the reeve and his supporters judged him *inculpabilem* and *illesum* ('not guilty' and 'uninjured').[63] Lantfred's description of the slave as *inculpabilis* picks up the wording of the liturgical rituals, and here, as in the legal and liturgical texts, what is described is perplexing: looking at the hand, the viewer sees a burn or not depending on perspective, and while this account is deeply problematic for a number of reasons,[64] it is important because it suggests again that even contemporaries were not quite sure what they expected to see.

I have recently argued that there were significant anxieties over the uses of ordeals in late Anglo-Saxon England, and that this is particularly clear in the case of certain individuals such as Archbishop Wulfstan of York (d. 1023), who seems to have systematically attempted to prevent or limit the use of ordeals in judicial process.[65] Uncertainty is also evident in the reworking of Lantfred's account by an earlier Wulfstan, a monk of the Old Minster, Winchester, in his verse rendition of St Swithun's miracles (*Narratio metrica de S. Swithuno*), probably between 994 and 996: the subtle changes made by Wulfstan of Winchester in his adaptation of Lantfred's account suggested that he was not actually comfortable with

---

[60] Lapidge, *Cult of St Swithun*, pp. 236–7 and 308, n. 229.

[61] Lantfred, *Translatio*, chap. 25, in *Cult of St Swithun*, ed. Lapidge, pp. 308–11.

[62] Lantfred, *Translatio*, chap. 25, ll. 19–20 (ed. Lapidge, p. 310): 'Sigillata est autem manus eius solito more in tertium diem'.

[63] 'Sanam ... palmam quasi penitus foruum non tetigisset ferrum'. Lantfred, *Translatio*, chap. 25, lines 35–6 (ed. Lapidge, p. 310).

[64] For full discussion of the issues, see D. Whitelock, 'Wulfstan Cantor and Anglo-Saxon Law', in *Nordica et Anglica: Studies in Honour of Stefan Einarsson*, ed. A. H. Orrick (Paris, 1968), pp. 83–92; and Foxhall Forbes, *Heaven and Earth*, pp. 168–72.

[65] Foxhall Forbes, *Heaven and Earth*, pp. 158–98.

the use of ordeals.[66] Importantly, even though miraculous preservation from harm is a fairly common trope in hagiographical ordeal stories, neither Lantfred nor Wulfstan suggests that the slave was miraculously kept from harm by St Swithun. However, in another hagiographical text, the *Life of Æthelwold*, Wulfstan includes a narrative that corresponds almost exactly to an ordeal of boiling water: he describes that the monk Ælfstan was instructed by his abbot to take some food from the bottom of a cauldron of boiling water, and Ælfstan achieved this without being injured or even feeling the heat.[67] This does not refer to a judicial ordeal, but it clearly demonstrates that in a context that mirrors the process of an ordeal the possibility of miraculous preservation from harm – which is precisely what is requested by the ordeal rituals – could fit into a hagiographical narrative. This raises questions about why Swithun's miracle is presented in the way that it is.

Recognising the complexity and ambiguity of all of these sources is particularly important because of the confusion that has arisen in modern scholarship over how judgement and interpretation of an ordeal might work. Recent studies have sometimes argued that 'reading' ordeals in the early Middle Ages involved determining whether the injury to the hand was healing rather than festering, while others suggest that a miraculous preservation from harm was what was sought and that the proband's hand should remain undamaged; however, the confusion is such that often scholars have argued (incongruously) for both options simultaneously. To take one example, Bartlett notes on the first page of his study of ordeals that when the proband's hand was examined after the ordeal of hot iron, 'if it was "clean" – that is, healing without suppuration or discoloration – he was innocent or vindicated; if the wound was unclean, he was guilty'; on the second page, however, he states that ordeals 'required that the natural elements behave in an unusual way, hot iron or water not burning the innocent'.[68] To point this out is not to criticise or to pick holes just for the sake of it: as I have shown, the evidence itself is confusing and seems to present both of these possibilities, and on the basis of the surviving texts, I do not think we can know either what ecclesiastics, law-makers or judges themselves thought they were looking for in the interpretation of an ordeal, or what they thought they were looking at when they unwrapped a sealed hand after three days, or even whether they knew that themselves. To my mind, this is significant because it calls into doubt the ways that ordeals might have been

---

[66] *Ibid.*, pp. 170–1.   [67] *Vita S. Æthelwoldi*, chap. 14 (ed. Lapidge and Winterbottom, p. 28).

[68] Bartlett, *Trial by Fire and Water*, pp. 1, 2; see also Lapidge, *Cult of St Swithun*, pp. 152, 308, n. 231; and C. Leitmaier, *Die Kirche Und Die Gottesurteile: Eine Rechtshistorische Studie* (Vienna, 1953), pp. 10–12.

used or understood; I am not sure in fact that they were 'understood' at all, or at least not in the way that some scholarship has suggested.

Practicalities

Ascertaining exactly how often ordeals were used in tenth- and eleventh-century England is virtually impossible owing to the nature of the surviving evidence. It is also quite possible that the threat of an ordeal could be intended to encourage a confession or, as Stephen White suggests for contemporary Francia, that 'using' the ordeal might mean the initiation of a process simply as a way of encouraging the accused to back down.[69] But assuming that ordeals sometimes did genuinely take place and that people found themselves looking at an unwrapped hand and being required to make a decision about failure or success, it is worth considering what contemporaries might actually have seen and how they might have understood what they saw (whoever was responsible for 'reading' the unsealed hand). This issue is explored by Margaret H. Kerr, Richard D. Forsyth and Michael J. Plyley, who note that it is possible that probands genuinely remained unharmed, since there are numerous instances of modern people managing to remain unburned despite close contact with extremes of heat and fire, such as fire-walkers or fire-handlers, and that these have been examined and verified by modern scientists, though ultimately it remains unclear why or how these people are not burned.[70] Another possibility they suggest is that contemporaries may have seen serious second- or third-degree burns inflicted by the glowing iron or boiling water: these burns often look white, pale or yellow-brown and may be dry and painless (because all the nerve endings are destroyed), so a proband with such a burn might have been considered unharmed because the redness and pain of more superficial burns were not present.[71] Finally, they consider the possibility that what was looked for was infection, which they suggest would not usually appear until about the fifth day after flesh has been burned: if the visibility of infection or pus after three days was

---

[69] S. D. White, 'Proposing the Ordeal and Avoiding It: Strategy and Power in Western French Litigation, 1050–1100', in *Cultures of Power: Lordship, Status and Process in Twelfth-Century Europe*, ed. T. Bisson (Philadelphia, 2005), pp. 89–123; see also Bartlett, *Trial by Fire and Water*, p. 160.

[70] M. H. Kerr, R. D. Forsyth, M. J. Plyley, 'Cold Water and Hot Iron: Trial by Ordeal in England', *Journal of Interdisciplinary History* 22 (1992), 573–95, at 589–91.

[71] *Ibid.*, pp. 592–3; see also L.-P. Kamolz et al., 'The Treatment of Hand Burns', *Burns* 35:3 (2009), 327–37, at 333.

what determined that someone had failed an ordeal, they suggest that this was 'very lenient'.[72]

It is worth considering further the effect of wrapping the hand and how this related to contemporary medical ideas about treating burns. Burns can become infected easily, so the cleanliness (or otherwise) of the bandage used to wrap the hand is significant.[73] Even now there is discussion over the best ways to treat burns, including whether or not wrapping a burn is helpful.[74] While a sterile bandage can be used to keep infection away from a burn, wrapping a burned hand in a non-sterile bandage might have had precisely the opposite effect, introducing bacteria and infection instead. It is noteworthy too that contemporary medical books have a range of (often rather dubious) remedies for burns but do not recommend that burns should be bandaged: instead, they suggest recipes that usually rely on food or plant ingredients, such as butter or grease and a selection of herbal or mineral additives. *Leechbook* I suggests remedies for burns including a mixture of goat droppings and wheat stalks, or fennel, or yarrow (with or without lily), or ribwort mixed with butter or grease.[75] Alternatives include mixing mallow and other herbs with grease and then mixing them into honey or wax or even putting egg white on the burn.[76] *Leechbook* III distinguishes between burns from fire, for which woodruff, lily and brook-lime are instructed to be boiled in butter and smeared on as an ointment, and from liquid, for which elm rind and lily roots boiled in milk are recommended.[77] In contrast, the *Old English Herbarium* recommends a mixture of oregano, verbena, silver and roses mixed with wax or (bear) grease.[78] Silver has long been used in the treatment of burns and is still, in the form of silver nitrate in silver sulphadiazine cream, but its efficacy in the ointment suggested in the *Herbarium* is not certain, particularly since it

[72] Kerr et al., 'Cold Water and Hot Iron', p. 593.
[73] B. Karaoz, 'First-Aid Home Treatment of Burns among Children and Some Implications at Milas, Turkey', *Journal of Emergency Nursing* 36 (2010), 111–14, at 113.
[74] With regard to hand burns specifically, see, for example, M. M. Al-Qattan and A. S. Al-Tammini, 'Localized Hand Burns with or without Concurrent Blast Injuries from Fireworks', *Burns* 35 (2009), 425–9; and F. Siemers and P. Mailänder, 'Die Behandlung Der Brandverletzen Hand', *Unfallchirurg* 112 (2009), 558–64.
[75] *Leechbook* I. lx. 1–3, in *Leechdoms, Wortcunning and Starcraft of Early England; Being a Collection of Documents, for the Most Part Never before Printed, Illustrating the History of Science in This Country before the Norman Conquest*, ed. O. Cockayne, 3 vols. (London, 1864–66), vol. II, pp. 130–1.
[76] *Ibid.*, pp. 130–3; the use of egg white on burns is apparently popular as a home remedy in some areas today (see Karaoz, 'First-Aid Home Treatment of Burns'), though presumably it just results in cooked egg white on the burn.
[77] *Leechbook* III. xxix (ed. Cockayne, vol. II, pp. 324–5).
[78] *Old English Herbarium*, CI.3, in *The Old English Herbarium and Medicina De Quadrupedibus*, ed. H. J. de Vriend (London, 1984), pp. 148–9.

may be that litharge rather than actual silver would have been used.[79] Recent research has suggested that some Anglo-Saxon medical treatments might in fact be less dubious and more effective than they seem at first sight, but even so, many of these recipes cannot have helped, and some of them may have hindered healing.[80] (Butter and eggs are still known as 'home remedies' in some places today, though they are not at all recommended by medical professionals, precisely because they can hinder healing.[81])

How often these recipes were used in practice is impossible to tell, and presumably those who underwent ordeals were not allowed recourse to such treatment. Though in some cases this may not have been to their disadvantage, we might question what contemporaries thought of treating burns or scalds received in the course of an ordeal differently from the surviving recommended medical wisdom and what they might have thought would have been the effect on the result. But, dubious though early medieval remedies for burns or scalds may be, their presence in medical books does demonstrate – to state the obvious – that early medieval people expected that fires, burning hot iron or boiling water would injure and damage them and that those injuries could be painful and might require treatment of some sort. Presumably, burns and scalds were in any case simply an unavoidable incidental hazard in the course of familiar activities such as cooking and smithing and therefore not especially unusual. A contemporary remedy for wounds (not caused by burns) where the edges are 'too high' (*to hea*) is also telling: the recommended treatment is to apply a hot iron very lightly so that the skin will whiten, suggesting perhaps that people did not necessarily expect the skin to redden after burning.[82] That early medieval people expected to be burnt or scalded in 'hot' ordeals should hardly be a surprise, but the miraculous preservation requested in the rituals for ordeals and the miracles of all kinds visible in contemporary hagiographical accounts seem to have left the impression that in the context of the early Middle Ages miracles might simply be

[79] J. H. Klasen, 'Historical Review of the Use of Silver in the Treatment of Burns. I. Early Uses', *Burns* 26 (2000), 117–30, at 117–18.

[80] F. Harrison et al., 'A 1,000-Year-Old Antimicrobial Remedy with Antistaphylococcal Activity', *mBio* 6 (2015), 1–7.

[81] Karaoz, 'First-Aid Home Treatment of Burns'; L. Cuttle et al., 'A Review of First Aid Treatments for Burn Injuries', *Burns* 35 (2009), 768–75; H. E. Graham et al., 'Are Parents in the Uk Equipped to Provide Adequate Burns First Aid?', *Burns* 38 (2012), 438–43; and S. R. Shah et al., 'Butter for Burns or for Bread?: A Dilemma', *Burns* 40:4 (2014), 777 (the authors of this last recommend butter for bread only, not for burns).

[82] *Leechbook* I. xxxviii. 8 (ed. Cockayne, vol. II, pp. 94–7).

expected as a matter of course. What we know about how miracles came to be recorded, however, suggests a far more complex process of mediation and interpretation from event to written record.[83] In addition, it is important to remember that early medieval scepticism may have been far more common than it is sometimes perceived to be in the surviving texts, and that early medieval narratives of the miraculous do not necessarily represent the only possible viewpoint on any given episode.[84]

Miracles

It is clear, of course, that many early medieval authors did genuinely believe in miracles; I am not suggesting that people believed only in the heat of burning iron and boiling water without any faith in the miraculous or in the possibility of divine intervention. However, it is briefly worth exploring in this context what can be learned about attitudes to the miraculous and the marvellous in late Anglo-Saxon England and how this might relate to ideas about ordeals. Authors in the twelfth century and later discussed in some detail how God's intervention in the affairs of the world should be understood and how such miracles related to 'nature'; while Anglo-Saxon writers do not seem to have examined miracles in this way, the scant evidence does hint at some concern over miracles in the contemporary world.[85] Patristic authors such as Gregory the Great had implied that the age of miracles was over, and this idea was picked up and asserted more explicitly by at least one late Anglo-Saxon author: Ælfric of Eynsham (d. 1009/10) stated that visible, physical miracles belonged to past times, when they had been required to convert people to Christianity.[86]

---

[83] Foxhall Forbes, *Heaven and Earth*, pp. 25–9.

[84] S. Reynolds, 'Social Mentalities and the Case of Medieval Scepticism', *TRHS* 1, 6th series (1991), 21–41.

[85] M. R. Godden, 'Ælfric's Saints' Lives and the Problem of Miracles', *Leeds Studies in English*, n. s., 16 (1985), 83–100; B. Ward, *Miracles and the Medieval Mind: Theory, Record and Event 1000–1215* (Aldershot, 1987), pp. 3–32; C. S. Watkins, *History and the Supernatural in Medieval England* (Cambridge, 2007), pp. 45–66; R. Bartlett, *The Natural and the Supernatural in the Middle Ages: The Wiles Lectures Given at the Queen's University of Belfast, 2006* (Cambridge, 2008), pp. 5–33; see also A. M. L. Fadda, 'Constat Ergo Inter Nos Verba Signa Esse: The Understanding of the Miraculous in Anglo-Saxon Society', in *Signs, Wonders, Miracles: Representations of Divine Power in the Life of the Church*, ed. K. Cooper and J. Gregory (Woodbridge, 2005), pp. 56–66.

[86] Gregory I, *Homiliae in euangelia*, 29. 4, lines 79–83, in *Homiliae in Evangelia*, ed. R. Étaix, CCSL 141 (Turnhout, 1999), p. 247; Ælfric, *Catholic Homilies* I, 21 lines 155–62, in *Ælfric's Catholic Homilies: the First Series*, ed. P. Clemoes (Oxford, 1997), pp. 350–1; see also M. Godden, *Ælfric's Catholic Homilies: Introduction, Commentary and Glossary* (Oxford, 2000), pp. 172–3, and the discussion of late Antique scepticism and debates about miracles in M. Dal Santo, *Debating the Saints' Cult in the Age of Gregory the Great* (Oxford, 2012), pp. 2–26.

However, this sits rather uneasily alongside Ælfric's inclusion of accounts of contemporary miracles in his *Lives of Saints*, some of which are not found in his sources and seem to have been added on the basis of his own knowledge, others of which he states explicitly occurred during his own lifetime.[87] Malcolm Godden has argued that the key distinction here is between miracles worked directly by God (which are acceptable) and miracles worked by people (which may not be): he notes that Ælfric seems particularly uneasy about the idea that even wicked people could work visible miracles, giving his own example of the miracles that Judas worked before he betrayed Christ.[88] This might suggest that Ælfric would have accepted miracles in the context of an ordeal, but it is worth remembering that ordeal rituals required people to perform them and did not involve God stepping in of his own accord. Ælfric also warned that physical (as opposed to spiritual) miracles which were performed by good and evil people alike should not be loved, only those which are uniquely the preserve of the good.[89] While Ælfric certainly believed in miracles, he was also aware that there was more than one kind of miracle and that miracles were not, in and of themselves, an unmitigated good.

That particular individuals could apparently alter the course of nature as if by a miracle was evidently a concern to other authors too. Archbishop Wulfstan of York urged awareness of Antichrist's ability to work miracles when he appears in the last days and warned that no one should be taken in by this, since Antichrist can only miraculously 'heal' people whom he has first injured.[90] In the same way, one of the Blickling homilies includes an account of Simon Magus and the 'miracles' that he was able to achieve through magical arts.[91] With this in mind, it is worth noting the concern shown in liturgical rituals that magic or diabolical means could be used to affect the results of ordeals, to conceal the truth in a process that was intended to reveal it: in one prayer, God is asked to bring out his truth in

---

[87] For example, his inclusion in his Old English account of the miracles of Swithun of a story about a man who mocked Swithun: Ælfric, *Life of Swithun*, chap. 19, in *Cult of St Swithun*, ed. Lapidge, pp. 600–1.

[88] *Catholic Homilies* I, 21, lines 178–82 (ed. Clemoes, p. 351); Godden, 'Ælfric's Saints' Lives and the Problem of Miracles', pp. 85–6; see also R. I. Moore, 'Between Sanctity and Superstition: Saints and Their Miracles in the Age of Revolution', in *The Work of Jacques Le Goff and the Challenges of Medieval History*, ed. M. Rubin (Woodbridge, 1997), pp. 55–67.

[89] *Catholic Homilies* I, 21, lines 187–93 (ed. Clemoes, pp. 351–2).

[90] Wulfstan, *Homily* 4, lines 37–70, in *The Homilies of Wulfstan*, ed. D. Bethurum (Oxford, 1957), pp. 131–2.

[91] Blickling Homily 15, in *The Blickling Homilies of the 10th Century: From the Marquis of Lothian's Unique Ms. A.D. 971*, ed. R. Morris, EETS, original series, 58, 63, 73, 3 vols. (London, 1874–80; single-volume reprint 1967), pp. 173–89.

the case that someone wanted to hide his theft or offence through *maleficium* or through *herbas maleficias*, which might be translated either as 'wickedness' and 'evil herbs' or, perhaps more appropriately, 'sorcery' and 'magical herbs'; there is also a reference to *causas diabolicas* ('diabolical means').[92] The statements in legal texts about possible invalidation of ordeals suggest too that correct performance of ordeals was considered critical, and that contemporaries were worried about a number of ways in which ordeals might go wrong.[93] It is worth remembering, then, that if ordeals could easily go wrong and if miracles themselves could be problematic, the demand for a miracle in an ordeal should not be passed off as a given or as 'rational' given the context, particularly if it could theoretically be attributed either to God or to the actions of the proband.

All the same, some tenth- and eleventh-century clergy certainly believed that God might step in to persuade nature to behave unnaturally, and to this end Wulfstan of Winchester adds a striking note in his account of the miraculous interpretation of the ordeal of Flodoald's slave. Wulfstan states that the miracle showed that the whole of nature was subject to Christ's orders, that it changes into different forms by Christ's command, so that whatever it will not do of its own accord, it will do with Christ as judge.[94] But this is a peculiar statement in the context of the miracle as described, since nature did not change into different forms in the way that we might have expected: hot iron still apparently burned the slave's hand, and he was not allowed to go unharmed. Wulfstan's story about Ælfstan, the monk who plunged his hand into boiling water but remained unharmed, would fit much better with such a statement, but in that account, the miracle is simply presented without further explanation. In the case of Flodoald's slave, Wulfstan does not explain whether the slave's hand was festering or 'clean', since the crucial point is the (in)visibility of the burn, depending on the viewer's perspective. Like Lantfred, Wulfstan echoes the language of the ordeal rituals in stating that the slave is reckoned to be *inculpabilis*, but he takes this further to state that the reeve and his supporters see that the slave has a *mundam ... manum* ('clean hand'), just as those present had looked for evidence of whether the slave was *mundus* ('innocent') of the offence and found him *mundatum domino mundante* ('cleansed by the

[92] See, for example, *Iud. Dei* II, 3.6 (ed. Liebermann, vol. I, p. 407).
[93] II Æthelstan 23.2; *Ordal* 6; *Northumbrian Priests' Law*, chap. 39 (ed. Liebermann, vol. I, pp. 162–5, 386–7 and 382); and Wulfstan, *Canons of Edgar*, chap. 63, in *Wulfstan's 'Canons of Edgar'*, ed. R. Fowler (London, 1972), pp. 14–15.
[94] Wulfstan, *Narratio*, lines viii, ll. 408–14, in *Cult of St Swithun*, ed. Lapidge, p. 512.

cleaning Lord').[95] In the end, it is not at all certain what the reader is supposed to make of the miracle and whether the way the slave is described is intended to refer to his physical or spiritual state, or to both. Unlike either Flodoald or the reeve, we as readers can see both the burn and its absence, but it remains unclear whether the slave is genuinely *mundus* in the sense of innocent; he certainly is not 'mundus' in the sense of whole and undamaged if the perspective of Flodoald is accurate. In addition, since we are told that *Deus . . . secreto examine mundat* ('God . . . cleansed [him] by a secret test'), if he is *mundus* at all, it may only be thanks to the actions of God, not to a lack of guilt on the slave's part: this may in fact be the real miracle rather than the outward appearance of the slave's hand.[96]

Other aspects of Wulfstan's reworking of the story suggest that he may have been uncomfortable with the use of this ordeal, though whether because the death penalty was demanded for failure or whether because he felt that ordeals themselves were problematic is unclear.[97] It is noteworthy too that Ælfric's Old English translation and adaptation of Swithun's miracles does not include the story about the ordeal, and though it is true that Ælfric left out a number of events described by Lantfred, it is worth remembering that if the case described took place in late 971 or 972, this will have been within Ælfric's lifetime and probably when he was a young monk at Winchester; he might well have heard about it firsthand, and his decision to leave out the episode may therefore be significant.[98] Ælfric's younger contemporary, Archbishop Wulfstan, also seems to have been concerned about ordeals, and it looks from the legislation that he wrote for Cnut and from other texts associated with him as if he tried to limit their use wherever possible.[99] To some extent this late-tenth- and early-eleventh-century Anglo-Saxon unease seems to echo the kinds of concerns that the Carolingian archbishop of Lyon, Agobard, had expressed in the ninth century: Agobard stated that ordeals were neither wanted nor commanded by God and that some things were simply meant to be known to God alone, whose judgements are impenetrable.[100] The line he took seems to have stemmed partly from concern over the idea that God would necessarily reveal by a miracle the truth in cases where it was hidden, though anxiety over the wrong sorts of

---

[95] Wulfstan, *Narratio*, lines viii, lines 378, 386 and 389–90 (ed. Lapidge, pp. 510–12).

[96] *Ibid.*, lines 419 (ed. Lapidge, p. 512).

[97] This is explored more fully in Foxhall Forbes, *Heaven and Earth*, pp. 170–1.

[98] J. Hill, 'Ælfric: His Life and Works', in *A Companion to Ælfric*, ed. H. Magennis and M. Swan (Leiden, 2009), pp. 35–66, at 44–51.

[99] This is explored in detail in Foxhall Forbes, *Heaven and Earth*, pp. 172–93.

[100] Agobard of Lyons, *Liber de divinis sententiis*, 2, in *PL* 104, cols. 251A–252B.

miracles can be found in Agobard's other writings too.[101] Later writers also worried about the issue of miracles 'on demand', such as the twelfth-century Petrus Cantor, who noted (among other reasons for objecting to ordeals) that God could not be compelled to step in to prevent a proband from harm, even if he was asked to in a liturgical ritual.[102]

Conclusion

In the end, therefore, I think we should be dubious of the idea that we can really know what contemporaries thought they were looking for if asked to pronounce judgement on ordeals or to take part in them in some way, whether as proband, reeve, witness or ecclesiastical officiator. Contemporary ideas about miracles sit somewhat uneasily alongside what was asked for by liturgical rituals, and the complexity of terminology and the variety in what is stated to be expected are so great that it seems unlikely that they were considered 'rational' even in the contexts in which they were used: in any case, as numerous scholars have noted, ordeals were a method of proof that was saved for cases of last resort.[103] It is clear too that within the tenth- and eleventh-century English kingdom(s), regional and chronological variation in the ways that ordeals were perceived and used are far more significant than scholars have usually recognised. A striking facet of the pre-Conquest English texts (in contrast to contemporary Continental evidence) is that the episode of Flodoald's slave is the only instance in which we seem to see a judicial ordeal that may have actually happened, even if the nature of the account makes it difficult to disentangle reality from rhetoric and hagiographical tradition, or to get much of a sense of what 'really' happened.[104] We

---

[101] S. Bosch Gajano, 'The Use and Abuse of Miracles in Early Medieval Culture', in *Debating the Middle Ages: Issues and Readings*, ed. B. H. Rosenwein and L. K. Little (Oxford, 1998), pp. 330–9. It is worth noting though that some people did support ordeals, for example Hincmar of Rheims: for discussion see A. Firey, *A Contrite Heart: Prosecution and Redemption in the Carolingian Empire* (Leiden, 2009), pp. 9–60.

[102] Petrus Cantor, *Verbum abbreviatum*, in *PL* 205, cols. 23–270. This is particularly interesting given that if we compare ordeal rituals to baptism rituals again, there is no sense that process would not work because God would not step in; in fact Hincmar explicitly compared ordeals to baptism (*De divortio Lotharii*, 6, in *PL* 125, cols. 664, 668, 669; *The Divorce of King Lothar and Queen Theutberga: Hincmar of Rheims's De Divortio*, trans. R. Stone and C. West (Manchester, 2016), pp. 151–3 and 156–61).

[103] Bartlett, *Trial by Fire and Water*, pp. 26–30.

[104] See, for example, J. W. Baldwin, 'The Crisis of the Ordeal: Literature, Law, and Religion around 1200', *Journal of Medieval and Renaissance Studies* 24 (1994), 327–53; White, 'Proposing the Ordeal'; and F. McAuley, 'Canon Law and the End of the Ordeal', *Oxford Journal of Legal Studies* 26 (2006), 473–513. It is worth noting that there are mentions of ordeals, and of people volunteering to undergo ordeals, in the records of the Domesday inquests, but it is not clear either whether any of

might therefore legitimately ask how often – or even if – they were really used in practice. That legislation connected with ordeals continued to be issued over the course of the tenth and eleventh centuries may indicate that their invisibility from non-normative sources does not mean that they did not happen, though it does also suggest concern and debate about ordeals as a judicial process. And, ultimately, accepting that ordeals were perhaps as puzzling in late Anglo-Saxon England as they seem now allows us to peek into a much more complex and nuanced world that included both belief and scepticism and one in which – despite what some of our sources suggest – God, God's presence and the visibility of God's judgements were never taken for granted.[105]

these took place or whether this represents standard Anglo-Saxon practice or Norman influence: see R. Fleming, *Domesday Book and the Law: Society and Legal Custom in Early Medieval England* (Cambridge, 1998), pp. 11–20, 51.

[105] I am grateful to the Leverhulme Trust for supporting the research for this article and to David Woodman and Rory Naismith for their suggestions and comments.

CHAPTER 13

An Eleventh-Century Prayer-Book for Women?
The Origins and History of the Galba Prayer-Book

Julia Crick

London, BL, Cotton Galba A. xiv, a small, charred, poorly written, and imperfectly reconstructed manuscript, attests a central but sparsely documented element of pre-Conquest religious life: private devotions.[1] While gospel-books from the period survive in quantity, and many manuscripts contain individual prayers, prayer-books themselves are a relative rarity.[2] Only six are known, four dating from *c.* 800 and two, including Galba, from the last generations before the Norman conquest.[3] If this meagre

---

[1] Simon Keynes is a scholar whose mastery of the field of Anglo-Saxon history is manifest in what he has written and how he has written it, in numerous highly important archival discoveries and in his apparently effortless technical proficiency in multiple fields and sub-disciplines. This chapter pertains to a period that he has made his own, the reign of Æthelred the Unready, and makes reference to a number of his own studies. It is offered as inadequate thanks for many kindnesses and as a token of appreciation for his brilliance as a teacher; his stature as scholar, historian and antiquary; and his advocacy of the disciplines that enable the critical study of Anglo-Saxon England in the twenty-first century.

[2] B. Raw, 'Anglo-Saxon Prayerbooks', in *The Cambridge History of the Book in Britain, I (c. 400–1100)*, ed. R. Gameson (Cambridge, 2012), pp. 460–7, at 460; H. Gneuss, 'Liturgical Books in Anglo-Saxon England and Their Old English Terminology', in *Learning and Literature in Anglo-Saxon England: Studies Presented to Peter Clemoes on the Occasion of His Sixty-Fifth Birthday*, ed. M. Lapidge and H. Gneuss (Cambridge, 1985), pp. 91–141, at 106–9 and 137–9; B. Günzel, *Ælfwine's Prayerbook (London, British Library, Cotton Titus D. xxvii)* (London, 1993), pp. 59 and 205–6; and T. H. Bestul, 'Continental Sources of Anglo-Saxon Devotional Writing', in *Sources of Anglo-Saxon Culture*, ed. P. E. Szarmach (Kalamazoo, 1986), pp. 103–26, at 124–6. See also D. N. Dumville, *Liturgy and the Ecclesiastical History of Late Anglo-Saxon England: Four Studies* (Woodbridge, 1992), pp. 96–152. For an evocation of the contents of these books, see H. Mayr-Harting, *The Coming of Christianity to Anglo-Saxon England* (London, 1972), pp. 182–90.

[3] Cambridge, University Library, Ll. 1. 10 (*c.* 820 × 840; Gn-L, *ASMss* 28); and London, BL Harley 2965 (s. viii/ix or ix[t]; Gn-L, *ASMss* 432); London, BL Harley 7653 (s. viii/ix or ix[in.]; Gn-L, *ASMss* 443); London, BL Royal 2. A. xx (s. viii[2] or ix[¼]; Gn-L, *ASMss* 450); London, BL Cotton Galba A. xiv (s. xi[t]; Gn-L, *ASMss* 333); London, BL Cotton Titus D. xxvi + xxvii (1023 × 1031; Gn-L, *ASMss* 380). Gneuss and Lapidge record a total of sixty-two manuscripts from pre-Conquest England that contain prayers (p. 926), although almost all contain only one or two prayers. Of the total, eighteen may be discounted as being of non-English or post-Conquest origin, whether the entire manuscript or the prayers within them (Gn-L, *ASMss* 30.3, 77, 148, 304, 334, 376, 423, 428.4, 474.5, 555.5, 592, 637–8, 655, 673.3, 754, 912.5, 914, 920). Only eleven of the remainder, including Galba A. xiv, include vernacular prayers or prayers with vernacular elements. Most groups of Latin and vernacular prayers have been

total reflects not just a high rate of obsolescence but, as has been suggested, a low level of production,[4] then special significance may attach to the fact that five of the six bear signs of female ownership or use.[5]

The Galba prayer-book is an enigmatic manuscript by any reckoning. It is a remarkably un-calligraphic production by multiple scribes, and yet its contents link it to a high-status centre of production: Winchester. It contains prayers in English and Latin for an audience of men and, apparently, women, but the institutional context in which it was produced and used remains elusive. Ker noted four prayers scattered through the volume bearing feminine singular endings, evidence that he interpreted as the adaptation of the volume 'for the use of a female member of a religious house'.[6] A fifth prayer names female as well as male supplicants (*pro fratribus et sororibus nostris*), and a sixth shows adaptation to female use: the scribe copied feminine endings inter-lineally above the masculine endings of the main text.[7] Michelle Brown and Barbara Raw have both cast the Anglo-Saxon private prayer-book as a particularly female genre, but the genesis of the surviving examples requires close consideration.[8] In Neil Ker's highly influential opinion, Galba A. xiv was originally compiled not as a women's book but for male use and only subsequently received additions adapting it to a female audience.[9] Bernard Muir has preferred to interpret its contents as those of a book produced 'for a religious institution which seems to have housed both men and women'.[10]

---

transmitted alongside liturgica; very few manuscripts contain as many as eight prayers (e.g. Gn-L, *ASMss* 104, 306, 363, all discussed by Raw, 'Anglo-Saxon Prayerbooks', pp. 460–1).

[4] Gneuss, 'Liturgical Books', p. 137.

[5] London, BL Cotton Galba A. xiv; London, BL Cotton Titus D. xxvi + xxvii; London, BL Harley 2965; London, BL Harley 7653; London,BL Royal 2. A. xx: see Dumville, *Liturgy*, pp. 101–2 and, on Titus, below. The Harleian and Royal manuscripts were discussed by M. P. Brown, 'Female Book-Ownership and Production in Anglo-Saxon England: The Evidence of the Ninth-Century Prayerbooks', in *Lexis and Texts in Early English: Studies Presented to Jane Roberts*, ed. C. J. Kay and L. M. Sylvester (Amsterdam, 2001), pp. 45–67.

[6] On 6v, the oblations prayer (ed. B. J. Muir (London, 1988), p. 31, no. 13); on 53v and 85v, the Latin prayers of confession (*ibid.*, pp. 70–73, 119, nos. 26 and 57); and on 125v, unidentified fragments (*ibid.*, p. 160, no. 78). N. R. Ker, *Catalogue of Manuscripts Containing Anglo-Saxon* (Oxford, 1957), p. 198.

[7] On 82r, the Celtic *capitella* (ed. Muir, p. 113, no. 54); and on 108r, the Latin prayer of confession (*ibid.*, p. 140, no. 66).

[8] Brown, 'Female Book-Ownership'; and Raw, 'Anglo-Saxon Prayer-Books'. For the association of later medieval women with a very different form of devotional book, see, for example, R. S. Wieck, *The Book of Hours in Medieval Art and Culture* (London, 1988), p. 35.

[9] Ker, *Catalogue*, p. 201.

[10] Muir, *A Pre-Conquest English Prayer-Book*, p. xiv. Muir printed its contents in full. On individual texts, for example, on fols. 104–106, 110, 112, 113v, see R. A. Banks, 'Some Anglo-Saxon Prayers from British Museum MS. Cotton Galba A. xiv', *N&Q* 210 (1965), 207–13. On Galba 3r–4v and Nero 10v–12v, see M. Lapidge, 'Some Latin Poems as Evidence for the Reign of Athelstan', *ASE* 9 (1981), 61–98, at 83–93. See also T. H. Bestul, 'A Note on the Contents of the Anselm Manuscript, Bodleian Library, Laud misc. 508', *Manuscripta* 21 (1977), 167–70, at 169 (87a, 39a).

Various scholars have proposed different male or female institutions in which the book might have been written. The Nunnaminster at Winchester has most frequently been cited as place of origin, adaptation or both, but Galba and its sister volume London, BL, Cotton Nero A. ii (fols. 3–13), have been associated with Truro, Exeter, West Wessex, St Germans, Sherborne, Leominster and, most recently, Shaftesbury.[11] The nature of the association between Nero A. ii and Galba has also occasioned debate. Ker identified at least one of Galba's scribes in Cotton Nero A. ii, but opinions have differed as to whether the two manuscripts should be treated as *membra disiecta*, or as independent products of the same scriptorium, or as written by itinerant scribes at different centres altogether.[12]

The level of controversy about Galba A. xiv has been sustained by ignorance of the construction of the manuscript. To some extent, the problem is insoluble. Galba was so badly burned in the Cottonian fire of 1731 that not only are parts illegible, but the physical structure of the whole has been irrevocably disrupted. Indeed, as late as 1840 it was presumed that the manuscript had been destroyed totally.[13] Subsequently, the remains were discovered, mounted and rebound, but the operation left some leaves upside down or out of order, and few clues remain as to their proper arrangement.[14] Wanley recorded the contents of the Old English part of the manuscript before the fire, but he said nothing about the Latin works that form the bulk of the contents.[15] A mid-nineteenth-century foliation that predates rebinding might promise

---

[11] Ker, *Catalogue*, p. 201 (Nunnaminster for Nero and Galba); D. H. Farmer, *The Oxford Dictionary of Saints* (Oxford, 1978), p. 327 (Truro for Nero); F. Rose-Troup, 'The Ancient Monastery of St. Mary and St. Peter at Exeter 680–1050', in *Report and Transactions of the Devonshire Association for the Advancement of Science, Literature and Art* 63 (1931), 179–220, at 196–7 (Nero A. ii copied from an Exeter exemplar); F. A. Gasquet and E. Bishop, *The Bosworth Psalter* (London, 1908), p. 152 ('from the most Celtic, backward, part of the country – the furthermost Wessex' for Nero); Lapidge, 'Some Latin Poems', pp. 84–5 (Winchester for Galba, St Germans for Nero), Günzel, *Ælfwine's Prayerbook*, pp. 204–5 (Winchester, Nunnaminster for Galba, Sherborne?, St Germans for Nero); J. Hillaby, 'Early Christian and Pre-Conquest Leominster: An Exploration of the Sources', *Transactions of the Woolhope Naturalists' Field Club* 45 (1987), 557–685, at 630 (Leominster for Galba and Nero); and *Anglo-Saxon Litanies of the Saints*, ed. M. Lapidge (London, 1991), pp. 69–70 (Shaftesbury for Galba).

[12] Ker, *Catalogue*, p. 201. See also Lapidge, 'Some Latin poems', p. 85; and Hillaby, 'Early Christian and Pre-Conquest Leominster', p. 629.

[13] F. Madden's 'List of the Injured Cottonian Manuscripts and Memoranda of Repairs 1837–184– (*sic*)' records Galba A. xiv as wanting (London, BL Add. 62576, 52r, 61v). The manuscript had been recovered by the time of Madden's revised list of 1866: London, BL Add. 62578, 69r. I owe this information to Tim Graham.

[14] As Ker observed: *Catalogue*, p. 200.

[15] Wanley, *Librorum veterum septentrionalium Catalogus*, p. 231. See Ker, *Catalogue*, p. 198.

to supply the deficiency, but in fact it conflicts with Wanley so much that its testimony must be doubted.[16]

Codicological indicators and written descriptions having proved inadequate, one must address the palaeography of the manuscript. Indeed, the distribution of the hands offers our only opportunity of gauging how and when the constituent parts of the manuscript were assembled. The most detailed and authoritative printed description of Galba A. xiv is that by Neil Ker:

> The oldest parts of it are probably of s. xi in., and may have been written for male use (ff. 7–37, 58–63^v, 65–70, 75), but the manuscript was extensively added to in s. xi[1] for the use of a female member of a religious house as appears from the feminine singular forms in texts on 6^v, 53^v, 85^v, and 125^v, and the mention of 'hoc monasterium' (89^v).[17]

Although this statement offers a masterly summary of the manuscript, the *Catalogue* did not provide a suitable place to discuss its complexities, not least because it was not the purpose of his catalogue to record Latin texts. The same focus on Old English materials has shaped the two most recent analyses of the script, which were not concerned with the parts of the manuscript copied in Latin or in Caroline minuscule and which arrived at slightly different conclusions about the identification of scribal stints.[18] Ker sketched only some of the details, describing five hands in Galba A. xiv, two of which he also identified in Nero A. ii,[19] but he did not relate them explicitly to stages in the construction of the manuscript.[20] Furthermore, he said almost nothing about the hands of what he had identified as the earliest phase.

This omission is readily explicable. The part of Galba A. xiv that Ker identified as the early section defies rapid survey, comprising disparate blocks of badly burned leaves written in at least five undisciplined, crude

---

[16] At the centre-foot or lower-lefthand corner of the folio, running from 89r to 132r (fols. 1–46) and 4r to 67r (fols. 48–109).

[17] Ker, *Catalogue*, p. 198. Folios 3–6 should be added to his list of the earliest parts of the book.

[18] D. Scragg, *A Conspectus of Scribal Hands Writing English, 960–1100* (Woodbridge, 2012), p. 40, hands 484–91; and P. A. Stokes, *English Vernacular Minuscule from Æthelred to Cnut, c. 990–c. 1035* (Woodbridge, 2014), p, 218, H1–H7: the Latin hands are discussed on p. 88.

[19] 'Arts IV–VIII are in the hand (1) which wrote ff. 37–38v, 45–49v, 64v, 71rv, 76–102, 104–17v, 120–5, 125v–6, 133, 137, 140, 141 . . . Art. I is in a better hand (2), also forward-sloping. Another hand (3) wrote ff. 3–4v, 39–45, 70, 74, 126v, 130, 131, 144–54, all Latin texts . . . Nero ff. 10v–12v are apparently in the same hand (4) as the collect for St Æthelwold, Galba f. 125 . . . The calendar, &c., in Nero ff. 1–10, appears to be in the same backward-sloping hand (5) as a *Computatio Grecorum* in Galba f. 2': Ker, *Catalogue*, p. 201.

[20] Compare D. N. Dumville, 'On the Dating of Some Late Anglo-Saxon Liturgical Manuscripts', *Transactions of the Cambridge Bibliographical Society* 10 (1991–5), 40–57.

and ugly hands. More than a dozen hands may be distinguished elsewhere in the volume. Clearly, given the importance of Galba A. xiv, a fuller description is needed, even if only to establish the limits of our ignorance about the origins and condition of the manuscript.

The analysis of the hands offered in Appendix 13A confirms several of Ker's observations. Most of the feminised sections of Galba were indeed copied by a scribe amplifying an existing manuscript, *viz.* Ker's hand (1). However, Ker's remarks need some modification and amplification. The work of hand 1 divides into two distinct sections (stints vii and xii), as does that of hand 4 (stints vii and xvii). The portions that Ker attributed to hand 3 must also be reassessed; folios 39–45 were arguably the work of more than one scribe, and the hand(s) of 126v and 130 cannot be assigned with any confidence to the scribe of 3r–4v.

The scribe who wrote hand 1 (stint xii), to whom Ker attributed the bulk of the additions, also copied folios 62v–63v, which Ker had listed as within the original part of the manuscript.[21] As these two folios form the end of a block of consecutive leaves (folios 58–63), they could originally have been left blank and have been first pressed into service at a later date when the manuscript was being expanded. However, doubts remain about Ker's identification of a separate 'female' phase in the history of the manuscript. The first of the feminised (and therefore presumably additional) sections that Ker noted, 6v, is written in large, rotund Caroline minuscule of the sort that characterises the presumed first phase of production, the part of the manuscript suitable for male use, reported by Ker as beginning at folio 7. Moreover, the textual evidence is less than clear-cut. The text found on 53v was copied in the feminine – *peccatrix miserrima* – but these words were glossed by a contemporary corrector with alternative masculine endings *-tor* and *-mus* (see Figure 13.1).

Despite the generally different appearance of, on the one hand, the bulk of the 'masculine' sections of the book and, on the other, the parts written for specifically female use (notably in stint xii), certain palaeographical idiosyncrasies link the two supposedly discrete units. Scribes in both parts of Galba A. xiv used Insular minuscule for Latin.[22] Several preferred the **et**-ligature to the ampersand when writing Caroline or the ampersand to the **et**-ligature when writing Insular minuscule for Latin.[23] Three scribes, including one

---

[21] The script is clearest on 63v. Stokes made the same identification, independently of mine: Stokes, *English Vernacular Minuscule*, p. 218.

[22] See stints v, vii, xii and xvii + xix. Examples of this practice were discussed by Stokes, *English Vernacular Minuscule*, pp. 200–1.

[23] See stints ii, iv, ix, xiii and v, vii and xii.

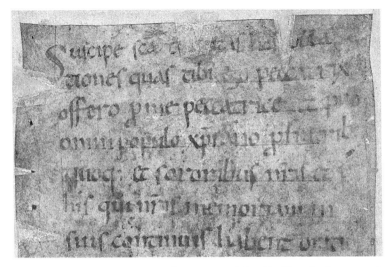

Figure 13.1 London, BL Cotton Galba A. xiv, 6v. (Noted by Ker, *Catalogue*, p. 198.)
Detail of Latin portion of bilingual oblations prayer in a first-person singular feminine
voice offered for *sorores* and *fratres* among others. (Crick stint iv.) (Image reproduced
with the kind permission of the British Library.)

identified by Ker as writing in the original part of the volume and one in the
additions, used a backwards-leaning round **s**.[24] Furthermore, the script on
folio 103r/v, in the supposedly additional part of the manuscript, closely
resembles that of stint xiii, in the supposedly original section. One can also
detect similarities between the usages found in stint xi ('original'), on the one
hand, and stints xvii and vii ('additional'), on the other.[25]

These observations lead to others. It is striking, for example, that the
part of the manuscript that Ker identified as having been written for male
use has large, crude, ugly script characterised by the intrusion of un-
canonical letter forms (so Insular **g** in Caroline minuscule, for example),
while much of the material for female use was copied in a more regular,
though equally undisciplined hand (stint xii). Furthermore, almost none of
our scribes used a purely Caroline- or Insular-minuscule alphabet despite
the fact that some houses maintained a rigorous distinction between the
two by the later tenth century, a period that (textual and palaeographical
indications show) Galba must postdate.[26] Indeed, many of Galba's scribes

---

[24] Stints vii, xi, xii and xvii.
[25] For example, the heavy pen strokes, the use of round **S**, the ticked foot of final **t** and the extended
abbreviation stroke on *pro*.
[26] Ker, *Catalogue*, pp. xxv–xxvi. See Dumville, *Liturgy*, pp. 146–52.

employed bizarre combinations of ostensibly outmoded usages. The tall-**e** ligature and the ampersand that imitates it seem to hark back to a form of Square minuscule seen in the middle years of the tenth century.[27]

The Scripts and Their Analogues

The peculiar combination of characteristics displayed in various stints in Galba merits some attention. The manuscript is notable for outsized, widely spaced script; lack of conformity to the canons either of Caroline or of Insular minuscule; and a peculiar treatment of ligatures, for example, the avoidance of the ampersand and the **st**-ligature in Caroline. However crude and uncouth the result, the possibility exists that these scribes were not simply ignorant of good scribal practice but were deliberately following unusual conventions. David Dumville, writing of Square minuscule in the context of liturgical books, has noted

> the continual pressure, which many scribes evidently felt, to upgrade their calligraphy by edging towards majuscule (that is, two-line) proportions, by increasing the size and weight of script, and by importing specific majuscule features or practices into their minuscule.[28]

These general principles well characterise the activity of several of Galba's scribes, both in Insular and in Caroline minuscule. The script of stint v, for example, I have already likened to the high-grade register of Square minuscule that Dumville was describing.[29] Stint ix looks like the application of similar principles of engrossment to Caroline minuscule.

Indeed, the various scribes who employed majuscule **S** and Insular **g** in otherwise unremarkable script may have been acting in the same spirit. The calligraphical late Half-uncial prayer-book, London, BL, Royal 2. A. xx, includes a decorative round **S**, a deliberately unligatured **st**, a rounded Insular **g** and a discreet **et**-ligature for the word *et* in Latin, all features found in Galba. Royal 2. A. xx also includes three of the same texts.[30] Another Half-uncial prayer-book containing texts found in Galba, the

---

[27] Style III. See D. N. Dumville, 'English Square Minuscule Script: The Mid-Century Phases', *ASE* 23 (1994), 133–64, at 144–51, esp. 145. See stint xi for the ampersand and stint xvii for the **et**-ligature. David Dumville reminds me that this reference back to earlier examples is a consistent feature of the history of Insular script.

[28] Dumville, *Liturgy*, pp. 146–7. For an earlier tenth-century example of this phenomenon, see S. Keynes, *Anglo-Saxon Manuscripts and Other Items of Related Interest in the Library of Trinity College, Cambridge* (Binghamton, 1993), no. 3, plate III.

[29] See above.

[30] *A Pre-Conquest English Prayer-Book*, ed. Muir, p. xxx; MS. R. London, BL, Royal 2. A. xx includes Galba's items 18, 22 and 67: *ibid.*, pp. xviii–xix.

'Book of Nunnaminster' (London, BL, Harley 2965), exhibits similar letter forms.[31] Galba's scribes therefore could have derived inspiration from the script of such high-grade exemplars.

Turning from letter forms to aspect, parallels closer in date to the writing of Galba can be found. The verso of a leaf inserted at the end of London, BL, Cotton Tiberius A. iii (folio 179), bears a Latin prayer (*Oratio post missam impletam*) written in the late tenth century in a Square minuscule as huge, ugly and peppered with majuscule letters as any of the script in Galba.[32] A comparable aesthetic may be found slightly later in a different context. Two charters of Lyfing, bishop of Crediton, Cornwall and Worcester (1027–46), one dated 1038, the other four years later, are in large, irregular Caroline and Insular minuscule, respectively.[33] Another example is the Exeter charter, D. & C. 2518, an eleventh-century copy of a document issued to St Petroc's, Padstow, in King Æthelstan's name (AD 670 for 925 × 939).[34] Such analogues may do little to localise our manuscript, but they suggest that its script should be regarded as uncommon rather than unique.

Scribes and Centre of Origin

The scribes of Galba A. xiv invite comment for their number as much as for the idiosyncrasy of their scribal practices. Although the shrunken and blackened state of the manuscript makes identification of scribal stints even more hazardous than usual, at least a dozen different scribes were probably involved in the copying of this manuscript, even allowing for the use of several registers of script by a single practitioner. This relatively high concentration of scribes necessarily bears on questions of dating and localisation. Three hypotheses can be proposed: that the manuscript was copied over an extended period of time or at a religious house with a particularly active (if not very skilled) scriptorium or at different times by scribes belonging to more than one centre.

The first option holds little attraction. Indications of absolute dating refer to the supplementary hands – Ker's hand 4, datable after the death of

---

[31] London, BL Harley 2965. See E. A. Lowe, *Codices Latini antiquiores: A Palaeographical Guide to Latin Manuscripts Prior to the Ninth Century*, 12 vols. (Oxford, 1934–72), vol. II, no. 199. On analogues with Galba, see *A Pre-Conquest English Prayer-Book*, ed. Muir, p. xxix.
[32] Ker, *Catalogue*, p. 248, no. 187.3. At the foot of 179v.
[33] S 1393 and S 1394. *Facsimiles of Ancient Charters in the British Museum*, ed. E. A. Bond, 4 vols. (London, 1873–8), vol. IV, nos. 22 and 23.
[34] S 388 (BCS 725).

Bishop Æthelwold in 984 (stint vii), and hand 1 (stint xii), datable after the death of King Æthelred in 1016 – but palaeography suggests a broadly similar date for the so-called original parts of the book, the late tenth or, better, the early eleventh century.[35] In other words, nothing encourages us to posit a substantial time lag between the copying of the various parts of the book. The third option also has little to commend it. As we have seen, the script of Galba's various components gives no grounds for supposing that the manuscript was written in two distinct centres. The contents may have led some commentators to suggest that Galba was begun at a male house and continued at a female monastery,[36] but palaeography links the two parts of the manuscript. I incline to the conclusion that Galba A. xiv was produced at a single centre within a single biological generation. The hand responsible for the bulk of the 'original' part of the manuscript, stint v, resembles that of the main hand of the 'additions' in many particulars (stints xii and xvii).[37] Indeed, additional and original material cannot be distinguished solely on the grounds of script. If this conclusion is correct, then Galba cannot be regarded as a prayer-book copied for male use and later *adapted* for female use. Instead, we should envisage a book that, from the start, contained material suitable for female use alongside that suitable for male use.

Such an observation brings with it some difficult problems of interpretation. Firstly, there remains the distinct possibility that the use of feminine or masculine endings might have been inherited from exemplars. Thus, in attempting to reconstruct a male or female audience for the various sections of Galba, we run the risk of reconstituting earlier audiences, those at whom those particular texts had originally been aimed. Secondly, even when a book can be firmly localised, the text may send out complicated signals. Recent commentators agree that BL Cotton Titus D. xxvi + xxvii was written between 1023 and 1031 at the New Minster, Winchester, by Ælfsige, a New Minster scribe (A), in collaboration with another, perhaps the dean, Ælfwine (scribe B);[38] the volume then remained at New Minster until 1057, perhaps until the end of the eleventh century.[39]

---

[35] The Insular minuscule of stint v belongs more happily in the eleventh than in the tenth century, for example.

[36] Dumville, for example, has suggested that the additions could have been made in Winchester but regarded the original core of the manuscript as un-localised: 'On the Dating', p. 46.

[37] See above.

[38] Günzel, *Ælfwine's Prayerbook*, pp. 1–3; it was Keynes' suggestion that Ælfwine should be equated with scribe B: S. Keynes, *The Liber Vitae of the New Minster and Hyde Abbey Winchester: British Library Stowe 944 together with Leaves from British Library Cotton Vespasian A. viii and British Library Cotton Titus D. xxvii*, EEMF 26 (Copenhagen, 1996), pp. 111–14.

[39] Keynes, *The Liber Vitae*, pp. 118–23. Ker, *Catalogue*, p. 266.

Despite this pedigree, Titus D. xxvi + xxvii contains more consistent testimony to apparent female use than does Galba. Scribe A copied no fewer than five prayers with feminine endings; a later scribe, perhaps in the latter part of the century, glossed the prayers extensively, adding feminine endings; finally, a twelfth-century scribe copied a lengthy prayer for female use.[40] This evidence has been interpreted in various ways. On the basis of the added prayer, both Ker and Keynes suggested that the manuscript was in a woman's hands by the twelfth century, while Wilmart and Birch argued that it had reached the Nunnaminster.[41] Barré and Günzel both tackled the question of the feminine endings copied or added in glosses in the eleventh century. Barré connected them with use by the nuns of the nearby Nunnaminster; Günzel thought that they derived from an exemplar. Whatever the solution, the example of Titus D. xxvi + xxvii raises complex questions about intention and use. Günzel's suggestion that Ælfsige derived feminised endings from his sources carries weight given that he worked at the New Minster; the hypothesis cannot be proved, however, as none of the prayers can be sourced.[42]

The question of the gender of the readership impinges particularly on discussions of prayer-books because prayers signal the gender of the intended user; almost all other texts, written in the third person, would bear no indications of female readership at all. This absence of evidence means that we should allow for the probability that, with the exception of prayer-books, books that originated at or were owned by a female house will bear no signs of female use. Likewise, it is equally possible that prayer-books associated solely with a male house may have inherited signs of female use inherited from an exemplar. The example of Titus shows that we cannot automatically assume that Galba, a book containing feminised texts and feminised glossing, was produced by female scribes or even at a female house.[43] However, scribes conscious of the gender of intended users did on occasion intervene to adapt the endings for particular audiences. Such texts served a practical function.

Galba presents a different set of problems from Titus. Firstly, its centre of origin cannot be established with certainty at the present state of our knowledge. Secondly, the evidence for the direction of travel of the manuscript is difficult to construe. On 53v the scribe of stint iii copied a Latin

---

[40] Günzel, *Ælfwine's Prayerbook*, pp. 3–4, 7, 128 and 186–8.   [41] Keynes, *The Liber Vitae*, p. 114.

[42] Compare Günzel, *Ælfwine's Prayerbook*, p. 207.

[43] But note the presence of nuns outside female communities: S. Foot, *Veiled Women, I: The Disappearance of Nuns from Anglo-Saxon England*; and *II: Female Religious Communities in England, 871–1066*, 2 vols. (Aldershot, 2000), vol. I, pp. 111–208.

confessional prayer with feminine endings, only to gloss them with masculine alternatives (Figure 13.2); on 108v, meanwhile, another Latin confessional prayer was copied by Ker's hand 1 with masculine endings (Appendix 13A, stint xii), only to gloss them with feminine alternatives (Figure 13.3). That said, some clear patterns do emerge. Only two hands were responsible for the copying of the prayers containing feminine endings. One was copied by the scribe of stint vii and four by Ker's hand 1, stint xii, the dominant hand in the manuscript. These hands, or hands closely related to them, recur in Nero A. ii (Appendix 13A). Moreover, the scribes in question copied texts that impinge on questions of dating and localisation: a prayer to St Dunstan and two texts invoking Saints Machutus and Hemma.

If we cannot always attribute the presence of feminine endings in prayer-books to sources, then perhaps we should allow that the book belonged at some stage to a female community. Indeed, both Galba and Titus have been assigned to the Nunnaminster. Critics have argued from the presence of a prayer copied on a blank leaf (74r) that Titus migrated there in the twelfth century. Such evidence may require a more complex explanation, however. Titus bears extensive eleventh-century feminising annotation despite the fact that the book remained connected with New Minster long enough for Ælfwine's obit, 1057, to be entered into the calendar. The circumstances

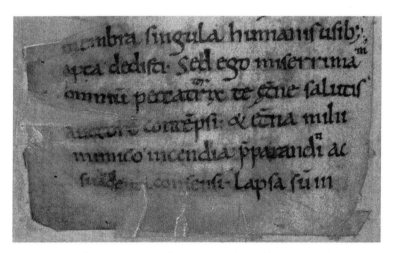

Figure 13.2 London, BL Cotton Galba A. xiv, 53v. (Noted by Ker, *Catalogue*, p. 198.) Latin prayer of confession copied with feminine singular endings and altered to masculine singular, possibly by the scribe. (Crick stint x.) (Image reproduced with the kind permission of the British Library.)

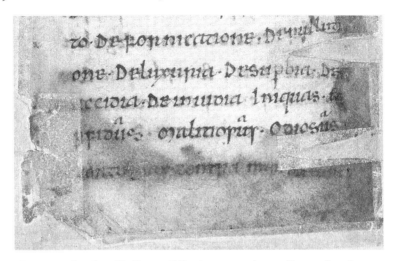

Figure 13.3 London, BL Cotton Galba A. xiv, 108r, line 13. Prayer of confession showing interlinear copying of feminine (singular) endings, apparently by the scribe of the text. (Ker's Hand 1; Crick stint xii.) (Image reproduced with the kind permission of the British Library.)

that inspired such annotations remain unclear. The annotator could have been adapting individual prayers to private or to institutional use; the manuscript could have been glossed while in Ælfwine's possession, or at New Minster itself, or of course after transfer to another house soon after 1057 – the hand is difficult to date. A range of options needs to be explored.

The task of locating a precise centre of origin must depend largely on the geographical range of the saints whose cults are mentioned in the kalendar, litanies and prayers; consequently, it lies beyond the scope of a palaeographical survey.[44] Some comments may be ventured on previous identifications, however. The litanies found in Galba include the names of saints culted at Winchester, which have made the Nunnaminster the most favoured point of origin,[45] although more recently Michael Lapidge has

[44] Although, for potentially fruitful comparative material, see M. Lapidge, 'Abbot Germanus, Winchcombe, Ramsey and the Cambridge Psalter', in *Words, Texts, and Manuscripts: Studies in Anglo-Saxon Culture Presented to Helmut Gneuss on the Occasion of His Sixty-Fifth Birthday*, ed. M. Korhammer (Woodbridge, 1992), pp. 99–129; and A. Corrêa, 'The Liturgical Manuscripts of Oswald's Houses', in *St Oswald of Worcester: Life and Influence*, ed. N. Brooks and C. Cubitt (London, 1996), pp. 285–324, at 286–7, n. 5.

[45] '"Machuti, Byrnst[ane], Aelf[ege], Grimbald, Haedda, Dunstani archi, Oswold archi, Athelwold, Byrnwold." Now we can recognize where we are – at Winchester': E. Bishop, *Liturgica historica: Papers on the Liturgy and Religious Life of the Western Church* (Oxford, 1918), p. 387. Ker, *Catalogue*, p. 201 (Machutus, Swithun). Lapidge, 'Some Latin Poems', p. 84 (Machutus, Ælfhead, Grimbald, Hæddi, Æthelwold).

cautioned against using certain major Winchester cults as localising evidence by *c.* 1000.[46] Winchester would certainly have housed a suitably extensive supply of scribes. However, as David Dumville has pointed out, one would have expected from that centre a more professional standard of calligraphy.[47] If, as he hinted, the Nunnaminster followed less stringent scribal practices, then we are faced with another surprise: the extensiveness of its scribal reserves. Twelve or more is no mean number of scribes for any house to muster, and the resources of the wealthiest nunneries did not match those of their male equivalents.[48] Nonetheless, others have suggested that Galba and Nero A. ii, folios 3–13, may have been copied at a nunnery. Joe Hillaby, arguing from the range of saints included in the kalendar in Nero A. ii, has made a case for Leominster as Galba's place of origin, an identification that has gained some acceptance.[49] One can easily imagine that such a centre produced some of the hybrid and provincial script found in Galba. It is more difficult to account for the presence of so many scribes there, however, especially as the lifetime of the house was short.[50]

Given that the book contained male and female material from its inception, we should widen the search for a provenance beyond known nunneries. In the absence of better indicators, the presence in Galba of a relatively newly introduced script type, Anglo-Caroline, could be taken as a guide to origin, though not a particularly reliable one given the number of un-localised examples of this kind of minuscule. Only a very few specialist centres have been identified as producers of Anglo-Caroline.[51] All these accommodated nuns in the tenth and eleventh centuries, however temporarily, and thus might provide a suitable context for the production of Galba.[52] Palaeographically, Bury St Edmunds makes a potentially attractive option – it has been identified as an active centre of book production in

[46] Specifically, that of Swithun and Iudoc: 'Abbot Germanus', p. 116.

[47] Dumville, 'On the Dating', p. 46.

[48] See J. C. Crick, 'The Wealth, Connections and Patronage of Women's Houses in Late Anglo-Saxon England', *Revue Bénédictine* 109 (1999), 154–85. On female scribes more generally, see R. Gameson, 'Anglo-Saxon Scribes and Scriptoria', in *The Cambridge History of the Book in Britain, I (c. 400–1100)*, ed. R. Gameson (Cambridge, 2012), pp. 94–120.

[49] Leominster has been endorsed as a possible place of origin: Gn-L, *ASMss* 333; Stokes, *English Vernacular Minuscule*, pp. 50–1.

[50] It was apparently dissolved soon after 1047: B. Kemp, 'The Monastic Dean of Leominster', *EHR* 83 (1968), 505–15, at 506. See now Foot, *Veiled Women*, vol. II, pp. 103–7.

[51] D. N. Dumville, *English Caroline Script and Monastic History: Studies in Benedictinism AD 850–1030* (Woodbridge, 1993), pp. 154–5: Canterbury, Winchester, Worcester, Exeter, ?Bury St Edmunds, ? Ramsey.

[52] See Foot, *Veiled Women*, vol. II, pp. 49–52, 84–8, 143, 243–53, 257–9. See also R. Gilchrist, *Gender and Material Culture: The Archaeology of Religious Women* (London, 1994), p. 33.

the century before the Norman conquest[53] – but the argument may founder on the saints' cults listed in the kalendar.[54] In any case, the unusual scribal practices found in Galba A. xiv impede identification with any known centre of Anglo-Caroline.

One further problem bears on the question of origin. When Ker identified two of the hands of Galba in Nero A. ii, he opened up a further controversy, this time about the nature of the connexion between the two manuscripts. Ker concluded that Galba and Nero were *membra disiecta*;[55] Michael Lapidge, on the contrary, has regarded them as two separate manuscripts;[56] Hillaby dissented from Lapidge and agreed with Ker.[57] As Nero A. ii contains a kalendar whose cults have been used as prime evidence for localising it and, by extension, Galba A. xiv, the relationship between the two requires some discussion here.

According to Ker, hands 4 and 5 of Galba reappear in Nero on folios 10v–12v and 11–10r, respectively. On examining the two manuscripts, I find that Ker's second identification is unassailable (stint i), his first looks extremely probable (stint vii) and a new point of comparison emerges (stint iv). The extent of stint vii bears most on the question of localisation. Within Galba, stint vii clearly belongs to the supposedly late, feminised phase of the manuscript's history, the script being almost indistinguishable from that of stint xii. Paradoxically, the litanies, which point to a place of origin quite different from that of Nero A. ii, folios 3–13,[58] belong to the same strongly feminised phase, within stint xii. Even if we do not follow Ker and equate the hands of stints vii and xii, strong affinity between them still exists. Thus there is some sort of connexion between the distinctive hand of Nero 10v-12v and the phase of Galba that includes the litanies.

If, as this observation suggests, the evidence of text is out of step with the evidence of hands, the nature of the association between the two manuscripts requires review. Palaeographically, nothing impedes the association between Galba and Nero. Indeed, on this criterion alone, they could, as Ker suggested, be *membra disiecta*. Three hands found in folios 3–13 closely resemble hands found in Galba: one of these is certainly the work a single scribe. Moreover, the dimensions of the manuscripts are at least compatible. Galba and Nero have been trimmed differently – the parchment of

---

[53] Dumville, *English Caroline Script*, p. 78, n. 360.

[54] The kalendar includes East Anglian saints, such as Æthelberht, martyred saint-king of East Anglia (20 May), Fursa (7 June), Botulph (17 June) and Neot (20 October), but note that St Neot also occurs in the kalendar of Sherborne.

[55] Ker, *Catalogue*, pp. 200–1.   [56] Lapidge, 'Some Latin Poems', pp. 84–5.

[57] Hillaby, 'Early Christian and Pre-Conquest Leominster', pp. 628–9.   [58] See above.

Galba measures approximately 11 × 14.5 cm and that of Nero 10.5 × 15.5 cm – but the ruled areas differ less widely – Galba's fall in the approximate range 8–9 × 11.3–12.5 cm and Nero's 7.5–9.0 × 12.2–13.3 cm. Given the level of variation within both manuscripts between the practices of individual scribes and the degree of distortion caused to Galba by fire damage, these ranges do not disturb Ker's hypothesis.[59] Lapidge first based on textual grounds his objections to taking Nero A. ii as a *membrum disiectum* of Galba: Galba's litany includes saints culted at Winchester who, in Nero's kalendar, are conspicuous by their absence.[60] Subsequently, he has suggested that Galba might be the product not of Winchester itself but of a female community within its 'liturgical ambit', for example, Shaftesbury.[61] However, if, as Ker hinted and as the present discussion suggests, Galba and Nero share not one scribe, as Lapidge reported, but at least two, then the likelihood that Galba and Nero originated from separate centres must be considerably reduced. Indeed, the duplication of shared scribes invites speculation that the different ranges of cults that the two manuscripts invoke derive as much from exemplars as from local habits of veneration.[62] Galba and Nero may indeed be separate manuscripts, as the repetition of at least one text suggests, but they probably issued from the same scriptorium, one located at, or associated with, a community partly or wholly made up of female adherents.

Conclusions

This study has not solved the problem of the place of origin of Galba A. xiv. That task lies most probably with a liturgist. However, I have suggested that we should be looking not for a series of houses but for a single point of origin for the whole of Galba A. xiv and probably too for Nero A. ii, folios 3–13. Moreover, such a centre is likely to have been a female community or a male community with an associated female congregation. One is reminded of the male and female readership 'in utroque sexu sagaces' to

---

[59] They neither prove nor disprove it.   [60] Lapidge, 'Some Latin Poems', pp. 84–5.

[61] Lapidge, *Anglo-Saxon Litanies*, p. 70.

[62] But note that even apparently local saints could be venerated in a surprisingly wide area. I owe to Professor Nicholas Orme the information that Petroc, though associated predominantly with the south-west, was culted in Winchester in the eleventh century: *Winchester in the Early Middle Ages: An Edition and Discussion of the Winton Domesday*, ed. M. Biddle (Oxford, 1976), p. 330. Petroc appears as no. 111 in the litany in London, BL, Arundel 60 (New Minster, Winchester, s. xi²): F. Wormald, 'The English Saints in the Litany in Arundel MS. 60', *Analecta Bollandiana* 64 (1946), 72–86, at 79; and Lapidge, *Anglo-Saxon Litanies*, p. 144.

whom Dunstan's biography was addressed, *c.* 1000.[63] A number of candidates present themselves. Hillaby's suggestion of Leominster remains viable but requires from the palaeographer a leap of faith: could an otherwise unattested, and presumably short-lived, scriptorium have mustered sufficient scribal resources? A western English solution would certainly satisfy both textual and palaeographical criteria.[64] Two charters of a western bishop, Lyfing, are written in comparably cumbersome script; Worcester, for example, certainly housed nuns at the time of Domesday Book.[65] The palaeographical link established here between the copying of the feminised prayers and that of texts invoking Machutus and Dunstan adds weight to the hypothesis of a Winchester origin and the association with a mixed community of some kind. However, nothing more than a working hypothesis can be arrived at until more textual work is done. One can only note that the apparent idiosyncrasies of Galba's script may reflect not so much the incapacity of scribes, female or male, but the devotional purpose for which the book was intended.[66]

APPENDIX 13A

Scribal Stints in Nero A. ii, Fols. 3–13, and Galba A. xiv

This list is incomplete; some sections of the manuscript are too badly burned to allow their script to be described, and the discoloration of many leaves impedes close comparison of their script.[67] Scragg has identified the hand of seven scribes writing Old English, and Stokes' analysis concurs with this, although he has revised the stint attributed to the first of them, Scragg 484.[68]

---

[63] 'B', *Vita S. Dunstani*, chap. 1. 3, in *The Early Lives of St Dunstan*, ed. and trans. M. Winterbottom and M. Lapidge (Oxford, 2012), pp. 4–5.

[64] Meaning a house west of the Pennine line. Note that no nunneries are recorded in the extreme southwest of England before the twelfth century: K. Cooke, 'Donors and Daughters: Shaftesbury Abbey's Benefactors, Endowments and Nuns *c.* 1086–1130', *ANS* 12 (1989), 29–45, at 40; and Foot found no evidence to corroborate later suggestions that Bodmin and Exeter housed female religious before the Norman conquest: *Veiled Women*, vol. II, pp. 43, 85–6.

[65] Foot, *Veiled Women*, vol. II, pp. 257–8.

[66] I am indebted to David Dumville, Tim Graham, Michael Lapidge, Nicholas Orme and the editors for their advice and assistance on a number of points in the course of the preparation of this chapter.

[67] A full digital surrogate of Galba A. xiv is available at www.bl.uk/manuscripts/Viewer.aspx?ref=cotton_ms_galba_a_xiv_f500r. Nero A. ii is reported to be scheduled for digitisation.

[68] Scragg, *Conspectus*, nos. 484–91; and Stokes, *English Vernacular Minuscule*, p. 218.

Stint i: Galba 2rv, Correction on 54r12, Nero 3r–10r

Ker: hand 5

Large and crude open hybrid script (for Latin), apparently based on Caroline minuscule but with majuscule proportions and square aspect, and written in dark ink. Majuscule letters are used to abbreviate the names of the months; Uncial **m** (with closed first compartment) and capital **P** and **R** occur; Caroline **a** resembles the Uncial form, and round-backed **d** occurs. Rustic-capital forms of **A** and **G** are found. Insular **g** is also used. **y** is straight-limbed and sometimes dotted. Certain letters take distinctive forms. **B** appears to have been written as an **L** and the two compartments then added (one is [?] lower case), Rustic **G** has the curled-C form favoured by Insular scribes and **k** was written as an **h** with a hook on the right shoulder. The lower-left quadrant of **x** sometimes ends in a foot. The **st**-ligature has a broken form. The script on Galba 2r, now darkened and faded, is difficult to compare closely with that on 2v. Red rubrics appear at the top of 2r.

Stint ii: Galba 3r–4v, ?6r8–6r13, ?130v

Ker: Hand 3

Large, upright Caroline for Latin with Insular features: over-tall ascenders, **et**-ligature rather than ampersand, and Insular form of **g** and **h**. **st**-ligature sometimes has the broken form. **y** is straight limbed and dotted. **s** falls well below the baseline. **a** has a large bow, and the eye of **e** is narrow. **r** tends to run into neighbouring **a, e** and **i**.

Ker regarded the folios as the work of the same scribe. Compare also stint iv (cf. below).

6r8–6r13

These few lines are written in the same upright Caroline but modified for Old English by the addition of Æ, round-backed **d** and thorn.

Stint iii: Galba 4v–6r7

Ker: Hand 2; Scragg: Hand 485; Stokes: Scribe 2

Large, relatively confident, upright, laterally compressed Insular minuscule (for Old English) with rightward slant and tapering descenders. Letter forms include Caroline **a** and **h**, tall round **d**, straight-limbed dotted **y** and attenuated round **s** in ligatures.

Stint iv: Galba 6v, 74r (Compare 70r and Nero 13v)

Medium-sized Caroline, mostly with correct usages, except that the **et**-ligature is used in preference to ampersand and **f** and **s** tend to fall below the baseline. Insular **g** is found. Stint iv may be the (Latin) work of the scribe of stint iii (Old English).

Stint v: Galba 7r–36r

Monumental round Insular minuscule (for Latin) with Caroline features, apparently a late and adapted derivative of Phase-V Square minuscule. The letters are heavy and widely spaced. Feet are found on some minims. Usages include Insular **g** with a half-closed loop, tall round-backed **d**, horned **e** and sometimes **c**, Insular long **r** and **s**, Insular **et**-ligature but eleventh-century features – round **a**, well-spaced **ct**-ligature (e.g. 16v5 *factos*), straight-limbed dotted **i** – also occur, as do curiosities such as Caroline **h**, an **st**-ligature that falls below the baseline and occasional use of the ampersand. The presence of clearly Caroline features – the *ct*-ligature and Caroline as well as Insular **h** – suggests that the scribe was very consciously modifying his script. Note the suspension of *supra* with a double-looped open **a** (resembling a **w**) above the **p** (15v9, 16r9, 17r9). A second scribe, writing in Style IV Anglo-Caroline, was responsible for corrections.

Stint vi: Galba 36v–37r7

Technically correct but awkward Caroline minuscule (for Latin); the letters are widely and irregularly spaced, but the script leans to the right, sits on the baseline and employs no non-Caroline letter-forms. **a** and **e** are upright, the crossbar of **t** sometimes just pierced, and the top-right quadrant of the ampersand rises up and finishes in a thickening. The Rustic Capitals used for display script at the top of 36v include a backwards-leaning round **S**.

Stint vii: Galba 37r8–38v, 45r–49v, 62r12–62r16, 125r, Nero 10v–12v

Ker: Hand 4: after AD 984; Hand 1

Competently written Insular minuscule (for Latin and Old English) with distinctive slightly angular aspect, long ascenders and descenders and some wedging. This scribe employs a pinched round **a**, a flat-topped round **d** no higher than neighbouring minims (but occasionally the straight-backed form), horned **e**, 3-shaped Insular **g** with a looped descender, a backwards-leaning round **s** that begins at minim height and descends below the baseline (occupying the same space as a g) and looped Insular **et**- and **st**-ligatures together with ampersand and **e**-caudata. The loop of **t** curls inwards.

Stint viii: Galba 39r–v4; Compare 132v

Large, round, crude Caroline minuscule (for Latin). **f, r**, and **s** trail below the baseline, but otherwise the script conforms to correct usage. The **st**-ligature respects the baseline. **a** has a generous bowl and tends to be linked to preceding **r**; Caroline **g** was used, as was dotted, straight-limbed **y**. **e**-caudata and the widely spaced **ct**-ligature found here occur elsewhere in the manuscript, but a form of ampersand, with the short top-right quadrant ending in a downward tick, is confined to this hand.

Stint ix: Galba 39v5–45r, 144v–146r, 147v–149v, 152–154v

Ker: Hand 3

Outrageously large Anglo-Caroline hand (for Latin) equated by Ker with hand 3 (folios 39–45 only; see stint ii). The scribe took over from stint viii in the middle of a text. Apart from its size, it is most conspicuous for **h** that loops noticeably below the baseline. This scribe employed an **et**-ligature, not the ampersand, and Insular **f, g, r** and **s** tend to fall below the baseline and trail leftwards. **s** and **t** tend not to be ligatured together. **y** is straight limbed and dotted.

Stint x: Galba 50–57v; Compare 70r7–70v, 126v

Caroline (for Latin) with an admixture of Insular features (Insular **et**-ligature and occasional Insular **g**). The script is less round and monumental than many others in the volume. **a** has a small head, Caroline **g** lacks any waist and the ampersand is disjointed in its construction. **e**-caudata occurs. The **st**-ligature has the broken form. Minim letters, for example, **m**, tend to be difficult to distinguish from one another. This scribe collaborated with Ker's scribe hand 1, for example, ligature 70v3 *intellegendum*.

Stint xi: Galba 58r–62r

Small, uneven Insular minuscule for Latin, employing round **a**; both
Caroline **d** and a flat-topped Uncial-like round form; 3-shaped Insular
g; Insular **r** and **t** finishing in a turned-in foot; also an ampersand with
a distinctive bulbous eye; the **or**-ligature; descending round **s**. The old
Insular abbreviation for -*ur* is also found after **t** (58r6, []-dit²). This
hand resembles Ker's hand 1 (above, stint xii) in its proportions, in
the angular approach strokes, the use of backwards-leaning round **s**
and the employment of a thick nib but differs from it in the use of
ampersand.

Stint xii: Galba 62v–63v, 64v, 71r/v, 76r–102v, 104–117, 120r–124v, 125v–126r, 133v, 137v, 140v–141v

*Ker: Hand 1: after AD 1016; encompasses the stints attributed by Scragg
to his Scribe 484*

Very similar to stint vii in usages and clearly related, but the script is
more upright and laterally compressed; minim letters are ticked; **a, d, e**
and **u** are more generously rounded; the curled form of **t** is absent; the
et- and **st**-ligatures less bulbous and the suspension mark is a continuous line, not angled at both ends as in stint vii. Initial letters are
frequently filled in red.

Stint xiii: Galba 65r/v, 66r–70rb, 75r/v, ?103r/v

Large, rotund Caroline with relatively correct usages, apart from the
employment of the Insular **et**-ligature. The script sits on the baseline. **a**
is upright with a relatively large bow, the eye of **e** is small, the tail of **g**
ends in an upward tick and is sometimes separated from the top compartment by a short stroke (e.g. 66r7 *agnitionem* but not 66r9 *Ego*), tall **s** is
thickened at the shoulder, **y** is dotted and of the curly limbed variety and
the ampersand is rotund. This script resembles late Style IV Anglo-
Caroline.

The usages and forms of **a, s** and, to a lesser extent, **g**, found on 103r/v,
resemble those on 75r/v, but the duct and details of the letters indicate that
this is the work of a different scribe.

Stint xiv: Galba 72r

Insular minuscule written with a thick nib: tall ascenders and long descenders, round **a**, tall round **d, et**-nota, an angled **g** and the **st**-ligature.

Stint xv: Galba 72v

Caroline minuscule written with a thick nib. **g** has a short waist. **f** trails below the baseline. Very probably the scribe of stint xiv writing Caroline minuscule.

Stint xvi: Galba 118r–118v7

Insular minuscule for Old English of a sort unlike others in the volume, with round **a**, two-line **d**, horned **e**, 3-shaped **g** with a marked angle in the descender and Insular (**h**, straight-limbed dotted **y**, and 7 for *ond*). Open, high tall-e ligatures occur. The descenders of **g** and **y** are strongly angled. The script bears some resemblance to that of the annal for 1001 of the Parker Chronicle (CCCC 173, folios. 29v–30r).

Stint xvii: Galba 118v, 119r, 132r

This Insular minuscule hand (for Latin) resembles Ker's hand 1 (stints vii and xii), notably in its angled approach strokes to minims and the tops of ascenders and descenders, flattened round **d**, occasional backwards-leaning round **s** and the bulbous Square-minuscule **et**- and **st**-ligatures. However, the script is generally more crudely written, small-eyed Caroline **e** predominates over other forms, straight-limbed dotted **y** was used and majuscule letters were given more mannered treatment (**T** is flourished, **R** has heavily ticked feet). This could be a higher grade of the script seen in stint xii.

Stint xviii: Galba 119v9–19

Round and stubby Caroline with majuscule proportions that otherwise follows correct usage and has a cup-shaped suspension mark, rotund ampersand and slightly cleft ascenders. Post-Conquest, ? twelfth-century.

Stint xix: Galba 127r–128v

Flat-topped and laterally compressed Insular minuscule (for Latin) of old-fashioned, almost Celtic appearance displaying pointed and shaded aspect, for example, with **ti**-ligature (e.g. 127v10 *orationes* and 127v13 *pollutione*), wedged ascenders and minims, employing flat-topped round **d** not ascending above minim height, and 3-shaped Insular **g** but unhorned round **e** and round **a**.

Stint xx: Galba 129v

Caroline minuscule reminiscent of the Insular minuscule of stint xvi: compare the aspect and the form of **g**.

CHAPTER 14

Writing Latin and Old English in Tenth-Century England:
Patterns, Formulae and Language Choice in the Leases of Oswald of Worcester

Francesca Tinti

From the Worcester archive of Anglo-Saxon charters there survive over 100 episcopal leases dating to the period between the eighth and the mid-eleventh century. The great majority of them, that is, seventy-six in total, were issued by Oswald, who held the bishopric between 962 and 991. His was an exceptionally important episcopate in the history of the church of Worcester, and his leases have been studied by several generations of historians, who have been able to reconstruct, among other things, the composition of the cathedral episcopal *familia* at the time of the Benedictine reform and the nature of the tenurial arrangements established by the leases themselves, as well as the social networks that were at the basis of (and were in turn reinforced by) such grants.[1] This chapter, by contrast,

[1] The numerous publications that deal with this material include I. Atkins, 'The Church of Worcester from the Eighth to the Twelfth Century. Part II', *AntJ* 20 (1940), 1–38 and 203–28; P. Sawyer, 'Charters of the Reform Movement: The Worcester Archive', in *Tenth-Century Studies. Essays in Commemoration of the Millennium of the Council of Winchester and 'Regularis Concordia'*, ed. D. Parsons (London, 1975), pp. 84–93 and 228–30; D. A. Bullough, *Friends, Neighbours and Fellow-Drinkers: Aspects of Community and Conflict in the Early Medieval West*, H. M. Chadwick Memorial Lecture 1, University of Cambridge, Department of Anglo-Saxon, Norse, and Celtic (Cambridge, 1991 for 1990); J. Barrow, 'The Community of Worcester, 961–c. 1100', in *St Oswald of Worcester: Life and Influence*, ed. N. Brooks and C. Cubitt (London, 1996), pp. 84–99; V. King, 'St Oswald's Tenants', *ibid.*, pp. 100–16; A. Wareham, 'St Oswald's Family and Kin', *ibid.*, pp. 46–63; S. Baxter, 'Archbishop Wulfstan and the Administration of God's Property', in *Wulfstan, Archbishop of York: The Proceedings of the Second Alcuin Conference*, ed. M. Townend (Turnhout, 2004), pp. 161–205; F. Tinti, 'The "Costs" of Pastoral Care: Church Dues in Late Anglo-Saxon England', in *Pastoral Care in Late Anglo-Saxon England*, ed. F. Tinti (Woodbridge, 2005), pp. 27–5; and F. Tinti, *Sustaining Belief: The Church of Worcester from c. 870 to c. 1100* (Farnham, 2010), pp. 25–38 and 75–150. I wish to thank Robert Gallagher, Jinty Nelson, Edward Roberts, Kate Wiles and this volume's editors for reading drafts of this chapter and providing valuable advice. Earlier versions were presented in 2015 at the Leeds International Medieval Congress and at the British Academy Anglo-Saxon Charters Symposium. I am grateful to participants in both events for useful

will look more closely at the language(s), the formulation and the diplomatic patterns that characterize these charters, features that have so far
failed to attract much attention among historians.[2]

Although leases had been in use at Worcester long before Oswald's
accession and continued to be produced after his death, those issued during
his episcopate represent a remarkably coherent group of charters. Their
exceptionally high number and distribution throughout Oswald's pontificate allow for close examination of the documentary practices of a cathedral scriptorium that seems to have made special efforts to provide regular
written reinforcement for the bishop's grants of small estates (ranging
between one and six hides) on a fixed-term basis, normally covering the
life of the beneficiary and that of two heirs. It should be remembered,
however, that the great majority of the surviving leases from Oswald's
episcopate have come down to us thanks to their having been copied en
bloc in the early eleventh century, that is, just a few decades after their
issue, in the earliest extant English cartulary, known as *Liber Wigorniensis*.[3]
In other words, one should not exclude the possibility that the presence of
such a high number of leases within the Worcester archive may be due to

discussion. In December 2015, I was also able to present some aspects of this research to this
volume's honorand when he came to give a lecture on Anglo-Saxon charters at the University of the
Basque Country without him knowing that the outcome of this work would be published in a
Festschrift in his honour. For his comments then, and for all that he has generously taught me
along the years about charters and Anglo-Saxon England, I am profoundly grateful. This chapter is
part of the activities conducted within the research projects HAR2013-44576-P and HAR2014-
51484-ERC funded by the Spanish Ministerio de Economia y Competitividad. For further
information on our work on the languages of early medieval charters, see our website at
www.ehu.eus/lemc.
[2] The linguist Herbert Schendl has written on the significance of these texts for providing some of the
earliest evidence of code switching in the history of the English language: H. Schendl, 'Beyond
Boundaries: Code-Switching in the Leases of Oswald Worcester', in *Code-Switching in Early English*,
ed. H. Schendl and L. Wright (Berlin, 2011), pp. 47–94.
[3] This is London, BL, Cotton Tiberius A. xiii, fols. 1–118, recently made available in digitized form at
www.bl.uk/manuscripts/FullDisplay.aspx?ref=Cotton_MS_Tiberius_A_XIII (accessed 15 January
2016). The leases can be found on fols. 57–101 and 111–18. For a tabular representation of the original
foliation of this section of the cartulary, see Tinti, *Sustaining Belief*, p. 112. For fundamental work on
the manuscript, which contains both *Liber Wigorniensis* and Hemming's Cartulary, see N. R. Ker,
'Hemming's Cartulary: A Description of the Two Worcester Cartularies in Cotton Tiberius A. xiii',
in *Studies in Medieval History Presented to F. M. Powicke*, ed. R. W. Hunt, W. A. Pantin and R. W.
Southern (Oxford, 1948), pp. 49–75, reprinted with additions in his *Books, Collectors and Libraries:
Studies in the Medieval Heritage* (London, 1985), pp. 31–59; and Baxter, 'Archbishop Wulfstan and the
Administration of God's Property'. Only two leases of Oswald survive as single sheets: S 1326
(London, BL, Additional Charter 19792) and S 1347 (London, BL, Additional Charter 19794), of
which the former was also copied into *Liber Wigorniensis*. The text of another lease (S 1315 (BCS
1204)) has been preserved thanks to the transcription that Humfrey Wanley made of the twenty-four
now lost charters that belonged *c.* 1700 to Lord Somers: see S. Keynes, 'Anglo-Saxon Charters: Lost
and Found', in *Myth, Rulership, Church and Charters: Essays in Honour of Nicholas Brooks*, ed. J.
Barrow and A. Wareham (Aldershot, 2008), pp. 58–9.

the special circumstances of their survival rather than to an exceptional production rate.[4] What is relevant for present purposes, however, is that this coherent and unusually large body of documents provides further evidence for the importance of the written word in tenth-century England.[5]

As will become apparent later, episcopal leases were modelled on royal diplomas, but when compared with royal charters, they often appear to record transactions involving individuals of lower social extraction.[6] Although their issuing agency was obviously an ecclesiastical one, many of the leases' extrinsic and intrinsic features point towards a documentary culture within which laypeople also played a role. The leases that survive as single sheets clearly indicate that the extant parchment is just one of the two portions of a chirograph, that is, a document that was issued in duplicate on a single piece of parchment that was then cut in two so that

---

[4] The preservation of such a high number of episcopal leases from Worcester can be contrasted with the lack of comparable material from York, the archiepiscopal see that Oswald held in plurality with Worcester from 971 until his death in 992. The only surviving evidence for Oswald's concerns with estate management at York is provided by an Old English memorandum about lands that had been lost and others that had been gained by Archbishop Oscytel, Oswald's immediate predecessor (S 1453 (*North* 6)). Given the extreme dearth of surviving Anglo-Saxon documents from northern England, it is very likely that more documents were produced in Oswald's time at his northern see, where, however, they had fewer chances to survive than those issued at Worcester. I am grateful to David Woodman for this observation. For further discussion of leasehold creation at Worcester and the possible impact of Oswald's episcopate on the employment of written documents to record fixed-term transactions, see Tinti, *Sustaining Belief*, pp. 151–5. Leases also survive from other Anglo-Saxon archives but in much smaller numbers, and while they certainly prove that several other ecclesiastical institutions leased out small estates to prominent individuals for a limited length of time, they do not give any indication that such transactions were as frequently recorded in writing as they were at Worcester in Oswald's time. It may be noted for comparative purposes that ten such leases, dating to the period between the mid-ninth and the mid-eleventh century, have survived within the archive of the Old Minster at Winchester (S 1274, S 1275, S 1285, S 1287, S 1444, S 693b, S 1391, S 1403, S 1476 and S 1402), whereas the otherwise exceptionally rich archive of Christ Church Canterbury has preserved just one episcopal lease, issued by Archbishop Plegmund in the early tenth century (S 1288 (*CantCC* 102)).

[5] Literacy and the uses of the written word in the early Middle Ages have attracted a great deal of attention in recent decades. From among the most important publications dealing specifically with the Anglo-Saxon documentary practice, see S. Kelly, 'Anglo-Saxon Lay Society and the Written Word', in *The Uses of Literacy in Early Medieval Europe*, ed. R. McKitterick (Cambridge, 1990), pp. 36–62; S. Keynes, 'Royal Government and the Written Word in Late Anglo-Saxon England', *ibid.*, pp. 226–57; K. A. Lowe, 'Lay Literacy in Anglo-Saxon England and the Development of the Chirograph', in *Anglo-Saxon Manuscripts and Their Heritage*, ed. P. Pulsiano and E. M. Treharne (Aldershot, 1998), pp. 161–204; and C. Insley, 'Archives and Lay Documentary Practice in the Anglo-Saxon World', in *Documentary Culture and the Laity in the Early Middle Ages*, ed. W. Brown, M. Costambeys, M. Innes and A. Kosto (Cambridge, 2012), pp. 336–62.

[6] For example, S 1344 and S 1365 were issued in favour of Wulfhelm and Æthelmær, respectively, both described as the bishop's *artifex* (craftsman). Vanessa King has suggested that they may have played an important role in the construction of the new cathedral church of St Mary: King, 'St Oswald's Tenants', p. 107.

the grantor and the beneficiary could obtain identical copies of the record.[7] The system thus ensured that all beneficiaries would be given a written record of the transaction, a document that demonstrated their title to the estate and that would later be passed on to his or her heirs together with the land. Kathryn Lowe has suggested that the chirograph acquired 'currency because of the increasing interest of the layman in the written document, and not merely because of the growth of bureaucracy in the Church'.[8] Lay interest in written documents would also be enhanced by another major feature of the Worcester episcopal leases, one that marks their departure from the royal diplomas on which they are at least partly modelled. I am referring to their frequent employment of the Old English language alongside the Latin, which extended well beyond the inclusion of a vernacular boundary clause, which was a customary feature of royal diplomas throughout the tenth century.[9] This remarkable body of material thus casts further light on the written bilingualism of Anglo-Saxon England, a field that has recently attracted a great deal of attention but that has so far failed to take on board the evidence provided by documentary production.[10]

Language Choice

Old English had made its appearance in the Worcester episcopal leases long before Oswald's appointment, but it only began to be employed beyond simple boundary descriptions during the episcopate of Wærferth, which lasted from 872/3 to an uncertain date between 907 and 915.[11] From Wærferth's time there survive seven reliable leases.[12] Of these, four have the main body of the text entirely in Latin, two are in Old English and a last one, S 1280, provides several instances of code switching between the two languages within the main body of the text. In other words, Wærferth's leases would seem to anticipate

---

[7] Surviving episcopal leases preserve, either in their top or bottom section, the lower or upper portion of the letters composing the word 'CYROGRAVVM', which had been written on the parchment between the two copies of the same text before the sheet was cut along the word itself. See Figure 14.1.

[8] Lowe, 'Lay Literacy in Anglo-Saxon England', p. 176.

[9] K. A. Lowe, 'The Development of the Anglo-Saxon Boundary Clause', *Nomina* 21 (1998), 63–100.

[10] One of the main recent publications on the multilingualism of pre-Conquest England is *Conceptualizing Multilingualism in England, c. 800–c. 1250*, ed. E. M. Tyler (Turnhout, 2011), in which, however, Anglo-Saxon charters are not considered.

[11] It must be noted, however, that other types of records preserved within the Worcester archive and presumably also written there, such as S 1432 (a memorandum concerning land at Inkberrow) and S 1437 (a record of a dispute settlement), were already produced entirely in Old English in the 820s.

[12] S 1278, S 1415, S 1416, S 1279, S 1280, S 1281 and S 1283. A further lease of the year 907 (S 1282) is likely to be a forgery and has not been considered here.

the various linguistic combinations that can also be seen in the much more numerous documents surviving from Oswald's time.[13] There are, however, also important differences. Of seventy-six leases issued by Oswald, seventeen are entirely in Latin, sixteen have the main text in Latin but also incorporate a boundary description in Old English, five are entirely in Old English, while in as many as thirty-eight documents (i.e. exactly 50 per cent of the surviving ones) both the Latin and the vernacular appear in a variety of combinations in the main text of the charter. In other words, Oswald's leases make much wider use of code switching.[14] They also demonstrate that by the second half of the tenth century the Worcester documentary production comfortably relied on two languages and that, consequently, language choice was an integral part of the drafting of every lease.

Although from these general observations one might deduce that the role of the two languages was roughly interchangeable, it is clear that it was far more common for specific component sections of the documents to be written in one rather than the other language. All the leases, irrespective of the language used, comprise diplomatic sections derived from royal diplomas. Though it should be stressed that not all leases include all such sections, it is possible to identify across the corpus the following components: verbal invocation, proem, date, dispositive section, request for ecclesiastical and/or secular dues and service, Old English summary, sanction, boundary clause and, of course, witness-list.[15]

Table 14.1 shows that it was much more common for the dispositive section to be written in Latin, as only twelve of seventy-six leases (i.e. *c.* 15 per cent) have such a section in Old English.[16] These twelve vernacular, or mostly vernacular, leases were issued between 962 and 991; in other words, they are distributed across the entire pontificate of Oswald. Their

[13] Three records of dispute settlements (S 1441, S 1442 and S 1446) and a number of charters of the Mercian and West Saxon leaders that are likely to have originated in the Worcester scriptorium also date from Wærferth's time. For the period between the end of Wærferth's episcopate and the beginning of that of Oswald, there survive only two episcopal leases issued, respectively, by Wilfrith and Cenwald. The former (S 1289) is almost entirely in English, and the latter (S 1290) is in Latin. For a detailed treatment of language choice in all these charters, see R. Gallagher and F. Tinti, 'Latin, Old English and Documentary Practice at Worcester from Wærferth to Oswald', forthcoming.

[14] See further Gallagher and Tinti, 'Latin, Old English and Documentary Practice'. Cf. Schendl, 'Beyond Boundaries', pp. 56, 60.

[15] The analysis that follows, however, will only take into account the linguistic features of the main text of the leases, leaving aside, because of space constraints, the treatment of the names of the cathedral community's members and their clerical grades in the witness-lists.

[16] These are S 1299, S 1305, S 1309, S 1326, S 1332, S 1372, S 1373, S 1374, S 1369, S 1362, S 1363 and S 1366. The chronological ordering of Oswald's leases in the footnotes and in Table 14.2 is based on S. Keynes, *An Atlas of Attestations in Anglo-Saxon Charters, c. 670–1066*, ASNC Guides, Texts and Studies (Cambridge, 2002), table LXXVI.

Table 14.1 *Language Use in the Main Component Sections*
of Oswald's Leases

Diplomatic sections	Latin	Old English	Latin and Old English
Verbal invocation	12	3	
Proem	12		
Date	58	5	7
Dispositive section	61	12	3
Request for church-scot and/or three common dues	29	8	
Old English summary		17	
Sanction	5	18	1
Boundary clause		39	

beneficiaries cover all the different categories of people to whom Oswald leased out land: mostly laymen, described as the bishop's *minister, cniht* (i.e. personal retainer) or simply 'man', but also one woman as well as members of the cathedral community. The latter included a *preost* named Goding, who, according to Hemming in his cartulary of a century later, had written many books for the community.[17] This would seem to exclude the possibility that Old English was used just for leases issued in favour of people who were not capable of understanding or reading Latin, thus providing further evidence for the role and potential of the vernacular in late Anglo-Saxon England, which, as several scholars have recently maintained, should not be considered as just a poor substitute for Latin employed to assist the *illiterati*.[18]

The Worcester leases also show that when it is possible to identify the same person as the beneficiary of several such documents, these follow different models, make use of either language and employ code switching in varied ways.[19] In other words, language choice does not seem to have

[17] The three leases in favour of members of the cathedral clergy are S 1372, S 1374 and S 1369. On Hemming's treatment of Goding, beneficiary of S 1369, see Tinti, *Sustaining Belief*, p. 34.

[18] Among the growing body of publications in this area, see most recently H. Gittos, 'The Audience of Old English Texts: Ælfric, Rhetoric and "the Edification of the Simple"', *ASE* 43 (2014), 231–66; and R. Stephenson, *The Politics of Language: Byrhtferth, Ælfric, and the Multilingual Identity of the Benedictine Reform* (Toronto, 2015).

[19] For example, this is the case for the leases issued in favour of a thegn named Eadric (S 1310, S 1334, S 1350, S 1358 and S 1366) as well as those for Wulfgar, a member of the cathedral community (S 1327, S 1372, S 1342 and S 1352). By checking the position of these charters further in Table 14.2, it is possible to appreciate their diversified typology. On Eadric and Wulfgar, see King, 'St Oswald's Tenants', pp. 105, 111. On the apparent lack of a relation between language choice and the status of the beneficiaries, see also Schendl, 'Beyond Boundaries', pp. 82–5.

been determined simply by the beneficiaries' linguistic skills or prefer-ences.[20] Other factors need to be taken into account: for example, the circumstances of the production of each lease, including the scribes' linguistic abilities, as well as the various models that would have been available in the course of Oswald's pontificate. In this respect, one has to bear in mind that the survival of only two original single sheets limits the possibilities of this analysis, as it does not allow one to connect individual scribes with specific linguistic preferences. For instance, for the first couple of years after Oswald's election to the Worcester see, there survive eleven leases dated 962 or 963[21] that display varied features and make use of different combinations of the two languages, but it is not possible to establish whether this variety is due to the contemporaneous activity of several different scribes or whether different languages and formulations were adopted by the same scribes because of the specific circumstances in which they were operating.

Patterns and Component Sections

By analyzing the structure of the documents, the ways in which the various component parts are combined and the formulation used in each of them, I have noted a trend to employ distinct models; these share the same wording in the opening sections of the leases and, more specifically, until the end of the passage stating that the estate leased must go back to Worcester after three generations of beneficiaries. After this point the scribes decided in each case what to do with the other sections: which ones to include and what formulation to employ. Taking the initial and main diplomatic sections of the leases as my guiding principle, I have been

---

[20] This appears to contrast with what has been suggested regarding the employment of the vernacular in a notable number of ninth-century charters from Christ Church Canterbury associated with laypeople. Old English would have been 'chosen for these documents specifically as the language that lay nobles and noblewomen might read, or to which they might listen': *Charters of Christ Church Canterbury*, Part 1, ed. N. P. Brooks and S. E. Kelly, AS Charters 17 (Oxford, 2013), pp. 126–30. See also N. Brooks, 'Latin and Old English in Ninth-Century Canterbury', in *Spoken and Written Language: Relations between Latin and the Vernacular Languages in the Earlier Middle Ages*, ed. M. Garrison, A. P. Orbán and M. Mostert (Turnhout, 2013), pp. 113–32. In both publications a case is also made for Old English being specifically chosen when women were involved in the transaction, a hypothesis that cannot be tested in the Worcester case because of a lack of sufficient evidence concerning women. However, it can be noted that the only lease that Oswald issued in favour of a woman (S 1309) was written in the vernacular.

[21] S 1298, S 1300, S 1302, S 1299, S 1301, S 1307, S 1297, S 1303, S 1304, S 1305 and S 1306. It is important to stress that these early leases of Oswald do not share significant features of their formulation with the earlier Worcester leases and that in this respect they represent a 'fresh start'.

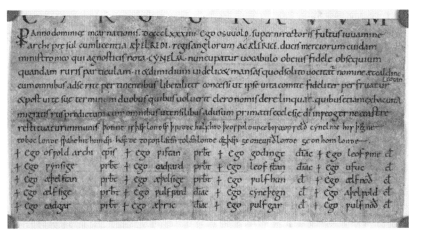

Figure 14.1 Face of S 1347. (London, BL, Additional Charter 19794; Image reproduced with the kind permission of the British Library and the Anglo-Saxon Charters
Project.)

able to identify distinct typologies of charters, which are represented in
chronological order in Table 14.2.[22]

The largest cluster, which I have called Group B, comprises sixteen
leases whose dispositive section is in Latin. They were issued between 962
and the mid-980s. They include the one lease of Oswald that survives in
single-sheet format, S 1347 (Figure 14.1).[23] Like all the other charters in this
group, it starts with the date (in this case 984), mentions the permission
obtained from the king and the ealdorman of the Mercians[24] and names
the beneficiary and the extent of the land leased, as well as the place where it
is located. As is often the case in Anglo-Saxon charters, the place-name
Caldinccotan is preceded by the preposition *æt*, although the syntactical Latin

<hr />

[22] It was only after finishing a first draft of this chapter that I discovered that Professor Simon Keynes
had already proposed in tabular form a typological classification of Oswald's leases in Keynes, *Atlas
of Attestations*, table LXXVII (3): Worcester leases, by type. Although our systems of classification
differ in aspects which depend on the features of the documents that have been given more
prominence in one or the other analysis, the main results broadly coincide. A similar exercise has
also been carries out by Schendl, though he only briefly refers to the two main typologies that he has
identified: 'Beyond Boundaries', pp. 85–6.

[23] London, BL, Additional Charter 19794.

[24] '[C]um licentia Æþelredi regis Anglorum ac Ælfrice ducis Merciorum.'

Table 14.2 *A Classification of Oswald's Leases Based on Their Formulation*

Leases with Latin dispositive clause	
Group A: Three leases, S 1300, S 1301, S 1311 (AD 962–6)	Mention permission obtained from king and ealdorman of the Mercians Share several features with leases in larger Group E, including dispositive verb *largitus sum*
Group B: Sixteen leases, S 1302, S 1323, S 1319, S 1325, S 1322, S 1327, S 1321, S 1333, S 1330, S 1335, S 1331, S 1336, S 1334, S 1347, S 1350, S1361 (AD 962–mid-980s)	Start with date Mention permission obtained from king and ealdorman of the Mercians Dispositive verb is *concessi* The land must be returned to the church of Worcester *ad usum primatis* Have several elements in common with the Group A charters
Group C: Two leases S 1298 and S 1313 (AD 962 and 967)	Share initial formulation until the dispositive verb *perpetualiter concedo*
Group D: Three leases S 1307, S 1310, S 1314 (AD 963–7)	Open with *Allubescente ac consentiente Eadgaro* … or a variation of that (*albuscente, albescente*) They all contain the Old English summary Dispositive verb is *æternaliter concessi* Date is at the end of the main text
Group E: Eleven leases S 1303, S 1304, S 1306, S 1312, S 1317, S 1320, S 1329, S 1337, S 1338, S 1339, S 1342 (AD 963–80)	Refer to permission obtained by the bishop from the community at Worcester, as well as the king and ealdorman of Mercians Dispositive verb is *largitus sum*
Group F: Two leases S 1315, S 1355 (AD 967 and 988)	Share exactly the same wording and deal with the same land The earlier one is in favour of Oswald's brother and the later one is in favour of the latter's son, that is, Oswald's nephew
Group G: Four leases S 1316, S 1318, S 1324, S 1352 (AD 967–85)	Start with date Mention only the consent of the Worcester *familia* for 'terram aliquam iuris nostri' Church-scot is requested in all cases Dispositive verb is *concedo* Restitution clause is as in Group E
Group H: Four leases S 1340, S 1346, S 1358, S 1360 (AD 979–89)	The Latin language is more elaborate Contain either a verbal invocation or a proem, which can be fairly long, as in S 1358 Dispositive verb is *libenti concedo animo* Mention permission of the Worcester *familia* Entirely in Latin, except boundaries

Table 14.2 (*cont.*)

Leases with Latin dispositive clause

Group I: Two leases S 1349, S 1356 (AD 984 and 988)	One has a verbal invocation; the other has a proem Both sees of Oswald (Worcester and York) are mentioned No mention of the king Dispositive verb is *largior* Entirely in Latin with the exception of boundaries and a few words on appurtenances in S 1356
Group J: Two leases S 1351, S 1365 (AD 985 and 991)	Verbal invocation is 'regnante in perpetuum domino nostro Ihesu Christo per uniuersa quadriflui orbis climata' Dispositive verb is *trado* Entirely in Latin with the exception of bounds
Group K: Two leases S 1353, S 1357 (AD 987 and 988)	Share initial formulation up until the verb *praebeo*
Group L: Two leases S 1354, S 1364 (AD 987 and 991)	Entirely in Latin except for the translation of *tributum ecclesiasticum* as *ciric-sceat* provided in S 1354 No mention of the king, but permission of the community Dispositive verb is *tradendo concedo*
Group M (miscellaneous): Eleven leases S 1297, S 1370, S 1328, S 1341, S 1343, S 1344, S 1345, S 1348, S 1367, S 1359, S 1308 (Apart from first three, they all date from AD 980 onwards)	Make more frequent use of elaborate proems than earlier leases Most of them are entirely Latin

Leases with Old English dispositive clause

S 1299, S 1309, S 1326, S 1332, S 1372, S 1373, S 1374, S 1369 (AD 962–980s)	Refer to permission obtained from the king, the ealdorman of the Mercians and the Worcester community Dispositive verb is *forgeaf* Seven of eight leases state that the land has to go back to Worcester for the use of the bishop
S 1305 (AD 963)	Text has the same meaning as those in previous group but different wording Dispositive verb is *geuþe*
S 1362, 1363, 1366 (AD early 990s)	Contain a verbal invocation that was not in earlier vernacular leases of Oswald The dispositive verb is *geboci(g)e* Neither the king nor the ealdorman of Mercia is mentioned Explicit clause of restitution is absent

construction would not require a preposition here.[25] The formulation common to all the sixteen leases that make use of this same model includes the dispositive verb *concessi*. The final words of the main section specify that the land must be restored to the church of Worcester *ad usum primatis*, that is, for the use of the bishop.

Group B can be contrasted with the second largest cluster of Oswald's leases (Group E), which make use of a separate set of distinct formulae. The eleven leases in Group E, which were issued between 963 and 980, that is, roughly over the same period when the formulation of Group B was also being employed, refer explicitly to the permission obtained by the bishop from the community of Worcester, as well as that of the king and the ealdorman of the Mercians (see Table 14.2). The dispositive verb for this group is always *largitus sum*, and the clause requiring the land to go back to the church of Worcester does not contain any specification about its use or allocation. In terms of content, the main difference that can be observed between leases in Groups B and E is the much more prominent place given to the cathedral community in the latter group. By contrast, as we have seen, in Group B, the bishop did not need to obtain permission from the cathedral clergy to lease out the estate, and more importantly, the land leased had to be returned to the church of Worcester after three generations of beneficiaries *ad usum primatis*. By comparing the location of all the estates dealt with in the charters in Group B with the evidence provided by Domesday Book and Hemming's Cartulary, I have been able to establish that none of those lands had become part of the monastic chapter's estate by 1066 or 1086.[26] It would seem, therefore, that the reservation of these estates for the use of the bishop reflected an awareness of their being set apart from the rest of the cathedral's estate. Conversely, Group E includes leases dealing with land that by the time of Domesday Book had been allocated to the monastic community. In this case, the evidence is less straightforward than it is for the leases in the other group, in that only some of the charters in Group E

---

[25] See Schendl, 'Beyond Boundaries', p. 78; and J. Bately, 'The Place Which Is Called 'at X': A New Look at Old Evidence', *Leeds Studies in English*, n. s. 37 (2006), 343–63. It can also be noted that the place-name was added afterwards, when the space that had been left blank for it proved to be too small.

[26] For a more detailed discussion, see Tinti, *Sustaining Belief*, pp. 35–8 and 214–22. It should be noted that the phrase *ad usum primatis* (or its Old English version) also appears in leases belonging to other groups. In other words, not all the estates reserved for the use of the bishop were leased out through charters making use of the formulation typical of Group B.

can be demonstrated to deal with estates that were later said to belong *ad uictum monachorum*.[27]

The separation of the cathedral chapter's estate from that of the bishop was a process that took place at all English cathedrals in the central Middle Ages and that is often referred to as the division of the *mensa*.[28] The second half of the tenth century was a crucial period for the start of that process at Worcester because of the growth of the community at the time of Oswald's monastic reform and the measures that were taken to ensure its sustenance. Changes and adjustments to the monastic estate took place throughout the late Anglo-Saxon period and were still occurring after 1066.[29] This process, which was still in its initial phases in Oswald's time, would seem to have played some role in the formulations used in these leases. The choice between the two most popular sets of formulae for the production of episcopal leases at Worcester between the 960s and the early to mid-980s appears to have been at least partly determined by the need to distinguish lands that were assigned to the use of the bishop from the rest of the estate. The fact that Oswald never had to ask for permission from the Worcester community to lease out the land in any of the sixteen leases of Group B would seem to carry some significance. These two major groups therefore seem to suggest that different models were used by scribes depending on the on-going process of assignment of the Worcester estates either to the bishop or to the cathedral community.

Over the same period in which the formulations typical of Groups B and E were used, the Worcester scribes produced other leases that display different patterns and that are also listed in Table 14.2. Groups A, C, D, and F–M comprise between two and four leases each. Like the charters in Groups B and E, they employ a Latin dispositive clause and

---

[27] Such a correspondence can be established, for instance, for S 1312, S 1337 and S 1342. S 1312 deals with Itchington in Tytherington (Gloucs.), which was part of the estate centred on Westbury-on-Trym, said by Hemming to have been assigned to the monks by St Wulfstan: *Hemingi chartularium ecclesiæ Wigorniensis*, ed. T. Hearne (Oxford, 1723), pp. 407–8; S 1337 concerns land at Blackwell in Tredington (Worcs.), about which see Tinti, *Sustaining Belief*, p. 19; and S 1342 is a lease of land at Waresley in Hartlebury (Worcs.), also assigned to the monastic community in the eleventh century (*ibid.* pp. 193–4).

[28] E. U. Crosby, *Bishop and Chapter in Twelfth-Century England: A Study of the Mensa Episcopalis* (Cambridge, 1994); and V. King, 'Share and Share Alike? Bishops and Their Cathedral Chapters: The Domesday Evidence', *ANS* 28 (2006), 138–52. For the earlier development of similar arrangements across the Channel, see the classic treatment in E. Lesne, *L'origine des menses dans le temporal des églises et des monastères de France au IXe siècle* (Lille, 1910).

[29] This is for instance the case for Alveston in Gloucestershire, about which see Tinti, *Sustaining Belief*, pp. 201–3. For further discussion of this topic see also *ibid.* pp. 214–24.

sometimes share some features with the formulations typical of the two main groups, as is the case with the leases in Groups A and G, which reproduce some of the wording of the Group E leases. One of the main features that these groupings demonstrate is that, as was to be expected, things changed over time. As mentioned earlier, the two main typologies stopped being used in the early to mid-980s, and, with very few exceptions, it is only in the later leases that we can see more varied formulations as well as a more confident employment of verbal invocations and proems.

The Leases' Latin and Their Relations with Royal Diplomas

The typologies identified among the leases containing a Latin dispositive clause give a clear idea of the formulaic nature of the language employed. It can also be demonstrated that the scribes responsible for the drafting of the charters in the early years of Oswald's pontificate adapted models that were also being used by the draftsmen of royal charters. For instance, the charters in Group B share some distinct formulation with royal diplomas of the 'Edgar A' type.[30] This is particularly evident in the clause detailing what was to happen to the leased estate after the death of the first beneficiary. The Worcester scribes responsible for the Group B leases adapted the 'Edgar A' formulation, which ensured undisputed succession to the land granted through the diploma to specify that succession was limited to two heirs after the first beneficiary's death. The connection between the formulae used can be seen by comparing, for instance, a single-sheet royal diploma from Westminster, written by 'Edgar A' and dated 962, with the above-mentioned S 1347.[31] The former reads

---

[30] Elements of the 'Edgar A' formulation can be found in two royal diplomas preserved within the Worcester archive: S 772 and 773, about which see S. Keynes, *The Diplomas of King Æthelred 'the Unready', 978–1016: A Study in their Use as Historical Evidence* (Cambridge, 1980), pp. 76–9. They are both dated 969 and by being later than the earliest leases in Group B cannot represent a direct source of inspiration for the drafting of the leases in this group. On the production of 'Edgar A', see also S. Keynes, 'A Conspectus of the Charters of King Edgar, 957–75', in *Edgar, King of the English, 959–975: New Interpretations*, ed. D. Scragg (Woodbridge, 2008), pp. 60–80. On these royal diplomas' formulation, see B. Snook, *The Anglo-Saxon Chancery: The History, Language and Production of Anglo-Saxon Charters from Alfred to Edgar* (Woodbridge, 2015), pp. 159–88. On 'Edgar A' and his possible association with Abingdon, see *Charters of Abingdon Abbey, Part 1*, ed. S. E. Kelly, AS Charters vii (Oxford, 2000), pp. cxv–cxxxi.

[31] The Westminster single sheet (S 702 (BCS 1085)) survives as London, Westminster Abbey, W. A. M. X. In quotations from Old English and Latin texts, I have tried to use as much as possible the original letter-forms, thus reintroducing, for instance, the manuscripts' original *u* for older editions' (such as BCS) *v* and *p* for *w*.

> *ut ipsa uita comite cum omnibus utensilibus*, pratis uidelicet, pascuis, siluis, uoti compos habeat *et post uite sue terminum quibus*cumque *uoluerit cleronomis inmunem derelinquat*;

while the latter, like all the other leases in Group B, has

> *ut ipse uita comite* fideliter perfruatur *et post uitę suę terminum* duobus *quibus uoluerit cleronomis derelinquat*, quibus etiam ex hac uita migratis rus predictum *cum omnibus utensilibus* ad usum primatis ecclesię Dei in Þeogerneceastre restituatur *immunis* [emphasis mine].

Moreover, all the leases in Group B that contain a Latin sentence to introduce a vernacular boundary clause make use of the formula also employed for the same purpose in the 'Edgar A' diplomas ('His metis prefatum rus hinc inde giratur').[32] Another early lease, S 1298 (dated AD 962), belonging to Group C (see Table 14.2), contains a Latin sanction that is the same as that found in contemporary 'Edgar A' charters.[33] By contrast, leases in other groups appear to make use of wording derived from 'Dunstan B' formulation. That is the case, for instance, for the unusual poetic verb *allubescere* (or variations of it such as *albescere, albuscere*, etc.) appearing in the leases of Groups D and H to refer to the king and his permission to lease out the estate (e.g. S 1314: 'allubescente ac consentiente Eadgaro basileo').[34]

This direct dependence on wording and formulae derived from con-temporary royal diplomas is typical of Oswald's early Latin leases. At this stage, scribes seem to have chosen to adhere to established models, espe-cially in the case of leases in Groups B and E; moreover, as mentioned earlier, formulation was rather straightforward and meant to provide just the main information about the land transactions, with verbal invocations being very rarely employed before the year 980.[35] In the remaining years of Oswald's episcopate, by contrast, Latin invocations and proems became more common.[36] Some of these proems contain biblical citations and display some stylistic ambitions in their use of occasional alliteration and

---

[32] This is the case for S 1321, S 1322, S 1323, S 1325, S 1327 and S 1333. The same sentence is also employed in S 1297, belonging to the miscellaneous Group M.
[33] Cf. S 690 (*Abing* 87). See also Snook, *The Anglo-Saxon Chancery*, pp. 173–4.   [34] *Ibid.*, p. 144.
[35] Out of forty-seven leases issued before the year 980, only two (S 1297 and S 1340) make use of a verbal invocation, and just one (S 1370) contains a proem.
[36] As well as in S 1370, a Latin proem can be found in S 1341, S 1343, S 1344, S 1345, S 1361, S 1353, S 1356, S 1357, S 1358, S 1359 and S 1308.

Aldhelmian vocabulary.[37] Moreover, what used to be a rather slavish adherence to established models became a more active and independent elaborative process, to the effect that eight leases issued from 980 onwards, included in Group M (miscellaneous), contain unique features that do not appear in any other surviving leases.[38] In sum, it can be maintained that the scribes of Oswald's leases were certainly competent Latin writers, though not particularly original. With the passing of time, the leases' use of Latin became slightly more elaborate, and although they cannot be said to rival the much more ambitious royal diplomas issued in the course of the tenth century, they certainly share several interesting features with them. It is tempting to see in these later developments the result of the monastic reform that Oswald promoted at Worcester. Although this cathedral church, unlike Winchester, did not produce any famous or representative writer, the educational programme that characterized the reform is likely to have contributed to the development of better standards of Latin learning and writing at Worcester too. Oswald himself, before being sent by his uncle – Archbishop Oda of Canterbury – to spend a few years at the pre-eminent Benedictine monastery of Fleury, was taught by the West Frankish scholar Frithegod, the foremost exponent of the so-called Anglo-Latin hermeneutic style, while he was staying in England at the household of Oda. As suggested by Michael Lapidge, the fruits of Frithegod's teaching can probably be seen in the Greek-based words and neologisms contained in the attestations of a couple of charters that are likely to have been drafted by Oswald.[39]

---

[37] See, for instance, S 1345 and S 1356, whose proem quotes Ps 113, and S 1308, which contains the sentence 'Date et dabitur uobis' from Lk 6, 38. S 1308 also makes use of several typically Aldhelmian words such as *panton, conditor, propatulus* and *paradigma*. Another interesting subgroup of leases is that comprising S 1341, S 1361 and S 1358, which share the same proem. This is relatively long, employs various polysyllabic words and such Aldhelmian phrases as *litterarum apicibus*, which by this time had become fairly customary in charters' formulation. See Snook, *The Anglo-Saxon Chancery*, p. 37.

[38] Before 980, there survive only three leases that belong to Group M, that is, unique charters that do not seem to follow the models identified for the other groups. Interestingly, one of these three is S 1328, an entirely Latin charter that is particularly anomalous. It was in fact issued in London in the year 973, during the course of a royal assembly summoned by Edgar. Although the general contents reflect those of the other leases issued by Oswald, it is interesting that its formulation departs significantly from them. It is clear that the models that were current at Worcester in the 970s were not available for the drafting of a similar lease while the bishop was in London.

[39] One of these two charters, S 690 (*Abing* 87), is an original royal diploma of 'Edgar A' for which Oswald would have drafted the attestations making use of what Michael Lapidge has described as 'florid language'. Incidentally, this charter would also provide evidence of the bishop's collaboration with the author of the royal diplomas which, as shown earlier, appear to have influenced the Worcester leases' formulation most directly. The other charter in which it seems possible to

Summaries, Sanctions and the Role of Old English

The twelve leases that are entirely in Old English or have at least their main dispositive section in the vernacular can be classified into three different sub-groups (see Table 14.2). The largest one comprises as many as eight charters sharing the same formulation; they all refer to permission being obtained from the king, the ealdorman of the Mercians and the Worcester community. Seven of these eight also state explicitly that the land has to go back to Worcester after three generations of beneficiaries for the use of the bishop, possibly confirming that, as in the case of the leases in Group B, this specific condition may have determined the choice of a certain set of formulae over others.[40] By the end of the period, however, things had changed noticeably, because, although we have three leases from the early 990s with dispositive sections in Old English, they display rather different features. They contain a verbal invocation that was not included in the earlier vernacular charters, while the mention of the permission from the king and the ealdorman of Mercia has disappeared;[41] interestingly, both features are also shared by the later Latin leases. It should be noted that none of these Old English texts is an exact translation of any of the surviving episcopal documents with dispositive sections in Latin, though, of course, they share many elements with them, and some specific passages can be seen to match exactly corresponding Latin ones.[42]

Attention has been focused so far on the initial and main clauses of Oswald's leases, up until the request for restitution to Worcester, since, as was mentioned earlier, these opening component sections seem to follow specific patterns that allow for the identification of clusters of charters

recognize Oswald's input is one of the leases belonging to the above-mentioned Group M (S 1341) in which the bishop's attestation makes use of the Greek-based word *aecclesiarches*, hitherto unattested: M. Lapidge, 'Æthelwold as Scholar and Teacher', in his *Anglo-Latin Literature 900–1066* (London, 1993), pp. 186–7. On the Anglo-Latin hermeneutic style, see M. Lapidge, 'The Hermeneutic Style in Tenth-Century Anglo-Latin Literature', also in his *Anglo-Latin Literature 900–1066*, pp. 105–49; M. Lapidge, 'Poeticism in Pre-Conquest Anglo-Latin Prose', *PBA* 129 (2005), 321–37; and Stephenson, *The Politics of Language*.

40 Interestingly, the only lease in this group (S 1326) not specifying that the land must be restituted to Worcester for the use of the bishop concerns land at Teddington and Alstone (Gloucs.), the former of which was assigned to the monastic chapter in the eleventh century. See Tinti, *Sustaining Belief*, p. 178.

41 It must be noted in any case that after the expulsion of Ælfric Cild in 985 there was no ealdorman in Mercia until 994. See A. Williams, *Æthelred the Unready: The Ill-Counselled King* (London, 2003), p. 66.

42 For instance, the most frequent Old English opening formula ('Ic Ospold bisceop þurh Godes gefe mid geþafunge 7 leafe Eadgares Angulkynincges 7 Ælfheres Mercna heretogan'), which also occurs in S 1326 (*Anglo-Saxon Charters*, ed. Robertson, no. 46), one of the two surviving single sheets, mirrors very closely the Latin opening of charters in Group A, such as S 1300 (BCS 1088): 'Ego Osuuald gratia Dei episcopus cum consensu ac licentia Eadgari regis Anglorum et Ælfhere ducis Merciorum.'

sharing the same formulation. But when considering what comes afterwards, one is bound to find other significant characteristics. For this purpose it is necessary to go back to S 1347, the one lease of Oswald that has only been preserved in single-sheet form (see Figure 14.1). After the restitution clause, the charter switches to Old English to provide a sort of summary of the main contents of the lease, with the addition of some more specific information that is not to be found in the Latin text:

> [Þ]onne is þæs londes þridde half hid þe Oswold arcebisceop selð Cynelme his þegne to boc londe swa he hit him ær hæfde toforlæten to læn londe ægþær ge on earð londe ge on hom londe.[43]

The Latin text that precedes this passage already contained the name of the beneficiary and the extent of the land leased. But what had not been stated before this point is that it consisted of both ploughland and meadowland and that Oswald had already leased out this estate to Cynelm as loanland, whereas he was now giving it to him as bookland. This is a very interesting piece of information that does not seem to have been much considered in the numerous studies published on the concept of Anglo-Saxon bookland.[44] It would seem to confirm that, during Oswald's episcopate, a significant effort was made to reinforce with written records the leasing out of landed estates; such records seem to add strength to the nature of the grant and the possible rights enjoyed by the beneficiary.

From the palaeographical point of view, it can be noted that the change of language is flagged through a change in the size and form of the script, with Caroline minuscule being used for Latin and Anglo-Saxon minuscule for the vernacular.[45] The shorter and slightly smaller Old English text thus

---

[43] 'Therefore this is this land's two and a half hides which Archbishop Oswald assigns to Cynelm his thegn as bookland as he had earlier leased it to him as loanland, consisting of both ploughland and meadowland'. Translation from Schendl, 'Beyond Boundaries', p. 57.

[44] This is not the place for a detailed discussion, but it may be tentatively suggested that in the case of this lease, as well as S 1334 and S 1350, which contain a vernacular recap to the same effect, Oswald was granting some of the privileges that were typical of bookland, albeit only for three generations of beneficiaries. He had already leased out to Cynelm the land at *Caldinccotan*, but only as loanland and without issuing a written document. For a short but useful discussion of bookland and loanland, see A. Williams, 'Land Tenure', in *The Wiley Blackwell Encyclopaedia of Anglo-Saxon England*, ed. M. Lapidge, J. Blair, S. Keynes and D. Scragg, 2nd edn (Chichester, 2014), pp. 282–3. A useful comparison may be drawn with the appearance in the ninth century of West Frankish charters issuing grants of *beneficia*, hitherto apparently just done orally: J. Martindale, 'The Kingdom of Aquitaine and the «Dissolution of the Carolingian Fisc»', in her *Status, Authority and Regional Power: Aquitaine and France, 9th to 12th Centuries* (Aldershot, 1997), II. 131–91. I am grateful to Jinty Nelson for this reference.

[45] For palaeographical discussion of this single sheet (London, BL, Additional Charter 19794) and comparisons with contemporary manuscripts, see N. R. Ker, *Catalogue of Manuscripts Containing*

can be easily distinguished from the more prominent Latin sections, which also employ display script for proper names. It is tempting to suggest that such a summary had an ancillary role, possibly one meant to assist those who may have had difficulties in understanding the Latin of the main dispositive clause. Vernacular summaries or recaps of this kind appear in seventeen leases of Oswald.[46] Of these, only two (S 1299 and S 1305) also contain a vernacular dispositive clause, thus making it more likely that the need for such vernacular passages was more typically felt when the details of the transaction had been provided in a Latin dispositive clause. It can also be noted that in S 1299 and S 1305 the recap is identical, except for proper names and the extent of the land leased, and that in neither case does the summary provide new information beyond that already contained in the dispositive clause.[47] Its nature seems more formulaic than that of the summary contained in S 1347, where, as we have seen, important information on both the nature of the lease and the composition of the estate was provided through such a passage.

In certain respects these seventeen vernacular summaries resemble Old English endorsements, an important element to bear in mind given that in the tenth century it was common for newly issued royal diplomas to be given a vernacular endorsement summarizing the contents of the charter.[48] There is no evidence, however, that these leases' summaries were ever conceived of as notes to be added on the dorse of the parchments. Although S 1347 is the only surviving single sheet to contain such a recap, it may be noted that in the copies of the leases that have been preserved in *Liber Wigorniensis*, summaries are always sandwiched between component sections of the charters that would have appeared on the face rather than the dorse of the original single sheets.[49] In three cases the summaries' contents can also be shown to

---

Anglo-Saxon, reissued with supplement (Oxford, 1990), p. xxvi; and D. N. Dumville, *English Caroline Script and Monastic History: Studies in Benedictinism, A.D. 950–1030* (Woodbridge, 1993), pp. 20, 22, 29, 56 and 75–6. A vernacular boundary clause for the land leased through this charter can be found on the dorse of the single sheet. It is edited, translated and discussed in D. Hooke, *Worcestershire Anglo-Saxon Charter-Bounds* (Woodbridge, 1990), pp. 307–10.

[46] S 1300, S 1299, S 1307, S 1297, S 1304, S 1305, S 1310, S 1311, S 1314, S 1316, S 1370, S 1318, S 1336, S 1334, S 1347, S1350 and S 1352. Some of the 'summaries' contained in these charters are printed and translated in Schendl, 'Beyond Boundaries', pp. 62–3. Vanessa King calls these leases' sections 'limitations': King, 'St Oswald's Tenants', p. 102.

[47] Cf. *Anglo-Saxon Charters*, ed. Robertson, nos. 34 and 36.

[48] *Charters of Christ Church Canterbury, Part 1*, ed. Brooks and Kelly, p. 41.

[49] When it is possible to compare the text of a lost single sheet that was transcribed before its disappearance with that preserved in *Liber Wigorniensis*, it can be demonstrated that the cartulary's scribes did not alter the succession of the various component sections of the leases. This is, for

lead to an introduction of the witnesses. For instance, in S 1336, the Old English text that precedes the attestations of the cathedral community's members reads

> Ðonne is þæs landes .iii. hida þe Ospald arcebisceop bocað Þynsige his munuce spa spa Þulfstan his fæder hit hæfde, mid þæs heorodes gepitnesse on Þiogornaceastre. Ðis is seo hondseten.[50]

The mention of the witnessing of the Worcester community here seems to lead naturally to the introduction of the same community's attestations. Similar recaps can also be found in S 1334 and S 1350, thus confirming that although it is possible that the inspiration for such vernacular summaries came from the endorsements given to newly issued royal diplomas, the Worcester scribes probably adapted that practice to create another component part for the main text of episcopal leases.

Old English was also normally used in these charters to provide information about the appurtenances of the estates leased, such as meadows, woods, mills or shares in some forms of open-field systems.[51] Such appurtenances tend to be listed immediately after the boundary clause;[52] occasionally they may be mentioned before the boundary clause (as in S 1327), and in at least two cases (S 1310 and S 1358) a detailed Old English description of the estate and its appurtenances is provided in the middle of a Latin dispositive section. These interesting cases of intra-sentential code switching, as the practice of alternating between two languages within the same sentence is called by linguists, seem to confirm that the vernacular was employed when the information to provide was too technical or contained too many Old English place-names for a sentence to be properly constructed in Latin.[53]

One should not think, however, that Old English was only used to describe technical, tenurial or agricultural arrangements. Spiritual matters

---

instance, the case for S 1370, one of the lost Somers charters transcribed by Humfrey Wanley and subsequently published in *Historiæ Ecclesiasticæ Gentis Anglorum Libri quinque, Auctore … Baeda*, ed. J. Smith (Cambridge, 1722), app. XXI, pp. 764–82, at 773–4; the Old English summary precedes the witness-list both in the lost single sheet's transcription and in the cartulary copy (London, BL, Cotton Tiberius A. xiii, fols. 70r–71r).

[50] 'Therefore this is this land's three hides which Archbishop Oswald grants by charter to Wynsige his monk, as Wulfstan his father had it, with the witness of the community at Worcester. This is the signature.' The lease is preserved in Cotton Tiberius A xiii, fol. 82 v. An edition of the whole text is provided in KCD 616.

[51] An interesting example is provided by S 1314, about which see Hooke, *Worcestershire Anglo-Saxon Charter-Bounds*, p. 268.

[52] Examples include S 1305, S 1314, S 1322, S 1370, S 1329 and S 1356.

[53] See Schendl, 'Beyond Boundaries', pp. 58–9 and 78–81.

could also be dealt with in the vernacular, as is made apparent by the frequent employment of Old English in the sanction of these episcopal documents, a linguistic feature that sets them apart from royal diplomas. As many as nineteen leases, of which eleven have their main dispositive clause in Latin, contain a sanction in Old English.[54] This is particularly significant when one bears in mind that, by contrast, Latin sanctions can only be found in five leases of Oswald (see Table 14.1). In one case (S 1370), the text contains both a Latin sanction at the end of the dispositive clause and a shorter Old English one following on from the summary, just before the charter switches again to Latin to introduce the witness-list. In general, it can be noted that Latin sanctions seem rather exceptional, and not surprisingly, when they are employed, they tend to be heavily dependent on royal diplomas. The earliest instance occurs in the above-mentioned lease dating from Oswald's first year of episcopate (S 1298), which reproduces the sanction of the contemporary 'Edgar A' charters.[55] A later example (S 1340, dated 979), whose sanction is not attested in any other surviving charter, contains some interesting infernal imagery and makes use of the word *Tartarus*.[56] More generally, it can be noted that the few Latin sanctions appearing in Oswald's leases are contained in texts that employ more elaborate Latin, contain an invocation or a proem and make use of biblical quotations.[57]

The much more frequent use of the vernacular for the sanction of the leases is one of the most striking linguistic features of the corpus. In seventeen of the nineteen documents containing an Old English sanction, this opens with an invocation to three saints (Mary, Michael and Peter), who are in fact named in Latin, before the sentence swiftly switches to English to invoke all of God's saints.[58] The earliest example dates from 966 and can be found in S 1309, one of the vernacular leases:

---

[54] S 1309, S 1315, S 1312, S 1313, S 1370, S 1317, S 1318, S 1326, S 1320, S 1332, S 1337, S 1338, S 1339, S 1372, S 1373, S 1374, S 1342, S 1369 and S 1355.

[55] See above, text corresponding to note 33.

[56] KCD 623: 'Si quis autem contumax ac rebellis hoc nostrum donum decreuerit peruersa frangere mente, sciat sese subinde dampnandum in tremendi examinis die, ex auctoritate principis aposto-lorum Petri, tartaribusque tradendum satellitibus, nisi in hac uita prius Deo hominibusque congrua emendauerit satisfactione.' The word *Tartarus*, which comes from classical mythology, was fairly common in medieval writings dealing with the Christian hell. It can be found in the sanction of several tenth-century royal diplomas (e.g., S 478, S 519 and S 724); S 1340 appears to be the only charter other than a royal diploma to use the word. See P. Hoffman, 'Infernal Imagery in Anglo-Saxon Charters' (unpublished PhD thesis, University of St Andrews, 2008), pp. 138–9 and 323.

[57] As well as S 1298, S 1370 and S 1340, a Latin sanction can be found in S 1345, S 1356 and S 1363.

[58] Of the leases mentioned earlier at note 54, only S 1370 and S 1318 do not contain an invocation to Mary, Michael and Peter.

Sancta Maria 7 sanctus Michahel cum sancto Petro 7 eallum Godes halgum gemiltien þis haldendum, gif hpa buton geprihtum hit abrecan pille God hine to rihtere bote gecerre. Amen.[59]

Sanctions addressing these three saints continued to be used throughout Oswald's episcopate, with the latest extant example being that contained in S 1355, of the year 988. It should be noted that while the first, 'positive' portion of the passage, also known as the blessing, remains the same in all the seventeen leases that make use of this sanction, the wording of the second part, that is, the anathema, is more varied. From the shorter version contained in S 1309, the formula can be found expanded slightly in other leases to incorporate an explicit reference to the Last Day, on which whoever attempts to change what has been established in the lease will have to account for it to God, unless he sets about making due amendments.[60] In one case the formula contains an even more interesting reference to the heavenly *lifes bocum* ('books of life'), from which God will blot out the name of those who try to interfere with the charter's dispositions. This reference occurs in S 1326, the other lease of Oswald that survives as a single sheet, although, unlike S 1347, this was also copied in *Liber Wigorniensis*. The whole formula reads

> Sancta Maria 7 sanctus Michahel, cum sancto Petro 7 eallum Godes halgum gemiltsien þis healdendum, gief hpa buton gepyrhtum hit apendan pille God adilgie his noman of lifes bocum 7 habbe him gemæne pið hine on þam ytemestan dæge þisses lifes butan he to rihtere bote gecerre.

It has been translated by Agnes Robertson as

> May St Mary and St Michael with St Peter and all the saints of God be merciful to those who uphold this. If anyone, without due cause, attempts to change it, God shall blot out his name from the books of life, and he shall have to account for it to him on the last day of this life, unless he set about making due amendment.[61]

---

[59] 'May St Mary and St Michael, with St Peter and all the saints of God, be merciful towards those who observe this. If anyone, without due cause attempts to break it, may God turn him to due amendment. Amen'; *Anglo-Saxon Charters*, ed. Robertson, no. 42.

[60] See, for instance, S 1372: 'gief hpa buton gepyrhtum hit abrecan pille hæbbe him pið God gemæne on þam ytemestan dæge þisses lifes buton he ær to dædbote gecyrre' ('if anyone, without due cause, attempts to break it, he shall have to answer for it to God on the last day of this life, unless he has set about making amends'); *Anglo-Saxon Charters*, ed. Robertson, no. 58.

[61] *Ibid.*, no. 46. This lease was issued in 969 in favour of Oswald's brother, Osulf, who was also the recipient of S 1370 (BCS 1139), an undated charter that is, however, likely to have been issued in the same year and which, as mentioned earlier, contains both a Latin and an Old English sanction. The shorter vernacular sanction does not provide a blessing but, like that in S 1326, refers to the Books of Life.

References to the heavenly Book(s) of Life, in which, according to the Scriptures, God writes the name of every person destined to go to Heaven, can often be found in Latin sanctions of royal diplomas, though it should be noted that Oswald's leases provide the only occurrences of the same motif in vernacular sanctions.[62] The mention of these three saints alongside the Book of Life also creates an interesting link with the eschatological culture of late Anglo-Saxon England. Mary Clayton has drawn attention to a couple of vernacular homilies (Vercelli homily 15 and an Easter homily contained in both Cambridge, Corpus Christi College 41 and 303) in which Mary, Michael and Peter appear together as intercessors for the souls of those led before Christ at the Last Judgement.[63] The three saints are also mentioned in the same order in which they appear in Oswald's leases in the Old English versions of the Sunday letter contained in Cambridge, Corpus Christi College 140 and 419, both of which date to the first half of the eleventh century.[64] Catherine Karkov has also explored the significance of the presence of these three saints in the illuminated pages depicting the Last Judgement in the New Minster *Liber Vitae*.[65] The context in which Mary, Michael and Peter are mentioned in the leases strongly suggests that in these cases too we should see a link with the late Anglo-Saxon belief in the saints' saving intercession, as they are asked to be merciful to those who observe the lease's dispositions, in contrast to what we find in the anathema portion of the sanction condemning those who do not respect what has been established in the lease and will have to account for that on the Last Day.[66]

---

[62] Examples from the Worcester archive include S 210 and S 402. The anathema in the former case reads: 'pax seruantibus et custodiantibus hanc nostram donationem et libertatem contradicentibus uero et negantibus atque frangentibus *deleantur de libro uiuentium et cum iustis non scribentur* et cum Iuda traditore Dei sint in eternum damnati, nisi ante hic emendauerint' (BCS 509; emphasis mine).

[63] M. Clayton, 'Delivering the Damned: A Motif in OE Homiletic Prose', *MÆ* 55 (1986), 92–102.

[64] *Sunday Observance and the Sunday Letter in Anglo-Saxon England*, ed. and trans. D. Haines (Cambridge, 2010), pp. 114–15 and 120–21.

[65] C. Karkov, 'Judgement and Salvation in the New Minster Liber Vitae', in *Apocryphal Texts and Traditions in Anglo-Saxon England*, ed. K. Powell and D. Scragg (Cambridge, 2003), pp. 151–63.

[66] Julia Barrow has linked the presence of the formula invoking the protection of the three saints with the dedications of the churches that then stood or were being built within the cathedral precincts and has used the evidence provided by the leases to suggest that construction of the church of St Mary started in 966, the date of the earliest lease containing the formula (S 1309). See Barrow, 'Community of Worcester', p. 98; and for further bibliography on religious buildings within the cathedral precincts, see Tinti, *Sustaining Belief*, p. 31, n. 88. However, the order and context in which the three saints are mentioned in the leases, together with the uncertain date of the foundation of a church of St Michael (first attested in the thirteenth century), suggest that the saints' invocation in the leases should be explained bearing in mind the intercessory role that was attributed to them as a group in later Anglo-Saxon England. This may of course have some bearing on the dedications of the churches that stood within the cathedral precincts, also considering the strong association

Connections can also be drawn with Latin prayers from several late Anglo-Saxon liturgical manuscripts, including Ælfwine's prayer-book, the Bury Psalter and the Portiforium of St Wulfstan. They all contain prayers invoking the intercession of Mary, Michael and Peter.[67] In some cases, as in the Bury Psalter, these are the first to be named in a slightly longer list of saints, whereas in a section of a more elaborate private prayer contained in the Portiforium of St Wulfstan, they are the only three named saints to be invoked within a context which refers explicitly to the time of death ('in illa hora tremendo quando anima mea egressa erit de corpore meo').[68] It is likely that the Latin opening of the leases' otherwise entirely vernacular sanction – calling upon the three saints ('Sancta Maria 7 sanctus Michahel, cum sancto Petro') – echoes Latin prayers like these. When appearing in Old English texts in the nominative case, saints' names were given their appropriate Latin declension, and the adjectives *sanctus* and *sancta* were also normally kept in their correct Latin nominative forms when preceding such proper names. However, the presence of the preposition *cum* followed by the Latin ablative *sancto Petro* makes this entire phrase stand out as a proper, unassimilated short Latin text, denoting a deliberate effort to keep the names of the three saints in Latin.[69] This seems to have been done because of influence from Latin prayers like those contained in

between those grounds, which hosted the only lay cemetery in town, and death. On the cathedral's undisputed control over urban burial, see J. Barrow, 'Urban Cemetery Location in the High Middle Ages', in *Death in Towns: Urban Responses to the Dying and the Dead, 100–1600*, ed. S. Bassett (Leicester, 1992), pp. 78–100, at 86–8. On the appearance of saints in charters, see more generally H. Foxhall Forbes, *Heaven and Earth in Anglo-Saxon England: Theology and Society in an Age of Faith* (Farnham, 2013), pp. 219–38.

[67] *Ælfwine's Prayerbook (London, British Library, Cotton Titus D. xxvi + xxvii)*, ed. B. Günzel (London, 1993), 76.7, 76.9, 76.60. The Bury Psalter's relevant prayer is edited in A. Corrêa, 'The Liturgical Manuscripts of Oswald's Houses', in *St Oswald of Worcester*, ed. Brooks and Cubitt, pp. 285–324, at 319–20. *The Portiforium of Saint Wulstan (Corpus Christi College, Cambridge, MS. 391)*, ed. A. Hughes, 2 vols. (London, 1958–60), vol. II, pp. 3–4.

[68] This is not the place for a comprehensive treatment of the private prayers and other liturgical texts in which Mary, Michael and Peter are invoked, but it is most probable that further research would easily lead to the identification of more manuscripts and prayers referring to them in this order and in similar contexts.

[69] This can be contrasted with the practice followed in the Old English texts mentioned earlier. For instance, Vercelli homily XV, in the passage dealing with the intercessory role of the three saints, contains the following forms to refer to them in dative constructions: 'þære halgan sancta Marian', 'þam halgan sancte Michael' and 'ðam halgan sancte Petre' (Clayton, 'Delivering the Damned', p. 93). The A version of the Old English Sunday Letter refers to the three saints in the genitive case, providing further examples of Old English inflections for the same names ('7 fela freccednessa synd gegearpod togeanes eop 7 gefyrn þære gif minre leofan moder þingung nære Sancta Marian 7 sancte Michaeles 7 sancte Petres 7 þære .XII. apostola' ('And many perils are prepared against you and would have happened long ago were it not for the intercession of my dear mother St Mary and St Michael and St Peter and the twelve apostles'): *Sunday Observance*, ed. Haines, pp. 114–15: CCCC 140, fol. 72r).

the above-mentioned manuscripts, though the combination of the saints'
Latin names with an otherwise entirely vernacular sanction must be interpreted as a deliberate and specific choice of the Worcester draftsmen. The
latter were clearly operating in a fully developed bilingual written environment, in which Old English could stand on a par with Latin.

Conclusions

The seventy-six leases issued by Bishop Oswald in the course of his episcopate represent both a continuation and a departure from earlier practices.
Leases were not a novelty at Worcester, but those issued in Oswald's time
display a number of remarkable features which cast important light on the
documentary culture of tenth-century England. The typologies of texts
which have been identified here point towards a systematized production
of chirographs, one within which draftsmen could choose among a number
of different models and different combinations of the two written languages
of late Anglo-Saxon England. Such choices must have depended on several
factors which cannot have been simply dictated by the linguistic needs of the
beneficiaries, since, as was shown above, when the same person can be
identified as the beneficiary of several leases, these display different characteristics, belong to different typologies and include charters written in
either language. While it is impossible to identify different scribes' abilities
or linguistic preferences because of the very limited survival of single sheets,
some of the patterns which have emerged point towards a possible role
played by the evolving system of organization of the church of Worcester's
landed property. This process – which was still in its infancy in Oswald's
days and which led to a division of the estate between the lands which
belonged to the bishop and those which were eventually set apart for the
cathedral chapter – can be seen as leaving its mark on the formulation of
these charters. The choice between the two most popular sets of formulae,
represented by the above-mentioned Groups B and E, seems to have been at
least partly determined by the need to distinguish the lands which had been
set aside for the use of the bishop from the rest of the estate.

In creating the various typologies of texts that have been identified, the
Worcester scribes relied on the formulation of contemporary royal diplomas, both for the Latin and for the Old English sections of their leases
However, they did so by adapting those formulae to describe a different
type of land grant and by ascribing to the vernacular language a much more
prominent role. This is particularly evident in the choice to employ Old
English for the sanction in the great majority of leases that contain such a

component section. Moreover, and perhaps even more significantly, they drafted documents that are more markedly bilingual than earlier leases or contemporary royal diplomas, as they swiftly switched between the two languages, even within the same sentence. Oswald's leases thus represent an exceptional body of material both in quantitative and qualitative terms, as they open an invaluable window onto documentary production at a late Anglo-Saxon scriptorium. As has been shown, they can be described at the same time as both homogeneous and diverse: the typologies identified point towards a fairly organized system, but the variety of linguistic choices made by their drafters when building the component sections of the texts demonstrate that the late Anglo-Saxon documentary bilingualism was a complex phenomenon that deserves more attention than it has so far received.

Index

Printed in Great Britain
by Amazon

31143855R00203